POPE FRANCIS

Pope Francis

Untying the Knots
The Struggle for the Soul of Catholicism

Paul Vallely

B L O O M S B U R Y

NEW YORK · LONDON · OXFORD · NEW DELHI · SYDNEY

Bloomsbury USA

An imprint of Bloomsbury Publishing Plc

1385 Broadway	50 Bedford Square
New York	London
NY 10018	WC1B 3DP
USA	UK

www.bloomsbury.com

BLOOMSBURY and the Diana logo are trademarks of Bloomsbury Publishing Plc

First published in Great Britain 2013
Revised and expanded second edition published in Great Britain 2015
First U.S. edition published 2015

ISBN: HB: 978-1-63286-115-3
ePub: 978-1-63286-116-0

Library of Congress Cataloging-in-Publication Data has been applied for.

2 4 6 8 10 9 7 5 3 1

Printed and bound in the U.S.A. by Thomson-Shore Inc., Dexter, Michigan

To find out more about our authors and books visit www.bloomsbury.com.
Here you will find extracts, author interviews, details of forthcoming events,
and the option to sign up for our newsletters.

Bloomsbury books may be purchased for business or promotional use. For information
on bulk purchases please contact Macmillan Corporate and Premium Sales Department
at specialmarkets@macmillan.com.

*What reviewers said of the first edition of
Paul Vallely's biography:*
Pope Francis: Untying the Knots

Peter Stanford, The Sunday Times:
'Paul Vallely's biography of Francis ... stands, in terms of seriousness of purpose and depth of understanding, head and shoulders above others.'

Mark Lawson, The Guardian:
'Reads like a lost, unexpectedly literate chapter of *The Da Vinci Code*...
Tough-minded analysis ... lifts the book well above the nervous reverence of much papal biography, and should recommend it to an audience broader than Catholics ... '

Michael Walsh, The Tablet:
'Read this book, forget the rest.'

Raymond A Schroth SJ, America, the US Jesuit magazine:
'At last a book has put both Jorge Mario Bergoglio, SJ, and Pope Francis in context, and explained the mystery of this man who seems to have come from nowhere to lead the Catholic Church at a critical time.'

Luke Coppen, editor of the Catholic Herald, in The Independent:
'Vallely skilfully unravels the competing narrative threads, without ever oversimplifying either Argentine politics or the new Pontiff's complex personality ... a sophisticated biography.'

John Wilkins, the Church Times:
' ... in a different class from other biographies ... a compelling account.'

The Economist:
'This book demonstrates that Pope Francis is a tougher, more complex figure than meets the eye. A turbulent life has given the pontiff a subtle sense of the realities of power, and the courage to act on it. Anybody who reads this book will eagerly await his next move.'

Tim Byron SJ, Thinking Faith, the online journal of the British Jesuits:
'"Untying the Knots" – is a stroke of genius. It expresses succinctly, but also with a certain profundity, the challenge at hand...an engaging and thoughtful read throughout.'

Tom Heneghan, religion editor, Reuters:
'Paul Vallely's *Untying the Knots* fills the gaps left by "instant books" on Pope Francis.'

John Cornwell, Times Literary Supplement:
'Vallely's book is a formidable achievement.'

James Carroll, The New Yorker:
'indispensable'

Julian Coman in The Observer:
A 'masterly biography'

Andrew Sullivan, The Daily Dish:
'The indispensable English-language biography of the Pope.'

Eamon Duffy, The New York Review of Books:
'Paul Vallely's *Pope Francis: Untying the Knots* was one of the earliest in the field. Admiring but keenly questioning, its judgments have worn well.'

About the Author

Paul Vallely has an international reputation as a commentator on religion, society and ethical issues. As a journalist he has produced award-winning reporting from thirty countries over three decades for which he was nominated for the UN Media Peace Prize. As an activist on international development he has worked with Bob Geldof and Bono and was co-author of *Our Common Interest*, the report of the Prime Minister's Commission for Africa. As a writer his books include *The New Politics: Catholic Social Teaching for the 21st Century* and *Bad Samaritans: First World Ethics and Third World Debt*. He co-wrote Geldof's best-selling autobiography *Is That It?*

He writes on political, cultural and ethical matters in the *Independent on Sunday*, the *New York Times*, the *Guardian*, the *Sunday Times*, *Newsweek*, the *Church Times*, *Third Way* and *The Tablet*. A former associate editor of the *Independent* and editor of the *Sunday Times* News Review, he is a regular broadcaster on television and radio. He is now Visiting Professor in Public Ethics and Media at the University of Chester. He is also a Senior Honorary Fellow at the Brooks World Poverty Institute at the University of Manchester. He has chaired the development agencies Traidcraft and the Catholic Institute for International Relations, and has been an adviser to the Catholic Bishops of England and Wales. He was awarded a CMG 'for services to journalism and to the developing world' in the Queen's 2006 Birthday Honours. He lives in Manchester with his wife and son.

www.paulvallely.com

For Christine
without whom
nothing would be possible

and for Thomas
faith in the future

In a higher world it is otherwise, but here below to live is to change, and to be perfect is to have changed often.

John Henry Cardinal Newman, 'On the Development of Ideas', from *An Essay on the Development of Christian Doctrine*

Abbreviations

€ means euros.
$ means US dollars.
Other currencies are spelled out in the text.

Contents

List of Illustrations

First plate section

1. Jorge Mario Bergoglio with his brother, Oscar in the early 1940s. (Rex Features)

2. Bergoglio, aged 13, at the *Wilfrid Barón de le Santos Ángeles* primary school in Greater Buenos Aires. (Rex Features)

3. Bergoglio and classmates, *c.* 1951. (Rex Features)

4. Family portrait, 1958. (Reuters)

5. *Mary Untier of Knots*, St Peter am Perlach Church, Augsburg. (Reuters)

6. St Peter am Perlach Church, Augsburg. (Alamy)

7. Bergoglio, Archbishop of Buenos Aires, *c.* 1992. (Reuters)

8. Bergoglio at a hospital in Buenos Aires, 1990s. (Rex Features)

9. Bergoglio is made cardinal by Pope John Paul II, February 2001. (Reuters)

10. Bergoglio and Pope Benedict XVI. (Reuters)

11. Bergoglio is elected Pope on 13th March 2013. (Getty Images)

12. Pope Francis with Argentina's president, Christina Fernández de Kirchner. (Rex Features)

13. Francis returns to pay his bill at the Vatican hotel he used before he became Pope. (Reuters)

Second plate section

14. Newly elected Pope Francis waves to the waiting crowd from the central balcony of St Peter's Basilica on March 13, 2013. (Alamy)

15. Francis bows his head to receive the blessing of the ordinary people before he gives his first blessing as Pope. (Getty Images)

16. Pope Francis's metal cross. (Alamy)

17. Francis greets the crowd at the end of his weekly general audience at St Peter's, February, 2015. (Getty Images)

18. Francis prays in the back pew in the chapel of the Casa Santa Marta. (CNS/*L'Osservatore Romano*)

19. Pope Francis carries his own bag as he disembarks in Rome on his return from Brazil in July 2013. (Getty Images)

20. Francis and US President Barack Obama in a private audience at the Vatican in March 2014. (Getty Images)

21. The Pope speaking during an audience with families at the Paul VI hall at the Vatican, December 2014. (Getty Images)

22. Francis dons a red nose to joke with a newly-wed couple. (Alamy)

23. Pope Francis prays at the separation barrier between Israel and Palestine in May 2014. (Getty Images)

24. The Pope at the Western Wall in Jerusalem's Old City, May 2014. (Getty Images)

25. Francis hugs and kisses Vinicio Riva. (Alamy)

26. Pope Francis meets Queen Elizabeth II at the Vatican, April 2014. (Getty Images)

27. Francis at the start of his homily during Mass at Manila Cathedral in the Philippines, January 2015. (Getty Images)

28. Pope Francis greets a young child in St Peter's Square. (Getty Images)

29. Pope Francis at Confession during Holy Week, March 2015. (Alamy)

30. Pope Francis greets the crowds in the rain in Tacloban, Philippines, January 2015. (Getty Images)

Foreword

'Where's my briefcase?' asked Pope Francis. The papal entourage had arrived at Fiumicino Airport in Rome for his first trip abroad. He had been Pope for just four months. He was bound for Rio de Janeiro where 3.5 million young people from 178 countries were waiting to greet him at World Youth Day which in 2013 was to be held in Brazil. The Pope and assistants had arrived from the Vatican by helicopter. And Francis could not find his briefcase. He looked preoccupied.

'It's been taken on board the plane,' a helpful aide explained.

'But I want to carry it on,' said the pontiff.

'No need, it's on already,' the assistant replied.

'You don't understand,' said Francis. 'Go to the plane. Get the bag. And bring it back here please.'

The press were already on the plane waiting, with the engines running, for the Pope to arrive so that Alitalia Flight AZ4000 could begin its 12-hour flight across the Atlantic. If anyone saw the bag being carried off they did not understand its significance. The journalists on board peered eagerly out of the windows of the Airbus 330 at the Pope on the tarmac below. He seemed engaged in desultory conversation with the Italian prime minister, Enrico Letta, who had come to see him off. Suddenly the press saw Pope Francis begin to move purposefully, with his characteristic rolling gait, through the crowd of functionaries to the aircraft. He was smiling and chatting with the prime minister now. In his left hand the Pope carried a black briefcase.

As Francis climbed the white aircraft steps, with a surprising steadiness for a man of 76 who suffers from sciatica, one reporter declared: 'Look, he's carrying his own bag.' An excited ripple ran around the journalists as they craned forward to catch a glimpse through the aeroplane windows, sensing a story. Popes had never before carried their own luggage. Here was another precedent being set by the first pope from Latin America, who seemed, with every day that passed, to find new ways of disregarding the old familiar expectations of how pontiffs are supposed to be behave.

An hour and a half later, when the breakfast debris had been cleared away, Pope Francis made his way to the back of the plane to hold an impromptu press conference. His predecessor Benedict XVI had spoken to the press on such journeys but in those days all the questions had to be submitted in advance. With Francis no notice was necessary; he would tackle any question on the hoof. He talked about young people who had no jobs and who felt discarded by a throwaway society in which old people had long been treated as similarly unimportant and disposable. Then he answered an array of questions from the reporters. What was in the black briefcase? one asked. 'The keys to the atomic bomb aren't in it,' Francis joked. So what did it contain? 'My razor, my breviary, my diary, a book to read – on St Thérèse of Lisieux to whom I am devoted ... I always take this bag when I travel. It's normal. We have to get used to this being normal,' he added. Normal for a pope.

It is a difficult business being normal if you are the leader of the world's biggest religious denomination and also a head of state. But Francis has presented himself to the world as an icon of simplicity and humility, eschewing papal limousines and the grand Apostolic Palace and instead being driven in a Ford Focus and living in the Vatican guest house, Casa Santa Marta. The lifestyle of the Pope who wants what he has called 'a poor Church, for the poor' is so simple it borders on severity.

But, as the story of the briefcase shows, it can be a complex business being simple. And there is much more to humility than mere self-effacement. 'Papa Francesco – there is no-one like you,' a man called out to him in St Peter's Square one day. With lightning speed the Pope riposted: 'And there's no-one like you either.' As Francis has shown, you can choose humility, even when it does not come naturally to you. There can be what you might call 'an option for humility'. It is one which, 25 years ago, Francis chose when he was cast into the wilderness after over a decade as the leader of Argentina's Jesuits.

If that sounds convoluted it is because there is a tortuous – and tortured – story behind the journey from the boy christened Jorge Mario Bergoglio in 1936 to the man anointed Pope by the Roman Catholic Church in 2013. To tell it I have avoided the reverential approach, and tried to see him as the normal man he is, with his share of human frailties. In the course of Bergoglio's journey, as he admitted in 2010, he made 'hundreds of errors' along the way. And, as he then revealed in his first interview as Pope, he 'lived a time of great interior crisis' when he was sent into exile by the Jesuits after a massive split developed among Argentina's Jesuits under his leadership more than two decades ago. Some biographers of Francis have produced accounts which emphasize the Pope's virtues, glossing over his self-confessed errors and weaknesses, and minimizing the areas in which he has changed over the years. They paint him as a cypher of Catholic orthodoxy and unflagging continuity with previous popes. By contrast Pope Francis himself is quite keen to be publicly critical of some of his own attitudes and actions in the past. Those errors, changes and that 'great interior crisis' in Córdoba – on which this edition throws new light – show how Pope Francis was reshaped and revitalized. Far from seeing the changes Francis has made in his life as a sign of weakness this book portrays them as a sign of strength. He has learned from his mistakes and from experience, a quality which is admirable rather than something which diminishes the man as hagiographers seem to fear. Francis changed himself and now he wants the Church he so loves to change in the same way.

The first two years of Pope Francis's papacy have been marked by a series of most extraordinary gestures, the first of which was that he became the first Pope in two thousand years to dare to take the name of the great saint of the poor, Francis of Assisi.

Some of those gestures have been characterized by a spontaneity which has taken the breath of the world away – as when he embraced and kissed Vinicio Riva, a 53-year-old man with a facial disfigurement so repellent that Riva later revealed mothers would cross the street to avoid their children having to get close to him.

Other gestures were carefully planned, like his decision to wash the feet of inmates in a young offenders' prison in his first Holy Thursday liturgy. Among the prisoners were two women, one of them a Muslim. The Pope's action violated a Vatican edict from the time of Pope John Paul II which decreed that only men were allowed to participate in the ritual. Francis showed the same kind of self-consciousness when he inaugurated a 24-hour Festival of Forgiveness in St Peter's in 2014. He was ushered by the master of papal liturgical ceremonies, Monsignor Guido Marini, to take a seat to hear confessions. But Francis avoided his guiding hand. Instead he moved to the penitent's side of another confessional. The leader of the global Church then made confession of his own sins, to a startled priest, in full public view of the entire basilica. Francis understands, as did his thirteenth-century namesake from Assisi, that actions speak more eloquently than words in delivering to believers, and everyone in the world with ears to hear, his message on how the Catholic Church must change.

His words have been more ambiguous, or at least have been read with ambiguity by different factions within the Church and the world. He gave comfort to liberals, and alarm to conservatives, with his early pronouncement that the Church has been too 'obsessed' with what he has called 'below the belt' issues like abortion, gay marriage and contraception. And when questioned about homosexuality he gave a response – 'who am I to judge?' – which induced the gay singer Elton John to suggest that Pope Francis should be canonized without having to go to the trouble of dying first.

Yet at the same time Francis praised the 'prophetic genius' of one of his predecessors, Pope Paul VI, for not overturning the ban on artificial contraception in the 1968 encyclical *Humanae Vitae* which has become an emblematic focus for dissent among huge numbers of Catholics in the Western world who ignore the Church's teaching on the issue. In a 2015 visit to the Philippines, where the Church has been involved in a prolonged disagreement with the government over reproductive health issues, the Pope departed from his prepared script to insist that, while priests should be 'particularly compassionate for particular cases', families nonetheless needed to maintain what he called an 'openness to life'.

These complexities and apparent contradictions have allowed Catholics of contrasting traditions to lay claim to Pope Francis as 'one of us'. Various groups spotlight what he does or says in highly selective ways so as to hijack him to seemingly support their particular view of the world. So the liberals underscore the way Francis puts personal kindness and the pastoral care of people before the upholding of doctrinal detail. And the conservatives highlight his matter-of-fact endorsement of traditional Catholic teaching. The secular media, meanwhile, has adopted a narrative about Francis which stereotypes him as 'modern' in contrast to his predecessors. The press then tends to play down anything which does not fit that storyline, as when the Pope talks about the Devil as a real person, something which the media ignores or reports in a throwaway manner without comment.

For all that, there are many ways in which the new Pope has already ushered in major change. The most striking example of this centres on the Church's traditional ban on Catholics who have divorced and remarried receiving the sacrament of Communion. Pope Francis used the idea of lifting this totemic ban to stimulate a debate within the Catholic Church which is unprecedented in modern times for its openness and candour. He began, extraordinarily, by issuing a questionnaire to ask ordinary Catholics their views on sexuality and the family. Then he provoked an outspoken debate among cardinals which became more heated at an Extraordinary Synod on the Family. Unruffled by the result he set the scene for more intense discussion at the Synod of Bishops in Rome in October 2015, a month after the Pope travels to Philadelphia for the World Meeting of Families.

It is far from clear what the outcome of this debate will be. But the process the Pope has put in place already constitutes a major gear change from the way such matters were handled in the previous two papacies. Francis has burst open the dam which was blocking free discussion on a range of issues within the Catholic Church. Over the last two decades open discussion had been discouraged by the Vatican. Dissent had been clamped down upon. Theologians had been silenced. Some subjects, like the ordination of women, were declared off-limits and no conversation was even allowed.

By contrast, Francis's first synod began with him declaring that all participants should speak boldly, and listen with humility. No-one should supress their thoughts for fear the Pope might not agree, he told them. The debate which followed was open and became passionate in its controversy. The Church is no longer talking in code but speaking plainly. Liberals hail the new freedom and candour as liberating. Conservatives are bewildered or outraged, with some even accusing Pope Francis of bringing division, confusion, uncertainty and anxiety. Some hardliners see the Pope as a Machiavellian bent on introducing liberalism by stealth. This book will examine those competing claims. But what is incontestable is that a battle has been joined in which the very future of the Church seems at stake. It is becoming a very public contest and, most particularly in the United States, an increasingly embittered one. A struggle for the soul of Catholicism has begun.

This second edition of *Pope Francis: Untying the Knots* makes significant revisions and additions to the first edition which was published within six months of the election of Francis on 13 March 2013. That focused largely on the life of Jorge Mario Bergoglio before he became Pope and hinted at what that augured for his papacy. The second edition has more on all that, throughout its early chapters. But the Francis pontificate is now in its third year. Clear lines are emerging about what is already in many ways a radical and even revolutionary papacy. But in many areas there is a distinct lack of clarity about Pope Francis's strategy. Does he have a stealthy long-term plan? Or is he just opening the doors and windows of the Catholic Church to let God's Holy Spirit blow where it will along corridors and through rooms which were stuffy and airless?

To explore that this second edition adds nine new chapters. One is an entire new chapter on the crisis in Córdoba but the rest tell inside stories behind the wide spectrum of activities which this whirlwind Pope is undertaking. One reveals the calculations beneath the big gestures of those early days in office. Another explores the programme for the papacy which Pope Francis set out in his first major piece of writing, *Evangelii Gaudium*. Another looks at his struggle to clean up the scandal-ridden Vatican Bank. Another uncovers the resistance he is encountering in his attempt to remake the Roman bureaucracy so that it becomes the servant of the Church rather than its master. Another analyses his revolutionary plan to elevate the Synod of Bishops to a new status to make the papacy less like a medieval monarchy and to return the Pope to the position of being a first among equals. It reveals the hidden resistance which Pope Francis is facing within the Vatican on all those fronts. And it analyses the conservative backlash through which opposition is growing and, in some quarters, threatening to become an open revolt, against this radical Franciscan revolution. Other new chapters analyse the areas in which this Pope has seemed less sure-footed: sex abuse by priests, and the place of women in the Church.

The final chapter reads the runes on what the future of the Catholic Church might be under this pope of contradictions – a man who wants the Church to decentralize but who seems to require everything important to pass across his desk; an advocate of collegiality who wants to direct the dispersal of power himself; a monarch who wants to abolish the papal monarchy. It concludes that to ask 'Is Francis a liberal or a conservative?' is to ask the wrong question of a man who is opposed to gay marriage on theological grounds, is in favour of same-sex civil unions as a matter of civil rights, and is against gay adoption on the grounds that a child has a right to a mother and a father – and that the human rights of children trump the rights of adults. Francis is a man of complexity in whom tradition and modernity are married in new ways. Pope Francis, liberal in many of his actions and conservative in many of his statements, represents a challenge to both sides in the old polarization. One side, he suggests, must change their hearts, while the other must change their minds.

This book tells stories to make sense of all this. Some are public stories like Francis's embrace of the disfigured man. Some are stories from behind the scenes, like the story of the briefcase which was told to me by one Vatican insider. Some are stories which sound true but which turn out not to be, like the urban myths which circulate about how Francis dons disguises and sneaks out into the streets of Rome at night to feed the homeless. Even myths reveal a truth of a kind.

Being simple can be a complicated matter. The pages that follow seek to untie some of the knots in the story of Jorge Mario Bergoglio and peel back some of the layers of the man who is now Pope Francis. When he was elected there were banners in St Peter's Square bearing the words which Francis of Assisi heard a crucifix speak at the moment of his conversion: 'Rebuild my Church which is falling into ruins.' Papa Bergoglio is about that task. He knows what needs doing. He is a man with a mission. He is an old man in a hurry.

You could be forgiven for thinking that there is nothing unusual about the suburban church of San Jose del Telar in Buenos Aires. Yet the steady trickle of women who enter it, on an ordinary weekday, make only the most cursory genuflection towards the rococo gold of the central altar and its sultry crucifix.

Then they immediately turn their backs on it. They move, instead, to the side aisle on the left, at the rear of the church, where the painting hangs.

It is a copy, and not a terribly good one, of the seventeenth-century original in a church in Augsburg where in 1986 it was discovered by a visitor from Argentina, Father Jorge Mario Bergoglio SJ. He could not have known then that some 27 years later he would surprise the world by appearing on the balcony of St Peters' in Rome. This virtually unknown priest would be elected the 266th Pope of the Catholic Church. More than that, he would break a number of precedents: as the first pope from the Americas, the first from the southern hemisphere, the first Jesuit pope, and the first to take the name of Francis – in a signal of his intent that henceforth things would be very different for the Church and its billion or more members.

He appeared a man of great confidence, in himself and in God. But he had been a man in turmoil on the day that he first came across the Baroque artwork in that German church. Painted in oils on wood panelling by one Johann Georg Schmidtner it bore the enigmatic title of *Mary Untier of Knots*. Behind it lay an intriguing story.

In 1610, as the tale was told, a Bavarian nobleman, Wolfgang Langenmantel, had travelled to the city to seek the sage counsel of a Jesuit priest named Father Jakob Rem. The aristocrat's marriage was in difficulties. He and his wife Sophia were on the brink of separating – which would have been a scandal of enormous proportion in Catholic Bavaria in those times. Rem had asked the nobleman to bring with him the long white ribbon which had been used to bind together the couple's hands in the celebration of their wedding. The Jesuit had in mind something which had been written by one of the first great Christian theologians and apologists, the second-century Church Father St Irenaeus who had written of how 'the knot of Eve's disobedience was loosed by the obedience of Mary'. Rem invoked the Virgin to intercede over the difficulties of Wolfgang and Sophia. 'In this act of piety,' he prayed over the wedding ribbon, 'I raise up the bond of marriage that all knots be loosed and resolved.' The couple subsequently overcame their problems and remained together. In 1699 their grandson, a canon in the Church of St Peter am Perlach in Augsburg, commissioned the painting and hung it as an altarpiece in the church in thanksgiving for the saving of the marriage. It shows Mary unravelling the entanglements in the ribbon, assisted by two angels and surrounded by cherubs, while her foot casually crushes the head of a serpent representing the Devil.

It is not difficult to understand why the Marian painting spoke so potently to the 50-year-old priest from Argentina. He had been sent to Germany purportedly to do research for a PhD on Romano Guardini, the Catholic philosopher who wrote in the 1930s about the moral hazards of power. But his superiors wanted him out of Argentina where his leadership of the Jesuit province over the previous 15 years – as Novice Master, then Provincial and finally as Rector of its seminary – had divided his religious order so deeply, and so bitterly, that the leader of the Society of Jesus in Rome eventually decreed that a Jesuit from outside Argentina must be sent in to heal the wounds. There were knots aplenty for the Virgin Mary to untie for Bergoglio.

Yet untied they eventually were. Within a few months he was back in Argentina. But after an unhappy period in Buenos Aires, the scene of his long years of controversy, he was exiled to the Jesuit community in that country's second city, Córdoba, some 400 miles from the capital. There he languished in penitential obscurity for two years before then being plucked by the Cardinal Archbishop of Buenos Aires to be made – highly unusually for a Jesuit, for Jesuits take a vow to avoid ecclesiastical preferment – an assistant bishop, back in the city of his birth.

An extraordinary journey had begun. It was to transform Jorge Mario Bergoglio into the Bishop of the Slums, a passionate defender of the disenfran-chised, an unwavering enthusiast for dialogue as a way to build bridges between people of all backgrounds and beliefs – and eventually a pope who announced his intention to transform the cultured silk-brocaded propriety of the Rome of Pope Benedict XVI into 'a poor Church, for the poor'.

There are still knots to be disentangled, not least for a Church and a world only just getting to know this pope of paradox. Jorge Mario Bergoglio is a doctrinal conservative but an ecclesiastical reformer. He is a radical but not a liberal. He seeks to empower others and yet retains a streak of authori-tarianism. He is theologically orthodox yet was on the far left of Argentina's reactionary bishops. He combines religious simplicity with political guile. He is progressive and open, yet austere and can be severe. The first Pope to have been ordained a priest after the Second Vatican Council, he nonetheless imposed a pre-Vatican II training on his novices. He has opposed same-sex marriage and gay adoption but he has kissed the feet of homosexuals with HIV-AIDS. He is of the South, yet has deep roots in the North: a Latin American whose parentage is Italian and who has studied in Spain, Ireland and Germany. He is a diocesan priest and yet also a member of a religious order. He is a teacher of theology but a pastor with the common touch. In him humility and power come together.

When he returned to Argentina from Germany he brought with him postcards of the Augsburg painting and distributed them to friends after his consecration as a bishop. The people of his native land took the image to their hearts. A decade later the parishioners in one church took it upon themselves to raise the money to have a full-size copy of the painting made by an Argentinian painter. It is to that painting, in the otherwise nondescript church of San Jose del Telar in Agronomía, a middle-class suburb of Buenos Aires, that pilgrims now flock. Later, in his time as Archbishop of Buenos Aires, the man who liked to be known only as Padre Bergoglio would slip in among them, dressed in the anonymity of plain clerical black, to sit in the pews before the painting, to unravel the knots of his own life.

'The copy has become more famous now than the original,' said Father Ricardo Aloe, as he sat in the right aisle, in a clear glass-sided confessional, on hand in case any of that steady trickle of pilgrims wanted to be shriven. 'People come from all over Argentina, indeed all over the world, to see it. On the eighth of every month we have ten thousand people here. On the eighth day of December, the Feast of Mary's Immaculate Conception, more than thirty thousand come. They all feel they are listened to and understood by the Virgin. As Mother she is very attentive to our problems. The knots are metaphors of the difficulties we have. She appeals to God to help us with them.'

A metaphor. Jorge Mario Bergoglio knew that only too well. And it seems he obtained the forgiveness he was seeking. Though it has never been enough.

Dirty Tricks in the Vatican

No-one admitted to sending the email. The ambassador said he did not do it. So did the lawyer. So did the journalist. So did several high-ranking officials of the Society of Jesus, the world's biggest and most powerful religious order. But the dossier that dropped anonymously into the inbox of senior cardinals as they gathered in Rome was damning. Or so it was clearly intended to be. Someone did not want Jorge Mario Bergoglio to be Pope.

When a pope dies cardinals from all over the world collect in the Vatican and begin to meet in what they call General Congregations. In April 2005 the first few days of these meetings were spent in absorbing the implications of the death of the man the Vatican swiftly dubbed John Paul the Great. *Santo Subito*, the crowds in St Peter's Square had cried: Make Him a Saint Now! The old Pope had died a long lingering public death, making himself an icon of suffering, as if to chastise a world which has become so fixated with the busyness of doing that it had forgotten about the business of simply being. But while in those Congregations the cardinals of the Roman Catholic Church were publicly deliberating on the details of what was to be the biggest funeral in human history, in private they were talking about something else: who should be the next Pope?

It was in the midst of this that the dossier arrived. Just three days before the 2005 conclave, a human rights lawyer, Marcelo Parrilli, in Argentina, filed a complaint charging Bergoglio with complicity in the kidnapping of two Jesuit priests, whose work with the poor in a Buenos Aires shanty-town was considered by Argentina's military death squads in 1976 to be subversive. The priests – whose dismissal from the Society of Jesus he had orchestrated a week before they disappeared, for disobeying his order to cease living with the poor in the slums – were tortured and held in hoods and shackles for five months before being released.

The allegations, which a spokesman for Cardinal Bergoglio in Buenos Aires in 2005 dismissed as 'old slander' – and which we will examine in detail in a later chapter – were based on the investigations of a campaigning journalist Horacio Verbitsky who had interviewed the kidnapped Jesuits after their eventual release. He had also compiled accounts from priests and lay workers which he claimed corroborated the accusations. And he had found documents in old government files implicating Bergoglio from his time as leader of the Jesuit province in Argentina. The lawsuit filed against Bergoglio in April 2005 was eventually dismissed, but the controversy surrounding it had raged on unabated.

Defenders of Bergoglio claimed that Verbitsky had an ulterior motive. He was a political ally of the previous and current presidents, Néstor and Cristina Kirchner, and once had been a member of the leftist guerrillas, the Montoneros. Verbitsky's most detailed allegations against Bergoglio had been published in a book, *El Silencio*, earlier that year. It had been written after Cardinal Bergoglio publicly criticized President Néstor Kirchner for his record on corruption and his failure to help the poor. The main Argentine newspaper *Clarín* claimed that the Kirchner government distributed the dossier to cardinals via its ambassador to the Holy See. In addition to the email version, some Spanish-speaking cardinals were said to have received a paper copy in an envelope hand-delivered to their Rome addresses. But both government and ambassador issued denials. Verbitsky countered by pointing out that he had begun investigating the allegations in 1999, four years before the Kirchners came to power.

There were other potential culprits in the frame. Alicia Oliveira, a former Argentinian human rights lawyer and judge who had been persecuted by the military junta – and who remained a close friend of Bergoglio until her death in 2014 – blamed conservative elements in the country's hierarchy linked to Opus Dei, the controversial independent lay movement within the Catholic Church, for the attempt to block his election to the papacy in 2005. Yet others laid the blame for the email at the door of fellow Jesuits who had fallen out with Bergoglio when he was the Provincial Superior, or leader, of the order in Argentina, and it is certainly true that there were heavy reservations among Jesuits about Bergoglio; they had complained about his behaviour many years before to the Jesuit Curia, the society's headquarters, in Rome. And there were emails in circulation from Jesuits complaining that Bergoglio was a man 'who never smiled'. Whoever sent the dossier to a large number of cardinals, there was clearly a Stop Bergoglio campaign in place. Bergoglio heard about the dossier but, after discussion with his confidants, decided to remain silent. Catholics like to say that, in the selection of a pope, the Holy Spirit guides the Church. Yet here there were clearly other forces seeking to steer the outcome. But did they succeed?

* * *

The cardinals met for the first of their General Congregations in the synod hall in the shadow of the great dome of St Peter's basilica. An undistinguished post-war building, with a boring beige interior like a university lecture theatre, it feels somehow suited to the dreary formality of ecclesiastical policy. But the real politics went on elsewhere, during the lunch breaks and at dinners hosted by several key cardinals who became conclave power brokers. 'Ever since the Last Supper, the Church has decided its most important affairs at the dinner table,' one cardinal-elector quipped. Some cardinals knew each other well beforehand. But they were in a minority. Pope John Paul II had over the years internationalized the College of Cardinals and new electors were arriving from all over the world. One cardinal's aide recounted seeing 'clutches of developing-world cardinals wandering around Rome as dazed as first-time tourists'. One even asked: 'Where are these dinners they are all talking about?'

Cardinal Cormac Murphy-O'Connor, then Archbishop of Westminster, hosted a gathering of the English-speaking cardinals in the Irish College. But he did his real business in a smaller group of European liberals, which included Cardinals Carlo Mario Martini of Milan, Walter Kasper of Stuttgart and Godfried Danneels of Brussels. The group had met at least once a year for many years and Martini – a Jesuit – had long been their candidate for the papacy. But by 2005 Martini was, at 78, felt to be getting too old; he was suffering from a rare form of Parkinson's disease and his health was so poor he had retired as a serving archbishop three years before. Bergoglio of Buenos Aires – also, coincidentally, a Jesuit – was another option for them. He and Murphy-O'Connor had been made cardinals in the same consistory in 2001. That meant, according to official Vatican seating plans, they always sat near one another at official Vatican events. The two men had become friends. Murphy-O'Connor nicknamed the small group of cardinals who regularly sat with Bergoglio and him *La Squadra*.

For many, though, Cardinal Joseph Ratzinger was the obvious candidate. He had been John Paul II's right-hand man for 24 years and had been watchdog of the Vatican's doctrinal orthodoxy in his job as Prefect of the Congregation for the Doctrine of the Faith. That post meant he was one of the few senior officials whom every cardinal saw on routine visits to Rome. He was also Dean of the College of Cardinals and therefore took the chair at the General Congregations, as well as presiding at John Paul II's funeral Mass and at the *Pro Eligendo Papa* (For the Election of the Pope) Mass on the morning the conclave began. At the General Congregations Ratzinger, a man with a phenomenal memory, called each cardinal by name and spoke to each in a language he knew they understood. For new cardinal-electors – who hardly knew one another, had poor Italian and had little sense of who to vote for – he seemed the obvious choice. He had, after all, been the closest aide to the late John Paul II of whom the conclave was in such awe. And he conducted himself with grace and purpose in the Congregations, and spoke with warmth in his homily at the funeral Mass and with analytical lucidity on the shortcomings of contemporary society at the pre-conclave Mass. Many of the cardinals who had arrived with the question 'if not Ratzinger, who?' began to ask 'why not Ratzinger?'

'Cardinal Ratzinger had a large number of votes before going into the conclave. He had chaired all the Congregation meetings as Dean and won over various people who were previously unconvinced,' said Cardinal Cormac Murphy-O'Connor, who is bound by the cardinal's oath of secrecy not to say what happened in the actual conclave thereafter. After 26 years of Pope John Paul II no-one wanted another long papacy, so it did not seem to matter that Joseph Ratzinger was 78. Somehow it seemed apt that on his birthday, shortly before the conclave, someone had presented the German cardinal with an arrangement of white and yellow tulips, the papal colours.

Had the Stop Bergoglio dossier not been circulated would it have made any difference to the election given the momentum which was building in Ratzinger's favour? On the first day of the conclave the cardinals began their solemn procession into the Sistine Chapel at 4.30 p.m. It took almost an hour for the 115 cardinal-electors to take their solemn oaths of seriousness and secrecy. Then all outsiders left to the formal cry of *Extra Omnes* (Everybody Out) and the doors were locked – *cum clave* is Latin for 'with a key' – so the voting could begin.

The outcome of all the formal Congregations, and informal meetings, was that attention was focused on four cardinals: Joseph Ratzinger, Carlo Mario Martini, Camillo Ruini (the papal vicar of Rome) and Jorge Mario Bergoglio. Other names were in the air too: Dionigi Tettamanzi who had succeeded Martini in Milan, Angelo Scola of Venice, and the African cardinal Francis Arinze of Nigeria. The Dean asked the assembly if they preferred to vote immediately or retire for the evening. They chose to vote.

On that first ballot, Ratzinger received 47 votes, 30 short of the 77 required to obtain the necessary two-thirds majority. But the real surprise of the first round was that the Argentine, Bergoglio, received 10 votes – one more than the liberals' candidate Martini. Ruini got six and the man who had been Pope John Paul II's chief minister, the Vatican Secretary of State, Cardinal Angelo Sodano, got four. The Honduran cardinal Óscar Rodríguez Maradiaga of Tegucigalpa had three and Tettamanzi of Milan just two. A few others received a single vote.

The cardinals closed the voting for the day and went to dinner. Across the tables in the dining hall, and in small knots in the corridor or in their private rooms, or smoking outside on the patio, the talk was of Bergoglio and how he had beaten his fellow Jesuit Martini. Those who knew a little about him began to exchange information. Some remembered him from the 2001 Synod of Bishops four years earlier. The Archbishop of New York, Cardinal Edward Egan, had been given the job of *relator*, or summarizer of the discussion and conclusions. But the 9/11 terrorist attacks had forced him to return to New York. Pope John Paul II had asked Bergoglio to take over, and some of his peers recalled warmly the collegial nature of his chairmanship. He had topped the poll when bishops elected the Synod Council at the end of the meeting to oversee the implementation of its conclusions. Latin American cardinals remembered the leading role he had played in their continent-wide gathering at Aparecida in 2007.

More intriguingly, the dining-room analysis noted something else. Bergoglio had over the years developed a relationship with one of the new movements of lay people within the Church, Comunione e Liberazione, on which Pope John Paul II had been so keen. Bergoglio had written a chapter in a tribute book to the Italian founder of the movement, Father Luigi Giussani; he had spoken several times at its annual mass gathering in Rimini. This had an additional significance since the movement had previously been seen as the main opposition in Milan to Bergoglio's Jesuit rival, Cardinal Martini.

Bergoglio was tight-lipped over whether or not he wanted to be Pope. Those who are still close friends in Argentina find him hard to read too. Some believe he wanted it, others not. 'Sometimes it's hard to know what a Jesuit is thinking,' one said. Certainly Bergoglio did not campaign behind the scenes. But Cardinal Karl Lehmann, president of the German bishops, began lobbying on his behalf. Cardinal Danneels, Archbishop of Brussels, persuaded a significant group of cardinal-electors from both the North and South Americas to back him. Two senior Vatican bureaucrats among the cardinals swung behind him. They argued that he was an effective unifying alternative to Ratzinger: conservatives could admire him as a man who had held the line against liberalizing currents among the Jesuits and opposed Marxist trends in Liberation Theology; on the other hand moderates could view him as a symbol of the Church's commitment to the poor and the developing world. And conservatives and moderates alike could respect his keen pastoral sense and his personal frugality – a prince of the Church who had given up a grand archbishop's palace for a simple apartment in his episcopal office-block, who cooked his own meals and eschewed a chauffeur-driven limousine in favour of taking the subway and the bus. He was also a man of deep prayer.

Next morning the voting recommenced at 9.30 a.m. Beneath the Latin legend *Eligo in summum pontificem* (I elect as supreme pontiff), each cardinal wrote his selection for Pope on a rectangular ballot paper, disguising his handwriting in accordance with the rules, and folded it lengthwise before posting it in a specially designed voting urn. The second round of voting showed that Ratzinger's votes had risen to 65 but Bergoglio's had more than trebled – to 35, a quarter of the votes. Martini and Ruini received none. The smaller votes of Sodano and Tettamanzi were unaltered.

At 11 a.m. the third round began. This time Ratzinger received 72 votes, 6 short of the 77 needed for the required majority. But Bergoglio got 40 – enough to constitute a blocking minority and prevent Ratzinger from attaining the two-thirds he needed to be declared Pope.

But there was another factor. In 1996 Pope John Paul II had issued a new Apostolic Constitution *Universi Dominici gregis*. It changed the voting system so that, in the event of deadlock, after 34 ballots a simple majority would be all that was required to win. Some of Ratzinger's supporters let it be known that all they had to do was persist in 13 days of inconclusive voting and their candidate would win anyway, for he had already passed the 58 votes needed for a simple majority.

At this decisive point the cardinals broke for lunch. What they shared in their whispered discussions was this question: would the next vote see Ratzinger become Pope? Or had his support peaked, in which case his votes might shift towards another candidate, perhaps Jorge Mario Bergoglio?

Away from the Sistine Chapel the Argentine cardinal knew that in every round he had received the second-highest number of votes. On every round his vote had increased. And the 40 votes he had won in the third ballot were the highest number ever obtained by a Latin American. But he also knew that if enough of Ratzinger's supporters took a hard line they could hold out until the simple majority kicked in. A conclave that long would be bad for the Church's image in the outside world. It would be read as a sign of discord. Later he told friends as much and said that he had felt uncomfortable at the fact that some cardinal-electors had tried to use him to block Ratzinger. This was not, he felt in his heart, the way things should be done.

Bergoglio let it be known – more in gestures than in words – that his supporters should switch their votes to Ratzinger. On the fourth ballot Bergoglio polled just 26 votes; Ratzinger received 84. Joseph Ratzinger was declared Pope and was taken off to the robing room for the new pontiff which is known as the Room of Tears, though it is never specified whether they be of anguish or of joy.

Bergoglio tried to follow, to talk to the new Pope, who had declared, as he accepted, that he would take the name Benedict. The guards would not let him in. The mechanism of the papal court had swung immediately into place to elevate and separate the new shepherd from his sheep. The bells pealed. Out on the balcony, before the waiting multitudes in St Peter's Square, Pope Benedict XVI beamed and raised his arms in clasped exultation like a triumphant prize-fighter.

The next morning in the Sala Clementina on the third floor of the papal apartments Cardinal Jorge Mario Bergoglio paused longer than almost any other cardinal to talk to the new pontiff as he made his obeisance and pledged his loyalty as cardinals have done since the Middle Ages. Some months later Bergoglio had an image of *Mary Untier of Knots* inscribed on a chalice and presented it to the German Pope. Without the dossier, might it have been a different story?

* * *

A pope is sometimes not like the cardinal he was before. As Prefect of the Congregation for the Doctrine of the Faith – the Vatican department previously known as the Supreme Sacred Congregation of the Roman and Universal Inquisition – Joseph Ratzinger had been an upholder of orthodoxy and the scourge of debate and dissent within the Church. But when he became Pope Benedict XVI the man who had infamously been called 'God's Rottweiler' turned into a gentler German shepherd. His views were as clear as before but he expressed them in a different tone. He displayed an unexpectedly gentle smile and, on his international travels, came across as a pope who was open to dialogue with the wider secular world. 'He made us sit up and think,' said Britain's prime minister David Cameron after Benedict's series of sensitively judged but thought-provoking speeches in the UK. But if he was a wise teacher and a gentle pastor, Benedict XVI was a weak governor and a poor politician.

His eight years in office were marked by a series of ill-fated judgements and public relations disasters. These began with his 2006 lecture at Regensburg which offended Muslims around the world, and went on to include the readmission to the Church of a Holocaust-denying bishop, the imposition across the globe of deeply conservative bishops more interested in culture wars than pastoral ministry, and the creation of an Ordinariate to woo traditionalist Anglicans to Rome without consulting the leaders of the Anglican Communion. That was not all. There were new allegations of money-laundering at the scandal-mired Vatican Bank, the imposition of controversial new translations of the Mass, and the disciplining of US nuns considered too liberal on issues such as homosexuality. Relations between the Vatican and Catholic theologians were reduced, in the words of one commentator, to their lowest point since the Reformation.

Hanging over it all was the continuing scandal of the cover-up of priestly sex abuse and a Vatican bureaucracy which was careerist and out of control.

The response of Jorge Mario Bergoglio in Argentina to all this was illuminating. His reaction to the Regensburg row brought him into direct conflict with the Vatican. The incident began with a thoughtful lecture on faith and reason given by Benedict XVI at his old university of Regensburg. In it the new Pope quoted a highly inflammatory remark by a Byzantine emperor linking Islam and violence which he appeared to endorse. Riots followed around the world and Christians died. The Pope, who had not consulted the Vatican's resident experts on Islam, apologized but seemed bemused that remarks which would have gone unnoticed when he was an academic now carried such power.

But Jorge Mario Bergoglio, over in Latin America, understood the implications well enough. Through a spokesman he told *Newsweek Argentina* of his 'unhappiness' with Benedict's words. 'Pope Benedict's statement doesn't reflect my own opinions,' the Archbishop of Buenos Aires declared. 'These statements will serve to destroy in 20 seconds the careful construction of a relationship with Islam that Pope John Paul II built over the last twenty years.' The Vatican was outraged; it demanded he sack his press aide, Father Guillermo Marcó, who had been Bergoglio's public spokesman for eight years and who had been the one to speak to *Newsweek*; Marcó took the blame and stood down, saying he had made the comments not as Bergoglio's spokesman but as president of the Institute of Inter-religious Dialogue. But few believed he had not reflected Bergoglio's thinking. Bergoglio responded by immediately organizing an interfaith meeting, though he demonstrated his political finesse by getting someone else to chair it.

He was similarly unimpressed with Benedict's 2009 decision to lift the excommunication of four schismatic Lefebvrists bishops of the Society of Pius X – one of whom, Bishop Richard Williamson, turned out persistently to insist that millions of Jews were not gassed in Nazi concentration camps. Benedict later admitted a simple internet check might have detected that fact – but so might a call to Bergoglio. Williamson lived in Argentina where he was considered so extreme that even the Lefebvrists expelled him as the head of one of their seminaries there. Bergoglio's friends in Buenos Aires reported that over the years he had numerous problems with the Lefebvrists, both ecclesiologically and politically. 'He saw them as supporters of the military dictatorship,' said Alicia Oliveira. 'He had a lot of problems with them.' It had emerged, during the trials of the military junta when democracy was restored to Argentina, that the founder of the breakaway group, Archbishop Marcel Lefebvre, had travelled to Buenos Aires. There he had congratulated the military on the repression of left-wing dissenters, tens of thousands of whom were tortured and killed by military death squads. Bergoglio saw the Lefebvrists as supporters of the junta.

Nor was Bergoglio enthusiastic about Pope Benedict's attempt the same year to persuade discontented traditionalists inside the Anglican Church to swim the Tiber. Not long after Benedict instituted the Anglican Ordinariate, the Cardinal Archbishop of Buenos Aires telephoned his Anglican counterpart, Gregory Venables, Bishop of Argentina and sometime primate of the Iglesia Anglicana del Cono Sur, and invited him to breakfast. Venables later said Bergoglio had 'told me very clearly that the Ordinariate was quite unnecessary and that the Church needs us as Anglicans'.

The Pope and Bergoglio were moving in opposing directions, too, on the legacy of the Second Vatican Council. For all his lip service to Vatican II, Benedict XVI, like his predecessor John Paul II, clearly felt that many of its reforms had gone too far. Both did their best to dampen the energy and expectation the spirit of the Council had generated within the Church. Benedict, as he grew older, retreated yet further into a sacristy bounded by traditional styles of liturgy, Gregorian chant, Latin and the monarchical robes of the pre-Vatican II Church. His decision to put Pope John Paul II on a super-fast track to sainthood was, in part, an attempt to consolidate the legacy of the past. Meanwhile, in Buenos Aires, the city's cardinal continued to celebrate the liturgy in a free and open style in contemporary vestments, interacting with the congregation in ways designed to connect with the ordinary people. Extreme traditionalists in Buenos Aires complained that Bergoglio had set such conditions around the saying of the Latin Mass that it was almost impossible to find one. Priests who disobeyed the limitations were personally ordered to stop by the man who would later describe Vatican II as 'a great work of the Holy Spirit' and insist there could be no 'turning back the clock'.

* * *

In 2005, when Ratzinger was elected Pope, there were many who hoped that he was the man to bring the necessary reforms to the Curia, which had grown unchecked in the 26-year pontificate of John Paul II. Pope Paul VI was the last pontiff properly to govern the Curia with its Secretariat of State, nine congregations, three tribunals, twelve pontifical councils and various other offices intended to provide support to the Pope. He placed significant power in the hands of the office of his chief minister, the Secretariat of State, and various other Vatican departments, but he required regular meetings of the heads of the different curial offices in the manner of the Cabinet style of administration found in many secular governments. But the practice had lapsed under John Paul II, who allowed the heads of the different departments to govern themselves like independent fiefdoms. So independent were they that the Congregation for Bishops, for example, routinely disregarded Bergoglio's recommendations on episcopal appointments in Argentina, much to his irritation.

At the conclave after the death of Pope John Paul II, who had been globe-trotting parish priest to the world but had let Vatican governance atrophy, cardinals hoped that Ratzinger – whom one described as 'the ultimate insider' – would know how to fix the problem. It did not happen. Instead the system collapsed further under Benedict XVI, who put his supporters in positions of administrative power because he knew and trusted them, rather than because they had the qualities required to do the job. His Secretary of State, Cardinal Tarcisio Bertone, was to come in for particular public criticism from cardinals during the General Congregations in 2013. He was regarded as a Yes man, with no diplomatic experience or linguistic skills, who saw his main job as protecting Benedict from bad news. While Benedict got on with writing his books and private prayer, the different departments of the Roman Curia formed policy and administered the various parts of the Church without consultation or coordination. Some department heads began to behave like medieval barons, jealous of their autonomy and resentful of what they perceived as interference. Rather than reform the Curia, Benedict just ignored it.

Eventually it all got too much for the German Pope. His health was deteriorating. His hearing had worsened. He could not see with his left eye. His body had become so thin that the tailors had difficulty keeping up with newly fitted clothes. By the end of 2012, his biographer the German journalist Peter Seewald said: 'I'd never seen him so exhausted-looking, so worn down.' In March 2012 on a trip to Mexico and Cuba he lost his balance in his room and fell, hitting his head on a bathroom sink. The accident was kept secret by the Vatican but for the failing Pope it was a decisive moment. When he returned from the gruelling trip he spent many hours praying before the large bronze figure of Christ which looked down from the wall of his small private chapel in his apartments in the Apostolic Palace. Before him, also, was the memory of how John Paul II had chosen to die in public; there was an almost carnivalesque atmosphere to those final dying days of which the austere reserved Bavarian disapproved. After long prayer he decided to do something which no Pope had done for 598 years, since Pope Gregory XII in 1415 stepped down to end the Western Schism between rival popes and anti-popes, each recognized by different factions and kingdoms within the Catholic Church. He would resign.

For a long time he kept the decision to himself. He wanted to time the announcement to cause minimum disruption to the liturgical life of the Church. After Pentecost or before Lent were the obvious times. But before he could make an announcement a new drama hit the Church, which had been reeling for years as it staggered from one crisis to another. It shook Benedict's already shaky confidence to the core.

On 23 May 2012 the Pope's personal butler, Paolo Gabriele, was arrested and charged with stealing sensitive documents from the pontiff's desk – and leaking them to the media. Gabriele was one of a handful of people who had a key to an elevator that led to the Pope's private apartments. He had been Benedict's butler for six years. The Pope, insiders said, regarded him like a son. The betrayal was devastating.

Much of the media reported the affair as if it were a comic caper. 'What the Butler Leaked' was just too good a headline. Yet when Gabriele was prosecuted, anyone who followed the court case more closely realized the affair was devastating in a different way. Gabriele had passed to a journalist papers that the Pope had marked 'to be destroyed' and he had done it not for venal motives, but out of a sense of violated loyalty because he was worried about the extent to which underlings were pulling the wool over the pontiff's eyes.

The leaked documents revealed scandalous intrigue and in-fighting, ambition and arrogance, greed and glory-seeking, clerical careerism and corruption, secrecy and sexual lapses in the Vatican civil service. And they showed the Pope to be an intellectual who, ill at ease with the day-to-day running of the Church, let himself become isolated in the Vatican. The butler was not so much a traitor as a whistle-blower.

The story which emerged was of a Pope who had begun to be out-manoeuvred by those who were supposed to serve him. It had started at least five years earlier when Benedict was persuaded by Rome's vested interests to move a Curia reformer, Archbishop Carlo Maria Viganò, formerly the Vatican City's second-highest ranking administrator, and 'promote' him to be papal ambassador to the United States. Viganò had been clamping down on internal waste and corrupt practices that cost the Holy See millions in higher contract prices. Projects were routinely being assigned to the same companies at twice the normal commercial cost. By putting an end to such practices Viganò had turned a Vatican City deficit of €8 million into a profit of €34 million in just one year. The corrupt Vatican old guard hated him for it. One of the leaked letters was a plea to the Pope from Viganò not to be moved before the job was done. But Viganò was smeared by his opponents, who got Benedict to move him out of their way to Washington. Other documents in the affair the media dubbed Vatileaks revealed the attempts of vested interests to resist efforts to reform the Vatican Bank by blocking proposals for greater financial transparency and complying with international norms to fight money-laundering. There were also tales of wealthy individuals and bodies paying large sums to secure an audience with the pontiff.

The impact of all this on Pope Benedict was shattering. 'He was never the same after that,' one intimate of the pontiff said. The Pope appointed a commission of three cardinals to investigate the leaks. They handed their 300-page report to the Pope on 17 December 2012. He locked it in a safe in the papal apartments for his successor to handle. Then Benedict visited his butler in jail, where he had languished since being convicted in October, and pardoned him. Gabriele was released three days before Christmas.

But if the Vatican's self-serving bureaucracy thought their entrenched resistance had defeated Benedict XVI they were wrong. Just after 11.30 a.m. on the morning of 11 February a group of cardinals gathered in the Sala del Concistoro in the Apostolic Palace to hear the Pope announce a new collection of saints. He spoke in Latin and many of the cardinals allowed their mind to wander to such an extent that they did not notice Benedict had appended an addendum. He had written the 350-word statement himself and sent it to a Latin expert in the Secretariat of State to make sure the grammar was correct. The translator had been sworn to secrecy. Benedict now read the words from the dead language in a weak but steady voice. To run the Church, it said, 'both strength of mind and body are necessary, strength which in the last few months, has deteriorated in me to the extent that I have had to recognize my incapacity to adequately fulfil the ministry entrusted to me'. The cardinals exchanged silent glances, some stunned, others unsure of what they had heard, as the pontiff left the room.

News of Benedict's resignation was so surprising that when an official from Rome called Cardinal Scola, who by now had been promoted to Milan, he refused to believe the news. Benedict had decided that heads in the Vatican should roll but he knew that he did not have the operational grip to know how to get rid of the Machiavellian characters who had been deceiving him for years. So he came up with a response none of them could have anticipated: that his own head should be the one to roll. By this device he checkmated his opponents entirely.

History may well determine Benedict XVI's resignation to be the defining act of his papacy – and his greatest service to the Church. Becoming the first Pope in modern times to stand down, he redefined the papacy as a job, rather than a vocation, with particular tasks and targets, which may be set aside when the time is ripe. He has set a benchmark. Future popes who find they are not up to the job will feel liberated, or indeed may come under pressure, to retire. His final act may turn out to be his most modernizing.

Had the Stop Bergoglio dossier not been sent, might things have been different? Perhaps a pope who was a true outsider would have been better placed to resist the machinations of the Curia. A man who had governed his own archdiocese as a distinctive leader for more than a decade might well have achieved what proved impossible to a man who had spent decades working as a faithful lieutenant to a charismatic master like John Paul II.

History has no answer to such speculations. But what was certain was that, even as Benedict floundered, Jorge Mario Bergoglio was consolidating his influence and reputation within the Church. Within seven months of coming runner-up in the 2005 conclave Bergoglio was voted head of Argentina's Conference of Bishops. Two years later he was elected president of the commission of his entire continent's gathering of bishops at Aparecida and given responsibility for writing that meeting's final summarizing document. It lamented the fact that a process of secularization in Latin America is arresting the faith which has animated the life of the continent for five centuries. And it endorsed firmly the 'preferential option for the poor' which those same bishops and their predecessors had set out at the seminal meetings of the Consejo Episcopal Latino Americano (CELAM), the Latin American bishops' conference, at Medellín in 1968 and Puebla in 1979. The 'unjust distribution of goods', it said, created a situation of 'social sin'.

The way forward, the Aparecida document set out, was to put 'poor people's culture' at the centre and get rid of all the 'transient structures that no longer encourage the transmission of the faith'. The people of South America would not receive the Good News 'from evangelizers who are dejected, discouraged, impatient and anxious' but from 'ministers who have primarily received the joy of Christ in themselves'. That means bishops who walk every day alongside their people. It means priests who do not live secluded in their parishes but who are to be found in the streets, in soup kitchens, in schools, in all the endless social and charitable works where they truly come across people's struggle to continue. 'Only within the concrete circumstances of daily life', it concluded, 'can one share in the faith and joy for the living presence of Christ.'

The conference lasted three weeks. In all that time only one homily provoked applause. It was given by Jorge Mario Bergoglio. During the conference breaks the other participants sought out the cardinal to talk and have their photograph taken alongside him as they would with a celebrity. But this was no rock star or sporting legend; it was a man who had crystallized a new vision for the Church, combining social justice, poor people's culture and spreading the good news of the Gospel to those outside the Church. Even as Pope Benedict was weakening, Bergoglio was going from strength to strength.

Perhaps in his heart he pondered with gratitude how fortunate he had been not to have been handed Benedict XVI's poisoned chalice. Or perhaps he thought how different things might have been had the outcome of the 2005 conclave been different. His friends are not so sure. 'Pope John Paul II was a hard act to follow,' one cardinal told me. 'Perhaps the Holy Spirit held off until the house was collapsing around our ears. God is good at writing straight with crooked lines.'

On his continuing visits to Rome Bergoglio stayed, as he always had, in the Domus Internationalis Paulus VI clergy house in Via della Scrofa in the heart of Rome. The floors are made of marble but the rooms are spartan. It is some considerable distance from the Vatican but it allowed Bergoglio a chance to walk through the cobblestone byways, past the shops and bars, homes and banks, monuments and churches in which the people of the city and its visitors live out the routine of daily existence with its chores, trials and small acts of kindness and love. His dark overcoat covered his pectoral cross and he did not wear his cardinal's red skull cap. He was among the ordinary people. When he returned from his Vatican meetings he would eat at the common table with the other visiting clergy. Most did not give him more than a glance. They knew he was the Nearly Man who, back in 2005, at the age of 68, had missed his chance. You didn't get a second chance, did you?

'Back then, in 2005, wasn't his moment,' said one close friend in Buenos Aires who still gets weekly phone calls from Bergoglio in Rome on a Sunday afternoon. 'Things needed to get a lot worse for the Church before they would be brave enough to choose Bergoglio. God knows what he's doing.'

2

The Common Touch

The crowd to see the new Pope was enormous. St Peter's Square was filled with an excited mass of people, shouting and laughing and pushing forward as the long white popemobile containing Francis swung through the roped-off pathways between the tens of thousands of visitors. Flags of many nations waved. Pilgrims and tourists shouted, giddy in the windy day. Parents held up their bewildered toddlers to be blessed as he passed. Some thrust their babies to security men to be raised aloft, so the Pope could ruffle their hair or kiss the top of their head. The joy was infectious.

How Pope Francis could have spotted a single individual amid the tumult is a mystery. But, all at once, he instructed his driver to stop. He climbed down to the line of people, waving and shaking the hands extended towards him. Then he stopped before a tiny woman in black with a walnut wizened face. Grabbing his arms she spoke volubly, a torrent of words gushing over him. She was too far away for me to hear what language she was speaking. But whether he knew her or not, whether her words made sense, he took her ancient face in his two great hands and cradled it with huge tenderness. His grandmother, Rosa Margherita Vassallo Bergoglio, had lived to see him ordained a priest. But how proud she would have been to see her eldest grandson as Pope. This, he must have known, is how she would have reacted.

It was Grandma Rosa who had taught him to pray and educated him in the faith. She had arrived in Argentina from Italy in 1929, just seven years before her grandson was born. Family legend has it she came down the gangplank of the steamship *Giulio Cesare* on a sweltering morning wearing a full-length fox fur, not because she had failed to appreciate that she would be arriving in the southern hemisphere where January would be high summer, but because sewn into its lining was the entire proceeds of the sale of the family's home and café back in Piedmont. With her in the third-class quarters of the ship had been her husband Giovanni and her son Mario José Bergoglio. They were late. The sale of their assets had been delayed and they had had to change their tickets in Genoa from those they originally had. Providentially, it transpired, for their original ship – the ocean liner *Principessa Mafalda* – had fractured a propeller shaft which pierced the hull. The ship sank in the Atlantic with the loss of 314 lives, most of them from the steerage class in which the Bergoglio family would have travelled.

Five years later Mario met a young woman, Regina María Sívori, an Argentinian whose family were originally from Genoa, at Mass in the San Antonio Chapel in the Almagro neighbourhood of Buenos Aires where they lived. Within twelve months they were married. The future Pope Francis was born Jorge Mario Bergoglio a year later on 17 December 1936 and was baptized eight days afterwards on Christmas Day.

Though he was born an Argentine, Jorge Mario Bergoglio was raised on pasta and in a culture and a faith tradition which were distinctively Italian. Since he was the first of five children Jorge was, in his early years, collected from his home by his grandmother every morning. He then spent the day at her home around the corner, returning only in the evening. As a result, of all his brothers and sisters, Bergoglio was the one who 'took the family's traditions most to heart', he later said. His grandparents spoke Piedmontese to one another and he learned it from them. 'They loved all of my siblings, but I had the privilege of understanding the language of their memories.' That is why today Pope Francis is completely fluent in Italian as well as Spanish, and can get by in German, French, Portuguese and English as well as Latin. He can also sing a few risqué songs in the Genoese dialect, thanks to a reprobate great uncle.

His father's brothers were confectioners and when they visited the family home his father would switch to Italian too, though he discouraged his children from speaking it; he wanted them to be fully Argentinian. Mario and his brothers were veterans of the First World War and would talk about their experiences and discuss the rise of Mussolini in their homeland, of which Mario disapproved.

Mario José Bergoglio was an accountant by trade. But, because his Italian qualifications were not recognized in Argentina, he took a lower-status job as a book-keeper in a hosiery factory. He earned less than he should have, but he was a cheerful man who did not show any resentment. The family was comfortably off though they had no luxuries. 'We had nothing to spare, no car, and didn't go away on holiday over the summer, but we still never wanted for anything,' Bergoglio has said.

Jorge, and his sister María Elena, who is his junior by over a decade, are the only two of the siblings still alive. They recall a happy childhood despite the fact that their mother was paralysed for more than a year after the birth of her fifth child. Jorge and his siblings would help with the cooking.

He recalls getting home from school to find her sitting, peeling potatoes, with all the other ingredients laid out on the kitchen table. She would then instruct them how to do the cooking. 'We all know how to do it, at the very least *cotoletta alla milanese*,' Bergoglio said. The skill has come in useful throughout his career; he cooked for the other students at seminary on Sundays when the chef was off; he fixed his own meals as an archbishop in Buenos Aires though in the Casa Santa Marta he usually eats in its cafeteria.

When he was 13 he was shocked to hear his father announce it was time for him to start work. He had just begun a six-year vocational course at the Escuela Nacional de Educación Técnica leading to a diploma as a chemical technician. The school hours were from 8 a.m. to 1 p.m. so his father arranged for him to work from 2 p.m. to 8 p.m. in the hosiery factory. After two years as a cleaner, and then a third doing clerical work, he got a job in a food laboratory. 'I had an extraordinary boss there, Esther de Balestrino de Careaga, a Paraguayan woman and communist sympathizer,' Bergoglio later told the interviewers Francesca Ambrogetti and Sergio Rubin who published *El Jesuita*, a book of autobiographical interviews with Bergoglio in 2010. Esther taught him a key lesson about work: that a job needs to be done properly. 'I remember that when I handed her an analysis she'd say, "Wow, you did that so fast" and then she asked "Did you do the test or not?" I would answer, "What for, if I've done all the previous tests it would surely be more or less the same." And she would chide me: "No, you have to do things properly." She taught me the seriousness of hard work. I owe a huge amount to that great woman.' Looking back he feels very grateful to his father for making him take those part-time jobs. 'The work I did was one of the best things I've done in my life. In particular, in the laboratory I got to see the good and bad of human endeavour.' Later, as a student, he had various other jobs, one as a bouncer at a Buenos Aires nightclub, an occupation which delighted the media when he became Pope.

It also taught him something about how work confers dignity upon an individual, a theme to which he regularly returned as an archbishop and as Pope. 'Unemployed people are made to feel like they don't really exist,' he has said. 'Dignity is not conferred by one's ancestry, family life or education. Dignity comes solely from work…It's very important that governments cultivate a culture of work.' That is, he says, a key part of Catholic Social Teaching. But so is the principle of work–life balance. 'One of the questions I would ask young parents during confession is whether or not they spend time playing with their children. Many go to work before the children wake up and come home after they've gone to sleep. And on weekends, overwhelmed by tiredness, they don't pay attention to them like they should. Too much work dehumanizes people. Man is not for work; rather, work is for man.'

Family leisure was a key part of his childhood. He treasures the memory of Saturday afternoons when his mother would make all the children listen with her to the 2 p.m. broadcasts of complete operas. 'She'd sit us around the radio and before the opera got underway, she'd explain what it was about. Saturday afternoons with my mother and siblings, enjoying music, was a wonderful time.' Today he still listens to classical music to relax before bed. Mozart, Beethoven, Bach and Wagner are favourites. He reads fiction too, with Dostoevsky, Manzoni and Borges among the authors he most frequently revisits.

* * *

But his family was, above all, where his deep faith was nurtured. When he was baptized it was his grandmother Rosa who came forward to be his godmother. It was she who taught the young Jorge how to pray. 'She had a big influence on my faith,' he recalled in a radio interview in 2012. His grandfather would tell him stories about the First World War but 'she'd tell me stories about the saints. She left a deep spiritual imprint in me.' His sister María Elena remembers she did not just go to church on Sundays: 'Grandma Rosa was very devoted; very, very devoted to the *Santisimo* (Jesus). We all used to pray the rosary with her. Jorge was particularly devoted to the Virgin.' María Elena is in no doubt that his grandmother was responsible at least in part for her brother's vocation to the priesthood. Bergoglio himself has quoted lines the nineteenth-century German poet Friedrich Hölderlin dedicated to his own grandmother; they end 'may the man not betray what he promised as a child'. For Bergoglio the poem reminds him that 'I feel a special devotion to my grandmother for all that she gave me in the first years of my life.' Bergoglio has regularly lamented the fact that the grandparent's role has 'gradually fallen by the wayside' in a society where we shove 'our elders into nursing homes with a couple of mothballs in their pockets as if they were an old overcoat'. Being with our grandparents, he said, brings us face to face with our past.

Grandma Rosa transmitted a similar strength of faith to her son, Mario, who in his own turn passed his on to his children. Mario would gather his family to pray the rosary before dinner. He encouraged his son, while still in primary school at Wilfrid Barón de los Santos Ángeles, to rise hours before his classmates so that he could serve Mass for one of the school's Salesian priests, a Ukrainian named Father Stefan Czmil, from whom he learned of the Eastern Rite used by Catholics in Orthodox lands Bergoglio later recalled, a puritanical streak to the religion he inherited; divorced or separated people were not allowed to enter the family home and the Bergoglios were suspicious of Protestants, though he recalls when he was about six years old being told by Grandma Rosa that two women from the Salvation Army were 'Protestants, but they are good'. The boy Jorge was sufficiently zealous that when he arrived in high school he sought permission to ask classmates if they had made their first Holy Communion. When it transpired that four had not, 13-year-old Bergoglio gave them catechesis in the sacrament. He was shocked, about the same time, when someone died from a heart attack at a family wedding, to hear a relative doubt the existence of God.

The religious worldview in which Bergoglio was enfolded as a boy was one of security and certainty. It took God for granted. Faith was as much about what you did as what you thought. His boyhood church, San José in the lower-middle-class Flores district of Buenos Aires, still shows that today. I visited it one Saturday afternoon and found a busy bustling place, high-vaulted and imposing, ornate and gilded in the rococo style, but bursting with colour and activity. At the front a couple of hundred people were gathered for a christening. The priest was engaging them with an interactive style of sermon in which he asked questions and the congregation shouted replies. I have seen Bergoglio do the same with a great crowd of children at his annual Mass for the children of the archdiocese. It is the style of the *porteños*, the slang-term which residents of Buenos Aires use of themselves; it has its roots in the fact that the city grew from a busy port and conveys something of the swagger and self-assurance found in dockers all over the world. 'We're the New Yorkers of Latin America,' one told me, laughing. In the side aisles of the church, individuals of all ages were engaged in private prayer, moving in and out of the dark confessionals, progressing down the side aisles in contemplation of the cornucopia of religious murals, brooding paintings, passionate crucifixes, golden effigies and brightly painted statues. The church was a burst of colour and sound, as busy as the notice board with the paraphernalia of rosaries, novenas, pilgrimages and processions.

In pride of place, near the door at the back of the church, was a statue of Nuestra Señora de Luján, the patron saint of Argentina, whose story summarizes the popular piety of the place. Copies of the celebrated icon of the Virgin, depicted with a long trailing gown of lace like the vapour trail of a rising rocket, have been replicated everywhere in Argentina since the day the original arrived in 1630. The image of Mary Immaculate had been made in Brazil and had disembarked in the port of Buenos Aires to be transported to a settler in Santiago. But the oxen pulling the cart stopped unaccountably in Luján and refused to move, despite all manner of cajoling. Only when the cart containing the statue was unloaded would they continue their journey with the rest of their cargo. A local peasant was so amazed at the miraculous determination of the Virgin to remain there that he set up a small shrine in her honour. Last year 1.5 million people went there in pilgrimage. Many intellectuals discount such legends as the residue of a superstitious peasant religion. Bergoglio never has, and that faultline was one of the subjects of the entrenched disputes he was to have in later years within the Jesuit order (see Chapter Three).

But as a young man there was more to life for Bergoglio than religion. As a boy he was a keen footballer – 'never seen without a ball at his feet', according to one of the nuns who were his first teachers. His father would take him to see San Lorenzo, the soccer team local to the Almagro neighbourhood in which Bergoglio senior had first settled on arrival in Buenos Aires. The team had originally been started by a priest to keep the local lads off the streets and out of trouble. Bergoglio has remained a lifelong supporter, attending matches for many years, though as he became busier with his pastoral work he tended to listen on the radio while doing routine administrative tasks. In 2011 he celebrated Mass for the club before posing with the players and holding up a team jersey for photographers. The Saturday after Bergoglio was made Pope the team trotted out for their next match with a photo of the new pontiff on the centre of their kit.

As a teenager he loved to dance. He was good at the tango, Argentina's celebrated national dance, but he preferred the *milonga*, its faster forerunner. He enjoyed the company of young women. Indeed, according to his sister María Elena, he was planning to propose to one of the girls at his school's annual Student Day picnic one spring morning in September – but something happened on the way. On impulse, passing the family church of San José de Flores, he popped in to say a prayer. There he encountered a new priest whom he had never met before. Bergoglio was struck by a sense of deep spirituality about the man and asked to go to confession with him. 'A strange thing happened to me in that confession,' he later told Rubin and Ambrogetti. 'I don't know what it was, but it changed my life ... It was a surprise, the astonishment of a chance encounter ... the astonishment of encountering someone who was waiting for you all along ... God is the one who seeks us first.' The priest to whom he made his confession, Father Carlos Duarte Ibarra, died within twelve months.

In later years Bergoglio reflected on that moment as one in which he had been chosen. When he became a bishop he adopted as his episcopal motto *miserando atque eligendo*. It comes from a comment by the Venerable Bede on the Gospel passage in which Jesus met the despised tax collector Matthew.

Translated it means 'unworthy but chosen', though Bergoglio likes to translate it rather more cumbersomely as 'he saw him through the eyes of mercy and chose him'. He now sees in that motto the moment he uncovered his vocation. 'That was how I felt that God saw me during that conversation. And that is the way he wants me always to look upon others: with much compassion and as if I were choosing them for him; not excluding anyone, because everyone is chosen by the love of God...It is one of the centrepieces of my religious experience.' Religion must contain such a measure of astonishment.

'I don't know what happened,' he later told an Argentine radio station. 'But I knew I had to become a priest.' He could not face the school picnic outing and the girl to whom he had intended to propose, so he went home instead.

But the 17-year-old did not act upon his decision for four years. 'My thoughts were not focused only on religious matters. I also had political concerns,' he has said. The young Bergoglio had become aware of politics early on. When he was at primary school something else happened which was to shape the churchman that Jorge Mario Bergoglio was to become. His mother's father was a carpenter. Once a week a man with a beard, named Don Elpidio, would come and sell him aniline dyes. His grandmother would serve the two men a cup of tea with wine as they chatted on the patio. One day, after the man had gone, his grandmother asked the young Bergoglio if he knew who the visitor was. It turned out that he was Elpidio González, who was once the vice-president of Argentina. Bergoglio was struck by the honesty and integrity of a man who had not corruptly profited from high office but had been content to return to the modest income of a dye salesman. 'Something has happened to our politics,' he later mused. 'It is out of ideas...'

As he became a teenager Bergoglio became fascinated by political issues. Elpidio González had been a member of Argentina's Radical Party. But the young Bergoglio was also intrigued by the ideas of communism. 'I had a political restlessness,' he later said, which was part of his growing intellectual exploration of the world. He devoured a Communist Party periodical *Nuestra Palabra y Proposito* and was particularly influenced by the articles of their celebrated cultural commentator Leónidas Barletta. 'It helped me in my political education, though I was never a Communist.' Yet he cherished too a Communist teacher at his high school. 'We had a wonderful relationship with him, he questioned us about everything and it was good for us, but he never lied to us. He always told us where he was coming from, what his hermeneutic and his worldview were.' As the years went by, however, the politics of Argentina polarized and as the Left became more atheistic and anti-clerical, Bergoglio more fully embraced Peronism (see Chapter Three), that peculiarly Argentinian political amalgam which sought to bring together the army, the unions and the Church in a vision of national unity with a distinctly authoritarian streak. Bergoglio was drawn to Peronism from when he was at school.

* * *

Throughout all this, Bergoglio's sense of vocation consolidated. When he graduated from technical school, with a diploma in applied chemistry, he told his mother that he intended to study medicine. Delighted, she cleared the attic overlooking the terrace of the family home 'so that he could study in peace, away from the rest of us', his sister María Elena recalled. Every day, after his morning job in the lab, he would arrive home and disappear into the room and work diligently. But one day, when he was out at work, his mother decided to clean his study. To her surprise she did not find text books on anatomy or pharmacology but only tomes on theology, many of them in Latin. When Jorge came home she confronted him.

'You said you were studying medicine,' she said, perturbed.

'I didn't lie to you,' Bergoglio responded coolly. 'I'm studying medicine – but medicine of the soul.'

His mother was angry and extremely upset. She told him to wait until he had finished university before making such a momentous decision. When, aged 21, he decided to enter a seminary, he told his father first and let him break the news to his mother. Mario could be stern but Bergoglio knew he would be pleased by his decision. But his mother was so upset she refused to go with her son when he entered the seminary. Bergoglio later put his parents' differing reactions down to the fact that his father was an immigrant, which had helped him understand that strength as well as pain can come from being uprooted. His mother, who had been born in Argentina, by contrast, he said, 'experienced it as a plundering'. It was four years before she was reconciled to his decision and he only knew she had fully accepted it when she knelt before him after he had been ordained a priest, 11 years later, and asked for his blessing.

Having come to the priesthood relatively late for that era, at the age of 21, he decided, not long after enrolling in San Miguel seminary in Buenos Aires, to join the Jesuits who ran the philosophy and theology courses there. He later explained the attraction: 'Three things in particular struck me about the Society: the missionary spirit, community and discipline. And this is strange, because I am a really, really undisciplined person. But their discipline, the way they manage their time – these things struck me so much.' As a teenager his spiritual director had been a Salesian, Father Enrique Pozzoli, but Bergoglio was now drawn to the military symbolism which has imbued the Jesuit order since it began in the sixteenth century. It was founded by the soldier-turned-mystic Ignatius Loyola as he was recovering from wounds received on the battlefield. Loyola conceived the order's charism as one of being 'contemplatives in action'. 'I was attracted to its position on, to put it in military terms, the front lines of the Church,' he said. He also liked the Ignatian tradition of intellectual and spiritual rigour and its emphasis on missionary work and had a hankering after becoming a Jesuit missionary in Japan.

It was not to be. Not long after entering the seminary the 21-year-old came down with a mysterious fever. For three days and nights he was on the brink of death. Eventually the worried doctors diagnosed that he had pneumonia caused by three cysts in his right lung. His life was saved only by the removal of the upper part of the lung. He recovered, but his impaired breathing capacity put paid to the idea of working overseas. The pain, he later said, was tremendous. The drainage tubes in his lung were also extremely uncomfortable. Visitors tried to cheer him up with the usual comforting banalities but he was not placated, until he was visited by the nun who had prepared him for his first Communion, Sister Dolores Tortolo. 'She said something that truly stuck with me,' he later recalled, 'and made me feel at peace'. 'You are imitating Christ,' he was told. Coming face to face with death strengthened his sense of what is important, and what is ultimately peripheral, in life. It strengthened his faith. It is, he later decided, a gift to understand and fully live through pain. 'Pain is not a virtue in itself,' he concluded, 'but you can be virtuous in the way you bear it'. Despite the severity of the experience it has not much impaired his physical ability, though breathing restrictions have produced some pain in the lower back, inducing sciatica, which is why today he needs special shoes and, occasionally, walks with a stick.

His was not an unswerving vocation. At one point in his seminary career he became besotted by a young woman he met at a family wedding. 'I was surprised by her beauty, the clarity of her intellect... and, well, I kicked the idea around for a while. When I returned to the seminary after the wedding, I could not pray during the entire week because when I prepared to pray, the girl appeared in my mind. I had to think about my choice again.' Eventually he reaffirmed his commitment to become a priest though he added: 'it would be abnormal for these types of things not to happen'.

In all this, Grandma Rosa, both before and after her death in the mid-1970s, was to Bergoglio a supportive and sustaining presence. His breviary is the first thing he opens in the morning and last thing be closes at night. Inside it he carries two pieces of paper. One is a letter she wrote in 1967, half in Italian and half in Spanish, two years before his ordination. It was written because she feared she might die before the great day arrived when he would become a priest and, in that event, she left it to be handed to him on the day. Fortunately she was there to give it to him in person. It read: 'On this beautiful day on which you hold Christ our saviour in your consecrated hands, and on which a broad path to a deeper apostolate is opening up before you, I bequeath to you this humble gift, of very little material but very great spiritual value.' With it came a personal creed she had written for herself in the form of a spiritual last will and testament. In one paragraph she wrote:

> May these, my grandchildren, to whom I gave the best my heart has to offer, have long and happy lives, but if someday sorrow, sickness, or the loss of a beloved person should fill them with distress, let them remember that a sigh directed toward the tabernacle, home to the greatest and noblest martyr, and a look to Mary at the foot of the Cross, can drop a soothing balm onto the deepest and most painful of wounds.

* * *

Jorge Mario Bergoglio has remained faithful to that, and to the style of spirituality with which Grandma Rosa imbued him. In an order as intellectual as the Jesuits he has had to find ways of reconciling to criticisms that he is pandering to the superstitions of folk religion. Another Argentinian Jesuit, Father Humberto Miguel Yáñez, who is now the head of the moral theology department at the Gregorian University in Rome, thinks Bergoglio has done that. 'He has always had a favourable attitude to popular religiosity,' said Yáñez. 'Some see it as including an element of superstition which is not part of the faith and some bishops were against that. But Bergoglio saw it as an important way that people linked to the spiritual. His influence gradually shaped a different culture among the bishops of Argentina, among other things pushing them to be much closer to their own priests.'

Any movement in that direction in the wider Church will be a significant departure. Benedict XVI was far more cautious about popular piety. 'Through it, faith has entered into men's heart, forming part of their sentiments, customs, feeling and common living,' he acknowledged to the Latin American bishops gathered at Aparecida in 2007. 'Faith has become flesh and blood. That is why popular piety is a great patrimony of the Church.' But he warned:

> It cannot be denied, however, that certain deviated forms exist of popular religiosity that, far from fomenting an active participation in the Church, create instead confusion and can foster a merely exterior religious practice detached from a well-rooted and interior

living faith. Popular piety can incline toward the irrational and perhaps also remain on the outside. Popular piety must certainly always be purified and point to the centre.

Bergoglio has always been a good deal less suspicious. His devotion to popular piety was, as we shall see in the next chapter, to cause a deep rift within Argentina's Jesuits.

The popular devotion to a woman named the *Difunta Correa* is a good example of the way popular piety is being accepted into the mainstream, Yáñez said. She died around 1840 in his own home province of San Juan in Argentina. 'She was a widow so consumed with grief when her husband died she walked into the desert carrying her infant child. She died of thirst but her breasts continued to produce milk to nourish her child.' Her body was found days later by *gauchos* driving cattle nearby. To their astonishment they found the baby still alive, feeding from the dead woman's 'miraculously' ever-full breast. Her devotees, who now number in their hundreds of thousands, believe she still intercedes for the living to perform more miracles. 'Her cult was for years not recognized by the Church,' said Yáñez. 'But nowadays the bishops do not discourage it. What Bergoglio thinks is that these are important ways through which the ordinary people express their spirituality and the Church should be part of that.' Bergoglio, he recalls, organized an international conference on the relationship between faith and culture towards the end of his time as leader of the province's Jesuits. 'Bergoglio understands that the attitudes of people like those who follow the Difunta creates a place where faith and culture meet.'

Bergoglio's frequent references to the Devil offer another example of his ease with combining the two approaches. After Vatican II many Catholic priests and theologians dispensed with the Devil, preferring to see evil in more abstract terms. But Bergoglio does not. He is what another Jesuit called 'a more concrete person with a more folksy religiosity' and yet the founder of the Jesuits, St Ignatius Loyola, very much saw the Devil as a person, a fallen angel. That idea still remains common in Catholic spirituality though some Jesuits tend to emphasize it more than others. 'Bergoglio's attitude to popular religiosity is that you don't judge it, you work alongside it,' said Father Augusto Zampini, a diocesan priest who taught at the Colegio Máximo where Bergoglio was once Rector. 'To disregard popular faith is in a way to disregard the option for the poor. Bergoglio would say: "This has to do with the Spirit; let's work with it, rather than against it."'

Argentinian Catholicism is replete with examples of this folk religion, which the nation's theologians prefer to call *teología del pueblo* – the Theology of the People. Cars carry bumper-stickers invoking *Gauchito Gil*, a legendary Robin

Hood character from the eighteenth century, whom devotees insist protects drivers. St Cayetano is upheld as the patron saint of bread and work. St Expedito is the saint of urgent cases. St Pantaleon, doctor and martyr, protects from the grippe, the flu and other illnesses of the winter season. 'There is a calendar of saints' days, a saint for health, a saint for work and so on. Father Bergoglio loves all that,' says Father Guillermo Marcó, who was for eight years Bergoglio's public spokesman in the archdiocese of Buenos Aires. The foreign incomers into the slums of Buenos Aires also bring with them their own Virgins – Nuestra Señora de Caacupé from Paraguay, Nuestra Señora de Copacabana from Bolivia and Nuestra Señora de Cuzco from Peru. Saints and manifestations of the Madonna appear through popular acclamation by simple folk who make bargains with them, like the woman in one shanty-town in Bergoglio's former diocese who has converted her home into a chapel and provides lunches for 40 hungry children a day because she promised St Cayetano she would do that if the saint found her husband a job.

In all this, Bergoglio is 'a man very close to popular devotion', said Father Francisco de Roux, the Provincial Superior of the Jesuits in Colombia. 'He is a man of popular piety. He captures the experience of God in the simplicity of popular practices, processions, shrines, the Christmas novena, the family saying the rosary. To him the strength of Catholicism is in the way simple people live their faith.' The approach is summed up in the chalice designed in Argentinian silver for Pope Francis by a local goldsmith, Juan Carlos Pallarols. It features images of Our Lady of Luján, Mary Untier of Knots, Jesuit symbols and an Argentine icon.

All this is not some strategy of Bergoglio's to keep close to the people; it goes to the core of his being. A small order named the Franciscan Friars of the Immaculate posted an item on their webpage after Pope Francis was elected. They had noticed, ten years previously, that whenever all the cardinals were in Rome, at 9 a.m. every morning a middle-aged man would come into their little church dedicated to the Virgin of the Annunciation in Lungotevere not far from St Peter's basilica in Rome. They were intrigued, not just by his clockwork timekeeping – Bergoglio is an extremely punctual man – but by the fact that he always went straight to a statue of St Thérèse of the Child Jesus and prayed before it with great devotion. 'At the end of the prayer,' they wrote, 'he used to do as many old ladies – who are sometimes looked down upon in this country – do; he touched the statue and kissed it.' Then one day they noticed the man had red buttons on his cassock. Alone and unobserved Cardinal Jorge Mario Bergoglio, Archbishop of Buenos Aires, was at prayer in the way that Grandma Rosa would have been.

* * *

'I remember two rhymes from my grandmother,' Bergoglio said in *On Heaven and Earth*, his book of conversations with the Argentinian rabbi Abraham Skorka.

See that God watches you,
See that He is watching you
See that you will have to die
And you do not know when.

'She had that saying under the glass top of her little nightstand, and each time that she went to bed she would read it. After seventy years I still have not forgotten it. There is another rhyme that she told me that she had read at an Italian cemetery:

Man who walks,
stop and think
about your pace,
your steps,
the final step.

'She impressed on me the awareness that everything must end, that everything has to be left behind in good order. With respect to the Christian life, death has to accompany you on the way. In my case, for example, I think every day that I am going to die. This does not distress me, because the Lord and life have given me the proper preparation. I saw my ancestors die and now it is my turn. When? I do not know.'

His thoughts turned to a previous pope. 'John XXIII, until the moment of his death, continued being a rural peasant. On his death bed, his sister placed on his head cold cloths with vinegar, just like they did in the country.' Had Bergoglio been elected Pope in 2005, he subsequently told a confidant, he would have taken the name John in honour of that good peasant pope. When the time came he chose a different name. But it is hard to believe that Jorge Mario Bergoglio, likewise, will ever leave behind the popular spirituality of his devotional roots.

3

Jesuit Secrets

It was not exactly an endorsement. As soon as the name of the new Pope had been announced the internet buzzed with emails. Who was Jorge Mario Bergoglio? What was he like? Members of the Jesuit order were particular targets for these inquiries. What many replied was far from flattering. One of the most senior figures in the Society of Jesus, a serving Provincial (regional Superior) in another Latin American country, wrote this:

> Yes, I know Bergoglio. He's a person who's caused a lot of problems in the Society and is highly controversial in his own country. In addition to being accused of having allowed the arrest of two Jesuits during the time of the Argentinian dictatorship, as Provincial he generated divided loyalties: some groups almost worshipped him, while others would have nothing to do with him, and he would hardly speak to them. It was an absurd situation. He is well-trained and very capable, but is surrounded by this personality cult which is extremely divisive. He has an aura of spirituality which he uses to obtain power. It will be a catastrophe for the Church to have someone like him in the Apostolic See. He left the Society of Jesus in Argentina destroyed with Jesuits divided and institutions destroyed and financially broken. We have spent two decades trying to fix the chaos that the man left us.

Given the otherwise universal acclaim that greeted the election of Pope Francis – the simple and humble Pope for the poor who would restore integrity to a compromised Church – this constituted an extraordinary counter-blast. And it was far from a lone voice inside the religious order in which Jorge Mario Bergoglio was formed and was a leading figure until the age of 50. Very soon an instruction went out from head office, the Jesuit Curia in Rome, ordering Jesuits around the world to be prudent in their recollections and keep to themselves any unhappy memories they had of the new Pope. Members of the Society of Jesus should not 'allow ourselves to be swept away by distractions from the past', wrote the Jesuit General Father Adolfo Nicolás, otherwise the past 'may paralyse our hearts and lead us to interpret reality with values that are not inspired by the Gospel'.

Even so, such was the strength of feeling within the order that some leading Jesuits put their names to critical comments. The leading English Jesuit, Father Michael Campbell-Johnston, a former Provincial, and a veteran of the persecution of the Church by the Western-supported military dictatorship in El Salvador where Oscar Romero was martyred, wrote in the Catholic journal *The Tablet* about how Bergoglio had been out of step with other Jesuit provinces on issues of social justice. And the distinguished Spanish theologian Father José Ignacio González Faus wrote in *El País* that Bergoglio's time as an archbishop offered great grounds for hope but that his time as a Jesuit – as 'a man with an amazing ability to charm, but with a passion for power' – raised real fears. What could create such strength of feeling among the ranks of those who might have been expected to applaud the first Jesuit pope as one of their own?

* * *

It takes 12 years' study and preparation to become a Jesuit. Given that, the progress of Jorge Mario Bergoglio through the ranks of the Society of Jesus was remarkably speedy. After entering the Society as a novice on 11 March 1958 he undertook a year of study in the humanities in Chile and then did two years of philosophy at the Colegio Máximo de San José in the San Miguel district of Buenos Aires. In his first interview as Pope, with Father Antonio Spadaro for a series of Jesuit publications, Francis reflected on this quite critically, particularly on the way he was taught the thought of the man who is perhaps the Church's greatest thinker, St Thomas Aquinas. 'Unfortunately, I studied philosophy from textbooks which came from decadent or largely bankrupt Thomism,' he recalled. But the Second Vatican Council began in 1962 in the young Bergoglio's second year of philosophy. He followed it avidly, posting notices about the latest developments on a board in the entrance to the Colegio Máximo.

Three years of teaching literature and psychology followed, in the Jesuit Colegio de la Inmaculada Concepción in Santa Fé, which was much sought after by Argentina's wealthy families seeking a traditional education for their sons, and then at the prestigious Colegio del Salvador in Buenos Aires. He was, said his pupils, a firm but enthusiastic teacher, with a great memory for his charges' names, home towns, acquaintances and interests. He brought all manner of outsiders into the classroom to enliven proceedings. The most famous of these was the great Argentinian novelist Jorge Luis Borges, whom the charismatic Bergoglio persuaded to write a foreword to a collection of the students' short stories. The literary heritage of Argentina, as we shall see, left a mark on Bergoglio theologically.

For the next three years, from 1967–70, he studied theology at the Colegio Máximo. In that time he was ordained a priest, on 13 December 1969, just a few days before his 33rd birthday, by Archbishop Ramón José Castellano. There others began already to remark upon the austerity of his lifestyle. He also earned a reputation for inscrutability, so much so that his fellow scholastics – as Jesuits in their second stage of formation training are known – teased him with the nickname *La Gioconda*, after the Mona Lisa, because it was impossible to know what he was thinking. His tertianship, the third stage of formation, was spent at the university of Alcalá de Henares in Spain from 1971 to 1972. He was so highly regarded, by his fellows and superiors alike, that on his return to Argentina he was made Master of Novices, which was not a post normally occupied by someone who had not yet taken his final vows as a Jesuit. He also served for a short time as vice-rector and professor of pastoral theology at the Colegio Máximo, again before his final vows. Indeed, within just three months of taking those perpetual vows, in April 1973, at the age of just 36, he was made Provincial Superior, the head of all the Jesuits in Argentina and Uruguay.

The tension which was to grow between what developed into *bergogliano* and *anti-bergogliano* factions would divide the province in two. There were two main areas of conflict. One was religious, the other political. The religious division was over the Second Vatican Council. Though Bergoglio went on to become the first Pope who had been ordained as priest after the Second Vatican Council, his formation was essentially pre-Vatican II in its style and content. As different sections of the Church began to explore how to put the insights of the Council into practice, a polarization occurred, and then deepened, between progressive and conservative factions within the Argentinian Jesuits. But there was another polarization growing in Argentina, in politics.

To understand Jorge Mario Bergoglio it is essential to understand something of the politics of Argentina, for Bergoglio is not comprehensible outside his own national context. Conventional paradigms of Left and Right do not greatly help here. Politics in Argentina is dominated by Peronism, a curious amalgam of forces not elsewhere associated with one another: the military, the trade unions and the Church. General Juan Domingo Perón was president of Argentina for a decade from 1946 onwards. An immensely skilled populist politician, he and the legend of his second wife Evita shaped the nation's politics for many decades more; in many ways his is still the defining model around which Argentinians do their politics.

Peronism had its roots in one of the major documents in the history of Catholic Social Teaching – an encyclical called *Quadragesimo Anno*. It was issued in 1931 by Pope Pius XI to mark the fortieth anniversary of the first Catholic social encyclical, *Rerum Novarum*, which in 1891 had set out to discover a third way between capitalism and communism. The idea was to increase social justice while dissuading Catholic workers from allying themselves with socialist movements. By 1931 Pope Pius XI had come to the conclusion that there was no alternative to capitalism; Pius gave it, implicitly, his blessing and exhorted it to behave more responsibly. But two years before *Quadragesimo Anno* was published there had been a worldwide collapse of money markets with the 1929 Wall Street crash. Clearly capitalism alone was not enough, the pontiff concluded. His encyclical addressed the fact of economic depression and the consequence of mass unemployment. The mechanism to control this which Pius XI proposed was a grand corporate plan for the reconstruction of the social order which would do away with class struggle between bosses and workers – and promote harmonious cooperation within industries and professions in its place. The problem was that the obvious vehicles for that in the 1930s were the fascist movements of Italy, Germany and Spain.

Though the Second World War had discredited fascism, its underlying principles lingered on in Argentina through Perón's holy alliance of Church, workers and the military which, he announced, was based on *Quadragesimo Anno*. His approach involved a new industrialization to boost the economy, nationalization and a substantial redistribution of wealth to ensure the new working class benefited from it. The physical might of the military and the moral authority of the Church were to enforce it, though in practice it also involved the authoritarian suppression of the opposition and the freedom of the press. Unfortunately Perón's approach led to a combination of economic stagnation, bloated state bureaucracy, inflation, falling living standards and rising unemployment. In 1955 the military overthrew Perón, who went into exile until 1973 when he returned to become president again, though only for a year until his death in 1974.

There is one final key factor to be grasped to understand the political worldview of the man who went on to become the first Pope from the Americas. Peronists thought of themselves as socialists but many of their policies were closer to the fascism of Mussolini's Italy or Franco's Spain. The lack of ideological consistency led the movement to split into dissenting factions. Some extreme Leftists known as the Montoneros took inspiration from Mao, Castro and Che Guevara and developed anti-clerical, anti-Catholic positions. Right-wing Peronists saw themselves as the defenders of the nation, private property and

Catholicism against the atheist communist hordes; the most extreme group on the Right was the murderous Alianza Anticomunista Argentina (also known as the Triple A) but there were a variety of other Peronist factions including the centre-right Guardia de Hierro (the Iron Guard), a name with echoes of the ultra-nationalist, fascist, anti-communist, anti-Semitic movement in Romania which claimed to be acting in defence of Orthodox Christianity. Puerta de Hierro (Iron Gate) was also the name of the area in north-west Madrid where Perón lived in exile.

These Peronist factions did not just disagree; eventually they set up death squads which roamed the streets in killing sprees targeted upon opponents at the other end of the Peronist spectrum. At one point, as we shall see, Bergoglio became a spiritual adviser to the Iron Guard. What pushed him in that direction was the other great polarization in his life – the religious split which developed between Catholics all across Latin America, and particularly in Argentina and inside the Society of Jesus there. It was over Liberation Theology.

* * *

Between 1962 and 1965 the Catholic Church had been shaken to its foundations by the Second Vatican Council. Before it, the Church had been an institution turned quietly inwards on its own inner sacramental life. Vatican II famously threw open the windows of the Church seeking greater interaction with, and influence on, secular society. In Latin America a number of theologians began to work out how the teachings of Vatican II should be applied on the ground.

A few individual priests took it upon themselves to move into the *villas miseries*, or 'misery villages', which Argentinians most commonly translate as 'slums'. Calling themselves the Movimiento de Sacerdotes para el Tercer Mundo (Movement of Priests for the Third World) they insisted the Gospel was about bringing good news to the poor and fought for the rights of their parishioners. The movement sought to achieve the economic, social, political and spiritual liberation of the poor in one single integrated activity. The idea was to teach the poor to read so that they could interpret the Bible and the key Christian doctrines through the reality of their own lived experiences. They would see not only the faith in a new way, but also the economic and social structures around them. The process would affirm their dignity and self-worth and inspire them to struggle together politically for a more decent life. Rather than just focusing on seeking salvation in the afterlife, Catholics should act in the here and now against unjust societies that breed poverty and need.

Jesuits were in the vanguard of this; one of the pioneers of Liberation Theology was a former Argentine Jesuit Provincial, Juan Marcos Moglia, who served in the slums for 20 years until his death. But the movement began to take greater shape in 1968. In May that year the provincials of all the Jesuits in Latin America met in Rio de Janeiro to reflect on their mission. They decided they must push for a greater involvement with social movements that challenged unjust structures. They drew up a mission statement which said: 'In all our activities our goals should be the liberation of humankind from every sort of servitude that oppresses it: the lack of life's necessities, illiteracy, and the weight of sociological structures which deprive it of personal responsibility over life itself.' They wanted to create 'a society in which all persons will find their place and in which they will enjoy political, economic, cultural, and religious equality and liberty'. Jesuits in Latin America became practically involved in many activities related to the defence of indigenous minorities, political refugees and migrants.

This was in line with a shift in consensus across the whole continent – apart from Argentina. That same year the Brazilian theologian Rubem Alves wrote a book called *Towards a Theology of Liberation* which set a template for the movement that was developed by thinkers like Gustavo Gutiérrez in Peru, Juan Luis Segundo in Uruguay, Jon Sobrino in El Salvador and Leonardo Boff of Brazil. The common ground was a perceived need to liberate the poor from unjust economic, political or social conditions in an underdeveloped continent where an elite class exploited resources and labour largely for their own benefit – and that of the rich world with which they traded. It was to be expressed in what Gutiérrez, in the movement's seminal work *A Theology of Liberation* (1971), called the 'preferential option for the poor' – the radical idea that in the Bible God takes sides and gives preference to the impoverished, the marginalized and the oppressed. The notion was endorsed at gatherings of all the continent's bishops at Medellín in Colombia in 1968 and again at Puebla in Mexico in 1979. The Medellín documents spoke of the 'institutionalized violence' of poverty. But Argentina's clerical establishment, which had come to identify the interests of the Church with those of the State, and which was deeply conservative, was notably unenthusiastic.

What the conservatives particularly disliked was that Liberation Theology allowed a critique of society, and of the Church, through the eyes of the poor. And it introduced a bottom-up model of Christian base communities where biblical interpretation and liturgy were designed by ordinary people – a notion which went down very badly in a top-down organization like the Catholic Church. The hierarchy in the Vatican objected to that, and also to the use by some liberation theologians of Marxist sociological analysis. The Church could not endorse notions of class struggle, Rome said. Most of all, it utterly rejected the idea adopted by a handful of Liberation Theology's most extreme enthusiasts that the Gospel offered a justification for the poor to engage in armed struggle against the rich.

There were a good number of liberation theologians who took such a view. Just before Medellín 1,500 priests from the Movement of Priests for the Third World signed a letter to Paul VI condemning 'the violence of the upper class' and 'the violence of the state' as the first violence. In the face of this, they argued, the violence of the poor was an understandable response.

But there was an element of deliberate and wilful misunderstanding of the basis of Liberation Theology by some in Rome. Much of the influence of Marxism on liberationist thinking was indirect. According to Enrique Dussel, the Argentine philosopher, Liberation Theology used Marxism in the same way that the great medieval theologian St Thomas Aquinas used the great pre-Christian thinker Aristotle or the hugely influential twentieth-century theologian Karl Rahner used the existentialist philosopher Martin Heidegger.

Most liberation theologians, when they talked about the need for revolution, were advocating a complete turnaround of existing exploitative economic and social structures. Opponents caricatured this as an endorsement of armed violence but most liberation theologians were not advocating that the poor should take up guns. What they wanted was that the Church should stand alongside the poor and help as they learned to organize themselves in unions and cooperatives to gain bargaining power. Liberation Theology proper was about giving the poor priority in their fight to overturn unjust relationships, bring about structural change, and the Church standing in solidarity with that.

But this was the time of the Cold War when the Soviet Union and, closer by, Fidel Castro in Cuba were intent on exporting revolutionary communism to what was then called the Third World. Elites in Latin America saw Liberation Theology as the first sign of the continent's slide towards Marxism. The United States took a similar view and deployed its Central Intelligence Agency (CIA) to galvanize the split of the Church into conservative and progressive elements – and back the conservatives. It even set up a special unit dedicated to working on the issue with the Vatican. Rome was happy to cooperate. It saw Liberation Theology as a threat to Catholic orthodoxy and the power of the Vatican hierarchy. Pope Paul VI was persuaded that Liberation Theology needed curbing. He appointed the Colombian bishop Alfonso López Trujillo, an Opus Dei supporter, to become its principal scourge. Cardinal Antonio Samorè, president of the Pontifical Commission for Latin America, was given the job of liaising between the Roman Curia and the Latin American bishops to stem the influence of this new theology of the poor.

What sharpened the significance of these religious and political distinctions was violence. In 1966 a military coup in Argentina had placed in power the authoritarian General Juan Carlos Onganía, who banned Peronism – along with mini-skirts and long hair on men – and presided over what its citizens later called a 'soft dictatorship' (in contrast to the horrors that were to follow). The Movement of Priests for the Third World issued a declaration supporting revolutionary socialist movements. In response Juan Carlos Aramburu, the acting Archbishop of Buenos Aires, forbade priests from making political declarations. Not long afterwards, Onganía's administration ended in a chaos of instability, discontent and demonstrations ushering in the first elections for a decade.

The return of the exiled Juan Perón which followed in 1973 was supposed to calm society's troubled nerves. It did exactly the opposite. The barely suppressed antagonisms between the Left and Right of Peronism erupted into open warfare with murders, kidnappings and bombings. Left-wing guerrillas battled the government, while right-wing death squads cruised the streets, murdering with impunity. Among those who died was the first of the 'slum priests' to be martyred, the charismatic Father Carlos Mugica, who was shot dead by the Alianza Anticomunista Argentina outside the church of San Francisco Solano where he had just finished celebrating Mass. He was talking to a couple of young people about their forthcoming wedding when the bullets struck. Between 1973 and 1976 a virtual civil war reigned on the streets of Buenos Aires. Some historians have suggested that as many people died in those three years as were killed by the military dictatorship in the so-called Dirty War in the years that followed the military coup that took place in 1976. Things were so bad that many ordinary citizens sighed with relief when the army stepped in.

* * *

It was against this background of a titanic struggle for the soul of Catholicism in Latin America that Jorge Mario Bergoglio became Provincial Superior of the Society of Jesus in Argentina. His predecessor was Father Ricardo 'Dick' O'Farrell, whose name discloses that the Irish were, along with Bergoglio's Italians, a major component in the melting pot of Argentinian immigration. O'Farrell was a sociologist who had embraced the changes of Vatican II. He was open to new ideas, including Liberation Theology. He supported base communities. He encouraged Jesuits like Father Orlando Yorio and Father Franz Jalics to work with the poor in the slums – from which they would be kidnapped by the military in an incident that cast a shadow over Jorge Mario Bergoglio's priestly ministry for many years. (see Chapter Four).

But O'Farrell presided over a dramatic decline in vocations. In 1961 there were 25 novices; by 1973 that had dropped to just two. The reason for this is disputed. The late Jesuit historian Jeffrey Klaiber has suggested it was merely a reflection of a general post-Vatican II crisis in vocations. Professor Fortunato Mallimaci, who runs the Society and Religion course at the University of Buenos Aires, suggests many Jesuits left at this time 'as an act of rebellion against the intellectual support the order had given to the regime of the dictator Onganía, who was one of a thousand members of the elite linked to Opus Dei'. But Marina Rubino, a theology student at the Colegio Máximo at the time, recalled that it was because O'Farrell and his teaching staff, which included Jalics and Yorio, were taking seriously the changes set out by the Second Vatican Council and Medellín – and this was driving old-style conservative seminarians away.

Whatever the explanation the order was in turmoil, according to Father Michael Campbell-Johnston, who was later sent on a visitation to Argentina on behalf of the Jesuit Superior General Father Pedro Arrupe in Rome. 'The Argentinian Jesuits had been going through a lot of trouble,' he recalled. 'A lot of people had been leaving the order and even the priesthood. Some 10 to 15 were leaving every year. That was quite exceptional.'

What was clear was that there were many Jesuits who were unhappy with the rapid pace at which things were changing in the order after the Second Vatican Council. They did not like the shifts of emphasis within Ignatian spirituality. Jesuits were supposed to be 'contemplatives in action'. The old guard preferred the contemplation to the action but some new progressives inverted the priority. All the progressive Jesuits wanted to downplay, or even abandon, the order's traditional role of educating the next generation of the nation's rich elite. Instead they wanted to move to working with the uneducated poor in the shanty-towns. The conservatives did not approve and, more than that, they were afraid that the progressives who were working politically in the slums would make all Jesuits targets for the right-wing anti-communist murder squads.

Something extraordinary then happened. The conservatives staged an unprecedented rebellion in which a number of them complained to the Superior General in Rome about their Provincial, Dick O'Farrell. They petitioned that he should be removed from office. The Jesuit Curia in Rome, fearful of the division that was being caused in the Argentinian province, acceded to their request. O'Farrell, who might have expected to serve for six years, as is the norm, found himself removed after less than four. The obvious candidate to replace him,

Father Luis Escribano, had just died in a car accident. So on 31 July 1973 Jorge Mario Bergoglio, one of O'Farrell's advisers, known as consultors, was made Provincial. O'Farrell, humiliatingly, was told to swap jobs with the younger man and become Novice Master, a post he then only held for 18 months.

As Provincial in charge of 15 Jesuit houses, 166 priests, 32 brothers and 20 students in their care, Bergoglio immediately set about reversing many of O'Farrell's changes and moving back to the traditional values and lifestyles in which his own formation as a Jesuit had been shaped. O'Farrell had had the chapel at the Colegio Máximo remodelled and replastered so that the once-traditional church now looked like an awesome giant white cave – the Vatican II enthusiast intended it to feel like the inside of Moses' tent in the desert – totally unadorned save for a great dark crucifix. It was a breath-taking transformation, as visitors to the Colegio Máximo can still see today. Entering the chapel is like emerging into an astonishing whitewashed catacomb. Bergoglio hated it, but knew he could not justify the cost of reordering the chapel again, so he swiftly installed a statue of the Virgin and what he felt was a more reverential tabernacle. But that was only the start.

* * *

The job of a Jesuit novice master is to test whether novices have a genuine vocation; some do that through gentle discernment, others through strict discipline. Bergoglio had been the latter. Now he used the same approach as Provincial. He made changes in the liturgy, setting aside modern post-Vatican II songs and replacing them with pre-conciliar songs, psalms and Gregorian plainchant. He introduced the service of Lauds, which is not part of the Jesuit tradition, and which many in the Society did not like. He brought the religious style of popular piety in which he had been brought up to the Church's most intellectual religious order. Novices were instructed to say novenas, traditional prayer cycles which devout lay Catholics like his Grandma Rosa prayed in the hope of acquiring special intercessory graces. Seminarians were encouraged to go into the chapel at night and touch or kiss statues and images. The rosary was said in the garden. Cerebral old-school eyebrows were raised. 'This was popular religiosity to which we Jesuits were unaccustomed,' one student of the time said. 'He tried to make us more like a religious order, wearing surplices and singing the office,' recalled one of his students, Miguel Mom Debussy, who joined the order in 1973 and was ordained a priest by Bergoglio in 1984. He moved the Provincial's office from the centre of Buenos Aires out to the Colegio Máximo in the suburb of San Miguel so he could keep a closer eye on the students.

Later, when his six-year term as Provincial ended and he was appointed as Rector of the college, he insisted on reverting to a more traditional formation for those training to be priests. He introduced a fixed schedule for the students and insisted on integrating manual labour into their formation in a Benedictine model, remembered another student, Father Humberto Miguel Yáñez, who is now the head of moral theology at the Gregorian University in Rome. O'Farrell had been a modernizing influence on everyday clothing, allowing students and priests to wear non-clerical clothing; Bergoglio put an end to that, insisting on clerical collars instead, Father Ignacio del Viso, a long-standing professor of theology at the Colegio Máximo recalled. Bergoglio himself routinely wore a cassock, something only older members of the community had done. He had about him the manner of an old-style authoritarian. He would stand tapping his watch if students were late, check their shoes for dust to make sure they really had been visiting the poor, or demand that they give up smoking in solidarity with poor people who couldn't afford cigarettes.

There were changes too in the curriculum. Bergoglio instructed the teachers of moral theology appointed by O'Farrell to work from an ancient textbook in Latin. 'That caused a problem because many of the novices had stopped learning Latin – or saying prayers in it – years before,' said Mom Debussy of Bergoglio's first few years as Provincial. 'We had to go to the older Jesuits, aged 45 or over, to get things translated. The teacher was a progressive type who obeyed the instructions given by the new Provincial but who would bite her lip with obvious disgust.' Bergoglio was unimpressed. He brought in more conservative lay professors to replace teachers he considered too progressive. Among those sacked was the theology lecturer Father Orlando Yorio, one of the two Jesuits later kidnapped and tortured by the military in 1976. Yorio had been one of Bergoglio's teachers. Books by the other Jesuit kidnapped alongside Yorio, Franz Jalics, who had taught Bergoglio philosophy, were withdrawn from the college library and a teacher using them on a student course was asked to remove them from its reading list. 'Before long,' said Mom Debussy, 'Bergoglio brought in an arch-conservative, the military chaplain from Moreno Air Base, to teach. He seemed unaware of any of the teachings of Vatican II. It was all St Thomas Aquinas and the old Church Fathers. We didn't study a single book by Gutiérrez, Boff, or Paulo Freire.'

'Liberation Theology was actually forbidden,' said another of Bergoglio's students, Father Rafael Velasco, who was until recently the Rector of the Catholic University of Córdoba. 'It was seen by him as very suspicious if you were interested in that. I had to wait to read it later in life.' Philosophy was similarly constrained. The course of study had begun with Pre-Socratic philosophers and then progressed through Descartes, Kant and Hegel to the modern period. Bergoglio put an end to that. 'Now it stopped with Nietzsche, of whom there was just a little with critical analysis from a Catholic perspective, and very little Kierkegaard or Heidegger,' said Mom Debussy. 'There was no Marx, Engels, Sartre, Foucault, structuralists, post-structuralists or postmodernists. Nobody who opposed one iota of traditional Catholic doctrine and dogma. All under the strict orders of Jorge Bergoglio.'

The resistance movement to key aspects of the reforms of Vatican II was being led within the foremost intellectual religious order in Argentina by Jorge Mario Bergoglio.

O'Farrell had encouraged seminarians to study a wide range of subjects outside their mandated philosophy and theology – sociology, politics, anthropology, engineering, even, in one case, solar engineering. Bergoglio steered novices and scholastics away from such an approach. 'There is a tradition in the Jesuits that you're encouraged to do political science as a sociology,' said Velasco. 'This was absolutely discouraged by Bergoglio.' Instead he encouraged the study of Argentine literature and history. He was particularly fond of the epic poem *Martín Fierro*, a work as iconic in Argentina as the *Divine Comedy* was in Italy or *Don Quixote* in Spain. Its hero was a *gaucho*, a cowboy on the Argentine pampas, and the tale celebrates the *gaucho* values of respect, loyalty, honesty and pride rooted in a code of ethics that valued work and brotherhood. Since *gauchos* played a key role in Argentina's independence from Spain the figure of Fierro was a touchstone of Argentine national identity, like a Latin American Robin Hood. In an essay on the poem Bergoglio has written of it as 'a way of letting the wisdom of our people speak to you, the wisdom that has been captured in this singular work'. And he continued: 'One thing is certain: we are historical people. We live in time and space. Every generation needs its predecessors, and owes itself to its successors.' Bergoglio wanted to reshape the formation of Argentina's Jesuits so that they embraced the religious values of the ordinary people rather than seeking to impose the educated vision of an elite. In the years that followed, Bergoglio began to be influenced by a handful of theologians who tried to embody this approach in what they called *teología del pueblo* – the Theology of the People. But the theologies of the *people* and of the *poor* turned out to be far from the same thing.

* * *

Although Bergoglio wanted to erase any trace of Liberation Theology inside the Argentinian Jesuits he was keen for them to maintain their contact with ordinary people. Much inspired by Pope Paul VI's 1975 apostolic exhortation *Evangelii Nuntiandi* – which said that the primary purpose of the Church was spreading the Gospel and that every Christian should be involved in that – Bergoglio set up a parish church on land owned by the Colegio Máximo in the suburb of San Miguel and sent his students out into the local working-class neighbourhoods to gather children to bring them in for catechism. On Saturday afternoons and Sunday mornings Jesuits were sent around the area to say Mass and offer religious instruction to children and to adults. Bergoglio encouraged them to keep their eyes open for any assistance the poorer people needed. The order of priority was always the same: Mass, catechesis and alleviating poverty. Food, medicines and blankets were distributed. Children were shown films after their catechism classes and on feast days given toys or taken on outings, with some seeing the sea for the first time that way. Bergoglio organized a missionary team of priests to venture far further afield, into the most remote parts of the country to take the Gospel and engage with popular piety. The roving priests travelled far and wide, often spending several months in each place.

But this was not to be confused with Liberation Theology. 'From Monday to Friday we were at the college but at the weekends students had to go out to parishes including poor areas,' said Velasco, 'but our only duties there were religious. We had nothing to do with unions or cooperatives or even Catholic NGOs. He was a very strict person with ideas about pastoral work at that time that I would consider today to be quite conservative – pastoral work with the people that didn't address the root causes of their social problems.' When students discovered a need in a parish, Bergoglio was swift to act. Yáñez, who was received into the order in 1975, recalled how Bergoglio dispatched him to a poor area to visit families and discover what they needed. In response the Provincial immediately set up a soup kitchen for 200 children in the district. Even so, according to Velasco: 'His relationship with the poor was pastoral but a little bit patronizing. It was to soften the consequences of injustice rather than to tackle the causes of injustice or poverty or to empower the poor.' The Bergoglio of those days would probably have agreed. Presiding at his first provincial assembly in April 1974, he told the gathered Jesuits that they should avoid what he called 'abstract ideologies mismatched with reality' and 'sterile conflicts within the Church' between factions characterized as 'progressive' and 'reactionary'. One of his then students, now a bishop, Father Hugo Salaberry recalled: 'Bergoglio has never had an abstract concern; he always is concerned about the concrete person, victim of injustices of poverty. He always knew people by name and because of this people love him a lot.'

Many in the province agreed with Bergoglio and found his changes helpful. 'He began to put the province in order; he did a good job,' said Father Andrés

Swinnen, one of his Jesuit contemporaries, but adding 'he handed himself a lot of authority; sometimes that was problematic'. Another Jesuit also recalled his legacy with ambivalence. 'He wanted to bring back certain elements of our formation that had been left aside after the Second Vatican Council, not for the sake of being pre-conciliar, but because he thought they reflected our reality,' said Yáñez. 'At the time, things like a fixed schedule seemed like going back to the past. But he wanted to create a certain discipline. Integrating manual labour into our formation struck me as a realistic way of living poverty.' It brought a certain coherence to their lives. But others disagreed. Students from rich backgrounds did not take kindly to being told to feed the pigs and other animals Bergoglio introduced to college life. They disliked mucking them out even more. Some objected to his re-imposition of clerical collars and cassocks. Others took it in their stride. 'The clerical dress was no big deal,' said another student of the time. 'In the 1970s in Argentina everybody – lawyers, doctors, priests – wore clothes appropriate to their job. It was not old-fashioned. It was just proper at the time. The people expected the clerical collar from a student priest in those days. I never found Bergoglio a control freak. As Provincial it was just about authority not control.'

The two views revealed the rift which began to deepen over Bergoglio's style. The points of difference were often over small things but they spoke to the deeper divisions within Argentine Jesuits. 'He was too much of a controversial figure among the young Jesuits, some were so absolutely pro him he couldn't do anything wrong,' said another contemporary, Father Michael Petty. The admiration began to be excessive and uncritical among the novices, said Rafael Velasco: 'He was greatly admired among the Jesuit students. In some cases there was even a cult of personality around him. Some even referred to him as El, like God.' But, added Velacso, 'he had a way of thinking that was very critical of those within the Jesuits that had a different way of seeing things'.

Then, as later when Bergoglio was an archbishop and now as Pope, many were impressed by his personal lifestyle. 'He was very austere,' said Velasco. 'He always wore the same clothes and he rejected luxurious food or drink.' He thought the order should also suit the action to the word, as his old friend the human rights lawyer Alicia Oliveira recalled. 'In those days the Jesuits ran a school for the wealthy, the Colegio del Salvador in Buenos Aires. My sons went there. It was actually two schools in one building with two separate entrances, for those who paid and those who didn't. When Bergoglio was Provincial he closed down the free school and moved all the poor children into the rich one. He did not tell the parents. No-one knew. He was always concerned about the poor.'

Already, in his late thirties, Bergoglio was a charismatic figure. 'His leadership was based on his personality,' said Velasco. 'He loved teaching the novices. He was not hierarchical in his style. He came across more as a brother than a father. You wanted to be very close to him.' The new Provincial was a dynamic force-of-nature figure who swiftly set about building a big new library for the Colegio Máximo. 'He was a marvellous leader,' recalled an Irish Jesuit, Father James Kelly, who was living in the house in those years while teaching scripture in Buenos Aires. 'In fact his leadership qualities were quite remarkable...A very spiritual man, humble but with strong convictions, he was responsible for attracting a large number of young men to join the Jesuits at a time when numbers had fallen.' But his charismatic style of leadership brought many problems. 'If you liked him and he liked you, you'd be in a good position,' recalled Rafael Velasco. 'But if he didn't like you, you were in for some kind of trouble. And if you didn't agree with him you'd be relegated outside the circle of power.'

That is what happened to Miguel Mom Debussy. 'For the first four years, from 1973 onwards, I had a really good relationship with Bergoglio. He often chose me as his driver,' he recalled, with a tart aside that the man who, in later years as Archbishop of Buenos Aires, was celebrated for taking underground trains and buses, earlier demanded that his juniors chauffeured him around: 'Even when he went to celebrate Mass in a parish church just ten blocks away he'd ask me to drive him. And nor was he simple in his approach to the liturgy in those days; he wore pre-Vatican II vestments of velvet embroidered in gold, saying that "ordinary people like a touch of Evita". But we got on very well in the early years and he shared a lot of confidences in the car, such as that he didn't like the fact that his brother was close to Opus Dei. We were quite close though we later fell out as Bergoglio became increasingly more conservative.'

Many of those who were first enthralled by Bergoglio's autocratic charisma eventually began to question it. 'There were those who remained loyal to Bergoglio and those of us who began to take a critical view of many of the things that had bothered us at the time,' said Velasco. 'I value many things about Bergoglio. He taught me how to get close to God and to relate the people. There are other things that I had to unlearn. His vision was marked by a very orthodox theology, definitely European, very critical of Liberation Theology.' Father Humberto Miguel Yáñez had slightly lost touch with Bergoglio after he moved to teach at the Gregorian, the Jesuit university in Rome. Now that they are back in the same city, the two men are in contact again. Yáñez had received a phone call from Pope Francis not long before I met with him to talk. The Argentinean Jesuit recalled Bergoglio as struggling to hold a divided religious order together in those days. 'These were years of a strong conflict between Left and Right,' he said, 'and I'd say that for the most part Bergoglio was in the middle'. But others told a different story and saw the young Provincial's injunctions about avoiding factional politics as distinctly one-sided.

* * *

By his own admission to his interviewers Francesca Ambrogetti and Sergio Rubin, Bergoglio was a political animal. As a teenager he had been interested in the relationship between faith and communism. But as Argentinian society polarized between an atheist anti-Church Left and a right-wing which claimed to be acting in defence of the Church and its values, Bergoglio was drawn inexorably to the worldview of the Right, if not with its tactics.

As he drove the Provincial's car through the streets of Buenos Aires, Miguel Mom Debussy gained insights into Bergoglio's political stance. 'I was a left-wing Peronist,' said Mom Debussy. 'Bergoglio was on the right of Peronism, he was linked with the Iron Guard, who were a traditional, right-wing, dogmatic group with an entryist strategy to various sources of power.'

Despite their name the Iron Guard did not have much in common with their violent fascist Romanian namesakes. Argentina's Iron Guard were an odd bunch of Peronist youth activists who liked to think of themselves as a secret order characterized by obedience, intellectual rigour and ascetic discipline – the Jesuit virtues – but whose intellectual influences were a mishmash of Lenin, the mystic Romanian philosopher Mircea Eliade and the sixteenth-century Jesuit missionary to China, Matteo Ricci. They had books on political and military strategy on their reading list, performed a fascist-style salute, wore paramilitary-style brown-shirt uniforms with diagonal belt across the chest and bore bracelets inscribed: *Aquí se aprende a amar a Perón* (Here you learn to love Perón). Their aim, as the *Wall Street Journal* put it, 'was to form political cadres schooled in a center-right version of Peronist ideology, deeply marinated in Catholic thought'. Their ideology borrowed from both Right and Left much as did that of Mussolini in Italy with whom they shared a 'corporate state' philosophy, so much so that they were called Trotskyites in the 1960s and fascists in the 1970s. But with their doctrine of preaching class harmony, they had the appeal of constituting a third way between the violent activists of the extremes of Left and Right. Bergoglio liked that idea; he had concluded that something in Peronism constituted Argentina's best hope for a solution to the nation's endemic problems of economic instability and political chaos. Various former members of the Iron Guard have confirmed that Bergoglio was from 1972 a spiritual adviser to the Peronist militia movement whose founder

Alejandro Álvarez later linked up with the Italian Catholic lay movement Comunione e Liberazione with which Bergoglio later developed links. The lawyer Alicia Oliveira acknowledged that Bergoglio had links to the Iron Guard: 'He was involved. He gave them spiritual help. But I never heard him say any of the stupid things that a lot of people in the Iron Guard said.'

The Iron Guard would have remained a mere eccentric footnote in the Bergoglio biography had it not been for an initiative from the Jesuit's Superior General, Father Pedro Arrupe. Just 20 days before Bergoglio was appointed Provincial an order had come from Rome. The 31st General Congregation of the Jesuit order, which had met while Vatican II was still in session, had decreed that the Society should reappraise its relationship with lay people in the Church. More responsibility should be passed to them. In pursuit of that, Arrupe had decided that in Argentina the order should pass one of the two universities in its control over to the hands of the laity. On taking over, Bergoglio put the matter in train. There was some urgency. In 1973 the finances of the Jesuit province were in a parlous state. Bergoglio decided to sell a number of under-used properties. But the university, which had large debts, was the biggest disposal – and it was more than just a building.

The Jesuit Universidad del Salvador in Buenos Aires, Bergoglio decided, would be given to the Iron Guard 'to facilitate the growth of the Kingdom of God'. It would represent a 'continuity of the Jesuit spirit' but in lay hands. It would also revitalize a demoralized institution, he argued. In August 1974 he appointed a leading member of the Iron Guard, Francisco José Piñón, as the university's rector. The Iron Guard's chief of staff, Walter Romero, and other leading figures in the Guard were also given senior university positions. Many in the Jesuits were furious at this decision, which was compounded three years later when the university awarded an honorary degree to Admiral Emilio Massera, the chief torturer in the military dictatorship's Dirty War (see Chapter Four). 'Handing the university to the Iron Guard,' said Father Guillermo Marcó, who was for eight years one of Bergoglio's closest aides, 'is something for which many Jesuits have never forgiven him'.

But the divisions within the province were set to worsen. And again Bergoglio was the focus. The following year Superior General Arrupe convened the 32nd General Congregation in the history of the Society of Jesus. It lasted from December 1974 to March 1975. The Superior General wanted the order's highest body to address the question of how the Jesuits were putting into practice the vision of the Second Vatican Council. It was to prove a watershed in the four centuries of the existence of the Society.

On the agenda was the mission of the Jesuits 'to engage, under the standard of the cross, in the crucial struggle of our time: the struggle for faith, and that struggle for justice which it includes'. The Society of Jesus had been founded 'principally for the defence and propagation of the faith' but now, the agenda said, there could be no genuine conversion to the love of God without conversion to the love of neighbour and, therefore, to the demands of justice. The promotion of justice was indispensable to the promotion of the Gospel. The Jesuit community was a community of discernment, it said, but final decisions would 'belong to those who have the burden of authority'. In other words the Congregation would decide on a possible change of direction and everyone else would have to do as they were told.

Arrupe knew that the decisions to be made would be controversial. He was keenly aware that a commitment to work for social justice would bring his priests and brothers into conflict, particularly in Latin America, where he knew right-wing dictatorships, with the backing of the United States, saw social justice as a back door to Cold War communism. The year before, he had travelled to Argentina, at the behest of the Holy See, to investigate the case of Bishop Enrique Angelelli in the diocese of La Rioja in the north-west of the country. Arrupe and the Archbishop of Santa Fé, Vicente Zazpe, had been asked by Pope Paul VI to adjudicate on a dispute between Angelelli, who had supported the formation of trade unions locally, and local landowners and merchants who had rioted in church when Angelelli arrived to say Mass. Arrupe and Zazpe had backed the bishop but it was clear to Arrupe what ire would be aroused by the Church siding with the poor. Revealingly, Bergoglio, who accompanied the official delegation, drew a different emphasis from the encounter; he later noted that 'many sectors of La Rioja society publicly expressed to us their discomfort with Jesuits working among the poorest'.

Many Jesuits, Bergoglio included, felt the changes Arrupe wanted to institute at the 32nd General Congregation would overly politicize the order. One group of ultra-conservatives in Spain objected so strongly to Arrupe's approach that they decided to propose they should be allowed to form a new congregation, a society within a society, to preserve the older traditions. They set out for Rome by train from Spain. Arrupe feared that the Spaniards' plea to the Congregation could prove destructively divisive. Someone, he decided, had to go to meet them off the train – and persuade them to turn around and head home without disrupting the General Congregation.

Just before the group from Spain arrived, Bergoglio landed in Rome at the head of the Argentinian delegation. Arrupe knew that the Spaniards would listen to Bergoglio since he shared many of their fears. One of the key dissidents was originally Argentinian so was bound by an oath of obedience to Bergoglio as his Provincial. So Arrupe asked the Argentinian Provincial to go to Termini Station to persuade the group from Spain to turn around and go home. Bergoglio, despite his own reservations, loyally obeyed and successfully persuaded the dissenters to get back on the next train. The Argentinian was apprehensive, but obedience is a prime Jesuit virtue.

* * *

Bergoglio did not have much to say in the discussions which ensued at the Jesuit congregation. 'He was very uneasy about putting justice on the same level as faith,' one top Jesuit in Rome told me, asking not to be named. 'He felt that the congregation worldwide was being taken over by radical perspectives from Latin America.'

The debate at the 32nd Congregation on Decree Four – the measure containing the decisive shift which would move the Jesuits from a focus on educating the elite to one of serving the poor – was intensely debated. So much so that a vote was not taken until the last day of the Congregation, 7 March 1975. When it came, the change was passed with an overwhelming majority among the delegates. Bergoglio was not happy with it, nor with the general direction of the 32nd General Congregation. He was against a number of the crucial decrees and in particular Decree Four on social justice, which he saw as flirting with Marxism. But he and Arrupe had a good relationship. 'He always took care to praise the Superior General in public,' one Jesuit contemporary said. 'There was much they agreed upon. They both shared a strategy to make the Society get involved in issues of the outside world. And the option for the poor was essential for both of them. But they disagreed on what exactly that meant.' Bergoglio wanted to alleviate the symptoms of poverty; Arrupe wanted to challenge them.

Bergoglio obediently returned to Argentina charged with the task of encouraging his priests to seek justice and defend and care for the poor. But on his return he warned senior members of the Argentine province that 'the price of violence is always paid by the weakest'. Seminarians found that Decree Four was not to feature in their studies. 'We never heard anything about it at all,' recalled Mom Debussy. 'Bergoglio did not have much sympathy for Decree Four,' confirmed Father Andrés Swinnen, who was Novice Master at the time and went on to succeed Bergoglio as Provincial when Bergoglio became Rector. 'When he was speaking to the novices he did not quote it.' Even three years later when, in 1978, Bergoglio made his address to the Province, although he referred several times to the Jesuit general meeting in Rome, he still did not refer once to Decree Four. The Vatican II document he preferred was *Evangelii Nuntiandi*, the encyclical Pope Paul VI published at the end of 1975 not long after the Jesuits had agreed on Decree Four. *Evangelii Nuntiandi* proclaimed that spreading the Gospel was the Church's deepest identity; the only point of its existence was to preach and teach and bear witness. This resonated much more with Bergoglio's view of the Church. It became, he later said, his favourite church document. *Evangelii Nuntiandi* spoke of liberation – but by that it meant, the document said, liberation through salvation – 'which is liberation from everything that oppresses people'. Liberation was not about changing economic or political structures but about 'a conversion of the hearts and minds of those who live under these systems and of those who have control of the system'. It hoped, through evangelization, to persuade the rich to surrender power rather than help the poor to take control of their own destiny. This was precisely Bergoglio's vision. Putting it into practice he sent priests and students alike from the Colegio Máximo to do pastoral work at the weekend. But he told them they were to work in conventional parishes rather than the new base communities which Bergoglio suspected would lead to a disregard of the authority of the mainstream Church.

For many in the Jesuits, Bergoglio's cautious and conservative approach was vindicated a year later. Fears that working in the slums would provoke a backlash were proved correct. In 1976 a junta comprising the heads of the army, navy and air force seized power and immediately instituted a terrifying crackdown on anyone it perceived to be a political opponent. Tens of thousands of people disappeared in a campaign of kidnappings, torture and murders. Among the victims were 150 Catholic priests as well as hundreds of nuns and lay catechists. Jorge Mario Bergoglio's personal behaviour during this so-called Dirty War – which was the subject of great controversy in Argentina, and globally after his election as Pope – is examined in detail in the next chapter. But here it is worth noting the impact all this had on the Jesuits of Argentina. The division in the province hardened. The violence underscored to traditionalists that for priests to become involved in politics was both wrong and dangerous. To the progressives, however, the sudden spasm of violence by the state reinforced the responsibility of the Church to speak out in prophetic witness as priests were doing under military dictatorships in Chile, Brazil, El Salvador and elsewhere. The upshot was that, in the words of the Jesuit historian Jeffrey Klaiber, 'during those years, the Argentinian province did not march in unison with the rest of the Society of Jesus in Latin America'.

The disparity was noticed in Rome. Superior General Arrupe sent one of his assistants out from Rome to Buenos Aires in 1977 to talk to Bergoglio.

Father Michael Campbell-Johnston's job was to monitor the work around the world of the Jesuits' social institutes, which were known as Centres for Investigation and Social Action (CIAS). Their job was to make sure issues of social justice were on the Jesuit agenda in every country. 'I was Aruppe's representative for the social apostolate,' Campbell-Johnston said. 'My job was keeping in touch with the social institutes. They needed a lot of support because in those days countries like Chile, Brazil and Argentina were ruled by harsh right-wing military regimes known as National Security States.' The governments in such countries, on the pretext of combating international communism, assumed total control over all dimensions of public life including education, the media, the unions and the judiciary. 'Anyone questioning the status quo was automatically considered subversive and such measures as arbitrary arrest and even torture were justified. In many of the countries our Jesuit institutes were facing opposition and even persecution.'

The social institutes were run by teams of Jesuits with expertise in the social sciences – economists, sociologists and political scientists. Typically there would be three to five Jesuits plus some lay academics, tackling issues like land reform and getting involved in the poorer parts of the communities. 'Throughout Latin America Jesuits in the social institutes were very critical of government,' the British Jesuit said. 'So much so that many had to go into hiding and continue their work underground. But this was not the situation for our institute in Buenos Aires which was able to function freely because it never criticized or opposed the government. As a result there were justice issues it could not address or even mention.

'At the time there were an estimated 6,000 political prisoners in Argentina and another 20,000 *desaparecidos* – people who had been "disappeared",' Campbell-Johnston said. 'And there was widespread evidence of torture and assassination. Yet in Argentina the institute was silent on all that. I discussed this at length with Father Bergoglio. He defended his position, trapped between the Catholic military and the very secularist anti-Church Left. I tried to show him how it was out of step with our other social institutes on the continent. Our discussion was lengthy but in the end we could not agree.'

Bergoglio was unrepentant. He cut back funding for the social institute and, when he ceased to be Provincial, attempted to persuade his successor Andrés Swinnen to do the same. Swinnen was very much Bergoglio's disciple and, as Provincial, continued to implement what Bergoglio desired. As Rector, with a compliant Provincial, in these years Bergoglio had unparalleled sway over the Society of Jesus in Argentina. At one point he tried to close the Centre for Investigation and Social Action entirely but Rome intervened and refused permission. Members of staff were sacked. Bergoglio's then aide Miguel Mom Debussy claims that one professor was dismissed in his absence. 'I helped Bergoglio clear the man's room and found in a drawer a file of denunciations of Bergoglio which the professor had been planning to send to Rome,' he claimed. Complaints from other Jesuits about Bergoglio did arrive in the Superior General's office in the Jesuit Curia.

In the years that followed, Bergoglio's stances became increasingly dogmatic, the more so after John Paul II became Pope, according to Mom Debussy. Certainly opposition to Bergoglio within the province began to grow as post-Vatican II attitudes consolidated within the order and as, in 1983, the military junta was replaced by a civilian government and investigations into the human rights abuses of the Dirty War began. 'Other members of the teaching staff were more open to new methods in philosophical and social matters,' said Rafael Velasco. 'Those opposed to him were in the majority by the 1980s. He was Rector but he was quite isolated.'

As his term of office as Rector ended in 1986 the polarization within the Jesuits of Argentina had crystallized into *bergoglianos* and *anti-bergoglianos*, with his opponents referring to his supporters as 'the dinosaurs'. By this time there had been a change at the top in Rome; Superior General Pedro Arrupe had been replaced in 1983 by Peter-Hans Kolvenbach who was alarmed at Bergoglio's divisive legacy. In the years up to his exile, more than a hundred young Jesuits who disliked the Bergoglio approach left the order. Bergoglio was blamed for the exodus.

'There's no doubt that in the years after he left, the style of formation was different than what it had been under Bergoglio,' said Father Humberto Miguel Yáñez, with diplomatic understatement. 'The new superiors felt it had been a little too conservative, and it needed to be renewed.' Professor Fortunato Mallimaci, of the University of Buenos Aires, said, more forthrightly: 'When Bergoglio left there was a huge crisis in the order in Argentina.' Twenty years on, the scars still had not fully healed. When Pope Francis was elected, the eminent Jesuit theologian Father José Ignacio González Faus wrote to the Spanish newspaper *El País* and said: 'He divided the Argentine province into two sides, sides that have not yet reconciled.' After two years of the Francis papacy that reconciliation is at last progressing, although even in a tribute book *Pope Francis: Our Brother, Our Friend* published by US Jesuits after Bergoglio became Pope, praise has been offset by guarded remarks hinting at the divisions. 'He had a plan but not everybody agreed with that plan,' wrote Father Carlos Carranza, the third-oldest member of the Jesuit province. 'I know that those confrontations caused Bergoglio to suffer a lot and that there were many who did not approve, who did not agree with the way he governed the province at that time. That is as much as I am able to say. We should not go into specific cases.' Carranza, sinful of his Superior General's injunction, was being prudent in his recollections.

* * *

When Bergoglio finished his term as Rector his superiors in Rome did not know what to do with him. It was decided that it would be best if he was removed from Argentina for a period. In 1986 Bergoglio was dispatched to Germany where he spent several months at the Sankt Georgen Graduate School of Philosophy and Theology in Frankfurt consulting the resident professors about possible topics for his PhD thesis. In the few months that he was in Germany, he travelled extensively and visited various Jesuit communities. He was supposed to be away for two years. But, just a few months later, he returned suddenly to Buenos Aires with piles of photocopies and books. Among the subjects he explored was the work of Romano Guardini, the German Catholic philosopher whose work in the 1930s criticized Nazi views of Jesus, emphasizing his Jewishness, and critiquing the relationship between religion and violence in ways which must have resonated with Bergoglio's recent experience with the terror in Argentina. Guardini also laid the groundwork for many of the liturgical reforms of the Second Vatican Council. But Bergoglio could not settle on a specific topic and returned to Argentina undecided.

It was while in Germany, in the church of St Peter am Perlach in Augsburg, that Bergoglio came across the eighteenth-century painting *Mary Untier of Knots*, which so moved him that he bought postcards of the image, and took them back to Argentina (see Foreword to the First Edition). The image of how Mary could help disentangle the knots of life spoke deeply to him. But he could not yet see how the tangles and snarls in his own life could be smoothed away. He was not happy in Bavaria, and not just because, as he later said, he always got homesick when away from the city of his birth Buenos Aires. Someone who came across him taking an evening walk in a cemetery near the airport one evening asked him what he was doing there. He replied: 'Waving to the planes. I'm waving to the planes bound for Argentina.'

There may have been another motive. The Argentinian journalist Elisabetta Piqué, who has had regular contact with Bergoglio since he became a cardinal in 2001, suggests in her book *Francisco: Vida y Revolucion* that he returned early for a reason. The following year a meeting of Jesuit procurators was due to take place in Rome. The job of a procurator is to report to the Jesuit Superior

General and offer a 'state of the nation' report on their province. In this way the Jesuit Curia in Rome gets information about each of its congregations independently of what it is being told by the Provincial. It is part of the order's system of governance checks and balances. Each procurator is elected by a provincial congregation, whose members are elected by every Jesuit in the province. In March 1987 Bergoglio was elected procurator. Piqué's source told her that Bergoglio had returned early from Germany specifically to make himself available. His intention was to blow the whistle on the counter-reformation in which the new leadership in Argentina were undoing the programme he had put in place over the previous 15 years as Novice Master, Provincial and then Rector.

The fact that Bergoglio was elected procurator in 1987 showed that the *bergoglianos* in the province were still strong in number. But his behaviour over the three years which followed steadily alienated his support base. On Bergoglio's return from Germany the new Provincial, Father Victor Zorzin, told him to take a room in the Colegio del Salvador and gave him a part-time job teaching theology there. He was asked to return to the Colegio Máximo one day a week to lecture in pastoral theology; he travelled to the college the night before his teaching day, had dinner with the students and stayed overnight in the San Miguel seminary. The rest of the time he was supposed to be working on his PhD, which he never finished, though he gave a draft of the thesis as an inaugural lecture at one of the Buenos Aires universities a couple of years later. He filled his time reading and writing and preparing speeches and homilies to give at various events around the country to which he had received invitations. In April 1987 Pope John Paul II visited Argentina for the inaugural World Youth Day and Bergoglio met him for the first time at a gathering organized by the papal nuncio – the Pope's ambassador in Argentina. The two men spoke only briefly. In September that year Bergoglio went to Rome for the procurator's meeting and had a lengthier exchange with the Jesuit Superior General. The meeting confirmed both men in their disapproving view of the other. The following year, in September 1988, Kolvenach travelled from Rome to Argentina for a meeting with all the Jesuit Provincials from all across Latin America. It was in the Colegio Máximo. He also had a lunch with Jesuits committed to social justice from the Centre for Investigation and Social Action to celebrate his fortieth year in the order. He pointedly never even met Bergoglio.

The new Jesuit leader in Argentina, Victor Zorzin, Bergoglio's former deputy, had also previously been an assistant to Father Ricardo O'Farrell, whom Bergoglio and his confrères had ousted as Provincial in 1973. Zorzin was far less sympathetic to Bergoglio than had been the previous Provincial, Andrés Swinnen. Under Zorzin the Bergoglio regime was being dismantled. Tensions were inevitable. But Bergoglio seemed incapable of adjusting to the fact he was no longer Provincial or Rector. He started to voice his disapproval of the way his peers ran the school in which he taught. The issues involved were petty details about courses and administration. But what rankled was the way that Bergoglio continually behaved as though he were not now just an ordinary Jesuit. He instinctively sought to exercise power as though he were what Swinnen called a 'parallel Provincial' in ways that Zorzin and the members of his advisory council found troublesome. Hardly a meeting of the group went by without some complaint about the ex-Provincial. 'Bergoglio wanted to continue to mould the consciousness of the younger Jesuits,' said Father Andrés Swinnen. By now even Bergoglio's loyal acolyte Swinnen had become disenchanted. 'He wanted to continue to lead them. There's something very unhealthy about this thirst for leadership that he has.'

An increase in the number of Jesuits leaving the Society was, fairly or unfairly, blamed upon Bergoglio, as most of them were in the *anti-bergogliano* camp. Gradually the support Bergoglio had had among the ordinary Jesuits ebbed away. Eventually his fellow Jesuits made it clear that Bergoglio's interference was intolerable.

Zorzin contacted the Jesuit Curia in Rome. After discussions he acted decisively on Bergoglio. He issued an instruction to the Rector to withdraw Bergoglio's teaching post at the Colegio Máximo. It was done immediately. Bergoglio was told to hand in the key to his room in the seminary at San Miguel which had been his home for most of the past 30 years. Publicly Zorzin was discreet, saying only that Bergoglio 'was getting into situations that weren't favourable or desirable for him'. But he, and the Jesuit leadership in Rome, had lost patience with the meddlesome Bergoglio. In June 1990 he was packed off to 'a more tranquil place' – Argentina's second city Córdoba, some 400 miles away. Privately his supporters were ordered not to contact him.

His duties in Córdoba, he was told, were simply to say Mass, hear confessions, act as a spiritual director to individuals who requested him, and continue work on his doctorate. He complied but, colleagues recalled, he also brooded. The man who had been for almost fifteen years the kingpin of the Jesuit province felt sidelined and belittled. 'Córdoba was, for Bergoglio, a place of humility and humiliation,' said Father Guillermo Marcó, who was later Bergoglio's right-hand man on public affairs in the archdiocese of Buenos Aires. And yet something happened in Córdoba, as we shall see in a later chapter, which changed Bergoglio radically.

'The Society of Jesus is an institution in tension,' Bergoglio was to say as Pope Francis two decades later, 'always fundamentally in tension.' Quite so. 'I lived a time of great interior crisis when I was in Córdoba,' he continued in his first interview as Pope.

So deep were the divisions in the Society of Jesus that Bergoglio's exile did not salve the problem. For the two years he was in his Córdoba limbo, and for many more after, the Bergoglio personality cult continued to divide the province. So much so that Kolvenbach, eventually, had to send in outsiders as both Provincial and Novice Master to sort out the deeply entrenched difficulties. When Father Álvaro Restrepo, a Colombian who had formerly been an assistant to Superior General Arrupe, arrived in 1997 he expected to find the Argentinian province divided between conservatives and progressives, he said. Instead he found a province bitterly divided over the personality cult that existed around Bergoglio. 'Some followed the formation of Jorge Mario,' Restrepo said, 'and others were a different generation.' Restrepo had to work hard to heal the wounds, which he did by fostering dialogue, being impartial, and making people with different opinions work together. But it was clear that, whatever the original cause of the divisions among the Jesuits of Argentina, the focal point of the deep rift had become Bergoglio himself.

* * *

Bergoglio's exile ended abruptly in 1992 when the Archbishop of Buenos Aires, Cardinal Quarracino, who was also an opponent of Liberation Theology, decided to rescue him. The cardinal recommended to Rome that Bergoglio be made one of his auxiliary bishops. Earlier in their careers, when Bergoglio was Provincial and Quarracino was Bishop of Avellaneda, the Jesuit had directed retreats for Avellaneda's priests. By 1990 Quarracino had been made Archbishop of La Plata and had again – twice, in the months before Bergoglio was sent into the Córdoba wilderness – asked the austere Jesuit to give retreats to his clergy there. He even went to Bergoglio himself to ask to be directed in the Ignatian Spiritual Exercises. 'Quarracino had been impressed by the depth of Bergoglio's spirituality and his cleverness,' said Marcó. He also admired how well Bergoglio related to his diocesan priests. 'When he heard about Bergoglio's penance in Córdoba he decided to rescue him.' In his interviews with Francesca Ambrogetti and Sergio Rubin for El Jesuita, Bergoglio told the story of how he had met the papal nuncio to Argentina, Archbishop Ubaldo Calabresi, thinking he was advising on the names of suitable candidates for the episcopacy, only to be told that it was he who was to become Auxiliary Bishop of Buenos Aires.

That too divided the Jesuits. 'His being a bishop was totally unexpected,' said Yáñez. 'We Jesuits must do what we can to avoid being bishops and only do so if the Pope expressly demands it.' One of the Jesuit callings is to radical sacrifice of personal ambitions. Another Jesuit undertaking is to avoid high ecclesiastical office. The Argentine Jesuit Father Michael Petty, nearly two decades later, was still unhappy with Bergoglio's decision to accept the post. 'I find it difficult,' he said, 'because that's not what Jesuits should do, and so lots of people were very cross about it.' But many saw Bergoglio's change of direction as a solution. 'It was a relief when he left the order behind and became a bishop,' said Velasco, 'a relief for him and for the order. I suppose there were some high up in the Jesuits who said: thank God, now he's the Church's problem.' More with hope than optimism one old Jesuit quipped: 'Perhaps a bad Jesuit can become a good bishop.' Others thought Bergoglio's decision to become a bishop reflected a problem of pride and ambition within the former Provincial. 'There was something about this more like a project for personal power,' said Velasco. 'When he could no longer get this power inside the Jesuits he looked outside.' Father Michael Petty went further: 'He must have had that interior battle to realise what it meant to become a bishop. It meant that he could become Pope.' Father Raphael Velasco agreed: 'When he came out on the balcony as Pope one of the things that came to my mind was: he got what he wanted.'

* * *

Yet even as a new direction opened up in the ministry of Jorge Mario Bergoglio the story of his problematic relationship with the Society of Jesus was not entirely over. When he moved back to Buenos Aires as a bishop, instead of moving into a house at the archdiocese, he went back into a Jesuit residence. There, colleagues from that period say, he began to meddle again. Once more, it was over small things. One Jesuit who shared the residence with him, who spoke on condition that he should remain anonymous, gave the example of a parcel of pastries which was sent to the house as a present by a friend of the order. 'Bergoglio grabbed it and carried it to the kitchen, so the maids and cooks could share the goodies,' he recalled. 'But we didn't need a bishop to teach us how to share.' After a few months, some Jesuits began to ask when Bergoglio would leave. Eventually the order formally asked him to move.

All of which may explain the Jesuit emails complaining about Bergoglio as 'a man who never smiles'. And it perhaps tell us why, over the two decades that followed in which Jorge Mario Bergoglio made countless visits to Rome, he never once stayed at a Jesuit house in the city. Bergoglio's spirituality and style of leadership was to develop but it needed to do so now outside the order which had formed him.

4

What Really Happened in the Dirty War

For six years the very name ESMA sent a shiver of fear through the hearts of the people of Buenos Aires. The initials stood for nothing more than a training place for navy mechanics, the Escuela de Mecánica de la Armada. But after the military coup toppled the democratic government in Argentina in 1976 it became something more sinister. The ESMA training centre was one of 340 clandestine concentration camps into which tens of thousands of individuals 'disappeared' and were never seen again.

It was here that two Jesuit priests, Father Francisco Jalics and Father Orlando Yorio, were brought one Sunday morning in May, hooded and shackled, and very frightened, after being arrested in the poor neighbourhood where they had worked for the previous six years. They were taken down to the basement, stripped naked apart from their hoods, and tortured for five days in a fruitless attempt to get them to confess that they were in league with the left-wing guerrillas which the military junta had seized power determined to extirpate. What made matters worse was that they were convinced they had been kidnapped after being betrayed by their Superior, the Provincial of the Jesuit order, Jorge Mario Bergoglio.

Today tours can be taken around the white-stucco red-tiled colonnaded building, rather grand in its colonial style. There are neatly trimmed gardens, painted kerb-stones, clipped conifers and beautiful deep pink Chinese hibiscus flowers by the door through which those about to die would enter. In May, which is autumn in the southern hemisphere, the trees turn rich shades of russet and chestnut.

The case for the prosecution was made, the day I visited, by a quietly spoken philosophy student who in his spare time guides visitors around ESMA. 'This is where they were brought in,' he said, indicating an elegantly proportioned entrance hall with stout wooden pillars, hooped top and bottom with bands of black iron. 'No photographs please; this is still a crime scene.'

Thirty years have passed since the first crime occurred in this building, and yet investigations are not considered complete. Prosecutions are still taking place now that the military's immunity from prosecution has been lifted. The wounds in Argentine society are not yet healed, which is why the controversy surrounding Jorge Mario Bergoglio is still alive and angry. There are many who do not like ESMA being a museum, with tours for members of the public and foreign tourists; they want to knock it down and create a park with a golf course 'so that society can forget'. As the debate around Bergoglio illustrates, there are still many alive in Argentina who are unreconciled with their past.

Four marble steps took the blindfolded prisoners up to El Dorado, the golden room, with its herringbone parquet floor; this main building was called the Casino de Oficiales, and was once the recreation centre of the naval officers training here. When ESMA was a detention and torture centre, a phone booth was installed in this room from which the *desaparecidos* – the disappeared – were forced to ring their relatives back home to say they were being treated well. To the left was the staircase, and to the right the elevator shaft, down to the basement, where the torture was done. Today neither can be seen; the building was altered by the military to mask the evidence when the Inter-American Commission on Human Rights visited to check out reports of abuse. Before the foreign commissioners visited, the prisoners were rounded up and taken off to El Silencio, an island in the Rio de la Plata which had been the weekend home of the Archbishop of Buenos Aires.

The offence of the 5,000 prisoners who were held in ESMA – of whom a mere 150 survived – was that they were branded 'subversives' by the military junta headed by the army's General Jorge Videla, the navy's Admiral Emilio Massera and the air force's Brigadier-General Orlando Agosti. The Proceso de Reorganización was the military dictatorship's name for what the rest of the world came to call Argentina's Dirty War. At that time relations between the United States and the USSR had warmed a little but the two super-powers had transferred their Cold War hostilities to proxy arenas. The dictatorships of Argentina, Chile, Brazil, Bolivia, Paraguay and Uruguay came together – with the backing of the United States – in a plan called Operation Condor. Its aim was to stamp out communism across Latin America through a continent-wide campaign of murder and incarceration of anyone suspected to be involved in terrorism. The Argentinian junta believed themselves to be engaged in one of the first battles of the Third World War. They reckoned that the Argentinian public, which had been terrified by the campaigns of violence of the extremists of Left and Right in the previous three years, would accept the extermination of the leftist troublemakers. People were dragged from their houses in the middle of the night or snatched brazenly from the streets in broad daylight and bundled into unmarked Ford Falcons, the vehicles of choice of the Argentinian security services. A climate of fear spread swiftly throughout the nation.

'As many people as is necessary will die in Argentina to protect the hemisphere from the international communist conspiracy,' Videla told army commanders the year before the coup. Videla saw the Proceso de Reorganización as a cleansing process after which politics could be handed back to a chastened civilian population. But others in the junta saw it as a permanent change which would keep the military firmly in charge. They began by picking up left-wing militants and activists but soon moved on to trade unionists, academics, students, artists, writers, journalists and psychoanalysts until, two years on, they were picking up hapless individuals who happened to be in the wrong place at the wrong time – and priests like Jalics and Yorio who had done nothing more subversive than work among the poor.

At the bottom of the marble staircase which led off the entrance hall was a massive iron door. There the prisoners waited as they heard a command passed via the crackle of a radio to the guard who controlled the door from the other side. They passed through it and then, still blindfolded, cracked their heads on the great concrete beam which spanned the entrance to the place where they would be tortured. The guards laughed mirthlessly as each skull took the self-inflicted blow. The massive basement had been partitioned off into individual cells. To the right was one in which a few prisoners with the necessary skills forged the fake ID documents the death squad members used to infiltrate the leftist groups where they would find their next victims. 'This was where the false ID was prepared for agents like Alfredo Astiz, the naval intelligence officer who infiltrated the Mothers of the Plaza de Mayo,' the guide explained. The Mothers of the Plaza de Mayo were a group of women who, for 30 years, gathered in the city's main square every Thursday afternoon to demand news of the whereabouts of their disappeared children, alongside a separate group the Grandmothers of the Plaza de Mayo. The handsome Captain Astiz, who became known as the Blond Angel of Death (and was later briefly arrested by the British during the Falklands War), had infiltrated the group, with a bogus identity card, pretending that his brother was one of the 'disappeared'. When he had worked out who the key figures were he marked them – in grotesque imitation of the Judas of the Gospels – with a kiss, watched from a distance by one of his death squads who then pounced and bundled the women into cars and took them away.

'One of his victims,' the guide explained, 'was Esther de Balestrino de Careaga, the woman who had been the first boss of the young Jorge Mario Bergoglio in his job in a chemistry lab.' She was kidnapped from Santa Cruz church in 1977 where she was working with other mothers to publish a list of disappeared family members. She had, very unusually, been successful in securing the release of her own daughter Ana Maria, who then fled to Brazil. But Esther insisted on staying in Argentina, despite her daughter's pleas. Other mothers have daughters who are not yet freed, she told Ana Maria. 'She was brought to ESMA and tortured for 10 days.' Secret United States government documents, declassified in 2002, showed that along with two French nuns and four other mothers she had been drugged, stripped naked, flown out to sea in a helicopter and thrown into the Atlantic Ocean. Her body was unrecognizable when it was washed ashore. When it was finally identified Bergoglio had her reburied in the garden of the church from which she had been kidnapped.

'For years the Mothers asked Archbishop Bergoglio for a private meeting but he always refused. Yet within a month of his election as Pope he met Estela de Carlotto, the leader of the Mothers,' my guide told me. With her was a young politician, Juan Cabandié, who was born in ESMA after his pregnant mother was kidnapped and imprisoned here. 'Pregnant women weren't exempt from torture,' the guide explained, 'but many were kept in isolation and then moved to small rooms to give birth. The babies were taken from their mothers almost immediately and priests and nuns found adopting families sympathetic to the military regime. Many of them were given to the torturers and other staff here.' When Cabandié found out that his father was one of the perpetrators of the horror he cut off all contact with him. 'Pope Francis told them he would open the archives of the Catholic Church so they could try to track their disappeared relatives. We will see if he does.'

In the middle of the basement was a row of cells in which prisoners were tortured. A sign on the wall leading to cells 11 to 15 read, with cruel irony, Happiness Avenue. The two Jesuits, Yorio and Jalics, were heavily tortured here for five days, naked apart from the hoods which blinded and disorientated them, fastened with shackles hand and foot. The methods of torture involved semi-drowning and shocks from electric cattle prods. Torture throws up its own moral dilemmas. The guide pointed to a room where the electric goads were repaired when excessive use wore them out. 'They brought in an electrician to fix them,' the guide explained. 'When he found out what they were used for he, very bravely, refused to do it. So the torturers used bare wires, which was far more dangerous.' The electrician was horrified by the quandary in which he had been placed. Should he collude with torture by fixing the goads? Or leave the victims to be subjected to even worse treatment? After an agony of indecisions he fixed the goads.

'The torture was extraordinarily effective,' the guide continued, matter-of-factly. 'Everybody talked. Although not everything they said was true. Prisoners will say anything to get the torture to stop. Some of the Montonero leftist guerrillas carried cyanide pills in their pockets to avoid torture and avoid betraying their comrades. They knew they would talk if they were tortured enough. People sometimes even named the innocent in an attempt to get the torture to stop.' There was a sadistic creativity to the forms of violence the perpetrators invented, torturing wives in front of husbands or children in front of their parents. They even lined one cell with egg cartons to muffle the victims' screams.

But Jalics and Yorio had nothing to confess. At one point Yorio was injected with some kind of truth drug which made him babble deliriously, but all he talked about was God and Jesus. After five days one of the torturers said to Yorio: 'We know you're not violent. You're not guerrillas. But you've gone to live with the poor. Living with the poor unites them. Uniting the poor is subversion.'

Death, when it came, was called a 'transfer'. In the roof space the prisoners lay in coffin-sized wooden cells when they were not in the torture basement. At 5 p.m. the guards would read out a list of those who were to be 'transferred' to another detention centre. Those chosen were taken down to the basement where they were given an injection which rendered them woozy but still able to walk. Then over their heads were placed black fabric hoods stuffed with cotton which pressed painfully tight on the eyes, thanks to the elastic at the sides. They were never washed so an unbearable stench came off them. Then the drugged prisoners were made to climb the 11 stairs, along a wall where the paint today is peeling, grey, cream, light blue as the layers of history are revealed. The steps led to the courtyard from where they would be taken to their final destination. Only a few, like Jalics and Yorio, were transferred to another jail – in their case to a country house in Don Torcuato, 30 miles from Buenos Aires. There, for five months, they were held – hooded, handcuffed and with their feet tied – but they were not tortured. Eventually they were taken by helicopter and dumped, drugged and naked, in a field. But most of the prisoners staggered up the stairs to lorries; they had been drugged sufficiently to prevent protest but not enough to inhibit faltering movement. At the airport they were loaded into planes or helicopters from which, dazed but conscious, they were pushed out into the Atlantic or the estuary of the River Plate. This was done in such numbers that eventually the friendly military dictatorship in neighbouring Uruguay complained about the number of bodies being washed up on its shores.

* * *

So was Jorge Mario Bergoglio complicit in all this, as Yorio and Jalics claimed on their release? To understand, it is necessary to grasp something about the role of the Church and the shocking extent to which it endorsed and colluded in the systems set up by the military junta. The repression, which began immediately the military seized power, was extraordinarily systematic. It had clearly been planned in advance. Enemies had been demarcated: the active ones, the potential ones, the associates and the sympathizers. Sector by sector, the repression was organized, with a division of labour among the armed forces. The navy seized the Peronists to bring to ESMA. The army went for the Leftists: Communists, Maoists, Trotskyists, Guevaraists and so forth. In ESMA there was even a store labelled The Spoils of War. 'When you were kidnapped the death squads looted your house for what they called booty,' said the guide. 'They would take everything, even washing machines and refrigerators.' The authorities even set up their own estate agent to sell the houses of the disappeared. It took 400 people, working in shifts, to staff the torture centre at ESMA alone – military, civilians, nuns and priests.

What could persuade those who had dedicated their life to Christ to work in a torture centre? An attempt to understand must begin with the political ideology of the era. Out of the Cold War there grew, in the United States, the concept of the National Security State. It was conceived within the Pentagon but proselytized by the CIA and spread throughout its sphere of influence in the Americas. The conflict with communism was to be waged as a total war. So the best allies for the US in that would be those right-wing military dictatorships who saw their military and economic interests as identical to Washington's. It was funded through a continent-wide strategy called Operation Condor. A separate building at ESMA was dedicated to the training of the Argentinian armed forces by military advisers from France and the United States sharing expertise in counter-insurgency tactics, including interrogation and torture techniques, learned in wars in Algeria and Vietnam. But it was not just the Argentinian military who were the focus of this preparation. The Church was drawn into the ambit of the strategy seen as defending Western Christian civilization against atheistic communism.

One of the prime toeholds of Marxism in Latin America was perceived to be Liberation Theology. The years 1973 to 1979 saw the full force of the counter-attack on this theology of empowerment of the poor by the CIA and the Vatican. In this period the CIA created a special unit devoted to working with the Catholic Church. It passed money to a large number of sympathetic bishops and priests. It also supplied information about hundreds of radical priests and nuns, who then became the victims of the military dictatorships. In Argentina discussions between the military junta and the Church took place at the highest level. The very day of the coup, 24 March 1976, members of the military junta met for a long time with Adolfo Tortolo, Archbishop of Paraná, who was president of the bishops' conference of Argentina and bishop to the military. Tortolo emerged from the meeting to urge his fellow citizens to cooperate 'in a positive way' with the new government.

Two months later the nation's bishops met to discuss the situation. In 2010 Bergoglio said in his interviews with Rubin and Ambrogetti: 'We have to keep in mind that, like wider society, the Church came to realize what was happening gradually. Nobody was fully aware of what was happening at the start.' But that was not true. Declassified documents now reveal that at a meeting on 10 May 1976 ten of the bishops gave chilling details to one another of incidents in their dioceses of persecution, harassment of priests, arbitrary arrest, looting of detainees' homes, and even torture. They then took a vote on what to do. Nineteen bishops wanted to issue a public condemnation of the government. But 38 voted against the idea. As a result the meeting issued a statement entitled 'Country and Common Good' which called for understanding towards the military government. The document said it was wrong to expect the security agencies to act 'with the chemical purity' they would in peacetime. This was a national emergency in which people were being killed or kidnapped on the streets. The moment required, the bishops said, that a measure of freedom be sacrificed.

Four of the 57 bishops stepped out of line. They publicly condemned what was going on. One of them, Bishop Enrique Angelelli, was killed in a fake car accident for his refusal to keep quiet. The vast majority of the Church remained silent. Some church leaders were afraid. Others felt it best to retreat into an inner life of worship and wait for better times. But some clearly shared the worldview and anxieties of the military about the need to defend Catholicism against the anti-Church atheist hordes.

But that was not the worst of the Church's behaviour. Some priests colluded with the military junta and its reign of terror. In the trials that took place after democracy was restored, the former dictator Jorge Videla said that the Church knew what was happening with the disappeared. He even claimed he consulted with the hierarchy. The former Peronist education minister Emilio Mignone, a devout Catholic who became a leading human rights campaigner after his daughter was seized in front of him by an army snatch squad, asserted in his book *Church and Dictatorship* that Dirty War rules of engagement had been agreed between the military and the military vicar Archbishop Totolo. He said that it had been agreed that the dictatorship, before detaining a priest, would inform his clerical superior and that some bishops actually took the initiative by sending a sort of 'green light'. This is the accusation that was to be levelled at Jorge Mario Bergoglio.

There is no doubt that some priests and nuns were active collaborators in the terror. One of the techniques of the torturers at ESMA and elsewhere was, after a session of violence was over, to send the victim to see a priest in another part of the prison. One of these was a qualified psychologist as well as a priest. Perhaps the most notorious was the prison chaplain Father Christian von Wernich, who actually held the rank of police inspector and frequently visited the regime's secret torture camps. There he encouraged political prisoners to provide information in order to avoid being tortured. One of them, Luis Velazco, revealed at von Wernich's trial how, after a torture session, he had begged the priest: 'Father, please, I don't want to die.'

To which von Wernich responded: 'Son, the lives of the men who are here depend on the will of God and the cooperation that you can offer. If you want to stay alive, you know what you have to do.'

Von Wernich was found guilty of complicity in 7 murders, 42 kidnappings and 32 instances of torture. He was sentenced to life imprisonment. But he has still not been defrocked as a priest.

In another trial a naval captain Adolfo Scilingo, who confessed to his part in ejecting 30 living people from aeroplanes over the sea, who had been previously drugged, told the court that he had been informed that such activities had been approved by the church hierarchy, as 'a Christian way to die'. Army and navy chaplains had told the men performing the killings that their actions were justified by the Gospel parable of the separation of wheat from chaff. The Church was also involved in the stealing of babies born to 'disappeared' women who had been pregnant when arrested. Both priests and nuns took the babies away to find 'good Catholic families' who would adopt them. Videla claimed that Catholic bishops endorsed this to prevent the infants being raised as 'a new generation of terrorists'. As many as five hundred babies were trafficked this way and their identities changed – and their mothers killed.

The victims and their relatives were outraged at the role of the Church in this. But many could not believe that priest and nuns would do such things. As Bergoglio later pointed out in conversation with Rabbi Abraham Skorka: 'At that time, I was 39 years old and I had been the Jesuit Provincial since 1973. I had a very limited vision of what was happening because it is very different from being a bishop with a jurisdiction.' So to what extent was Jorge Mario Bergoglio complicit in any of it?

* * *

Three years before Jorge Mario Bergoglio became Provincial Superior of the Jesuits in Argentina his predecessor, Father Ricardo O'Farrell, had given his blessing to the setting up of a new Jesuit community in the Bajo Flores district of Buenos Aires. The four priests – Franz Jalics, Orlando Yorio, Luis Dourrón and Enrique Rastellini – were to live in a new area of social housing known as Rivadavia alongside a shanty-town known only by the number given it by some city council bureaucrat: Slum 1.11.14. During the week they would continue their work as university lecturers and writers but at the weekends they would minister to the neglected peoples of the slum next door. Among those with whom they worked in the slum were activists from the Peronismo de Base movement, a group with Marxist leanings working among the underprivileged. It was just one of what the Jesuits had come to call 'insertion' communities in which priests inserted themselves into the lives of the poor.

This was precisely the kind of activity which Bergoglio, when he became Provincial in 1973, was determined the Jesuits should stop. The new Provincial had a double motivation in this. Such work was dangerous, and drew the attention of men of violence towards the Jesuits. But it was also the kind of Liberation Theology which he had been appointed to purge from the order. By the end of 1974 he had closed all the Jesuit 'insertion' communities except this one. Using the scriptures to politicize and empower the poor, he felt, was giving scandal to traditional Catholics who saw this 'preferential option for the poor' as subversive and degrading to the traditional Ignatian spirituality. He told the four priests to move out of the slum and return to live in the main Jesuit community house.

A long dispute ensued. Bergoglio was the Superior. But two of the priests, Jalics and Yorio, were not just older than him – Bergoglio was only 36 when he assumed the leadership position – but had been his teachers when he was in his Jesuit formation. Jalics had taught him philosophy and Yorio theology. But after a protracted internal process that lasted more than a year – during which Yorio was sacked from his teaching post in the Colegio Máximo – Bergoglio ordered them to dissolve the Rivadavia community. Jalics and Yorio refused. Matters came to a head in February 1976. Bergoglio met the two priests and told them he was getting 'tremendous pressure from Rome and sectors of the Argentine Church' to dissolve the community. In Italy the Vatican, which was entering its most aggressive anti-Liberation Theology phase, was pressing the Jesuit Superior General to crack down on theologians who associated with Marxist groups like Peronismo de Base. The Superior General in Rome, Father Pedro Arrupe, had told the men to choose between the Rivadavia community and the Society of Jesus, Bergoglio informed the four priests. Yorio had his doubts about whether the order came from Rome. A month later, on 19 March 1976, they met again. What happened then is a matter of dispute. Yorio and Jalics thereafter maintained that the Provincial told them they were being expelled; Bergoglio has ever since insisted that the two men had resigned, albeit at his suggestion, as did Father Dourrón. Bergoglio said that the resignation of Yorio and Dourrón was accepted but that Jalics' resignation could not be as he had taken his final solemn vows – and only the Pope could release him from those. What seems actually to have happened is that Bergoglio told the men that unless they left Rivadavia they would be deemed to have resigned from the Jesuit order.

There was another point of disagreement. The two men had announced they wanted to start a new religious order and had drawn up rules for it, Bergoglio asserted. They had given him a copy of the rules which he had kept. No, said Yorio, the document they had given him was not a demand for a new order but a critique of Bergoglio's claim that what they were doing was incompatible with Jesuit practice. It set out, he later said, 'a structuring of religious life in case we couldn't continue in the Society of Jesus' but it was not a desire to leave the order. Clearly that was, to Bergoglio, a moot distinction. He concluded the meeting with a warning. 'In view of the rumours of an imminent coup d'état,' he said, 'I told them to be very careful.'

Five days later the military junta overthrew the democratically elected government. 'Everyone knew the coup was coming,' recalled the human rights lawyer Alicia Oliveira, who had been a friend of Bergoglio's since before he was Provincial and was one of those in Buenos Aires with whom he remained in touch as Pope until her death in November 2014. 'The newspapers, the month before, were speaking about who would be the ministers in the military government. The civilian government was really bad. Most people were happy when the coup happened. As one of Bergoglio's Jesuit contemporaries, Father Michael Petty, put it: 'It was an absolute mess. We were all very pro-military at first. I remember very clearly we were thrilled that the military should have taken over. But then the disappearing started...'

Oliveira and Bergoglio had foreseen something bad would happen. 'Bergoglio and I weren't happy at all. We both felt that the coup could be really bad,' she said. Both lawyer and priest had seen early on what she called the military's penchant for 'friend/enemy logic' – and their dangerous inability to distinguish between political, social or religious activism and terrorist insurgency. 'As we talked in the weeks before the coup I could see that his fears were growing, especially with regard to Yorio and Jalics.' Two years earlier another Jesuit, Father Juan Luis Moyano, who had been working on literacy programmes with the poor, had been held by the security forces and then deported. And a right-wing Triple A death squad had murdered the slum priest Father Carlos Mugica.

Fellow Jesuits said that Bergoglio was well versed in local politics and would sometimes get tips about pending military sweeps and alert colleagues to avoid them. Three of the Jesuits inside the Colegio Máximo were military chaplains; they supplied their Provincial with what inside information they could. More specifically he had particular information about Yorio and Jalics. He knew that they were generally under threat. But he had been told more than that. 'Bergoglio knew from a source that they were to be kidnapped,' Father Andrés Swinnen revealed in 2015.

'He and I met often and we constantly exchanged with each other all the information we had,' Oliveira told me. 'A friend of mine worked with Yorio and Jalics in the slum. She was a catechist. I gave her the same advice Bergoglio gave his priests. I told her to leave. I told her she was not just putting herself in danger but also the poor people she worked with. They could be killed because of her presence. Eventually she listened and she and her husband left. But Yorio and Jalics did not, and we know what happened.'

Someone who did take Bergoglio's advice was the Spanish Jesuit José Caravias, who was active in Buenos Aires in the last months of the democratic government. He had fled to Argentina from Paraguay four years earlier where he had been imprisoned by the Stroessner dictatorship for his work helping loggers organize a union. In Buenos Aires he worked in the slums. 'Bergoglio came and told me he'd heard that the Triple A had decreed my death and that of Jalics. I felt that it was not worth being a hero. But Jalics was brave and stayed, and it nearly cost him his life. Bergoglio encouraged me to flee to Spain. I think he was relieved when I left; he did not agree with my organizing among the poor, and perhaps police reports made him doubt me, but he was noble and helped me.'

Yorio and Jalics, however, were now in a kind of limbo. Their Rivadavia community had been dissolved but they continued to live in the area without any official status so far as the Jesuit order was concerned. What they needed, under church law, was to be attached to another order, or placed under the authority of a bishop. The men had approached the Bishop of Morón, Miguel Raspanti, who had participated as one of the Church Fathers in the Second Vatican Council. He agreed to bring them under his jurisdiction so long as their Provincial gave them appropriate references. He even assigned parishes to the priests. Bergoglio promised the men he would provide the necessary references. But when the documents arrived Raspanti became alarmed. They contained allegations which meant the men were not fit to exercise the priesthood. One said that Yorio was a communist who had subverted the members of female religious orders. Yorio went to confront Bergoglio. The Provincial denied it all, saying his references had been entirely favourable. Raspanti was elderly and perhaps confused, Bergoglio suggested.

Whatever Bergoglio's references said, the Bishop of Morón was sufficiently concerned to travel to the Colegio Máximo to see the Jesuit Provincial in person. A catechist from his diocese, Marina Rubino, who was studying theology at the college at the time, bumped into the bishop as he waited to see Bergoglio. He told her he was very worried. He had had an appropriate reference for Dourrón, who would now transfer to Morón, but he could not accept Yorio and Jalics. Rubino said: 'With the bad references Bergoglio had given them, he told me, he could not accept them into the diocese.' Both Yorio and Jalics had taught Rubino, who told the bishop they were both fine priests with spotless reputations. That only made the bishop more agitated. 'He was very distressed because he knew that left the two priests stranded without any ecclesiastical authority.' Raspanti told the catechist: 'I've come to ask Bergoglio to withdraw the report saying such very serious things.' Unless that happened, he said, the two priests would be left in the air, without a manager, without hierarchy, and he was afraid they would disappear. Several days later they did.

But there was another factor which may have played into that. Whether they had resigned or been expelled in Bergoglio's eyes, Yorio and Jalics were no longer members of the Jesuit community. He informed the Archbishop of Buenos Aires, Juan Carlos Aramburu, who withdrew their licences to say Mass. It was, Yorio later said – based on what he had been told in ESMA – 'like a green light' to the military to move against the two Jesuits. Three days after they lost their licences to say Mass the men were snatched by a naval death squad.

* * *

The kidnapping took place at 11 a.m. on Sunday 23 May 1976. The day before Yorio had telephoned Bergoglio and asked what they should do about the usual Sunday Mass. Bergoglio told them they could say Mass in private at their homes and sent another priest, Father Gabriel Bossini, to say Mass in the church. As Mass was being said in the church 200 naval storm troops moved into the Bajo Flores area. They snatched the two priests in their homes and also four catechists and two of their husbands. Father Bossini was left unharrassed. Father Dourrón, who was cycling around the area at the time, managed to escape on his bicycle. The six people taken with the priests were never seen again.

Bergoglio heard the kidnapping had taken place that same day when a resident of Bajo Flores rang him. The men responsible had been from the navy, he was told. 'The very night I learned they had been kidnapped, I set the ball rolling,' he said. He informed the Jesuit Superior General in Rome 'from a phone box on Corrientes Avenue, so as not to use the phone in the Curia'. He rang the church hierarchy. And he contacted the families of Yorio and Jalics to inform them about the actions he was taking. To Yorio's brother Rodolfo he later wrote: 'I have lobbied the government many times for your brother's release. So far we have had no success. But I have not lost hope that your brother will soon be released...I have made this affair *my* thing. The difficulties that your brother and I have over the religious life have nothing to do with it.' On 15 September 1976, when the two priests had been missing for almost four months, he wrote to Jalics' family in similar terms: 'I have sought in many ways to bring about your brother's freedom, but thus far we have been unsuccessful', began the letter written almost entirely in Latin. 'But I have not lost hope that your brother will be released soon. I have decided that the matter is my task.' Alluding to his disagreements with Jalics, he continued: 'The difficulties that your brother and I have had between ourselves concerning the religious life have nothing to do with the current situation.' Then, he added, in German, 'Ferenke [Franz] is a brother to me...I'm sorry if I started writing in German, but this is the way I think about it...I have Christian love for your brother, and I will do all in my power to see him freed.'

Those close to Bergoglio insist that the kidnapping caused him great distress. 'Jorge suffered great anxiety in the months after the disappearance of Yorio and Jalics,' his friend Alicia Oliveira said. 'He did a lot to try to release them. He visited the head of the junta, General Videla, and Videla told him it had been done by the navy. So he went to see the head of the navy, Massera. He talked to the Jesuits in Rome. He talked to the Vatican. He has since constantly reproached himself for not doing enough but he worked like crazy to get them out.' That was confirmed by Father Juan Carlos Scannone, an elderly Jesuit in the Buenos Aires community who had been one of Bergoglio's teachers. 'When they disappeared Bergoglio was informing me on an on-going basis about everything he was doing,' Scannone said.

Bergoglio went twice to see both Videla and Massera. Bergoglio made public details of the meetings when he was in court in 2010 where he was a witness in the trial of individuals accused of crimes against humanity in the ESMA torture centre. He described his first meeting with the army chief, who was the de facto president: 'It was very formal. He took notes and he said that he would make enquiries. I told him that it was said that they were in the hands of the navy. The second time, I managed to find out which military chaplain was going to celebrate Mass in the residence of the Commander in Chief. I persuaded him to say he was sick and to send me in his place. That Saturday afternoon, after the Mass, which I said before the whole Videla family, I spoke with him. There I had the impression that he was going to take action, and take things more seriously.' The conversation with Vidal was verified by an official from the US embassy who was present.

His meetings with Emilio Massera, the Commander of the Navy, were, by Bergoglio's account, more problematic. 'The first time he listened to me, and he told me that he would look into it. I told him that these priests were not involved in any odd activities. And he said he would give me an answer. But when he didn't answer, after a few months I asked for a second interview. By this time, I was almost certain that the navy had them. The second interview was very nasty.'

'I've already told Tortolo what I know,' said Massera, making curt reference to Archbishop Adolfo Tortolo, president of the bishops' conference and bishop to the military.

'Monsignor Tortolo,' corrected Bergoglio.

'Look here, Bergoglio,' Massera began, annoyed at being corrected.

'Now you look here, Massera,' Bergoglio replied in the same manner before repeating that he knew where the priests were and he wanted them freed.

The verbatim transcript of their conversation came from Bergoglio himself in a rare interview with the Argentinian journalist Horacio Verbitsky in 1999. At that time Verbitsky, a former intelligence chief with the Montoneros, had written sympathetically of Bergoglio, then the newly appointed Archbishop of Buenos Aires; he has since become his fiercest critic. 'I never felt this dialogue rang true as it was with one of the most powerful and cruel members of the government, who would have had no scruples in kidnapping Bergoglio,' he wrote in 2013. But many others believed Bergoglio's account.

* * *

It took five months for the two Jesuits to be freed. On 23 October 1976 the telephone rang in the Provincial's office in the Colegio Máximo. It was Yorio. Bergoglio assumed the phone line was tapped by the military. He later told the court in the ESMA trial: 'I told him: "Don't tell me where you are, and don't move from where you are. Send me a person to tell me where we can meet." At that point one had to take all possible precautions.' Bergoglio then contacted the papal nuncio, Archbishop Pio Laghi, to ask him to accompany Yorio and Jalics to the police headquarters. Laghi played tennis with the head of the navy, Massera. Accompanied by the Pope's chief representative to Argentina, Bergoglio told the ESMA trial, 'nothing bad could happen to them inside there'. It was decided that it would be best if the two Jesuits left the country. Yorio was packed off to Rome to study canon law. Jalics was sent to the United States where his mother was living. Later he went to live in a retreat house in Germany where he set up a specialism supervising retreats using the Jesus Prayer – 'Lord Jesus Christ, Son of God, have mercy on me, a sinner.' Jalics had survived psychologically in captivity by reciting it over and over.

Various accounts were given of why they were released rather than being murdered like most of the 'disappeared'. Bergoglio's friends insisted that it was his intervention which was decisive. Others said the human rights campaigner Emilio Mignone secured the Jesuits' release; his widow maintained he had done so through contacts in Rome who put pressure on the Argentinian regime. Yorio's brother Rodolfo put it down to a deal that secured a meeting between the junta's economic minister and the Vatican, which took place within days of the men being freed. But some in Argentina made links with the granting of an honorary degree to the ESMA boss, Admiral Massera. A year after the two Jesuits were released the Universidad del Salvador, which was run by the Iron Guard to which Bergoglio had links, made Massera an honorary professor. In accepting it, in November 1977, Massera – newly returned from a visit to the Vatican where he had been honoured with an audience with Pope Paul VI – made a bizarre speech in which he lauded the sacred nature of private property and called for Marx, Freud and Einstein to be excluded from the university curriculum on the grounds that their Jewishness meant they were not part of the great Western Christian tradition. Bergoglio later denied responsibility for the award, saying: 'I received the invitation to the ceremony, but I did not go. Furthermore, the university is not part of the Society of Jesus and I had no authority there.' But he did send his Jesuit deputy, Father Victor Zorzín, in his place. Most Jesuits blamed Bergoglio for the debacle. 'We were very angry about it,' said Father Michael Petty, 'because we knew who Massera was, of course' – and the torture for which he had been responsible.

Yet even then the saga was not over. In 1994 Jalics published a book *Kontemplative Exerzitien* (Meditation Exercises) in which he claimed that, before the kidnapping, he had confronted Bergoglio – to whom he refers in the text as 'the person in question'. He wrote:

Many people who held far-right political beliefs frowned on our presence in the slums. They interpreted the fact that we lived there as a support for the guerrillas and proposed to denounce us as terrorists. We knew which way the wind was blowing and who was responsible for these slanders. So I went to talk to the person in question and explained that he was playing with our lives. He promised that the military would know that we were not terrorists. From later statements of an official, and thirty documents which

I was able to get hold of later, we saw without a doubt that this man had not kept his promise but, on the contrary, had filed a false report with the military.

Bergoglio must have known, he wrote, that his life, and that of Yorio, were put in mortal danger by his 'credible libel'. In the book Jalics said that he had burned the incriminating documents in 1980 to free himself of bitterness and move on. But he clearly had not moved on that far, as was evidenced by the fact that 15 years later he still felt sufficiently agonized to want to write a book. Jalics was to say more later, after Bergoglio became Pope.

It also transpired that in 1977 Yorio had written a 27-page letter to the Jesuit Curia in Rome with similar complaints. Bergoglio's actions, at a time when the junta was trying to 'cleanse' the nation of Liberation Theology, were tantamount to a death sentence on his fellow Jesuits. All they had been doing, Yorio said in his letter to Rome, was entirely in line with Vatican II.

Yorio also told friends that his interrogators had asked questions based on theological information and spiritual confession he thought only his Provincial could have known. He was so upset when Bergoglio was made a bishop in 1992 that he moved to Uruguay, where he lived until his death. In 1996 the Jesuits' new Superior General Peter-Hans Kolvenbach offered to accept Yorio back into the Society of Jesus. Yorio said he would only accept if he was given access to the documentation in which Bergoglio had filed charges against him. Kolvenbach replied that this could not be done. Yorio died of a heart attack in 2000 after suffering from years of what appeared to be post-traumatic stress disorder. In court at the ESMA trial Bergoglio said that Yorio had been 'conditioned by the suffering that he had to go through'. Whether his evident resentment supports or undermines his testimony is a matter of judgement.

There is one further twist in this tragic tale. In 2005 the investigative journalist Horacio Verbitsky was in the archives at the Argentine Ministry of Foreign Affairs. He was rootling through box after box of old papers in search of a story. He found one. It was in a note bearing the letterhead of the Society of Jesus, with the stamp and the signature Father Bergoglio, dated 4 December 1979. Jalics was in Germany at this point but the dictatorship was still in power back home. His passport was about to expire – he had been born in Hungary but had become an Argentinian citizen – and he did not think it safe to return to Buenos Aires to renew it. So he asked his old Provincial to do it for him.

Bergoglio wrote the requested letter to the Foreign Ministry, asking if the passport could be renewed by post to save Jalics a long and expensive trip. But there was a second sheet in the folder, signed by one Anselmo Orcoyen, the ministry's Director of Catholic Worship. It noted that 'Fr Francisco Jalics' had been involved in subversive activities at female religious congregations provoking conflicts of obedience and that he had been held in ESMA, together with Yorio, on suspicion of contacts with guerrilla groups. What followed sounded as though it might have been the kind of account Bergoglio would have given, for it tallied exactly with his version of events rather than that of Yorio or Jalics. They lived, it said, in a small community that was dissolved by the Jesuit Superior in February 1976; they declined to obey and were asked to leave the order on 19 March; Yorio had been expelled, but not Jalics because he had already taken his final perpetual vows; no bishop in Argentina would accept the two priests thereafter. At the end was a note saying that all this information had been given to Orcoyen by Bergoglio – who admitted as a witness at the ESMA trial that he had delivered the letter to the Foreign Ministry by hand. At the same time, Orcoyen's note claimed, Bergoglio made a verbal recommendation that the passport application be rejected.

To Verbitsky what the two pieces of paper revealed was clear. 'The documents close the case, in my opinion, on Bergoglio's attitude to the junta,' Verbitsky wrote. 'He publicly asked for a favour for his priest, Father Jalics, but behind his back accused him of activities that could cause his death.' What he had done with the passport was clearly what he had done in all his dealings with Yorio and Jalics from the outset, Verbitsky concluded. 'While he seemed to be helping them, he was also accusing them behind their backs.'

The story made a compelling coda to the earlier accusations of bad behaviour by Bergoglio in the Yorio and Jalics case. Within a month of Verbitsky publishing them in his newspaper *Página/12* the allegations were to form the central plank of the Stop Bergoglio dossier which was sent to a large number of cardinals ahead of the 2005 conclave to elect a successor to Pope John Paul II.

Bergoglio offered a clear answer to this in the Rubin and Ambrogetti interviews: 'The civil servant to whom I gave it asked me what had caused Jalics to leave so suddenly. "He and his friend were accused of being guerrilla fighters, but they had nothing to do with any such thing," I answered.' The civil servant made a note of the first part of the sentence but not the second. Why, Bergoglio asked, would he have bothered to intercede for Jalics in the first place if he had been trying to hinder him? 'I wrote the letter making the request. I was the one sticking my neck out for Jalics.'

What all this means is that the only actual evidence on which to make a judgement on Bergoglio's behaviour is a note which is open to several possible interpretations. Perhaps the civil servant was sloppy in his note-taking. Perhaps he misunderstood or over-interpreted what was said. Perhaps he might have been wilfully selective in order to curry favour with his superiors. Perhaps the official could have had other motives. It is hardly conclusive proof on a charge which goes to the integrity of a man who was to become Pope. To find an answer we must look elsewhere.

* * *

It is beyond doubt that during the years of the Dirty War Jorge Mario Bergoglio did much to protect the victims of the military junta's violence. Indeed he had begun to assist those being persecuted even before the coup. At the Provincial headquarters in Bogotá Street in downtown Buenos Aires he had sheltered individuals on the run from the dictatorship in neighbouring Uruguay. A few weeks before the military seized power he decided to close down the house, having heard that it was 'marked' by the security forces. 'He knew the inside story on lots of things,' said a contemporary Jesuit, Father Michael Petty. Bergoglio transferred the fugitives hiding there to Colegio Máximo, more than ten miles away in the suburbs, where he told members of the community that if anyone asked, they were to say that the newcomers were undergoing a 30-day silent spiritual retreat. Bergoglio gambled that the military were less likely to interfere with a Jesuit house of higher learning.

One of the Uruguayans, Gonzalo Mosca, who was not religious, though his brother was a Jesuit, recalled: 'I had novels to distract me, and a portable radio, but it was very tense. I had four days without sleep while Bergoglio made the preparations for me to fly to the city of Puerto Iguazú and then cross from there into Brazil. Bergoglio drove me to the airport and escorted me almost to the plane.' He was both 'personally and institutionally brave,' said Mosca who escaped successfully to Europe. 'The repression in Argentina was very strong. I kept wondering if the priest [Bergoglio] knew what he was playing with.'

If he did not, he soon learned. Within six months of the coup one of the few bishops to speak out against the dictatorship, Enrique Angelelli, was killed in a bogus car crash; Bergoglio took three of Angelelli's seminarians into hiding soon after. They suffered from guilt by association because they had, like Yorio and Jalics, been working in the slums. One of them, Father Miguel La Civita spoke out in support of Bergoglio after he became Pope to counter the suggestions being be made that the new pontiff had collaborated with the military during the dictatorship. Bergoglio hid La Civita and his friends in Colegio Máximo while documentation was prepared so that they could leave the country. 'This is not something someone told me. I saw it and lived it,' La Civita said. 'The Jesuits had an organization to help people leave the country. Bergoglio acted like a father to us to fill the space that had been left by the death of Angelelli.

He took us under his protection at a time when we were being closely watched. Father Bergoglio never took the time to answer the criticisms of those who said he collaborated. But the reality was the opposite.' Any suggestion that Father Bergoglio collaborated with the dictatorship, he said, was 'a barbarity that reflects a lack of ethics on the part of the accusers'.

The human rights lawyer Alicia Oliveira offered similar evidence. 'The Jesuits had a retreat house called St Ignatius,' she told me. 'Every weekend there, for many, many Sundays, Bergoglio invited me. They were often farewell meals for people who had been protected by Bergoglio and who were then being smuggled out of the country. After a small Mass and meal they would leave.' She corroborated the account Bergoglio had given to the interviewers Rubin and Ambrogetti about how he had given his own ID card to a fugitive who looked like the Jesuit Provincial. 'He bought a clergyman's suit and dog collar for the man and gave him his own ID papers,' she said, 'and the man fled to Brazil disguised as a priest.'

Bergoglio did what he could by way of public gestures of support, Oliveira said. She had been a judge before the coup but was sacked immediately when the military took power. That was not all. 'My four-year-old was approached by people who said: "We are going to kill your mother." Two days afterwards, someone sent me a bouquet of flowers with a letter saying how good I had been as a judge. It was unsigned but I recognized Bergoglio's handwriting.' When she went into hiding Bergoglio would come to take her by a secret route to a Jesuit school where she could meet her children. He offered her safe haven at the Colegio Máximo but she turned him down. 'I'd rather be taken by the military than live with priests,' she joked in response. Oliveira was a single mother; shortly afterwards Bergoglio made a point of baptizing her younger son. It was not public prophetic witness, but it was very supportive personally, she said.

But most of the acts of resistance Bergoglio offered were clandestine, like the time he received a call from his former boss Esther de Balestrino de Careaga, asking him to call to give her mother-in-law the last rites. Bergoglio knew that the family were not Catholic but he went anyway. When he arrived de Careaga explained that her daughter had recently been arrested and she feared her house would soon be searched. The security forces would be bound to find a number of books on Marxism. 'Bergoglio took them and hid them in the new library he had had built at Colegio Máximo. Among the books was *Das Kapital*,' Alicia Oliveira later told me, laughing at the thought of Bergoglio taking Marx to a library he had earlier purged of the writer's influence. Later Esther brought another woman to Bergoglio for help. 'She had two sons, who were both communist militant worker delegates who had been kidnapped,' Bergoglio himself recalled. 'She was a widow, and her sons were all she had left. How she cried. It was a scene I will never forget. I made some inquiries but got nowhere, and I often reproach myself for not having done more.' Bergoglio resisted the junta, not in public but in dark places, like the shadowy back staircase at the college. Bergoglio told the students to use that to avoid the scrutiny of government agents in the public lobby by Colegio Máximo's main marble staircase. Throughout all this Bergoglio displayed considerable personal courage.

But he did not speak out publicly. Bergoglio, despite his charismatic leadership qualities, was younger than Argentina's other church leaders. He was 40 years of age at the time and had no real means of challenging the authorities without the support of the Argentinian bishops – and the then Archbishop of Buenos Aires, Cardinal Juan Carlos Aramburu, repeatedly insisted that the military could not be behind the disappearances and other violations of human rights. When relatives of the disappeared approached Aramburu he ignored their complaints. Bergoglio 'might have done more to protect political prisoners', adjudged Professor Mario I. Aguilar, author of *Pope Francis: His Life and Thought*, but the real blame 'should be placed upon the Argentinian bishops: they should have spoken openly and with a common voice about the political situation'.

'It was a very tense time,' recalled Father Juan Carlos Scannone, a theologian then and now at Colegio Máximo, 'you had to be careful of every move you made. When the military took over in 1976 everything related to Liberation Theology was seen as Communist and Marxist. I was labelled Marxist which I never was.' Another Colegio Máximo resident, Father Andrés Swinnen, said: 'It was a time of panic. Anything could happen. Everyone was in danger'. Scannone calls himself a liberation theologian, though of a non-Marxist strain. During the Dirty War he would often show Bergoglio his articles on Liberation Theology before publication 'to protect me from bad interpretations'. Bergoglio asked him to post them from a different address because he suspected the military were scrutinizing the Jesuits' mail but he made no attempt to censor the writing of Scannone who was, developing the *teología del pueblo* which embraced Bergoglio's respect for the popular piety of the ordinary people. And he advised Scannone and others doing work in poor neighbourhoods to avoid travelling back alone after dark, to avoid government kidnappers.

But he felt very limited in what he could do publicly, he told Oliveira, who was later Human Rights Ombudsman for the City of Buenos Aires. She urged him to speak out during the dictatorship. 'He was anguished,' she recalled. 'But he said he couldn't, that it wasn't an easy thing to do.' It is important to take into account the limitations Bergoglio faced at the time, said Scannone: 'He wasn't even a bishop yet, and could act only in his capacity as head of the country's

Jesuits. His job was to protect the Jesuits, and all of the Jesuits made it through the period alive, which tells you he did his job.'

But Bergoglio always thereafter, he told friends, felt he could have done more.

Some 30 years later when Pope Francis stood in the Hall of Remembrance at the Yad Vashem Holocaust memorial in Jerusalem he said something which seemed full of resonance for his time as a leader during the Dirty War. He confirmed that he intended to open the Vatican archives on Pius XII, the Second World War Pope who was accused of not speaking out to condemn the Nazi genocide against the Jews. Like Bergoglio in Argentina, Pius kept public silence but worked behind the scenes to save thousands of Jews. But Pope Pius too has never shaken off the accusation that, had he spoken out, he could have saved many more. Commenting on the controversy, which has put a strain on Catholic–Jewish relations for decades, Pope Francis said: 'I don't want to say that Pius XII did not make any mistakes – I myself make many – but he has to be seen in the context of that era. Was it better for him not to speak out so that more Jews were not killed, or that he speak out?' Papa Bergoglio might have been asking the question about himself.

* * *

There is one other grave accusation that must be addressed in making a judgement on how Bergoglio acquitted himself during Argentina's Dirty War. As we have already seen there were around 500 pregnant women among the tens of thousands who disappeared at the hands of military death squads. Their babies were taken from them and passed via priests and nuns to 'good Catholic families' – a euphemism for those sympathetic to the right-wing junta. One of the women who had their babies taken in this way was Elena de la Cuadra. The 23-year-old was five months pregnant when she was kidnapped in 1977.

Elena's father Roberto Luis de la Cuadra was well connected. He got Elena's brothers to visit Father Pedro Arrupe, head of the Jesuit order in Rome, to appeal for help. Arrupe asked his Provincial in Argentina to assist the family. In 1977 Bergoglio met Elena's father twice and gave him a diplomatically worded letter to take to Mario Picchi, the auxiliary bishop of La Plata, who had contacts in the military. It said simply of Mr de la Cuadra: 'He will explain to you what this is about, and I will appreciate anything that you can do.' Several months later the bishop told the family that Elena had given birth to a daughter who had been christened with the bitterly ironic name of Ana Libertad – Anna Freedom. The child was 'now with a good family', the bishop said. The situation was 'irreversible' the family were told. Elena's body was never found.

In 2010, during Argentina's crimes-against-humanity trial, Cardinal Jorge Mario Bergoglio was asked to testify as a witness. He told the court that it was only about ten years earlier that he had heard of babies being stolen and their mothers killed. Really, said one of the prosecutors; ten years ago? Well perhaps it was 25 years, Bergoglio said. But it was after the return of democracy. So what about the case of Elena de la Cuadra whose family had a photocopy of Bergoglio's handwritten letter dated 1977? Horacio Verbitsky promptly accused the cardinal of lying under oath. Many in Argentina suspected Bergoglio was not telling the whole truth.

Once again the evidence is inconclusive. The letter does not mention Elena or that she was pregnant. It simply asked the bishop to speak to Mr de la Cuadra on a matter which Mr de la Cuadra would explain. 'He told me that his daughter had been kidnapped,' the cardinal told the court. 'I don't recall him telling me if his daughter was pregnant.' And yet copious numbers of press reports in the late 1970s show that the issue of the 'stolen babies' was well in the public domain. It was inconceivable, Elena's sister Estela told the court, that Bergoglio couldn't have known.

This is a charge which many feel Bergoglio has not satisfactorily addressed. Fellow Jesuits have talked about how well informed he was as Provincial in the 1970s, with intelligence from his three Jesuit military chaplains and his friends in the Iron Guard and the tip-offs he seemed to receive about impending military sweeps. His friend Alicia Oliveira admitted: 'He always seemed to know more than me when we met to exchange information.' And Bergoglio's loyal disciple, Father Swinnen, has said that the young Provincial had had a specific tip-off about the kidnap of Yorio and Jalics. Father Michael Campbell-Johnston, the assistant Arrupe dispatched to Buenos Aires in 1977 to pull Bergoglio into line over the work of the Jesuit social institute (see Chapter Three), returned to Rome to receive 'a copy of a letter addressed to the Pope and signed by over four hundred Argentinian mothers and grand-mothers who had "lost" children or other relatives and were begging the Vatican to exert some pressure on the military junta'. And Alicia Oliveira told me: 'The Jesuit retreat house called St Ignatius was right across the road from a secret maternity hospital where kidnapped women who were pregnant were taken to have their babies – the babies that were then taken away from them and the women "disappeared".'

The evidence proves none of these surmises. Even so, many in Argentina agree with Lisandro Orlov, a leading Lutheran theologian in Argentina who, in all other aspects, defends Bergoglio's record during the Dirty War, but who said this is the area in which Bergoglio has most questions to answer. 'None of us who were around in those years can say we didn't know what was going on. He can't sustain the argument that he didn't know about the missing children.'

The issue goes to a wider point. Many of the families of the victims of the Dirty War in Argentina have asked why Bergoglio did not speak out later when he could have done, as a bishop, archbishop and cardinal. Only as Pope has he agreed to meet the Grandmothers of the Plaza de Mayo who regularly, and always fruitlessly, petitioned him to meet them when he was in Buenos Aires, requesting that he open the Church's archives to help trace the stolen babies so they can be put back in touch with their blood relatives – something it was announced that he had finally done in April 2015. (After a meeting with another Argentine human rights activist, Lita Boitano, the 83-year-old mother of two sons who were "disappeared" during the dictatorship, the Pope agreed to the opening of the Vatican archives for the period covering Dirty War when the papal nuncio Pio Laghi played tennis on a regular basis with Admiral Emilio Massera, considered to have been the bloodiest member of the three-man military junta that ruled Argentina. The Pope also ordered a meeting between Boitano and Monsignor Giuseppe Laterza, an official in the Secretariat of State, to discuss the possibility of the Vatican issuing a statement of self-criticism regarding its role during Argentina's dictatorship, Boitano said.) It may have been prudent for Bergoglio to decide that, during the dictatorship, it was too dangerous to confront the military openly. The case of Bishop Angelelli offered a salutary reminder of what happened to Church leaders who spoke out; the military said he died in a car crash but a post mortem showed that he had been beaten to death. But what is the explanation for Bergoglio's reticence, once the dictatorship was over, in condemning the wrongdoing by priests who were so closely involved in the illegal incarceration of political prisoners and even their torture?

It did nothing for his reputation that when he was asked to testify at the 2010 ESMA trial Cardinal Bergoglio refused, exercising a provision in Argentine law allowing senior church officials to decline a summons to court. So the court went to him. When the court decamped to the Archbishop's office, prosecuting lawyers repeatedly expressed their frustration at Bergoglio's minimalist replies. One of the prosecutors, the human rights lawyer Myriam Bregman, accused him of avoiding giving straight answers. 'Bergoglio's reticence and the brevity of his replies,' she said, 'was consistent with the church hierarchy's attitude of silence and concealment during the whole post-dictatorship period, systematically refusing to hand over files or documentation.' Anyone watching videos, or scrutinizing transcripts, of his evidence would be hard put to disagree that his performance looked evasive. 'That is hardly surprising,' one parish priest from Buenos Aires told me. 'They weren't out to get the truth, they were out to nail him.' He was not being quizzed as a neutral witness, said one neutral diplomat, 'he was definitely under attack'. He also admitted that when Jalics and Yorio were released and told him that there were still kidnapped people in ESMA, he did nothing about that. For all that, Germán Castelli, one of three judges in the trial, later insisted: 'It is absolutely wrong to say that Jorge Bergoglio delivered these priests [to the military]. We've heard this version, analysed the evidence presented and concluded that his actions had no legal involvement in this case. If this was not the case, we would have prosecuted.'

* * *

In the end, diligent examination of Bergoglio's conduct leaves unanswered questions. But if there is, finally, a shortage of definitive facts there is no lack of opinion among those most intimately involved. Yorio died convinced Bergoglio was a duplicitous traitor. The devout Catholic establishment man Emilio Mignone agreed. Yet Jalics, who once thought the same, has resiled from that view. He announced in March 2013 that, years after his grim ordeal, he and Bergoglio had met and concelebrated Mass together and shared what Jalics called 'a solemn embrace' after which he was reconciled with Bergoglio. When Bergoglio's critics pointed out 'you don't pardon somebody that didn't offend you' Jalics issued a second statement five days later which said: 'I myself was once inclined to believe that we were the victims of a denunciation but...after numerous conversations, it became clear to me that Orlando Yorio and I were not denounced by Father Bergoglio.' He now believed that a female catechist, who had at first worked with the two priests but later joined the guerrillas, had given the names of Yorio and Jalics to the military under torture. For some that was a plausible explanation but others, like Yorio's sister, Graciela, insisted that to say 'that the reconciliation happened indicated that there was something that had to be reconciled. We are absolutely convinced that Francisco (Jalics) was pressurised' into making his emollient statements about the new Pope.

Those on the periphery are similarly divided. Bergoglio's only surviving sister, María Elena, said she could not conceive that her brother would have colluded with the junta, betraying everything his father had taught them about the need to resist the fascism he had fled Italy in 1929 to escape. Bergoglio's former Jesuit driver, Miguel Mom Debussy, who is largely critical in his memories of his old Provincial, declared: 'During the Seventies I saw his attitude as repressive but looking back I think he was trying to protect us.' Father Michael Petty agreed;

Bergoglio had sent him away from Buenos Aires to Córdoba, in retrospect, 'to save my life'. The Vatican, not unexpectedly, has insisted: 'There has never been a credible, concrete accusation against him.' Instead Vatican spokesmen have talked of slanders on the new Pope's past by 'anti-clerical left-wing elements' used by the Kirchner government in Argentina to attack the Church.

The investigative journalist Horacio Verbitsky has countered by pointing out that the first accusations were levelled by Mignone in 1986 when Bergoglio was largely unknown outside Argentinian church circles – and that Verbitsky himself began to investigate Bergoglio long before the Kirchner government, which he supports, came to power. Verbitsky is convinced that the man who went on to become Pope, while far from the worst of the church leaders colluding with the junta – 'the degree of complicity of the highest hierarchy of the church at that time was enormous' – is guilty of lying and 'a duplicitous *modus operandi*'. To which Alicia Oliveira, who was once both friend and lawyer to Verbitsky, shrugged her shoulders and said: 'Each of us is in charge of our own madness.'

Opinion is fragmented too in Argentinian society and the wider Church. The Jesuit theologian Father José Ignacio González Faus has insisted: 'Franz Jalics has written things about him that cannot be overlooked, particularly, since these things were written in a very respectful way. And when they met each other, many years later in Germany, they fell into each other's arms crying.' Faus sees ambiguity in that act. And Father Eduardo de la Serna, coordinator of the Movement of Priests for the Third World, has said: 'Bergoglio is a man of power and he knows how to position himself among powerful people. I still have many doubts about his role regarding the Jesuits who went missing under the dictatorship.'

By contrast Father Angel Centeno, the current Secretary of Religious Matters in the Argentinian Jesuit headquarters, has said: 'It was a very difficult time for the Society but if he had not been at the forefront the difficulties would have been much worse.' And Adolfo Perez Esquivel, who was awarded the Nobel Peace Prize for the defence of human rights in Argentina, has insisted: 'There were bishops that were accomplices to the dictatorship, but Bergoglio was not one of them [though] I think he lacked the courage to accompany our struggle for human rights in the most difficult times.'

'Maybe, as a pastor, he didn't do enough to protect those priests,' said Father Ignacio Rafael García-Mata, who has served as Provincial of the Jesuits since Bergoglio. 'But he couldn't imagine what was going to happen. You can say the same against me or any other priest. Maybe we didn't have the courage to express our rage against the dictatorship.'

'All of us,' concluded Lisandro Orlov, 'could have done more during the dictatorship.'

Bergoglio, the astute church politician, has picked a very careful path through all this. He chose his words with great precision in the set of interviews he gave to Rubin and Ambrogetti. 'It's true that there were some more perceptive pastors who took great risks,' he said. 'There were others too who immediately began to take strong stances in defence of human rights. There were others who did a lot but spoke out less. And, finally, there were a few who are naïve or lazy. On the other hand, sometimes, subconsciously, an individual doesn't want to see things that could become unpleasant. Any organization has both saints and sinners. There were also men that are a mix of both of those characteristics ... It cannot be assumed that there was a simplistic complicity.'

Yet this kind of careful diplomacy cannot avoid the clear fact that the pastoral relationship broke down between Bergoglio and the priests in his care. Emilio Mignone understood that back in 1986 when he asked: 'What will history say about these pastors who allowed the enemy to take their sheep without defending them or rescuing them?'

Argentine society was polarized during the Dirty War. Many on the Left were not just secularist but very anti-clerical and anti-Church. By contrast the Right espoused Catholicism. According to Professor Fortunato Mallimaci: 'Like the great majority of the leaders in the Catholic Church he [Bergoglio] believed that the dictatorship would bring order to the country in the face of so many subversives. The bishops and Bergoglio also believed that priests who lived with the people in the slums dissolved the Jesuit identity, broke with authority and gave a bad example to the rest of Argentinian society'. For a churchman of traditional spirituality as Bergoglio very much was in those days it undoubtedly seemed natural to side with the worldview of the Right, if not with its tactics. His links to the Peronist Iron Guard movement will undoubtedly have reinforced that. So will his antipathy to Liberation Theology and the crackdown the Vatican was, in those years, beginning to impose upon those who saw the empowerment of the poor as a key part of the Gospel mission. Yet a Jesuit of his intelligence ought to have seen the danger of his opposition to Liberation Theology in the context of the military's anti-communist agenda. Being politically perceptive, and also well informed about the tactics and even occasionally the timing of the military's repressive behaviour, he ought to have realized in May 1976 the danger that Yorio and Jalics were in.

Obedience is a key virtue for Jesuits. It is one of their prime vows, along with poverty, chastity and particular loyalty to the Pope. Bergoglio was clearly outraged by the refusal of Yorio and Jalics to obey his order as Provincial to end their work in the slums. When he told them the order had been reiterated by Rome, and they still resisted, he locked horns with them. Disobedience for a Jesuit was a cardinal offence. To this was added the affront to the deeply authoritarian streak then within his leadership style. The idea that they wanted to set up a new order, as he saw it, deeply offended him. It is hard not to suspect that all this coloured his judgement and made him careless of the level of risk to which the men were being exposed.

There is no evidence that Bergoglio informed the military that he had disowned Yorio and Jalics but he informed other clerics, including officials in the archdiocese of Buenos Aires. The military will have known how to read Bergoglio's views, without being told, once they heard that the Archbishop of Buenos Aires had withdrawn the two Jesuits' permission to say Mass. The anxieties of Bishop Miguel Raspanti, who was prepared to offer alternative ecclesiastical supervision in his diocese of Morón to the dissenting Jesuits, add to the doubts as to the propriety or wisdom of Bergoglio's actions in the volatile political climate of the day – of which, indeed, he had warned Yorio and Jalics. A man of Bergoglio's intelligence, political acumen and contacts ought to have known what he was doing. But he allowed his anger with the men to cloud his judgement. But Bergoglio had done enough to trouble his conscience. Reflecting in later years Bergoglio knew he had behaved recklessly and determined to atone for his behaviour.

Whether he had a duty to speak out publicly is more problematic. Many have recently, from the comfort of their armchairs, looked back to the example of Oscar Romero in El Salvador who confronted a similarly brutal right-wing dictatorship. Romero was shot at the altar for it. But martyrdom is not a calling to which all Christians are summoned, nor do the rest of us have a right to expect that of others. Closer to home Bergoglio had before him the example of Enrique Angelelli. The Bishop of La Rioja met his death within weeks of denouncing the military for abducting two of his priests; the men were found shot dead in response and within a month Angelelli was dead too. Bergoglio may well have felt that he could achieve more working secretly behind the scenes while keeping his public lines open to the government. And he had limited influence; he was the Provincial of a religious order, not a bishop or cardinal archbishop. That is not a judgement which it is apt for those who sit in safety to overturn in hindsight.

Yet if Bergoglio the politician has delivered one verdict, Bergoglio the priest has offered another more penitential one: 'I don't want to mislead anyone – the truth is that I'm a sinner who God in His mercy has chosen to love in a privileged manner,' he told his interviewers Rubin and Ambrogetti. 'From a young age, life pushed me into leadership roles – as soon as I was ordained as a priest, I was designated as the Master of Novices, and two and a half years later, leader of the province – and I had to learn from my errors along the way, because, to tell you the truth, I made hundreds of errors. Errors and sins. It would be wrong for me to say that these days I ask forgiveness for the sins and offences that I might have committed. Today I ask forgiveness for the sins and offences that I did indeed commit.'

He reiterated that even more forcefully in his first interview as Pope when he told his Jesuit interviewer, Father Antonio Spadaro: 'My style of government as a Jesuit at the beginning had many faults...I found myself Provincial when I was still very young. I was only 36 years old. That was crazy. I had to deal with difficult situations, and I made my decisions abruptly and by myself...' It was an interview of shocking frankness – the first such interview any Pope had every given – and it had begun with the question: 'Who is Jorge Mario Bergoglio?' Pope Francis had stared at his interlocutor in silence and then replied: 'I am a sinner. This is the most accurate definition. It is not a figure of speech, a literary genre. I am a sinner.'

Whatever judgements others have made of the role of Jorge Mario Bergoglio during the Dirty War it probably does not match the one he has made of himself before God in prayer. His conduct in that time of crisis – along with the deeply divided legacy he had left the Jesuits in Argentina – were just two of the knots with which the exiled priest wrestled as he sat before the Marian painting which so moved him in the church of St Peter am Perlach in Augsburg in 1986. The themes of mercy and forgiveness – so dominant in his homilies in his early days as Pope – speak of something far more personal than many suppose.

5

The Bishop of the Slums

The slum was not even graced with a name. The locals called it by the number which the unimaginative bureaucrats of Buenos Aires city had designated it. Welcome to Villa 31. Villa comes from the term *villas miserias* which translates as 'misery villages'. The taxi driver would only take us to the edge. The potholes in the alleyways between the ramshackle houses, built of crudely cemented terracotta breezeblock, would have ruined his suspension. Or perhaps worse. Police cars would not enter here either. There was a fortified building on the periphery, but the security guards there looked more concerned with keeping any crime or gang violence from spilling outside the shanty-town rather than tackling the problems within. This was a place where the law was as crooked and chaotic as the townscape of criss-crossed water pipes, dangling electricity cables and lanes down which open sewers run like streams when the rain comes.

But Sunday 12 May 2013 was a fine and sunny autumn morning here south of the equator – and the weather matched the mood of the people of Villa 31 who were spilling out of their homes and crossing the bridge over the railway that cut though the slum. They were making for the church. But they did not go inside. There were too many of them for that. Instead they gathered on a grassy bank that rose to the motorway over-pass under which their homes squatted. Before them, on a stage in the yard before the church, was a makeshift altar on which 17 of the 24 priests who serve the slums of Buenos Aires assembled. They had come to celebrate a murder, not one of the slum's routine gangland killings, but the death 39 years ago that weekend of the first *curas villeros* – slum priests – to be martyred. Father Carlos Mugica was killed by a right-wing paramilitary terror group, the Alianza Anticomunista Argentina, in 1974 outside the church where he had just finished celebrating Mass and was talking to a young couple about their forth-coming wedding. In 1999 his remains were transferred here, to the tiny church of Cristo Obrero (Christ the Worker) in the slum where he spent his priesthood. At that ceremony Jorge Mario Bergoglio, by then Archbishop of Buenos Aires, had prayed: 'For Father Mugica and all those involved in his death – for his actual killers, for those who were the ideologues of his death, for the complicit silences of most of society and for the times that, as members of the Church, we did not have the courage to denounce his assassination, Lord have mercy'. Bergoglio was the only one of the Argentine bishops to attend the ceremony.

And yet the anniversary of Carlos Mugica's death was a cause for celebration rather than sadness for the sons and daughters and grandchildren of the slum-dwellers the martyred priest had served. Mugica had left a legacy. It had brought the faith back into their daily lives, restored a self-esteem to people who had felt marginalized by society and energized them to do battle with the city authorities to improve the basic living conditions in the *villas*, like clean drinking water, electricity and improved sanitation. In recent years all this had been accelerated by Jorge Mario Bergoglio, the man who had – twenty years earlier – recalled priests from the slums for doing exactly that work. And now Bergoglio had gone to Rome and become Pope.

* * *

After Jorge Mario Bergoglio became Archbishop of Buenos Aires the number of priests working in the slums of the vast city had quadrupled, though that is still not many to serve the needs of the estimated 700,000 poor people who pack into around 110,000 makeshift dwellings in the cramped slum where the only way to build is up – so that new rooms are piled on top of one another, like stacked containers at a port, in precarious teetering towers within sight of some of the most desirable residential areas in the Argentine capital. Slum landlords nonetheless demand exorbitant rents for these basic facilities.

Behind the open-air altar was a giant banner bearing the name of the dead priest and two huge portraits. At one end was a black-and-white photograph of Mugica, blond-haired and 1970s film-star handsome. To the left was a colour portrait of Papa Francisco, the first Pope of the Americas, in papal yellow and white. Between them a chequerboard flag of different colours represented all the different nationalities living in the slum: economic migrants and refugees from Paraguay, Peru, Bolivia and Brazil. Propped against the front of the altar was a poster of Mugica bearing the legend: 'A priest has died, who dares to follow him?' And another carried a quote from the murdered man: 'Nothing and nobody will prevent me from serving Jesus Christ and his Church, fighting with the poor for their liberation. If the Lord offers me the privilege, which I don't deserve, of losing my life, I am at his disposal.'

Behind the altar, facing the huge crowd on the grassy bank, stood a priest with long hair, a dark beard and a shy smile. Quietly, through a hand-held microphone, he said: 'You are all welcome here, all you in the slums and all those who want a better society.' The crowd hushed, hanging on his every word. There was an extraordinary charisma about him, even if you did not know that he had been working here in the slums for 27 years. His name was Father José María Di Paola though everyone called him Padre Pepe. One of the other priests took the microphone. 'What he won't tell you,' he told the crowd, 'is that it's his birthday. And he's 51!' There was a huge cheer and the crowd began at once to sing Happy Birthday.

The music was from Bolivia and Peru and Paraguay as well as Argentina. A band of acoustic guitars of many sizes and shapes shifted from the birthday song into an opening hymn and then a Gloria in which there was much call and response and rhythmic clapping. Faith in Villa 31 is a two-way process. During the prayers of intercession, after Padre Pepe had led the formal prayers, the congregation shouted out prayers in the names of their favourite saints. Religion here is immediate and about everyday life. Faith is strong and of the people.

A younger priest in his early thirties stepped forward to give the sermon. It was about how Jesus had a simple faith like the people in the slums, a faith nourished by the Virgin and protected by St Joseph. The slum-dwellers stood enrapt, a motley collection: some looked well, others pinched and unhealthy; some too thin, others too fat; some in clothes washed translucently threadbare, others city-smart in stylish pants, glitzy sunglasses and high boots.

The sermon continued. 'Faith is not selfish or individual,' the priest said. 'It must be shared with everyone, including immigrants. We have to develop things for ourselves. We have to cut through the bureaucracy. We have to fight against *paco* [the cheap cocaine of the poor]. This is the faith of Jesus. It is the faith of Father Mugica – the same faith he felt in his heart and that made him offer his life to be a martyr for our people. It is the faith Pope Francis will renew by asking for a poor Church for poor people.'

Paco is the bane of life in the slums. It is the chemical residue left over from the processing of the high-quality cocaine which is sent to Europe and the United States and the lower-grade coke which is sold to the affluent of Buenos Aires. Once it was thrown away. But then in the economic crisis which hit Argentina in 2001 someone had the idea of mixing the residue with pesticides, fertilizers, kerosene, rat poison or even crushed glass and selling it for a dollar a dose to the people of the slums. It is so addictive that one day's free supply is enough to get people hooked, creating a very short-lived high followed by an intense craving and then paranoia and hallucination. The dealers targeted adolescents and children.

Padre Pepe led other slum priests in a campaign against *paco* which was far too effective for the liking of the drug dealers. The priests set up Hogar de Cristo, an addicts' recovery centre, and two farms where the recuperating addicts could live and work. Even more disturbingly for the drug dealers, in slums where 44 per cent of the residents are under the age of 16, they launched an education campaign, a church Scout group called the Explorers, and an apprentice scheme to give kids an alternative to aimless unemployment; instead they could train to become electricians, stone-masons, car-mechanics, metalworkers, tailors, cooks or bakers. Suddenly *parroquia* (the parish) looked an alternative to *paco*.

Then one evening in 2009, when Padre Pepe was coming home to his church in Villa 21 and 24, on his bicycle, he was stopped by a well-dressed stranger and told that if he did not stop his anti-drugs activities: '*vos vas a ser boleta, te la tienen jurada*' – 'they have their knives out for you, you're doomed'. The frightened priest contacted his archbishop. They met, just the two of them, in Bergoglio's room in the archdiocesan offices. Padre Pepe recalled: 'He told me "If someone has to die, I would prefer it be me." He said that to me personally. He didn't say it somewhere else in order to look big. He just said it to me.'

Bergoglio showed up in Pepe's parish unannounced. He walked slowly through the entire slum and chatted to people, blessed them and drank *mate* (Argentina's national tea drink) as he often did. He said nothing but the message was clear: 'if you touch him, you touch me'. He even offered to sleep in Padre Pepe's house in the slum. 'Bergoglio showed great courage when Padre Pepe was threatened,' said Father Pedro Velasco, who took over as chaplain in Slums 21 and 24 when Pepe was moved to another slum parish.

The next day, the archbishop held an outdoor Mass in the Plaza de Mayo, the city's main gathering point between the cathedral and the Presidential Palace. Television crews had been briefed that Archbishop Bergoglio had something to say. When he reached the sermon Bergoglio delivered a bold denunciation of the drug traffickers and their death threats. He called them *los mercaderes de las tinieblas*, the merchants of darkness. In defiance he elevated Padre Pepe to a new position as Vicar for All Slums. 'At that time we were all afraid,' said Velasco, 'and when it was time to celebrate Mass, the fear was still very present. Just like the Bible says, if a pastor is hurt, the flock will disperse. Bergoglio understood this and the fact that he said the Mass spoke volumes.'

Padre Pepe is in no doubt that he could not have done what he has without Bergoglio. 'My relationship with Bergoglio is very deep,' he said, eschewing the past tense. 'We spoke every week and he came a lot to this slum. When we started he would show up by surprise. But then he left us to work freely. He didn't impose things. He let us get on with things as we saw fit. He felt comfortable here.' The archbishop would wander the alleyways alone, talking with people, drinking tea and eating biscuits in the *villa*'s homes, posing for photographs when requested. Bergoglio was, the locals said, *campechano* (matey). Some called him, instead of Father, *El Chabon* (The Dude). He was at home with those he felt had been tossed on what one of his aides said he referred to as life's 'existential garbage pile'.

'He came and washed the feet of the kids who were addicted to *paco*,' recalled Padre Pepe. 'We wrote two important documents here in the slums and Bergoglio included them in the official magazine of the local church. He was trying to show that the slums were not just important for the people who live here but for the whole Church. The documents said that the culture of the slums and the people who live here have to be respected. The state and the local city authorities should not just impose changes on what the people here have decided. The people here need not to be helped but to help themselves. Our theology is not theoretical. Its main idea is to respect people's choices. Liberation has to start, not with an ideology nor with charity, but with people.'

Yorio and Jalics and the other Jesuits whom Bergoglio once ordered out of the slums for saying such things would have been astonished to hear that, almost forty years on, the same man would not just be tolerating such sentiments but endorsing and blessing them.

* * *

It had been two decades earlier that Jorge Mario Bergoglio, then aged 55, had arrived in the slums of Buenos Aires. It was 1992 and he had just left behind the community life of the Jesuits and arrived back in the city of his birth as one of five auxiliary bishops chosen by the Archbishop of Buenos Aires, Cardinal Antonio Quarracino. The canny old veteran had chosen five different assistants to help him manage the 12 million people who lived or worked in the Argentine capital. Bergoglio was given Flores, the area where he was born. 'That's where I met him,' recalled Guillermo Marcó, the man who would later be Bergoglio's close aide for eight years. 'I was the curate to a parish priest who was a friend of his. He'd come to our parish a lot and he would ask me to walk home with him so, he said, he could get to know his diocese and what a young priest like me was thinking.' From the outset his style was markedly different from that of other bishops. In addition to fulfilling the tasks given him by the archbishop he acted on his own initiative to get to know the priests and people on his patch. And his first approach was to listen and consult. He gave the impression that the views of the ordinary clergy and laity counted. And the slums in his area were his first focus. When he visited more affluent parishes he invariably asked them what they were doing to help their poorer neighbour in the *villas*. Everywhere he ended his visits by asking people to pray for him. Something had happened which had changed utterly the man who had been so self-certain and domineering with the Jesuits.

'Quarracino was a very different man,' remembered Marcó. 'He wasn't humble or austere like Bergoglio. When we went to Rome he would stay in the best hotel. But he liked Bergoglio who was very faithful and loyal to Quarracino. So much so that within a year he named Bergoglio as his vicar general which put the Jesuit in charge of the day-to-day administration of the diocese. After four more years Quarracino, whose health was failing, wanted to choose a successor and decided upon Bergoglio, whom he felt had been outstanding as a bishop in all departments – pastoral, administrative and financial. Outgoing archbishops usually leave such appointments to the Vatican but Quarracino flew to Rome and told the Congregation of Bishops, which makes the selection, that Bergoglio was the man. He asked for him to be made coadjutor of the diocese, which would give him automatic right of succession when Quarracino retired or died. The powerful Curia officials said no. Since they also controlled Quarracino's access to the Pope it seemed that was that. But the wily old cardinal, who had been born in Italy, was not defeated. He then wrote a letter of appointment for the Pope to sign and went to see the Argentinian ambassador to the Holy See, Francisco Eduardo Trusso, who was an old friend. 'Give the Pope this when you next see him,' the cardinal told the diplomat. As Quarracino knew, Trusso was due to see Pope John Paul II quite soon; when he did, he gave the Pope the letter. He signed it there and then and gave it back to Trusso who sent it on to Quarracino. The Vatican bureaucrats were furious. But the deed was done. In June 1997, Bergoglio was appointed coadjutor. Eight months later, on 28 February 1998, Quarracino died of a heart attack and Bergoglio, aged 61, became Archbishop of Buenos Aires.

It was from this point that the reputation of Bergoglio began to grow outside church circles. The main residence of the Archbishop of Buenos Aires was an elegant house in one of the capital's most exclusive neighbourhoods, Olivos, close to the presidential estate. But instead of moving there Bergoglio chose to remain in the four spartan rooms – an office, bedroom, library and chapel – he had occupied in the archdiocesan office next to the cathedral in downtown Buenos Aires. (He did not even move into Quarracino's study with its antique furniture, old paintings and fine carpets but instead used it as a storeroom.) In part his decision was pragmatic. It was 14 miles from official residence to the city. Archbishops had a chauffeur-driven limousine but the traffic jams in Buenos Aires were, and are, horrendous. But Bergoglio also knew the symbolic significance of rejecting the palace and chauffeur. The building he turned into a hostel for priests and nuns; the driver was redeployed to other work in the diocese. Bergoglio used public transport – the subway train and then the bus – for his visits to parishes around the city. In his apartment he cooked his own meals and he wore a normal dark clerical suit and dog collar in preference to an archbishop's purple. His personal belongings were so few that when someone gave him a gift of some CDs he asked a friend to record them to cassettes, as he did not have a CD player. Shortly after becoming archbishop he was invited to have dinner at the Metropolitan Seminary; at the end of the meal, when the rector asked if he wanted to say something to the seminarians, Bergoglio stood up and said: 'I'll wash the plates tonight.' When he was made a cardinal in February 2001 he refused to order new robes but had his predecessor's garments altered to fit him. When as an archbishop people addressed him as Your Grace, or as a cardinal Your Excellency or Eminence, he asked them instead to call him Father Jorge. Those who wanted to fly to Rome to see him elevated were told by him to save the money for use among the poor at home.

Within the Church his priests were finding him unusually accessible. He woke each day around 4 a.m., without an alarm clock, to pray. After breakfast he would read the papers and then from 7 a.m. to 8 a.m. he would sit by a landline to take calls from any priest in his charge. 'There was no secretary,' said Marcó. 'They would get straight through to him. Every priest in the diocese was given his number.' After a morning of meetings, and a frugal lunch at 12.30 p.m., he would take a 40-minute siesta and then visit parishes. Back home he would often have just an apple and tea for dinner – 'he avoids invitations to dinner,' said Marcó – and then listens to classical music on the radio before bed around 11 p.m. 'He's always been quite a solitary person. He looks after his interior life and doesn't really have a social life.' But his days were flexible. He would spend nights in any parish attending to a sick priest if necessary. One of the Jesuits with whom he kept in contact from his old days at the Colegio Máximo, the theologian Father Juan Carlos Scannone, recalled how as auxiliary bishop Bergoglio travelled 250 miles on one occasion to be by the side of one of his priests who had gone to Mar del Plata and fallen ill, so that the man was not alone. 'He did things that were striking, that bishops normally didn't do, with all that he gave to the slums, to the poor and to the priests in the slums,' said Scannone. 'He would make himself available till late in the evening,' said Padre Pepe, who talked endlessly with the archbishop when as a young priest he had a vocational problem. 'Bergoglio wasn't preaching a particular message,' he recalled. 'I was in a crisis. He just listened and gave me the space to make my own decisions.'

He was revolutionary when it came to administrative matters too. He put an end to the traditional system of young priests starting in poor parishes and then being promoted over the years to larger and wealthier ones. 'Nor did he like the idea that the best priests would go off to jobs in Rome; he saw that as careerism,' said Marcó. 'It had a downside though. He put young priests in their twenties and thirties with no experience in important places. It was not a good idea. They found it difficult to manage. It also meant there was a generation of older priests who were stuck in smaller parishes. Bergoglio was never a parish priest, so he didn't understand that.'

Perhaps he did, and did not care. If there were administrative disadvantages he could undoubtedly see the symbolic importance the gesture sent to ordinary members of the Church – and the message it sent to priests about where their priorities should lie. Where previous archbishops had left the pastoral care of priests to auxiliaries, Bergoglio insisted on doing that job himself. 'He didn't delegate much to his auxiliaries,' said Marcó. 'So everyone went straight to Bergoglio. He's a man with a strong sense of power.' He also kept very well informed. 'He would sometimes ring you and chat away asking innocent questions,' one Buenos Aires priest told me, 'and then when you had said every-thing was OK he would ask the killer question which showed that he knew all along what your problem was.' Priests who were not toeing the line were offered a chance to change, but then could be removed.

In other matters he was more collegial. He delegated a lot of administrative and finance work to his six auxiliary bishops with whom he held fortnightly meetings. All the detailed public affairs work was entrusted to Guillermo Marcó, though the pair would speak daily about policy and strategic issues. At the twice-monthly meetings with his bishops, Bergoglio would routinely go around the table and solicit advice. He considered it carefully but when it came to decisions, said Marcó, 'he would do that himself'. There was no vote. When he was facing a tough call, said Federico Wals, a layman who succeeded Marcó as the archbishop's PR man, 'he'd pick up the phone and ask opinions from different people and get different points of view, and then he'd make his own decision'. But auxiliaries, priests and the laity were all involved.

'The way he implemented change was consultation, long process, partici-pation – parishes, priests, deaneries,' said Augosto Zampini, a diocesan priest from Greater Buenos Aires. 'At the beginning people didn't believe it. He made it clear he did not want to impose; he wanted things to emerge.' And new emphasis was given to the ordinary people in the Church. 'It wasn't just about priests doing the job,' said Wals. 'He was also concerned with getting the laity active inside these movements, and letting them take charge. Priests were just one leg of the stool, along with the religious and the laity. He felt that if you didn't do it that way, you would end up with a Church that's too focused on itself. It's not just about what priests do, but above all the laity.'

Yet Bergoglio also knew when unilateral executive action was necessary. When he took over as archbishop the diocese of Buenos Aires was facing not just a financial crisis but a banking scandal. His predecessor, Cardinal Quarracino, had been very close to a prominent family of Argentinian bankers, the Trusso family – of which the Argentine ambassador to the Holy See was a member. 'Quarracino was very dependent on the Trusso family for money,' said Marcó. 'At one point there was a run on the Trusso family bank. So one of the sons went to an insurance company and said the Archbishop wanted to borrow $10 million.' The money was to be used by the Trusso elite to prop up their failing bank. It was 1997; Bergoglio was Quarracino's appointed successor but the old man was still in charge. The company was the Sociedad Militar Seguros de Vida – an insurance company for military veterans – and the loan was underwritten by the Trusso family bank, the Banco de Crédito Provincial. 'When the lenders went to see Quarracino to get him to confirm this, and get the necessary paperwork signed, the Archbishop's secretary, Monsignor Roberto Marcial Toledo, told them Quarracino was busy. He took the paperwork and said he would get the Archbishop to sign it. He came back a few minutes later with the signed papers. But out of sight he had simply forged Quarracino's signature.' When the Banco de Crédito Provincial became insolvent, and the military veterans asked the archdiocese to return the money, it turned out that the cash had never appeared in the church accounts. A year later, after the Banco de Crédito Provincial went bust, it was discovered that the bankers had been paying Quarracino's credit card bills, and taking advantage of the two churchmen's political influence. More than that, $700,000 had been transferred from the archdiocese's account to the bank – without being registered in the archdiocese's records. Toledo and two of the Trusso sons went to prison.

'Bergoglio immediately called in the international accountants Arthur Andersen to get to the bottom of the affair,' said Marcó. 'The judge in the case tried to make political capital out of it all, in an attempt to embarrass the Church. But Bergoglio's thoroughness in the paperwork he handed over to the court meant his reputation was enhanced by the way he handled the whole affair.' The new archbishop did not leave matters there. He then sold off the archdiocese's shares in several banks, in order to sever any inappropriate links, and placed the church funds in banks in which the Church held no shares. This abolished the grey area, said Federico Wals, by which the archdiocese was a partial owner of the banks and allowed to borrow on favourable terms. The old system had encouraged fiscal indiscipline. 'It was a black hole, so there were basically no limits on what we could spend,' Wals said. Bergoglio acted swiftly and had no hesitation in bringing in outsiders to help sort out the archdiocese's chaotic finances.

* * *

But money matters were never at the top of Bergoglio's agenda. 'His vision was for the Church to reach out,' said Wals, 'to those for whom society didn't seem to care, such as single mothers, the poor, the elderly, the unemployed.' But if they were his top priority, from the outset Archbishop Bergoglio was keen to reach out to the widest possible range of groups outside the Catholic Church which, in a metaphor to which he returned again and again, he felt was sick from spending too long turned in on its own interior sacramental spirituality when it ought to be reaching out to the world. 'A Church that stays in the sacristy too long gets sick,' he repeatedly said.

Bergoglio was admirably comprehensive in those he included as he reached outwards – he embraced everyone, from Christians of other denominations, and believers of other faiths, to those who were none of those. Drawing on his boyhood experiences serving Mass for the Ukrainian priest Father Stefan Czmil he now took on the title and role of Ordinary for Eastern Catholics in Argentina, who did not have their own archbishop. His relations with Argentina's Anglicans were so good that their leader, the Archbishop Gregory Venables, described him, in a back-handed compliment, as not so much a Catholic as 'more of a Christian, Christ-centred and Spirit-filled'. Venables called him 'a friend to Anglicans'. As if in confirmation, when Pope Benedict XVI set up the Ordinariate – to attract disaffected Anglicans into the Catholic Church – Bergoglio told Venables he disapproved and insisted the wider world needed the diversity in Anglican witness.

Bergoglio, similarly, reached out to evangelical Protestants, whom many in the Catholic Church viewed as rivals, enticing away the faithful to more colourful and charismatic styles of worship. Once Bergoglio too had been suspicious of that; indeed in his time as Provincial he had banned the Jesuit leading the Catholic Charismatic Renewal, Father Alberto Ibáñez Padilla, from being involved. Now the changed Bergoglio took the opposite view and went to pray with them. He particularly outraged Catholic traditionalists when in 2006 he asked a stadium full of Catholic and Protestant charismatics to pray for him. 'Archbishopric of Buenos Aires *sede vacante*' roared the headline from an ultra-traditionalist Catholic magazine the following week using the Latin phrase to indicate that a bishop has died or retired leaving the episcopal chair empty. To make matters worse, apparently, he had knelt down to receive the blessing from those he had asked to pray for him. 'What's the problem?' Bergoglio shrugged in response. At one joint prayer gathering some Catholic protesters arrived brandishing a poster bearing an image of the Virgin Mary. When they tried to divide pastors from priests by requesting a response to the poster Bergoglio gently requested they gave him the poster. When they did he simply folded it, and put it inside his briefcase.

Bergoglio is no Protestant. He is deeply Catholic in the colour, richness and sacramentality of his being in the world; one of his favourite films is *Babette's Feast* in which a severe Puritan community is confronted by a meal which is a metaphor for the staggering cornucopia of gifts God has provided for humankind. Bergoglio had always intuitively comprehended that there are deeper poetic qualities to religion which go beyond doctrine; that was what lay behind his love for the popular piety of plain people. But over the years he became a man intent on seeing the good in others, and their common ground, rather than defining himself by the singularity of his religious identity.

He made particular efforts with other religions too. He held several inter-faith gatherings in his cathedral. He visited a mosque and an Islamic school and he took part in several Jewish ceremonies in synagogues. In the cathedral he commemorated the anniversary of Kristallnacht. He even produced a book of conversations with one of Argentina's leading Jewish scholars, Rabbi Abraham Skorka, *Sobre el Cielo y la Tierra* (On Heaven and Earth). In it Bergoglio said:

> Dialogue is born from a respectful attitude toward the other person, from a conviction that the other person has something good to say. It supposes that we can make room in our heart for their point of view, their opinion and their proposals. Dialogue entails a warm reception and not a pre-emptive condemnation. To dialogue, one must know how to lower the defences, to open the doors of one's home and to offer warmth.

Bergoglio might have been talking about himself, Skorka later told me. 'He's very open-minded,' the rabbi said. 'He can dialogue with anyone who speaks with honesty and respect even if he does not agree with them. He'll listen to a woman tussling with abortion and suffer with her. He has empathy. He has a very important listening capability. That doesn't mean he will change his mind. He is a conservative priest. But he's not got a dogmatic attitude. So he will dialogue too with opponents.'

Skorka and Bergoglio's conversations ranged across God and the Devil, through Death and Old Age to Communism and Globalization. 'We had a good dialogue because the roots on which we stand are the same roots. Our ethics are the ethics of the Prophets of Israel. Bergoglio has a special feeling for the Synoptic Gospels and when you analyse Jesus's words there you find many parallels between them and the principles developed by the Prophets.' They even agreed on the controversy around Pope Pius XII and Europe's Jews during the Holocaust. 'There are two views,' Rabbi Skorka said. 'One is he did all he could to save Jews without confronting the Nazis which could have accelerated the killing of Jews. The other view asks how could Pius XII stay silent and not shout to all the winds: "Stop killing innocent people." Bergoglio said: "We must open the Vatican archives and find out the truth." Now he has the chance to do that. I'm confident he will.' Again right-wing Catholics in Argentina protested at Bergoglio's openness to inter-faith dialogue; they particularly complained about a display in the cathedral, near where Cardinal Quarracino is buried, containing fragments of Hebrew prayer books saved from the different concentration camps along with other documents relating to the Holocaust. Bergoglio ignored them and called the Jews 'my elder brothers'.

But Bergoglio has shown himself most anxious to reach those outside the traditional religious institutions. Sometimes at 11 p.m. he was to be found in the Plaza de Flores talking to the prostitutes who worked there. Occasionally he would even hear a confession sitting on a park bench. 'No doubt I will one day appear in the newspapers,' he joked to a colleague. He went out of his way to embrace those marginalized by society, using the symbolism of Christ's washing his disciples' feet which the Church celebrates each year on the Thursday of Holy week. In 2001 he surprised the staff of Muñiz Hospital in Buenos Aires by asking for a jar of water and then proceeding to wash the feet of 12 patients hospitalized with AIDS-related complications. He then kissed their feet. In 2008 he celebrated the Holy Thursday Mass of the Lord's Supper in the *villas miseries* where he washed the feet of 12 youths from the Hogar de Cristo rehabilitation centre for drug addicts. And Bergoglio also sought to offer greater acceptance to those marginalized within the Church. While not departing from the Church teaching that remarried Catholics should not take Communion he went as far as he could to reach out to them saying: 'divorced members who have remarried...are not excommunicated – even though they live in a situation on the margin of what indissolubility of marriage and the sacrament of marriage require of them – and they are asked to integrate into the parish life'. He went out of his way to protect Argentine theologians under investigation by Rome, like Marcelo Gonzalez and Gustavo Irrazabal, even where he didn't agree with what they had said or written.

His befriending of the widow of Jerónimo José Podestá was particularly bold. Podestá was a progressive Catholic bishop from the 1960s whose radical teachings had irritated the Vatican. He was exactly the kind of priest Bergoglio himself would have condemned at the time. He made outspoken attacks on the government's economic policies, made stirring speeches at trade union rallies, and enthusiastically supported the reforms of the Second Vatican Council which the conservative Catholics in Argentina's hierarchy so doggedly opposed. Rome found the perfect opportunity to get rid of him when he began a relationship with his secretary Clelia Luro, a single woman with six children, in 1967. Worse than that, Clelia, a feminist as radical as was imaginable on the Catholic spectrum, used to concelebrate Mass with her husband. Podestá fled Argentina after death threats from the Alianza Anticomunista Argentina and returned in 1983 after the overthrow of the military dictatorship but by the time of his death in 2000 he was poor and living in obscurity. He had continued to be president of the Federación Latinoamericana de Sacerdotes Casados (Latin American Federation of Married Priests) however and on his deathbed, on impulse, he contacted Archbishop Bergoglio to talk about the movement. Bergoglio not only received him but was the only church official to have any contact with the disgraced bishop before his death. Indeed Bergoglio visited the dying cleric in hospital to give him the last rites and hold his hand as he neared death. For the rest of the church hierarchy Podestá was, like anyone who left the priesthood, to be ostracized. For Bergoglio it was a pastoral issue; Podestá was, like everyone else, a child beloved of God. And the archbishop was confident enough in his own faith to be able to reach out pastorally to his widow.

Sitting in a grand colonial house with pink colonnades which had seen far better days, his feisty widow told me before she died – eight months after Bergoglio became Pope – that over the 13 years since her husband's death Bergoglio had become a close friend. 'After Jerónimo's death he kept in touch,' she said. 'Whenever I had a problem he would help – with economic issues, with the house, and my pension, because everything was complicated for me. At nights when I couldn't sleep I would write letters to Bergoglio and every Sunday, faithfully, he would call me. He did this every week until he left for Rome, and he has rung me from the Vatican too. We talk about all manner of things. He was very respectful of our marriage, of myself, of women in general. I told him: "Celibacy is a law that has to be changed. It's a law made by men, not by Jesus." Bergoglio said to me: "It's a cultural issue; change may well be accepted at some point."'

On gay marriage too Bergoglio acted from a perspective of pastoral inclusion. Like other bishops in Argentina he was opposed to the concept of marriage being applied to same-sex partnerships. But when in 2010 Marcelo Márquez, a gay rights leader, devout Catholic and a former seminary theology professor, delivered a critical letter to him on the subject the activist was surprised to hear the phone ring within the hour and find Cardinal Bergoglio on the other end of the line. The men met twice. 'He listened to my views with a great deal of respect,' said Márquez. It was not perhaps what he expected. This was a church in which Bergoglio's predecessor as Archbishop of Buenos Aires, Cardinal Quarracino, had said that homosexuals should be 'locked up in a ghetto'. Bergoglio adopted a very different tone. Despite the strong public criticisms church officials had been making for months of the government's plans to legalize same-sex marriage, privately Bergoglio told Márquez that 'homosexuals need to have recognized rights, and that he supported civil unions but not same-sex marriage'. A political row inside the Church broke out over Bergoglio's stance but here again dogmatic principle did not overcome pastoral concern.

The same approach governed Bergoglio's position on a wide range of subjects. Some of his toughest criticisms were for conservative legalists who put obedience to church rules above everything else. 'There are sectors within the religions that are so prescriptive that they forget the human side,' he said. He once said of Catholics obsessed with sexual ethics that they wanted to 'stick the whole world inside a condom'. He excoriated priests who refused to baptize the children of unmarried mothers, calling them hypocritical clericalists who were hijacking baptism in a kind of sacramental blackmail. When it comes to the confessional, he told his priests to be neither too severe nor excessively indulgent. '"And so Father what should we do?" they ask me. And I tell them: "be compassionate".' In confession, Bergoglio admitted, he is more likely to ask parents whether they are too busy with work to play with their children; it is not the kind of sin they are expecting to be quizzed about.

Once a mother who lived in a slum rife with crime, unemployment, drugs and poverty apologized to him for the fact that her son had stopped going to church. He replied: 'Is he a good kid? That's what matters.' Or as he put it elsewhere: 'The most important thing is the person in front of you.'

In all this the Church must go to people and not expect the people to come to the Church, Bergoglio insisted. 'He used to say that we need to learn from the model of the Evangelicals, meaning that we have to knock on doors and talk to people,' said Federico Wals. 'He wanted to make the Church visible outside its buildings, which is why Buenos Aires developed some very interesting outdoor events. For instance, the Via Crucis procession during Holy Week moves through the entire city, going on for miles and miles. There are also lots of open-air Masses. The most important Masses here don't take place inside the cathedral, but in the square.' It was why Bergoglio, who in his earlier years had been an avid fan of San Lorenzo football team, would go to say Mass in the club's stadium on special occasions.

But it was more profound than that. When fire swept through the Cromañon nightclub in Buenos Aires in 2004 Bergoglio was one of the first on the scene, arriving before many of the fire engines. Some 175 people had died, with the tragedy being compounded by the fact that the club owners had locked the emergency exits to keep out freeloaders Bergoglio accompanied the grieving relatives to the morgue. He said nothing. 'He was quiet and respectful,' recalled the father of one of the victims. 'But he was one of the few authorities that was with us that day. He accompanied us with his presence.' In the face of a cruel death, Bergoglio later said: 'I stay silent. The only thing that occurs to me is to remain quiet and, depending on the trust they have in me, to take their hand. And to pray for them because both physical and spiritual pain are borne from within where no-one can enter ... What people need to know is that someone is with them, loves them, respects their silence and prays that God may enter into this space that is pure solitude.' What Bergoglio showed that night, wrote Alberto Barlocci of the Buenos Aires monthly magazine *Ciudad Nueva*, was that the Church wanted to accompany people in their moment of sorrow: 'For many his close presence was a consolation; for some it was nothing less than the rediscovery of a faith they seemed to have lost. For all it was an encounter with a Church that is near, like a friend, a sister and mother.'

* * *

There were two groups with whom confrontation rather than inclusion was the dominant model of Bergoglio's years as archbishop. With both the government and the conservatives in the hierarchy of the Catholic Church relations were more problematic. Bergoglio had not cast a vote in a political election since the late 1950s during the mid-term of the government of Arturo Frondizi, which was overthrown by the military in 1962, but throughout his life he has been a highly political animal. When he became Archbishop of Buenos Aires the president of Argentina was the Peronist Carlos Menem. On 25 May each year, to celebrate one of Argentina's two national days, the president traditionally attends an annual Te Deum and Mass in the capital's cathedral at which the Archbishop of Buenos Aires preaches. In his first year Bergoglio spoke from the pulpit about Argentina as a society where all sat at the table but only a few benefited and where the social fabric was being destroyed. Menem's face registered clear discomfort at the words. It was only the start of Bergoglio's robust interaction with the political class. Menem's successor as president, Fernando de la Rúa, was told that under him 'the system has fallen into a period of dark shadow'.

But it was under a later president, Néstor Kirchner, that Bergoglio's relationship reached its nadir. At the Te Deum in 2004 Kirchner had to sit and listen to the nation's most senior cleric criticize political exhibitionism and slander, intolerant populism and propaganda, and the bastardization or elimination of institutions as part of what Bergoglio called 'a long list of stratagems which conceal and protect mediocrity'. The next day, when the press asked if Bergoglio had been referring to Kirchner, the Church's spokesman, Father Guillermo Marcó, replied: 'if the shoe fits, wear it'. Kirchner riposted that 'the Devil also reaches everyone – those who wear trousers and those who wear cassocks'. The president refused ever again to attend a Te Deum where Bergoglio was preaching. Since Kirchner's supporters could not accuse Bergoglio of ignoring the poor, or the broader concerns of Latin America, they began to raise accusations about his failure to defend human rights during the period of the military junta. By 2007 a US diplomat in a cable to Washington was describing the Archbishop of Buenos Aires as the 'leader of the opposition' to the government.

Relations hardly improved when Néstor Kirchner was succeeded in that year as president by his widow Cristina Fernández de Kirchner. In 2008 when Bergoglio called for national reconciliation during disturbances in the country's agricultural regions, Mrs Kirchner interpreted his words as support for anti-government demonstrators. The two went on to fight further political battles. Bergoglio had already objected to government plans in 2006 to legalize abortion in some cases and in 2010 he unsuccessfully sought to oppose Mrs Kirchner's plans to legalize gay marriage, a position she derided as 'medieval', while he continued sharp criticisms of the government's failures to address corruption and poverty. The latter particularly rankled. Kirchner is a Peronist who projects herself as pursuing left-wing policies on social justice – though critics attack her government for crony capitalism and economic mismanagement. Bergoglio's criticisms of her bolstered that, for they came not from the Right but the Left saying that Kirchner's policies did little for those in extreme poverty.

Not all Bergoglio's interaction with politicians has been oppositional. As archbishop he had good relations with many in the government and was active in dialogue with politicians of all parties. 'In truth,' said Federico Wals, 'there are plenty of government ministers who came here to talk to Bergoglio about human trafficking, about poverty, about trying to channel government funds for urban development through Catholic charities because they know it will be done well.' The idea that the whole government was at war with the Church was a considerable exaggeration. Bergoglio once lamented to Wals that politicians from the Right complained about him being on the Left but that those of the Left saw him as right-wing. 'He said, "I'm trying to be a bishop of the centre, who talks to both parties and takes the best from each."' The reality, Wals said, is that Bergoglio is much more interested in concrete situations than ideological theories. 'As part of that, he was always open to talking with anyone.' Bergoglio often took the initiative of approaching politicians himself, though Mrs Kirchner, it is said, turned down the offer of meeting with Bergoglio no fewer than 14 times.

One area where they did find a measure of agreement was over the 30th anniversary commemoration of the invasion of the Falklands Islands – or the Malvinas as they are known in Argentina. Mrs Kirchner marked the occasion with an international appeal for the Argentinian claim of sovereignty over the islands to be upheld. Critics abroad rebuffed the idea, saying that it was an attempt by Mrs Kirchner to divert the attention of the voters of Argentina away from her mismanagement of the country's economy. But Bergoglio attended a ceremony marking Argentina's defeat in the Falklands War and he said: 'We come to pray for those who have fallen, sons of the homeland who set out to defend their mother, the homeland, to claim the country that is theirs and that was usurped.' Such sentiments led Mrs Kirchner, who changed her attitude to Bergoglio markedly once he was elected Pope, to hope that he might intervene from Rome in the sovereignty dispute. But those hopes were quashed by Vatican officials who announced, after a meeting between the Argentinian president and pontiff, that the Pope would be remaining remain neutral on the Falklands issue.

Perhaps the most significant dimension of Bergoglio's interaction with politicians in his time as Archbishop of Buenos Aires was the way it focused his attention on the issue of poverty in a different way. The man who was once the scourge of Liberation Theology began to see, as national leader, that there was weight to aspects of the liberation theologians' analysis that sin could reside in structures as well as in the bad behaviour of individuals in positions of power. The great Argentinian economic crisis of 2001 was perhaps a turning point.

During the 1990s Argentina's constantly changing governments had done what they could to reverse the decline in the economy and build-up of national debt which had taken place under the military dictatorship. Some 400,000 companies of all sizes went bankrupt under the junta. Reforms recommended by the International Monetary Fund included privatization, deregulation and trade liberalization but Argentinian politicians pursued these without success.

Throughout the years that followed, the Argentinian economy staggered from one crisis to another. A decision to peg the currency, the peso, to the US dollar to control inflation proved disastrous when the dollar was revalued internationally in 1997. Argentina had got stuck in a spiral in which higher interest rates constantly increased its national debt and the cost of servicing it until, in December 2001, the country announced it would stop paying the interest on the $94 billion it owed. It was the biggest debt default in world history.

The impact on ordinary people was devastating. Banks closed, accounts were frozen, the value of wages was slashed, one in four people lost their jobs and the savings of millions of people were wiped out. More than half the population was plunged below the poverty line (compared with just 7 per cent before the dictatorship). A quarter of the Argentine people were destitute and hungry and the economy suffered its sharpest decline since the Great Depression. Riots broke out in Buenos Aires. Angry Argentinians took to the streets marching, protesting and looting. President Fernando de la Rùa resigned and was succeeded by four presidents in just 11 days. At least 25 people were killed as the police responded so brutally that, looking out of his window overlooking one riot, Archbishop Bergoglio rang the Minister of the Interior protesting that the police, who were beating people outside his window, seemed unable to distinguish between looters and ordinary people who only wanted to withdraw their savings from the bank.

In his pleas to the public throughout the crisis Bergoglio urged the people of Argentina to avoid violence. Later he castigated the rich as those who wanted to keep their 'privileges, their rapacity and their share of ill-gotten gain' even as the country was 'on the verge of national dissolution'. But he also turned his attention to the need for structural change: 'In becoming involved in this common attempt to overcome the crisis in Argentina, keep in mind what is taught by the tradition of the Church, which regards oppressing the poor and defrauding workers of their wages as two sins that cry out to God for vengeance,' he warned. And he said on behalf of the bishops who had responded to the emergency by opening a network of parish food programmes for the needy: 'We are tired of systems that produce poor people who the Church then has to support.'

It was a theme he was to continue to explore at the milestone meeting of all of Latin America's bishops at Aparecida in 2007 where he noted that the economies of South America had 'grown the most, yet reduced misery the least' – creating a situation of 'social sin'. In 2009 he expanded the same line of thinking, condemning 'extreme poverty and unjust economic structures' as violations of human rights. Something had changed in Jorge Mario Bergoglio.

He was talking the language of the Liberation Theology he had once vehemently rejected. How that change came about is something we shall uncover in the next two chapters.

The other significant group with whom Bergoglio had problems throughout his 15 years as Archbishop of Buenos Aires were to be found, ironically perhaps, within his own Church. For all his growing sense of the need for social justice Jorge Mario Bergoglio was doctrinally orthodox. But that placed him, in the words of one informed outside observer, the prominent Argentinian Lutheran theologian Lisandro Orlov, 'on the left in what is a deeply reactionary and right-wing collection of bishops'. Almost all the serious opposition to Bergoglio in his time as archbishop came from the Right rather than the Left in the Catholic Church.

In some areas, of course, there was no division. When Néstor Kirchner's government in 2006 proposed that abortion be legalized in certain cases, the Argentine episcopal conference was of one mind in its opposition. It was a delicate political atmosphere because there was rising public concern over the rapes of two mentally disabled women. Both had been denied abortions after pressure from religious organizations. The health authorities then demanded a change in the law and the government proposed abortion should be made legal in some circumstances. Opinion polls suggested that 76 per cent of Argentinians supported abortion being legalized for the victims of rape. Bergoglio intervened robustly, describing it as an attack on the Catholic values of the Argentinian people. When the Supreme Court ruled, in 2012, that abortion is legal in the case of rape or where a woman's life is threatened Bergoglio spoke for all the bishops when he condemned it as a 'backdoor attempt' to bring abortion to Argentina. 'Abortion is never a solution,' he said. 'We listen, support and offer understanding from where we stand to save two lives' – one of them 'the smallest and most defenseless' of human beings.'

But in other areas there were tensions inside the Argentine bishops' conference where the hardliners were led by Héctor Rubén Aguer, the Archbishop of La Plata, a cleric widely linked in Argentina to Opus Dei – and a supporter of the ultra-traditionalist groups Miles Christi and the Instituto del Verbo. One central issue which Bergoglio was never able to resolve because of the factionalism within the conference was the extent to which the Church should respond to its collusion with the military dictatorship during the dark days of the Dirty War. At the turn of the millennium Pope John Paul II called upon the Church worldwide to examine its conscience and make apology for its historic sins in preparation for the Jubilee that was held in 2000. The bishops of Argentina responded with a statement in which they acknowledged that the Church needed 'to put on garments of public penance for the sins committed during the years of the dictatorship'. It continued:

> We share everyone's pain and once again ask the forgiveness of everyone we failed or didn't support as we should have. We were indulgent towards totalitarian positions. Through actions and omissions we discriminated against many of our brothers, without exerting ourselves sufficiently in defence of their rights. We beseech God to accept our repentance and to heal the wounds of our people.

It was a big step forward but many in Argentina were not satisfied, pointing out that the Church was not taking responsibility for institutional complicity but instead placing the blame on the mistakes of individual Catholics.

The situation was compounded in 2012 when the unrepentant ex-dictator General Jorge Rafael Videla gave a rare interview to the Spanish political magazine *Cambio16* in which he claimed:

> My relationship with the Church was excellent. It was very cordial, frank and open. Don't forget that we even had military chaplains assisting us, thus not allowing our partnership and friendship to falter… The Argentine Church in general, thankfully, was not carried away by the leftist Third World tendencies of other churches of the continent. Even though certain members of the Argentine Church fell for this game, they were a minority group that was hardly noticeable.

The attitude of the Argentine Church was in stark contrast to the church leadership elsewhere. 'There was much clearer leadership in Brazil,' said the late Professor Jeffrey Klaiber, author of *The Church, Dictatorships, and Democracy in Latin America*, 'where Dom Helder Camara, Aloisio Lorscheider, and Paulo Arns of Sao Paulo were very vocal and took a strong stance, denouncing the military. The Catholic Church in Argentina was the black sheep of Latin America in the passive way they dealt with the military dictatorship.'

But Bergoglio insisted the picture was not so black and white. 'In the Church there were Christians from different groups,' he said in 2010. 'There were Christians killed as guerrillas, Christians who helped save people and repressive Christians who believed that they were saving the Homeland. There were different types of clergy… It cannot be assumed that there was a simplistic complicity.' Even so Bergoglio was instrumental in organizing another apology from the bishops, which was released in 2012 after he had ceased to be chairman of the episcopal conference. It expressed sorrow to all those who had been let down or felt unsupported by the Church. But critics expressed the same reservations as before, saying the apology was woolly and unspecific.

Delivering an apology deemed adequate by the families of the victims defeated Bergoglio. Lisandro Orlov said he thought he knew why. 'People have asked, "Why did it take so long for Bergoglio to get the Catholic Church to apologize?" But the fact is that it was not up to Bergoglio alone. There had to be a consensus within the bishops' conference of the Church. He had to negotiate with people who wanted to remain silent. The more progressive elements were in a minority. So they never apologized as a Church but just asked forgiveness for the behaviour of individuals.'

That fact was emphasized by the fact that eight years after the former police chaplain Father Christian von Wernich was sentenced to life in prison – for complicity in 7 homicides, 42 kidnappings, and 32 instances of torture during the Dirty War – he has still not been penalized by the Catholic Church. In 2010 a church official said that 'at the appropriate time, von Wernich's situation will have to be resolved in accordance with canonical law'. But it did not happen and von Wernich was allowed to continue to celebrate Mass in prison. Professor Fortunato Mallimaci, a researcher on Catholicism at the University of Buenos Aires, believes that is because 'the great majority of the bishops believe von Wernich has not committed any crime' but simply 'fulfilled his role as a priest, which at that time was to support the military during a terrible time caused by the attack from Marxist subversives'.

The Archbishop of La Plata had more than a theological disagreement with Bergoglio. The two men had both been auxiliary bishops to Cardinal Quarracino at the same time; indeed Aguer, though younger in years, was the senior bishop by a few months. The younger man had wanted to be Archbishop of Buenos Aires after Quarracino and had thought he had the better chance. He was a favourite of Cardinal Angelo Sodano who, as the papal nuncio in Chile, had become a friend of the Chilean dictator Augusto Pinochet. Sodano had a strong influence on Latin American affairs at the Vatican, where he was Secretary of State under Pope John Paul II. Aguer was also smiled upon by the Argentine cardinal Leonardo Sandri, who was Sodano's deputy. In Bergoglio's circle it was assumed that it was through the influence of these men that, whenever Bergoglio made a recommendation to Rome on who should be created a bishop in Argentina, his suggestions were repeatedly ignored. The supporters of Aguer, who travelled regularly to Rome, were appointed instead. Bergoglio's appointment of one of his chief theological collaborators, Father Victor Manuel Fernández, as Rector of the Catholic University of Buenos Aires was blocked for two years. One of Bergoglio's first acts as Pope was to make Fernández an archbishop.

'Bergoglio didn't get along with Opus Dei,' said his long-time friend, the human rights lawyer, Alicia Oliveira. 'It was people associated with that group who spread the slanderous stories about Bergoglio in the 2005 conclave. There were all kinds of murky dealings about money-laundering and the Vatican Bank.'

'There were certain bishops in the episcopal conference who were always complaining to Rome behind Bergoglio's back,' said Guillermo Marcó, who worked closely with Bergoglio' for eight years. One regular gripe was that vocations to the priesthood had fallen in Buenos Aires in his time whereas they were rising in other dioceses. But in 2010 the conservative faction saw a much greater opportunity to unseat Bergoglio, who would be 75 in December 2011 and therefore obliged to tender his resignation to the Pope. The Pope did not have to accept it, but if pressure could be applied by Bergoglio's enemies there would be a chance for Aguer to succeed to Buenos Aires and become the nation's senior churchman. It was at this point that Argentina's politicians decided to introduce a law permitting same-sex couples to marry. Various conservative bishops and rabbis protested. 'Bergoglio kept out of it,' said Alicia Oliveira. 'He was angry at the shocking things the conservatives were saying, linking homosexuality with paedophilia. When the law was issued he started talking about it. But he left it too late.'

Bergoglio went to the bishops' conference with a strategy. The Church should offer to back same-sex civil unions as the 'lesser of two evils' so long as gay marriage was ditched. He persuaded a prominent evangelical parliamentarian, Congressional Representative Cynthia Hutton, to make the same proposal in the legislature.

'Bergoglio was against same-sex marriage but in favour of a law for equal rights for gays,' revealed Marcó. 'The hard-line conservatives were in the minority but they were supported by the papal nuncio and by Rome. The nuncio was at the meetings every week. The hard-line traditionalist bishops and supporters of Opus Dei had complained to Rome about Bergoglio.' It looked as though the bishops would say no to Bergoglio's proposal. Matters were only complicated by a letter he wrote a month before the parliament was due to vote. It took the orthodox line on gay marriage and used extremely vivid language. Sent to a closed order of Carmelite nuns, asking them to pray for the right outcome in the vote, it said: 'Let us not be naïve: this is not a simple political struggle; its intention is to destroy God's plan. It is not merely a legis-lative project but rather a move by the Father of Lies [the Devil] who wishes to confuse and deceive the children of God.'

Some commentators have discerned in such language that Bergoglio was using the language of the spiritual retreat rather than the public political forum. Others felt it had a more wily intention. 'He thought a closed order would not make the contents public but that he could send a copy of it to Rome to show he was doing what was required,' said Marcó. 'But it was published. The strategy backfired on him. He lost the vote among the bishops. The law was passed. And the traditionalists denounced him in the Vatican for not speaking out soon enough.' In the six years that Bergoglio was president of the bishops' conference it was the only time he was unable to broker consensus.

But Aguer had not done enough to unseat his rival, and his supporters in Rome were not able to land him the job he craved as the Vatican's chief doctrinal watchdog, the head of the Congregation for the Doctrine of the Faith, when its Prefect, Cardinal William Levada, stood down in 2012. Aguer had played out his career in the shadow of Bergoglio but he continued in petty ways to attempt to thwart his rival, as he had done when he offered to post bail of one million pesos for the release of the disgraced banker Francisco Trusso – who had been jailed in the fraud Bergoglio had exposed when he took over as Archbishop of Buenos Aires. Aguer 'had been a thorn in Bergoglio's side,' Clelia Luro claimed she had learned from her weekly conversations with Bergoglio. 'He was a constant problem.' The Argentine journalist Elisabetta Piqué wrote a number of reports for *La Nación* on the various plots by Bergoglio's opponents; for her pains she was summoned to see a senior conservative bishop in Rome and told that if she continued writing her 'too fanciful' articles on the conflict between Bergoglio and the Curia she might find her Vatican press accreditation withdrawn.

But all this politicking, both secular and ecclesiastical, was merely an irritant to Jorge Mario Bergoglio, those close to him said. His main concern was to turn the Church outwards to those who needed to hear the Good News rather than allowing it to remain turned in on itself and its own spirituality. To him one of the defining moments of his time as Archbishop of Buenos Aires was the meeting of all the bishops of Latin America at Aparecida in Brazil in 2007. It encapsulated his conviction that his duty was 'to proclaim the Gospel by going out to find people, not by sitting [around] waiting for people to come to us'. More than that, there was a *sensus fidei* (sense of the faith) among the everyday lives of ordinary men and women which helped them grasp the reality of the faith with more clarity than that of many specialists, theologians and priests. 'To remain faithful we need to go outside,' Bergoglio concluded. 'That is what Aparecida says at bottom. That it is the heart of the mission.'

As Cardinal Archbishop of Buenos Aires he put that into practice most obviously in the slums of the city – including the one where Yorio and Jalics had worked 20 years before. Then he did not want his priests living in places like Villa 1-11-14 at Bajo Flores. Two decades later he was sending priests to work in the exact same place. The slum priest there, in the parish of at Santa María Madre del Pueblo (Holy Mary, Mother of the People) was Father Gustavo Carrara when I visited. It was still one of Buenos Aires's largest and most dangerous slums, though the risks now come from drugs and gang warfare rather than military death squads. Father Gustavo is another of 'the Bergoglio generation' of hand-picked dedicated strong young priests who do not just visit the slums but live and work there, sharing the lives of the poor. 'It was Father Bergoglio who suggested I came here,' Carrara said. 'And it has been a great experience.' He works long hours, seven days a week, hearing confessions, giving Communion, baptizing children, visiting the sick and conducting funerals. But his day is also filled with the practicalities of life among the unemployed and hungry: soup kitchens, health centres for teenage mothers, job training for unemployed youth, even running community radio to give the people a voice.

'Bergoglio was in a way like my father,' Carrara said. 'He was very close to me. He trusted me. He let me do things my own way. And he was always there when I needed him. I could visit or call in whenever I wanted. He'd always return the call immediately. "Hi, this is Bergoglio, how can I help?" Once I wanted to set up a project to help kids who are drug users. I found a good place but told him I needed $180,000 to buy it and set it up. He said, OK, and a few days later the money arrived. He would come here whenever he could, incognito, travelling on the bus. He doesn't like fuss but he loves talking to the ordinary people.'

'The poor are the treasure of the Church and we must care for them,' Bergoglio said in his conversations with Rabbi Abraham Skorka. 'If we lose this vision of things, we will have a lukewarm, weak and mediocre Church. Our true power must be service. We cannot adore God if our spirit does not include the needy.'

In that service the religious and the political are indivisible to the slum priests like Gustavo Carrara. 'The biggest problem we face is marginalization of the people,' he said. 'Drugs are a symptom, violence is a symptom, but marginalization is the disease. Our people feel marginalized by a social system that's forgotten about them and isn't interested in them. Popular faith is very important to them. It is the culture of the people that religion is not just for one day a week. God has to do with all life, and vice versa. When there's a market in the slum you can take the Virgin there. People will ask in the marketplace to be blessed, for a visit to the sick at home, to bless holy water. This is our life – everyday things like lobbying the city authorities to provide better water pressure in the neighbourhood and blessing holy water.'

Priests and people alike will miss their Bishop of the Slums, said Carrara, 'but we were having to get used to the idea of missing him anyway'. When he turned 75 in December 2011, Bergoglio submitted his resignation as Archbishop of Buenos Aires to Pope Benedict XVI as required by canon law. It had not, at the time of the 2013 conclave, been accepted but Bergoglio had already selected his room in a priests' retirement home in the place of his birth, Flores. 'He'd started to give away his books and to say goodbye,' Carrara said. In his frugal set of rooms in the archdiocesan office he had begun throwing out papers saying: 'I want to leave as little as possible behind me when I take my leave from this world.'

He left it behind. But not in the way he expected. 'He has gone to Rome, but at least,' said one woman happily in the *villa miseria*, 'he takes the mud of the slums with him on his shoes.'

6

Exile in Córdoba

Hello?

Hello? Yes. Who is it?

Jorge Bergoglio...

Pardon me?

Jorge Bergoglio.

Is this for real? Holy Father?

Yes! Do you want me to say it in *cordobés*?

Cordobés is the accent of Spanish spoken in the city of Córdoba, the place to which Jorge Mario Bergoglio was exiled for two years by the Jesuit leadership in Rome when he came to the end of 15 years of leadership of the Society of Jesus in Argentina. In 1971 he had become Novice Master; in 1973 Provincial; and in 1979 Rector of its ceremony. From 1971 to 1986 he had been the most influential figure in the religious order but by the end of that period Argentina's Jesuits were deeply riven between those who loved him and those who loathed him.

In an attempt to heal the wounds the Jesuit Superior General in Rome, Father Peter-Hans Kolvenbach, ordered that he be removed from the capital Buenos Aires and sent into the deep interior of the country to Córdoba. The plan was to take him away from the centre of the Society's activity where, despite having stepped down from his leadership position, he had been continuing to act as an alternative source of authority for those Jesuits who mourned the end of his regime.

Just four months after Bergoglio was elected Pope, two journalists in Córdoba decided to write a book about the pontiff's time in the city. He had spent two periods there. The first was two years from 1958 to 1960 during his Jesuit training. The second was from 1990 to 1992 – the two years when his fellows cast him into the wilderness.

The two writers, Javier Cámara and Sebastián Pfaffen, had been researching their book for eight months when, in February 2014, just before noon Argentine time, the phone rang on Cámara's home number. The journalists had told the Archbishop of Córdoba, Carlos Ñañez, about their project. Ñañez told the Pope. And the Pope picked up the phone and rang.

Two months earlier Ñañez had informed them that, having heard about their project, the Pope had decided to collaborate with the writers. The archbishop had produced a small piece of paper with an email address which Francis had given Ñañez to pass on to the two men. They were told to send questions, and comments about what they were doing, to the Pope in Rome. The Pope called not once but several times and there were numerous email exchanges over several months. 'What emerged was not an interview,' the authors explained, 'but he clarified many doubts and offered us some comments and important memories.'

What was so special about the Córdoba years which made Francis care so much about how they were portrayed to the world?

* * *

When Jorge Mario Bergoglio was exiled so suddenly to Córdoba in June 1990 a strict set of instructions was given by the Jesuit Curia in Rome. The man who had been the charismatic young leader of the Jesuits at the age of just 36 was now, aged only 50, stripped of all responsibility. In Córdoba he was to live in the Jesuit residence, pray, hear confessions, and work on his doctoral thesis. He was not placed on the rota to celebrate Mass in the Jesuit church. He could only go there to hear confessions. Kolvenbach forbade him from visiting other Jesuit communities. The order's houses and communities elsewhere were told they could not receive him. He was not allowed to make phone calls without permission. His letters were controlled. His supporters were told not to contact him. The ostracism from his peers was to be complete.

And yet that ostracism was reinforced by Bergoglio himself. There was one Jesuit at Córdoba, Father Michael Petty, whom Bergoglio had known well from Buenos Aires. The exiled former Provincial refused to talk to him. 'I used to try to see him,' said Petty. 'I'd go into the dining room and he'd go out the other door. We thought he was mad. I remember thinking clearly that. Because he wouldn't speak to anybody.'

The book by Cámara and Pfaffen, called *Aquel Francisco* (That Francis) claims that Bergoglio's exile came about as the result of a 'smear campaign' against him and 'bullying by Jesuit superiors' who spread slanders about Bergoglio outside the province. This account, they disclosed, was 'reconstructed from a series of conversations with members of the order' rather than having been offered to them by Pope Francis. They deduce that Argentinian critics of Bergoglio poisoned the mind of the Jesuit Superior General in Rome, the Dutchman Kolvenbach, with allegations that Bergoglio was 'brilliant but insane'. But Petty's testimony revealed that there was genuine concern in the Córdoba Jesuit community for Bergoglio's mental health.

Cámara and Pfaffen's account is a more lurid version of the claim that Bergoglio was undermined by a small group of leftist Jesuits who ran the Centre for Social Research and Action (CIAS) of the Argentine province. There may have been liberationists sympathetic to Marxism in the CIAS in the 1970s. But that was not the case in 1990 when Bergoglio was banished. And there were plenty of Jesuits in Rome who believed Bergoglio's approach to the poor was weak on social justice. Nor did Kolvenbach have to rely on second-hand reports about Bergoglio; the two men had met when Bergoglio attended the procurators' conference in Rome and had not seen eye to eye. The Jesuit General knew that the problem was not confined to a small cabal of opponents but that the Argentine province had been for years split down the middle between *bergoglianos* and *anti-bergoglianos*. And although Bergoglio had been sufficiently popular among Argentina's Jesuits in 1987 to be elected procurator, by 1990 his support had been eroded by his incorrigible inability, in the words of Father Frank Brennan SJ, 'to let go the reins of office once a Provincial of a different hue was in the saddle'. Another senior Jesuit told me: 'He drove people really crazy with his insistence that only he knew the right way to do things. Finally the other Jesuits said: "Enough".' Bergoglio failed to comprehend 'his impact on the common life' of the community, said another Jesuit, Father Arthur Liebscher, chair of the history department at Santa Clara University in California. By the time he was sent into exile, according to one senior Jesuit in Rome with an overview of the whole Argentine province, around two-thirds of its Jesuits had lost patience with him.

Pope Francis does not share this conspiratorial view of the past. In *Aquel Francisco* he tells Cámara and Pfaffen: 'I cannot say that I have been wronged, although others believe it. A religious should never say: "I suffered an injustice", because he must always find within himself, in all cases and under all circumstances, the path of God, the way to an inner purification.' For all that, Bergoglio was stung by the way his fellow Jesuits had rejected him. One of those who knew him in Córdoba remembered him saying afterwards: 'I've got nothing to do here. They give me no work. My letters are intercepted, they read my letters. I don't get phone messages. I feel completely shunned. I thought my life was finished when I was in that place. I was doing penance.' Cámara and Pfaffen's book returns to the theme of 'purification' over and over again.

There is an echo there of what Francis told Father Antonio Spadaro in his first interview after becoming Pope. In that, Francis spoke of the need for 'humility, sacrifice and courage, especially when you are misunderstood or you are the subject of misunderstandings and slanders'. But when asked specifically about his time as Jesuit Provincial, the Pope said: 'My style of government as a Jesuit at the beginning had many faults. That was a difficult time for the Society: an entire generation of Jesuits had disappeared. Because of this I found myself Provincial when I was still very young. I was only 36 years old. That was crazy. I had to deal with difficult situations, and I made my decisions abruptly and by myself. My authoritarian and quick manner of making decisions led me to have serious problems and to be accused of being ultra-conservative. I lived a time of great interior crisis when I was in Córdoba.'

But on the nature of that inner crisis Cámara and Pfaffen, despite their access to Pope Francis – who tells them the story of how as a child he once met Eva Perón – have few insights to offer. They paint a picture of how Bergoglio, who in Córdoba essentially cut contact with most Jesuits, hardly speaking to most of those with whom he was living, increased engagement with the world of ideas and with ordinary lay people. Francis directed them to individuals like Lucila Tejeda, a receptionist who manned the porter's lodge, who recalls Bergoglio bringing in bags of food to be given to beggars who called at the Jesuits' door. He always set some aside, Lucila told them, for her and her children. Then there was Irma Peralta, a poor woman he met to whom he gave the money to put a roof over her head. And Ricardo Spinassi, a janitor and cleaner; Bergoglio gave him money to buy a very modest house in Córdoba, but he got very angry when he realized that Ricardo had built a small pool by his new home.

Apart from his conversations with ordinary people, Bergoglio engaged mainly with the world of ideas. He spent long hours in his room at the residence. There he read and reread the works of the theologian Romano Guardini in preparation for his doctoral thesis. The deep influence of Guardini's thinking – which he described as 'challenging and exciting'– was later to surface in the key piece of writing that was to set the tone for his papacy, the apostolic exhortation *Evangelii Gaudium*. The document includes a quote from Guardini's prophetic work *Das Ende der Neuzeit* (The End of the Modern World) but the thinking of the German Catholic philosopher is in evidence through whole sections of the papal document. Of the thesis, he told Cámara and Pfaffen: 'I never managed to finish it, but it helped me a lot later.'

Paradoxically his exile in Córdoba stimulated in Bergoglio an interest in politics and the outside world. He started to read the Argentine national newspaper *La Nación* and think about wider society. A story in the paper about the brutal rape and murder of Maria Soledad Morales by a group of youths in Catamarca preoccupied him. The youths were from rich and powerful local families. A blanket of silence descended over the region and the case. But the cover-up of the murder was exposed by a nun, Sister Marta Pelloni, who became the leader of street rallies of local people demanding justice. The affair compelled Bergoglio to write a small book, *Corrupción y Pecado* (Corruption and Sin), a theme he has returned to on several occasions throughout his career. Its core reflection is that sin is weakness of which the sinner is aware and is able to seek forgiveness, but corruption makes people blind to their own failings, and to God, and is a growing and creeping infection which spreads to others and creates a wider culture that makes sin seem inevitable and acceptable. He also produced in his Córdoba period a collection of articles, speeches and sermons called *Reflexiones en Esperanza* (Pondering on Hope), which was published in 1992.

* * *

In Córdoba Bergoglio turned in on himself. He said Mass privately since he was not asked to say Mass routinely in the Jesuit church. His main public spiritual engagement was the hearing of confessions. He spent a lot of time looking out of the window and walking the streets. He would walk from the Jesuit residence to the church along a road that passed through many different areas of the city. People from all walks of life – academics, students, lawyers and ordinary folk – visited the church for the penitential sacrament. He found particularly moving those of the poor whom, he discovered, came from Traslasierra, the valley where a hundred years earlier Argentina's famous 'gaucho priest' the Cura Brochero had worked. 'Through confessions one learns a lot about human nature,' said Father Guillermo Marcó, who was perhaps Bergoglio's closest confidant in the eight years immediately after the Jesuit left Córdoba in the period in which Bergoglio's relationship with the poor deepened into a new dimension.

But there was one person who came regularly to confess whom Pope Francis did not mention to his Córdoba journalists. Roberto Juan Yannuzzi, a conservative young Catholic, had first met Bergoglio in 1973 when the Jesuit said Mass in Yannuzzi's home parish of Our Lady of Sorrows in Buenos Aires. Yannuzzi was 17 and in his last year of secondary school with the Betharramite Fathers at the Colegio San José. Bergoglio became the boy's confessor. Yannuzzi wanted to be a Jesuit but the order did not admit him and instead, the following year, he entered the Buenos Aires Metropolitan Seminar at Villa Devoto and trained to become an ordinary diocesan priest. When he was eventually ordained, Bergoglio preached at Yannuzzi's first Mass.

Yannuzzi visited Bergoglio often in Córdoba. By then Yannuzzi had become a highly conservative priest who was filled with admiration of the strict and disciplined restorationist regime Bergoglio had imposed on the Colegio Máximo. Yannuzzi, having been rejected by the Jesuits, now wanted to found his own ultra-traditionalist religious order based on the Spiritual Exercises of the Jesuits' founder, St Ignatius of Loyola. He claimed to have received, on the Feast of the Assumption in 1984, the inspiration to found an association of priests dedicated to 'the sanctification of the laity', particularly of college students. He wanted to call his order Miles Christi, Latin for Soldier of Christ.

He already had 10 seminarians enlisted as secret members, he told Bergoglio. Yannuzzi, it transpired, had persuaded the Metropolitan Seminary to start accepting the men two years earlier. When the most recent were admitted he had given the new Archbishop of Buenos Aires, Antonio Quarracino, undertakings that he had no intentions of founding a new congregation. But Yannuzzi was clandestinely meeting the 10 seminarians every week to correct anything they had learned in the seminary of which he disapproved. In return they were feeding him information on what was going on in the seminary. At the same time Yannuzzi was frequenting the city's colleges and the philosophy faculty of the Catholic University of Argentina, UCA, in search of disciples. Staff there still have painful memories of Yannuzzi's divisive influence, using recruiting tactics they compared to Opus Dei or another ultra-conservative movement, the Instituto del Verbo Encarnado. Yannuzzi's style was highly authoritarian and, his critics say, he repeatedly revealed an inability to accept orders from his superiors when he did not agree with them.

It was while Bergoglio was still in Córdoba that Quarracino found out what Yannuzzi was up to. The archbishop was furious and confronted Yannuzzi. The Miles Christi founder defended himself saying that Bergoglio was his mentor, confessor and friend. Bergoglio could not deny that, but he told Quarracino he did not support what Yannuzzi had been doing.

Something happened between the two men, for Bergoglio broke off the spiritual relationship abruptly. Yannuzzi later complained that Bergoglio had abandoned him. Miles Christi followers accused the Jesuit of betrayal. Bergoglio said nothing, though later the future Pope's supporters laid the fault at the door of Yannuzzi. Either way the bond between the two men was sundered. That may have been a simple collapse of trust and a two-way breakdown in loyalties. But there may be another explanation, as we shall consider.

Yannuzzi fell into a deep depression. The break-up with Quarracino deprived him of a seminary for his followers. He felt that everything he had worked for had collapsed around him. But eventually he rallied and moved himself and his 10 seminarians from Buenos Aires to the diocese of La Plata just across the River Plate, where he secured the support of a more conservative prelate, Carlos Galán, the Archbishop of La Plata. In 1994 Galán established Miles Christi as 'a Public Clerical Association of the Faithful'. Galán was succeeded by an even more conservative coadjutor bishop in 1998, Héctor Rubén Aguer, who, a year later, elevated Miles Christi to the status of Clerical Religious Order.

Bergoglio's hostility grew. When he became Archbishop of Buenos Aires the Miles Christi Institute, which those close to Bergoglio described as 'a sect', found itself the subject of a de facto ban. So did several other extreme conservative orders, which had ordinations stopped, a seminary closed and restrictions placed upon their founder. Miles Christi concentrated its activities in La Plata and a few other Argentine dioceses, though it continued to work secretly in Bergoglio's Buenos Aires. Since then it has spread to parts of Mexico and the United States, where it chants plainsong Masses *ad orientem* – with the priest's back to the people as in the days before the liturgical reforms of the Second Vatican Council. At the invitation of the conservative Jesuit Father John Hardon – who was forbidden by his own order from teaching in any Jesuit-run institution in the 16 years before his death – Miles Christi estab-lished itself in Michigan in 2000 and later in the archdiocese of Detroit and the diocese of San Diego. Among its activities it runs silent retreat on Ignatian lines for college students and others. The most prominent conservative bishop in the United Sates, Cardinal Raymond Burke, is one of its US supporters. Back in Argentina, Archbishop Aguer continues to ordain Miles Christi priests.

Father Roberto Yannuzzi remains the Superior General of Miles Christi based in Argentina. But he does not give interviews, said Father Luis María Recúpero, the executive secretary of the institute, especially not about Bergoglio and the relationship of the two men in the Córdoba years. 'The figure of the Holy Father is too big for him and enormously exceeds whatever Father Roberto may be able to contribute about him,' Recúpero told me.

Bergoglio has spoken of the experience but has done so obliquely, as he so often does. In his series of conversations with Rabbi Abraham Skorka he says:

Yes, some small restorationist factions have continued to multiply; I call them fundamentalists. They tell young people: 'Do this, do that.' So a seventeen- or eighteen-year-old guy or girl gets excited and they push them forward with rigid directives. And to be honest, they mortgage their lives and at thirty, they burst because they were not properly prepared to overcome the thousand and one crises in life, or the thousand and one shortcomings that everyone has, or the thousand and one wrongs that they are going to commit. They do not have the proper criteria to know and understand the mercy of God, for example. This type of rigid religiosity is disguised with doctrines that claim to give justifications, but in reality deprive people of their freedom and do not allow them to grow as persons. A large number end up living a double life. Restorationist fundamentalism is an opiate as well because it takes you away from the living God. Opium is an idol that alienates you, as any idol does. They reduce God to a being that you can manage with prescriptions: 'If I do this everything will be fine, if I do this I will not lack anything.' It is a form of buying comfort, wellbeing, fortune and happiness, but it leaves behind the living God, He that accompanies you along the way.

Yannuzzi and his followers knew that he was talking about them.

Yet the breakdown of the relationship between Bergoglio and Yannuzzi could have been symptomatic of something deeper. Yannuzzi's machinations may well have been for Bergoglio a trigger to rethinking his own yearning for orthodoxy and order. Or, conversely, thinking through, and praying through, the failures in his own leadership style may appear to have brought him to a clearer perception of the spiritual and political mind-set of ultra-traditional pietists like Yannuzzi. Bergoglio had not been that kind of traditionalist as leader of the Jesuits. But he had certainly been reactionary in his analysis of Liberation Theology, an authoritarian in his style. That was clear from the changes which followed when he became Archbishop of Buenos Aires. Certainly Pope Francis dropped a hint of a spiritual dimension to the experience of Córdoba in his interview with Spadaro when he spoke of it as being 'a time of great interior crisis'. Francis later told Cámara and Pfaffen: 'I felt the two years I spent in Córdoba as a priest, between 1990 and 1992 ... helped me to consolidate as a pastor.' What could that mean?

* * *

Something happened to Jorge Mario Bergoglio which changed him dramatically. Before Córdoba his leadership style was that of a strict, severe, dutiful, disciplinarian authoritarian who rarely smiled, was happy to be driven around by a priest-chauffeur and who cared for the poor as people who needed charity. Afterwards he became gentler, more forgiving, more concerned to preach mercy, more listening – and more anxious to empower the poor, acknowledging that they needed not merely charity but justice. And he got rid of his episcopal mansion and chauffeur and took the bus. Clearly something happened in Córdoba. 'He must have done a lot of discerning there,' said his fellow Córdoba resident, Father Michael Petty. 'It's not easy to change that sort of style. But he changed. And he changed when he was in Córdoba.'

There seemed more to this than learning from experience. Certainly he contemplated the mistakes of his past, the 'hundreds of errors' to which he later admitted. As he told Spadaro: 'Over time I learned many things. The Lord has allowed this growth in knowledge of government through my faults and my sins.' But something deeper also changed. He underwent a dramatic transformation from authoritarian self-certainty to profound humility. Cámara later recalled that, after many conversations on the phone, Bergoglio told him that re-examining his 'years of shadows and inner purification' brought back to the surface feelings that 'were deep in his heart and that this made him feel well'. Cámara told me: 'He remembers having made some mistakes in the past and asks forgiveness for this. He knows that the hand of God was present in all the things he had to face in his life.' One of the few visitors Bergoglio had from Buenos Aires was his old teacher Father Juan Carlos Scannone who took one look at Bergoglio's face in Córdoba and was alarmed. 'I said to myself: "He's going through a dark night". So it was a difficult time in his life, a time of purification.'

When Bergoglio arrived back in Buenos Aires, as its new auxiliary bishop, after his exile in Córdoba in 1992, he had totally remodelled his approach to being a leader. He began as a bishop in an entirely different way to how he had acted as head of the Jesuits. Bergoglio had lost none of his steely sense of purpose. But his style was consultative, delegatory and participative. And his manner was distinctly different. From the outset humility was his watchword. It was there he developed what became one of his most familiar habits – of ending all encounters by asking the other person to pray for him. He had previously done that occasionally but, he revealed in his first airborne press conference after he became Pope, it only developed into a habit after his exile in Córdoba. It was then, he revealed, that 'I began to ask with greater frequency while I was working as a bishop, because I sensed that if the Lord does not help in this work of assisting the People of God to go forward, it can't be done. I am truly conscious of my many limitations, with so many problems, and I am a sinner – as you know! – and I have to ask for this. But it comes from within! I ask Our Lady too to pray to the Lord for me. It is a habit, but a habit that comes from my heart and also a real need in terms of my work. I feel I have to ask... I don't know, that's the way it is... '

Humility is a much misunderstood quality in the contemporary world where it is a quality in short supply. It is not, as is often assumed, some kind of synonym for shyness, reticence, bashfulness or lack of ambition. Humility is not a character trait with which some are born; it is the orphaned virtue which our age has publicly forgotten how to embrace. For Bergoglio in 1992 humility was more like an intellectual stance than a personal temperament. 'He's worked out that to be a good Shepherd he needs to be humble,' said the Buenos Aires priest and theologian Augusto Zampini. 'It's calculated. That's not to suggest it's fake but it is thought-through.' More than that, it has been nurtured, suggested Bergoglio's friend Rabbi Abraham Skorka: 'He's developed it through spiritual exercises'. Bergoglio's humility is a religious decision, according to Bishop Jorge Eduardo Lozano of Gualeguaychú, who was Bergoglio's auxiliary in Buenos Aires for six years. His humility and simplicity are 'actually an expression of his magisterium'.

Bergoglio's critics have claimed there is something cynical in the change. Too humble is half proud, as the Yiddish proverb has it. Or they quote St Augustine saying that 'false humility' is 'grievous pride'. Bergoglio's nemesis, the investigative journalist Horacio Verbitsky, has gone so far as to suggest that the series of interviews Bergoglio gave in 2010 to Rubin and Ambrogetti for El Jesuita were a Machiavellian attempt by Bergoglio to clean up his image after the dossier at the 2005 conclave had so damaged his chances of rivalling Joseph Ratzinger for the papacy. Bergoglio's political opponents in Argentina have seen many of the great gestures he has made since becoming Pope – paying his own hotel bill, driving a small car, carrying his own bags – as gimmicky or even hypocritical PR stunts.

This is too conspiratorial. Pope Francis's decision to take the bus with the cardinals after his election, instead of taking a chauffeur-driven official limousine, was just a reprise of his routinely taking Linea A on the Buenos Aires subway for years. Sitting in his papal white in the back row in the Vatican church of Santa Anna merely continued his long-standing habit as a bishop of always taking a seat in the lowest place. Bowing his head for the blessing of the people of Rome at his first appearance on the balcony of St Peter's was no different to kneeling for a blessing from a stadium full of Argentinian evangelical Protestants.

Certainly Bergoglio in all phases of his life has been a shrewd politician but there has been more to that than sheer ambition. Throughout his career Bergoglio has shown significant courage. It was a bold tactic to ask a priest to feign illness so Bergoglio could gain access to the leader of the military junta during the Dirty War. It took strength of character to stand by Clelia Luro, the widow of the ostracized bishop, Jerónimo Podestá, when no other bishop would, after her husband died. There were repeated examples of his personal bravery smuggling out victims of the military dictatorship, standing up to the drug gangs in the slums and sticking to his principles on inter-faith dialogue despite accusations of heresy, apostasy and disloyalty by ultra-traditionalists in

Argentina and Rome. At the same time it is clear that his decision to embrace radical humility was a tool or technique he developed in his struggle against what he had learned were the weaknesses in his own personality with its rigid, authoritarian and egotistical streaks. There is evidence of that in a whole range of incidents. At its most trivial was the row over the cakes in the Jesuit residence on his return from Germany. At its more grave was his uncooperative and even evasive performance in the witness-box during the ESMA trials, where he appeared to put the defence of the institutional Church before the pursuit of the full truth. On the Church and the Dirty War he clearly felt that the collusion in the dictatorship by members of the Church, to a very senior level, was so deep and wide that individual accusations and recriminations would damage, rather than help, wider Argentinian society. Some things are best left buried, he believed, because too many people are guilty in some degree. Many suspect that he is wrong about that. He may yet change his view. As Pope he has already given instructions to open the Vatican archives on the behaviour of the papal ambassador to Argentina during the Dirty War. After a brief meeting with representatives of the Grandmothers of Plaza de Mayo, and sent along his successor as Archbishop of Buenos Aires to their offices. The women are hopeful he will instruct that the records of the Argentinian Church be opened to outside scrutiny, even as Rabbi Skorka hopes he will do the same with the Vatican archives on the role of Pius XII. The journey from Bergoglio to Francis may mean that change is not yet complete.

* * *

The change in Jorge Mario Bergoglio may not have been triggered by an event so much as by a process. Bergoglio's key decisions are all made during his long sessions of daily prayer. It is difficult to overstate the importance of prayer in his life, says his former aide Guillermo Marcó: 'He likes to wake at 4.30 a.m. to 5 a.m. every morning to pray. He makes decisions while he prays.' Prayer, Bergoglio has said, 'should be an experience of giving way, of surrendering, where our entire being enters into the presence of God'. In *El Jesuita* he said:

> This is where dialogue, listening, and transformation occur. Looking at God, but above all sensing that we are being watched by Him. This happens, in my case, when I recite the rosary or the psalms or when I joyfully celebrate the Eucharist. But the moment when I most savour the religious experience is when I am before the tabernacle. Sometimes I allow myself to fall asleep while sitting there and just let Him look at me.

I have the sense of being in someone else's hands, as though God were taking me by the hand.

In Buenos Aires he often prayed for two hours before the start of his day. He still does in Rome.

As a bishop one of the first things he did when he visited priests in their parish was to ask them about their prayer life. How did they pray? When and where? How much time did they make to pray? Without prayer, he has repeatedly said, priests are just social workers, without Christ the Church is just another NGO (non-governmental organization or charity). It was because prayer was so important to him, said Marcó, that he would rarely accept invitations to dinner as Archbishop of Buenos Aires. 'He knew that if he accepted invitations for evening events he wouldn't get up early. And he did not want to miss that prayer time. He has a very strong relationship with God. He doesn't have very many friends. He's a solitary man. In the eight years I worked with him I only ate with him about five times though I saw him every day. He's always been, I'd say, monkish in his lifestyle. His main relationship is with God.'

The many people with whom Bergoglio stays in touch, particularly those in Buenos Aires who still receive weekly phone calls from him, might be surprised to hear Bergoglio described as a solitary man. But Marcó is adamant. 'He has a pastoral care for people,' his former aide said. 'He keeps dates and numbers in his little work book and rings people on their birthday, on the anniversary of a loved one's death. Or with a few people [he rings] every Sunday afternoon. He keeps in touch. He has an interest in people. He worries about them. But it's a kind of pastoral concern rather than friendship. If you define friendship as having fun with people then he has no friends. Friendship is a symmetrical relationship. His relationships are not like that. People believe they are his friends but he never goes to dinner at their homes. He doesn't even see his family at Christmas. He is quite happy after the Christmas service to go to cook for priests and people in the slums and then go home to his room on his own. He is quite content. It's the life he has chosen. It's not mawkish. In his own time he wants to be alone.'

Except that he is not alone. He is with God. 'Prayer is talking and listening,' Bergoglio has said, 'Prayer is an act of freedom but sometimes it emerges as an attempt at control, which is the same as wanting to control God.' Yet there are also 'moments of profound silence, adoration, waiting to see what will happen'. In prayer, 'this reverent silence coexists together with a sort of haggling'. In the end what Bergoglio does, he said, is 'put myself in the presence of God and, aided by His Word, go forward in what he desires'.

In prayer Jorge Mario Bergoglio struggled against his own personality to become the person he believes that God wants him to be. One of the techniques used in the standard 15-year Jesuit formation is a series of Spiritual Exercises devised by the order's founder, St Ignatius of Loyola. Over the years the Ignatian exercises had honed and refined Bergoglio's instincts and opened his capacity to change. Examination of conscience, exercises in empathy, and a cultivated process of discernment are at the heart of Ignatian spirituality. The Exercises are meditations and contemplations whose aim is 'to conquer oneself and to regulate one's life in such a way that no decision is made under the influence of any inordinate attachment'. The goal is to create a spiritual detachment or indifference to an individual's own 'likes, dislikes, comforts, wants, needs, drives, appetites and passions' so that they may be able to discern what is God's will for them.

One of the key techniques of discernment in Ignatius's Spiritual Exercises is called *Las Dos Banderas* – The Meditation on the Two Standards. It is used to clarify motives. It asks whether we are deluding ourselves that what we say we do in the service of God is in fact a disguised version of the values of this world with its illusions of security, reputation and power. Such discernment has helped Bergoglio strip away his layers of self-justification and self-delusion, and penetrate through to the inner core of his behaviour and motivation. In Córdoba Bergoglio had two long years to reflect on his divisive leadership of the Jesuits in Argentina – and on what he had done wrong or inadequately during the Dirty War. He had to confront the fact that, in his inexperience as a young leader, he had allowed the breakdown of the pastoral relationship between himself and priests in his care. Learning from experience might have changed Bergoglio's head. But something also changed his heart.

Almost 25 years after Franz Jalics and his fellow slum priest Orlando Yorio had been released from their illegal detention, there was a meeting, in Germany, between Jalics and Bergoglio who was by then the Archbishop of Buenos Aires. As disclosed earlier, the two men met and concelebrated Mass together, ending with what Jalics later called 'a solemn embrace'. What actually happened, an eyewitness said, was that when the two men met they fell into each other's arms and cried. There was more than a change of politics or of style about the encounter. It was the visceral intermingling of relief, remorse and repentance. The change within Jorge Mario Bergoglio, it seemed, sprang from deep within his soul.

* * *

It is not possible for us to see into another's soul, but the years in Córdoba made it possible for Jorge Mario Bergoglio to see further into his own. And the clues to what he has seen, and continues to see, have been evident in what he has said, as well as done, over the years. He learned from the hundreds of errors he committed as Provincial, to which he admitted in his interviews with Rubin and Ambrogetti. Ambrogetti taught him, as he said to Spadaro: 'I am always wary of the first decision, that is, the first thing that comes to my mind if I have to make a decision. This is usually the wrong thing. I have to wait and assess, looking deep into myself, taking the necessary time. The wisdom of discernment redeems the necessary ambiguity of life and helps us find the most appropriate means, which do not always coincide with what looks great and strong.'

Guilt, Bergoglio said in his conversations with Rabbi Skorka, can be just a psychological feeling which is not a religious experience. 'Guilt by itself... is just another human resource. Guilt, without atonement, does not allow us to grow.' He returned to the subject in *El Jesuita*. 'There's no clean slate,' he said. 'We have to bless the past with remorse, forgiveness, and atonement.' Regret is not sufficient; there has to be change. By changing his style of spiritual leadership so radically Bergoglio was saying to the world that he had made a change of heart – and a change of behaviour was its fruit. Just before he left for Rome and the conclave, Bergoglio penned what turned out to be his last Lenten message to the people of Buenos Aires. Morality, he said, is not a 'never falling down' but an 'always getting up again'. And that is a response to God's mercy.

The need for forgiveness and for God's mercy have been his dominant theological refrains, both before and after he became Pope. Mercy was the subject of his homily on the first Sunday after his election as Bishop of Rome. 'Mercy is the Lord's most powerful message,' he told the congregation in the little Church of Saint Anna located within the Vatican. 'It is not easy to trust oneself to the mercy of God, because [God's mercy] is an unfathomable abyss – but we must do it.' From Jesus, he said, we will 'not hear words of contempt, we do not hear words of condemnation, but only words of love, of mercy, that invite us to conversion. "Neither do I condemn you. Go and sin no more!"... The problem is that we get tired of asking forgiveness. Let us never get tired. He is the loving Father who always forgives, who has that heart of mercy for all of us.' Bergoglio has changed, is the message, but changes will continue for Francis too who has called the Catholic Church to a Holy Year of Mercy beginning in December 2015. The man who is now Pope remains, he is telling us, a work in progress.

'After his exile in Córdoba', said Elisabetta Piqué in her biography, 'Bergoglio feels he is a man reborn.' In their book, Cámara and Pfaffen suggest that Bergoglio was depressed when he arrived in Córdoba, but Guillermo Marcó, the man who was the Jesuit's aide for eight years directly after Córdoba, disagrees.

'Bergoglio was not depressed in Córdoba, but in pain for this degradation. He thought that the rest of his life was going to be like this: punished and isolated.' He was aged just 50 and he felt finished. He felt he had been disposed of.

The man who sent Bergoglio into the wilderness, the then Jesuit Provincial, Father Victor Zorzín, has since said: 'It cost him a lot to accept the change. But pain can ripen into something else.' Over time he learned many things.

One of the emails sent to Pope Francis by Cámara and Pfaffen asked the pontiff whether Córdoba had been 'a dark night'. They were alluding to the phrase of the sixteenth-century Spanish mystic St John of the Cross who used the words 'dark night of the soul' to describe the bleakness and sense of abandonment which can be induced by a spiritual crisis. One of Bergoglio's favourite saints, the nineteenth-century French Carmelite, St Thérèse of Lisieux, among other holy figures from history, underwent such an experience. 'That would be an overstatement,' replied Bergoglio, with characteristic humility. 'Dark nights are for saints. I am just an ordinary guy. But it was a time of inner purification.' Córdoba, he said, had 'engendered spiritual solidity'. The two years had been 'like a night, with some inner darkness' which 'allowed me to do apostolic work which helped consolidate me as a pastor'.

More than a decade later, Bergoglio, then Cardinal Archbishop of Buenos Aires, was approached by a politician seeking advice. The man had been defeated in an election and did not know how to cope with the rejection. Bergoglio told him: 'Live your exile. I lived mine. And afterwards you will be back. And when you do come back you will be more merciful, kinder, and will want to serve your people better.'

7

How Bergoglio Changed

There are books on Liberation Theology for sale in the foyer of the Colegio Máximo today. To the side of the seminary's grand entrance, with its stone arches, marble floor with diamond squares and heavy smell of polish on the dark mahogany, is a glass-fronted case containing titles like *Labour and Capital* and *Democracy, Human Rights and the Political Order* and *The Theology of Liberation and the Social Doctrine of the Catholic Church*. They would not have been allowed there when Jorge Mario Bergoglio was Provincial Superior of the Jesuits or Rector of the college. But if the Colegio Máximo has changed so has the authoritarian conservative who has been transformed from the scourge of Liberation Theology to a Pope for the poor.

The extent of the change took many people by surprise, and not just those who had not been paying attention. Hebe de Bonafini is one of the leaders of Mothers of the Plaza de Mayo whose members for years protested in the square between Buenos Aires cathedral and the Casa Rosada, the official residence of the president of Argentina. It was a public witness to the disappearance of their children and grandchildren at the hands of the death squads of the military dictatorship in the years from 1976 to 1983 – and to the lack of information which was forthcoming from the files of official organizations including the Catholic Church. Priests and nuns were involved in the disappearances of their victims and the children they bore in captivity. Hebe de Bonafini once famously left a bucket of urine in the cathedral, accusing Bergoglio of being in league with fascism. But after his election as Pope she diplomatically wrote to him: 'Father Francis, I did not know about your pastoral work; I just knew that a top leader of the Argentinian Church lived in that cathedral. When we marched and passed by the cathedral we used to scream: "You kept silent when they were being taken away."' But since, she said, she had found out about his commitment to the slums and was overjoyed at the prospect for change in the Vatican. And even one of Bergoglio's former Jesuit pupils, Father Rafael Velasco, a former Rector of the Catholic University of Córdoba, said: 'Bergoglio was so very conservative that

I was rather shocked years later when he started talking about the poor. It wasn't something which seemed at the top of his agenda at the time but clearly became so as a bishop. Something changed.'

Those who dealt with him at a more intimate level agree. But they differ in their views of how that metamorphosis came about. 'He has changed. He was pretty conservative,' said Father Michael Campbell Johnson, who in 1977 was sent by Jesuit headquarters in Rome to persuade Bergoglio to adopt the social justice agenda which characterized the order throughout the rest of Latin America. He added: 'He has clearly grown in his witness for the poor'. Father Miguel Yáñez, who was received into the Jesuits in that same year by Bergoglio, has watched Bergoglio over almost four decades. 'He did change,' Yáñez said. 'It was mostly when he was a bishop and an archbishop. But it was not a sudden change, so much as a gradual evolution. Being outside the tensions and complex atmosphere of the Society [of Jesus] he possibly became more open to dialogue and more open generally. Looking at him now I recognize he's the same person; he's always had a strong personal authority. But his relationship to the poor has deepened.'

The change goes wider than that, according to Rabbi Abraham Skorka, with whom Bergoglio had a series of conversations for a book and television series. 'Bergoglio has changed over the years,' the Jewish leader said. 'He's a very dynamic person. He's a person who is learning from life. He's very sensitive and has great empathy. He has changed according to his life's experience.' Bergoglio himself, talking to Skorka, added this gloss: 'Religious truth does not change, but it does develop and grow. It is like with the human being, we are the same as a baby and in old age, but in the middle there is a whole journey. In this way ... something that was once seen as natural, is not seen like that, today.'

In the middle there is a whole journey. Bergoglio's own words – and the testimony of those who know the new Pope well, and over many years – hint at how deeply Bergoglio's experiences have affected him and how profound has been the change they have wrought. But it is his own words, definite but slightly opaque, which are intriguing enough to want to unpack more explicitly. In the middle there is a whole journey.

What changed Bergoglio? In Córdoba it seems something happened deep within his soul. But the change, and its extent, came from more than that. External events played their part. So did regular contact with the poorest of the poor in the slums of Buenos Aires. So did a growing understanding of the theology of liberation which he found too disturbing as a young man. Ironically, 40 years on, he found he had arrived at a similar understanding of social justice to that of Yorio and Jalics, the two Jesuits with whom he had fallen out because of their work in the slums in 1976, leaving them exposed to the violent predations of a military torture squad.

* * *

History has been a major factor in the transformation of Bergoglio, for the world has changed significantly around him. His opposition to Liberation Theology was very much rooted in the mind-set of the Cold War and the fear that atheistic Soviet-style communism would supplant both capitalism and Catholicism in Latin America, with Cuba as its toehold. But then the Berlin Wall came down. The Soviet Union and its empire collapsed. A new international *realpolitik* was ushered in. It was not quite 'the End of History' predicted by the American academic Francis Fukuyama, but the globalization of the world's economy – and the seismic economic crisis which seized Argentina in 2001 – prompted Bergoglio to think differently about extreme poverty. To criticize the exploitation of the poor, or their wilful marginalization, was no longer to risk being seen to side with anti-religious Marxism. Rather it began to sound like bringing the good news to the poor. After the end of the military dictatorship in Argentina the shocking extent of its brutality was revealed in all its gory details. Also revealed was the extent of the collusion by prominent figures in the Argentinian church with the junta. All that created the emotional and intellectual space in which Bergoglio could examine his conscience over his own role in it. Even those who had committed no crimes were forced to face up to sins of omission once democracy returned. The Church too had lessons to learn; after its disastrous endorsement of the military dictators, and of Perón before them, it backed away from endorsing politics and gradually became critical of successive governments. The final changed context was that Bergoglio – who had been very much rooted in Argentina for most of his life – travelled more as a bishop, and particularly as an archbishop. He also had more contact with other Latin American bishops and international figures. That brought home to him how out of step the Church had been in Argentina by comparison with the rest of Latin America, where church leaders had stood out prophetically against military dictatorships.

But there was not just change in the outside circumstances; there was change within Bergoglio too. Looking back on his earlier days as a schoolmaster, Bergoglio recognized, in conversation with Rubin and Ambrogetti in 2010, how much he had learned from his students. 'I thank them for all the good they did me,' he reflected, 'particularly for the way they taught me how to be more a brother than a father'. Something similar happened to him when he first became a bishop. He learned from the poor in the same way that he had learned from his students. In that, he was very similar to Archbishop Oscar Romero of El Salvador according to Professor Mario I. Aguilar, author of *Pope Francis: His Life and Thought*. Like Romero he was 'a traditional priest who was changed and educated by the people around him, and who wrestled with those challenges in prayer,' said Aguilar. As Bishop of the Slums he learned about the impact of drugs and prostitution on poor people – and he learned to see those involved in crimes not simply as the creators of problems but as their victims too. He learned more of the broken realities and frailties of human lives – and that broadened his understanding of the complexity of poverty and its structural causes.

'In Buenos Aires he came across more concrete problems,' said Father Augusto Zampini, a diocesan priest in Greater Buenos Aires. 'When you're working in a shanty-town 90 per cent of your congregation are single or divorced. You have to learn to deal with that. Communion for the divorced and remarried is not an issue there. Everyone takes Communion.' Bergoglio never altered his doctrinal orthodoxy on such matters but he did not allow dogma to overrule the priority of pastoral concern. 'He was never rigid about the small and stupid stuff,' said Father Juan Isasmendi, the parish priest in Villa 21 slum, 'because he was interested in something deeper.' Bergoglio's visits to the slums brought him into contact with a huge number of ordinary people in their everyday situations. Over his 18 years as bishop and archbishop in Buenos Aires, one priest estimated, Bergoglio must have personally talked to at least half the people in that slum in visits where he would just turn up, wander the alleyways, and chat to the locals and drink *mate* tea with them. 'It is when we are involved in ministry that we discover who we are,' Michael Campbell-Johnston said of him. And the man who was Bergoglio's close aide for the first eight years of his episcopal ministry had no doubt about that either: 'He doesn't see the poor as people he can help but rather as people from whom he can learn,' said Father Guillermo Marcó. 'He believes the poor are closer to God than the rest of us; they have a very personal experience of Him.'

All this developed a new openness in Bergoglio. As he said in *El Jesuita*:

I don't have all the answers; I don't even have all the questions. I always think of new questions, and there are always new questions coming forward. But the answers have to be thought out according to the different situations, and you also have to wait for them. I confess that, because of my disposition, the first answer that comes to me is usually wrong. When I'm facing a situation, the first solution I think of is what *not* to do. Because of this I have learned not to trust my first reaction. When I'm calmer, after passing through the crucible of solitude, I come closer to understanding what has to be done... You can do a great deal of harm with the decisions you make. One can be very unfair.

Clearly he was there looking back to the *modus operandi* of the younger Bergoglio. As a young priest in powerful leadership positions he did not have the maturity he needed to cope in the 1970s with the competing pressures of the Jesuit Curia in Rome, the Vatican and a ruthless military dictatorship. He had only taken his final Jesuit vows months before he was thrust prematurely into the top leadership role among Argentina's Jesuits. His experience led to some bad judgements. 'When you're young, you believe you can change the world, and that is good, that's the way it should be,' he told Rubin and Ambrogetti. 'But later, when you seek this change, you discover the logic of patience in your life and the lives of others... A good father, like a good mother, is one who intervenes in the life of the child just enough to demonstrate guidelines for growing up, to help him, but who later knows when to be a bystander to his own and others' failures, and to endure them.' Shortcomings, he concluded, act as a springboard for growth.

A key part of Bergoglio's growth has been in the development of an understanding that what the poor need is not charity but justice – an insight at which the two Jesuits Yorio and Jalics had arrived two decades earlier. The quality of Bergoglio's commitment to help alleviate the consequences of poverty was never in doubt from the outset; his provision of food, medicine and blankets to the needy in the 1970s, even as he was expunging Liberation Theology from the Jesuit province, was testimony to that. But in the early days his concern for the poor never went beyond the impulse of Gospel-inspired philanthropy. He worked *for* the poor rather than *with* them. 'His theology was traditional and conservative,' according to Mario Aguilar, who is editor of the De Gruyter three-volume *Handbook of Liberation Theologies*, 'but his pastoral openness to other people [was] enormous, warm and empathetic.'

Some of that impulse survived into his years as a bishop. If only the rich would behave with more decency, he thought at first, then things would be much better for the poor. So in Argentina's massive economic crisis in 2001, which plunged half the population into poverty, he castigated the rich for 'rapacity' in attempting to maintain their privileged position as the rest of the nation descended into an economic maelstrom. A year later in a sermon he chastised 'golden-mouthed' politicians who were making unrealistic promises to voters to fix the nation's economy. 'Go and fix yourself,' he told them. 'Have a change of heart. Get to confession, before you need it even more!' The *Wall*

Street Journal, not unreasonably, concluded of Bergoglio that 'his Christianity is less political than personal'.

What happened next sowed seeds in Bergoglio's mind which would change the personal into the political. The 2001 economic crisis forced Argentina to tell the world that it would refuse to pay the $94 billion it owed to foreign banks and investors. The economy spiralled uncontrollably and life became incredibly tough for ordinary Argentinians. In the years that followed, the International Monetary Fund did its job as the guardian of world financial stability but the austerity its medicine imposed fell cruelly upon the poorest people in the land. Bergoglio began to be highly critical of the economic formulae of modern capitalism; he was particularly critical of how it creates speculative financial markets which damage the real economy. He attacked the way that the debt-restructuring process was being paid for – by cutting services on which the poor depended. He began to make use of the insights of Liberation Theology with regard to economic structures which were so corrupt that they constituted structures of oppression which were themselves sinful. He attacked 'unbridled capitalism [which] fragments economic and social life'. What was needed instead, he said, was a solidarity which brought people together. The 'unjust distribution of goods', he lamented, was creating 'a situation of social sin that cries out to Heaven and limits the possibilities of a fuller life for so many of our brothers'. That was not all. 'Unjust economic structures,' he thundered, were violations of human rights. The build-up of debt on restructured debt was 'immoral, unjust and illegitimate'. Homelessness he described as 'structural slavery'. Bergoglio was beginning to sound like a liberation theologian.

More radical liberation theologians, like Lisandro Orlov, an Argentinian Lutheran, were unconvinced as to how far Bergoglio really understood the concept of sin residing in structures. 'He talks about the imperialism of money and the tyranny of the market, but that's not Liberation Theology, it's just Catholic Social Teaching,' said Orlov. 'It's strong on analysis, but without real proposals or a programme for an alternative. Bergoglio does not go on to the next step – the empowerment of the poor. Bergoglio has moved from the right to the middle not the left.' And the Chilean economist Olga Larrazabal Saitua has said of Bergoglio: 'I don't believe that he thinks of Christ as a liberator, not only from poverty but from the historical oppressions of culture, as do the liberation theologians... Rather he sees Christ emotionally as Saviour and Comforter, who can be approached through the pious rituals of the charcoal burner, if it's the poor we are talking about, and by charity if it's the wealthy.'

Perhaps that was true then. But Bergoglio's political journey was not over, as was to become clear when as Pope he set out to shift the whole of the Catholic

Church from the Right, not to the Left, but rather to a radical middle. He wanted to bring to the Church the personal revolution he had undergone. Leadership was not about authority and discipline, he now saw, but about service and mercy.

* * *

Bergoglio's thinking was more sophisticated on Liberation Theology than many supposed. Bergoglio had always cared for the poor. He sought to address both their spiritual and material needs with his soup kitchens and other works of charity. He loved their simpler faith; as people became more educated he feared there was a danger they moved further away from God. That was why, as leader of the Jesuits, he wanted his seminarians to stay in touch with simple people. He believed the educated have something to learn about faith from the poor. Bergoglio's priorities for the Jesuits in poor neighbourhoods was always, in this order, to say Mass, to teach the catechism and then to address the physical needs of the people. He was suspicious of both the priorities and the Marxist analysis used by some leftist theologians and felt that the concern for the poor in Liberation Theology was driven by a socialist ideology rather than Christian love.

For that reason he was attracted to the theology being developed in the late 1970s and 1980s in the Colegio Máximo by a senior Jesuit theologian, Father Juan Carlos Scannone. Called *teología del pueblo*, or the Theology of the People, it grew initially out of Liberation Theology. It kept elements from the more political original. It liked the idea that the Gospel displayed a 'preferential option for the poor'. It too believed that working among the poor should come first and that theological reflection must grow from that, and was therefore of secondary importance. But Liberation Theology wanted to help the poor use politics to gain control over their own destiny. The Theology of the People, by contrast, did not want to shake the political and economic status quo; instead it wanted to transform the culture of society.

It is important to understand that there is not a simple division between Liberation Theology and the Theology of the People here. Right-wing opponents of Liberation Theology like to characterize it as purely Marxist – this was a caricature which the CIA and the Vatican played on during the early part of the pontificate of Pope John Paul II. But there were a variety of non-Marxist strands of Liberation Theology and even some of the Marxist types did not support armed uprisings as opponents liked to suggest.

Even so there was a distinct difference between Liberation Theology's emphasis upon political activism and the Theology of the People's emphasis on the culture and religious devotion of the common people. For Scannone local culture was an essential part of a Theology of the People which was to be rooted in all the qualities of folk religion – the shrines, statues, processions, medals, rosaries and novenas – which Bergoglio so valued from his upbringing. Scannone told me: 'Some people think Argentinian Theology of the People isn't Liberation Theology at all and class it just as popular theology. But others see it as a current within Liberation Theology; the father of this theology Gustavo Gutiérrez and I wrote an article to that effect in 1982.' Certainly when the Vatican crackdown on Liberation Theology came in 1984, in a document entitled *Instruction on Certain Aspects of the 'Theology of Liberation'*, it did not object to all Liberation Theology, Scannone emphasized, but only that which laid a Marxist template on society and history. 'Argentine People's Theology does not use Marxist analysis, but a historical and cultural one. It pays attention to social structures, but it does not consider class struggle as the main principle.' Rather it concerns itself with how to change culture in line with Gospel values, but also with how the Gospel should be read differently in different cultures.

What Scannone and his peers were fighting was a view handed down from Argentina's colonial masters which saw local culture as 'barbaric' in contrast to European culture, which it presented as 'civilization.' So much so that the history of the Jesuit *reducciónes* – the missionary settlements in Latin America in the seventeenth and eighteenth centuries which allowed the Gospel to speak through the culture of the local people – was then not even taught in Argentina's schools. The Argentine establishment still held to the disdainful dismissal of indigenous culture which they had inherited from the rapacious Spanish colonial authorities.

All of this resonated deeply for Bergoglio for it offered an intellectual underpinning to his sympathy for the forms of popular religiosity with which he had been brought up by his Grandma Rosa and which had been all round him in the lower-middle classes among whom he was raised. As early as 1974 Bergoglio, as the new young Provincial of Argentina's Jesuits, had called on his fellow Jesuits to face up to 'the recognition of the sense of religious reserve that the faithful people possess'. And in his essay, 'Meditaciones para religiosos' (Mediations for the Religious), written in 1982 when he was Rector of the Colegio Máximo seminary, he spoke of how 'the faithful people are infallible in believing', adding that the experts of the Vatican could teach who the Virgin Mary was but that only the ordinary faithful people could 'teach you how to love her'. Bergoglio thought that Liberation Theology imposed a European ideological straitjacket which patronized the faith and culture of the Argentine people. That was why he made it compulsory for Jesuit seminarians to study Argentinian history and literature. He wanted them to be proud of the history of inculturation of the Jesuit missions. He wanted them to understand the reverberations which the legend of Martín Fierro – a kind of gaucho Robin Hood – had in the minds of ordinary Argentinians, as a text which suggested a unified identity for immigrants to Argentina, and how all that interacted with their faith. It was a culture which had as much to teach as to learn. Looking back in 2012 Bergoglio told a radio interviewer how: 'little by little I started to talk about the holy people of God, the faithful people. The expression that I really like is *santo pueblo fiel de Dios*: the holy faithful people of God.'

Unlike Scannone, Bergoglio was not at the centre of the theological debate. But on the fringes he listened avidly. 'He adopted a position of maintaining dialogue with everyone without getting involved,' said Father Enrique Laje, who had been one of Bergoglio's professors. A younger Jesuit, Father Fernando Cervera, recalled: 'Bergoglio participated in these reflections' though his role was 'more one of pastoral application, as can be seen in his homilies'.

One of the distinctive qualities of this first phase of the Theology of the People was that it thought social activism must be rooted in concrete acts of mercy arising from the demands of ordinary people rather than some political paradigm suggested to them from outside. Cultural change would eventually bring about structural change. Bergoglio, writing in an article entitled *Criteria of Apostolic Action* in 1980, put it thus:

> Walking patiently and humbly with the poor, we shall learn how we can help them, after having first accepted that we receive from them. Without this slow walk with them, action in favour of the poor and the oppressed would contradict our intentions and impede the poor from making their aspirations heard and acquiring for themselves the tools they need for an effective assumption of their personal and collective destiny.

In practice what that meant was, as the Jesuit historian Father Arthur Liebscher has put it, 'this "theology of the people" emphasized the faith experience of ordinary folk while trying to avoid the class conflict, social theorizing or political activism implied in other movements'.

* * *

More than a decade later this was the vision which Bergoglio, as Archbishop of Buenos Aires, tried to put into practice when he created a new generation of *curas villeros* – priests working in the slums. When Father José María Di Paola, who later became the anti-drugs campaigner known as Padre Pepe, first arrived in Villa 21 and 24 he decided that the best way to ignite some interest in the Church was to find some symbol of the local people's faith. Most of the slum-dwellers, he discovered, were refugees from Paraguay. So, with funding from Bergoglio, he sent a group of local people to Paraguay to bring back an icon of that country's patron saint Our Lady of Caacupé – an image originally carved by a Guarani Indian and credited with miraculous properties. Padre Pepe then paraded the icon around the alleyways of the shanty-town.

Cheering crowds gathered on such a scale that Archbishop Bergoglio held a special Mass for the people of the slum – but invited them into the city's cathedral to celebrate it. As the children of the slum clambered all over the formal high-backed chairs normally occupied by Argentina's elite, Bergoglio said delightedly: 'Look how far the children from the *villa* have come!' When the people paraded back to their slum with the icon, Bergoglio, wearing a poncho and carrying his rosary beads, slipped surreptitiously in among the procession.

The arrival of the icon of the Virgin created a new mood in the shanty-town. Amid a new sense of common heritage among the slum-dwellers the fierce fighting between rival gangs reduced. Cooperation on schemes to improve the neighbourhood increased. In part what Padre Pepe had done was in the tradition that the desert hermit, Charles de Foucault, called *presence* – being present among the poor and sharing their lives with great emphasis on symbolic gesture. To that, Pepe had added an affirmation of local culture by bringing the statue of the Virgin to the slums.

What Padre Pepe and his fellow slum priests – and also Bergoglio – discovered was that learning was a two-way process. The priests were changed by the simple devotion of those they had arrived to help. Father Jorge Vernazza, one of the slum pioneers, who died in 1997, wrote a book on his experiences in which he confessed 'our ignorance about the real feeling of the people' when he and his peers arrived expecting that 'authentic faith' would be defined more by evangelical think-tanks than by 'the richness of the devotion of the people'. The reality of life in the slums brought them to do battle with what Padre Pepe called the 'misunderstood progressivism' of liberation theologians educated in Europe who arrived 'from outside to give lessons' and looked askance at the statue-kissing, processions, and the like. The slum priests, by contrast, had 'seen and followed the faith of the people, their way of living it and expressing it' and been changed by it. 'Liberation has to start with people, not an ideology and not with charity,' Pepe said. Augusto Zampini, a diocesan priest who has taught at the Colegio Máximo where Bergoglio was once Rector, went further: 'To disregard popular faith,' he said, 'is, in a way, to disregard the option for the poor.'

* * *

But the Theology of the People had its limitations. For a start it created a false dichotomy in suggesting that liberation theologians did not value the faith of the ordinary people. In many cases the opposite was true. And it created a significant shift in emphasis. Liberation Theology had the *poor* as its primary focus and placed great emphasis on the stark contrasts between the rich and the poor in the Gospel. The Theology of the People focused on the *people* and their pious practices. The poor and the people were not the same. That was particularly true in Argentina where popular politics were embodied in the politics of Juan Perón and his glamorous wife Evita. Peronism talked of social justice but imbued it with a messianic quality which sometimes seemed more akin to a fascist than a Christian understanding. And there was a temptation within the Theology of the People to romanticize the ordinary man and woman.

There were other differences. Liberation Theology tended to direct the poor to the Bible where the Theology of the People was more concerned with traditional Catholic practices and devotions. Liberation theologians were more likely to teach poor people to read and write and organize self-help groups, whereas the Theology of the People in Argentina tended to insist on a great deal of government intervention. Liberation theologians were more likely to concentrate on raising the self-consciousness of the poor; the Theology of the People was unlikely to see the Church as part of an unjust social order.

Some critics went further. They saw the Theology of the People's obsession with culture and pious popular practices as an unhelpful diversion. Popular piety could so turn poor people's attention to the next world that they succumbed to a fatalist resignation instead of pressing for improvements in the economic and social structures or pressing politically for power to be transferred from privileged elites to ordinary people. Some, like the Uruguayan Jesuit Father Juan Luis Segundo, a leading force in Liberation Theology, thought that the Theology of the People was incapable of fostering real change. Worse still it was actually an obstacle to it. All theologies are political, he argued; it is just that some are not sufficiently self-aware to understand what their political stance is. Others are more severe. Hugh O'Shaughnessy is a prize-winning journalist who has written on Latin America for over forty years. He describes the Theology of the People as 'a theological figleaf to disguise the fact that the church in Argentina stood out from other Latin American churches in its failure to tackle the structural economic and political issues which kept the poor oppressed'.

Advocates for the Theology of the People disagreed. One influential exponent today is Miguel Yáñez, one of Bergoglio's former students who now teaches at the Gregorian University in Rome. The Theology of the People embraced the notion of the preferential option for the poor, but from a distinctly Argentine perspective, the Argentine Jesuit insisted. He said: 'Liberation Theology in Argentina is not as it is understood elsewhere in Latin America by thinkers like Gutiérrez, Sobrino and Boff. Those who embraced aspects of Marxist thinking saw elements like culture and religion as tools of alienation rather than liberation. In the more distinctly Argentinian strain, both philosophically and theologically, there was a strong appreciation of culture, in particular the culture of popular religiosity.'

What was clear, however, was that some of the tensions between these two strains of theology were resolved over the decades that followed. With the end of the Cold War and the collapse of communism in Europe, both Liberation Theology and the Theology of the People developed in ways that brought them closer together. The Catholic Church began to absorb elements of Liberation Theology into mainstream Catholic Social Teaching. Bergoglio, who was put in charge of the Jesuits in Argentina in 1973 to wipe out Liberation Theology, began to appreciate some of its strengths.

In 1985, towards the end of his 15 years in leadership roles among the Jesuits, he and Scannone organized a four-day international conference. Its title was 'The Evangelization of Culture and the Inculturation of the Gospel' and its subject was the relationship between faith and culture. It was Bergoglio's final year as Rector of the seminary at the Colegio Máximo. He combined it with a large popular mission to local communities in Greater Buenos Aires to commemorate the 450th anniversary of the arrival of the Jesuits in Latin America. 'The theme was about contact with poor people and re-establishing the popular piety,' recalled Yáñez. But Bergoglio's thinking was clearly developing at this point for he invited to the conference Father Jean-Yves Calvez, a French Jesuit who was an expert on Karl Marx and who had been one of Jesuit Superior General Arrupe's four chief advisers. It was the first time that Bergoglio allowed discussion on Decree Four, the controversial measure the Jesuits had passed a decade earlier insisting that the fight for justice was an integral part of the Jesuit mission to spread the Gospel. Thereafter Calvez was invited back to teach a course at Colegio Máximo every year.

What also influenced Bergoglio into a deeper appreciation of the need to move from charity to justice was the publication of three major papal documents that significantly developed Catholic Social Teaching. In 1987 Pope John Paul II published the encyclical *Sollicitudo Rei Socialis* (The Social Concern of the Church) which borrowed from Liberation Theology the terms 'structures of sin' and 'option of preference for the poor' in analysing the widening gap between the rich and the poor under the emerging 'turbo-capitalism' of the 1980s. In 1991 the same Pope in *Centesimus Annus* (The One Hundredth Year) condemned the excesses of capitalism, speaking of the 'idolatry of the market' and the 'insanity of the arms race'. Then in 2009 Pope Benedict XVI in *Caritas in Veritate* (Charity in Truth), writing after the global economic and banking crisis of 2008, tackled issues of global poverty and the arms race but also introduced strong environmental concerns and the concept of 'intergenerational justice'. All of these documents were to modify Bergoglio's thinking on questions of social justice and shift the balance for him on the relationship between the Theology of the People and Liberation Theology.

He still continued to be dismissive of socialism. Later, as Archbishop of Buenos Aires, he published a small book after Pope John Paul II visited Cuba in 1998. It was called *Diálogos entre Juan Pablo II y Fidel Castro* and he authored it as chair of the Grupo de Reflexión Centesimus Annus. It spoke of the 'anthropological error' of socialism and insisted that communism in Cuba had destroyed a popular culture which had passed values and virtues from one generation to the next. That was pure Theology of the People, with a touch of Aristotle's virtue ethics. But in condemning Cuba's failure to uphold 'the transcendent dignity of the human person' he also highlighted Catholic Social Teaching's vehement condemnation of the market ideology which the modern world saw as the only alternative to communism.

The influence of this increasingly critical Catholic Social Teaching, combined with Bergoglio's years of direct contact with the poor in the slums, brought Bergoglio to see the value of what had been done by the followers of the Liberation Theology of which he had once been so afraid. With the ideology of the Cold War drained away, Bergoglio's distrust slowly evaporated. He began to respect and pay homage to the sacrifice of those of whom he had once been so suspicious. In 1999, just a year after he became Archbishop of Buenos Aires, on the 25th anniversary of the murder of Father Carlos Mugica, Bergoglio gave instructions that the remains of the priest should be disinterred from a fashionable cemetery near his parents' home and brought back to the poor district where he had exercised his ministry. The cardinal celebrated Mass on the occasion, and made his prayer for 'the complicit silence' of the Church at the time. In 2005 he authorized a request for the beatification of six members of the Pallotine community murdered by a military death squad in the shrine they served. In 2006 he travelled to La Rioja to say Mass for the anniversary of the murder of Bishop Enrique Angelelli – a church leader who had spoken out against the junta when Bergoglio had remained silent. In his sermon Bergoglio for the first time publicly acknowledged that Angelelli had 'preached the

Gospel, and shed his blood for it'. At the service Bergoglio quoted Tertullian's maxim that the blood of the martyrs is the seed of the Church. In 2011 Bergoglio authorized the process to recognize as a saint Father Carlos Murias, a Franciscan priest killed under the military dictatorship, despite reservations among conservative Argentinian bishops against canonizing priests who were killed for 'social' causes.

'History has its ironies,' Bergoglio said when he went to the Faculty of Theology in Buenos Aires that same year to honour the memory of Rafael Tello – one of the Argentine founders of Liberation Theology, who was in his day silenced by the Church. Tello, who developed the thinking on the synergies between Liberation Theology and the Theology of the People, had made 'one of the most important contributions' to the Church in Argentina, Bergoglio told the faculty. He was there to vindicate Tello, he announced, saying: 'There was a time when the hierarchy had problems with him; now the hierarchy comes here to present his book.' And he observed wryly: 'Nobody who has opened up new paths leaves without scars on his body.'

By 2010, in his conversations with Rabbi Skorka, Bergoglio was directly addressing the issue of helping poor people to take control over their own lives. He said:

> In the Social Doctrine of the Church it took quite some time to assimilate the concept of social justice, though now it is accepted everywhere. When someone takes up the manual of the Social Doctrine of the Church, they are astounded by the things it denounces. For example, the condemnation of economic liberalism. Everyone thinks that the Church is against communism, and yet it is as against communism as it is against the wild economic liberalism we see today. We have to seek equal opportunities and rights and strive for social benefits, dignified retirement, vacation time, rest, and freedom of unions. All of these things build social justice. No one should be dispossessed and there is no worse dispossession – and I want to emphasise this – than not being able to earn one's own bread, than being denied the dignity of work.

Perhaps the most significant coming together of the Theology of the People and Liberation Theology came when the bishops of Latin America gathered together in the Brazilian town of Aparecida for their fifth general conference. Bergoglio was the pivotal figure at that event. The meetings of the Consejo Episcopal Latino Americano (CELAM) have over the decades been the milestones in the development of Latin American theology. The second CELAM meeting, at Medellín in Colombia in 1968 – where the continent's bishops worked out how to interpret Vatican II 'in the light of Latin American reality' – called for

Christians to be involved in the transformation of society. It denounced 'the implicit violence of institutions' which the bishops called a 'situation of sin'. It called for an approach to evangelization which raised the consciousness of the poor – and it saw Liberation Theology's idea of 'base communities' among the Christian poor as crucial in that. The third CELAM gathering, at Puebla in Mexico in 1979, was the high-water mark of the influence of Liberation Theology. Puebla endorsed the idea of a 'preferential option for the poor'. It was after this that conservative forces in the Vatican began to try to curtail the influence of the liberationists. One of the founding theoreticians of Liberation Theology, Father José Comblin, lamented: 'After Puebla there began the Church of Silence. The Church began to have nothing to say.' The fourth CELAM meeting, at Santa Domingo in 1992, which was highly controlled by Rome and conservatives in Latin America, was described by the leading liberation theologian Father Jon Sobrino as 'a shaky step' after Medellín's 'leap forward'.

But then in 2007 came Aparecida, the fifth CELAM meeting, at which the driving force was Jorge Mario Bergoglio, the Archbishop of Buenos Aires. Under his chairmanship the continent's bishops agreed a final document which called for a missionary drive to inspire the Church to take the message of the Gospel back to the streets. It included the primary impulse of the Theology of the People – to celebrate the 'precious treasure' of popular piety. But Aparecida also embraced four key elements from Liberation Theology: the preferential option for the poor, the idea that sin could reside in unjust social structures, the need for base Christian communities, and the 'see-judge-act' method (of moving from social analysis through biblical reflection to political action) which was fundamental to Liberation Theology's way of working. Anyone who had read the Aparecida document would have found few surprises in the priorities of Pope Francis in setting out the mission of his papacy.

* * *

The measure of the reconciliation Bergoglio has forged between the Theology of the People and liberationism was made clear by an important event in Rome not long after Francis became Pope. The man who coined the phrase 'Liberation Theology', Father Gustavo Gutiérrez, held a joint press conference with the head of the body that is the guardian of Rome's doctrinal orthodoxy, Archbishop Gerhard Ludwig Müller, Prefect of the Congregation for the Doctrine of the Faith. The meeting of the two men came just six months into the Francis papacy. At it, Müller announced that Liberation Theology should 'be included among the most important currents in twentieth-century Catholic theology'.

After three decades of hostility from the conservative pontificates of John Paul II and Benedict XVI this was an extraordinary turnaround.

Cardinal Müller even went so far as to attack the right-wingers in the United States who had been the Vatican's allies in the war on Liberation Theology in the past. He disclosed a secret document prepared by a group of President Ronald Reagan's advisers known as the Committee of Santa Fé. It requested that the US government take aggressive action against the Liberation movement. Written in 1980 – four years before the Vatican published its first official attack on Liberation Theology – the Santa Fé group accused Liberation priests of transforming the Catholic Church into 'a political weapon against private property and productive capitalism by infiltrating the religious community with ideas that are less Christian than communist'. In revealing the existence of the document, Rome's chief doctrinal watchdog tartly riposted: 'The impertinence shown by the document's authors, who are themselves guilty of brutal military dictatorships and powerful oligarchies, is disturbing. Their interest in private property and the capitalist production system has replaced Christianity as a criterion.' The Vatican's semi-official newspaper, *L'Osservatore Romano*, backed Müller, announcing that Liberation Theology can no longer 'remain in the shadows to which it has been relegated for some years, at least in Europe'.

The role of Pope Francis in all this has been clear. Within a month of him becoming pontiff Vatican officials were saying that he had 'unblocked' the canonization process for the murdered Archbishop of San Salvador, Oscar Romero. To Bergoglio the public martyrdom of Romero had long stood as a silent rebuke. Romero had been shot dead at the altar after sermons telling the ordinary soldiers in El Salvador's army that they should not obey immoral orders to kill their fellow citizens. Romero had chosen to speak out publicly when Bergoglio, in his time of national crisis, had chosen to remain silent, albeit working to save individuals behind the scenes, in the face of the injustices of Argentina's military junta. Romero's beatification – the final step before being made a saint – had been put in the deep freeze for decades because conservatives in the Vatican thought that making Romero a saint would give succour to Liberation Theology. It eventually took place, in the third year of the Francis pontificate, in May 2015 in San Salvador.

Not long after that unblocking, Pope Francis privately got in touch with one of the liberation theologians most reviled by Rome – the former Franciscan priest Leonardo Boff – who had previously been condemned to 'obsequious silence' and suspended from his religious duties by the Congregation for the Doctrine of the Faith for his theology. Francis asked Boff to send him his writings on eco-theology to help the new Pope prepare his encyclical on the environment, *Laudato si*. Setting that in train was one of his early priorities.

Then in September 2013 Francis had a private meeting with Gutiérrez. In August 2014, on the plane back from Korea, Pope Francis told journalists that he wanted to see the beatification of Romero happen quickly. The month after, the Pope lifted a ban imposed by Rome on another liberation theologian; Father Miguel d'Escoto Brockmann had been forbidden from saying Mass for 30 years after the Vatican suspended him as a priest for serving as foreign minister in Nicaragua's revolutionary Sandinista government around the same time that Romero was murdered. Father d'Escoto was an unapologetic liberationist who once called President Ronald Reagan a 'butcher' and an 'international outlaw' and condemned US 'acts of aggression' in Iraq and Afghanistan. The 81-year-old had written to Pope Francis asking to be allowed to celebrate Mass before he died. The cumulative impact of all these moves by Francis clearly signalled that the war between Liberation Theology and the Vatican was over.

Certainly the chief exponents of liberation think so. Leonardo Boff, not long after the election of Francis, said: 'Francis will teach a lesson to the Church. We are coming out of a bitter and gloomy winter. With him comes the spring.' In *Francis of Rome and Francis of Assisi: A New Springtime for the Church* Boff addressed the question of whether or not the new Pope was a supporter of Liberation Theology. The Brazilian brushed the question aside, writing:

> The important thing is not to be for Liberation Theology but [to be] for the liberation of the oppressed, the poor, and the victims of injustice, and that he is without question...This was always the purpose of Liberation Theology. Real liberation from hunger, poverty, moral degradation, and distance from God comes first...Pope Francis has lived Liberation Theology among us...Pope Francis is fulfilling the primordial insight of Liberation Theology and promoting its registered trademark: the preferential option for the poor and in favour of life and justice...For him, this option is not just rhetoric but a life choice and a spirituality.

The man who once told his Jesuits to keep out of politics has now said the exact opposite to an audience of young students in Rome. 'Getting involved in politics is a Christian duty,' Pope Francis said in June 2013. 'We Christians cannot be like Pilate and wash our hands clean of things. We need to get involved in politics because it's one of the highest expressions of charity. It takes the common into consideration. Lay Christians must work in politics. That's no easy task you might say. But it isn't an easy task becoming a priest either! Politics is dirty but the reason it has become dirty is that Christians didn't get deeply enough involved in the evangelical spirit. It's easy to find excuses for this...but what do I do? Working for the common good is a Christian duty.'

In Bergoglio is to be found a figure who bridges one of the great divides in Catholicism, said the 2012 Nobel Peace Prize nominee and Argentinian social activist Juan Carr. The faith is split, he said, between 'a Church completely focused on the spiritual side' and 'a Church that's completely committed to the social issues but without addressing the devotional needs of the people. Bergoglio is a rare figure who transcends that divide.'

What shines through all this change is that Bergoglio is a pragmatist rather than an ideologue. In his more conservative younger years he adopted pre-Vatican II styles of worship, discipline and theology because he thought they worked better, said his 1975 student Miguel Yáñez. But as a bishop and archbishop he embraced many of the central doctrines of Liberation Theology – especially those relating to poverty, inequality and economic justice – because they now fitted his changed priorities. His contact with the popular piety of ordinary people made him embrace the plain and popular styles of worship he had opposed when he was Jesuit Provincial in the 1970s. In the slums he saw clearly that worship in the vernacular, with guitars, clapping and the liturgical reforms of Vatican II, appealed more directly to the plain people who became his priority in his later years. Anyone who doubts that should watch the videos of his interactive almost pantomimic *porteño* style of preaching in his Masses in the slums. That lingers on in the homeliness of his papal homiletics.

Bergoglio is a pastor who has been unafraid to embrace change. In line with the quip attributed to the economist John Maynard Keynes – 'When the facts change, I change my mind. What do you do, sir?' – Bergoglio has not been afraid to perform an about-turn when necessary. As Provincial in the 1970s he was severe in his instructions to his Jesuits that they must serve only in parishes and not in Liberation Theology's smaller bottom-up base communities where lay men and women took the place of priests, and the poor learned to read and interpret the Bible for themselves. In those days he had felt that raising the consciousness of the people by giving them a broader perspective on their place in society was politicizing the Gospel; base communities, he had believed, did not fit into the traditional structure of the Catholic Church so he had ordered Jesuit priests and students to ignore them and work only through parishes. But now as archbishop he gave exactly the opposite instructions. When religious sociologists discovered that a parish had a zone of influence that typically radiated 700 metres around its church, Bergoglio told his priests – knowing that Buenos Aires churches were on average 2,000 metres apart – to set up something in between the churches.

'If you can, rent a garage and find some willing layman, let him go there, do a little catechesis, and even give Communion,' he instructed his priests.

'But if we do this people won't come to Church any more,' one priest replied.

'Do they come to Mass now?' Bergoglio inquired pointedly.

The result was something very like the base Christian communities he had once so firmly opposed.

The new Bergoglio would have shocked the old Bergoglio with the scathing critique he delivered in 2010 of a clericalism which put the clergy at the centre of the Church in a way that infantilizes the ordinary people where they need empowering. 'Priests and bishops [are] falling into clericalism, which is a distortion of religion,' he told Rabbi Skorka in one of their conversations: 'The Catholic Church is the entire People of God, including priests. When a priest leads a diocese or a parish, he has to listen to his community, to make mature decisions and lead the community accordingly. By contrast, when the priest imposes himself, when in some way he says "I am the boss here", he falls into clericalism.'

In his years in Buenos Aires Bergoglio was anxious to put that into practice. A strong example of that, said Bergoglio's spokesman Federico Wals, was his work supporting the *cartoneros* – some of the poorest people in Buenos Aires who make a living sorting through the city's garbage to find and sell recyclable materials. 'Bergoglio helped them to form a union and to turn this work into something from which they can make a decent living,' said Wals. 'He wanted to help them to protect their rights.' This was exactly the kind of work for which two decades earlier he had condemned Yorio and Jalics. Yet it was just one of many similar schemes Bergoglio introduced, working with government, city authorities and a variety of community organizations.

'He was also concerned with getting the laity active,' as his aide Federico Wals has said, 'and letting them take charge.' This was in line with the classic Liberation Theology vision of all the Latin American bishops assembled at Puebla in 1979 that the poor should be agents and not merely recipients.

And where he had once told Jesuits like Yorio and Jalics that they must close the 'insertion' communities in which the order had inserted itself into the lives of the poor, now, as Pope, he said in the Spadaro interview: 'The word *insertion* is dangerous because some religious have taken it as a fad, and disasters have occurred because of a lack of discernment. But it is truly important.' And he added:

Ours is not a 'lab faith,' but a 'journey faith,' an historical faith. God has revealed himself as history, not as a compendium of abstract truths. I am afraid of laboratories because in the laboratory you take the problems and then you bring them home to tame them, to paint them artificially, out of their context. You cannot bring home the frontier, but you have to live on the border and be audacious...

When it comes to social issues, it is one thing to have a meeting to study the problem of drugs in a slum neighbourhood and quite another thing to go there, live there and understand the problem from the inside...

There is a brilliant letter by Father Arrupe [former Superior General of the Jesuits] to the Centres for Social Research and Action on poverty, in which he says clearly that one cannot speak of poverty if one does not experience poverty.

The crowning example of the transformation of Bergoglio over the years can be found in the major teaching document he has published as Pope. His apostolic exhortation *Evangelii Gaudium* is primarily concerned with spiritual liberation. But where it touches on issues of the economy it passes from the Theology of the People into a liberationist theology of the poor. '*Evangelii Gaudium* and all that Francis is saying go beyond the Theology of the People,' said the Buenos Aires theologian Father Augusto Zampini. When right-wing critics condemned the document for being Marxist the Pope replied: 'There is nothing in the Exhortation that cannot be found in the social doctrine of the Church.' But Zampini sees something more in the document. 'It goes onto the territory of Catholic Social Teaching, particularly the Latin American version of it, which includes, officially, a lot of Liberation Theology.' Father Juan Hernández Pico, a Jesuit theologian based at the Romero Pastoral Centre in El Salvador, agreed. 'It is my understanding that few from the perspective of the Theology of the People talk about money as a fetish and about the worshipping of money as true idolatry,' he said. 'In *Evangelii Gaudium* his theology is certainly much more than a people's theology; in my opinion it is a truly Liberation Theology.'

Jorge Mario Bergoglio's time spent among the poor took him on a journey of change. Now he wants the Church to change in the same way. And to those in Argentina who found it hard to forget the past, Leonardo Boff offered wise counsel: 'What matters isn't Bergoglio and his past, but Francis and his future.'

8

Francis – a Name to Alter History

'He can't go in those shoes,' said one of the priests in the Metropolitan Cathedral at Buenos Aires to a colleague. Cardinal Jorge Mario Bergoglio was about to set off for Rome and the conclave to elect a successor to Pope Benedict XVI. On his feet were an extremely shabby pair of plain black shoes. He had had them for years but he liked their simplicity with their smooth toe and no decorations. They were exceedingly comfortable and helped with the pain in his leg. And who needs, he said, more than one pair of shoes? But it would be embarrassing if the Archbishop of Buenos Aires turned up in the Vatican wearing those, the priest said, and persuaded several friends to club together to raise the cash to buy their cardinal a new pair. Bergoglio was duly grateful. 'Thank you very much,' he said and promptly put the new shoes away and set off to catch the bus to the airport wearing his old ones.

The Vatican had sent him a first-class ticket but he refused to use it and travelled in economy for the 13-hour flight to Rome. The only concession to comfort he made was to request a seat by the emergency exit where there was more leg-room. He had a bad knee and hip, he explained. On a previous trip to Rome the journey had provoked an attack of sciatica so bad he had to stay in bed and miss the meeting he had gone for. He did not want that to happen this time. The Alitalia crew put him in Row 25 and he settled in for the long flight.

* * *

He arrived in Rome one day before the date that Pope Benedict XVI had designated that his resignation would take effect and the See of Rome would become vacant. Bergoglio had booked a room, as he always did, at the international clergy hostel, the Domus Internationalis Paulus Sixtus in Via della Scrofa, whose occupants were still coming to terms with the first resignation by a pope in 600 years – and already indulging in speculation about who were the likely candidates to succeed him. The Italian press were pretty clear that the next pope would be Cardinal Angelo Scola of Milan. He had as many as 50 votes already committed, said *Corriere della Sera*. And only 77 were needed to reach the necessary two-thirds majority. And Joseph Ratzinger had coasted to the papacy last time after reportedly starting with 47 cardinals backing him in the first ballot of the conclave.

The talk around the city was that Pope Benedict wanted one of two cardinals to succeed him, and had shown this by how he had recently promoted them. The first was the Canadian cardinal, Marc Ouellet, whom he had transferred in 2010 from the archdiocese of Quebec to the Vatican to run the Congregation for Bishops. As the man in charge of the appointment of new bishops, that post would mean he would have cardinals from all over the world vying for his attention. He would make the necessary contacts. The second man was Cardinal Scola. Benedict broke the usual conventions by moving him from the prestigious post of Patriarch of Venice in 2011 to become Archbishop of Milan, which for centuries had been seen as a staging post to the papacy. The three popes before Pope John Paul II had all come from Milan or Venice. Many saw it as the anointing of a successor for, surely, after a Polish then a German Pope it was time to return to an Italian. Both Ouellet and Scola had in earlier days worked on *Communio*, the journal Ratzinger had founded to stem the liberal spirit unleashed by Vatican II.

The Italian press was sure it would be Scola. They all agreed he had dozens of votes in the bag. But to make the race sound more interesting they tossed in a few other candidates. As well as Ouellet there were Odilo Scherer of Brazil, Peter Turkson of Ghana, Francisco Robles Ortega of Mexico and Luis Antonio Tagle of the Philippines. Longer shots were said to be Sean O'Malley of Boston, Timothy Dolan of New York and Christoph Schönborn of Austria. Some even floated Francis Arinze of Nigeria even though he was over 80 and not eligible to vote for the new Pope. In the days before the start of the conclave various cardinals were being quoted in the Italian newspapers saying there were half a dozen to a dozen possible candidates. It was going to be a long conclave, they suggested.

Hardly anyone even mentioned Jorge Mario Bergoglio. Some did not realize he had been the runner-up last time. Most of those who did shrugged that you didn't get a second chance at the papacy. At 76 he was thought too old because many cardinals had suggested that they would not vote for anyone over 70 after watching Pope Benedict, who had been elected at the age of 78, increase swiftly in infirmity. Bergoglio was so off the radar of the media that, when he slipped into the synod hall for the first of the cardinals' pre-conclave meetings, he went largely unnoticed. Anyone who had been reckless enough to put a bet on him would have got odds of 30 to 1 against him being elected.

The international media read the election so poorly because they tend to take their lead from the seemingly well-informed Italian journalists. The problem was that, with a few exceptions, the resident press got most of their information from Italian cardinals, which created an entirely misrepresentative picture.

Inside the hall were gathered most of the 115 cardinals who would vote. Also there were a significant number of cardinals over 80, and thus ineligible to vote but able to make a contribution in the seven pre-conclave assemblies known as General Congregations. These would not discuss individual candidates but would explore the general issues thought to be facing the Church. Two cardinals were noticeably absent: Julius Darmaatmadja, from Indonesia, was too ill, and the disgraced Keith O'Brien from Scotland had stayed away after being accused of sexual misconduct towards priests.

The Church's maladroit handling of the scandal of sex abuse by priests – and the hierarchy's bungled attempts to cover it up – was one of the issues uppermost in the minds of the cardinals. But that was only part of what was widely seen as a dysfunctional Vatican bureaucracy in which various Curia departments were operating in an autonomous and high-handed manner, issuing instructions to bishops around the world with the authority of the Pope but without his knowledge. The Vatileaks scandal – which saw the leaking of confidential documents that Pope Benedict had marked to be destroyed – had only made public what individual bishops abroad knew from personal experience. By the morning of the first General Congregation there was already a clear consensus that the new Pope needed to be a strong administrator – and probably a Vatican outsider – to clear up the mess. 'There was a sense of crisis in the air,' Cardinal Cormac Murphy-O'Connor, the Archbishop Emeritus of Westminster, told me.

* * *

Usually the first days of a pre-conclave General Congregation are taken up with organizing the funeral of the Pope who has just died. After a long papacy, like that of John Paul II, there is a need for cardinals, many of whom have not met before, to get to know one another. But this time was different. Some cardinals had to resort to Googling one another, but 50 of the 115 cardinal-electors who had been novices at the 2005 conclave now knew one another and also had views on how things should be done. Pope Benedict had put into their minds a new possibility: that a pontiff could resign. That altered many cardinals' thinking about the age of the next pope; an older man could be elected because he could resign if he became too infirm to do the job. And because the previous pope was not dead, and there was no mood of grief, so it became easier for the electors to scrutinize the previous papacy without emotion. They concluded that for all Benedict XVI's strengths as shepherd and teacher he had been lamentably weak as a governor. Some unusually frank public discussions followed.

There was a pointed exchange of views on the running of the Roman Curia, the Church's central administration. The Brazilian cardinal João Bráz de Aviz was widely applauded after criticizing Benedict XVI's de facto prime minister Cardinal Tarcisio Bertone, the outgoing Secretary of State, for his poor management, inept diplomacy, inadequate supervision of the Institute for Works of Religion (the official name of the Vatican Bank) and general lack of coordination. Some senior cardinals had gone to Pope Benedict a few years earlier and asked him to sack Bertone but the Pope had refused; now they said in public what Benedict XVI had refused to heed in private. The report of the three cardinals commissioned by Benedict to investigate the Curia in the light of the Vatileaks scandal was, one cardinal told me, 'like an additional elector in the room'; its contents were not available to cardinals – Benedict XVI had locked it away in a safe for the eyes of his successor only – but the three authors of the report, all cardinals over the age of 80, were in the Congregations and made themselves available for some discreet one-to-one conversations with their peers as requested. Other cardinals used more coded language about the need for the new Pope to govern in a more collegial manner, but beneath the cautious language, as Cardinal Cormac Murphy-O'Connor told me, 'everyone knew what the message was': the Curia should have less say, and bishops around the world should have more.

There was a second key area around which consensus began to emerge among many electors. It was a shared sense that the Church needed to leave behind the old-fashioned culture wars over which Benedict XVI had presided in his attempts to reinforce Catholicism's identity, particularly in its historic home, Europe, following the collapse of the Church's influence in the face of a rising and sometimes aggressive secularism. The German Pope had tried to foster in Catholics a siege mentality in which a 'creative' remnant of the Church would nurture a purer doctrine to resist the tide of secularism across the Western world. 'Cardinals felt that after Benedict they wanted to press the reset button and go back eight years,' another insider said. The speakers were not openly critical of Benedict but were clear on the areas in which they thought he had been deficient.

Cardinals had begun to divide into two main camps. One wanted a pope who would reform the Vatican. The other wanted to defend the Curia and keep it in the hands of a Roman insider. But who should be the champion of each cause? This was where Cardinal Scola began to run into difficulties. There were cardinals on one side claiming that he would be an effective reformer because he knew well how the system worked. And there were electors on the other side insisting he would defend the interests of the status quo. Geography proved not to be so much a factor in the election as some had predicted. There were 28 cardinals from Italy and 11 from the United States compared with just 19 from the whole of Latin America, the region with the world's largest Catholic population. But the Italians were not united behind Scola. Some were backing Cardinal Odilo Scherer; the Archbishop of São Paulo in Brazil was widely seen not as a candidate to unite the developing world so much as a representative of the curial old guard, since he had worked for many years in the Vatican and was of German extraction. He defended the Curia when his fellow Brazilian João Bráz de Aviz attacked it. Scherer looked an option to some conservatives. But a number of other cardinals began to become convinced that the next pope should not only come from outside Europe but also be among those who had not spent years working in Rome. Some electors began to look to Cardinal Luis Antonio Tagle of Manila in the Philippines – a media-savvy intellectual with a man-of-the-people touch – but he was just 55 and a very new cardinal, so he was ruled out as too young, this time.

The 11 cardinals from the United States had a particular influence on events. In part this was because they were the biggest single bloc outside the disunited Italians; in part it was because of their shrewd use of the media. They held daily press conferences – until they were stopped, apparently on the instructions of Secretary of State Bertone. But that development only further strengthened the general agreement for reform. It was symptomatic of the problems with the Vatican that transparent communication was curbed, leaving the Italians to carry on their backdoor briefing and leaking.

The man assumed to be the front-runner, Cardinal Scola of Milan, however, did not shine in the Congregations. His complex Italianate way of speaking made little impact. But one speech did. It was from Jorge Mario Bergoglio. Towards the end of the week Bergoglio took the podium and, speaking in Italian, offered a short contribution in which he made one simple point in several striking phrases. The cardinal from Argentina said:

> The only purpose of the Church is to go out to tell the world the good news about Jesus Christ. It needs to 'surge forth to the peripheries', not just geographically but to 'the existential peripheries' where people grapple with 'sin, pain, injustice, ignorance, indifference to religion and misery'.
>
> Instead the Church has got too wrapped up in itself. It is too navel-gazing. It has become 'self-referential' which has made it sick. It is suffering a 'kind of theological

narcissism'. When Jesus said: 'Behold I stand at the door and knock' people assumed he was outside, wanting to come in. But sometimes Jesus knocks from within, asking us to let him out into the wider world. 'A self-referential Church wants to keep Jesus to itself, instead of letting him' out to others.

The Church is supposed to be 'the *mysterium lunae*' – the mystery of the moon is that it has no light but simply reflects the light of the sun, and the mystery of the Church is that it reflects the light of Christ. The Church must not fool itself that it has light of its own; if it does that it gives in to 'spiritual worldliness' which is what Henri De Lubac in *The Splendour of the Church* called 'the worst evil that can befall the Church'. That is what happens with a self-referential Church, it believes it has its own light.

Put simply, there are two images of Church: a Church which evangelizes and comes out of herself or a worldly Church, living within herself, of herself, for herself. The next Pope should be someone who helps the Church surge forth to the peripheries, like a sweet and comforting mother who offers the joy of Jesus to the world, bringing 'changes and reforms' for the salvation of souls.

The speech lasted just three and a half minutes – instead of the five allotted to each cardinal – but it electrified the synod hall. 'Bergoglio was the first man not to be introspective about the problems of the Church but to be outgoing,' said Cardinal Cormac Murphy-O'Connor; 'he was more spiritual and more theological'. As several cardinals said in the same shared phrase afterwards, 'he spoke from the heart'. It was very simple, very spiritual and it touched on the urgent necessity for renewal. Cardinal Schönborn turned to a neighbour and said: 'That's what we need.'

The Archbishop of Havana, Cardinal Jaime Ortega y Alamino, was so struck by the force of the speech that he asked Bergoglio for the text. Bergoglio had spoken only from a few scribbled notes but overnight he transcribed from memory what he had said and gave the text to Ortega. The Cuban asked if he could distribute it and, when Bergoglio gave his consent, Ortega put it on his diocesan website. Cardinals found the text repaid study. The *mysterium lunae* was a concept which originated with the Church Fathers: '*fulget Ecclesia non suo sed Christi lumine* – the Church shines not with its own light, but with that of Christ', St Ambrose had said. But it was an image which had been used by both popes John Paul II and Benedict XVI. So it spoke of both continuity and change. There was a rich ambiguity too in a phrase like 'the periphery', which in Italian had resonances of the *periferia* – the parts of Europe's cities where the poorest residents, including the immigrants, live. The echoes of the indignities of poverty and the needs of social justice were clear. It was a speech,' said Ortega, which seemed 'masterful, enlightening, challenging and true'.

* * *

In the final days, as Congregations gave way to conclave, the discussion moved, according to Cardinal Cormac Murphy-O'Connor of Westminster, 'from just the need for good governance to the need for a pope deeply rooted in the Gospel – a new style in the Church and a new style of papacy'. The Bergoglio candidacy began to take shape. Cardinals began to examine his background. The liberals highlighted a personal lifestyle that rejects the modern consumerist vision of life. The conservatives decided that his family background and culture made him 'Italo-compatible'. As a cardinal who had never worked in the Roman Curia, with a track record of criticizing careerism and ambition, Bergoglio appealed to those who saw reform of the Vatican bureaucracy as a top priority. The more assiduous looked into the 2007 Aparecida document, produced following the Fifth General Conference of the Latin American bishops' conference, which Bergoglio had the main hand in writing. They found it spoke of the same themes of taking the Gospel out to where people were – instead of waiting, in vain, for them to come to the Church. It was also strong, they noted, on collegiality, which was a repeated theme of the pre-conclave Congregations, with the idea being floated that perhaps the next pope needed to create a group of cardinals that he could consult with regularly as a sort of 'council of elders'. (Pope Francis was to set this up after just one month in office.) Bergoglio maintained a low profile, as had long been his habit, but in the meetings, lunches, dinners and coffee breaks that followed, his name became part of the wider conversation.

Yet, despite all this, the talk in media circles was still of Scola as the man who could attract votes from both camps. What the press failed to pick up was that leading European moderates, Cardinals André Vingt-Trois of Paris, Cormac Murphy-O'Connor, formerly of Westminster, and Walter Kasper, the man previously in charge of promoting Christian unity for the Vatican, had begun lobbying their closest peers – who counted for 15 to 20 votes – saying Bergoglio was the man. Among the Latin Americans, Cardinal Oscar Rodríguez Maradiaga of Honduras, who had once himself been considered a contender to be Pope, was briefing on behalf of Bergoglio.

Bergoglio began to suspect that he would be going into the conclave on Tuesday 12 March as a candidate. Two days before, he had been walking through the Piazza Navona not far from the clergy house in the Via della Scrofa when he met Father Thomas Rosica, a Canadian broadcaster who helped out in the Vatican press office when times were busy. The Argentine, Rosica said later, looked agitated.

Bergoglio stopped and grabbed Rosica's hands.

'I want you to pray for me,' the cardinal told the priest.

'Are you nervous?' Rosica asked.

'A little bit,' Bergoglio confessed.

Next morning Bergoglio was up early for Mass in the Domus. It was the last day of the General Congregations. The conclave would start 24 hours later. It was 6.30 a.m. A young priest was preparing to say Mass in the chapel. Bergoglio did not pull rank and take the altar. The priest said the Mass with the man who would next day be Pope as his altar server.

* * *

There was just one vote on the afternoon of the first day of the conclave. Black smoke coming out of the Sistine Chapel's chimney indicated that the first ballot was inconclusive. Cardinals in a conclave are sworn to secrecy but enough reports eventually emerge, via non-voting cardinals and well-informed vaticaniste journalists, to piece together a good idea of what transpired. Inside, the front-runner Scola had not done anywhere near as well as the Italian press had anticipated. He had topped the poll, but only with 35 votes, it was said. Bergoglio had 20 votes and Ouellet 15. The 28 Italians, it turned out, had split over Scola. Big figures like Angelo Bagnasco of Genoa, president of the Italian bishops, and Carlo Caffarra of Bologna had backed him. But Bertone, and the Dean of the College of Cardinals, Angelo Sodano, had rallied significant numbers of the Italians to an 'anyone but Scola' stance. The Italian contingent were in chaos, with some seeing Scola as a threat to the vested interests of cardinals serving in the Curia and others insisting he was too close to the centre of power to initiate thoroughgoing change. There was talk of 'betrayal' in the Italian camp as the conclave ended for the day and the cardinals went off for dinner.

Over the tables of the Casa Santa Marta, and afterwards in huddles over coffee, or smoking outside on the patio, the chief theme was that Scola could not make it. The Brazilian Scherer, who had been the preferred candidate of Bertone and many in the Curia, had performed far more weakly than anyone expected, perhaps because cardinals had been alerted to a group lobbying on his behalf after a story appeared on the *Vatican Insider* website just before the conclave began. His candidacy had been adversely affected by his defence of Bertone in the final Congregation after the attack on the Italian by Scherer's fellow Brazilian Bráz de Aviz, who reportedly had a quite vocal spat with Bertone during the last day of General Congregations, on Monday. Many expected Scherer to tell his followers to now back Scola but, over dinner, it was said Scherer was directing his support to Bergoglio. The reform camp had already begun to coalesce about Bergoglio. In the American camp the moderate Archbishop of Washington, Donald Wuerl, began pressing the 11 cardinals from the United States, some of whom had voted for Cardinal Timothy Dolan of New York in the first round, to swing behind Bergoglio.

Next morning, when the second ballot was counted, Scola's candidacy had stalled and support for Dolan had fallen. Votes started to converge around Oullet as the conservative candidate and Bergoglio as the man for reform, though Scola still retained a significant number of electors' support. By the third ballot it looked as though Bergoglio might be the next pope. When they broke for lunch Bergoglio seemed 'very weighed down by what was happening', said the Archbishop of Boston, Cardinal Sean O'Malley, who sat by him. In the dining room over lunch Oullet told his supporters to back Bergoglio. So did Scola, whose support had remained steady until the third ballot but who could by then see he had entirely lost momentum. By the fourth ballot, the first after lunch, Bergoglio took the lead in the voting and was not far off the required two-thirds majority. With each round his vote had grown. As the fifth ballot was being cast, and then counted, Bergoglio sat looking serious and slightly dazed. At his side his old friend Claudio Hummes, the former Archbishop of São Paulo, sat supportively.

The votes were counted by three cardinals randomly chosen to act as Scrutineers. As the votes were unfolded each Scrutineer read the vote and made a record of each individual result on a tally sheet. The final Scrutineer read the name each time aloud. When the 77th vote for Cardinal Jorge Mario Bergoglio, the Archbishop of Buenos Aires, was read aloud the cardinals knew he had reached the number of votes required. Applause broke out in the Sistine Chapel. But there were still other votes to be read out. When the final vote was read aloud Bergoglio had 90 of the 115 possible votes. The Catholic Church had a new Pope.

Finally, when the tally had been made, the assistant Cardinal Dean, Giovanni Battista Re, approached Bergoglio.

'*Acceptasne electionem de te canonice factam in Summum Pontificem?*' he asked. (Do you accept your canonical election as Supreme Pontiff?)

'*Accepto*' is the normal response. But Jorge Mario Bergoglio replied, echoing a Jesuit phrase from the Society's 32nd General Council after Vatican II, which Bergoglio had attended. He said: 'I am a sinner, but I trust in the infinite mercy and patience of our Lord Jesus Christ, and I accept in a spirit of penance.' Even at this moment, or perhaps especially now, the remorseful awareness of his past was in his consciousness. 'Many times I think of Saint Peter,' he was later to say. 'He committed one of the worst sins, that is he denied Christ, and even with this sin they made him Pope.'

'*Quo nomine vis vocari?*' (What name do you take?)

'*Vocabor Franciscus.*' (I will be called Francis.)

At the name the cardinals cheered. But no Pope had ever taken the name Francis before. None, perhaps, had dared to. Some eyebrows were raised. More than a few wondered what they had let themselves in for.

* * *

It did not take them long to begin to work it out. Over the centuries a comparatively small list of standard papal names has evolved. At one time popes simply used their baptismal name but when a pagan convert to Christianity became Pope in 533 he changed his name from Mercury to John II. Over the years John has been taken 21 times (excluding anti-popes and numbering errors), Gregory and Benedict 16 times each, Clement 14, Leo 13, Pius 12, Stephen 9, and Boniface, Alexander and Urban eight times. Not since the tenth century has a pontiff – Pope Lando – ventured right outside this nominal mainstream and since the eleventh century only two popes have not changed their names on election. Over those years the choice of name has come to represent either an indication of intended direction or a gesture of continuity, gratitude or respect to their predecessor. John Paul I chose his as a joint tribute to his two predecessors – John XXIII and Paul VI – and added the numeral I to his name, something Francis has chosen not to do. He will remain plain Pope Francis until some successor might chose to become Pope Francis II. The Polish Pope, Karol Wojtyla, who it is said had to be dissuaded from taking the name Stanislaus, after the eleventh-century Polish martyr bishop, took John Paul II to acknowledge the untimely death of his predecessor who was Pope for just 33 days. Bergoglio, by choosing Francis, indicated that he intended the trajectory of his pontificate to be a radical break with the past. Not many of the cardinals would have read his book of conversations with Rabbi Abraham Skorka. Had they done so they would have known that he once said of St Francis of Assisi: 'He brought to Christianity an entire new concept about poverty in the face of the luxury, pride and vanity of the civil and ecclesial powers of the time. He changed history.'

A few days later Pope Francis gave a clear indication of his programmatic intent when he explained his choice of name to the media. 'Some people wanted to know why the Bishop of Rome wished to be called Francis,' he said. 'Some thought of Francis Xavier, Francis de Sales, and also Francis of Assisi. I will tell you the story. During the election, I was seated next to the Archbishop Emeritus of São Paulo and Prefect Emeritus of the Congregation for the Clergy, Cardinal Claudio Hummes: a good friend, a good friend! When things were looking dangerous, he encouraged me. And when the votes reached two-thirds, there was the usual applause, because the Pope had been elected. And he gave me a hug and a kiss, and said: "Don't forget the poor!" And those words came to me: the poor, the poor. Then, right away, thinking of the poor, I thought of Francis of Assisi. Then I thought of all the wars, as the votes were still being counted, till the end. Francis is also the man of peace. That is how the name came into my heart: Francis of Assisi.'

But when the white smoke ascended from the chimney of the Sistine Chapel at 19.06 (Rome time) on 13 March 2013, announcing that a pope had been chosen, the huge crowd gathered in the heavy rain in St Peter's Square were unaware of the name. They cheered rapturously at the smoke and waved flags from all around the globe as the great bells of the basilica rang out. *Habemus papam* – we have a pope – the crowd began to chant, happy that there was a new pope even if they did not know who he was.

* * *

Inside the Vatican they were beginning to learn exactly who Bergoglio was. The new Pope was led by the Papal Master of Liturgical Ceremonies, Monsignor Guido Marini, to the robing area in a small sacristy to the left of the High Altar just off the Sistine Chapel. The vestibule is known as the Room of Tears. It is the first place in which a new pope is accorded a degree of privacy after the long and public process of the conclave. It is in this time and space that the burden of the high office can make itself felt. Bergoglio saw papal vestments in three different sizes hanging from a rail and red papal shoes resting in tissue-papered boxes in five different sizes. The rest of the world was waiting, thinking of a new chapter in the history of the Church. But the thoughts of the new pontiff often cling to the old life they realize they have left behind. Bergoglio will have known that he might never again see the little room in Buenos Aires that had been his Spartan home for 18 years with his modest music collection of classical music, tango and opera; his poster of his beloved San Lorenzo football team signed by all the players; his individual photographs of recovered drug addicts from the slums; and the crucifix of his Grandma Rosa hanging over the simple wooden bed. He would not deliver the sermon he had prepared for Easter Sunday which was lying on his desk there. He would never use the return portion of the airline ticket on which his journey home had been booked for 23 March.

At the rail of papal vestments Pope Francis changed from his scarlet cardinal's robes into a plain white cassock with a watered silk sash. Then the Master of Ceremonies offered the new Pope the traditional ceremonial elbow-length red velvet cape, trimmed with ermine – the *mozzetta*. Benedict XVI had been keen on papal fashions. He wore violet copes, blue chasubles and a furry white paschal mozzetta not seen since the days of Pope Paul VI for the spring season. He rediscovered the stripey papal collar known as the *fanon* and a faintly preposterous hat called the *camauro*, dating back to the twelfth century, but which would look at home on one of Santa's gnomes. In the days after the Pope's election a story began to circulate in Rome that Francis had spurned the mozzetta, when it was offered by Marini, with the words: 'No, thank you, Monsignor. Carnival time is over.' What he actually said was: 'I prefer not to.' Humiliating a papal servant is not Bergoglio's style. But the message was the same. 'He doesn't like the trappings of monarchy that surround the papacy,' his old friend Rabbi Skorka told me. 'He rang the other day. He's feeling very at peace with himself.'

The other signals to the papal courtiers were clear. He declined a jewel-studded gold pectoral cross and pulled on the old pewter-coloured cross he had worn since he became a bishop in Argentina. There would be no papal cuff links. Then an assistant asked his shoe size and pointed to the boxes of red shoes which represented another tradition Benedict XVI had revived. Red shoes for the papacy go back to the Byzantine era and a time when only three individuals were allowed to wear red footgear – the Emperor, the Empress and the Pope. Francis looked down at his dilapidated old black shoes. 'These are fine with me,' he said. The papal outfitters were to have no more success than the friends back in Buenos Aires cathedral who had given him their new pair.

Outside, St Peter's Square was thronged, despite the wind and rain. A great cheer went up as the long red curtains on the balcony opened and Cardinal Jean-Louis Tauran, Protodeacon of the College of Cardinals, emerged on to the loggia. Blinking in the bright lights, he proclaimed the ancient '*Habemus Papam*' – We have a Pope. The crowd roared once again but fell silent as he announced the identity of the 266th successor of St Peter: '*Eminentissimum ac Reverendissimum Dominum, Dominum Georgium Marium Sanctae Romanae Ecclesiae Cardinalem Bergoglio qui sibi nomen imposuit Franciscum*' – the most eminent and most reverend Lord, the Lord Jorge Mario, Cardinal of the Holy Roman Church, Bergoglio, who has taken the name Francis.

A sudden silence fell upon the drenched revellers. Who was he? The name sounded Italian. And the Jesuit cardinal from Buenos Aires had been on hardly any of the lists of Vatican-watchers' *papabili*. The crowd began asking one another: Who is he? Where is he from? On television channels across the globe, commentators began Googling his Wikipedia entry. Jorge Mario Bergoglio had taken the world by surprise.

But though few apart from Argentinians knew the name Bergoglio, everyone seized upon his chosen name: Francis. No Pope had ever before taken the name of the great saint of the poor, Francis of Assisi. Any new Pope, like any New Year, prompts within the faithful a renewed sense of promise and optimism but this was a new departure. Might it mean that the era of the institutional Church, with its power and pageantry, scandal and silk-brocaded vestments, was over – and that one bearing the Franciscan virtues of poverty, simplicity, humility, charity, obedience and wisdom was being ushered in? Among the crowd, smartphones and radios were being used to check out the new man. The excitement mounted as the word went around of the number of precedents being broken: the first non-European Pope for a thousand years, the first Pope from the southern hemisphere, the first Jesuit Pope, the first Pope from the Americas where more than half of the planet's 1.2 billion Catholics live. It was, said one US citizen in the crowd, 'an Obama moment – the arrival of the first Pope from the Third World was like the arrival of the first black President in the White House'. Francis was a name to change history. A new chapter in the story of the Church had begun.

* * *

Inside the Apostolic Palace the College of Cardinals was beginning to discover what that might mean. They lined up to offer their congratulations and pledges of fealty to the new pontiff in the traditional manner. But as they did so they found that Francis had determinedly declined to sit on the papal throne, which is a centuries-old symbol of a past in which the papacy saw itself as the equal of imperial power, purloining temporal trappings like the triple-crown tiara and the highest pagan religious title *Pontifex Maximus*. This pope would not even stand on an elevated platform when fellow cardinals approached but greeted them, one by one, on an equal footing. And before he did that he darted over to the two cardinals, one in a wheelchair and one with a walker-frame, who were unable to rise to greet him. Gone was the notion of Pope as Prince in the pyramid model of spiritual authority which destroyed the unity between the east and west of Christendom. It was the first sign many of the cardinals had that change was really now afoot. Francis was saying: the old model of autocratic feudal monarchy has gone; this Pope will gain his status as a first among equals; collegiality has returned. He addressed them as 'brother cardinals' rather than

'Lord cardinals'. He offered to greet them with a hug and when one insisted on bending to kiss his ring, he bent to kiss the ring of the man paying homage. He had hardly begun when someone told him it was raining heavily outside. 'I can't keep the people waiting in such weather,' he announced and broke off, telling his fellow cardinals that he would see them all that night at supper.

But as he made his way to the upper corridor of St Peter's façade to address the waiting crowd another thought occurred to him. First, he decided, he should ring his predecessor in Castel Gandolfo. An aide put a call through to the residence of the man who had styled himself Pope Emeritus. There was no reply. It turned out that Benedict and his entourage were glued to the television, waiting for the new Pope to appear on the balcony and were ignoring the phone in case they missed his emergence. Eventually an aide answered and the new Pope spoke to the old, exchanging good wishes and assurances of mutual prayer. Then the red velvet curtains parted on the central balcony.

What happened next was, in the richness of its symbolism, like a programme for the new papacy. When the figure in white appeared on the balcony, he was not wearing the traditional scarlet and ermine cape which is a symbol of pontifical authority. Nor did he raise both arms as Benedict XVI had done in 2005, clasping his hands together above his head like a victorious boxer. Pope Francis stood there, arms straight by his sides, and made a simple blessing with his right hand towards the 150,000 people crowded in the piazza below. He looked dazed, which he may have been; he had once said that his mind went blank after any shock, good or bad. Or he may have intended his actions to look as simple as possible. On his chest was the old metal cross he first used as a bishop in Buenos Aires.

He spoke in Italian, in a halting Spanish accent which was modestly engaging rather than hesitant. He was the Bishop of Rome presenting himself to the people of Rome and he spoke their language. He had also, of course, chosen the name of perhaps the most famous of Italian saints. At his side he brought with him the Vicar of Rome, Cardinal Agostino Vallini. Here was the Bishop of Rome speaking to his diocese before addressing the world. He began with the most quotidian words possible: 'Buona Sera' – Good Evening. The greeting sounded refreshingly informal, even intimate, for this most momentous of occasions. Then he made a gentle joke. 'You know that the task of the conclave was to give Rome a bishop. It seems my brother cardinals went almost to the ends of the earth to find one.' His voice was quiet and gentle too, and yet somehow more compelling than had he spoken with physical power or energy. The world seemed to lean forward to listen. It was the first indication of the power that resides inside humility.

He prayed first for his predecessor, pointedly referring to him not as Pope Emeritus but as the Emeritus Bishop of Rome. He prayed the prayers best known to Catholics in all languages: the Our Father, the Hail Mary and the Glory Be. And then he said: 'Now let's begin this journey, bishop and people, this journey of the Church of Rome, which is the one that presides in charity over all the churches – a journey of brotherhood, love and trust among us.' Only the church scholars would have realized that 'presides in charity' was a quotation from the first-century saint Ignatius of Antioch. Decoded this amounted to a call to restore collegiality inside and between the churches. 'He is undermining a thousand years of papal monarchy,' said Father Timothy Radcliffe, the former Master of the Dominicans after the event. 'It's a shift in our understanding of Church. The community which presides in love: that is putting the Pope back in the college. It is ecclesiastically radical. He has thought through what he is doing. It is the product of the many years of practical theology.' The Patriarch of the Greek Orthodox Church realized it too; the words allowed him to become the first head of the Orthodox Church since the Great Schism in 1054 to attend a papal installation.

What was more immediately evident to the ordinary listener was the extraordinary mutuality in his next gesture. He said: 'Let us pray for one another' and he meant it. Tradition has it that a new pope offers a blessing, *urbi et orbi* – to the city and the world. But before he did that he said to the people: 'First, I need to ask you a favour. Before the bishop blesses his people, he asks that you pray to the Lord to bless me.' Another departure. And he asked them to do it in silence. Yet another. Then he lowered his great head towards the balcony rail and bowed down to the people of God for their prayer, a new and unprecedented gesture: a bishop asking for the prayers of his people, reasserting the fundamental relationship of the bishop to the community of the baptized: they should pray for one another.

Italian crowds are notoriously noisy but the silence was complete. It was as if, a commentator later said, for a few precious seconds a desperately needed spiritual silence had fallen upon our frenetic and distracted world. So powerful was the silent prayer that, the tale was later told, the technicians in one TV studio momentarily panicked, thinking they had lost the sound-feed. The story walked the line between urban myth and parable.

When the blessing came, the Pope placed a rich red embroidered stole around his neck and spoke, though he did not sing, in Latin. But the blessing was addressed not just to the Church but to 'all people of goodwill'. This was the language of Vatican II. It sent out another ripple of shock after the retrenchments of popes John Paul II and Benedict XVI. And then, at the end, more demotic language for the plain people. 'Brothers and sisters, I'll leave you. Thank you so much for the welcome. Pray for me. We'll see each other soon. Good night and sleep well.' In a few short moments, packed with symbolism of so many kinds, Pope Francis had set out a whole programme of governance in miniature and signalled that things were going to be rather different from now on.

So they were. After his first public appearance the official papal limousine – registration SCV1, for Stato della Citta del Vaticano – was waiting to take the new Pope to dinner. The Pope declined to use it and climbed aboard a mini-bus taking his fellow cardinals back to the Casa Santa Marta. 'We have come together, we go together,' said Francis. The papal limousine drove away empty. After the meal the Pope responded to a toast from the cardinals by saying, 'May God forgive you for what you have done.' They laughed.

* * *

Back in Buenos Aires there were tears among the cheers as crowds thronged the streets, car horns hooting in delight, to greet an Argentine Pope. Bergoglio's great rival there, Héctor Aguer, the Archbishop of La Plata, who knew he would now never ascend to the post of Archbishop of Buenos Aires which he had so coveted, instructed that the bells in his cathedral should not be rung, as they traditionally are to greet a new pontiff. There was no need to have a sort of 'soccer stadium celebration' just because a fellow Argentinian was elected, he later told his congregation grumpily. In a little corner café in the Argentine capital Bergoglio's friend of 40 years, the human rights lawyer Alicia Oliveira, had watched it all on the television behind the bar. 'When I saw the white smoke on TV and I heard it was Bergoglio I burst into tears,' she said. 'Someone in there asked me why. I said: "He's my friend and I'm missing him already." I was thinking of myself. Real friends like him are very few. I'm lucky to have had such a great friend. He is a very good man. I'm very happy he's running the Church, and I am happy for him. He wanted to be Pope. He tells me he's having a great time. But I'm sad too because I won't see him any more.'

Bergoglio will miss Argentina too. The evening before his installation a huge crowd began to gather in the main square of Buenos Aires, Plaza de Mayo, where four huge screens had been erected to carry the live broadcast from Rome. They spent a sleepless night, apart from the young children who dozed in their parents' arms, but the atmosphere was joyous and buoyant. Through the night the screens displayed the first images of the new Pope with extracts from the most famous of his past homilies. Priests and rock singers took to the stage to keep the crowd company. Amid the throng, priests wandered chatting and even hearing confessions. Suddenly at 3.32 a.m. – which was 7.32 a.m. in Rome – the loudspeakers crackled with a long-distance call. Bergoglio had phoned the Rector on his mobile phone and an enterprising TV technician who was nearby patched the call through to the loudspeakers in the square. A huge wave of cheering and applause swept the crowd as they recognized the voice from the other side of the world. It was Papa Francisco. He spoke:

> Dear sons and daughters, I know you have gathered in the square. I know that you are saying prayers; I need them very much. It is beautiful to pray because we look to heaven and know that we have a good Father who is God.
>
> I want to ask a favour of you. I want to ask for us to walk together, to care for one another, for you to care for each other. Do not cause harm. Protect life. Protect the family; protect nature; protect the young; protect the elderly. Let there not be hatred or fighting. Put aside envy. *No le saquen el cuero a nadie* [don't take the skin off anyone's back with your gossiping tongue – the crowd laughed affectionately at his use of porteño slang]. Talk with one another so that this desire to protect each other might grow in your hearts. And draw near to God. God is good. He always forgives and understands. Do not be afraid of him. Draw near to him and may the Virgin bless you. May she, as a mother, protect you. And don't forget that this bishop who is far away loves you very much. Pray for me.

The whole square broke into riotous applause. At the other end of the phone Francis could hear them. 'Now be silent and pray,' he said, 'and I will bless you. "Through the intercession of Mary, ever Virgin, and each of your guardian angels, the glorious patriarch St Joseph, St Thérèse of the Child Jesus, and each of your protector saints, may God Almighty, Father, Son, and Holy Spirit, bless you."'

As the Pope departed to prepare himself for Mass in Rome, and the applause in Buenos Aires died away, a priest from the city's slums took the microphone and said: 'There is still extreme poverty and slavery here; people take advantage of others, of children and make money by forcing women to give up their dignity and sell their body. Change needs to come from within us, if we really want it.' In the crowd a young woman wrapped in an Argentinian flag, with tears in her eyes and a smile stretched across her face, told a local news agency: 'I'm also happy to share this man with the rest of the world because he is the change our Church needs.' He was Argentina's gift to the world. Dawn came just after

Communion had been given and received, in Rome and Buenos Aires alike, but in Argentina the crowd remained in the square. No-one wanted to leave.

* * *

Bergoglio was by no means finished with his phone calls back home. He rang, and continued to ring, friends like Alicia Oliveira, Rabbi Abraham Skorka and Clelia Luro, the widow of the former bishop to whom no one else in the church hierarchy would speak. 'When he left for Rome I told him: you won't be back,' recalled Luro. 'When he called me after he had been elected he laughed and said: "You're a witch". He didn't want to be Pope in 2005. He didn't want the power. But I think he's very happy now. He's very serene, quiet, happy.' He also rang his newsagent to cancel his paper order and his dentist to say he wouldn't be making his appointment there. And he rang the man who made those battered old black shoes. 'He wanted to know if I could repair them,' said 81-year-old Carlos Samaria who had for the previous 40 years made shoes specially to suit Bergoglio's bad knee and hip. The cobbler said he would try but that he would also send him some new ones. Reluctantly Jorge Mario Bergoglio saw sense. 'But not red ones,' he insisted. 'Make them black, like usual.'

9

A Pope of Surprises

He could not sleep the night he was elected Pope. After a celebratory dinner in the Casa Santa Marta, his brother cardinals, as he had continued to call them, retired to their beds. But not long after they had settled down for the night, Francis opened the door to his room and stepped into the corridor. He had changed from his papal white and was wearing the black trousers and black overcoat he habitually wore to travel the subway in Buenos Aires. Startled officials found themselves being asked if there was a car available. The new Pope wanted to go for a drive, he said. A driver was summoned and, in a small unmarked car, the man who hours earlier had pointedly styled himself only as Bishop of Rome, toured the streets of that city watching the celebrating crowds.

The next morning, at 5.45 a.m., he emerged from his room for a second time, in black pullover, trousers and shoes. He made his way to the chapel of the Vatican hostel. Security staff looked on bemused. Where was his papal garb? Perhaps he had forgotten he was Pope? He had not. Rather he had embarked upon a process by which the staff of the Vatican would have to learn that the Pope now did what Bergoglio had always done. And Bergoglio's day began with up to two hours' prayer before the tabernacle. After prayer, and a breakfast with six other early-rising cardinals, he again took an ordinary car – rather than the papal limousine – to arrive just before 8 a.m. at the fifth-century Basilica of Santa Maria Maggiore. He carried a small wreath of yellow and white roses. There, in the oldest church in Rome dedicated to the Virgin Mary, Francis prayed for the people of the city, as he had promised them from the balcony the night before that he would. He stopped first before the Byzantine icon of the Salus Populi Romani – Protectress of the Roman People. He prayed too at the altar where the founder of the Jesuit order, St Ignatius of Loyola, celebrated his first Mass and at the tomb of Saint Pius V, the Dominican Pope who established the tradition that the pope should wear white because he would not give up his Dominican religious habit. When the security officers tried to close the church to the public, Francis protested: 'Leave them alone. I am a pilgrim too.' But behind his back his security officials ushered the public away. The Vatican machine will not end its old ways without a fight. As he left the church, he met the priests about to hear confessions and urged them: 'Be kind. Be merciful, the souls of the faithful need your mercy.' He stopped finally at a nearby schoolyard to greet the children who thronged to see him.

On the way back to the Vatican, Francis asked his driver to stop at the Domus Internationalis Paulus VI, the hostel for visiting foreign clergy in the centre of Rome where he'd stayed for the two weeks before the conclave. Alighting in the arc-cobbled courtyard of the gold-stuccoed building he climbed the few stairs, past the copper-green bust of Pope Paul VI, to the mahogany desk in the reception and asked for the house-keeping staff. He wanted to thank them all for their kindness over the previous two weeks, he said. Then he handed them a credit card to pay for his stay. 'Don't forget to add on the phone calls,' he said. The flummoxed staff protested that, as Pope, it was unnecessary that he should pay. 'On the contrary,' said Francis. 'That is precisely why I must set a good example.' While they prepared his bill, he said, he would just go upstairs and pack his things. And then he asked a man behind the desk if he had a bulb for the bedside lamp which, he recalled, had blown. A bulb was produced. When staff went up to the room after Francis had descended with his battered black suitcase and old briefcase, paid his bill and returned to the Vatican, the bulb had been changed.

* * *

A year later one of the Pope's most senior Vatican aides looked back on that day. 'We didn't realize it at the time but paying that hotel bill was perhaps the single most important of the great gestures he made when he became Pope,' the aide said. 'By paying that bill, and paying it himself, he was signalling a mighty blow to the heart of the clerical privilege which has lain at the heart of the Catholic Church for centuries.'

When he got back to the Vatican the new Pope was given the keys to the papal apartments in the Apostolic Palace, just to the right of St Peter's basilica. In accordance with tradition the rooms had been sealed after the departure of Benedict XVI. Francis broke the seals on the door in order, the papal courtiers assumed, to take possession of his new home as every Pope had done throughout the century since Pius X moved there in 1903. The papal apartments accommodated offices for the Pope and two private secretaries, a chapel and living quarters for the pontiff, his secretaries and household staff – four consecrated women from the lay movement Comunione e Liberazione had run

Born in Flores, a suburb of Buenos Aires in 1936,
Jorge Mario Bergoglio (*left*) was the eldest of five children.
He is pictured here with his brother Oscar in the early 1940s.

Bergoglio attended the *Wilfrid Barón de le Santos Ángeles*
primary school in Greater Buenos Aires until he was aged 13.

Bergoglio, *circled*, with his classmates, *c.* 1951.

Bergoglio poses for a family portrait in 1958: (*back row, from left*) his sister María Elena, mother Regina, brother Alberto, Jorge Mario Bergoglio, brother Oscar, sister Marta, and Marta's boyfriend Enrique. (*Front row, from left*) His grandfather Juan, grandmother Rosa – the woman responsible for Bergoglio's spiritual upbringing – and father Mario.

While studying in Germany, Bergoglio saw the painting *Mary Untier of Knots* (*above*) at the St Peter am Perlach Church in Augsburg (*below*); it so spoke to the turmoil in his life, after presiding over a deep rift among Argentina's Jesuits, that he took copies of the painting back to Argentina where a cult has since developed around the image of the Virgin as the solver of problems.

Bergoglio came out of years in the wilderness to be made a bishop in 1992 and then Archbishop of Buenos Aires. He changed his authoritarian leadership style and became humbler and more listening, particularly among the poorest people. He quadrupled the number of priests in the shanty-towns and earned himself the title 'Bishop of the Slums'.

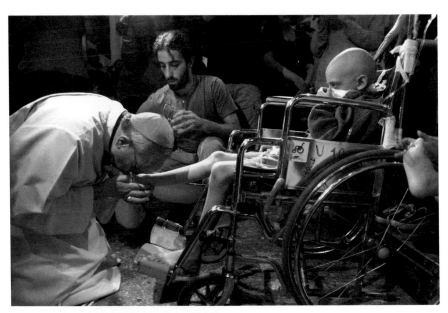

During his time as Archbishop of Buenos Aires, Bergoglio made it his custom to celebrate the Holy Thursday ritual by washing the feet of the poor or the marginalised including drug addicts and people with AIDS; he is pictured here at a hospital in Buenos Aires.

Jorge Mario Bergoglio was made cardinal by Pope John Paul II (*above*) in February 2001. Five years later, the Argentine attended the funeral of the Polish Pope but a Stop Bergoglio campaign was launched to prevent him being elected Pope and he was the runner-up in the conclave which made Joseph Ratzinger (*below*) Pope Benedict XVI.

Following Benedict XVI's retirement, Jorge Mario Bergoglio was elected Pope on 13th March 2013, becoming the 266th head of the Roman Catholic Church and the first to take the name Francis.

Old adversary, Argentina's president Christina Fernandez de Kirchner (*above*), was the first politician Francis met as Pope.

Francis returns to pay his bill at the hotel he used before he became Pope – one of the bold early gestures of humility and integrity with which he signalled that major change must come in the Vatican.

the place in Benedict's time. Francis shocked Vatican staff by his response. As he looked around he said: 'There's room for 300 people here. I don't need all this space.'

He provoked a similar response among some cardinals later in the day at the Mass for the closure of conclave that evening in the Sistine Chapel. In his homily he told them: 'If we walk without the Cross...then we are not our Lord's disciples. We are worldly people. We may be bishops, priests, cardinals, popes. But we are not disciples of the Lord.' Cardinals were not used to anyone suggesting, particularly not the Pope, that they were not proper disciples of Christ. It was not just his words that ruffled some. He had had the freestanding altar moved in the Sistine Chapel so that he would say Mass facing the congregation. Pope Benedict had, in recent years, reverted to the old practice of saying Mass there, *ad orientem*, with his back to the congregation, as was the norm in the days before the Second Vatican Council. Francis made plain that this practice had been overturned for good reason: to make the people feel more included in the Church's liturgy. If he had ever doubted that, he had learned its truth in the slums of Argentina.

Francis used the occasion of his first public Mass as Pope to send other signals. He carried Benedict's pastoral staff, as a sign of continuity, but declined one of his elaborate mitres in preference to a simple one trimmed in brown, in honour of St Francis. Most strikingly he set aside the homily in Latin which the Secretariat of State had prepared for him (in accordance with another old tradition) and spoke off the cuff in Italian reflecting on the Gospel passages that had just been read – and did so from the lectern, as any parish priest would do, instead of from the papal throne as previous popes had done.

* * *

The days that followed gave an insight into what would be the priorities of the new papacy. On the Friday, two days after he had been elected on Wednesday 13 March, he rang the Superior General of the Jesuits, the order in which he was formed. Rome, and the rest of the world, had to accustom itself to the precedent of a pontiff who made his own phone calls. The receptionist at the Jesuit house in Borgo Santo Spirito was disbelieving when a voice came on the line saying: 'Good morning, this is Francis, the Bishop of Rome, here. I would like to speak with the Father General.' The Pope was ringing in response to the letter of congratulation which he had just received from the head of the Jesuits, Father Adolfo Nicolás. He had written to the Pope with particular warmth in an attempt to assign to the past the tensions between the order and the man who had become the first Jesuit Pope. 'Hello, it's Bergoglio…' became the prelude to a number of reports recounting how Pope Francis had made calls to old friends in Rome or Argentina to cancel the papers or his dentist's appointment back in Buenos Aires. This was a pope with an unprecedentedly common touch.

Later that morning he articulated both the intensity and optimism which characterized his faith, in an address to the College of Cardinals to mark the end of the conclave. In it he praised Pope Benedict, describing his decision to resign as a 'brave and humble gesture'. The cardinals, he said he had been told, were 'the Holy Father's priests'. The community, friendship and closeness that had developed among them in recent days would serve the Church well in the future. They should return to their dioceses – never giving in to the bitterness, pessimism and discouragement with which the Devil would try to entrap them every day but, rather, to continue their ministry 'enriched by the experience of these days that have been so full of faith and ecclesial communion'.

The next day, Saturday, he broke another precedent. He invited the world's media, who had been in Rome to cover the conclave, to a post-election papal press conference. As Archbishop of Buenos Aires he had taken care to develop a good relationship with the media, which he saw as essential to the dissemi-nation of the Church's message. Though he had hardly ever given interviews, he often gave off-the-record briefings and briefed his press aide daily, sometimes twice a day. The head of the Vatican press office, Father Federico Lombardi, another Jesuit, who had seen Benedict XVI rarely, was now getting direct access to the Pope. Francis had let the Vatican communications personnel know that he regarded what he intended to say at this first press conference as particularly important. It was to this assembly of around two thousand journalists that he revealed the story of how he had come to choose the name Francis. It was here that he announced what was to be the main theme of his pontificate: 'How I would like a poor church for the poor,' Francis said.

He concluded with an additional signal. Francis, who has spoken in the past of his respect for atheists, ended by saying: 'Since many of you don't belong to the Catholic Church and others are non-believers, I offer this heartfelt blessing in silence, to each one of you, respecting the conscience of each person, but knowing that each one of you is a child of God.' His words were instead of the traditional blessing which Catholic journalists had expected. Many non-Catholics lauded the change as a welcome increased sensitivity towards them. Some Catholics felt disappointed and a few conservative bloggers complained on the internet.

* * *

The next day he sent out a further important token of intent. Sunday was the new Pope's first Angelus from the balcony of St Peter's on the Sunday, two days before his official installation. Previous custom had it that the pontiff should speak in many languages. But although, as mentioned before, Francis has several languages – Spanish, Italian, French, German and a little English and even Ukrainian – he spoke at the noontime gathering only in Italian. The message this was intended to convey was underscored two weeks afterwards when he gave his first Easter blessing. The Vatican had prepared greetings in 65 languages, as was traditional. Francis chose not to read them. Again he spoke only in Italian, underlining his repeated presentation of himself not as 'Pope' but as the 'Bishop of Rome', as if to reflect a less monarchical conception of the papacy and a return to the role's historical roots.

That worldview was reflected even more clearly in the style of installation with which Francis chose to begin his papacy. For a start, it was to be an installation, not an enthronement. 'There is no king here,' the Pope's press spokesman told the media. And the new Pope declined to select special readings for his inaugural Mass. Fortuitously a date was approaching which had great personal resonance for him: the following Tuesday, 19 March, was the Feast of St Joseph, the patron saint of both Bergoglio's boyhood church, in which he had first heard the call to become a priest, and also of the Colegio Máximo in which he had spent much of his Jesuit formation. But the idea of sticking with the ordinary readings of the day fitted with Francis's love of the calendar of the saints and also with his sense that God is to be found in the everyday rather than in the special. Though political and religious leaders attended from all around the world – including six sovereign rulers, 31 heads of state, three princes and 11 heads of government from 132 states and international organizations – Francis did all he could to play down the pageantry. He chose a mitre and chasuble that he had had since he was a bishop. He selected a recycled papal ring based on one which had belonged to a former secretary of Pope Paul VI – and which was gold-plated silver in contrast to those of his predecessors' which were all solid gold. He wore a second-hand *pallium*, the woollen scarf which symbolizes pontifical office. He pared down the liturgy and kept the music far more simple and plain than had been the norm under Benedict XVI, who had a predilection for Latin and lace. Instead of requiring every cardinal to profess their obedience to him at the ceremony he asked for a symbolic six, two of each rank – cardinal bishops, cardinal priests and cardinal deacons.

Far more important to him was the fact that this was the first papal installation ever attended by a Chief Rabbi of Rome; Francis had sent an invitation to the Jewish leader, Riccardo Di Segni, mentioning Vatican II, on his first full day in office. He had also invited Bartholomew, the Ecumenical Patriarch of Constantinople, who became the first head of the Orthodox Church in nearly a thousand years to attend the installation of a pope – a bold step, on both sides, for Bartholomew accepted. The initiative augurs a major warming of ecumenical relations between the Orthodox and the Roman Catholic churches. To show his thanks Francis directed that the installation Gospel be sung in Greek rather than the usual Latin. 'Let us never forget,' Francis said during his inaugural homily, 'that authentic power is service, and that the Pope too, when exercising power, must enter ever more fully into that service.'

His sermon moved many to tears. One of them was Cardinal Christoph Schönborn, the Archbishop of Vienna. So affected was he that at the end he turned to the cardinal next to him, Archbishop Timothy Dolan of New York, and whispered as they stood up for the Creed: 'Tim, he speaks like Jesus.' To which Dolan replied: 'Chris, I think that's in the job description!'

* * *

As the days turned to weeks in the infancy of his papacy Francis showed, time after time, through signs and symbols, that change had come in a big way. Perhaps the most dramatic was his decision not to move into the Apostolic Palace – the space in which he had said 300 people could live. Instead he would remain in the Casa Santa Marta, the spartan modern guesthouse for priests and bishops visiting the Vatican for meetings and conferences. It was, like his decision to use the bus and subway had been in Buenos Aires, in part pragmatic. It allowed him to live in community with other priests and bishops – the hostel has rooms for 128 visitors – and not risk being cut off from outside influences by Vatican officials. As he later told Antonio Spadaro in *La Civiltà Cattolica* in his first public interview as Pope:

> I did not see myself as a priest on my own. I need a community. And you can tell this by the fact that I am here in Santa Marta. At the time of the conclave I lived in Room 207. (The rooms were assigned by drawing lots.) This room where we are now was a guest room. I chose to live here, in Room 201, because when I took possession of the papal apartment, inside myself I distinctly heard a 'No.' The papal apartment in the Apostolic Palace is not luxurious. It is old, tastefully decorated and large, but not luxurious. But in the end it is like an inverted funnel. It is big and spacious, but the entrance is really tight. People can come only in dribs and drabs, and I cannot live without people. I need to live my life with others.

But if Francis was staying at the Casa Santa Marta for the good of his own psychological health, the move also sent a powerful signal to the world about Francis's hope for 'a poor church for the poor'. It said to the Church that here was a pope for whom authenticity was a touchstone of the Gospels. He reinforced that message with his decision to remain in Rome during the hot and sticky city summer, rather than decamping to Castel Gandolfo, the cooler papal summer residence in the hills to the south of the city. It was, Lombardi said, a sign of his solidarity with the poor who cannot afford to take holidays.

The gestures followed one on another. He invited the Vatican's cleaners and gardeners to attend his early morning Mass. On Sundays he led the worship at the little church of Santa Anna attended by Vatican staff, and stood outside to greet them like a normal parish priest. He was photographed by someone with a surreptitious mobile phone sitting humbly at the back of a congregation, rather than on the altar, in prayer after Mass. He walked around the Vatican instead of taking cars. He would spend an hour after his Wednesday audience greeting people in wheelchairs, or order his popemobile to stop so he could leap out to embrace a disabled man. When the crowds chanted his name he told them to chant the name of Jesus instead. He chose a simple papal coat of arms and then conspicuously declined to have it emblazoned all over the place as his predecessors did. He briefly met members of the Grandmothers of Plaza de Mayo, the group that works to locate children and grandchildren who disappeared during Argentina's military dictatorship – and which he had declined to meet when he was Archbishop of Buenos Aires. Inside the Vatican he signalled his unease at society's contemporary bonus culture by axing the €1,500 lump sum which Vatican staff were traditionally paid at the transition from one Pope to the next. He ended the annual stipend of €25,000 awarded to each of the five cardinals who make up the supervisory board of the Istituto per le Opere di Religione – the Vatican Bank. He lifted the block the Vatican had placed on the murdered Salvadorian Archbishop Oscar Romero becoming a saint. He addressed the Vatican's trainee diplomats and warned them against ambition and careerism. Almost every week there was another story in the press about a 'Hello, it's Bergoglio ... ' phone call he had made.

* * *

Not everyone was impressed. His political opponents in Argentina dismissed it all as gimmickry. Estela de la Cuadra and her family had appealed to Francis for help when he was Jesuit Provincial in 1977. Her pregnant sister, Elena, had been kidnapped by the Argentine military dictatorship but Bergoglio had declined to get involved. She said: 'He's not really humble. All this paying the hotel bill is just a publicity stunt.' And the new Pope's rejection of Benedict's revivals of tradition outraged Catholicism's ultra-conservatives. The head of the Lefebvrist Society of Saint Pius X in South America, Christian Bouchacourt, denounced Francis's simple style as humiliating and undignified for the Church.

A traditionalist blog, *Rorate Caeli*, catalogued the extremity of the ultra-conservatives' indignation: Francis took off his stole in public; he removed the wall of candles Benedict had placed between celebrant and congregation; he said, rather than sang, certain prayers; he didn't make the deacon kneel before him for a blessing before the Gospel; he preached without wearing his mitre; he folded his hands during the liturgy instead of pressing his palms piously together; he did not genuflect at the Consecration; and he gave the kiss of peace to deacons not just concelebrants. His solecisms were not just confined to liturgy, they bemoaned. He asked cardinals to wear black instead of red; he conversed with the Patriarch of Constantinople seated on an armchair rather than a throne; he used the phone, contrary to protocol; he drank *mate* tea in public when receiving the Argentinian president, when popes should never be seen publicly consuming food or drink, except the Eucharist; he insisted the Jesuit Superior General should use the informal Italian form 'tu' instead of Your Holiness; he signed himself plain Franciscus without the usual PP suffix, for *pontifex pontificum*; he didn't wear red shoes or white stockings – or cuff links! This catalogue of 'miserablist' errors was downright Protestant, the scandalized ultra-traditionalists complained.

Francis, however, had greater scandals in his sights. Each morning he established the custom of inviting different guests and Vatican staff to his 7 a.m. Mass in the 50-seat Casa Santa Marta chapel. There he would deliver an extemporized homily based on the readings of the day. Each was characterized by his spontaneous thinking-aloud and his homely turn of phrase, a technique he carried over to sermons elsewhere. So he complained about the 'babysitter Church' which only 'takes care of children to put them to sleep' instead of acting as a mother with her children. Then he ridiculed 'God spray', the New Age idea of an impersonal 'spiritual bath in the cosmos' God 'that is a bit everywhere but one does not know what it may be'. He issued warnings to those who did not share his belief that evil, like good, is embodied in a personal force: 'whoever does not pray to God, prays to the Devil'. Next he criticized 'satellite Christians' whose conduct was governed by 'common sense' and 'worldly prudence' instead of the Gospel. Then there were priests who become 'collectors of antiques or novelties' instead of being shepherds who take on 'the smell of the sheep'. Priestly vestments at Mass are 'not so much about trappings and fine fabrics' as about 'the glory of our God'. The Second Vatican Council was 'a beautiful work of the Holy Spirit' on which there could be no 'turning back the clock' and those who resisted change should instead be asking themselves: 'Have we done everything the Holy Spirit was asking us to do during the Council?'

In one sermon, with staff from the Vatican Bank in the congregation, he described their organization as 'necessary up to a certain point' but told them to take care not to get its work out of proportion in the 'love story' the Church had to tell. In front of staff from the Congregation for the Doctrine of the Faith (CDF), the Vatican's enforcers of doctrinal orthodoxy, he made a joke about the CDF which did not amuse some of those present as much as it did those who heard the remark later reported on Vatican Radio. The Vatican's official newspaper *L'Osservatore Romano* edited out some papal asides which the radio station happily reported in the new spirit of *glasnost* that was abroad in Rome.

These off-the-cuff morning homilies were variously reported from the transcripts that Vatican Radio made available. Different media outlets reported them according to what suited their political agenda, ecclesiological or secular. Interpretations were sometimes partisan, ignorant or deliberately mischievous, as when Francis declared that Jesus had redeemed everyone, including atheists, to whom he said: 'Just do good and we'll find a meeting point.' The media responded with all manner of jumbled nonsense about salvation, infallibility and heaven and hell. But the new Pope seemed determined not to let the risk of misinterpretation deter him from a style that St Augustine called the *sermo humilis* – which insists that even the most humble or homely phrases can be made holy when harnessed to the service of God. To Francis his risky on-the-hoof language embodied his preference for 'a Church that gets out in the street and runs the risk of an accident' to a Church that 'doesn't get out [and] sooner or later, gets sick from being locked up'.

* * *

All this altered the mood in Rome significantly. 'Today Rome is easy and smiling,' one cardinal told me in the early weeks of the new pontificate. 'The whole atmosphere is changed.' An archbishop in the Curia said something similar: 'Many members of the Church now feel able to say things they wouldn't dare say before.' A theologian said the same: 'We moral theologians were afraid of who would be the new Pope; now we are relieved.'

But Francis was about more than changing the mood just in Rome. The new Pope's gaze was directed outwards too. Greeting four new ambassadors to the Holy See two months after his election, Pope Francis raised the issues of the growing chasm between the rich and poor throughout the world, warning: 'while the income of a minority is increasing exponentially, that of the majority is crumbling'. The following week, visiting a soup kitchen run by Mother Teresa's Missionaries of Charity, he inveighed against our modern 'savage capitalism' which seeks 'profit at all cost' without looking at the people it exploits or discards. The month after, on UN World Environment Day, he attacked the rich world's 'culture of waste' which consumerism had come to make feel normal. And at one official dinner in Rome, for the Italian members of the Legion d'Honneur, he persuaded the host, the French ambassador, Alain LeRoy, to greatly simplify the dinner and place by the plate of each guest a papal note warning that 'food wasted is food stolen from the poor'. The wider world began to wonder what all the changes in the Vatican might portend.

Yet many commentators also began to ask whether the Pope was all style and no substance – 'all sizzle and no steak', as the veteran Vatican-watcher John Allen graphically put it in the *National Catholic Reporter*. In truth, the hints were there that Francis was preparing something more substantial. One clue lay in the fact that he did not, even several months into office, confirm most members of the Curia in their existing positions. When a pope dies, or retires, all the heads of the various administrative departments in the Vatican automatically lose their jobs until a new pope is elected. One of the first acts of new popes, traditionally, is to reappoint the vast majority of these Curia bureaucrats and politicians to their old jobs for five-year terms. But Francis did nothing for several days. The Curia was held in abeyance. Then, when he did make an announcement, it was that the heads of the various congregations and pontifical councils should continue in office *donec aliter provideatur* – 'until other provisions are made'. The Pope's press secretary, Federico Lombardi, issued a communiqué which said: 'The Holy Father wants, in fact, to give himself a certain amount of time for reflection, prayer and dialogue before any appointments or definitive confirmations.' Dialogue was the key word in the statement.

What commentators should have brought to mind was the unwritten rule among Jesuits that a new superior should spend his first 100 days in office learning about the community before making any changes. But Pope Francis was already clear about some of what needed doing. After just one month spent meditating he announced that – 'taking up a suggestion that emerged in the course of the General Congregations preceding the conclave' – he was setting up an unprecedented cabinet of eight cardinals from all around the world to advise him on the running of the Church and the reform of the Vatican. The official announcement spoke of a project 'of revision of the Apostolic Constitution

Pastor Bonus on the Roman Curia'. Decoded, that meant reforming the Curia from top to bottom.

But the new group of eight cardinal advisers – which was dubbed the C8, and later the C9 when the Pope added another adviser – had a wider brief than curial reform. They were also charged with the task of advising in 'the government of the universal Church'. Close scrutiny of the eight men Francis had chosen suggested that their advice would be radical. They were not all of like mind, they numbered conservatives and moderates, but they all shared a fierce independence of thinking. None had ever served in the Curia, seven had wide experience of running dioceses and only one was Italian. Some of them had been among the most outspoken critics of the current Vatican system in the pre-conclave discussions. And they came from every continent in the globe so that they could feed the Pope with perspectives from local churches all around the world which previously had had no conduit to reach the Pope. Though the first meeting of the C8 was not to be for six months, views from the grassroots churches began to be fed immediately to the chosen eight for onward trans-mission to Pope Francis.

The new Council of Cardinal Advisers was significant in a number of ways. It was a suggestion that Rome would henceforth be accountable to the local churches rather than the other way around. (We shall look at the importance of the C8 to Pope Francis's developing reform of the Roman Curia in Chapter Twelve.) But the C8 was noteworthy for another reason. As the Pope made clear, by deliberately articulating the fact that the new body was in direct response to the concerns cardinals had voiced in the pre-conclave discussions, it was a concrete move in the direction of greater collegiality within the Church. Some commentators saw the implication of the C8 immediately. Alberto Melloni, Professor of the History of Christianity at the University of Modena, and an expert on the Second Vatican Council, called it the 'most important step in the history of the church for the past 10 centuries'.

Nor was this the only indicator that change would be more than symbolic. Pope Francis said he plans to make changes to the international Synod of Bishops to make it more collegial as Vatican II intended. That intention had been undermined by the insistence of Benedict XVI, when he was head of the Congregation for the Doctrine of the Faith, that episcopal conferences 'had no theological significance' being mere collections of bishops whose collective weight was theologically no more than the sum of their parts. By contrast Francis told the 15-member coordinating council of the synod in June 2013: 'We trust that the Synod of Bishops will be further developed to better facilitate dialogue and collaboration of the bishops among themselves and with the Bishop of

Rome.' We shall consider Francis's revolution in the synod process – and the strong conservative backlash against it – more fully in Chapter 13.

There were other hints of future directions in which the new Pope wanted the Church to go. He intimated his desire for greater subsidiarity – the notion enshrined in Catholic Social Teaching that decisions and action should be taken at the lowest level possible. In May 2013 Francis addressed the Italian bishops' conference (after letting it be known that he wants to reduce it in size from its existing 225 dioceses, a figure which is proportionately far higher than for any other part of the world). Breaking with tradition yet again, Francis made no reference to Italian politics, as popes have usually done on this occasion. His speech was the shortest on record by a pope – just 12 minutes – prompting the Vatican-watcher Andrea Tornielli to dub the event the 'end of the era' in which the Church saw itself as a political power broker. The focus was to return to pastoral essentials.

A concrete example of the kinds of issue which could be dealt with by local churches rather than Rome was the way the Church engaged with national politics. 'Dialogue with the political institutions [of Italy] is up to you', not the Pope, the bishops were told by Francis. This explained why, a month earlier, just after he was elected, Francis had refrained from commenting on the vote by politicians in Uruguay to legalize gay marriage – even though most commentators predicted it would be the tipping point for the rest of the Latin American continent to do the same.

But, Francis intimated, the principle of subsidiarity should cascade down further than local bishops. After Francis addressed the Italian bishops' conference one of its members declared that henceforth it would be the job of the laity rather than the bishops to speak out when Catholic values were under threat. 'As far as political life [is concerned] it would be better for us bishops to keep out of it,' said Archbishop Luigi Negri of Ferrara-Comacchio. 'The autonomy of the laity has to be respected.' The shift, according to the Italian sociologist Luca Diotallevi, reopened 'an enormous space for the laity' to take the lead on the intersection of faith and politics.

* * *

The new Pope threw other straws into the wind which revealed that it was blowing in the direction of change. Those engaged in rethinking the future of the Vatican Bank noted Francis's remark, on several occasions, that neither St Peter nor St Paul had needed a bank account. More significantly in those first three months he set up two separate task force think-tanks to review not just the Vatican Bank (with a body in June known by the Italian acronym CRIOR[1]) but the whole economic structure of the Vatican State and the Holy See (with another group set up in July abbreviated to COSEA[2]). They were given powers to summon any documents and data they deemed necessary and told to report directly to Pope Francis, bypassing the Vatican bureaucracy.

There were indications of change too for the body which guards the orthodoxy of church teaching, the Congregation for the Doctrine of the Faith. It was told it should be expanding rather than restricting the interpretation of the Second Vatican Council as it had done under the previous two pontificates. And when Pope Francis met representatives from the Confederation of Latin American and Caribbean Religious (CLAR) within his first months in office he told them, according to notes they circulated to their orders afterwards, not to take too much notice of the intrusive Vatican bureaucracy. He reportedly said: 'Perhaps even a letter of the Congregation for the Doctrine [of the Faith] will arrive for you, telling you that you said such or such thing. But do not worry. Explain whatever you have to explain, but move forward. Open the doors, do something there where life calls for it. I would rather have a church that makes mistakes for doing something than one that gets sick for being closed up.'

Another early key indicator was of the new Pope's warmth towards other denominations and faiths. That was evidenced by the cordiality and frankness of his discussions with the new Archbishop of Canterbury, Justin Welby. The Pope was so relaxed that he teased the archbishop, who was installed on 21 March 2013, just two days after Francis's own installation. The Pope looked seriously at the man who leads the church which grew out of the Protestant breakaway from Rome at the Reformation. He leaned down to whisper in Welby's ear:

'You must remember I am senior to you ... ' the Pope said.

'Yes,' said the man from Canterbury slightly taken aback.

' ... by two days,' said Francis and broke into a hearty chuckle.

Over the past century different popes have had different attitudes towards other Christian denominations and other faiths. At their most conservative the template has been that ecumenism and moves towards Christian unity must be premised on the principle that other Christians must convert to Catholicism or at least acknowledge the supremacy of the Bishop of Rome. But for Francis unity does not require uniformity. Diversity is something Bergoglio has long

---

[1] Commissione Referente sull'Istituto per le Opere di Religione.

[2] Commissione Referente di Studio e di Indirizzo sull'Organizzazione della Struttura Economico-Amministrativa della Santa Sede.

embraced, rather than feared. Better relations with other religious traditions is one of the areas at the heart of Francis's approach to the papacy.

* * *

In those first few weeks Francis, Bishop of Rome, broke tradition after tradition in his attempt to strip away accretions to return to authenticity. Perhaps the most significant of the new Pope's breaches of precedent came with his decision in Holy Week not to celebrate his first Maundy Thursday in the church of St John Lateran as popes customarily do. The Papal Archbasilica of St John Lateran is the oldest and highest ranking of Rome's cathedrals and the official seat of the Bishop of Rome. The Holy Thursday ritual commemorates the night before Christ's Crucifixion when Jesus washed the feet of his 12 disciples in a daring reversal of the usual relationship between leader and followers. Since the late twelfth century, at least, popes have marked the night by washing the feet of 12 priests or deacons. The tradition that only men should have their feet washed was embedded in canon law by a 1988 edict from the Vatican Congregation for Divine Worship under Pope John Paul II which excluded women from the ritual.

But Pope Francis, for his first Holy Thursday, spurned the ancient basilica and went to the Casa del Marmo juvenile prison. There he washed the feet of 12 prisoners. On his knees on the stone floor the 76-year-old Pope, vested like a deacon, washed feet which were black, white, male, female, tattooed and untattooed, and then kissed each one. The owners of the feet were Catholics, Orthodox Christians, Muslims and atheists. And two of them were women.

No Pope had ever washed the feet of a woman before, and the debate sparked by Francis's decision was like the debate surrounding his entire papacy in microcosm. Liberals welcomed the gesture as a sign of greater inclusiveness in the Church. Conservatives were aghast at the setting aside of tradition and the breach of church law involved. 'The rubric says *viri* – men,' said the liturgist Monsignor Andrew Burnham who served on the Liturgical Commission of the Church of England before he converted to Catholicism. 'The Bishop of Rome setting aside the rubrics is a serious matter, with many consequences, some highly undesirable.' Conservatives lamented the Pope's 'questionable example'. But one senior Curia bureaucrat, who could see which way the papal wind was blowing, shrugged at the response. 'The Pope does not break the rules,' he told me. 'He just remakes them.'

Francis – who as Archbishop of Buenos Aires had washed and kissed the feet of drug addicts and hospital patients with HIV-AIDS – spoke to the young offenders before getting down on both knees at their feet. 'This is a symbol, it is a sign. Washing your feet means I am at your service; he said. 'Help one another: this is what Jesus teaches us. This is what I do. And I do it with my heart. I do this with my heart because it is my duty; as a priest and bishop I must be at your service.' After the ceremony he gave each of them a chocolate egg and an Easter cake in the shape of a dove. The detainees gave the Pope a wooden crucifix and prayer-kneeler they made in the prison workshop. As he left, Francis told the young people: 'Do not let yourselves be robbed of hope.'

That was his message not just to the young offenders of Casa del Marmo. It was his message to the wider world. 'He's totally aware that he must in some sense be a revolutionary pope, not only for the Catholic Church but for the whole of humanity,' I was told by Rabbi Abraham Skorka, who had known Jorge Mario Bergoglio for almost two decades. But the rabbi spoke in the future tense. After Pope Francis had been in office for 100 days, many Vatican commentators, in preparing the usual pieces of journalism to mark the milestone on 20 June 2013, declared that for all the signs and symbols, semiotics and signifiers, there had been little shift in substance in the Franciscan pontificate.

Some were unsurprised. Father Antonio Spadaro, editor of the Jesuit magazine *La Civilta Cattolica* – who was, two months later, to conduct the first interview with Pope Francis – declared that the new Pope was still in a 'listening phase', as he got to know the people around him and evaluated the issues facing the Church. It would be premature, he said, of those who had great expectations of change, 'to pass judgement on his capacity for reform just now'. It would come, he said, not abruptly but deliberately and after long consideration.

10

Signs of His Times

'Would you like to come to the Pope's birthday party?'

Marczin looked up.

In front of him was a man in his fifties with a shock of wiry grey-white hair. He wore a black jacket over a long cassock and a white dog collar. He was unmistakably a priest.

Marczin is an unemployed truck driver from Poland. He was homeless and had travelled to Rome where at least the nights were warmer for someone who was sleeping rough. He was rearranging his bags, sacks and blankets in a desultory way, searching for something without disturbing his dog, a small brown and black mongrel named Marley. 'Named after Bob Marley,' he offered without waiting to be asked, the night I met him. It was 17 December 2013, the day Jorge Mario Bergoglio celebrated his first birthday as Pope.

That morning Marczin had been to Pope Francis's birthday breakfast. He had been gathering together his belongings after bedding down on a hard marble floor in the portico of a Vatican building just outside St Peter's Square where the Christmas crib was being erected. He and a homeless companion, with their dog, looked like a modern-day equivalent of those for whom there was no room at the inn. But that morning the man with the wiry hair, Archbishop Konrad Krajewski, had invited him and two other homeless men – along with Bob Marley – to Casa Santa Marta to the Pope's party.

The men – itinerants from Poland, Slovakia and the Czech Republic – loaded all their belongings in the archbishop's car for the short journey to the Vatican guesthouse where Pope Francis lives. The dog rode in the middle. The archbishop had bought them a bunch of flowers to give to the pontiff for his birthday. They were sunflowers, Krajewski said, because they always turn towards the sun like the Church should always turn to Christ. The archbishop knew his boss was keen on symbols and gestures. The Pope invited the men to have breakfast with him in the hostel's dining room, where they talked and shared a few laughs.

Krajewski is the Pope's almoner, the man whose duty it is to give alms to those in need. It used to be a desk job, concerned with the raising of money and the organizing of charitable disbursements. Francis changed the job. 'The Holy Father told me at the beginning: "You can sell your desk. You don't need it. You need to get out of the Vatican. Don't wait for people to come ringing. You need to go out and look for the poor,"' Krajewski said. Every morning a papal messenger walks from Pope Francis's quarters in the Casa Santa Marta across the Vatican gardens to the almoner's office. He takes with him a bundle of letters that the Pope has received asking for help. On the top of each letter Francis has scribbled an instruction about what he wants done and the almoner hits the streets. On the morning of Francis's birthday he had not needed to wait for instructions. He knew what the Pope would want.

'The Pope,' Marczin told me that evening, was 'a top man'. He formed a circle with his fingers and kissed them in a universal gesture of approbation. 'It was a top breakfast. There were herrings, and everything.'

* * *

As Francis settled into the early months of his papacy the big gestures which surprised, and even shocked, continued. He had clearly taken to heart the words attributed to his namesake St Francis of Assisi: 'Preach the Gospel at all times, and if necessary use words.' But it became clear that the gestures were not spontaneous or random responses to situations in which he happened to find himself. They were being planned to set out what was in effect the programme of his papacy. Some were directed to the world and drew the attention of the media but others were aimed at the clerical establishment and at the ordinary faithful.

On his first Holy Thursday as pontiff, just one month after his election, the Pope also set down a marker on the kind of priests he wants to see in the Catholic Church. Immediately before his unprecedented washing of the feet of the women Francis addressed more than a thousand priests, bishops and cardinals at the annual Chrism Mass, in which the sacramental oils for the year ahead are blessed. In the service priests each year renew their ordination promises. Francis spoke to them in what was to become his characteristic mixture of admonition and exhortation. He focused his homily on what it means to be anointed with oil, most particularly for those who are ordained, underlining Holy Thursday as the day Jesus shared his priesthood with the apostles.

A priest who does not go out and live with his flock 'misses out on the best of our people, on what can stir the depths of his priestly heart', he said. 'This is precisely the reason why some priests grow dissatisfied, lose heart and become in a sense collectors of antiquities or novelties – instead of being shepherds living with "the smell of the sheep".' He looked up from his prepared text to survey the priests before him. 'This is what I am asking you,' he said with emphasis, 'be shepherds with the smell of sheep'. It was a metaphor – that a priest should be above all a pastor who is close to his people – to which he would repeatedly return. The same criteria must apply when the Church is appointing new bishops, he later told an assembly of nuncios, the papal ambassadors based in national churches all around the world who produce the shortlists from which Rome selects bishops.

It was only the first of a succession of remarks directed at those whom he suspects regard themselves as a privileged clerical caste. 'It hurts my heart when I see a priest with the latest model car,' he said on another occasion. He denounced clerical careerism as 'a form of cancer'. He warned new bishops that they must avoid the 'psychology of princes' and told new cardinals not to let their red hat go to their head. They were not being promoted, honoured, or decorated – rather they were being asked to serve with greater intensity, self-effacement and humility. He told religious orders not to allow redundant convents or monasteries to be turned into hotels but rather to use them as shelters for refugees. He told seminarians and novices that they must be consistent and authentic since the Gospel was best preached by example rather than words. Priests, monks and nuns should not be 'bachelors and spinsters' but full of 'pastoral fruitfulness'.

* * *

To Catholics in the pew he had a different message. When he made his first visit to an ordinary parish in the diocese of Rome, at the Church of Saints Elizabeth and Zachariah about 30 miles from the Vatican, he arrived unannounced 40 minutes early. He was just two months into his papacy. He was scheduled to say Mass and give 26 of the parish's children their first Holy Communion. But the Pope told the parish priest, Father Benoni Ambarus, that he would like to hear some confessions.

Ambarus rushed through the crowd inviting parishioners to the sacrament of Penance. They were unenthusiastic.

'We'll lose our place at the front of the crowd to see the Pope,' one said.

'Oh, believe me, you'll be seeing the Pope,' the priest said, ushering them into the confessional inside the church.

Pope Francis, who has taken forgiveness and mercy as his main preaching theme throughout the first two years of his pontificate, wanted to emphasize the liturgical dimension of that by being seen to administer the Church's primary sacrament of mercy. Two months later, on the plane back from World Youth Day in Brazil, he told an impromptu airborne press conference: 'I believe this is the time of mercy. The Church...must go down this path of mercy. It must find mercy for everyone. When the Prodigal Son returned home, his father didn't say: "But you, listen, sit down. What did you do with the money?" No, he held a party. Then, maybe, when the son wanted to talk, he talked. The Church must do the same...I believe that is a *kairos* of mercy,' he said using the Greek word which speaks of a special moment in history when a particular aspect of God's plan for salvation is unfolding. What ordinary believers – and the world in general – need to hear from the Church above all today is a message of compassion.

* * *

But if this is to be a papacy of forgiveness, mercy and compassion it will also not be one that shies away from strong condemnations of evil in the world. That same month – on May Day, which is both International Labour Day and the Feast of St Joseph the Worker – he issued a fierce denunciation of the sins of unregulated capitalism after the collapse of a Bangladeshi sweatshop factory in which more than a thousand people died. The workers had been working for wages so low that it constituted 'slave labour' in an unbridled quest for profits, which 'goes against God'. A few weeks later, in a ceremony to receive new ambassadors to the Holy See, he chose the occasion to launch a strong attack on 'ideologies which uphold the absolute autonomy of markets and financial speculation'. Referring to himself for the first time not as the Bishop of Rome but as the Pope he called for a reform of the world financial system along ethical lines for the benefit of everyone. Francis was signalling that social justice was to be a major plank of his pontificate.

His excoriation of the evil that springs from 'the worship of the golden calf of old' was not restricted to what the liberation theologians called the 'structural sins' of an international economy biased against the poor. Francis revealed that he was not afraid to confront depravity in its den. In the fourth month of his pontificate the new Pope flew by helicopter to Cassano all'Ionio in the southern region of Calabria in the very toe of Italy. The Calabrian town is the heartland of the 'Ndrangheta, one of the most dangerous of Italy's Mafia gangs which controls the flow of cocaine into Europe. There Francis comforted the jailed father of a three-year-old boy killed in a Mafia ambush, and condemned the crime syndicate as an example of the 'adoration of evil and contempt of the common good'. Those who 'in their lives follow this path of evil, as Mafiosi do, are not in communion with God. They are excommunicated.' And he was later dismissive of those gang members who see themselves as religious and attend church ceremonies – often using the position of *padrino* (godfather) to create bonds between crime families. Commenting on a Marian procession in Calabria, when hundreds of people paused and bowed in front of the house of a local Mafia boss, Pope Francis reportedly said: 'All this is changing and will change. Our denunciation of the Mafia will not be just once, but constant.' The local church has been galvanized by the Pope's words. When a procession in one Calabria diocese, Oppido Mamertina, ignored the Pope's instruction, the local bishop banned all processions. Training on how to stand up to the Mafia was introduced for seminarians in Calabria in 2015. After the Pope's visit Cardinal Paolo Romeo, the Archbishop of Palermo, banned the confirmation of the 17-year-old son of a jailed Mafia killer from the city's famous Norman cathedral and told the boy he would have to be confirmed in an ordinary church. To show his continuing support, Pope Francis in 2015 made a cardinal of Archbishop Francesco Montenegro from the little town of Agrigento, which had not had a cardinal since the eighteenth century, after Montenegro denied a church funeral to a Mafia leader.

Evil was condemned in new guises as well as old. A key characteristic of the Aparecida document, of which Bergoglio was the chief author (see Chapter Seven), was that it extended Liberation Theology's 'preferential option for the poor' to specific new categories of people. The 'new faces of the poor' could be seen in 'migrants and victims of violence, displaced persons and refugees, victims of abduction and human trafficking, disappeared people and drug addicts, girls and boys who become victims of prostitution, pornography and violence or child labour, to abused women who are socially excluded and victims of the slave trade for sexual exploitation'. All of these increasingly prominent contemporary evils were to become hallmark concerns of the Francis papacy.

* * *

For his first trip outside Rome the new Pope chose, in the fifth month of his pontificate, to travel to Lampedusa, the tiny Italian island on whose shores are frequently washed up the bodies of dead migrants who fail in the desperate journey across the Mediterranean from the north coast of Africa. Their flimsy craft find Lampedusa – midway between Tunisia and Sicily – the easiest part of Europe to reach. To Francis the island stood as a symbol of the locked door between the worlds of affluence and poverty. He said Mass there using altar furnishings made from the wood of wrecked migrants' boats and called for a 'reawakening of consciences' in a world that has 'forgotten how to cry' for refugees, displaced persons and victims of human trafficking. 'In this globalized world, we have fallen into globalized indifference,' he said there. 'We have become used to the suffering of others.' The Pope also prayed with police divers as they worked to raise the dead from the sea floor.

The politicians of Europe were discomfited by his actions and his words. The trip ruffled feathers in the Vatican, too. The new Pope did not consult Cardinal Tarcisio Bertone, the man who still held the position of Secretary of State to which he had been appointed by Pope Benedict XVI. Demonstrating his determination not to follow old protocols, and to assert his independence, the Pope even, according to one report, tried to book his own flight on Alitalia. Vatican officials were said to have only discovered his intentions when the airline contacted them to ask if it was really the Pope who had been making the enquiry. When he got back to Rome Francis sent his almoner, Archbishop Krajewski, to Lampedusa with 1,600 phone cards so that the latest arrival of refugees could contact their relatives back in Eritrea to tell them that they had made it to the island safely.

Pope Francis drew the world's attention to another group of marginalized people when in the autumn of 2013 he visited the shrine of the saint whose name he had taken as Pope. Before he arrived at Assisi, home to the saint the Italians call *il poverello* – the poor one – the media predicted that the new Pope would stage some dramatic gesture of renunciation. It would happen, they forecast, in the room in which his namesake had cast off his pampered life as the son of a rich merchant, stripping himself of his costly garments, and set out in defiance of his wealthy father to serve the poor. No Pope had ever before visited the room, in what is now the home of the Bishop of Assisi. But the new Pope made his first visit to the shrine memorable for a different reason.

What was most memorable about his visit was that he chose, at the start of the day, to visit a group of profoundly sick and disabled children in the city's Serafico Institute. Forgetting about the various dignitaries who awaited him in a packed 11-hour schedule the Pope stopped to greet every child – more than a hundred individuals – kissing some, bending to hear a whispered greeting, embracing those unable to speak. By the time he left this first appointment he was 45 minutes behind schedule. Itineraries do not matter so much as people, was the implied message.

Once inside the room where the saint had stripped himself of his fine clothes to embrace a life of poverty, the senior local prelate, Archbishop Domenico Sorrentino, asked the Pope to say the Lord's Prayer there, as St Francis had eight centuries before. 'The Our Father?' the Pope replied. 'But I want to talk about what the Church today needs to strip away to emulate the gesture Francis made.' Such myth-making, the world and the Church were learning, was a conscious part of the Jesuit pontiff's spiritual armoury. The figure on the cross in Assisi's Church of San Damiano – which reputedly spoke to St Francis telling him to rebuild the ruined church 800 years ago – was one, the Pope noted, on which Jesus is depicted not as dead, but alive, his eyes open to a world in which we all need to live more simply. The Church, Francis said, now needed to strip itself of 'worldliness [which] leads us to vanity, arrogance and pride'. The eyes of Jesus today were alive, not to the sumptuous basilica of Assisi, the new Pope's actions suggested, but first to the needs of individuals like those disabled children. Setting aside his prepared text he recalled that after Christ was resurrected the wounds on his hands and feet did not disappear but rather he 'brought them with him to heaven'. Today the wounds of Christ could be seen in the wounds of these children. 'These are the wounds of Christ,' he said, and 'we care for the scars of Jesus here and he from heaven shows us his scars and tells all of us "I am waiting for you."'

It was a message which was reinforced powerfully a month later when Pope Francis hugged and kissed a man whose body was covered with such repellent tumours that mothers in his home town made their children cross the road to avoid seeing him up close. Vinicio Riva suffered from neurofibromatosis, a disease which has covered his body with disfiguring growths. When the Pope saw him, during one of his weekly public audiences in St Peter's Square, he stopped to embrace the 53-year-old man. Afterwards Riva said: 'He didn't even think about whether or not to hug me. I'm not contagious, but he didn't know that. He just did it. He caressed me all over my face, and as he did I felt only love.' Photographs of the encounter flashed around the world prompting widespread comparisons of the new Pope's actions with the incident in which Francis of Assisi had embraced a leper. The emotional power of this unqualified act of love was evident to all who saw the photographs but the Dominican friar Father Timothy Ratcliffe later articulated the theological potency of the act: 'One of the ways Jesus embodied the love of God was by touching people, by holding them – and now we're all terrified of touch. Everybody is afraid of intimacy and friendship. And that subverts one of the ways in which the faith can be transmitted. Pope Francis has begun to restore that trust. Because his touching of people is inseparable from a much wider display of love.'

* * *

Yet it was another incident that most drew the eyes of the world to the new Pope's embrace of those Church or society has marginalized or excluded. It occurred on the papal plane as Pope Francis flew back to Rome from World Youth Day in Brazil. At his final Mass there he had given three million worshippers the message that spreading the Gospel should be a joyous business. Catholics, he said, should go out on to the streets to 'stir things up'. The Pope, it seemed, was determined to do the same thing on his in-flight press conference. No questions were to be off-limits, reporters were told, in contrast to similar airborne encounters with Pope Benedict XVI where the questions had to be submitted in advance so Curia officials could vet them. Francis was asked if it was true that there were coteries of gay priests in the Vatican, as had been widely reported during the Vatileaks scandal during which these groups had been referred to as 'the gay lobby'. The new Pope, with characteristic frankness, replied: 'We must make the distinction between the fact of a person being gay and the fact of a lobby, because lobbies are not good. They are bad. If a person is gay and seeks the Lord and has good will, who am I to judge that person?'

Those five words 'who am I to judge?' reverberated around the world. They did not change Catholic doctrine, which had long stated, nominally at any rate, that being gay was not an issue even if homosexual sex acts were considered sinful. The 80 minutes of questions which the Pope answered for the travelling journalists sent signals of change in many areas. But it was the remark about not judging gays which grabbed the attention of the media. The *New Yorker* headlined its account: 'Francis Redefines the Papacy'. Doctrine may not have changed but Francis had replaced the old cold compassion, which hid a thinly veiled distaste and hostility, with a human warmth. 'Who am I to judge?' was a brilliant response to the question, said Cardinal Cormac Murphy-O'Connor. What was so subtle about it, said the American Catholic commentator Michael Sean Winters, was that it was not just a message about homosexuality. 'That was incidental', Winters said. 'Pope Francis was really telling us something about what he thinks it means to be a Christian, and especially a Christian leader.' That Christians should be 'content to leave judgment to God, determined to walk alongside those who struggle, and trusting always in the merciful judgement of God'.

* * *

The secular world loved the new Pope and the signals he was sending out – of joy, love, compassion, social justice and firm judgement tempered with forgiveness and mercy, and in which the poor and vulnerable were prioritized but from which no one was excluded. He exuded authenticity. 'He walks the talk,' one pilgrim said to me in St Peter's Square. (Indeed he does. When I shook hands with him I noticed he wore a cheap plastic wristwatch.) On top of that he was warm and had a sense of fun. He posed for selfies with teenagers on their mobile phones. He put on a variety of hats and headdresses offered to him by visitors – 'something politicians are told never to do for fear of compromising their dignity', one foreign diplomat to the Holy See told me. He donned a red nose with two newlyweds who use clown therapy in their work with sick children. He ruffled the hair of a little boy who invaded the stage and clung to the papal leg despite repeated attempts by aides to remove him. And he was funny. When he met a crowd of young adults at the end of his long day in Assisi, having said Mass and given five speeches, he nonetheless stopped to talk to them and soon had them roaring with laughter with the story of a woman who could not get her 30-year-old son to marry his girlfriend and set up his own home. 'I told her: "Ma'am, stop ironing his shirts,"' the Pope joked.

'The only people not charmed by the new Pope,' wrote the doyen of Vatican correspondents John Allen, 'were his security personnel, who found themselves scrambling to keep up with a pontiff determined to escape the protective bubble in which major world leaders usually move.'

Francis's approval ratings soared in opinion polls. By the end of 2014 the Pew Research Centre showed that only 11 per cent of people throughout the world viewed him unfavourably. In Europe, the United States and Latin America around 80 per cent expressed a positive view, even if he appeared less well known in Africa, Asia and the Middle East. *Time* magazine made him their Person of the Year. He was the most talked-about person on Facebook in 2013. Gay magazines lauded him; Elton John wanted to canonize Francis despite the fact that the Pope was still very much alive. He appeared on the cover of *Rolling Stone* for what it called his 'gentle revolution' after the 'disastrous papacy' of his predecessor with its decade of scandal over sexual abuse and the leaking of the Pope's private papers by his own butler revealing intrigue and in-fighting in the Vatican. *The Economist* said that the Harvard Business School should study Francis alongside IBM's Fou Gerstner and Apple's Steve Jobs as an example of 'turnaround CEOs' who breathe new life into dying organizations, describing him as 'the man who has rebranded RC Global in barely a year'.

Catholics knew that this was a very particular view of the new Pope. And it was not always a fair one, as the international Catholic weekly *The Tablet* noted: 'The first six months of the papacy of Francis have seen perceptions of the Catholic Church transformed beyond recognition. Its image when Pope Benedict stood down was dire. Catholicism was regarded as narrow-minded, corrupt and sclerotic. This was unfair to the millions of ordinary Catholics, laity and clergy, who were none of these things, nor was it fair to Benedict, and it concealed a burgeoning desire for renewal.' One commentator, Luke Coppen, editor of the *Catholic Herald*, said that some in the secular world had created a Fantasy Francis in their own image, highlighting all the characteristics of which they approved and ignoring all those which did not fit with their worldview. But even so, it was clear to Catholics what it was about Pope Francis that the world took to its heart. 'This is a Pope,' continued *The Tablet*, 'who, rather than wag his finger, puts his arm around the shoulder. That says a great deal about his understanding of human beings. They need to be loved; they need to know that God loves them. And like the love of a parent for a child or each spouse for the other, such love is unconditional. It is also reciprocal; love freely given generates love in return.'

* * *

The idea of Fantasy Francis was, however, not confined to some outside the Church. The story of Francis and the Swiss Guard shows that. One night, not long after his election as the Catholic Church's 266th pontiff, Pope Francis came out of his bedroom in the guesthouse of Casa Santa Marta. It was just before dawn and a young Swiss Guard was on duty by the door. Discovering he had been standing there all night the Pope went back into his rooms and brought out a chair. He told the young soldier to sit down. The guard said he could not. The rules did not allow it. 'Whose rules?' asked the Pope. 'My captain's orders,' the soldier replied. 'Well, he is just a captain and I am the Pope and my orders are that you sit down.' The soldier sat down. The story has a coda. A few minutes later Francis reappeared with a slice of bread and jam – *panino con marmellata*, to add a little Italian verisimilitude – which the leader of the world's billion Catholics gave to the soldier with the words: '*Buon appetito*, brother.'

The tale went viral in the Catholic blogosphere, despite the fact that there appeared to be no serious news source from which it could be verified. To the re-tellers of the story that did not matter. It worked as parable or poetic truth to illustrate the authenticity of the humble Pope, a man whose greatness lay in his mastery of the smallest things. And yet, even as a myth, it contains some of the ambiguity which surrounds the real man, as was pointed out to me by Guillermo Marcó, a close advisor when Bergoglio was Archbishop of Buenos Aires. 'The story demonstrates a man with the common touch, true,' said Marcó. 'But it also reveals him as a man with a strong sense of power. It shows him saying: "I am the Pope, I will decide. You do what I tell you."'

What became clear was that this was the kind of story people wanted to hear because it confirmed their hopes of the new Pope, or their view of the world into which he fitted. In another airborne press conference Francis had to dismiss an urban myth about his having gone to the airport in disguise to meet a doctor from Buenos Aires who had arrived at the airport in Rome. His almoner, Archbishop Krajewski, repeatedly fields questions from the press about rumours that the Pope has been slipping out on to the streets of Rome at night to feed the needy. If it is not true, some journalists clearly felt it ought to be. Francis had little patience with the notion. Asked about 'Francis-mania' in an interview with Ferruccio de Bortoli, the editor of Italy's biggest-selling daily newspaper *Corriere della Sera*, just before the end of his first year as Pope, Francis replied: 'I don't like the ideological interpretations, a certain "mythology of Pope Francis". If I'm not wrong, Sigmund Freud said that in every idealization there is an aggression. Depicting the Pope to be a sort of superman, a type of star, seems offensive to me. The Pope is a man who laughs, cries, sleeps calmly and has friends like everyone. A normal person.'

* * *

If the first year of the Francis pontificate generated almost universal appeal it was also marked by division – in the form of attempts by opposing factions within the Church to claim the new Pope for their interpretation of the faith. Liberals insisted Francis was one of them; conservatives asserted the opposite. Both sides began spinning the facts to suit their inclinations. The problem was that, for someone so celebrated for his simplicity, Jorge Mario Bergoglio was turning out to be a man of considerable complexity.

A number of signals convinced the liberals that the new Pope was one of them. Social justice, clearly one of the real priorities for Francis, as we have seen, was one of the prime emphases among progressives in the Church. There was a fresh coinage about the way the Pope expressed himself in the informal folksy sermons he delivered at his 7 a.m. Mass each morning which suggested he was an innovator as well as someone who put the pastoral before the doctrinal in his teaching. Then, within a month of taking office, Francis gave a homily to mark the 50th anniversary of the Second Vatican Council. In it he described Vatican II as 'a beautiful work of the Holy Spirit' and criticized 'those who wish to turn the clock back' on the council's reforms. Half a century on from the great renewal of the Church, he asked whether 'we have done everything the Holy Spirit was asking us to do during the Council?' Pope Francis said the answer was: No. That was because, he suggested, we resist the movement of the Holy Spirit. 'We celebrate this anniversary, we put up a monument but we don't want it to upset us,' he said, and yet 'the Holy Spirit upsets us because it moves us, it makes us walk, it pushes the Church forward'. The Church's liberal theologians stopped looking over their shoulders and began once more to speak freely. A cloud of fear and caution was lifted. Some bishops began to be more outspoken. The liberal wing of the Church was re-invigorated by the arrival of the new Pope. They felt that, in the words of one commentator in the *New York Times*, 'after 35 years left out in the cold during the papacies of Benedict and his predecessor, John Paul II,' their Church was once more 'a home for all'.

More conservative Catholics, temporarily silenced by the whirlwind that was the new pontiff, soon began to rally to suggest that Jorge Mario Bergoglio, for all his dramatic new style, was one of them. He was, they announced, on the issues taken as totemic in Catholic orthodoxy, thoroughly mainstream. He was uncompromisingly anti-abortion. In his daily homilies and elsewhere, Francis repeatedly referred to the need to value human life from conception until natural death. And when thousands of US anti-abortion activists held a protest he sent a message to his 11 million followers on Twitter announcing: 'I join the March for Life in Washington with my prayers.' He told a conference of Catholic doctors: 'Each child who is unborn, but is unjustly condemned to be aborted, bears the face of Jesus Christ.' He took a conventional line on the other 'culture wars' litmus tests. He was against gay marriage. He ruled out women priests, saying on the flight back from Brazil: 'with regards to the ordination of women, the Church has spoken and says no ... That door is closed.' And he had not acted to overturn a Curia decision to excommunicate an Australian priest, Father Gregory Reynolds, who advocated women's ordination. His frequent references to the Devil, they said, made clear he was very traditional. In the United States the leading conservative intellectual George Weigel, the biographer and confidant of John Paul II, began to assert that Francis was making no break with the two previous pontificates and was merely advancing the Polish Pope's New Evangelization. The Argentinian Pope was, he said, 'in full continuity' with the German and Polish pontiffs who preceded him. The new Pope was changing no doctrine but merely offering a different style. It was only Francis's tone that was different.

Pope Francis abetted this 'liberal or conservative' confusion by sending mixed signals on a variety of issues. Having called Vatican II 'a beautiful work of the Holy Spirit' he then wrote a letter to Archbishop Agostino Marchetto telling him, 'I consider you to be the best interpreter of the Second Vatican Council.' Marchetto took a position which supported Benedict XVI's view that Vatican II was not the revolution proclaimed by the Council's enthusiasts.

Rather it was merely a development in the Church's understanding of its mission. Pope Benedict had invented two ideological terms to describe these contrasting views of the great council. Traditionalists saw in the Council what Benedict called a 'hermeneutic of continuity'. By contrast those who perceived Vatican II as a revolution had adopted a 'hermeneutic of rupture', he argued. This was a false polarity since the Fathers of the Council were quite clear at the time that they were about renewal not revolution. They saw one of Vatican II's biggest changes – a switch from an imperial to a collegial form of government – not as something new, but rather as a recovery of the style of governance which had characterized the early Church before the medieval papacy began to adopt a monarchical model of running the Church. Collegiality was undoubtedly part of what Francis had in mind when he asked 'have we done everything the Holy Spirit was asking us to do during the Council?' Pope Paul VI had in the end been afraid of collegiality, John Paul II had sidelined it, and Benedict XVI had undermined it. So it was odd that Pope Francis should have chosen to praise Marchetto – whose argument was essentially that it was wrong to speak of a 'spirit of Vatican II' and who insisted that the great Council had to be understood only through the documents it had produced. This was a way of doing theology which was more Protestant than Catholic. So what Francis was up to, sending such contradictory signals? Many concluded that he was trying to preserve unity by making all sides feel listened to and included. 'Papa Bergoglio is a very shrewd political operator,' said the veteran Vatican reporter Robert Mickens, editor of globalpulse.com. Others took a different view. It was more than politics, it was theology, one senior Vatican insider countered: 'This isn't a tactic, to maintain unity. It it is a principal, to usher in collegiality.'

* * *

Catholic teaching on contraception is perhaps the area in which Pope Francis has created greatest ambiguity. In his interview with *Corriere della Sera*, to mark his first year in office, Francis praised the prophetic genius of Pope Paul VI in 1968 in publishing *Humanae Vitae*. That document had declined to lift the ban on Catholics using artificial contraception which had been enshrined by Pope Pius XI in 1930 in his encyclical *Casti Connubii*. *Humanae Vitae* became a milestone in relations between the Vatican and the ordinary Catholic faithful in the developed world. Pope John XXIII had put in place a commission of six clerics to consider whether or not the ban on contraception should be lifted and Paul VI had greatly extended that to a body of 72 members, among whom were six married couples as well as experts in theology, demography, sociology, psychology and psychiatry. The commission recommended the ban be lifted. But Pope Paul VI decided not to take their advice for fear it would undermine the moral authority of the papacy if he overturned the ruling of Pius XI. But *Humanae Vitae*, ironically, itself undermined the authority of the papacy in the eyes of the majority of Catholics in the Western world who refused to accept the teaching by ignoring it in practice. Many lay and clerical leaders were in open revolt against the authority of Rome. 'And at least half of the world's bishops agreed with their people,' wrote Robert Blair Kaiser, an historian of the commission. Some even wrote open letters to the faithful telling them to follow their own consciences. 'Paul VI knew when he was licked. In his 10 remaining years as Pope, he did not write another encyclical.'

So for Pope Francis to endorse *Humanae Vitae* was striking. It seemed in contradiction of the secular world's image of him as a 'modern' pope. Francis said of Pope Paul: 'His genius was prophetic, as he had the courage to go against the majority, to defend moral discipline, to apply a cultural brake, to oppose present and future neo-Malthusianism.' (Thomas Robert Malthus was the eighteenth-century English clergyman who first suggested that population control was needed if the world was not to run out of food, or find that nature controlled population by famine and disease.) But Francis prefaced those remarks by saying: 'It all depends on how the text of *Humanae Vitae* is interpreted. Paul VI himself, towards the end, recommended to confessors much mercy and attention to concrete situations.' And he ended by adding: 'The object is not to change the doctrine, but it is a matter of going into the issue in depth and to ensure that the pastoral ministry takes into account the situations of each person and what that person can do.'

What exactly did that mean? Most Catholics were no clearer when he returned to the subject on his visit to the Philippines in 2015. The context there was that, in the teeth of opposition from the local Catholic hierarchy, the Philippines government had recently passed a health law which established sex education for schoolchildren and adults and subsidized birth control for women in a country where 81 per cent of the population is Catholic. Pope Francis addressed crowds of more than six million people. Departing from his prepared text – always an indication that Francis is saying something that is important to him – the Pope offered a strong defence of *Humanae Vitae*, saying of Paul VI: 'He had the strength to defend openness to life at a time when many people were worried about population growth.' Pope Francis warned Filipino Catholics that the family was under threat from 'growing efforts on the part of some to redefine the very institution of marriage, by relativism, by the culture of the ephemeral, by a lack of openness to life'. The Argentinian Pope said that an 'ideological colonization' was trying to destroy the family, a phrase that was seen as reference to the passage of gay marriage rights in countries around the world and other liberal views.

But then on the plane back to Rome the Pope qualified what he had said in Manila. He reiterated that Paul VI had spoken of 'particular cases' where the prohibition on artificial contraception may not apply. The contraception ban 'does not mean that the Christian must make children in series', he said. He even told reporters that experts said that only three children per family were needed to maintain the population. And he mocked the idea that 'good Catholics' had to breed 'like rabbits'. Echoing a phrase used by Pope Paul, and wagging his finger, he insisted that what was required was: 'Responsible parenthood'. He even revealed that during a parish visit some months before he had 'rebuked' a woman who was pregnant again after having seven children, all delivered by Caesarean section. 'But do you want to leave seven orphans?' Francis told her. 'That is to tempt God!'

This broadside of mixed messages only heightened the sense of ambiguity. Conservatives asserted he was restating orthodox doctrine. Liberals said he was prioritizing commonsense compassion. Catholics with big families were so upset at what they perceived as criticism from the pontiff that the Vatican had to assemble the media to say that Francis had not been saying 'three is enough' and that he 'absolutely did not want to disregard the beauty and the value of large families'. Archbishop Giovanni Becciu, Substitute at the Secretary of State, apologized on Francis's behalf saying 'the Pope is truly sorry' that his remarks about large families 'caused such disorientation'. Admirers of the two previous popes began to complain about what they saw as Francis's 'lamentable fuzziness' in his off-the-cuff remarks in his daily homilies and irregular press conferences. One even called him 'the blabbermouth Pope' and suggested he needed to think more carefully before he spoke.

Others, however, began to wonder whether Pope Francis was engaging in some astute political positioning in an attempt to keep everybody happy, or at any rate, to keep all feeling as though their viewpoint was heard, recognized and included. It brought to mind the politics of balance which Pope John XXIII embodied when he said: 'I have to be Pope both for those with their foot on the accelerator and those with their foot on the brake'. There certainly seemed an element of that in his decision to accelerate the canonization of Pope John XXIII so that it took place on the same day that Pope John Paul II was made a saint. It was an adroit balancing act to bring together the two popes who had become emblematic figures for the liberal and conservative camps within the Church – the man known as 'Good Pope John' who had convened the Second

Vatican Council and the man who had been called 'John Paul the Great' who had sought to bridle what he saw as the breakneck progress of 'the Spirit of the Council' rushing the Church towards sloppy relativism.

But perhaps it was not balance but nuance that drove the Bergoglio shifts of emphasis. Those who knew him from his time in Buenos Aires were aware of the subtlety with which he could freight his opinions. As an archbishop and cardinal he did not at all demur from the Church's official teaching against abortion but his track record showed he was more likely to speak out on child trafficking and sex slavery. He opposed the Argentinian government's distribution of free contraceptives but abhorred the tendency to reduce the faith to its precepts on sexual morality.

On family issues he was more likely to ask parents whether they make the time to play with their children properly. He has long opposed same-sex marriage, which as Archbishop of Buenos Aires he called an 'anthropological regression', but he spoke out strongly in favour of civil unions and equal rights for homosexuals – a position he was unsuccessful in persuading his fellow bishops in Argentina to adopt but which, in his *Corriere della Sera* interview, he has said that as Pope he will consider. 'Each case must be looked at and evaluated in its diversity', he said.

On euthanasia his public pronouncements were chiefly about how contemporary society's neglect of the elderly constitutes a form of 'covert euthanasia' – with frequent references to the shame of a society where old people are hidden away in care homes like unwanted overcoats shoved into a closet. On the place of women in the Church, though he has long upheld church teaching that women cannot become priests because Jesus was a man, he routinely emphasized that women, not men, were chosen by God to be the first witnesses of the Resurrection. As one cardinal rather colourfully put it to me: 'The new Pope plays for the same team but kicks the ball in an entirely different direction.'

There was one other way to read the runes of the first stage of the Bergoglio papacy. It was that there was clearly sometimes tension between what the new Pope said and did. Whatever he said to Marchetto, about admiring his conservative interpretation of the Second Vatican Council, the new Pope's actions have demonstrated that Francis is in favour of the changes ushered in by Vatican II. That was clear from his very first Mass in the Sistine Chapel when he had the altar reoriented so that he faced the congregation rather than turning his back on them as Pope Benedict had done in his final days. But the changes went well beyond the liturgy, as we shall see in the coming chapters. In certain significant areas, though not all, Bergoglio consistently adopted a style, in word and act, which Eamon Duffy, the Emeritus Professor of the History of Christianity at the University of Cambridge, has described as 'manifestly at odds with the ethos of the previous two pontificates'.

* * *

Evidence of the Bergoglian mastery of ambiguity was afforded by the pilgrimage which Francis made to the Holy Land early in his second year as Pope. It offered important insights into his way of working. Nominally the purpose of the trip was to commemorate a watershed in relations between the Catholic and Orthodox churches. Pope Francis, the successor of St Peter, was to meet the head of the Orthodox, Ecumenical Patriarch Bartholomew, the successor of St Andrew. The occasion was the 50th anniversary of a meeting between a previous pope and patriarch. In 1964 Pope Paul VI had held a reconciliation with the Ecumenical Patriarch Athenagoras on the Mount of Olives in Jerusalem. They prayed together and exchanged the kiss of peace and subsequently lifted the Anathemas of 1054 – mutual decrees of excommunication which had split the churches causing a thousand years of Great Schism. Bartholomew, the spiritual leader of the 300 million Orthodox Christians worldwide, had suggested the meeting when he met with the new Pope after becoming the first Patriarch for a millennium to attend a papal installation.

But if the stated purpose of the visit in May 2014 was to take another step in ecumenism, towards the eventual goal of Christian unity, Francis also had a number of other interlocking concerns. He arrived in the Holy Land at yet another delicate point in Israeli–Palestinian relations. Peace talks had broken down and the Palestinian leadership had been taking unilateral steps in the international arena which the Israelis did not like. More significantly, a pact had been signed a month before between the rival Palestinian factions Fatah and Hamas in an attempt to repair the rift between them. There was talk of a Palestinian unity government being formed within weeks. The Pope stressed that his mission was religious not political. His message was of the need to improve relations between Christians, Jews and Muslims. But the semiotics of his visit sent out more complex signals, with actions and words sometimes acting in counterpoint rather than as complements to one another.

When the previous two popes went on pilgrimage to the Holy Land they went first to Jordan, then to Israel, and then to the Occupied Territories. Pope Francis altered the order. He arrived in Jordan but then insisted on crossing into the Occupied Territories before visiting Israel. Francis, a man known for the potency of his symbolism and gesture, was making a point. The official itinerary issued by the Vatican confirmed that. The first thing the Pope would do, it said, on crossing into the Israeli-occupied West Bank was to call on 'the president of the State of Palestine'. The wording was significant. Francis was announcing that he was visiting a country which Israel, and the United States, insisted does not exist. But in 2012 the United Nations had declared that Palestine was a member state. The Vatican was one of the many countries which had officially recognized the status of the Palestinian state. The Pope seemed determined to make that recognition real on the ground. There was also symbolic significance in the fact that he based himself in the residence of the papal nuncio in annexed east Jerusalem before arriving, via helicopter, in Tel Aviv. He met the Israeli prime minister Benjamin Netanyahu at the Notre Dame complex, which is Vatican sovereign territory, on the border between the Israeli and Arab sectors of Jerusalem, before travelling to visit Israel's president and two chief rabbis and pay his respects at the Yad Vashem Holocaust memorial.

Having made that point Francis took great care to be even-handed in his travels. After saying Mass at the Church of the Nativity in Bethlehem he had lunch with Palestinian children from the Aida and Dheisha refugee camps. But then he made an unscheduled stop to pray at the separation wall that divides Israel from the West Bank. He stopped at a point where the concrete of the wall was covered in political graffiti: 'Apartheid wall', 'Free Palestine' and 'Bethlehem look like Warsaw Ghetto'. Next to that was the message 'Pope: we need someone to talk about justice'. The potency of the Pope, stock still for four full minutes, praying with his forehead pressed wearily against the controversial wall, created a photograph that flashed around the world. The Israeli authorities complained vehemently to Vatican aides. They felt he had gifted their enemy a propaganda coup. Proving himself to be a shrewd diplomat, Pope Francis the next day reached out to Israelis with a spontaneous gesture at the Yad Vashem memorial to Nazi genocide. There he met six elderly Holocaust survivors who shared with him their stories of survival. The Pope bent and kissed their hands, one by one. And he was compliant when Netanyahu requested, as a counterweight to the unscheduled stop at the separation wall, that the pontiff add into his itinerary an unplanned stop at an Israeli monument to commemorate the civilian and military victims of terror attacks.

* * *

There was another dimension to the Pope's agenda which saw the 77-year-old pontiff attend more than 30 events in 55 hours in a marathon schedule. Francis was much exercised by the growing religious persecution in parts of the Middle East and the resulting exodus of Christians from a region that was the birthplace of the faith. A century ago 20 per cent of the region's population were Christians; today that is down to just 4 per cent. The situation had deteriorated rapidly over the previous decade with the invasion of Iraq, the Arab Spring uprisings and civil war in Syria. Attacks on Christians were also happening in Israel, with fire-bombings and murders by Muslims, and with Jewish extremists spraying 'Death to Arabs and Christians' and 'Jesus is Garbage' graffiti on Christian sites. In Bethlehem the Christian population had plummeted from 60 per cent in 1990 to only 15 per cent at the time Francis visited. The Pope's increasing anxiety about all this was reflected on the Vatican-run website dedicated to the Pope's trip, with several sections about the persecution of Palestinian Christians who were, it said, 'faced by an exclusivist Islamic movement that often refuses to recognize Christians as co-citizens with equal rights, equal obligations, and equal opportunities'. If the trend continued, the Holy Land could become a spiritual Disneyland, full of pilgrim tourist attractions but devoid of local believers.

Pope Francis raised the issue with both communities. Addressing a Muslim group that included the Grand Mufti of Jerusalem, Muhammad Ahmad Hussein, Francis called for an intensified 'fraternal dialogue' between the two faiths, based on respect and love, and pleaded: 'May no one abuse the name of God through violence!' To a group of Jewish leaders, including the two chief rabbis of Israel, David Lau and Shlomo Amar, again he spoke of dialogue and kinship, emphasizing the shared theological heritage of Jews and Christians and pleading for 'a continued and even growing interest in knowledge of Christianity in this holy land to which Christians trace their origins'.

But if Francis believes, as he told the Vatican diplomatic corps not long after he was elected, that 'it is not possible to establish true links with God, while ignoring other people' he also gave a clear example of the way in which he thinks that can be achieved. His trip to the Holy Land broke papal precedent by including an inter-religious element in the official entourage. With the Pope throughout were a Jew and a Muslim – old friends from Argentina – Rabbi Abraham Skorka, Rector of the Latin American Rabbinical Seminary, and Omar Abboud, president of the Institute for Inter-religious Dialogue in Buenos Aires, Both men were long-time collaborators from Francis's days as Archbishop of Buenos Aires. Both had become personal friends of Francis.

* * *

Jorge Mario Bergoglio's first approach to inter-denominational and inter-faith religious dialogue was through friendship. It began with an invitation to meet over a cup of coffee. All three men shared an interest in Argentinian football. They did not all support the same teams but that only offered the opportunity for affectionate banter. It was from personal closeness that religious encounter grew and relations between communities improved.

Interestingly there was a precedent for this in his namesake Francis. The ambitious missionary from Assisi set off for Egypt in 1219 with the intention of converting the infidel to bring an end to the Crusades. But the thirteenth-century saint was changed by what his twenty-first-century namesake repeatedly refers to as 'the culture of encounter'. Entering into enemy territory St Francis was arrested and taken to Sultan al Malik al Kamel. The monarch, perceiving his captive to be a holy man, received him with courtesy. After three weeks of dialogue he left Egypt. Thereafter Francis of Assisi was respectful of Muslims to the point that he encouraged Christians to emulate them in prayer and prostration, and to join Muslims – and others – in service to all, setting aside the differences in their religions. And the saint specifically told his followers not to try to convert the followers of the Prophet. Ten years later, incidentally, the Sultan voluntarily ceded control of Jerusalem and Bethlehem – and a corridor from there to the sea – to Christian worshippers. He reserved the Dome of the Rock and the al-Aqsa Mosque for the Muslims, and the Temple area for the Jews.

It was by the only remaining Western Wall of that Temple that Pope Francis and his two companions, Abraham Skorka and Omar Abboud, embraced in celebration of the pilgrimage they had long dreamt of making together. The three old friends wept in a tableau of Jewish, Christian and Muslim harmony in the city they shared as holy. But though it was a singular moment it was built on long years of friendships cultivated patiently over decades in Buenos Aires.

At the end of the visit the Pope invited the Israeli and Palestinian presidents 'to my home in the Vatican' to pray. When the meeting happened a month later in Rome the secular press were disappointed at the lack of outcome. Some had hoped it would help restart the stalled peace process. But it was a low-key event. The Israeli president Shimon Peres and the Palestinian president Mahmoud Abbas arrived separately to join the Pope and Ecumenical Patriarch Bartholomew. The men did not recite a joint prayer but sat together while separate prayers were offered in the chronological order of the founding of the world's three great monotheistic religions: first Judaism, then Christianity and Islam. There were prayers to give thanks for creation, to invoke forgiveness and entreat for peace. Music from the three cultures was played. Afterwards the two politicians together planted an olive tree as a symbol of peace in the Vatican Gardens. It was the first inter-faith event ever held in the Vatican.

'This is a pause from politics,' said Father Pierbattista Pizzaballa, the Franciscan Custodian of the Holy Land who had organized the event. 'The Pope wanted to look beyond, upwards. Nobody is fooling themselves that peace will break out in the Holy Land, that this will bring peace closer. But this time to stop and breathe has been absent for some time.' Peace begins with friendship, Pope Francis was saying, and friendship begins with mutual respect, and respect begins with encounter. It was not just a model for one pilgrimage. It was a programme for a papacy.

11

If Necessary Use Words

Room 201 on the second storey of the Casa Santa Marta feels an austere place. The flooring is a shiny wooden parquet but the furnishings are spartan. There are a couple of scallop-back chairs and a sofa, upholstered in a blue velveteen. There is a desk, a bookcase and a crucifix. There is no touch of luxury. It is a room of bare simplicity. When the door to the right of the sofa is open a dark wooden bed can be seen next door. An image of Christ's face is carved into the mahogany headboard. These are the two rooms in which Pope Francis lives.

The outsider with the privileged access to Room 201 was Father Antonio Spadaro SJ, the editor of the Jesuit magazine *La Civiltà Cattolica*. Just five months after the new Pope was elected, Spadaro was granted an interview with the first Jesuit Pope in the history of the Catholic Church.

There were few books, few papers, few objects, Spadaro noted – just an icon of St Francis, a statue of Our Lady of Luján, patron saint of Argentina, a crucifix and a statue of St Joseph asleep similar to the one that can still be seen in the room Jorge Mario Bergoglio occupied when he was Rector of the Colegio Máximo back in Buenos Aires. Bergoglio's spirituality is drawn from human faces – the faces of Christ, St Francis, St Joseph and Mary.

The Pope offered Spadaro one of the armchairs but chose for himself a higher stiff-backed chair, explaining that he had problems with his back. Talking to Pope Francis, Spadaro observed, was like being enveloped in 'a volcanic flow of ideas that connect up together'. Even taking notes seemed intrusive and gave him a disagreeable sense of interrupting a wellspring. 'It's clear,' Spadaro said afterwards, 'that Pope Francis is more accustomed to conversations than to giving lessons.'

What followed was what one veteran religious affairs reporter, Andrew Brown of *The Guardian*, called 'one of the most sensational interviews of my lifetime'. Pope Francis startled the world, and the Church, in three ways. He talked with unprecedented frankness about the errors of his own past. He set out a stark analysis of what he thought ailed the Catholic Church as he took over as its global leader. And he set out an uncompromising recipe for how the

Church needed to change. On each he spoke both boldly and with a bluntness that seemed outside the parameters of what the world had come to expect from papal discourse. 'The Pope's language,' said David Willey, who has covered the Vatican for the BBC for more than forty years, was 'unlike anything heard coming out of the Vatican during recent papacies'.

* * *

In his time as Cardinal Archbishop of Buenos Aires the man who was to become Pope Francis spoke more often through actions than words. He was fluent in the pulpit, though even there he could be oblique and elliptical. But he very rarely gave interviews. Homilies aside, those who wanted to work out his message were left to deconstruct it from his actions and example, which could be bold and direct. But something changed in the transition from cardinal to pope, just as changes had come in earlier transitions in his life.

In his first year as pontiff Francis produced a veritable deluge of unscripted reflections – and not just from the papal dais during his crowd-pulling weekly audiences or on major church ceremonies and feasts. He delivered homely homilies at his daily morning Mass. He talked off the cuff in airborne press conferences. He spoke frankly to gatherings of clerics, diplomats, nuncios, bishops and cardinals. But two of his reflections set out dramatically what looked like a road-map for his pontificate. The first came with a series of three interview sessions he gave to Spadaro for a group of Jesuit magazines all around the world led by the US Jesuit magazine *America*. The second came from his own pen in the form of an apostolic exhortation which he entitled *Evangelii Gaudium* – the Joy of the Gospel. The first shattered many of the preconceptions which the world and the Church assumed they could take for granted in a pope. The second set out the vision that he wanted to put in its place.

The opening question from Spadaro was 'Who is Jorge Mario Bergoglio?' It was not what the Pope was expecting. He sat and stared at his interviewer in silence, and for so long that Spadaro began to wonder whether he had asked something inappropriate. Was he allowed to ask that? he asked the pontiff to cover his embarrassment. The Pope nodded and then said: 'I do not know what might be the most fitting description ... I am a sinner. This is the most accurate definition. It is not a figure of speech, a literary genre. I am a sinner.' It was the first line in an interview of extraordinary candour. The spiritual quality he most valued from his Ignatian training, he said, was discernment – the process of deep reflection and self-analysis through which a Jesuit tries to work out what it is God wants of him. It showed in what followed. 'I am a bit astute, I can adapt to circumstances, but it is also true that I am a bit naïve,' the Pope began. He then went on to ruminate on the difficult period in his life in which he was the leader of Argentina's Jesuits – a time of deep division and bitterness – and to think aloud about how that period had prepared him for the task as Pope of governing the universal church. The Jesuit style, said Spadaro, was that the Superior made the decisions but after extensive consultation with his official advisers. Francis replied:

> In my experience as Superior in the Society, to be honest, I have not always behaved in that way – that is, I did not always do the necessary consultation. And this was not a good thing. My style of government as a Jesuit at the beginning had many faults. That was a difficult time for the Society: an entire generation of Jesuits had disappeared. Because of this I found myself Provincial when I was still very young. I was only 36 years old. That was crazy. I had to deal with difficult situations, and I made my decisions abruptly and by myself. Yes, but I must add one thing: when I entrust something to someone, I totally trust that person. He or she must make a really big mistake before I rebuke that person. But despite this, eventually people get tired of authoritarianism.
>
> My authoritarian and quick manner of making decisions led me to have serious problems and to be accused of being ultra-conservative. I lived a time of great interior crisis when I was in Córdoba. To be sure, I have never been like Blessed Imelda [a goody-goody], but I have never been a right-winger. It was my authoritarian way of making decisions that created problems.
>
> I say these things from life experience and because I want to make clear what the dangers are. Over time I learned many things. The Lord has allowed this growth in knowledge of government through my faults and my sins. So as Archbishop of Buenos Aires, I had a meeting with the six auxiliary bishops every two weeks, and several times a year with the council of priests. They asked questions and we opened the floor for discussion. This greatly helped me to make the best decisions. But now I hear some people tell me: 'Do not consult too much, and decide by yourself.' Instead, I believe that consultation is very important.

His fellow Jesuits, who had been so divided by his behaviour in Argentina, were astonished by the Pope's candour – and deeply touched by it. As Father James Martin, editor-at-large of *America*, said: 'The most moving part of the interview was when Pope Francis looked back on his time as Provincial, or regional superior, in Argentina. He says some of the decisions he made were authoritarian, hasty and rash. I don't think I've ever heard a religious leader speak so bluntly about his failures and the things he regrets in the past. People might say "mistakes were made" in general but the Pope is really frank about what went wrong, and he talks about himself as a sinner. So this interview is really blunt.' It was also, he said, very prayerful and a helpful vehicle for spiritual reflection.

* * *

But Bergoglio did not only put his own past under intense scrutiny. He applied equally concentrated thinking to the Church and where and why it has been failing in recent years.

> The Church sometimes has locked itself up in small things, in small-minded rules. The most important thing is the first proclamation: 'Jesus Christ has saved you'. And the ministers of the Church must be ministers of mercy above all. The confessor, for example, is always in danger of being either too much of a rigorist or too lax. Neither is merciful, because neither of them really takes responsibility for the person. The rigorist washes his hands so that he leaves it to the commandment. The loose minister washes his hands by simply saying, 'This is not a sin' or something like that. In pastoral ministry we must accompany people, and we must heal their wounds.

Instead the Church has become stuck in old formulations of thought. But a formulation of thought ceases to be valid, Pope Francis said, 'when it loses sight of the human, or even when it is afraid of the human, or deluded about itself'. And even when old teachings are valid they have to be taught with a sense of proportion. 'The dogmatic and moral teachings of the Church are not all equivalent,' he said. 'The Church's pastoral ministry cannot be obsessed with the transmission of a disjointed multitude of doctrines to be imposed insistently.' The example he gave shocked many in the Church, particularly the sections which had dedicated themselves to fighting what in the United States are called 'hot-button culture wars' issues:

> We cannot insist only on issues related to abortion, gay marriage and the use of contra-ceptive methods. This is not possible. I have not spoken much about these things, and I was reprimanded for that. But when we speak about these issues, we have to talk about them in a context. The teaching of the Church, for that matter, is clear and I am a son of the Church, but it is not necessary to talk about these issues all the time ... We have to find a new balance; otherwise even the moral edifice of the Church is likely to fall like a house of cards, losing the freshness and fragrance of the Gospel.

The proclamation of the love of God should come before moral and religious imperatives, he said, but 'today sometimes it seems that the opposite order is prevailing'. The phrase 'son of the Church' was a masterpiece of *bergogliano* ambiguity. It allowed conservatives to assume that he accepted unconditionally the doctrinal positions of previous popes. And it allowed those who hoped for change to suggest that he was neatly sidestepping the question in a way which meant: 'I don't want to talk about that just now.'

He then returned to the subject of gays and lesbians. Some commentators had previously suggested that Pope Francis was referring only to gays in the priesthood when he asked his headline-grabbing question: 'Who am I to judge?' But it became clear from his interview with Spadaro that his desire to welcome homosexuals into the Church was wider than that:

> A person once asked me, in a provocative manner, if I approved of homosexuality. I replied with another question: 'Tell me: when God looks at a gay person, does he endorse the existence of this person with love, or reject and condemn this person?' We must always consider the person. Here we enter into the mystery of the human being. In life, God accompanies persons, and we must accompany them, starting from their situation. It is necessary to accompany them with mercy.

God is to be encountered in the world of today, he said. But God is always a surprise, so you never know where and how you will find him. And he offered a warning to those who looked for God in the sacristy rather than in the street, or in the past rather than in the present:

> If the Christian is a restorationist, a legalist, if he wants everything clear and safe, then he will find nothing. Tradition and memory of the past must help us to have the courage to open up new areas to God. Those who today always look for disciplinarian solutions, those who long for an exaggerated doctrinal 'security', those who stubbornly try to recover a past that no longer exists – they have a static and inward-directed view of things. In this way, faith becomes an ideology among other ideologies.

Individuals have to be open to change, he said, and so does the Church. Human self-understanding changes with time and human consciousness deepens. Once slavery, and the death penalty, were universally accepted as legitimate. Not any more. 'We grow in the understanding of the truth. Exegetes and theologians help the Church to mature in her own judgment. Even the other sciences and their development help the Church in its growth in understanding. There are ecclesiastical rules and precepts that were once effective, but now they have lost value or meaning. The view of the Church's teaching as a monolith to defend without nuance or different understandings is wrong.'

* * *

Pope Francis then set out for Spadaro how the Church should change to bring the joyful proclamation of the word of God as good news for the people of the world. The preaching of the Gospel must be 'more simple, profound, radiant':

> I see clearly that the thing the Church needs most today is the ability to heal wounds and to warm the hearts of the faithful; it needs nearness, proximity. I see the Church as a field hospital after battle. It is useless to ask a seriously injured person if he has high cholesterol and about the level of his blood sugars! You have to heal his wounds. Then we can talk about everything else. Heal the wounds, heal the wounds... And you have to start from the ground up.

Reform of church institutions was essential but it was not the first priority:

> The structural and organizational reforms are secondary – that is, they come afterward. The first reform must be the attitude. The ministers of the Gospel must be people who can warm the hearts of the people, who walk through the dark night with them, who know how to dialogue and to descend themselves into their people's night, into the darkness, but without getting lost. The people of God want pastors, not clergy acting like bureaucrats or government officials. The bishops, particularly, must be able to support the movements of God among their people with patience, so that no one is left behind. But they must also be able to accompany the flock that has a flair for finding new paths.

By way of examples the Pope touched on a number of specific issues. The running of the Church needs to be devolved from Rome to local diocese. 'The dicasteries of the Roman Curia are at the service of the Pope and the bishops. They must help both the particular churches and the bishops' conferences. They are instruments of help. In some cases, however, when they are not functioning well, they run the risk of becoming institutions of censorship. It is amazing to see the denunciations for lack of orthodoxy that come to Rome. I think the cases should be investigated by the local bishops' conferences, which can get valuable assistance from Rome. These cases, in fact, are much better dealt with locally.'

Francis also flagged up the need to 'investigate' further the role of women in the Church. Prefacing his remarks with the words 'a woman has a different make-up than a man', he said: 'We have to work harder to develop a profound theology of the woman. Only by making this step will it be possible to better reflect on their function within the Church. The feminine genius is needed wherever we make important decisions.' He touched on the issue of the Latin Mass, saying that it had been right for Pope Benedict to allow a wider use of the old Tridentine rite for those who loved it but warned against it becoming what he called 'an ideology'. (The month before, Francis forbade the traditionalist Franciscan Friars of the Immaculate from saying the Latin Mass and launched an investigation into their finances.) On the sacrament of Reconciliation he said: 'the confessional is not a torture chamber, but the place in which the Lord's mercy motivates us to do better'.

Above all his message was that 'we must not reduce the bosom of the universal Church to a nest protecting our mediocrity'. The Church 'is the home of all, not a small chapel that can hold only a small group of selected people'. And it is a place for collective rather than just individual salvation:

The image of the Church I like is that of the holy, faithful people of God. This is the definition I often use, and then there is that image from the Second Vatican Council's 'Dogmatic Constitution on the Church' (No. 12). Belonging to a people has a strong theological value. In the history of salvation, God has saved a people. There is no full identity without belonging to a people. No one is saved alone, as an isolated individual, but God attracts us looking at the complex web of relationships that take place in the human community. God enters into this dynamic, this participation in the web of human relationships.

The job of the pontiff in all this, Francis said, quoting a previous pope, John XXIII, was to 'See everything; turn a blind eye to much; correct a little.'

* * *

It was a startling interview. The world's secular media, which largely failed to understand the nuances, said things like 'this amounts to a wholesale repudiation of the policies and priorities of the last two popes'. They were not correct in that. But they were right to sense that something seismic was taking place. Pope Francis did not change any church doctrine but he had utterly transformed the tone in which the Church spoke – and the way it was perceived. Where Benedict, the previous pope, had suggested that the rise of secularism would mean a smaller and purer Church, Francis was calling for a Church that saw its task as joyfully taking the message of the Gospel out across the globe with an embrace that was open to all. Benedict's Church had turned in on itself, with its back to the people; Francis wanted the Church to turn outwards and fling its arms open wide. The words were not changed but the Church was singing a different tune. 'Pope Francis has added sharps and flats to papal teaching,' said the BBC's David Willey, 'which show that, far from claiming infallibility, he is a person of great humility who has grown accustomed to living with his own past personal failings and mistakes.'

Reaction within the Church was swift. Liberal Catholics who had felt left out in the cold under the two previous papacies were filled with hope and excitement. Conservative Catholics, most particularly those who had devoted themselves to campaigning on abortion and other issues of sexual morality, were alarmed. 'They feel like their general has deserted them,' said Edward Pentin, the Rome correspondent of the *National Catholic Register*, who has good contacts with conservatives and traditionalists. 'They do not like his theological vagueness, his lack of precision.' The papal historian, Eamon Duffy, was clear on how this fitted into a longer perspective. Pope Francis's 'pastoral emphasis on the missionary proclamation of the mercy of God to fallible people in difficult situations', wrote Duffy, 'seemed to point away from sterile preoccupation with ritual and doctrinal niceties, bureaucratic obstructionism, and the ignoble protection of the Church's institutional interests'.

What Pope Benedict made of it all, sequestered away in his retirement home within the former monastery Mater Ecclesiae, just a few minutes' walk from Pope Francis's quarters, we do not know. But Francis does. The new Pope sent the old Pope a copy of the Jesuit magazine containing the 11,000-word interview with Spadaro. 'You will see the first page after the table of contents is empty,' Francis told Archbishop Georg Gänswein, who is personal secretary to the Pope Emeritus. 'Please ask Pope Benedict to write there any comments, suggestions and criticisms he has on the contents and pass it back to me.' There was not enough room on the blank page. Three days later Francis received four pages of comments back from Benedict. Gänswein, who mischievously revealed the story of the exchange, would not be drawn on what they said. Benedict's remarks were 'interesting' was all he would say. But Francis was not finished yet. In fact he had only just begun.

* * *

Just a few weeks after the Jesuit interview the Pope granted another. But this time his interlocutor was about as far removed from a fellow Jesuit as could be imagined. Eugenio Scalfari was a 90-year-old atheist intellectual who had been the founder of the leading centre-left Italian daily newspaper *La Repubblica*.

In the summer of 2013 Scalfari had published in the paper two articles on religious and philosophical topics publicly addressed to the Pope. To Scalfari's surprise the Pope not only replied with a letter to the newspaper in September that year, he also telephoned the writer to suggest they should meet to discuss the issues further. It was as if Francis was demonstrating his intention to dialogue with the whole spectrum of society from a fellow Jesuit to a prominent atheist.

The fruits of their ensuing conversation were published by Scalfari in his newspaper. They continue the themes Francis had set out in his interview with Spadaro but the Pope's language was this time even more graphic. Francis reportedly described the court that formed around pontiffs in previous periods of history as a 'leprosy of the papacy'. Previous popes, he was quoted as saying, 'have often been narcissists, flattered and thrilled by their courtiers'. Ambitious careerist priests were said to be 'vain' butterflies, 'smarmy' idolators and 'priest-tycoons'. The Church had a 'Vatican-centric vision' which 'neglects the world around it and I will do everything to change it'. The most urgent problem that the Church is facing,' he said, was youth unemployment and the neglect of the elderly. On economics 'savage liberalism only makes the strong stronger and the weak weaker and excludes the most excluded,' he said, which meant the world needed greater restraints on market forces.

Highly unusually for a journalist, Scalfari, as was his habit, conducted the interview without a notebook or voice recorder and wrote the 80-minute conversation up from memory afterwards. He had sought the Pope's permission to publish his account and offered to send Francis the text for his approval before publication. The Pope told him not to 'waste time' in sending him the text, saying, 'I trust you.' After the interview was published in *La Repubblica* it was also reproduced on the Vatican website, suggesting that the Pope was happy with the account. The broad thrust of what it reported was clearly in line with the kind of thing Francis had said to Spadaro. But there were several egregious errors in the account, such as the atheist's suggestion that the Pope had said that he no longer believed that sin existed, because God's mercy and forgiveness were eternal. Individuals who did not like the kind of things Francis had been saying complained that the account was inaccurate and after a small cloud of controversy the interview was removed from the official Vatican website. There was, however, little doubt that what Scalfari had written reflected the general tenor of the new Pope's thinking. The official Vatican press spokesman, Father Federico Lombardi, told the media that the interview 'should be considered faithful on the whole to the mind of the pope, but not necessarily in its particular words and the accuracy of its details'.

What was particularly significant about the episode was how it affected the way that many in the Church regarded papal utterances. Lombardi suggested that a whole new genre of papal speech was now emerging. The traditional forms of papal communication involved written documents, the highest level of which were encyclicals; canonical decrees which carried the force of church law; and official speeches and sermons. In previous papacies the text of such documents had been weighed, word by word, by teams of sedulous civil servants. But in addition to these traditional forms, Lombardi said, Pope Francis was developing a new 'conversational' genre arising out of off-the-cuff homilies at his 7 a.m. daily Mass – of which the Vatican publishes only summaries with verbatim quotations – and the increasing number of ad hoc press conferences and interviews with journalists he was conducting. When the Pope speaks spontaneously, his words should carry correspondingly less weight than in more traditional forms and contexts, Lombardi said.

In practice the opposite of this was happening. In July, just four months into his papacy, Pope Francis had published his first encyclical. It was largely the work of his predecessor Benedict XVI, who had not quite finished the first draft when he resigned. The document *Lumen Fidei* (The Light of Faith) was the concluding part of a trilogy of documents Pope Benedict had produced during his time in office. The encyclical on faith complemented the previous documents on the other two theological virtues, charity and hope. But *Lumen Fidei* had received relatively little public attention when compared to Francis's impromptu remark 'who am I to judge?' on gay relationships. This meant that the highest level of papal pronouncement was making far less impact that the conversational. As if to confirm that, the day after the Spadaro interview was published (in which Pope Francis said that the 'Church's pastoral ministry cannot be obsessed' with certain moral issues, including abortion, adding, 'it is not necessary to talk about these issues all the time') there was an occasion on which the Pope did deem it apt to affirm the work of Catholics who defend the sacredness of unborn human life. Speaking to a group of Catholic doctors and gynaecologists he praised them for 'going against the tide' and sometimes 'paying a personal price' to oppose the injustice of abortion. But this official speech did not create the same stir in the international media and so reached a far smaller audience.

The response of the Vatican press spokesman, Father Lombardi, to all this was to suggest that a 'new hermeneutic' – church jargon for a method of interpretation – was needed so that regard was paid to the overall sense of the Pope's casual remarks rather than analysing the significance of individual words. 'This isn't *Denzinger*,' he said, referring to the famous German collection of official church teaching, 'and it's not canon law.' It should not be regarded as part of the official church teaching known as the magisterium. The media was not much interested in advice containing words like hermeneutics and magisterium.

* * *

Conservative critics of the new Pope felt that what was needed was not a new method of interpretation but a greater sense of care and restraint by Pope Francis. The moral philosopher Germain Grisez, the defender of the conservative theology of the previous two popes, attacked Francis for 'letting loose with his thoughts' as self-indulgently 'as he might unburden himself with friends after a good dinner and plenty of wine'. It was not just conservative Catholics. One seasoned foreign ambassador to the Vatican worried privately to me: 'Francis is ceding to the press the power of interpretation and that's a very big power. After something the Pope said about abortion I was contacted by someone senior in my government who said: "So the Catholic Church is changing its position on abortion." His loose style means he repeatedly lays himself open to misinterpretation.'

Some highly traditionalist Catholics began to worry aloud that the new Pope's liking for extemporizing could undermine the carefully laid foundations of Catholic doctrine. A US Catholic convert from Anglicanism, Father Dwight Longenecker, blogged: 'In almost every impromptu press conference, personal phone call, informal conversation, and unscheduled event the Pope's candid and relaxed style has caused confusion, consternation, and bewilderment among the faithful.' This informal and often ambiguous method of communication 'cannot help but erode the more solemn teaching authority of the papacy'. In the UK another caustic convert, Father William Oddie, suggested that 'a period of papal reserve' was now overdue.

Francis was unfazed by all this, if he even noticed it. 'He loves to set hares running,' one senior Vatican insider told me. Another leading cleric, in the higher ranks of one department of the Curia who had recently been promoted by Pope Francis, used another metaphor. 'He likes to fly a kite – which is what he was doing with Scalfari,' the official said. 'There is no innocence about it. But rather like a secular politician he will say, "Let's float the idea and see what happens." He's launching ideas. It suits him to have the ideas floated without being pinned down on the specific.' The head of one Roman institution told me: 'Francis has deliberately set out to lower the status of papal pronouncements. He has developed the interview as a form of teaching. This approach is both a strength and weakness but it deals with the person immediately before him. It is all part of his strategy to demystify the imperial papacy and make it more normal. "We must be normal. We must be normal." He says that all the time.' So much so that the Argentinian journalist Elisabetta Piqué, who has known Bergoglio for over a decade, has coined the phrase 'the scandal of normality'.

* * *

There was no ambivalence about what Francis did next. Just six months into office he published, in November 2013, what amounted to a manifesto for his mission. *Evangelii Gaudium* (The Joy of the Gospel) is an apostolic exhortation – the type of document a pope publishes in response to a Synod of Bishops, like the one in 2012 on 'The New Evangelization for the Transmission of the Christian Faith'. Exhortations are also published to encourage the faithful to do something particular. In this document Pope Francis ticked both those boxes. It had, he insisted 'a programmatic significance and important consequences'. It was a call to action.

Evangelii Gaudium was an updating of an apostolic exhortation, Pope Paul VI's 1975 *Evangelii Nuntiandi* – the document that Bergoglio had most treasured throughout his career, as Provincial of the Jesuits, as an auxiliary bishop in Flores, as Cardinal Archbishop of Buenos Aires and now as pontiff. (Pope Francis has cited Paul VI's text at least 31 times on at least 11 different occasions, including 13 times in *Evangelii Gaudium*.) Both documents begin with the premise that spreading the Gospel must be the primary and deepest purpose of the Church.

What Catholics must do, Francis wrote, was live the Gospel joyously and with such enthusiasm that the Good News about Jesus Christ would spread to the rest of the world by being caught not taught. It was unlike any previous papal document. It was mainly written in plain language but was bold, passionate, direct, energetic and accessible. At times sharply critical, it was in places lyrical, often warmly affectionate and occasionally even witty. At 50,000 words it was the length of a short book but it was easy to read. He wrote as he spoke, peppering the text with folksy phrases, many of which like 'the smell of the sheep' were familiar to his followers worldwide but particularly in Argentina. Francis was serving notice that he was not going to change but intended to behave in Rome as he had for the previous 18 years in Buenos Aires – as a pastoral bishop, close to the concerns of ordinary people, who put the pastoral before the doctrinal and placed reality before philosophy or theology. Proclaiming the Gospel wasn't about preaching, he said; rather it should feel more like inviting others to a delicious banquet. To do that, the Church – which was not the hierarchy but the whole people of God – needed to change its priorities and its practice.

Joy was the keynote. The document used the word 110 times, a figure surpassed only by the word love, which appeared 154 times. There were 65 references to the poor, 58 to peace, and 37 to justice. Interestingly there were 120 references to Christians as against only 25 to Catholics. The only heavily used piece of Church jargon was the word 'evangelization', variants of which appeared 190 times. But if *evangelizing* – spreading the Gospel – was the key verb, *joyful* was the key adjective. 'An evangelizer must never look like someone who has just come back from a funeral!' the Pope wrote near the beginning of the document. But he also included early in the text a stark warning about the failings of today's consumer society in which so many people suffer from 'the desolation and anguish born of a complacent yet covetous heart, the feverish pursuit of frivolous pleasures, and a blunted conscience'.

* * *

The authorship of the document was significant. It was shot through with salty and homely turns of phrase which could only have come from the pen of Francis himself. But *Evangelii Gaudium* also bears the hallmarks of two Argentinian priests – Father Victor Manuel Fernández and Father Carlos Galli. They had helped Bergoglio write what had been, until *Evangelii Gaudium*, the most important work the new Pope had authored – the concluding document of the meeting of bishops from all over Latin America in Aparecida in 2007. One of Francis's first acts as Pope had been to make an archbishop of Fernández, whom he had earlier appointed as Rector of the Pontifical University of Buenos Aires. *Evangelii Gaudium* pointedly quotes that Aparecida text along with writings of the Latin American bishops from their Puebla meeting. It also quotes from previous papal documents, decrees from the Vatican Council and from the documents of the national episcopal conferences of Brazil, India, United States, Philippines, France and the Congo. With this wide range of authorities Pope Francis was underscoring his idea that all the faithful have a role to play in defining and cherishing the repository of the Catholic faith. Religion, he said cannot be 'relegated to the inner sanctum of personal life'. He wrote: 'An authentic faith – which is never comfortable or completely personal – always involves a deep desire to change the world, to transmit values, to leave this earth somehow better than we found it...The earth is our common home and all of us are brothers and sisters...The Church cannot and must not remain on the side-lines in the fight for justice.'

Bergoglio's experience providing charity to the poor in his years as leader of Argentina's Jesuits and helping them to fight for justice when he was Archbishop of Buenos Aires bore direct fruit in *Evangelii Gaudium*, which reiterated the Church's 'preferential option for the poor'. Francis wrote: 'God's heart has a special place for the poor, so much so that he himself became poor.' He was born to 'a lowly maiden from a small town on the fringes of a great empire'. He was 'raised in a home of ordinary workers and worked with his own hands to earn his bread'. And he began his ministry by reading the words: 'The Spirit of the Lord is upon me, because he has anointed me to preach good news to the poor.' This is why, said Francis, 'I want a Church which is poor and for the poor'.

The Pope's debt to *teología del pueblo* – the Argentine Theology of the People – was clear. 'For the Church, the option for the poor is primarily a theological category rather than a cultural, sociological, political or philosophical one', *Evangelii Gaudium* said. It echoes the Aparecida teaching by extending the definition of the poor to include people with a range of vulnerabilities – 'the homeless, the addicted, refugees, indigenous peoples, the elderly who are increasingly isolated and abandoned, and many others'. A Church which is poor and for the poor must learn from those who are poor. They have much to teach us, he wrote, because in their difficulties they know the suffering Christ. We must 'let ourselves be evangelized by them'. Once the Gospel has become part of the culture of the people they find new ways and new forms through which to transmit the faith. Different peoples will express the faith in different ways which each accord to their particular genius. So the Church in Rome must take care not to impose a European model on people with different cultures. 'It is not essential to impose a specific cultural form, no matter how beautiful or ancient it may be, together with the Gospel.' The Church should not be afraid, he said, to re-examine 'certain customs not directly connected to the heart of the Gospel, even some which have deep historical roots.'

What poor people need is a Church which gets out of the sacristy and onto the streets. Priests should go to the people, rather than expecting the people to come to them. Francis wrote:

I prefer a Church which is bruised, hurting and dirty because it has been out on the streets, rather than a Church which is unhealthy from being confined and from clinging to its own security... My hope is that we will be moved by the fear of remaining shut up within structures which give us a false sense of security, within rules which make us harsh judges, within habits which make us feel safe, while at our door people are starving and Jesus does not tire of saying to us: Give them something to eat.

But *Evangelii Gaudium* went beyond the preoccupations of the Theology of the People and embraced some of the thinking of Liberation Theology. In additional to the bias to the poor, *Evangelii Gaudium* looked at the working of the global economy, employing the liberationist notion that sin can reside in social structures as well as being the responsibility of individuals. If the Church was to listen to the cry of the poor for justice, he wrote:

> it means working to eliminate the structural causes of poverty and to promote the integral development of the poor, as well as small daily acts of solidarity in meeting the real needs which we encounter. The word 'solidarity' is a little worn and at times poorly understood, but it refers to something more than a few sporadic acts of generosity. It presumes the creation of a new mind-set which thinks in terms of community and the priority of the life of all over the appropriation of goods by a few.

Pope Francis in the document castigated the workings of the contemporary economy in much more vivid terms than had his papal predecessors. In a section headed 'No to an economy of exclusion' Francis wrote: 'Such an economy kills. How can it be that it is not a news item when an elderly homeless person dies of exposure, but it is news when the stock market loses two points?' He continued:

> Some people continue to defend trickle-down theories which assume that economic growth, encouraged by a free market, will inevitably succeed in bringing about greater justice and inclusiveness in the world. This opinion, which has never been confirmed by the facts, expresses a crude and naïve trust in the goodness of those wielding economic power and in the sacralized workings of the prevailing economic system. Meanwhile, the excluded are still waiting. To sustain a lifestyle which excludes others, or to sustain enthusiasm for that selfish ideal, a globalization of indifference has developed. Almost without being aware of it, we end up being incapable of feeling compassion at the outcry of the poor, weeping for other people's pain, and feeling a need to help them, as though all this were someone else's responsibility and not our own. The culture of prosperity deadens us; we are thrilled if the market offers us something new to purchase. In the meantime all those lives stunted for lack of opportunity seem a mere spectacle; they fail to move us.

The worship of the golden calf for which Moses condemned the Israelites has returned in a new and ruthless guise in the idolatry of money, Pope Francis wrote, while under the laws of competition the powerful feed upon the powerless. 'Behind this attitude lurks a rejection of ethics and a rejection of God. Ethics has come to be viewed with a certain scornful derision.'

Strong criticism of the working of unrestrained and unregulated capitalism was nothing new in Catholic Social Teaching. But previously popes like Pope John Paul II had made some genuflection, amid their forceful criticism of the excesses of global capitalism, to the fact that wealth creation can benefit society, creating jobs and thus alleviating poverty on a large scale. *Evangelii Gaudium* acknowledged none of that, which is perhaps why, as we shall see, aspects of Francis's teaching were not well-received in advanced market economies like the United States.

* * *

But the Pope's fire was directed primarily on the Church rather than the world. In a reprise of his concern in the Spadaro interview Francis inserted into *Evangelii Gaudium*, almost word for word, the line that had so upset conservative Catholics with the suggestion that they were 'obsessed' with abortion, gay marriage and contraception. He wrote: 'Pastoral ministry in a missionary style is not obsessed with the disjointed transmission of a multitude of doctrines to be insistently imposed.' Some of that multitude of doctrines, he said, were more central to the key message of the Gospel. He then quoted the Second Vatican Council's reiteration of the ancient tradition that there is 'an order or a hierarchy of truths' in church teaching, with mercy, in the judgement of St Thomas Aquinas, being the greatest of all the virtues. Thus, said the Pope:

> in preaching the Gospel a fitting sense of proportion has to be maintained. This would be seen in the frequency with which certain themes are brought up and in the emphasis given to them in preaching. For example, if in the course of the liturgical year a parish priest speaks about temperance ten times but only mentions charity or justice two or three times, an imbalance results, and precisely those virtues which ought to be most present in preaching and catechesis are overlooked. The same thing happens when we speak more about law than about grace, more about the Church than about Christ, more about the Pope than about God's word.

Later in the exhortation Pope Francis offered four principles to help the Church prioritize within the hierarchy of truths. They were yardsticks which he had developed from various sources throughout his priestly career. Now he offered them as coordinates for the construction of a society that puts the common good before the demands of a materialist individualism and that would build peace, justice and fraternity which would overcome the divisions that arise from diversity. The four yardsticks were:

- time is greater than space;
- unity prevails over conflict;
- reality is more important than ideas;
- the whole is greater than the part.

His account of the first axiom – time is greater than space – was almost mystical. He spoke of the way people live 'poised between each individual moment' and the prospect of a 'greater brighter horizon' of the future. We live in a tension between the present and what is to come, he said, between trying to possess the space around us and trying to initiate processes that will bear fruit in an unknown future. Francis was challenging the Church to guard against short-termism. Christians should work 'slowly but surely, without being obsessed with immediate results'. God works in history and his people walk forward to the unknown destinations to which the Holy Spirit might lead us. We do not walk alone, but together. And we walk in hope, 'to make the kingdom of God present in our world'.

This was not easy reading. But many found it inspirational. The liberal theologian Tina Beattie, Professor of Catholic Studies at the University of Roehampton, said of it: 'Francis is not an intellectual lightweight as some critics have suggested. *Evangelii Gaudium* is the work of an amazing mind. The passage on the politics of time and space is really profound. It is saying: I have to start here and trust the future to the seeds I plant now. But it is much more. It shows Pope Francis has a mystical intellect.'

The second maxim – unity prevails over conflict – set out to address the perennial question of how we resolve disagreements. Conflict cannot be ignored or concealed, Francis wrote. It has to be faced. 'When conflict arises, some people simply look at it and go their way as if nothing happened; they wash their hands of it and get on with their lives. Others embrace it in such a way that they become its prisoners; they lose their bearings, [and] project onto institutions their own confusion and dissatisfaction.' But there is a third way, which is what Jesus was talking about when he said, 'Blessed are the peace-makers'. If we acknowledge that unity is greater than conflict then 'conflicts, tensions and oppositions can achieve a diversified and life-giving unity'. Then there can be communion amid disagreement because 'peace is not about a negotiated settlement'. Rather it is 'the conviction that the unity brought by the Spirit can harmonize every diversity'. *Evangelii Gaudium* speaks of 'reconciled diversity'. It quotes the bishops of the war-torn Congo, who have said: 'Our diversity is our wealth.'

The third guideline – reality is more important than ideas – illustrated the differences between Francis's pastoral pragmatism and the philosophical precision of previous popes. There exists a constant tension between ideas and realities. A continuous dialogue is needed between the two. Without that, ideas become detached from reality and can begin to mask it. When that happens, according to Francis, in one of the denser passages in the document, the result is 'angelic forms of purity, dictatorships of relativism, empty rhetoric, objectives more ideal than real, brands of ahistorical fundamentalism, ethical systems bereft of kindness, intellectual discourse bereft of wisdom'. Ideas should be at the service of reality, as aids to communication and the spread of good practice. They should not call the tune. They should not twist or obscure reality or reduce it to rhetoric or ideology. There is no better example of how realities are greater than ideas than God becoming man in Jesus Christ – the word becoming flesh.

The final Bergoglio principle – the whole is greater than the part – brings together the global and the local. 'We need to pay attention to the global so as to avoid narrowness and banality,' *Evangelii Gaudium* says. 'Yet we also need to look to the local, which keeps our feet on the ground.'

> There is no need, then, to be overly obsessed with limited and particular questions. We constantly have to broaden our horizons and see the greater good which will benefit us all. But this has to be done without evasion or uprooting. We need to sink our roots deeper into the fertile soil and history of our native place, which is a gift of God. We can work on a small scale, in our own neighbourhood, but with a larger perspective. Nor do people who wholeheartedly enter into the life of a community need to lose their individualism or hide their identity; instead, they receive new impulses to personal growth.

Characteristically Francis came up with a striking image to illustrate the relationship between the whole and the parts. We should not think of the whole as if it were a sphere, he said. Instead, think of it like a polyhedron – a modern-style football, which is made up of many individual shapes sewn together, would be a good example. The whole is a multifaceted reality to which the diverse parts make distinct contributions. As *Evangelii Gaudium* puts it, the shape 'reflects the convergence of all its parts, each of which preserves its distinctiveness'.

In spreading the Gospel, Francis said, the Church should bring together the global and the local, but with each part growing in its own way. One of the things he was defending here was the popular piety of the Argentine religious culture in which he grew up and which, throughout his life, he felt he had had to protect from intellectual snobs who devalued and derided the piety of what he called the ordinary holy faithful people of God. Bergoglio had previously used the image of the polyhedron to suggest that local and national cultures did not have to have imposed upon them the European cultural model which had been imposed on them by Rome. The Gospel can be 'inculturated' so that it speaks through the culture of the local people. And then these local cultures can become wellsprings which can renew the faith of the wider Church: 'Its fullness and richness embrace scholars and workers, businessmen and artists, in a word, everyone. The genius of each people receives in its own way the entire Gospel and embodies it in expressions of prayer, fraternity, justice, struggle and celebration.' They come together. But the whole is not just greater than the part. It is even greater than the sum of the parts.

* * *

Evangelii Gaudium also reinforced another Franciscan preoccupation which had been evident from his time in Buenos Aires but also on his 2014 pilgrimage to the Holy Land in the company of Muslim and Jewish friends. The new Pope wanted to bring a wide range of interlocutors into dialogue with the Church. Religious people must engage with wider society in a constant attempt to find a synthesis between faith and reason. The Church should be attentive to the advances of science, philosophy and the empirical fields of knowledge. Oppositional stances were unhelpful, though the Church should bring its ethical wisdom to bear upon the conversation. But dialogue could open new horizons for thought and new possibilities. The second area of dialogue mentioned was with other Christians and in this Pope Francis singled out the Orthodox and the Anglicans, naming the Patriarch Bartholomew of Constantinople and Rowan Williams, the former Archbishop of Canterbury, as 'a true gift from God'. Judaism, the Pope made clear, was to be held 'in special regard', with the two faiths able in part to pray the same scriptures. He expressed sincere regret for Christian persecutions of the Jews throughout the ages. But perhaps most arresting was the section on Islam. Francis wrote:

> Christians should embrace with affection and respect Muslim immigrants to our countries in the same way that we hope and ask to be received and respected in countries of Islamic tradition. I ask and I humbly entreat those countries to grant

Christians freedom to worship and to practise their faith, in light of the freedom which followers of Islam enjoy in Western countries!

There was a replied rebuke in that. But he warned Christians to 'avoid hateful generalizations' about Muslims. Despite 'disconcerting episodes of violent fundamentalism' we should remember that 'authentic Islam and the proper reading of the Qur'an are opposed to every form of violence'. And he added that to sustain dialogue with Islam 'suitable training is essential for all involved'.

* * *

In his exhortation Pope Francis quoted from the Second Vatican Council's Dogmatic Constitution on the Church, *Lumen Gentium*, which in 1964 had famously characterized the Church as 'the People of God' – a phrase which came to be identified with the reforming spirit of Vatican II. *Evangelii Gaudium* consciously reconnects to that with extensive references in its footnotes to the documents of Vatican II. It repeatedly weaves into its main text key words, phrases and themes from the Second Vatican Council. One of these is the idea that the Church needs to 'read the signs of the times', a phrase Francis used several times in *Evangelii Gaudium*. He quoted Pope Paul VI, who presided over Vatican II, as saying that 'the Church must look with penetrating eyes within herself' and with 'vivid and lively self-awareness' examine the gap between the ideal which Christ embodied and 'the actual image which the Church presents to the world today'. Many of the signs he was reading, Francis suggested, reveal a need for serious change within the Catholic Church.

Parts of the Church had become infected, Pope Francis said, with 'spiritual worldliness, which hides behind the appearance of piety and even love for the Church' but which actually consists of individuals seeking 'human glory and personal well-being'. This was the sin for which Jesus had reprimanded the Pharisees. Francis was scathing about those in the Church who 'feel superior to others because they observe certain rules or remain intransigently faithful to a particular Catholic style from the past'. Their 'supposed soundness of doctrine or discipline' was in fact a 'narcissistic and authoritarian elitism'. It was not hard to see why conservative cardinals in the United States and elsewhere were unhappy with Pope Francis's thinking.

Change was needed from the top down, he said, starting with 'a conversion of the papacy'. It was his duty as Bishop of Rome to be open to suggestions which could change his job so that it was closer to the kind of leadership which Jesus modelled. Pope John Paul II had asked for suggestions on how that should be done, Francis noted, but 'we have made little progress in this regard'. Church structures needed conversion too. The Second Vatican Council had said that bishops' conferences should play a much greater role in governance, as they had in the early Church. But measures to allow bishops 'genuine doctrinal authority' had not been put in place. Instead the Church is excessively centralized, which hampers its mission to spread the Gospel. He stated baldly: 'It is not advisable for the Pope to take the place of local bishops in the discernment of every issue which arises in their territory. In this sense, I am conscious of the need to promote a sound "decentralization".'

Widely varying situations throughout the world meant, he said, that the Christian community in each country was better placed to make judgements about what was needed there than was Rome. The papal magisterium, he said, should not be expected to offer a definitive or complete word on every question which affects the Church and the world. The Roman Church had much to learn from the Orthodox Church on more collegial styles of government and on the role of synods of bishops in running the Church.

Pope Francis was indicating his intention to make big changes in the Catholic Church. That, along with his excoriation of uncaring global capitalism, was what made the headlines when *Evangelii Gaudium* was published. But it also revealed the Pope's intention for change to pass throughout the Church right down to parish level. The parish, he insisted, was not an outdated institution but one capable of great flexibility. It could be adapted to the needs and abilities of both priest and people to become a real force in its local community. It was important that new lay movements and other associations which were bringing a new enthusiasm to the Church did not bypass the parish, or set up systems in parallel; rather they should strengthen the parish. Sermons should be short and designed to draw attention to the faith rather than to the cleverness of the preacher. Baptism should be open to all. (Francis was here perhaps thinking of the priests he had condemned when he was Archbishop of Buenos Aires because they refused to christen the babies of single mothers.) And the Eucharist was 'not a prize for the perfect but a powerful medicine and nourishment for the weak'. The Church, he said, is 'the house of the Father, where there is a place for everyone, with all their problems'.

Yet if Pope Francis was anxious that the Church should modernize he was also clear on what that did not mean. Turning to the issue of abortion he said: 'I want to be completely honest in this regard. This is not something subject to alleged reforms or "modernizations". It is not "progressive" to try to resolve problems by eliminating a human life.' The Church wishes to care with particular love for the vulnerable and there is no one who qualifies for that description more than 'unborn children, the most defenceless and innocent among us'. Taking an uncompromising stand against abortion was a human rights issue, he said. Of unborn children, he added:

> Frequently, as a way of ridiculing the Church's effort to defend their lives, attempts are made to present her position as ideological, obscurantist and conservative. Yet this defence of unborn life is closely linked to the defence of each and every other human right. It involves the conviction that a human being is always sacred and inviolable, in any situation and at every stage of development. Human beings are ends in themselves and never a means of resolving other problems. Once this conviction disappears, so do solid and lasting foundations for the defence of human rights, which would always be subject to the passing whims of the powers that be. Reason alone is sufficient to recognize the inviolable value of each single human life, but if we also look at the issue from the standpoint of faith, every violation of the personal dignity of the human being cries out in vengeance to God and is an offence against the creator of the individual.

Having said that, Pope Francis was anxious to stress that 'it is also true that we have done little to adequately accompany women in very difficult situations, where abortion appears as a quick solution to their profound anguish, especially when the life developing within them is the result of rape or a situation of extreme poverty. Who can remain unmoved before such painful situations?'

Another area in which there would be no 'modernization', he insisted in *Evangelii Gaudium*, was in the continuing demand, from inside and outside of the Church, for the ordination of women. 'The reservation of the priesthood to males, as a sign of Christ the Spouse who gives himself in the Eucharist, is not a question open to discussion', the apostolic exhortation stated. Sacramental power was not the same as power in general. Pope Francis wrote:

> The Church acknowledges the indispensable contribution which women make to society through the sensitivity, intuition and other distinctive skill sets which they, more than men, tend to possess. I think, for example, of the special concern which women show to others, which finds a particular, even if not exclusive, expression in motherhood. I readily acknowledge that many women share pastoral responsibilities with priests, helping to guide people, families and groups and offering new contributions to theological reflection. But we need to create still broader opportunities for a more incisive female presence in the Church. Because the feminine genius is needed in all expressions in the life of society, the presence of women must also

be guaranteed in the workplace and in the various other settings where important decisions are made, both in the Church and in social structures.

Demands that the legitimate rights of women be respected, based on the firm conviction that men and women are equal in dignity, present the Church with profound and challenging questions which cannot be lightly evaded, he wrote. 'This presents a great challenge for pastors and theologians, who are in a position to recognize more fully what this entails with regard to the possible role of women in decision-making in different areas of the Church's life.' But if he was acknowledging that there were big questions about the role of women in the Church, and how it should be improved, he did not give any concrete indication of what he thought the answers might be.

Notably absent from *Evangelii Gaudium* – the first major document for which Pope Francis had been the primary author since his election – was any mention of clerical sex abuse and the institutional cover-up for which many of its bishops had been responsible. Nor was there any mention of the place of gay people in the Church, though there was a footnote revealing that one quotation Francis used – on secular society's rejection of the idea of objective moral norms – was taken from a 2006 document by the US bishops' conference named 'Ministry to Persons with a Homosexual Inclination: Guidelines for Pastoral Care'.

But overall *Evangelii Gaudium* signalled that the new Pope was intent upon, at the very least, a distinct change of tack. His determination to foster what he called a 'culture of encounter' would promote dialogue – both between the Church and the world, and also within the Church – 'to devise a means for building consensus and agreement'. But in some areas he seemed to be set on turning things upside down.

The document ended, as many papal documents habitually do, with an invocation for assistance from Mary the Mother of God. But even here Francis was unconventional. Making reference to the appearance of Our Lady of Guadalupe to the indigenous saint Juan Diego, Pope Francis concluded:

Whenever we look to Mary, we come to believe once again in the revolutionary nature of love and tenderness. In her we see that humility and tenderness are not virtues of the weak but of the strong who need not treat others poorly in order to feel important themselves. Contemplating Mary, we realize that she who praised God for 'bringing down the mighty from their thrones' and 'sending the rich away empty' is also the one who brings a homely warmth to our pursuit of justice.

What *Evangelii Gaudium* made clear was that the Catholic Church had embarked on a new chapter in its modern story. The era of the beleaguered Church, the defensive Church, the fortress Church was over. Pope Francis went on to deliver a number of other major programmatic addresses at the European Parliament and the Council of Europe among others. But it was *Evangelii Gaudium* which set the parameters for his papacy, offered a route-map for the Church to follow and gave it the compass to point the way.

* * *

Many in the Church were excited. Liberals saw it as a return to Vatican II. 'Pope Francis has gone back to basics to proclaim the joy of the Gospel – which had been lost in the previous 30 years in a lot of obsessive (to use Francis's word) anxieties about sexual ethics,' said Tina Beattie, a theologian who was out of favour under the Benedict papacy after challenging Church teachings on contraception and women's ordination. 'He has relocated the Gospel message in issues of poverty and social justice, recognizing the destructive potential of neo-liberal economics and of cultures driven only by market values and lack of care for the environment. Pope Benedict XVI was terribly pessimistic anthropologically; he didn't have great faith in human nature where Francis has a high level of trust and hope in human ability to get things right eventually.' Some inside the Curia were also excited by the challenge. 'Pope Francis sees his mission not as strengthening the institutional Church (though that might be a side effect) but ministering to the world,' one cleric high in the Vatican bureaucracy told me. '*Evangelii Gaudium* also underscores what Pope Francis doesn't want from us: clericalism, arrogance, ambition, power and the rest.'

More conservative Catholics received *Evangelii Gaudium* respectfully but without notable enthusiasm. Some were still trying to reconcile Francis to their old world. Francis was changing no doctrine but merely offering a different style, they said. Many of his comments could have been made by Pope Benedict – it was only Francis's tone that was different. The leading conservative Catholic George Weigel, a devotee of both John Paul II and Benedict XVI, still attempted to cling to the idea that Jorge Mario Bergoglio – 'a radically converted Christian disciple who has known the mercy of God in his own life and who wants to enable others to share that experience' – was 'in full continuity' with his two predecessors, the Polish and the German popes. 'He puts the New Evangelization at the very centre of the Church and orients everything else around it,' Weigel said. 'This exhortation demonstrates the seamless continuity between John Paul II, Benedict XVI and Francis and the continuity between the John Paul–Benedict interpretation of Vatican II and Francis: It's all about recovering the missionary vocation of everyone.'

But this was an increasingly difficult position to maintain, as the Cambridge historian of the papacy, Eamon Duffy, pointed out. Weigel's view, he wrote 'carefully ignores the significance of Bergoglio's consistent adoption of a rhetoric, in word and act, manifestly at odds with the ethos of the previous two pontificates. For admirers of the "dynamic orthodoxy" (a euphemism for the vigorous exertion of central authority) that characterized the pontificates of John Paul II and Benedict XVI, Bergoglio's frank acceptance of clerical fallibility and the perils of authoritarian leadership are both startling and deeply unappetising.'

Others began to shift uneasily in their episcopal seats after seeing in *Evangelii Gaudium* aspects of Pope Francis's teaching which they found uncomfortable. Bishop Robert Morlino of Madison, Wisconsin, in an interview on the conservative EWTN TV network, tried to downplay the significance of the exhortation saying it was not a teaching document of the Church but merely 'a call to a personal encounter with Jesus Christ'. In an interview which one commentator described as 'astonishingly condescending' he also attempted to diminish the intensity of the Pope's attack on unfettered capitalism by suggesting Francis was referring to an abstract concept rather than the actual workings of the economy in the United States. The Pope's view on economics, he said loftily, was not binding on all Catholics in the way that statements on faith and morals are.

Lay reaction was more stark. The media had focused much of its coverage on the Pope's critique of trickle-down as an economic solution to poverty. Rush Limbaugh, host of the most listened-to talk show in the United States, told his 15 million listeners that *Evangelii Gaudium* was 'dramatically, embarrassingly, puzzlingly wrong' and 'just pure Marxism coming out of the mouth of the Pope'. The former vice-presidential candidate Sarah Palin announced that she was taken aback by the Pope making 'statements that to me sound kind of liberal'. In the US business magazine *Forbes* a British free-market Catholic, Tim Worstall, a Fellow at the Adam Smith Institute, announced that his reaction to the papal document was 'barely controlled rage' since market-based economics were actually lifting millions out of poverty across the globe, and were the solution rather than the problem. More subtly, the American Catholic philosopher Michael Novak, celebrated as the author of *The Spirit of Democratic Capitalism*, suggested that *Evangelii Gaudium* made sense in Argentina but did not apply so well elsewhere. There were also translation problems. Francis had written in Spanish and had not used the words 'trickle-down' or 'inevitably' in the section which had outraged the American Right (see page 217).

The US billionaire Ken Langone was so upset at the Pope's suggestion that the rich can 'end up being incapable of feeling compassion' for the poor that he suggested wealthy Catholics might stop giving to the Church. Langone, a major donor to the Republican Party, was working with Cardinal Timothy Dolan, the Archbishop of New York, to raise $180 million for the restoration of St Patrick's Cathedral there. He told Dolan that the rich were feeling ostracized by the Pope. In response Dolan penned a controversial op-ed article in the *Wall Street Journal* headlined 'The Pope's Case for Virtuous Capitalism', which was widely seen as diluting the Pope's trenchant critique of the free market and ignoring Francis's analysis of structural sin. The Pope, Dolan seemed to want to reassure the citizens of America, was not trying to march the Church towards socialism.

Pope Francis took all this in his stride. There had been too little debate in the Catholic Church in recent decades, was his view. A little heated discussion was all to the good. In any case he had got his retaliation in first. Towards the end of *Evangelii Gaudium* he had written:

> If anyone feels offended by my words, I would respond that I speak them with affection and with the best of intentions, quite apart from any personal interest or political ideology. My words are not those of a foe or an opponent. I am interested only in helping those who are in thrall to an individualistic, indifferent and self-centred mentality to be freed from those unworthy chains and to attain a way of living and thinking which is more humane, noble and fruitful, and which will bring dignity to their presence on this earth.

Shrugging off the controversy he told an interviewer, Andrea Tornielli of the Italian daily paper *La Stampa*, that there was nothing in *Evangelii Gaudium* which could not already be found in the social teaching of the Church.

> I wasn't speaking from a technical point of view; what I was trying to do was to give a picture of what is going on. The only specific quote I used was the one regarding the 'trickle-down theories' which assume that economic growth, encouraged by a free market, will inevitably succeed in bringing about greater justice and social inclusiveness in the world. The promise was that when the glass was full, it would overflow, benefitting the poor. But what happens instead, is that when the glass is full, it magically gets bigger; nothing ever comes out for the poor. This was the only reference to a specific theory. I was not, I repeat, speaking from a technical point of view but according to the Church's social doctrine. This does not mean being a Marxist.

As to the accusations of Marxism, he said: 'The Marxist ideology is wrong. But I have met many Marxists in my life who are good people, so I don't feel offended.'

* * *

The wind of change was blowing through the Vatican. Yet still no-one could be quite certain which way it would take the Church. As these last two chapters have shown, the new Pope in his first year was sending out signals and also using words that spoke of disturbance and renewal – two fruits that Christians see as characterizing the inspiration of the Holy Spirit. Francis was indeed a pope of surprises, conservative on doctrine but distinctly the opposite in style.

Some were contemptuous of this. One prominent secularist described the new head of the Catholic Church as 'business as usual, with smiles'. But those who thought about the Church more deeply knew that something seismic was stirring. 'The little tiny things that are terribly important,' said Father Timothy Radcliffe, the former Master of the Dominican order. 'The gestures of the Pope – washing the feet of the prisoners, especially the Muslim girl, and hugging that chap with those terrible tumours on his skin – they changed our perception of the world. And this is a very Catholic way of changing things because at the centre of our faith is a great gesture – taking the bread and breaking it. Gestures are pregnant. They say more than we can say in words.'

This is profound. And it answers the questions of those who asked whether Pope Francis was all style and no substance. In a Church which has at the heart of its tradition the idea of sacrament – an outward sign of inward grace – for a Pope to so radically transform a monarchical papal style, hardened by centuries of history, was itself revolutionary. Sacrament insists that outward signs are freighted with a deep internal significance and a reality of a different order which makes the distinction between style and substance artificial. As befits a Church in which sign and symbol are far more than mere emblems, and which has as its core the idea that God was incarnated as a human being, the semiotics were substance. As another perceptive priest and theologian, Father James Alison, in Brazil, put it: 'what Francis has essentially shown is that witness matters more than message. Or rather that witness is message. With him it's always been the little castaway phrases rather than the formal messaging that makes the difference. And that's what you would expect in Christianity. Christianity is a religion of witness and when people see someone happily doing something good – and not being particularly bothered about what the media or their critics say – that is a very way effective way of communicating their mission.'

All this was deeply disturbing to those – on all sides – who had become steeped in the old expressions of how the Church should behave. They were unsettled by Pope Francis's suggesting that the ways they took for granted – and found comfortable or beautiful – had become stale and ineffective. 'It is very challenging from a theological point of view,' said Father Augusto Zampini, a priest and theologian from Buenos Aires. 'Not just because of Francis's insistence that a pastoral approach always prevails over a doctrinal one, and that people always come before institutions. What unnerves some people even more is the fact that, in Francis' style, you don't need to use words – or complex theological arguments – to be challenging. His symbols promote changes in a more rapid and effective way than would a mere formal theological or institutional approach. Most people will now expect the next Pope to follow this style, and his idea of the hierarchy being humbled. There is no road back now he has shown another way.'

Pope Francis would find it apt, and unexpected, that ordinary members of what he loves to call the holy faithful people of God understand this intuitively. I began these last two chapters – on the actions and words with which Pope Francis set out his mission – with a story about Marczin, the homeless man, sleeping rough in a Vatican porchway, who was surprised one morning by the joy of being invited to the Pope's birthday breakfast. That same night I had come across him, back in his porchway with his dog and his companions and his huddle of blankets and bundle of earthly possessions. Despite his encounter with the Supreme Pontiff of the Universal Church, Marczin still had no bed and no job. Yet there was no contradiction in that to Marczin. 'Was breakfast enough?' I asked him. That was when he replied: 'Yes, there were herrings and everything,' misunderstanding my question. Couldn't the Pope find him a hostel or some work? Marczin replied: 'No, that's not his job. Anyway we like to move around. And the Pope has millions of other people to look after – with bigger problems.'

It was a salutary corrective – and a reminder, as Pope Francis routinely told his priests and seminarians, that the educated should go to the poor to learn and not to teach. After all, the Catholic Church is a body that's big on sacrament – which, translated from theological jargon, is merely the insistence that outward signs and symbols carry a deep internal significance. It's not about style or substance, Marczin was telling me. The medium is the message. The style is the substance. Gestures that change the way we see the world are what the Gospel is all about. The homeless truck driver had understood that where I had not. So too had the journalist James Carroll when he wrote in the *New Yorker* about watching Francis pray over Vinicio Riva, the man with the tumours in the St Peter's Square crowd. Carroll wrote: 'I realised, as the Pope pressed his hands on the bowed head of the stricken man, that curing and healing are not the same thing. To cure is to remove disease. To heal is to make whole.' Those of us who are healthy perhaps need to understand that more than those who are sick.

* * *

There was one final lesson in all this which Francis wanted to teach the world. Not long after the new Pope was elected, the Director of News at the BBC, James Harding, went to Rome to make the case to the head of the Vatican press office, Father Federico Lombardi, for the Pope to give an interview to the BBC, which has an audience of 250 million people around the world. The newsman later recalled: 'Father Lombardi, plainly inundated with such requests, smiled and with some charm left me with the impression that the Pope was having no trouble reaching a global audience.'

Yet how did the Pope do this? He used an unexpected route to communicate with the world. As the weeks and months went by he personally picked up the phone and rang a variety of ordinary individuals in answer to letters they had written to him. He offered to baptize a child in Italy whose father wanted the child aborted. He counselled a woman in Argentina who had been raped by a police officer. He comforted an Italian man whose brother had been murdered. He rang another woman in Argentina, who had written to ask his advice after her parish priest refused to give her Communion because she had married a divorced man – and apparently told her to ignore the priest and find another parish where she could take Communion. He dialogued with an atheist newspaper editor – and in the process made it clear that establishing a personal relationship with the man was more important than being guarded about what he said.

The most interesting reflection on this came not from a theologian but from a business guru. John Baldoni, an executive coach and author of books with titles like *The Secret to Bold and Gutsy Leadership*, wrote an article in the business magazine *Forbes* with the headline 'The Pope on the Phone: A Leadership Lesson'. What the Pope was doing, he wrote, was 'directly contacting a variety of stakeholders and interacting with them'. In this, Baldoni said, Francis was giving senior leaders everywhere a lesson in how to connect to their followers. 'Too often senior executives get cut off from the folks they lead', he wrote. Their aides, ever mindful of the chief's time, husband it shrewdly. They schedule time with the boss only for those closest to the top. Pope Francis does the opposite of that. He contacts the ordinary people. He keeps his own diary. He never stands on ceremony. He lives simply and travels as much as he can without an entourage. The business guru continued:

> 'The point is that people need to see and hear their leaders. Too many of us, especially in management positions, do the bulk of our communicating via email. That's fine for expediency but it does not make up for face-to-face, or voice-to-voice communication... We humans are meant to connect personally. It is important to see how people receive a message, even if it's interpreting intonations over the phone. Using the phone is personalized. When a senior leader dials up a front-line staffer, it implies that the person on the other end is worth speaking to. [It] demonstrates that the executive views them as important and their issue as urgent.

And it means the leader gets to find out how things are going on the front lines and gets the information unfiltered. Chris Lowney, a former Jesuit seminarian turned managing director for JP Morgan & Co. has explored similar ideas. His book *Pope Francis: Why He Leads the Way He Leads* concludes that the new Pope probably does not have a leadership philosophy, but only a focus: that of being a follower of Jesus. But Francis has also learned from bitter experience, substituting the stern authoritarianism which failed him as the leader of Argentina's Jesuits with the gentler pastoral tolerance and compassion he adopted when he became a bishop after his exile in Córdoba. At the end of his first year in Rome it had become clear that he had brought that style, which had further developed over his years as Archbishop of Buenos Aires, to the papacy. He had begun recalibrating the model of what leadership should look like in the Catholic Church. He had instituted a new way of being Pope.

On his next birthday as well as receiving gifts from his friends he had one to give. He asked volunteers to distribute 400 sleeping bags, bearing the papal crest, to homeless people around the Vatican and on the streets of Rome. Soon after, he installed three bathrooms in the public toilets in St Peter's Square – and also in ten parishes in the areas in which homeless people congregate around Rome – to which rough-sleepers could go to shower and even get their hair cut by barbers volunteering on their day off. Marczin, wherever he was one year on, would have been pleased. But he would also have known that Pope Francis had yet bigger tasks to accomplish.

12

Reforming the Vatican Bank

The arrest of the priest changed everything. At 6.30 a.m. on 28 June 2013 – just three months into the pontificate of Francis – officials of the Guardia di Finanza pulled up in front of a rectory in Palidoro, a town west of Rome. They rang the bell. The cleric who had been sleeping inside opened the door and was told that he was under arrest. A few hours later, wearing an elegant grey suit, Monsignor Nuzio Scarano entered a cell in the Regina Cæli, the most crowded prison in Rome.

He was not just any priest. Scarano was the director of the accounting analysis service at the Amministrazione del Patrimonio della Sede Apostolica (APSA) – the body that controlled the finances for the Vatican's property, purchasing and personnel departments, and much else. Regina Cæli is Latin for Queen of Heaven, and the name of one of the most ancient hymns of the Catholic Church. Once the building was home to a contemplative order of Carmelite nuns. But the Italian government had confiscated it after the collapse of the Papal States and in 1881 turned it into the city's biggest jail. The name resonated with a double irony for the imprisonment of the high-profile Catholic clergyman.

The Roman world knew Scarano by another name. Father Nunzio Scarano was a suave handsome high-living priest who had been dubbed 'Monsignor Cinquecento' (My Lord Five Hundred) from his penchant for flashing €500 banknotes. His arrest made front-page news. 'Scandal at the Vatican Bank' proclaimed the headline in the leading Italian daily *La Repubblica*. The top church accountant was accused of trying to smuggle €20m in a private plane across the border from Switzerland in a conspiracy which involved an agent of the Italian secret services and a dubious financier.

The details of the case added a touch of spice to the story. The suspicions of the police had first been alerted six months earlier after Scarano reported a burglary on his apartment in the city of Salerno, one of the centres of Mafia activity in the Naples region. Paintings from his art collection had been stolen, he complained. When the police arrived at the 17-room luxury apartment on

Via Romualdo Guarna in one of the city's most up-market neighbourhoods they were startled by its opulence. A spectacular collection of art lined the walls in hallways divided by mock-Roman columns. Scarano's art collection included six works by Giorgio de Chirico, one by Renato Guttuso, one attributed to Marc Chagall and various pieces of religious art. It was also furnished with valuable antiques. The missing paintings alone were worth €6m, police estimated. There was no sign of breaking and entering apart from a broken window, which investigators thought could not have given the thieves access. Police believed the thieves had entered with a key.

How could a bureaucrat priest on a stipend of just €36,000 a year afford such luxuries? They were all gifts or 'donations', the urbane cleric told them. The police also accused him of corruptly accepting gifts from banks which were soliciting Vatican business. These included 'trips, cruises, five-star hotels, massages, etc.' When he was arrested Scarano had €2.3m in his various personal accounts.

But this was a story that had much deeper implications than the scandal of naughty Father Nunzio. Investigators suspected that the high-society cleric had been operating APSA as a 'parallel bank' for Italian VIPs to use to dodge taxes. There was talk of Mafia money-laundering. Scarano denied it all but within a few days the Vatican Bank's second- and third-in-command suddenly quit their jobs.

* * *

A month later Pope Francis was on his way back to Rome after World Youth Day in Brazil. On the papal plane he held an impromptu in-flight press conference. Some asked him about Scarano. Wasn't it time, the reporter asked, to close the Vatican Bank?

The Pope made a joke. 'For sure he did not enter prison because he acted like the Blessed Imelda,' said Francis, using an irreverent Argentinian expression which makes comparison with a fourteenth-century virgin who died in ecstasy after receiving Holy Communion for the first time and whose body was said to be so pure it never decomposed. But Francis did not attempt to dismiss the Scarano affair. 'These are scandals,' he said, 'and they do harm.' The finances of the Vatican were a long-standing problem which had been raised by many cardinals in the discussions in the General Congregations that took place before the conclave which had elected him. But they had not been his top priority. 'The financial part I was planning to address next year, because it is not the most important thing that needed to be done,' he told the Vatican press corps. But the agenda changed. 'These things happen when you're in governance: you try to go in one direction, but then someone throws you a ball from another direction, and you have to bat it back.'

But things were not quite as simple as Pope Francis was making out.

* * *

The Vatican Bank is housed in a medieval tower that once served as a dungeon. Its lower floors have no windows. To gain admittance you have to leave Italy and go through the gate of the Porta Sant'Anna, be checked by two Swiss Guards, and pass through a two-door security kiosk set in a plate-glass window. Once inside you encounter, by the manned reception desk, a cash machine in the wall. The language which flashes up asking you to insert your cashcard is Latin: *Insertio scidulam quaeso ut faciundam cognoscas rationem.* The semiotics of all this are clear: communication between what is inside this place and the outside world will be made as difficult as possible.

I was there by invitation. The email had come as something of a shock. The bank's new press officer – it had never before had such a person – wrote to invite me to enter what has been for generations one of the world's most secretive institutions. And not just to look around. Someone inside the bank had heard I had begun work on this much-expanded second edition of my biography of Pope Francis. The offer was that officials would talk me through the financial reforms which were just part of the revolution in which the first non-European Pope for a millennium was turning the Church of Rome upside down.

Beyond the reception area, up a short flight of curved stairs, was a cream and brown marble rotunda. Round the edges stood eight highly polished tellers' desks at which representatives of religious orders, wealthy dioceses and Catholic charities deposit funds for onward transmission to pay clergy and build churches, schools and hospitals in the developing world. The official name of the bank is the Istituto per le Opere di Religione (the Institute for Religious Works), known in Rome as the IOR.

Since much of its money came from collection plates the IOR handled unusually large amounts of cash. And much of the money was wired out covertly to poor countries and failed states without functioning banking systems. Transparency and accountability have, therefore, never been high on the IOR's list of desiderata. Small wonder that, over the years, the Vatican Bank had become a byword for clandestine and dodgy dealing.

Markus Wieser was one of two high-powered crisis communications experts brought in to manage the bank's PR. A director of Communications & Network

Consulting, with offices in all the world's main financial centres, Wieser alternated between bases in Berlin, London, Rome and Munich. 'It is largely a very simple service,' he said airily. 'It is used mainly by religious orders which are too small to have their own finance department, by employees and pensioners of the Holy See, and by accredited diplomats.' The Holy See is not the same organization as the Vatican State, but we shall come to the significance of that later.

'They can deposit or send money very quickly and cheaply,' Wieser continued. 'The other function of the IOR is to safeguard the patrimony of the religious orders who own 85 per cent of the bank's funds.' In 2013 that patrimony consisted of religious orders depositing around $3.1 billion for safekeeping. The IOR paid out around 1 per cent in interest on that but, on average, invested the money deposited in government bonds at an average of 3.3 per cent. That generated profits of more than $70 million. 'In banking terms it's a rather pedestrian service,' said Wieser, adding jocularly: 'The sex and crime was only a little aspect. Incompetence was the main problem.'

There was rather more to it than incompetence.

* * *

On the top floor of the Vatican Bank is a board room with a dark mahogany floor and a massive table. An allegorical fresco looks down from the vaulted rococo ceiling above. In it the figure of a woman, Mother Church, wearing the long-gone three-crowned papal tiara, receives a gold platter of crowns and sceptres from a regal figure kneeling in tribute. Again the message – that temporal power and wealth must defer to the Church – is unmistakable. But that was before the Francis revolution began to take effect.

Opposite the door, set in an alcove of green marble, is a window which looks down on St Peter's Square. From it you can see the backs of the massive Bernini statues of evangelists, martyrs and popes which top the great semi-circular colonnade surrounding the elliptical piazza. The rows of columns enclose the gathering pilgrims in a symbol of the embrace of the Church for multitudes who assemble there. But between the window and the backs of the statues you can see something that is hidden from the rest of the world.

From the streets a crenellated battlement can be seen atop the Vatican walls. But from this privileged vantage point you can see that there is, in fact, a double wall, inside which runs a secret pathway. This is the Passetto, the hidden escape route down which popes would flee when the Vatican was under siege in the days of the Papal States. The Swiss Guards keep the key at the ready to this day. The top two floors above the bank have housed the private quarters of every pontiff until the present Pope rejected them in favour of two rooms in the Vatican guest house, the Casa Santa Marta on the other side of the great basilica. Indeed there is a narrow elevator from the ground floor, by the bank's back door, which was installed when Pope John Paul II became too infirm to take the stairs. It is a symbol of how the reputation of the papacy and the scandal-plagued bank have become enjoined.

* * *

Vatican finances have fascinated historians for centuries but the Vatican Bank itself is a comparatively recent institution. Until 1887 Pope Leo XIII hid the Vatican's ready wealth – a trunk full of gold coins – under his bed. That year he decided to found the Amministrazione per le Opere di Religione to gather money to do good religious works. It was only in 1942 at the height of the Second World War that Pope Pius XII gave the organization a new name and a clear banking mission. Its job was to protect church assets from both Nazi and communist threats. But it was also used to hide from the British and the Americans the deals that the Church in Germany was doing. Some reports suggest that the Vatican was dealing in German insurance policies which benefited from the fact that German insurers did not have to pay out on policies of Jews who died in the Holocaust – because their relatives could never certify the deaths. And one 1946 memo from a US Treasury agent reported that about $225 million in stolen Nazi gold had ended up at the Vatican. To prove their loyalty to the Church the bank's depositors in early years were required to produce their baptismal certificates to prove they were Catholics.

The confidentiality which was built into the organization from the outset has proved double-edged. In the 1980s Pope John Paul II used the IOR to send money to Solidarity, the Polish trade union movement which played a key role in triggering the fall of communism in Eastern Europe. With the Polish Pope's approval, millions of dollars of covert US aid passed through the Vatican Bank to Solidarity. William Casey, the director of the US Central Intelligence Agency, used to fly to Rome regularly to brief the Pope on the fight against communism in Eastern Europe. There were suspicions too that the bank was used to fund the Contras in El Salvador, and other anti-communist guerrillas in Latin America as part of the anti-Liberation Theology liaison unit established between the Vatican and the CIA during the Cold War. Most recently the bank has been used to channel cash to vulnerable Christian groups in Egypt and Cuba.

* * *

A system aimed at getting money speedily and secretly to difficult places had obvious operational advantages. But it had a big downside too. It became an easy target for those who wanted to use it for criminal purposes. Around the same time the then chairman of the bank was an American, Archbishop Paul Marcinkus. This native of Cicero, Illinois – the one-time base of the gangster Al Capone – clearly got involved with the wrong people. In the 1970s Marcinkus started doing business with Roberto Calvi, president of the Banco Ambrosiano of Milan, who turned out to have links with the Sicilian Mafia and a Masonic Lodge called Propaganda Due (P2) which was also active in Argentina involving members of the military junta at the time.

What was going on might never have been disclosed. But then in 1982 the Banco Ambrosiano dramatically collapsed. In the revelations which followed it publicly emerged that its main shareholder was the Vatican Bank. Behind the scenes Calvi had set up ten shell companies in Panama, nominally controlled, via a Luxembourg subsidiary, by the Vatican Bank. He had borrowed $600 million from 120 foreign banks and lent it to the shell companies and used the money to manipulate the share price of the Banco Ambrosiano. Marcinkus was found to have been a director of Ambrosiano Overseas, which was based in the Bahamas.

After the bank collapse a $1.3 billion black hole was found in the Banco Ambrosiano accounts. Calvi fled the country on a false passport. He was then found hanged under Blackfriars Bridge in London. Prosecutors in Rome saw it as a murder by P2, whose nickname was the Black Friars; four years later another P2 member and Vatican financial adviser, Michele Sindona, died after he drank cyanide-laced coffee in prison. The Vatican insisted it had no responsibility for the collapse of the bank but nonetheless in 1984 the Vatican agreed to make a $244 million 'goodwill payment' to Ambrosiano creditors. Three years later investigating magistrates in Milan issued a warrant for Marcinkus's arrest for 'complicity in fraudulent bankruptcy'. The warrant was never executed, because the archbishop hid away in the sovereign Vatican State.

The scandal came as a severe shock to Catholics around the world. It cost the Vatican hundreds of millions of dollars in a series of legal battles with the Italian authorities. But it did immeasurable damage to the moral authority of the Church.

For three months Marcinkus had to remain inside the Vatican for fear he would be arrested if he stepped onto Italian soil. This was one area in which the Catholic hierarchy evidently decided that confession was not good for the soul. The Church got off the hook some months later when Italy's Supreme Court nullified the warrant on the grounds that it violated the 1929 Lateran Pact under which Mussolini had agreed to respect the territorial autonomy of the Vatican as a state. Marcinkus, who once observed: 'You can't run the Church on Hail Marys', kept silent about what really happened until his dying day. But one Mafia expert, Umberto Santino of the Sicilian Centre for Documentation, afterwards went so far as to say: 'The Vatican financial system has been the protagonist, not the victim, of the criminalization of the [Italian] economy.' That may have overstated the case but the shadow of shame which fell across the Vatican Bank has never fully lifted since.

* * *

The bank more or less kept its nose clean after the Marcinkus era, according to the leading expert on Vatican finances, Cambridge academic John Pollard, author of *Money and the Rise of the Modern Papacy: Financing the Vatican, 1850–1950*. 'The heavy Mafia-related activities took place in the 1970s and 80s, though I suspect that some money laundering may have gone on since then,' he said.

He was not the only one to think that. After the terrorist attacks of 11 September 2001 the world's financial authorities began to crack down on money-laundering, which had ceased to be seen as a merely criminal matter and had become an issue of national security. The fear was that it disguised the financing of terrorism. The 2009 Euro crisis intensified the scrutiny to which it was subjected globally. International authorities steadily turned the screw on off-shore havens that failed to comply with the new standards. The Vatican Bank, with 25 per cent of its business done in cash and so much of its dealings conducted in the shadows, was a classic suspect. A major investigation by the *Financial Times* showed that officials in the European Union persuaded the Bank of Italy, then headed by Mario Draghi, later President of the European Central Bank, to launch a crackdown on the IOR.

It did not take long. Soon afterwards a routine Bank of Italy anti-money-laundering investigation at a UniCredit Bank branch, just down the road from the Vatican, found payment slips from unnamed holders of the Vatican Bank. But when the authorities asked IOR officials to identify the senders of the money they were told: 'Our laws don't require us to tell you.' The Vatican was a natural tax haven. It was an off-shore bank in the middle of Rome which Italians could enter merely by waiting for the traffic lights to change from red to green. In line with the Catholic Church's instinctive aversion to transparency the bank authorities adamantly refused to cooperate.

So the Bank of Italy switched its pressure to the 40 commercial banks – known as 'correspondent banks' – around the world through which the IOR moved billions of euros a year. Investigators discovered funds were being transferred from an IOR account at the Rome branch of Credito Artigiano to another IOR account with the Banca del Fucino. The Vatican Bank had failed to furnish information on the origin or destination of the funds, as Italian law required. So Italy's financial police seized €23m from two IOR accounts.

Other banks, under pressure from regulators to provide information, asked more and more questions about IOR transactions. The 112 staff at the Vatican Bank, mainly Italians, couldn't or wouldn't answer them. In March 2012 American bankers forced the IOR to close the account it held with the US bank JP Morgan. The IOR had moved €1.5 billion through that one account in the previous 18 months. In July the Council of Europe's anti-money-laundering body, Moneyval, announced the Vatican Bank was non-compliant on 7 of its 16 core standards. 'Bank officials proclaimed that it had passed on 9 of the 16,' said Markus Wieser, 'but the situation was clear.'

The international bankers tightened the screw. The Bank of Italy forced all banks in Italy to close their IOR accounts. The crunch came when the German banking giant Deutsche Bank acted. Its Italian subsidiary managed the Vatican City State's 80 cash machines and credit card terminals. On 1 January 2013 Deutsche Bank closed them all down. With tourists only able to pay in cash, the Vatican lost €40,000 a day. The Vatican Bank was on the brink of total collapse.

The world did not know that. In any case its attention was soon elsewhere. Just a month later Pope Benedict XVI dramatically announced that he was to become the first pope to resign for over 500 years. He was, he said, 'no longer physically, psychologically, and spiritually capable of handling the duties of office'. The turmoil at the Vatican Bank – along with the dysfunctional nature of the Vatican bureaucracy known as the Curia, which had been laid bare in the Vatileaks court case – was high on the list of burdens Benedict felt he was no longer able to carry.

His resignation wrong-footed those in the Curia and the Bank who had been taking advantage of the old pope's frailty and of his earlier inclination to turn his back on such matters in favour of theology. Benedict had been aware of the problems; he had just not known how to handle them. But he had tried. Three years earlier, on the last day of 2010, he had created the Autorità di Informazione Finanziaria (AIF) as a regulator to be a watchdog over Vatican finances. It was Benedict who had invited Moneyval into the Vatican to report on its accounting procedures. And he had appointed a conservative banker, Ettore Gotti Tedeschi, a member of Opus Dei, to take over the presidency of the bank in 2009. At the time it was hailed as the dawn of a new day in Vatican finances.

It had not been enough. When Moneyval arrived it found the AIF lacked legal powers to demand access to the books of various Vatican bodies. Gotti

Tedeschi had arrived demanding greater transparency in the bank but he was regarded with suspicion by some of the council of cardinals who supervised the Vatican Bank. He could not devote himself to the job full-time; he was only in the office two days a week. He was eventually out-manoeuvred by those in the Vatican who wanted no change. They even pushed through a law in January 2012 removing the independence of the AIF watchdog, forcing it to report to the Secretary of State, Cardinal Bertone. Bertone became so powerful as Benedict's prime minister that insiders called him the 'Deputy Pope'. Moneyval declared this 'a step backwards'. Gotti Tedeschi revealed in 2015 – speaking out for the first time since his sacking, in an article for the UK weekly the *Catholic Herald* – that at this point the international banking system began refusing to work with the Vatican Bank altogether. After three years of power struggles those cardinals on the IOR's supervisory body who had all along resisted change passed a motion of no confidence in Gotti Tedeschi. He was fired two months later in March. Pope Benedict declared himself 'very surprised' according to an interview later given by papal secretary Gänswein. But Benedict XVI was not the man making the decisions.

Curial conservatives had done everything they could to block reform. 'The old guard passed an amendment softening the provisions Pope Benedict had installed,' said Wieser. 'Everything took a step back.' But Benedict was not quite finished. After the announcement he was to quit, but before he actually stood down, the outgoing Pope appointed a new director of the Vatican Bank. Ernst von Freyberg was not an Italian. He was a German aristocrat and devout Catholic who organized pilgrimages to Lourdes – but he was also a mergers and acquisitions banker. Freyberg swiftly hired an American compliance and auditing firm, Promontory Financial Group, to review all the bank's accounts. It was not the only card Benedict had in his closing hand. He also appointed a new broom as head of the AIF. René Brülhart, a 40-year-old Swiss lawyer, had made his name tracking down the assets hidden by Saddam Hussein. He had then helped take Liechtenstein off the blacklist of countries which did not comply with banking standards. Once inside the Vatican the debonair lawyer – whose good looks swiftly earned him the nickname the Vatican's James Bond – swiftly set up a crisis management team. Its job was to review accounts across the Curia. It was told particularly to track money transfers to smoke out money-laundering scams.

'Such a danger exists everywhere where there are large numbers of cash transfers,' Brülhart told *Der Spiegel*. 'That's why it's so important to know where the money comes from and where it's going.' But the Swiss 007 found that he, too, faced stiff resistance from the office of the Vatican's Secretary of State and the man who had been the power behind the Benedict papacy, Cardinal Tarcisio Bertone.

Benedict's resignation changed all that.

* * *

Before a pope is elected the cardinals gather for several days to discuss what kind of leader the Church needs. It required someone with a very different skillset from the shy theologian Ratzinger, they decided this time. Cardinal after cardinal stood up and criticized Bertone for his poor management, inept diplomacy and inadequate supervision of the Vatican Bank. The new pope would have a strong mandate for reform.

The man the conclave chose was someone with a track record of tackling financial malpractice in the church. Jorge Mario Bergoglio, as Archbishop of Buenos Aires, had inherited his own banking scandal which ended in a collapsed bank with two bankers and a priest jailed. Bergoglio, as we saw in Chapter Five, had acted swiftly, decisively and transparently – on several levels at once. And that is exactly what, as Pope, he proceeded to do with the opaque finances of the Vatican and its scandal-tarnished bank.

* * *

Pope Francis was being disingenuous when he told the reporters on the plane back from Brazil that he had been planning to leave the Vatican finances for a year in order to deal first with more urgent matters. The new Pope had actually gone into action long before the Scarano scandal broke.

Within weeks of taking office Francis immediately set about tackling the problem of the Vatican Bank at three levels. First, he moved swiftly to curb obvious excesses. Second, he strengthened existing organizations and brought in no fewer than five firms of top-level management consultants to scrutinize every aspect of the Vatican operations. And third, on 24 June 2013, four days before Scarano was arrested, he set up a special Commission of Reference on the IOR (known in Vatican jargon as the CRIOR) with an invited group of outsiders to work out what should be done with the Vatican Bank. They were told to think the unthinkable – including whether the Vatican Bank should be simply shut down. A month later, in July, he set up a second group of expert outside financiers to look at the rest of the financial and economic portfolio of the Vatican State and the Holy See – the Commission of Reference on the Economic-Administrative Structure of the Holy See (COSEA). They too were told to begin with a blank sheet and decide what fundamental structural reforms were required in Rome. The clerical stranglehold on Vatican finances was being broken with this huge influx of lay people. So was the domination of the universal Church by Italians.

As in so much he did in the early days, the new Pope moved first on the symbolic level. Having chosen to take the name of the great saint of the under-privileged, Francis of Assisi, the pontiff who had once been called the Bishop of the Slums declared he wanted a 'poor church for the poor'. In a sermon at a Mass for bank staff he pointedly described their organization as 'necessary up to a certain point'. He ended the practice of the Pope giving special audiences to big donors. In speeches he attacked the 'idolatry of money', trickle-down economics and global tax evasion and commodity speculation that compromised ordinary people's access to food. 'St Paul did not have a bank account,' he noted.

But there was more to this wily Pope than symbolic gestures and rhetorical flourishes. One of his first moves on taking office was to strip the bank's five supervisory cardinals of their €25,000 annual stipend. When it became clear to him, some months later, that this clerical establishment was not up to the job, he removed four of the five men he had inherited from Pope Benedict – just 11 months into what were supposed to be five-year terms. Among those removed was the man who had run the Benedict bureaucracy, Cardinal Bertone. Another who went was Cardinal Domenico Calcagno, the head of the finance ministry APSA, under whose supervision Scarano had worked as a senior accountant. In their stead the Pope appointed cardinals from big dioceses with extensive experience of financial affairs – Thomas Christopher Collins from Toronto and Christoph Schönborn from Vienna. Another member was a close friend of the Pope's. Only one man survived from the existing board – Cardinal Jean-Louis Tauran, from France, who had previously been the Vatican's top diplomat and was the cardinal who had made the 'Habemus Papam' announcement from the Vatican balcony when Francis was elected. It was to be chaired by Cardinal Santos Abril y Castelló, who was well known to Bergoglio having served as nuncio in Buenos Aires. Other immediate action by the new Pope included strengthening and broadening the supervisory powers of the Vatican's financial watchdog and regulator, the AIF.

At the third level he decided upon a complete philosophical rethink. The two Commissions of Reference, CRIOR on the Vatican Bank, and COSEA on wider Vatican finances, were made up of outsiders who were told to act like blue-skies think-tanks. They were to work from first principles rather than beginning with existing structures.

* * *

For such a small state the Vatican has a financial set-up that is unduly complex. This is, in part, because it consists of two separate administrations – the Vatican and the Holy See.

The Vatican City State is the last remnant of what was once the powerful Papal States. It administers the 108-acre Vatican enclave within the city of Rome, running the highly profitable Vatican Museums and the 200-man security force known as the Swiss Guards – whose martinet chief, Colonel Daniel Rudolf Anrig, was fired by Pope Francis at the end of 2014 after being accused of a lack of compassion to his troops. The Vatican owns 18,000 works of art which would fetch billions if they ever went on the market but which in its books are valued at just one euro on the grounds that 'they belong to humanity'. The finances of the Vatican State, with its steady flow of tourists, are stable.

The Holy See runs the Catholic Church, overseeing the 40 ministerial departments of the Curia, operating 116 diplomatic missions around the world, organizing the Pope's overseas trips, and running the Vatican's radio station and daily newspaper. The finances of the Holy See are unpredictable. It has income from the money it invested after Mussolini paid it 1.75 million lira in compensation for Italy's confiscation of the Papal States, covering much of central Italy, 60 years earlier; low interest rates have reduced the annual yield on this to between €15m and €25m in recent years. It holds some very expensive property in Rome and elsewhere, but this produces comparatively little income since the 2,000 palaces and apartments are largely used to house clergy. So the annual donation of around €70m from the Vatican Bank to the Holy See has been a significant element in its finances, exceeded only by donations from the faithful around the world which the US business magazine *Fortune* estimated to top $85 million in 2013.

All this is controlled by the Administration of the Patrimony of the Apostolic See (APSA) in which the alleged fraudster Monsignor Scarano was a key figure until his arrest. According to a 2012 Moneyval report it has €680m on deposit with the Bank of England, the US Federal Reserve, the Deutsche Bundesbank, the Bank for International Settlements and others. Sacrano has told prosecutors it also has over €600m in more liquid assets. Its operations, and those of the Vatican's various other departments, are so opaque that at the end of 2014 the Pope's new money-man, Cardinal George Pell – of whom more later – announced that he had found 'hundreds of millions of euros...tucked away in particular sectional accounts [which] did not appear on the balance sheet'.

* * *

It did not take Pope Francis long after his election to see that this sprawling complex was beyond his control or even comprehension. This was despite the fact that he had demonstrated he was a canny financial manager when he was Archbishop of Buenos Aires. The new Pope soon realized, Pell told me, that 'the Vatican's financial systems had evolved in such a way that it was impossible for anyone to know accurately what was going on overall'.

Within weeks of his election Francis invited Peter Sutherland – chairman of Goldman Sachs International, the multinational investment bank, and a practising Catholic – to the Vatican to talk with his newly appointed cabinet, the Council of Cardinal Advisers (now known as the C9). The banker told the cardinals that a shift to transparency was essential if Rome was not to be isolated from the modern financial system.

How would that best be put into effect? Pope Francis decided to bring in two teams of external experts. For CRIOR, the commission to reform the Vatican Bank, he picked a team of five whose members were selected not so much on the basis of expertise in the subject-area, but rather because of their reputation for 'moral rectitude' and because Francis had personal confidence in them. To head it he chose an Italian, Cardinal Raffaele Farina, who had formerly been head of the Vatican Secret Archives. Another member was Cardinal Jean-Louis Tauran, the only cardinal on Pope Benedict's Vatican Bank supervisory body not purged by Francis in January 2014. The three other members were an Opus Dei prelate, Bishop Juan Ignacio Arrieta, and two Americans, Monsignor Peter Wells, the No. 3 in the Vatican foreign ministry, and Mary Ann Glendon, a Harvard law professor and a former US ambassador to the Holy See.

The commission was to bypass the Curia and report direct to Francis alone, indicating that the Pope intended to take a personal interest in the Vatican Bank rather than leave it to others to make decisions in his name. It was given powers to summon any documents it required and to interview any officials it desired. It could make spot-checks without notice and demand answers to its questions in the same way. Curia officials were told in a personal chirograph – signed in the Pope's own hand – that they could withhold nothing on grounds of confidentiality. The members were told by the Pope to 'trust with reluctance' and to 'verify deeply'. Whistle-blowers, the Pope let it be known, could approach the commission in complete confidence.

The following month, in July 2013, Pope Francis summoned a group of top Catholic moneymen from all round the world and handed them a brief to restructure the Vatican's wider finances. The group met just a few days after Francis returned from World Youth Day in Brazil. They gathered in a conference room on the first floor of the Casa Santa Marta where Francis now lived. The Pope, who had said the first time that he met the world's media that he wanted 'a poor Church for the poor', now confronted the paradox that to work for the poor he needed money. He knew, he told the group, speaking directly and plainly, that the Church's spiritual message would not be credible unless its finances were seen to be in order. The bankers and financiers included Joseph Zahra, a former chairman of the Bank of Valletta; Jean-Baptiste de Franssu, the former head of the European asset-management giant Invesco; Jochen Messemer, one of Germany's leading insurers; and George Yeo, the man who turned around the Singapore economy.

His approach was 'highly managerial', one of the group told *Fortune* business magazine. 'You are the experts,' the Pope said, 'and I trust you. Now I want solutions to these problems, and I want them as soon as possible.' With that Francis exited the room and left the financiers to work on the detail. 'In finances, he's not a micromanager but an inspirational leader,' said Zahra, who was appointed the review group's leader. The Pope's approach, like that of the CEO of any big corporate multinational company, is to set the strategic vision, then choose and motivate the right people to make it work.

The group became the Pope's second external advisory group, COSEA. Their brief was to look at the whole horizon of papal finances, outside the Vatican Bank. They began by hiring a raft of outside consultants to complement the work the US compliance company Promontory Financial Group was already doing inside the Vatican Bank. On their recommendation Pope Francis asked KPMG to bring the Holy See's wider accountancy systems up to international standards. Deloitte were hired to review management systems and to conduct audits, Ernst & Young to scrutinize the Holy See's property holdings, McKinsey & Co to reform its communications and Spencer Stuart to recruit top management talent from around the globe.

The work of the two reform think-tanks was to proceed in parallel.

* * *

Meanwhile things were moving apace inside the Vatican Bank. Four months after Francis became Pope the bank's new boss Ernst von Freyberg, who had been appointed by Pope Benedict just before he resigned, gave up his grand office. Its expensive leather furniture and fine oriental rugs were pushed to one side. Beneath its crystal chandeliers and heavy gilt-framed oil paintings, rows of desks were crammed in. At each place three individual computer terminals were set up for the team who were taking over.

This was the work of Elizabeth McCaul, the partner-in-charge of the New York office of Promontory Financial Group, the US financial consultancy which sells itself as one of the world's leading specialists in 'strategy, risk management and regulatory compliance'. McCaul had flown in 25 regulatory specialists from the United States. They had been given six months to trawl through every single one of the Vatican Bank's 19,000 accounts.

'It has been a huge cleaning effort,' the bank's new communications man, Markus Wieser, told me as we toured the high-security building. The team began by sorting through computer scans of the passports of every account holder, which were painstakingly cross-checked against the names and faces of bank records. 'The activities were designed to make this place compliant with Vatican law and align Vatican law to international standards.'

The Promontory specialists worked in seven work streams, checking the account of each and every customer to ascertain whether all the required information was there. They set up new standard rules. They established an IT system to automate the rules by running an algorithm over every transaction in each account to see whether it fitted the usual profile of the customer. They trained the bank's full-time Italian employees to operate the new system. Later they did the same with the accounts of APSA, Monsignor Scarano's old stamping ground, the Administration of the Patrimony of the Apostolic See.

The Promontory team started with the highest-risk accounts and worked their way down. What they found was embarrassing for the Italian bankers who had previously been in charge. The US banking experts found poor cash-flow checks, inadequate documentation, ignorance about correct due diligence procedures and a complex system of proxies which clouded who really controlled many accounts. When senior IOR officials were asked by Promontory staff how – amid such chaos – they answered to the regulator, they replied: 'We answer to God.' Well now, they were told, you will answer to more earthly authorities.

The Americans worked through 16,900 accounts before they returned to the US, leaving two thousand in the final low-risk group – 'close to zero risk', according to Wieser – which were checked by the retrained IOR employees. Within six months 3,300 accounts were shut down. 'The vast majority were dormant accounts with a negligible balance,' said Wieser. 'Or were held by individuals no longer eligible to hold an account under the new rules introduced by Promontory. But some have been frozen in the course of regulatory or criminal proceedings.' The team found 200 serious irregularities. Each of those cases, under a new system introduced by Promontory, triggered a 'suspicious transaction' report which was sent to the bank's regulator, the Autorità di Informazione Finanziaria.

One case Promontory referred to the regulator, Markus Wieser revealed, was an investment the Vatican Bank made, against the advice of its staff and supervisory board, on the insistence of Pope Benedict's No. 2, Cardinal Bertone. In 2012 the IOR invested €15m in Lux Vide, an Italian film and television company that made films about popes and produced a series about a bike-riding priest who helped police solve rural crimes. The company was founded by a friend of Bertone, a Catholic with links to Opus Dei, Ettore Bernabei. In May 2014 the Vatican spokesman Father Federico Lombardi denied that the 79-year-old cardinal was under investigation by Vatican magistrates. But, according to Wieser, a 'suspicious transaction' report on the case has been made by Promontory and the case remains with the AIF. The watchdog could yet refer Bertone to the Vatican prosecutor.

The circumstances surrounding the deal were undoubtedly shadowy. The board of the IOR refused to make the investment when Bertone first asked. But, when Gotti Tedeschi was fired as director of the bank, the Vatican's second most powerful man proposed it again. 'The message was: the boss wants this,' a Vatican source revealed. The boss was Bertone. This time the transaction was approved. The IOR eventually wrote off the money – but a month later, in August 2013, Pope Francis sacked Bertone from his post as Secretary of State. Francis then reconfigured the job so that Bertone's successor in the post would have no direct power over Vatican finances.

Few in Rome expected the Bertone case to advance to the Vatican prosecutor. The cardinal continued to insist that the investment in the film company was an appropriate one. But the fact that a pope's former second-in-command was under the scrutiny of the regulator was a measure of how far the Francis revolution had advanced.

At the end of 2014 the Vatican regulator reported that it had examined 200 'suspicious transactions'. In some cases, said Wieser, the AIF 'began liaising with the appropriate foreign authorities'. But five were reported to the Vatican prosecutor, the office of the Promoter of Justice. The most high profile of these, in December 2014, were the cases of two former Vatican Bank managers who were charged with embezzlement and €16m in their accounts was frozen as part of an investigation into the sale of Vatican properties. A former president of the IOR, Angelo Caloia, and a former director general, Lelio Scaletti, were accused, with a lawyer, of embezzling money while managing the sale of 29 buildings sold by the Vatican bank to mainly Italian buyers between 2001 and 2008. Such prosecutions at the very top were a measure of how deeply the Francis reforms were biting.

* * *

Monsignor Cinquecento was no longer in jail. His health had deteriorated so, after several weeks, he had been released from the overcrowded Regina Cæli prison and was put under house arrest. Prosecutors in Rome charged him with corruption. Their counterparts in Salerno charged him with money-laundering. As the investigations into him continued they threw up more and more revealing detail about both the Vatican Bank and the Amministrazione del Patrimonio della Sede Apostolica (APSA) which oversaw the rest of the Roman curial economy.

It turned out that, although the suspicions of the police in Salerno had been aroused by the theft of €6m-worth of his art works, the police in Rome had had their eye on him for a little longer. Officers of the Guardia di Finanza, who police financial crime in Italy, had received an anonymous note many months earlier. It had asked: 'How could this man, in just a few years, buy a whole floor of a prestigious building in Salerno's city centre, worth at least $4 million?'

The tax police began to dig into Monsignor Scarano's bank accounts, property deals and investments. The luxury 700-metre seaside pad in Salerno was not the only property the high-living cleric owned. They discovered he was also part-owner of three Salerno property companies. They began monitoring all his bank transactions. But it was when they started wiretapping his phone that they learned of the plot to smuggle €20m by private plane across the border from Switzerland – and began to suspect he was conniving to whitewash money for businessmen from Mafia havens in the Naples region.

Scarano, who was aged 61, had worked in APSA for 22 years. He had been a late entrant to the priesthood and was ordained only at the age of 35 after a career in banking. He had worked as an executive for several Italian banks and for Deutsche Bank before becoming a priest. From his childhood he had known members of the D'Amico family, whose patriarch Antonio D'Amico had founded a Salerno shipping company which grew to own a large fleet of oil tankers and an empire with offices in Rome, Genoa, Monte Carlo, Dublin, London, Singapore, Mumbai, Vancouver, New York and Tokyo. Through the family the young bank executive became acquainted with D'Amico's wealthy friends: bankers, entrepreneurs and members of the nobility. Scarano built up high-society friends and maintained the relationships after he became a priest and went to work in the Vatican finance offices. What the court documents compiled by the investigating magistrates showed was that over nine years members of the D'Amico family transferred more than €5 million via off-shore companies into Scarano's accounts at the Vatican Bank: his personal one and the one he called 'account for the elderly'. All the transfers were labelled donations.

What finally led to Scarano's downfall was a deal involving a financial broker from Pompeii named Giovanni Carenzio, who was running an investment scheme which purported to offer investors returns of up to 20 per cent in just three months. Spanish investigators alleged this was Ponzi fraud. Whatever the truth of that, the wiretaps on Scarano's phone recorded a call in which he referred to a suspicious transaction he had made with two of the D'Amico family. Scarano asked Carenzio to keep the D'Amico family name out of any investigation by the Spanish prosecutors. The men discussed how to get the €22 million which the D'Amicos had invested with Carenzio back from Switzerland. All this was admitted by Scarano's lawyers but they claimed he was merely trying to help his friends recover their money as an act of generosity.

A secret meeting was set up by Scarano with Carenzio with the help of another friend, Giovanni Zito, who was a member of the Italian secret service. But, when Zito went to Switzerland to get the money, Carenzio and the cash never materialized. The Italian police, however, did.

Another deal emerged which showed how Scarano had been manipulating the Vatican system. According to papers filed with the Italian court, Scarano allegedly withdrew 555,248 euros from his Vatican account in cash in 2009 and carried it across the road into Italy. But he knew he could not deposit it in an Italian bank without arousing suspicion. So he selected 56 high-society friends and gave them euros in cash; in return they gave him a cheque or made an electronic transfer for the same amount, which ranged from 2,000 to 20,000 euros. When Scarano paid them into his Italian bank account he labelled the payments as 'donations'. But he used the money to pay off the mortgage on his Salerno apartment. Scarano, through his lawyer, admitted all this, but said he intended to sell the luxury flat to raise the money to buy a home for the terminally ill.

The scandal-ridden monsignor maintained this line when an enterprising reporter for the *New York Times*, Davide Casati, managed to secure an interview with him while he was under house arrest – before the court banned him contact with the media. 'I spent my whole life doing good deeds,' Scarano told him in his vast apartment furnished with white and gold Baroque furniture and filled with decorative china and hundreds of books. 'Sometimes I took advantage of the rich to help the poor – I behaved somewhat like Robin Hood...Sometimes I told some lies, too,' he continued. 'But what mattered to me was to help someone.' And he concluded: 'I am no saint, no. I am a sinner, like everyone else. I trusted the wrong people. I have been stupid. I made a mistake. That's it.'

The Vatican Bank was happy to help catalogue Scarano's mistakes. In previous eras the Vatican would have closed ranks at the levelling of accusations against one of its number. It would have refused to help the police. No longer.

'As soon as Freyberg learned about it he got Promontory to compile a 90-page document tracking Scarano's every transaction from 2003 to 2013,' revealed Wieser. The information was sent to the police via the AIF. The Vatican was at last giving evidence instead of hiding it. 'It was the first time the Vatican had collaborated with the Italian authorities,' said Wieser. 'This was a game changer.'

A few days after Scarano's arrest the director of the Vatican Bank, Paolo Cipriani, and his deputy, Massimo Tulli, resigned. Promontory officials took over their posts. And they created a new job – that of Chief Risk Officer.

* * *

Not everyone was happy with the changes the new Pope was introducing. To keep the Vatican Bank on its toes the Pope did not ease the pressure for reform. Indeed he increased it. Monsignor Battista Ricca was a priest he had come to trust. Ricca was a former papal diplomat but he was back in Rome and had been given the job of running the Casa Santa Marta where the Pope had made his home. But previously he had run the Domus Internationalis Paulus Sixtus, the clerical guest house in Rome where Bergoglio used to stay when he was a cardinal – the one to which he famously went back to pay the bill on his first day as Pope. Francis liked Ricca and placed great confidence in him. The director of the Vatican guest house seemed just the man for Francis to have as his eyes and ears inside the Vatican Bank. On 15 June, two weeks before the Scarano scandal broke – and when Bertone still presided over the IOR's board of supervisors – Pope Francis named Monsignor Battista Ricca as the new Prelate of the IOR, giving him authority to access all documents. Nominally the job was to be the link between Bertone's board and the Vatican Bank's managers. But it was clear that Ricca's real job was to keep the Pope alive to what was going on.

Just a month after Ricca's appointment the respected Vatican writer Sandro Magister – who has particularly good contacts among conservatives in the Vatican – published a story in the weekly news magazine *l'Espresso* claiming that Ricca had been involved in homosexual affairs while serving as a papal diplomat in Uruguay a decade before. It claimed that Ricca had had an affair with a male captain in the Swiss army on an earlier posting to Berne and had taken his lover with him when he was sent to Uruguay. That was not all. Lurid headlines followed: 'Catholic bishop in charge of cleaning up Vatican finances "got stuck in a lift with a rent boy"', read the heading over a story that Ricca had once been trapped in a lift and when firemen rescued him they found a young man in the elevator with him. On another occasion in the same year, 2001, the priest was reportedly beaten up in a gay bar and had to call for help, arriving back at the Vatican embassy with bruises to his face. The Vatican denied the claims. But it was widely assumed that Ricca would have to resign.

Indeed, it later emerged, Ricca did submit his resignation to the Pope three days before Francis left Rome for World Youth Day on 23 July 2013. The Pope refused to accept it. He saw the leaks behind the story as a deliberate attempt by conservatives to undermine his reform programme for the Vatican Bank by trying to discredit one of his key reformers. On the plane on the way back to Rome a journalist asked the pontiff about the Ricca story and about a meeting a month earlier at which Francis had confirmed to nuns and priests from Latin America that there was indeed a 'gay lobby' or clique in the Vatican and a 'current of corruption' within the Roman Curia.

This was the context in which Pope Francis made what was to become the totemic phrase of the early part of his papacy: 'Who am I to judge?' It came after the Pope made a distinction between a sin and a crime:

> People search for 'sins from youth', for example, and then publish them. They are not crimes, right? Crimes are something different: the abuse of minors is a crime ... But if a person, whether it be a lay person, a priest or a religious sister, commits a sin and then converts, the Lord forgives ... When we confess our sins and we truly say, 'I have sinned in this', the Lord forgets, and so we have no right not to forget, because otherwise we would run the risk of the Lord not forgetting our sins ...
>
> I believe that when you are dealing with such a person, you must distinguish between the fact of a person being gay and the fact of someone forming a lobby, because not all lobbies are good. This one is not good. If someone is gay and is searching for the Lord and has good will, then who am I to judge him?

The Pope was not talking only of Ricca; subsequent signals from the Vatican made that clear. But Ricca was the trigger for the remark and the indication of where Francis's sympathies lay. Ricca remained in his job at the Vatican Bank and reform there continued. Pope Francis ordered it to publish an annual report, which it did in October 2013 for the first time in its 125-year history. The IOR president Ernst von Freyberg described the 100-page report as an attempt to meet the commitment to transparency that Catholics around the world 'rightly expect'. The revolution continued. Four months later, in January 2014, Pope Francis removed the old hidebound president of the AIF, Cardinal Attilio Nicora, and replaced him with Bishop Giorgio Corbellini, who had once worked alongside the only serious Vatican reformer from the Benedict era – Archbishop Carlo Maria Viganò, who had been 'promoted' by his enemies to be papal ambassador in Washington to end his rigorous anti-corruption campaign in Rome.

* * *

Perhaps the most dramatic example of Francis's determination to root out obstacles to change came in June 2014 when, in one swoop, he dismissed all five members of the supervisory board of the regulatory watchdog, the AIF. The drastic move came after a year of in-fighting between the establishment reactionaries and the AIF's modernizing director, René Brülhart. The Swiss anti-money-laundering expert had tried repeatedly to implement the kind of restructuring he had put in place when he was head of the financial intelligence unit in Liechtenstein. But he found his agenda for change continually frustrated by resistance from a Vatican old boys' network. Eventually he complained direct to the Pope, who acted decisively. 'It had become clear the old guard were being wilfully obstructive to Brülhart,' one Vatican insider told me. 'So the Pope swept them aside.' The five *ancien régime* Italian bankers who were in post were replaced by an international team of financial experts, including a Switzerland-based philanthropist Marc Odendall; the man who had turned around the economy in Singapore, Joseph Yuvaraj Pillay; and a former counter-terrorism adviser to President George W. Bush, Juan Zarate, who was perhaps the world's leading expert on how to fight financial crime.

But Pope Francis was not finished with the Vatican Bank. A month after he sacked the AIF board he made another big change at the IOR. He removed the man at the top. Out went Ernst von Freyberg, the German banker appointed by Pope Benedict to clean up the bank. In came Jean-Baptiste de Franssu, a member of Francis's top financial advisory group, COSEA. Publicly it was announced that there was to be a smooth handover because Freyberg wanted to return to his family shipping business. The Pope wanted a full-time president for the IOR, the press was told, and Freyberg wanted to work only part-time.

There was more to it than that. What had become clear was that Francis wanted reform to move more quickly and more radically than Freyberg felt comfortable with. There had been tensions between the banker and Monsignor Battista Ricca, the Pope's eyes and ears inside the IOR. The cleric felt that Freyberg had not kept him sufficiently informed about some operations at the bank. Freyberg wanted to clean up the existing operation at the IOR but did not want to change the bank's structure. The Pope disagreed.

The timing of these big changes, at both the bank and the regulator, was significant. Francis's third level of reforms were kicking in. The two blue-skies review bodies he had put in place to rethink papal finances, CRIOR and COSEA, had worked swiftly. It was acting on their reports that Francis had changed those at the top of both bodies after concluding they were incapable of implementing what his two reform commissions were proposing.

The commission on the Vatican Bank had reported first, in April. It had recommended that the IOR should not be abolished. Rather it should continue but with a role restricted to current accounts for Vatican employees, 147 religious orders and other approved Catholic institutions. All accounts held by foreign embassies accredited to the Holy See would close, a principle made more pressing by concerns about large cash deposits and withdrawals by diplomats from Iran. The IOR should be stripped of its function of managing investments and told to concentrate on transferring funds to dioceses, religious orders and missionary outposts around the world. Its investment activities would transfer to a new body, Vatican Asset Management. The Pope accepted the plan. And the CRIOR committee was disbanded a month later.

The work of the commission on the wider Vatican economy, COSEA, was more complex. The various external consultancy firms it had put in place were still active. It made a raft of recommendations but it was clear that its work was not complete and it still had much more to do. Even so, the thinking it had done allowed the Pope to put in place an initial radical restructure. In July 2014 Pope Francis announced the creation of a new over-arching finance ministry, the Secretariat for the Economy, which would have the same status as the Secretariat of State – underscoring the fact that the department which used to be the centre of power in the Vatican had been stripped of its control of the papal finances. The new super-finance ministry would be headed by Cardinal George Pell, who was a doctrinal conservative but who had been vehemently critical of the dysfunctional Roman Curia in the past. Pell was a member of the Pope's new Council of Cardinal Advisers, the C9. He was a tough Australian who had knocked the finances of the diocese of Sydney into shape during his time as archbishop there. A Council for the Economy – made up of eight cardinals and seven lay members, five of them members of COSEA – would oversee Pell. The office of Secretary of State, formerly held by Cardinal Bertone, was stripped of its financial power. APSA was to confine itself to its original function of managing the Vatican's property, purchasing and personnel portfolio, and would hence-forth do so as part of the Secretariat for the Economy under the eagle eye of Pell. The new Vatican Asset Management body would take over all the investments previously controlled by the Vatican Bank and APSA. 'The aspiration is that Vatican Assent Management will become a major international player,' said Markus Wieser. 'At present both the Vatican Bank and APSA involve themselves in investing in both government bonds and money market accounts. The new body will end duplication and also bring in a more professional approach.'

It was to accommodate all this that the incorrigible recidivists of the Vatican establishment had been so comprehensively sent packing by the Pope.

* * *

It was not hard to see why Pope Francis chose Australia's Cardinal George Pell to be the first-ever prefect of the newly created Secretariat for the Economy of the Holy See with the job of reordering the way money is spent and managed in the various offices of the Vatican. The 73-year-old cardinal had left assets of nearly 1.2 billion Australian dollars in the archdiocese of Sydney after his 12 years of leadership there. And despite payments related to lawsuits over clergy sex abuse, the archdiocese showed a 9.1 million Australian dollar surplus during Pell's last full year there. It was not a one-off. Before his elevation to Sydney in 2001, where he became a cardinal, he had headed the much larger archdiocese of Melbourne for four years and he had balanced the books there, earning a reputation for effective fiscal management which had not gone unnoticed in Rome.

There was another reason for choosing Pell. Francis was determined to eradicate the Italian dominance over the central administration of the Catholic Church. Previous attempts at reform had always foundered because of a culture of self-serving petty corruption and nepotism within the Curia. 'It's hard to overstate how deep-rooted it is,' one non-Italian curial official told me. 'Jobs are for life, and are passed on from father to son. In so many areas they do not look for the best person for the job; they look for somebody's relative who could be trusted – an attitude which is very much a hangover from a courtly mentality. In my department there are three people whose job it is to answer the door, even though we often don't get a visitor more than once every couple of days. That's replicated throughout the Curia. What starts with the doorman goes all the way up. It's been ingrained, not just for generations but for centuries.' Indeed the very word nepotism comes from the Italian for nephew from the dubious practice of popes in previous times appointing their nephews to be cardinals.

There was more to this than anecdotal prejudice. Italy was only 69th in the list of least corrupt nations in the 2014 Transparency International Corruption Perceptions Index – worse than some African and Middle Eastern countries. Though there are many 'truly holy people', in the Roman Curia, Pope Francis has admitted, there is also 'a current of corruption' which featured in the 300-page report written by three senior cardinals for Pope Benedict XVI after the Vatileaks revelations.

'Half of the trouble of the Vatican Bank is that it is in Italy and largely staffed by Italians, clerical and lay,' said Professor Pollard, the leading authority on Vatican finance. 'It is thus inevitably affected by Italian cultures of nepotism and cronyism. I fear that Scarano is the tip of the iceberg. People talk about the "gay lobby". The real lobby is the Italian lobby.'

One of the most striking of Francis's reforms has been his conscious attempt to replace this with an Anglo-Saxon model of business practice. Almost all the consultants he brought in were rooted in US business models. English replaced Italian as the language of finance in the Vatican. Cardinal Pell brought in other beady-eyed antipodeans with him. He set up a new project management office to do the detailed financial work for him; as its head he hired Danny Casey, his former business manager from Sydney. Monsignor Brian Ferme, the Secretary of the new Council for the Economy to which Pell was answerable, was also an Australian, who had trained in the UK and taught in the US. Many others were English-speaking; Pell's No. 2, Monsignor Alfred Xuereb, a cleric, and Joseph Zahra, the head of the Pope's financial reform think-tank, COSEA, were both from Malta where English is one of two official languages and the business *lingua franca*. René Brülhart, the head of the Financial Information Authority, invariably answered in English when questioned in Italian at press conferences. Most of the members of the AIF's supervisory board, of COSEA, and of the new Council for the Economy were English-speakers.

Many Italian veterans were distinctly unhappy at this Anglophone takeover. Reports of opposition within the Curia were common. Cardinal Pell appeared untroubled by the phenomenon. 'Certainly there is some [resistance],' he told me over breakfast at his base in the Domus Australia in the centre of Rome. 'But surprisingly little in comparison with what you might have been led to expect. There are small elements – some who just don't like change, some who feel their special interests should be protected, and some who might have been keen in the past to exploit loopholes for undesirable purposes. But most people are cooperating. The great majority of the Italian people working there are very fine people and most of them recognized that changes needed to be made.' He tried to play down the Anglo-Saxon emphasis in the new regime. It was not anti-Italian, he insisted; rather, he maintained, 'we're internationalizing', adding 'we shouldn't insert too many Anglos into the process so it doesn't become a complication'.

The Italian diehards were finding other ways of fighting back. There were dirty tricks, with facts and fictions leaked to the Italian press. They were not so lurid as they had been in the Ricca affair but stories appeared with headlines like 'The dark side of Cardinal Pell', cataloguing Pell's less than happy record on handling sex abuse cases back in Australia – where he provoked outrage after claiming that the Catholic Church should be no more responsible for the abuse of children than a trucking company is for a driver who picks up and molests a woman while on the job. There were no new facts in the articles, which led commentators to suggest that the details, dating back to 1996, had been dug up by those whose interests were threatened by reform. Later, the Italian curial old guard, began to leak stories suggesting that Pell was as secretive and prone to cronyism as those he was trying to replace. After that they leaked inaccurate accounts claiming Pell had over-spent on the fittings of his new office – and made out that a business-class seat for a tall 73-year-old man on the 21-hour flight from Australia to Rome was some kind of abusive luxury. Pell shrugged his shoulders when I asked him about it. 'That's part of the game,' he said. 'It doesn't greatly cause me concern.'

* * *

Pope Francis was careful not to place too much power in one man's hands. Though Pell had been given unprecedented reach over all Vatican finances he has been overseen by a Council for the Economy, chaired by another of the Pope's trusted C9 cabinet, Cardinal Reinhard Marx, the Archbishop of Munich. The council sets the policy which Pell is mandated to implement. 'It's a separation of powers,' Pell said, 'designed so there will be no unique focus of power.' Nor is it exclusively clerical. 'Half the members are lay people who have an equal vote with the cardinals.' It is the only decision-making body in the Vatican where cardinals and laity enjoy full parity as voting members. The experts do not just bring technical know-how; they bring a lay perspective into senior church governance – an area which was unhealthily dominated by clerics. A third element in this system of checks and balances will be an auditor general who will be a non-cleric and who will have powers to go 'anywhere and everywhere' in the Vatican to certify that the entire financial system is operating correctly. Libero Milone, a former chairman and CEO of the global auditing firm Deloitte in Italy was appointed in June 2015. He will report direct to the Pope and will conduct spot-checks as well as annual audits. A new supervisory board was planned for APSA. And all Vatican departments, for the first time in their history, were told they must produce quarterly reports comparing actual spending to budgeted expenditure – as was standard in the departments of every big company in the business world.

Not everyone was impressed with the detail of the new system. John Pollard, whose research on Vatican finances goes to the nineteenth century and beyond, said: 'When you stand back, for such a very small bank and a very small state, these mechanisms of regulation seemed very heavy-handed.' The Vatican, he added, has always been 'an over-duplicating organism'.

But there was no doubting the ambition of Pope Francis's intent. There was an irony in that. The man who began his pontifical ministry demanding 'a poor church for the poor' responded to that challenge by setting up Vatican Asset Management. But anyone acquainted with Bergoglio's track record from his time in Buenos Aires would recognize in this the combination of an audacious prioritizing of the poor and a canny understanding of the politics of how change is achieved in this world.

Francis told his financier advisers at their first meeting in July 2013 that 'sound financial management was a pillar of his greatest mission: aiding the poor and underprivileged'. What that meant, said Cardinal Pell was: 'The Pope wants to maximize the amount of money coming in so that it could be spent on the poor and the works of the Church. Because we're trying to help people is no reason why we should be inefficient, or not transparent, or open to being robbed.' A church for the poor should not be poorly managed, he insisted.

The idea of Vatican Asset Management was a strategy that made sense, too, to those well versed in the mechanics of the money markets. Martin Hall – an asset-management expert who has worked with Morgan Grenfell, Norwich Union, Morley Fund Management, Fidelity Investments and AXA – said: 'Concentrating all asset management in one place will give the Vatican more buying power and will provide more control with lower costs.' The reforms would also act, said Hall, as 'a kite-marking exercise, a rebranding and ring-fencing to tell the world that they have learned the lessons of the past. It gives them a better cleanliness rating in the outside world.' But the shift would have practical benefits too. 'It may enable them to hire their own fund managers and bring them in-house, which will again increase control.'

What Pope Francis wants next, said Cardinal Pell, is for that control to be exercised by choosing investments which are ethical. 'Initially we might have about €8 billion invested,' he said, 'some of it from the IOR and some from APSA.' But Pell's plan is that Vatican Asset Management could become a market leader in ethical investment. He hopes it will attract money from across the world and raise millions in annual fees for Pope Francis's work among the poor. 'There will be a variety of options from which investors can choose,' Pell told me. 'There will be different levels of risk according to what they want within their portfolio but all the options will be ethical.' So how will the Vatican define ethical? 'We haven't spelled it out fully yet,' he admitted, 'but we will have an ethical investment policy in place within 12 months.'

Again the world of money sees this as eminently practicable. 'The bigger their portfolio the more they will be able to dictate better terms for ethical investment,' said Martin Hall, a former Bank of England economist now with Leadenhall Consulting. 'The more money you have the more you can dictate terms rather than just taking what's on offer in the market.'

There is even talk of a Sovereign Wealth Fund. The Vatican needs to find ways of securing its pension pot for the medium to long term. Its pension plan guarantees 80 per cent of final salaries to staff who retire after 40 years of service. Pope Francis sees it as a matter of social justice that the Vatican should provide its 1,750 existing pensioners, and staff who are yet to retire, with pensions better than those in Italy generally. 'We have had a good look at what Singapore have done with their Sovereign Wealth Fund,' said Pell. 'Technically this is separate from pensions but it's very likely the two will come together or cooperate.' Reports have suggested that the Vatican pension fund is short by 'a few hundred million dollars' but Pell sounded sanguine. 'Like everybody else the Vatican lost money in 2008 [in the global financial crisis]. But there is no black hole. We've already announced we're OK for the next 10 to 15 years but we've got to take substantial steps to make sure we're secure after that. Everybody's pension at the moment is secure. There's no risk to that. But there will need to be a substantial injection of funds for the middle and longer term. For the future, pensions investments won't be foolishly conservative but they will be risk-averse.'

* * *

The new system was not to be wrinkle-free. Individual departments within the Curia had, over the decades, grown used to operating like independent fiefdoms. They resisted Pell's attempts to bring them under control. At the end of 2014 he announced in an article written for the *Catholic Herald* that he and his fellow reformers had 'discovered hundreds of millions of euros...tucked away in particular sectional accounts which did not appear on the balance sheet'. Officials in other departments resented the announcement. They thought Pell was inviting the world to infer that there was something 'illegal, illicit or poorly administered' about the funds when they were just being kept separately as they had been for decades. They leaked documents to the Jesuit magazine *America*, which showed that the funds had never been 'lost' and that information on them had been made available to the Pope's reform commission

COSEA before Pell's Secretariat for the Economy had even been established. Much of the money was a reserve fund established by Pope Paul VI and held in the Secretariat of State to be used for extraordinary expenditures or shortfalls. The Italians clearly resented what they saw as Pell's insinuation that they had been fiddling the books.

Pell responded with a counter-blast at the meeting of the Pope's Council of Cardinal Advisers in February 2015 when he told Francis and his fellow members of the C9 that he had discovered that the Vatican actually had more than $1.5 billion in assets it didn't previously know it possessed. There were around $500 million in various accounts which had been deliberately excluded from an overall 2013 balance sheet, he said in a meeting behind closed doors, as well as $1 billion in assets that should have been included in that report but were not. But the discrepancies were not the result of illegal activity, he said, so much as an over-compartmentalized and unwieldy reporting system. He might, he said, yet find more. On top of that the Vatican's real estate holdings might well be undervalued by a factor of four, meaning that the overall financial health of the Vatican was considerably better than was previously believed. 'It's been muddled,' Pell said afterwards, 'there's been inadequate information, but we're far from broke.' There is, however, some shortfall in Vatican pensions to address in the medium to long term. That could be $1 billion short.

Opposition from other departments – including the other most powerful ministry, the Secretariat of State, the base of papal diplomacy – was diminishing, Pell told the Pope's cabinet. Those who imagined that Pope Francis's reforms would never actually be put into operation – and that 'after some huffing and puffing the world would return to way it was' – had had their hopes or illusions shattered. The change came after Pope Francis approved a 45-page manual to all Vatican departments which outlined the international standards of accounting and budgeting that the 200 Vatican departments and allied bodies answerable to Pell had to follow from the start of 2015. 'The penny dropped after that,' Pell said. 'People realized the game has changed.'

But the resistance had not evaporated entirely, whatever Pell believed. Cardinal Wilfrid Fox Napier of South Africa, one of the cardinals on the Council for the Economy to which Pell reports, tweeted after the same meeting: 'Council for the Economy Meeting yesterday was rather tense, reflecting that we've reached a decisive stage in setting up checks and balances for better management of Vatican finances. Clearly Council is grasping the nettle and taking charge of the reform issues entrusted to it!' The C9 was running into resistance, he said, from some departments which had earlier enjoyed financial autonomy and whose senior staff were now shocked at having to account for their spending. The

fightback was led by Cardinal Francesco Coccopalmerio, the president of the
Pontifical Council for Legislative Texts, whose office has the job of scrutinizing
the statutes of Pell's new Secretariat for the Economy. He proposed constraints to
curb Pell's power and even to scrap English as a working language in the finance
departments, to return everything to Italian. 'It's a culture shock to have to report
to somebody other than themselves,' he said, adding that getting used to what
are standard practices in most companies requires 'a mind shift and a change of
heart'. But Pope Francis rejected Coccopalmerio's proposal to curb Pell's power.
Francis was clear that no compromise could be permitted in the pace of change.
Those close to him had already known that. One of the reformers appointed by
Francis to clean up the Vatican finances went to the Pope early on and reported
that he was encountering huge resistance from the self-interested old guard
within the Roman bureaucracy who did not want to see change. What should
he do? the reformer asked the Pope. Pope Francis responded with a single Italian
word: *fretta*. It means faster, stronger, more.

* * *

Will it all work? The jury is still out on the efficacy of Pope Francis's financial
transformation. Professor John Pollard remains quizzical about some of it. 'I'm
not so impressed with the reforms of the other Vatican financial agencies, I
didn't think APSA needed reform but the IOR has been a scandal for years now.
And the reform which Francis has brought in there is really significant.' Sceptics
among veteran Vatican reporters, like Robert Mickens, editor-in-chief of *Global
Pulse* magazine, warn that reforms have been tried many times in Rome over
the decades and always fail. 'The Roman Curia is around 500 years old and it's
hard to change a culture like that. In the end it overwhelms the reformers and
stifles them,' he said.

But others are more optimistic. Shawn Tully, a US business journalist who
has followed Vatican finances for three decades for *Fortune* magazine, insists
of Francis: 'His rapid overhaul of the Vatican's finances is both one of the most
unusual case studies in the annals of business and one of the more instructive.'
John Ringguth, executive secretary of Moneyval, the anti-money-laundering
body of the Council of Europe, said: 'The Holy See has made substantial
progress since 2011. It has introduced in a very short time a significant number
of reforms in legislation and practice.' Inside the Vatican Bank there is a new
self-confidence. 'New systems are in place which make us feel confident that
we'd find out if there was something dodgy going on,' said its communications
man Markus Wieser. 'It's not all done but the revolution has been put in place.'

The reforms might really work this time said Cardinal Daniel DiNardo of Houston, who also serves on the 15-member Council for the Economy – half of whose members are now laymen. 'Pope Francis does follow-ups,' DiNardo has said. 'He'll take part in a meeting about a project, and a week later you'll get a phone call to find out where things stand.' And George Pell, he believes, will make a difference. Pell, the son of a heavyweight boxing champion, is so driven and unyielding that during his time in Sydney he was dubbed Pell Pot. Talking of the Curia recidivists DiNardo said: 'If there's one person capable of confronting them it's Pell. He doesn't back down, he keeps moving.'

Cardinal Pell himself is in no doubt that the great driver of reform is Pope Francis himself. Financial transformation was top of the Pope's list of issues for immediate action when he took office, Pell said. But Francis did not just set the wheels in motion and turn his attention elsewhere. 'We speak every fortnight,' Pell revealed, and more often if the Australian prelate requires help or advice. 'He understands money and he's interested in it. Honesty, efficiency and transparency are his priorities.' The Pope had supported the reform effort at every turn. 'Whenever there were things we couldn't clean up on our own, he's been there to support us.'

The reforms are already past the point where it would be possible to return to the bad old days, insisted Pell. Much remains to be done but the primary structural reforms have now been put in place. Pell was able to give a detailed presentation of the overall financial position to the Consistory of Cardinals in February 2015. Such a report had never been given before. 'By the end of the year it will all be finished or dangerously close to being finished,' concluded Pell who, at the end of 2014, moved into the Vatican Bank and took over the big top-floor office which had once belonged to the bank's presidents. Not long afterwards the Bank of Italy announced the return of the €23 million in IOR assets which it had frozen in the money-laundering investigation in 2010. The Vatican Bank, so far as the international regulatory authorities are concerned, had come in from the cold.

Cardinal Pell once said he would only be happy when the Vatican Bank was 'off the gossip pages'. As he rose from the breakfast table and headed off to meet the Pope I asked him if he has managed that yet. He smiled grimly: 'Not quite.'

Through all this, one thing is clear. The new Pope's relentless pursuit of reform – and his appetite to confront, and to remove, individual after individual he found obstructing that – have revealed the political steel that lies behind Francis's avuncular pastoral smile.

13

Cleansing the Curia

Every year, just before Christmas, the Pope assembles all the top people who run the Vatican bureaucracy, the Roman Curia, in the richly frescoed Sala Clementina inside the Apostolic Palace. Traditionally he delivers a 'State of the Church' speech, reflecting on the events and issues of the last 12 months and looking ahead to the challenges of the coming year. It is the preamble to the Vatican top people's Christmas festivities. But last year Pope Francis had a rather different idea.

On 22 December 2014, with almost two years behind him as pontiff, Francis set aside the traditional festive formularies and subjected his audience of cardinals and archbishops to a withering critique of what, since arriving full-time in Rome, he had discovered were their shortcomings. In an excoriating address, the man who had called himself 'the Pope from the ends of the earth' berated his audience with a list of the many spiritual 'illnesses and temptations' which he had encountered in the Vatican. Many of those who sat before him were guilty of some or all of them. 'They are illnesses and temptations that weaken our service to the Lord,' he admonished.

Archbishop Georg Gänswein, the Prefect of the Papal Household, sitting to the side of Francis, lost count when the Pope got to Fault No. 9 – in what turned out to be Fifteen Failings. Gänswein had been given a copy of what Francis was about to say just before the session began. But he had not had time to read it. The text lay burning a metaphorical hole in his briefcase. The Pope, in his blistering broadside, accused the churchmen around the great hall of an exaggerated sense of self-importance, a lust for power and control, the building of personal empires, sucking up to their superiors and preening themselves when their juniors did the same to them. That was not all, Francis had detected calumny and defamation, cliques who tried to discredit others through leaks to the media, a lack of empathy for others and a general opposition to the movement of the Holy Spirit in the Church.

The senior churchmen, in their black cassocks with their red and violet skullcaps and sashes, sat with stony faces and furrowed brows. Some put their hands to their mouths to cover their reactions. The Pope went on for more than thirty minutes. Unusually Francis hardly looked up from his written text to catch any one eye. He added only a couple of very minor unscripted remarks. His delivery was slow and deliberate. He did not smile.

As he continued his figures of speech became more graphic. He condemned the 'terrorism of gossip'. He accused some of leading a double life and called it 'existential schizophrenia'. Many had forgotten the experience of God that had brought them to the Church in the first place and had suffered 'a progressive decline of the spiritual faculties and an increase in a false self-reliance' which he dubbed 'spiritual Alzheimer's'. To cap it all, he told the assembled of faces before him, some by now as dark as thunder, that they were insufficiently joyful. Holiness was not revealed in faces of funereal solemnity or pained melancholy, he said. 'A heart full of God is a happy heart that radiates with joy and infects all who are around him: you can see it right away!' They should pray, as Francis did every day, the prayer of St Thomas More – to ask the Lord for a good sense of humour.

The prelates were not amused. Some agreed. Some were perplexed. Others were angry. All were shocked. When the Pope finished, the assembled men of God applauded politely but without enthusiasm. This was not their idea of how the annual Christmas party with the Successor of Peter should begin. Nonetheless – as if in ironic confirmation of the court mentality and clericalist ethos the Pope had been attacking – they were all smiles afterwards as Francis walked around the room and greeted each of them individually.

'To be honest, nothing like this has ever happened before,' said one Curia old-timer, Cardinal Giovanni Lajolo, who in his time had been the Holy See's foreign minister under Pope John Paul II and governor of the Vatican City State under Benedict XVI. 'Never before had a Pope set us in the Curia a series of pathologies that we must examine ourselves on ... The exchange of Christmas wishes has been a customary occasion, that follows a usual pattern ... So you could have expected Francis to talk about his travels to the Holy Land and Turkey ...' But, the old cardinal concluded, 'Tacitus' question is extremely current; what do we need good laws for, if we do not have good values?'

Others were less sanguine. Gänswein, who had once been the private secretary to Pope Benedict, said days later that cardinals were 'still reeling' from what they felt was an act of public humiliation by the Pope. Responding to a question from a German journalist – on what Pope Francis could have hoped to achieve by this demotivating 'act of flagellation' – Gänswein replied: 'That is a question that many of my colleagues also asked.' To many in the Curia what Pope Francis had done felt like a declaration of war for the soul of the Catholic Church.

* * *

Just ten days after he had been elected Pope, Francis had travelled to Castel Gandolfo, traditionally the summer residence for popes, up in the cool hills above an overheated Rome in the months of July and August. The papal palace there was now the temporary home of his predecessor, Benedict, the Pope Emeritus.

Wearing a white quilted jacket over his white cassock to guard against the spring chill, Benedict greeted Francis in the Castel Gandolfo gardens as soon as the papal helicopter landed. The media made much of the historic encounter, unprecedented in 500 years, as new Pope met old pope. They noted how Benedict acknowledged Francis to be supreme pontiff by offering him the right-hand side of the car, the traditional place of the Pope – but how Francis treated his revered predecessor as an equal by refusing the papal kneeler in the chapel and kneeling side by side with Benedict in the front pew, saying, 'No, we are brothers.' But what few if any reported at the time was that, when the two men met in the Castel Gandolfo library, with Benedict taking a high-backed chair with arms and Francis sitting relaxed on a banquette, there was a large white cardboard box on the low table between them. On top of it was a large envelope. Inside the box was the report compiled by three senior cardinals, at Benedict's request, after their investigation into the Vatileaks affair when the Pope's butler had leaked to the media documents revealing intrigue and in-fighting, careerism and corruption among the Curia. Those were the very same diseases for which, two years later, Francis was to scold the same Roman officials. The big box contained all the statements of the witnesses quizzed by the three cardinals. The envelope contained their summary and conclusions. They were what had proved the final straw for the frail Benedict, who resigned within just a few weeks of reading it.

In the General Congregations – the meetings of cardinals in the run-up to electing a successor to Benedict XVI – cardinal after cardinal had referred to the contents of this box, though only the three who compiled it knew exactly what it said. But there was an almost universal consensus that the Curia was 'dysfunctional' and in need of a radical shake-up. Francis was elected because it was thought he was the man to do that. Now as Pope he made great play of the mandate for reform his fellow cardinals had set out in the General Congregations. 'Last March, I didn't have a project to change the Church,' he said in his interview with *Corriere della Sera*. This somewhat stretched credulity given the things he had said when he was Archbishop of Buenos Aires on how the Curia needed to change. But he was anxious to stress that what was to follow grew not merely from his own ideas but from a wide consensus among the College of Cardinals. 'I began to govern,' he told the *Corriere della Sera*, a year later, 'trying to put into practice that which had emerged in the debate among cardinals in the various Congregations' before the conclave.

From his very first minutes in office, Pope Francis had been trying to change the culture of the institutional Church. From the moment on the balcony when he bowed for the people's blessing he was setting out a different model of leadership. Priesthood was about service rather than symbolic status or the exercise of sacramental power. He was setting out an alternative to what the historian Eamon Duffy has called 'the exalted doctrine of priesthood that has been in favour during the last two pontificates' – and which had undoubtedly contributed to the resurgent clericalism which Francis found so problematic in the Church. To the new Pope it got in the way of communicating the Gospel. So did curial careerism. Reform, he realized, required a conversion of hearts and minds. But that would not come without changes in personnel and changes in culture. And that required changes in structure.

* * *

It took Pope Francis just a month to make his first revolutionary change. The eight cardinal advisers he selected from all around the world were to work not within the Curia but outside it, subjecting it to independent scrutiny. Six months later he formally constituted the group as the Council of Cardinals. He gave them two jobs: to aid him 'in the government of the universal Church' – and to revise the constitution known as *Pastor Bonus*, drawn up by Pope John Paul II in 1998, which defined how the Roman bureaucracy should work. He told them he wanted a thorough revision. The move generated both excitement and consternation. So much so that few commentators initially paid attention to the first part of the job. And yet in some ways that was the more radical change.

What was so far-reaching about advising on the general running of the Church was that this had previously been the function of the Curia. The new group would operate *above* the Roman Curia rather than being part of it – and certainly not taking orders from it. Inside the Vatican bureaucracy those who had always called the shots on church governance knew what that meant. 'It was immediately sending out a sign about collegiality, about sidestepping the Curia, making the Curia irrelevant,' one long-time Curia insider told me. 'He knew that if he was to affect real change he must not be hamstrung by the Curia. He was, as ever, playing a very canny long game.'

The eight advisers did not all share similar views. The coordinator of the group was Cardinal Oscar Rodríguez Maradiaga, the Archbishop of Tegucigalpa in Honduras, a moderate figure with a passion for social justice and a long-standing critic of economic inequality. But another crucial figure was George Pell, the Archbishop of Sydney, who was solidly conservative politically, socially and doctrinally and was a supporter of the Latin Mass. The others were: Cardinal Reinhard Marx, the Archbishop of Munich; Cardinal Laurent Monswengo Pasinya, Archbishop of Kinshasha; Cardinal Oswald Gracias, Archbishop of Bombay; Cardinal Francisco Javier Errázuriz Ossa, of Chile; Cardinal Sean Patrick O'Malley, Archbishop of Boston; and Cardinal Giuseppe Bertello, a career diplomat, who ran the Vatican City State. Bertello was the only member of the Curia to be asked to join. The Council of Eight swiftly became dubbed the C8, until the new Secretary of State, Cardinal Pietro Parolin, joined and it became known, a year later, as the C9. Between them the advisers covered a range of opinions and approaches.

But they all had one thing in common. They may have had different views on politics. They may have had different views on traditional and modern styles of worship. The conservatives may have wanted to interpret doctrine with judgemental precision, and the liberals with a pastorally flexible compassion. But there is another axis which runs through the Catholic Church: at one end are those who want a firm centralizing control of the Church from Rome and at the other are those who want to see authority and decision-making dispersed far more widely across the globe through a college of bishops, each of whom understands and responds to the needs of his particular flock. In this last area the Council of Eight were all of one mind. They all shared the conviction of Pope Francis that in recent times the Catholic Church had become far too centralized and inflexible to the needs of the ordinary holy faithful people of God. All wanted a return of what church jargon calls collegiality.

Collegiality was one of the great upheavals advocated by the revolutionary Second Vatican Council in the 1960s. But its vision was never properly implemented. Indeed it was wilfully undermined in the decades that followed Vatican II by the popes and curial bureaucrats who followed. They did not want to see authority dispersed. The last two popes had both increased centralization within the Church. But Francis was a pope of the periphery.

The eight cardinals were all fiercely independent in their thinking. None of the C8 had ever served in the Curia; by contrast seven had wide experience of running big dioceses far from Rome. Only one was Italian. All were used to working collegially as central figures in their bishops' conferences back home; even before the Council of Cardinals had its first meeting its members were bombarded with suggestions from their local churches on how things should be improved at the Vatican. The Eight also all shared one disposition: each had previously been critical of the way that Vatican officials had behaved in the past as though they were the masters of the Church around the world rather than its servants. Some of them were among the most outspoken critics of the current Vatican system in the pre-conclave discussions. Pell had been a blunt public critic of the Curia in the past. And Rodríguez Maradiaga had had a bruising encounter with the Curia in 2011. He was president of the Church's aid agency network Caritas Internationalis when the Vatican's Secretary of State Cardinal Tarcisio Bertone decided to refuse permission for the organization's secretary general, Mrs Lesley-Anne Knight, to stand for a second term because she saw the Church's 165 aid agencies' primary task as assisting the poor rather than pushing Catholic doctrine. Her unpardonable offence was having allowed Catholic aid agencies to work alongside secular agencies which promoted contraception. Rodríguez Maradiaga defended her, but lost the internal Vatican power struggle with Bertone. Loyalty oaths were imposed on Knight's successor. Now that balance of power was reversed. 'We had all assumed that Rodríguez was toast,' a senior member of Caritas told me, 'but within six months it was Bertone who had vanished from the scene.'

By setting up the C8 Pope Francis gave notice to the Curia's clerical careerists, who had spent the last two papacies arrogating power to themselves. The Church, he told them, should be less of a top-down hierarchy and more of a horizontal community. He instructed his new cabinet of cardinals to suggest more collegial ways in which the Church could make its decisions so that it reflected the needs and views of the Church of the peripheries.

The Pope made clear that the advice of the Council of Cardinals would be an effective part of the way he governed the Church. In his interview with Spadaro he said:

> As Archbishop of Buenos Aires, I had a meeting with the six auxiliary bishops every two weeks, and several times a year with the council of priests. They asked questions and we opened the floor for discussion. This greatly helped me to make the best decisions. But now I hear some people tell me: 'Do not consult too much, and decide by yourself.' Instead, I believe that consultation is very important.
>
> The consistories [of cardinals], the synods [of bishops] are, for example, important places to make real and active this consultation. We must, however, give them a less rigid form. I do not want token consultations, but real consultations. The consultation group of eight cardinals, this 'outsider' advisory group, is not only my decision, but it is the result of the will of the cardinals, as it was expressed in the General

Congregations before the conclave. And I want to see that this is a real, not ceremonial consultation.

Outside observers at once understood the implications of that. The C8 created an embryonic structure for a more collegial system of government. It shifted the balance of power from the Curia towards regional or national conferences of bishops. 'This move represents a highly significant rebalancing of forces within the government of the Catholic Church, and may pave the way for a form of representative Cabinet-type government instead of the model of an absolute monarchy that many believe has gone beyond the end of its useful life,' said the international Catholic weekly, *The Tablet*. 'The Pope's intention appears to be to translate into action the Second Vatican Council's desire for a realignment of forces within the Church that has remained largely theoretical over the last half-century.' Commentators from across a wide variety of opinions in the Church seemed agreed on the heft of the change. The Italian traditional liturgist Professor Mattia Rossi, editor of *Liturgia Culmen et Fons*, disapprovingly described the new group of advisers as a step towards the 'demolition of the papacy' which replaced the divinely instituted authority and stability of the apostolic hierarchy with a quicksand swamp of collegiality. At the other end of the spectrum Alberto Melloni, Professor of History of Christianity at the University of Modena called it, as we have heard, the 'most important step in the history of the Church for the past 10 centuries'.

* * *

The Catholic Church has been run for centuries as an absolute monarchy. Its governance template is still essentially as it was set by Pope Sixtus V in 1588. Officials in a series of departments, known as dicasteries, act as papal courtiers. In theory the members of this Curia discharge the wishes of the pontiff. But in practice they are largely autonomous, sometimes even working at cross-purposes or intriguing to advance their own careers or departmental interests.

Attempts at reform have been made in the past. But this self-serving bureaucracy has usually managed to undermine them. When, in the 1960s, the Second Vatican Council decreed new models of collegiality which would cede power to bishops and their local synods, the Curia connived to emasculate the plan and draw power back to itself. This was the problem that Francis and his Council of Cardinals set out to address. They needed to find ways of reversing the process by which this monarchical model of the papacy had replaced the earlier model of collegial government in which the Pope was not an autocrat but only 'first among equals' in the company of bishops. Francis, as the first Pope from the New World, was clear that a truly collegial Church would better reflect the fact that the global make-up of the Church has changed dramatically even since the Second Vatican Council. Today more than two-thirds of Catholics live in the southern hemisphere, yet Italy had more cardinals in the last conclave than the whole of Latin America.

All this had been a source of irritation to Bergoglio as Archbishop of Buenos Aires. He had had a number of unhappy experiences with the Curia when he was an archbishop. His recommendations for new bishops were routinely disregarded by comparatively junior Curia officials who treated cardinals from around the world with what Bergoglio had seen as infantilizing disdain. He had been unhappy with Rome's response to what he saw as his constructive criticisms of Benedict XVI's ill-judged remarks about Islam at Regensburg which impacted on inter-faith relations in Argentina. He was irritated by the high-handed advice of what his former aide Guillermo Marcó called 'Italians with emptying churches…telling bishops in countries with growing congregations what they should and should not be doing'. All this instilled in him the importance of the Church being run more collegially, which is how he ran the Argentinian bishops' conference during his six years as their president – even when their decision was not one with which he agreed, as when he wanted the Church to back same-sex civil unions while opposing gay marriage.

But the transformation Francis wanted to bring was not simply a question of abandoning the style the papacy had adopted from a Renaissance Italian court – with its finery, courtly patronage and Machiavellian manoeuvring. And it was more than switching the Church from a centralized to a more federal model. Change was needed deep within the entire culture of the Vatican.

Conservatism, caution and self-preservation had become part of the curial DNA. The Curia was a self-selecting organism. Popes had to endorse appointments but they were generally presented with candidates and with options from a palette selected by men well schooled in curial ways. The Curia had become a self-perpetuating bureaucracy in which individuals saw it as their job to propagate the institution, or their part of it. (There are around thirty dicasteries of varying statuses, as is reflected in their differing titles: secretariats, congregations, pontifical councils, pontifical commissions, tribunals.) 'As someone who has worked four years inside the Curia I can say there's a lot about it that is good,' I was told by a middle-ranking curial officer who had recently chosen to return to a senior pastoral position back in his home country. Despite now being away from Rome he thought it best to speak anonymously, as so many in the Church did in conversation with me. 'The

Curia is full of very talented, multilingual, fine theologians but the mechanisms of the bureaucracy are such that many of them are never allowed to make a proper contribution. It is seen as a career ladder with new recruits told who to cultivate and who to ignore.'

When dealing with the rest of the Church, he said, 'we were told never say Yes or No. We were taught to answer not just in Italian but in a kind of opaque eighteenth-century Italian. The whole idea was not to box yourself in.' The aim was to protect the interests of their curial department rather than to think about the good of the Church or the wider common good. 'The Italians use the word "*bo*". It's a Roman word. It means "I don't know, I don't care, why ask me?" It comes with a shrug of the shoulder. It is heard very commonly in the Curia.'

There is another popular phrase in the Vatican, a senior serving member of the Curia told me. 'It is "loro hanno deciso" – it means "they have decided". But who is they? No-one really ever knows.' Pope Francis is impatient with all that. 'His differences with the mainstream Vatican are as much temperamental as ideological. The Vatican has traditionally been concerned, to use a football metaphor which Francis would understand, with whether the team is "keeping its shape". But Pope Francis is a Latin. He's not worried about the team's shape, but about whether it is scoring goals. He is not looking for consistency and coherence – which is why he has said he prefers an accident-prone Church to a safe one.' But if Pope Francis was clear on the changes he wanted, the question remained: how best to bring it about?

* * *

There are four ways to bring about organizational change. You can shift the people in the top jobs. You can bring in new people. You can make the people in existing jobs start to behave differently. And you can change the structures of the organization to promote different behaviour. Francis has set about doing all that, and something more subtle.

'Is Pope Francis purging the Curia of conservatives?' asked a headline in the *Catholic Herald* six months into the papacy. It was easy to see why traditionalists might fear that. Top of the list of those cleared out in the first six months was Cardinal Tarcisio Bertone, the man who had for the previous seven years been the 'deputy pope' to Benedict XVI. Bertone departed with bitterness, lashing out against the 'crows and vipers' who had undermined him. In his stead Francis placed Archbishop Pietro Parolin, a talented and respected Vatican diplomat who had been responsible for handling some of the Vatican's most delicate relationships, with Israel and China. In the previous era he had fallen foul of Bertone and was shunted off to be papal nuncio in Venezuela to get him out of the way. Parolin was clearly a reformer who was on record as having described Catholicism under Pope Benedict as 'a Church under siege with thousands of problems, a Church that seemed, let's say, a little sick'. Aged only 58 he represented 'a clear throw of the dice on where Francis sees the future,' one senior cardinal told me.

Bertone was not the only major conservative figure from the previous papacy to make a swift departure. One of Pope Francis's first significant changes was to remake the Congregation for Bishops, the body in Rome which appoints bishops for local churches all around the world. In the era of Pope John Paul II – and his doctrinal watchdog Cardinal Joseph Ratzinger, who went on to be Benedict XVI – it had been dominated by hardliners who oversaw the selection of a slew of conservative and traditionalist men including what the leading American Catholic commentator Michael Sean Winters called 'a string of "culture warrior bishops" elevated to metropolitan sees in Philadelphia, Denver, San Francisco, Baltimore and Portland'. The Congregation, as moulded under the influence of the long Ratzinger era, was never going to provide bishops with the characteristics Francis required. The new Pope had set these out early on, when addressing 108 nuncios gathered in Rome from their postings as papal ambassadors all around the world. Nuncios are responsible for drawing up the shortlist of three candidates for every bishop's post. These three, known as a *terna*, are sent to the Congregation of Bishops in Rome. From now on, Francis told the nuncios in June 2013, candidates should be 'pastors who are close to their people, fathers and brothers, who are meek, patient and merciful'. A good prospective bishop should 'love interior poverty' and demonstrate that externally with a simple lifestyle; he would not have the 'mind-set of a prince', the Pope said, warning: 'Beware of those who are ambitious, who seek the episcopacy.'

Six months later, clearly unhappy with the work of the Congregation for Bishops, Francis cleared out half its members, replacing conservative ideologues like the Italian cardinal Mauro Piacenza and US cardinals Justin Rigali and Raymond Burke. In their place he appointed moderates like Washington's Cardinal Donald Wuerl and Westminster's Vincent Nichols, men whom the Pope regards highly – both are orthodox but pastoral by inclination and far more likely to provide Francis with what he wanted: bishops with the smell of their sheep.

The Pope rapidly began to make his mark not just on membership of important committees but also on pivotal posts within the Curia. Francis had Parolin in mind as his first minister from early on. He mentioned him to his chief adviser Cardinal Rodríguez Maradiaga at a private lunch the two men had just four days after he was elected Pope. But, true to his word, he consulted widely on the key appointment. 'He asks many people's advice,' one Cardinal told me. 'But he is strategic about it; he triangulates everything.' On other appointments he was more intuitive. He made an archbishop of his closest theological collaborator, Victor Manuel Fernández, the man he had nominated to be Rector of the Catholic University of Argentina, but whose appointment had been blocked for years by the Curia. (The Pope also demoted the cardinal who had blocked the nomination.) But generally he took advice, and from a wide range of sources Fernández revealed: 'He has a broad circle of people from whom he asks advice on various issues. He listens to more people than just those in the dicasteries of the Curia, and in this way he is closer to the different voices in the Church and in society.'

A series of more moderate appointments followed. The post of Secretary General of the Synod of Bishops was to be a key job for Pope Francis if he was to enhance the status of bishops in the running of the Church; into that job he put the reformist Archbishop Lorenzo Baldisseri. Another strategic position was running the department which looks after religious orders; a previous incumbent, Archbishop Joseph Tobin, had been removed from the job for being too sympathetic to the US nuns who were being investigated by the Vatican on accusations of being too feminist. Again Francis appointed a respected moderate, the Franciscan friar, José Rodríguez Carballo. And as Secretary for Relations with States, the Vatican's foreign minister, he installed Archbishop Paul Gallagher, originally from Liverpool, who was described as a 'refreshingly non-ideological thoroughly Vatican II man'.

The old regime was cleared out not just at the very top level. Cardinal Piacenza – who was once described as one of Pope Benedict's most conservative appointments in the Roman Curia – lost his job as head of the Congregation for Clergy. But with him went a whole raft of his acolytes. Archbishop Beniamino Stella, the career diplomat who replaced Piacenza, dismissed half the priests serving in the congregation in less than a year. They were sent back to work in their home dioceses. It was a similar story in the Congregation for Divine Worship – which had been at the heart of the Ratzinger project to re-translate the Mass into an English that was nearer to the original Latin text but which was wooden and convoluted as a result. Benedict's central figure there, Cardinal Antonio Cañizares – a traditionalist known as 'little Ratzinger' – was removed by Francis and sent back to Spain to become archbishop of his native Valencia. Soon after, his two undersecretaries – one an enthusiast for the pre-Vatican II Tridentine Mass, the other a key figure in that translating of the Mass into clumsy English – were sent packing too. And on the changes went.

Conservatives were alarmed. One traditionalist blog spoke about 'de-Ratzingerization'. The conservative Vatican-watcher, Sandro Magister, noted how ironic it was that when Francis spoke to the world he 'loves to call himself Bishop of Rome' but when he was 'within the Leonine walls' he acted '100 per cent as supreme pontiff of the universal Church'.

And yet nowhere near all the prominent conservative figures were defenestrated. Many others remained. Francis kept the man Benedict XVI had just appointed as Master of Pontifical Liturgical Celebrations, even though Monsignor Guido Marini demonstrated a high-church formality, and taste for lace-trimmed surplices, which the new Pope clearly did not share. Similarly Francis left in place, nominally at any rate, Archbishop Georg Gänswein, who had been made Prefect of the Papal Household by Pope Benedict just before he retired. 'The plan was that he was to have been the conduit between Benedict and Scola,' one insider told me. But it was not Scola who was to become Pope.

To have swiftly replaced these two figures who embodied so much about the Benedict era would have shown disrespect to his predecessor, Francis decided. The new Pope had genuine affection for the 87-year-old Pope Emeritus whom Francis called, fondly, in private, 'the old man'. It is 'like having a wise grandfather at home', Francis once said to a crowd of elderly people in St Peter's Square. So Marini has had to accommodate himself to Francis's less elaborate liturgical tastes. And Gänswein is allowed to coordinate formal papal audiences, and acts as a messenger between new Pope and old pope, but is simply bypassed by Francis on all matters of substance. 'It's an arm wrestle, not a boxing match,' one Vatican insider said. Certainly Pope Francis understands about taking time.

But there was more to it than that. George Pell is one of the avowedly more conservative figures in the College of Cardinals. Yet Francis has hugged him close, both as a member of the Council of Cardinals and by giving him a massive job overseeing the reform of all the Vatican finance. Some, especially those who remember Bergoglio the masterly political operator from Argentina, are cynical about this. 'Francis has played it very cleverly,' said one seasoned diplomat. 'It was a masterstroke to get Cardinal Pell involved. He is a really tough nut. And it is far better to have him in the tent shouting out than outside shouting in. Given the absence of theological issues around money it gave Pell a really big job to do in an area on which there will be no friction. It also ties him to Francis. If he succeeds it will reflect well on the Pope's reforming vision; if he fails it will be Pell's fault.'

That is very much a politician's analysis however. And Francis clearly has a deeper ecclesiological agenda. He wants to create an inclusive Church in which a wide range of opinions and interpretations blossom. One pivotal role in the

Catholic Church in recent decades has been that of the head of the Vatican's guardian of orthodoxy, the Congregation for the Doctrine of the Faith. Pope Francis has left in place the man appointed by Pope Benedict, Archbishop Gerhard Müller. Müller's views are generally conservative and he values doctrinal clarity with some rigour. In the past his approach has leaned more to the judgemental than the compassionate. Müller was a personal friend of Pope Benedict and the editor of his theological writings. Yet he has views of some theological nuance. He is also a friend and admirer of the liberation theologian Gustavo Gutiérrez. Francis decided to confirm Müller in this most important of posts and then made him a cardinal.

The most high-profile firing of the Francis pontificate has been that of the fiery arch-conservative Cardinal Raymond Burke. The former Archbishop of St Louis, a canon lawyer, and one of the most forceful exponents of a traditionalist conservatism in the Church in the United States, had for the previous five years been the Catholic Church's most senior judge as Prefect of the Supreme Tribunal of the Apostolic Signatura. He was noted not only for his hard-line views on the interpretation of doctrine but also for his predilection for high-church liturgy and extravagant vestments including the *cappa magna*, a five-metre-long silk cloak sometimes worn by bishops in bygone times. None of this was to the liking of Pope Francis, who prefers plain vestments, direct liturgy and sees the Gospel as a greater priority than canon law. Some months after being dismissed from the committee that oversees the appointment of bishops, Burke was removed from his position on the Catholic supreme court and made chaplain to the Order of Malta, a ceremonial post usually given to a retired cardinal. It was a striking public demotion. The American cardinal was stunned, his friends said privately.

The move came after the Extraordinary Synod of Bishops on the Family in October 2014 at which Burke led a rearguard action by those who want to keep the ban on remarried Catholics taking Communion. Burke was characteristically pugnacious in his opposition. The US cardinal, who had previously dismissed Francis's manifesto *Evangelii Gaudium* as 'the Pope's personal thinking' and not 'official doctrine', now denounced the synod process as 'controlled and manipulated'. He openly criticized the Pope. Francis's decision to open up discussion on pastoral responses to difficult issues around family and sexuality, Burke said, had only spread 'confusion'. At this critical time, Burke said, 'there is a strong feeling that the Church is as a ship without a rudder'. The Catholic faithful 'are feeling a bit seasick because they feel the Church's ship has lost its way', he added. 'It seems to many that the Church's ship has lost its compass.' And, in an extraordinary public attack on the Pope for a lack of leadership,

Burke demanded that Francis should break the silence he had maintained as he listened to the synod discussions. He should stand up and make an unambiguous statement on the issues. A clear affirmation of Catholic doctrine by the Pope, Burke said, was 'long overdue'.

Pope Francis was just as extraordinary in his response. In an interview with the Argentine newspaper *La Nación* the pontiff denied that Burke had been demoted as a punishment for his outspoken behaviour at the synod. The move, the Pope said, was part of a broader restructuring of the Vatican legal system. Burke had been informed of this long before the synod. The Pope added: 'I said to him, "This will take place after the synod because I want you to participate in the synod as a dicastery head." It is therefore not true that I removed him because of how he had behaved in the Synod.'

Few were fooled by this papal 'restructuring' nicety. Conservatives were outraged. They felt, said Edward Pentin, the Rome correspondent of the *National Catholic Register*, that 'Burke has been treated fairly shamefully. He is a gentle holy man who always wants to be loyal to the Pope and the Magisterium.' The ultra-traditionalist blog *Rorate Caeli* described Burke's defenestration as 'the greatest humiliation of a curial cardinal in living memory, truly unprecedented in modern times'.

Burke's opponents were also not fooled by the Pope's attempt to defuse the row over Burke's demotion. 'Burke is a mischievous man,' said one leading Jesuit in Rome. 'It was not his vanity of vanities that got too much for Pope Francis but his obstructive aggressive opposition.' It is in this that lies the distinction Francis makes between a conservative like Cardinal Müller and one like Cardinal Burke. 'Francis wants an inclusive Church. Whatever your view, unless you're a really awkward plotter, like Cardinal Burke, he wants you inside the tent.' It was a judgement shared by a senior Vatican official close to the Congregation for the Doctrine of the Faith. 'Müller is a conservative but he's much more open-minded than Burke,' he said. 'Müller is very collegial internally. He is part of the team. Burke is not; Burke goes to the media a lot. All the stories about Cardinal Burke come direct from Cardinal Burke. Müller is part of a loyal opposition; Burke has a touch of disloyalty about him. Jesuits have a very clear idea of where the line is on these matters.'

Revealingly Cardinal Müller himself gave an interview to a German Catholic news agency underscoring that point. 'I am not his conservative opponent,' Müller told Kathpress, disclosing that he was not happy about being presented as an internal antagonist of Pope Francis. The two men had differences in terms of formation and approach but, he insisted, 'these complement each other, they are not contradictory'. What all this suggested was that, although the trend in

Francis's appointments was steadily away from the conservatism of the previous three decades, it was not a move towards liberalism. Rather it was an attempt to restore a balance which Francis felt had been lost within the Church under the two previous pontificates. He wanted both liberals and conservatives in the Curia.

It was for the same reason that, he had wanted to link the canonizations of Pope John Paul II and Pope John XXIII. The message was that both wings of the Church are needed. One of the core elements of the Francis vision was that he wanted to let a thousand flowers bloom. The new Pope was asserting his profound belief that diversity and inclusion needed restoring to a church whose very name – catholic – means universal.

* * *

Appointing new bishops fulfilled a double function for Francis. He was able to install in crucial positions across the Church men who personified the different elements of catholicity which made up the complex Bergoglio worldview. He was also able to send clear signals to the Church's existing 4,938 bishops around the world about the approach they should adopt to obtain his approval. He had spelled out his idea of a good bishop to the Church's nuncios, and also to trainee Vatican diplomats at the Pontifical Ecclesiastical Academy where he uttered one of his memorable phrases: 'Careerism is leprosy!' But his selection of individuals for major bishoprics undercut suggestions that the Francis revolution was about a clearing out of conservatives.

In Cologne, one of the largest and wealthiest Catholic sees in the world, the retiring bishop was the arch-conservative Cardinal Joachim Meisner, a long-time adviser of Benedict XVI. The two men would sometimes speak as often as twice a week on the phone. Francis chose, to replace Meisner, someone who had once been seen as a Meisner disciple. Rainer Maria Woelki had gone to be Archbishop of Berlin three years earlier with the reputation of being a doctrinaire conservative. He had done his doctorate at an Opus Dei university and described homosexuality as an 'offence against the order of creation'. It was thought he would be a disaster in the cosmopolitan capital with its large gay community. But Woelki had developed such a pastoral dialogue with them that they nominated him for their annual Respect award. Woelki developed into 'a sort of Francis before his time' in the words of Vaticanista John Allen. Berlin's *Tagesspiegel* newspaper called him 'the prototype of a new generation of bishops...not grumpy and dogmatic...these men speak of mercy and mean it'. Woelki was theologically conservative but was a spiritual shepherd who could reach out to people and had a heart for the disadvantaged.

Sydney was the next indicative appointment. This was the archdiocese vacated by Cardinal Pell when he left for Rome to head the Pope's reformed Economic Secretariat. There Francis chose a Dominican theologian, Anthony Colin Fisher, another conservative but one cut from a far softer cloth than his combative predecessor Pell. Fisher was as gracious and erudite as Pell was belligerent and blunt. Fisher took the view that an approach of 'out-and-out confrontation' to the culture wars issues of abortion and gay marriage hardened the hearts of opponents and 'made them write off Christians as fanatics or single-issue people'. Maybe, he said, 'we need a different rhetorical register and a different strategy'.

In the United States the Pope's bellwether appointment suggested that he thought more than a softening of style was required to restore equilibrium to the culture-war-riven episcopal conference. In Chicago the outgoing archbishop was the staunchly conservative Cardinal Francis George, who died in April 2015. His episcopal style had done much to set the confrontational tone of debate within the US Church. To succeed him, as shepherd of Chicago's two million Catholics, Pope Francis chose a bishop of the opposite orientation, 65-year-old Blase Cupich. He was orthodox but no conservative nor a traditionalist. Early in his episcopal career he had banned a traditionalist Catholic community from celebrating the Easter Triduum in the pre-Vatican II rite. As Bishop of Spokane in 2011 Cupich asked his priests and deacons not to take part in prayers in front of abortion clinics since this could indicate disdain rather than care for the women entering the clinics. His pro-life statements, controversially in the United States – though less so elsewhere in the world – invariably couple opposition to abortion with opposition to the death penalty. Nor did he accept the desire of hard-line conservatives to refuse Communion to politicians who vote in favour of abortion, insisting 'we can't politicize the Communion rail'.

The common denominator in these tone-setting appointments was not, as some conservatives said, a drift to liberalism. Pope Francis's appointments were doctrinally orthodox. Two of the three key appointments were of men generally regarded as conservative. But there was a clear move towards men who were more inclined to dialogue than to diatribe. The approach Francis wanted prioritized was pastoral compassion over doctrinal precision. He preferred moderates to ideologues. And he wanted bishops with a particular concern for the marginalized. The Francis template was for shepherds who were, in the words of one commentator, as 'interested in loving their flock as teaching it, let alone hectoring it'. This was a matter of some urgency to Francis, as could be seen by the fact that he also speeded up the process of filling vacant dioceses.

* * *

There was a more subtle level on which Pope Francis was at work to reshape the dynamics of the papacy. He was encouraging debate with a freedom that stood in contrast to the way that John Paul II and Benedict XVI had striven to restrict debate and diversity. Their strategy was to reassert a particular Catholic identity as a bulwark against what they saw as a sea of secularist relativism. Those two popes had attempted to suppress views that were outside the parameters they had set. Francis appeared to want the opposite.

When Pietro Parolin became Francis's new Secretary of State he gave an interview which unleashed a discussion on whether priests might be allowed to marry. Priestly celibacy was a topic which was off-limits under previous popes but Parolin publicly speculated about the idea. Compulsory celibacy for priests was not an immutable Church dogma but merely a Catholic tradition which 'can be discussed', he said. This was not exactly the line Francis had taken before he became Pope. 'It can change,' said the then Cardinal Bergoglio but, 'I am in favour of maintaining celibacy, with all its pros and cons, because we have ten centuries of good experiences rather than failures.' For all that, he was clearly happy for the issue to be raised.

It was the same with the ban on remarried Catholics taking Communion. In private Francis gave clear indications to his cardinals that he wanted to relax the prohibition. His aim was to find ways of guarding the doctrine of the indis- solubility of marriage without excluding those with failed marriages from the sacraments. Indeed he had written in *Evangelii Gaudium* that the Eucharist 'is not a prize for the perfect but a powerful medicine and nourishment for the weak'. But he wanted to bring the Church round to his view rather than imposing it by papal fiat; he saw the stimulation of debate, rather than its suppression, as the way to progress the mind of the Church. So he was content to allow Cardinal Müller of the Congregation for the Doctrine of the Faith to speak vehemently in public against lifting the ban – while at the same time smiling as the opposite was argued by other leading figures, like Cardinal Rodríguez Maradiaga, to whom the Pope was far closer.

What Francis was also doing was endeavouring to shift the balance of power between the different Vatican departments. Müller could have his say, the Pope seemed to be suggesting, but so could other cardinals. This was a departure. Under previous popes the opinions of the head of the Congregation for the Doctrine of the Faith were given particular weight. No longer.

Francis signalled this in a number of ways. A few weeks after he was elected he held a private meeting with a group of nuns and priests from Latin America.

It was the meeting in which he reportedly admitted to the representatives from the Confederation of Latin American and Caribbean Religious that there was 'a stream of corruption' and 'a gay lobby' in the Curia. But he also told them – according to notes of the meeting the religious orders posted on a Catholic website *Reflexión y Liberación* and which the Vatican, pointedly, did not deny – that they should not take too much notice of intrusions into their work by the Roman Curia. He told them: 'Perhaps even a letter from the Congregation for the Doctrine (of the Faith) will arrive for you, telling you that you said such and such a thing. But do not worry. Explain whatever you have to explain, but move forward. Open the doors, do something there where life calls for it.' This was a telling indication, I was told by one of the Jesuits closest to the Pope, who said: 'Muller can write letters, but who cares. In my opinion Francis is very smart. He wants to avoid martyrs.'

It was far from the only signal. Müller was not asked to become a member of the Congregation for Bishops at the end of 2013 – though all his four predecessors at the CDF had become so. A month later, Pope Francis went to address Müller and his staff at the CDF. He affirmed their role in 'promoting and protecting the doctrine of the faith' but then warned them to guard against the temptation to domesticate the faith or reduce it to abstract theories. He called for a kinder and gentler CDF which seeks always to have 'a constructive dialogue, respectful and patient with authors' and he told them their work should be 'distinguished for the practices of collegiality and dialogue'.

When Francis announced his first batch of cardinals, Müller's name was not, as expected, second to Parolin's in the pecking order but third – below that of Lorenzo Baldisseri, the Secretary General of the Synod of Bishops. The detail was not lost on Vatican reporters, who concluded that strengthening a democratizing process in the Church was a bigger priority for Pope Francis than was the patrolling of doctrine.

Evidence that this was not journalistic speculation soon followed, with an unprecedented barrage of criticism of Müller from the Pope's closet allies. The man said to be Francis's favourite theologian, Cardinal Walter Kasper, described Müller's views as 'narrow'. Baldisseri contradicted Müller, saying the Church's teaching on family and marriage can and must be 'updated', a position echoed by Archbishop Robert Zollitsch, the chairman of the German bishops' conference. Cardinal Marx, of the Pope's council of nine cardinal advisers, publicly reproved Müller for trying to clamp down on new ideas on Communion for the remarried, saying: 'The Prefect of the Congregation for the Doctrine of the Faith cannot stop the discussions.' Cardinal João Bráz de Aviz, head of the Vatican congregation for religious orders, openly complained that the CDF was planning to conduct a doctrinal assessment for his department without proper consultation.

But what raised most eyebrows was the boldness of the rebuke by the coordinator of the C9, Cardinal Rodríguez Maradiaga, who declared that most Catholics were 'behind the Pope' and that Müller needed to become less absolute in his approach. 'I understand it,' Rodríguez said. 'He's German and a German professor of theology on top of it. In his mentality, there is only right or wrong, that's it. But I say: The world, my brother, isn't like that. You should be slightly flexible when you hear other voices, instead of just listening and saying, "No, no, this is fixed and final". I believe he'll get there, and understand other views. But for now he's still only at the beginning.' The Congregation for the Doctrine of the Faith, which was the department once known throughout the Roman Curia as *La Suprema*, was supreme no more. Under Francis it would be merely one among equals.

* * *

From Day One the Roman Curia was unsure how to read Francis. Two years later it was still unsure. That was the way the Pope from Argentina liked it. Down in his unconventional lodgings in the Casa Santa Marta he would refer to the Apostolic Palace – in which traditionalists thought he ought to be living – as 'La Su' (Up There). His day soon adopted a settled pattern. He would rise before 5 a.m. and spend two hours in prayer and in preparing the sermon for his daily Mass at 7 a.m. in the Casa Santa Marta chapel, at the end of which he would sit in the back pew with the congregation to pray. After breakfasting at 8 a.m. in the Casa cafeteria the workaholic pontiff would make his way La Su for a morning organized by officials of the papal household. Even on Wednesdays when he had public audiences at 10.30 a.m. he would get through prodigious amounts of official paperwork before climbing into the popemobile to tour St Peter's Square for 40 minutes to wave at the crowds before the official audience began. 'His mornings are planned and structured,' one bureaucrat told me. 'A lot goes across his desk. He's keen to get reports. He picks up the phone and says Yes, No, I like this, I don't like that. He's good at giving brief instructions. He really expects follow-up.' He swiftly established a distinct and personalized way of working which bypassed official systems, depending on close relationships with individuals he trusts. 'He's got quite good antennae for people who are just trying to please him,' one close collaborator revealed. He appreciates frankness and honesty and dislikes unclear speech, ambiguity and hypocrisy. Officials of the papal household arranged the morning, with paperwork and meetings with foreign dignities, but Francis kept a close control.

But if in the mornings he was 'up there', in the afternoons he was 'down here' – in his small suite of rooms in the Casa Santa Marta. If his mornings were planned and structured, his afternoons were just for him. 'He controls them entirely,' the insider told me. 'The household know nothing about them. When he invited Scalfari [the atheist newspaper editor], for example, no one in the household knew anything about it.' He kept very few things on his desk and very few papers. He booked his own appointments and made his own phone calls. He rang individuals whose letters had personally moved him, and occasionally called friends back in Argentina, though he mainly reserved Sunday afternoons for social calls. In the early afternoon he would take a short nap but afterwards went straight back to work on activities of his own control.

This *modus operandi* did not just unsettle members of the Curia. It left outsiders uncertain too, as one foreign ambassador to the Holy See explained: 'The Vatican has always been a court and in the past you always knew where your best route through to the Pope was. Now there is no route through. There is no privileged conduit. His private secretaries are just secretaries, they are not decision-makers.' The effect, the No. 2 in one Vatican department told me, was that 'there has been a significant change in Curia priorities. There is a new determination and directness in the air.' Francis is a pope at ease with power. His Jesuit training – and the mistakes of his own personal past – have given him a penetrating insight into community dynamics and also developed in him the self-sufficiency of a lone wolf. It is a formidable combination, as is his holy simplicity and his steely political wiles – as the vested interests in Rome are beginning to understand. Francis was both using the Curia and imaginatively bypassing it. But how would that help him bring about the fundamental reform of the system that he had set out to achieve?

* * *

The Roman Curia is one of the oldest institutions of government in the world. Over the years it has proven extraordinarily resistant to change. It was created by the medieval papacy to govern, not just a church, but the substantial territory that popes controlled as medieval monarchs. To do that they needed a tax system, a police force, and army, a judicial system and all the appurtenances of a state.

It was fixed in its present format in 1588 by Pope Sixtus V, who organized the consistories of cardinals into 15 standing congregations, each with a specific area of competence. Later Popes tinkered with the system but did not alter the basic bureaucratic structure Sixtus had put in place. In 1908 Pius X undertook a significant reorganization to take account of the loss of the Papal States after the unification of Italy – and to accommodate the declarations of papal primacy and infallibility made at the First Vatican Council in 1870. A second reform took place in 1967 when Paul VI greatly expanded the system by adding 12 pontifical councils to work on the new issues Vatican II had highlighted – the laity, Christian unity, the family, justice and peace, migrants and refugees, inter-religious dialogue, culture, and communications. But paradoxically the 1967 reform, according to the church historian Massimo Faggioli, in practice strengthened the centralizing tendencies in the system – of which so many bishops had complained at Vatican II, as they did before the conclave that elected Pope Francis. The two popes who followed, John Paul II and Benedict XVI, had even less time for the Vatican II notion of collegial government and turned the Synod of Bishops into a mere talking shop, and then controlled what they were allowed to talk about. Pope John Paul II set aside Paul VI's idea that the major heads of curial offices should stay in office for only a five-year term. And he shifted the focus of curial power from its traditional place in the office of the Secretariat of State to that of the Congregation for the Doctrine of the Faith where Cardinal Joseph Ratzinger was the man in charge for 23 years.

This was the system against which cardinals of all doctrinal persuasions were united in the General Congregation discussions before they elected Jorge Mario Bergoglio as Pope. The centralizing model had brought scandal, self-serving intrigue, lethargy and dysfunction. It was time for a change. The overwhelming consensus in the debates gave Pope Francis the mandate to bring radical reform.

Radical reform was the brief Francis gave to his hand-picked advisers on his Council of Cardinals in his first month in office. Pope John Paul II's constitution, *Pastor Bonus*, had set out the responsibilities and rights of more than thirty departments, known as dicasteries, which included one secretariat, nine congregations, twelve pontifical councils, seven pontifical commissions, three tribunals and an array of commissions, academies, institutes and other offices. Pope Francis told his C8 not to amend *Pastor Bonus* but to scrap it and write 'something completely new, not just a modification or adaptation'.

What the new Pope wanted, said Cardinal Sean O'Malley, one of the eight cardinal advisers, was for 'The Curia to be at the service of the universal Church and that means great efficiency, greater transparency, collaboration among the different departments, a great focus on collegiality and involvement with the bishops through the world and the local churches.' It was such a priority for Francis that on his first day in Brazil in July 2013 – when he was supposed to be resting after a 12-hour flight – the new Pope instead held a meeting with the C8's coordinator Cardinal Rodríguez Maradiaga. Francis began consulting regularly with Cardinal Rodríguez, and others on the C8, long before the advisory council came together for its first actual meeting in October. By the time they convened, on their advice, Francis had already set up a number of papal committees and commissions, and hired outside companies, to audit and review the financial and administrative entities of the Holy See – including the notorious Vatican Bank.

With so many dicasteries at present, Rodríguez said later, 'How can a leader regularly bring together all of his ministers? In the past, meetings took place once or twice a year. How can an institution go on like this? Meetings and consultations need to be more frequent. Then we will be able to say that simplification fosters collegiality. And this is important.' Other members of the C8, in those early days, fired out all kinds of ideas for the kind of reform required. 'Bishops have their own dicastery,' Rodríguez said. 'Religious people and the clergy have theirs, but the laity is the majority of the Church, and they only have a council.' Perhaps the Pontifical Council, which has only the status of a think-tank in the Vatican, could be upgraded to a Congregation, which is a decision-making body – and perhaps, suggested O'Malley, it could be led by a woman. Perhaps a lot more lay women were needed in the Curia. Perhaps curial congregations could be staffed entirely by diocesan bishops; the Congregation for Divine Worship, for example, could be staffed by the chairs of liturgical committees in bishops' conferences. Perhaps the job of the Secretary of State should be redefined to avoid the problems produced under Cardinal Bertone. Perhaps, said another C8 member, Cardinal Oswald Gracias, the idea of a set term of five years should be brought back. Bishops would be willing to send their best men to Rome if they knew they would get them back in five years, he said. That would also have the advantage of reducing careerism, one of the besetting sins of the Curia, added Cardinal Rodríguez.

All this set high expectations of change running in the Church. Around the same time the retired Archbishop of San Francisco, John Quinn, revealed that he had bumped into Bergoglio a few days before the conclave. The Pope-to-be had said to him: 'I've read your book and am hoping it will be implemented.' The book of which Bergoglio so approved was called *The Reform of the Papacy: The Costly Call to Christian Unity*. In it Quinn had said that the election of a pope should be transferred from cardinals to representatives elected by the world's bishops. Bishops should be elected by their fellow bishops in each nation and not be appointed by Rome on the recommendation of the nuncio, as at present; Rome should only have a veto. The Curia should be run by civil servants who should not be elevated to the rank of bishop, which was 'an abuse of the office of bishop' because a bishop was a teacher and a pastor not a bureaucrat. The Synod of Bishops should not be responsible to the Curia; the system should work the other way round, with the bishops making the decisions and the Curia merely implementing them. Heads of curial dicasteries should not be members of the synod as at present. All this would restore 'the synodal model of the Church of the first millennium' which saw the Pope not as monarch but as 'first among equals' in the college of bishops.

This was heady stuff. Other prominent figures added their voices to such radical ideas. 'Francis could abolish the conclave – it only dates from 1059,' said the papal historian Michael Walsh, the former Librarian of Heythrop College. 'He's got to repatriate authority to the diocese. Rome should just be an appeal system on annulments, the liturgy and doctrinal orthodoxy. The traditional role of a pope, if you go back to the great Innocent III (1198–1216), was to be an adjudicator.' 'It would be very possible to restructure the Curia so the cardinals didn't have to be in it at all,' said another prominent Catholic historian, Professor Eamon Duffy. 'The idea that popes should appoint all bishops in the Latin rite only goes back to the 1917 code of canon law,' said Nicholas Lash, Emeritus Professor of Divinity at the University of Cambridge. 'We need to give over the appointment of bishops to the episcopal conferences. It's through their control of the appointment of bishops that the Curia control the Church. De-centralizing the church has its dangers, and we need to be alert to them, and to the possibility of too much diversity. But at present the pendulum has swung far too far the other way. Bishops are supposed to be teachers but at present they do not teach, they just give orders. Commanding is not the same as teaching.' The Jesuit Father Thomas Reese, author of *Inside the Vatican: The Politics and Organization of the Catholic Church*, suggested that the Pope introduce 'a greater separation of powers' so that the CDF could no longer act as 'prosecutor, judge, jury and executioner' when trying theologians it arraigned, alleging a lack of doctrinal orthodoxy. 'The whole system needs more checks and balances.' Francis should change the language of the Vatican from the minority language of Italian to a world language like English or Spanish, said one serving member of the Curia, who asked not to be named, adding: 'He could even move the Vatican from Rome to the developing world'. The Pope's chief theological adviser, Archbishop Victor Manuel Fernández, who wrote the first draft of *Evangelii Gaudium*, has even gone so far as to say: 'The Roman Curia is not an essential structure. The Pope could even go and live away from Rome, have a dicastery in Rome and another one in Bogotá, and perhaps link-up by teleconference with liturgical experts that live in Germany.'

Compared with talk like that progress on the reform seemed slow, which only led commentators to assume that the change would be radical. After all, Pope Francis had said to Spadaro: 'Discernment takes time. Many think that changes and reforms can take place in a short time. I believe that we always need time to lay the foundations for real, effective change.' But as the second anniversary of Francis's election approached, rumours began to circulate that the process had stalled or run aground. In the cardinals' meeting at the creation of Francis's second batch of cardinals in February 2015 the talk was that the C9 reform was amounting only to a merger of the main pontifical councils into two new Congregations – one for the Laity and the other for Justice and Peace. Francis appeared to confirm this in an interview for the Argentine newspaper *La Nación*. Asked by Elisabetta Piqué if a married couple might be the head of the new dicastery for lay people, the Pope replied: 'The head of a dicastery like the Congregation for the Doctrine of the Faith, the liturgical dicastery or the new dicastery encompassing laity and family as well as justice and peace will always be a cardinal. This is best because of his closeness to the Pope as a collaborator in a given sector. But dicastery secretaries do not necessarily have to be bishops.'

Reform optimists opined that the Pope was suggesting that only the heads of the Congregations need be cardinals, thus opening the way for more lay people in lesser roles. Pessimists concluded that Pope Francis seemed to be rowing back on earlier radical ideas with his rather tame proposal merely to create two new congregations. Yet even such a modest proposal met with objections from some cardinals. When the issue of term-limits for curial officials was raised some argued against that too. The tentative proposals received far more criticism than had been expected.

It may have been that this was just a first step in the Francis revolution. But many long-standing Vatican observers seemed disappointed. John Thavis, who was for 25 years the head of the Rome Bureau of the Catholic News Service, concluded that the Vatican press office was trying to 'downsize expectations'. It briefed that the cardinals were offered only 'a vague outline' of the proposal to combine six or seven pontifical councils into two new congregations and that 'the cardinals were told it could take years to complete the reforms'. Certainly the Secretary of the C9, Archbishop Marcello Semeraro, seemed to be outlining a protracted process when he referred to the process used, by Pope John Paul II. Then a first group of cardinals wrote a draft, he said, which was then discussed by each episcopal conference. The suggestions were then analyzed and incorporated into a second document, written by cardinals and canon law experts. Pope John Paul's modifications to the Roman Curia took 10 years to design and implement, with multiple stages of consultation and approval. 'I'm not sure Pope Francis has 10 years to dedicate to this project,' Thavis observed. The Vatican spokesman, Father Federico Lombardi, had said that it was 'unthinkable' for any Vatican congregation – even one for laity – to be headed by a lay person. 'That tells me,' concluded Thavis, 'that whatever the Pope's advisers have in mind, Curia reform is not going to touch the fundamental clerical framework of decision-making in the Vatican.' The plans might not even get beyond the 'endless study' phase without 'some forceful leadership moves by Pope Francis' to advance the reform agenda.

The Jesuit Father Thomas Reese, who writes for the liberal *National Catholic Reporter*, was even more gloomy at the glacial pace. 'That it took the Council of Cardinals two years to come up with this reshuffling of boxes on the organizational chart,' he wrote, 'simply shows they really don't know what they are doing. It should have taken two months to develop this plan, not two years. At this pace, Pope Francis will be dead before real reform hits the Curia.'

Reforming the Vatican, he suggested, needed to begin with a vision rather than a desire to improve efficiency. If the Pope was seen as an absolute monarch in whom all wisdom resides then a structure was required which referred all important decisions to the Pope or to those to whom he has delegated decision-making power in the Curia. But if the Pope was seen as a first among equals, acting collegially with his fellow bishops, then the Church needed a system for encouraging discussion and consensus-building. Francis in his words had called for the latter, yet the reforms being proposed in his name seemed to fit into the old monarchical model. The proposed reform felt it still belonged in a court rather than a civil service, Reese said. The plan did little to address the problem of clericalism or careerism within the Church. The reform of the Roman Curia was intractable precisely because there was no practical consensus on this vision.

'If Francis doesn't transform the Curia,' warned Quinn, 'not only will everything else come to nothing, but he himself will also be affected by it. I know a lot of very holy humble people in the Curia but as a system, as a structure, it has long been a great obstacle to the life of the Church.' Perhaps what was needed was some input from an outside secular agency, suggested the Jesuit Father John W. O'Malley, a professor of theology at Georgetown University and author of *What Happened at Vatican II*. 'The commission of cardinals that Pope Francis has appointed for this task is a step in the right direction,' he wrote. 'But the cardinals are themselves churchmen who work inside the system.' Outside advisers, he proposed, would be 'much more likely to ask questions that do not even occur to Church members.'

* * *

Reform in the Church always meets serious resistance. Perhaps the most persistent and radical advocate of reform after the Second Vatican Council, the theologian Father Hans Küng, wrote of Pope Francis not long after he was elected: 'Doubtless, he will awaken powerful opposition, above all in the power-house of the Roman Curia, opposition that is difficult to withstand. Those in power in the Vatican are not likely to abandon the power that has been accumulated since the Middle Ages.'

At first those who were wary of the Pope who had taken the name of that most radical of saints, Francis of Assisi, kept quiet and watched. They were uneasy that they, and their allies, had been confirmed in their jobs only provisionally – *donec aliter provideatur* – but they decided to say nothing in the hope that that would keep them out of the line of fire. 'They thought that all they had to do was keep their heads down and wait for the next pontificate,' said an Argentine theologian who makes frequent visits to Rome. 'Then in a few years everything would go back to how it was before.'

But gradually unease hardened into discontent. Conservatives looked around and saw that many of their fellows who had been provisionally confirmed in their jobs were being steadily removed. Curia officials grew more nervous and began to worry that all the talk of closing offices and cutting staff might cost them their high-status positions. Biding their time seemed a less attractive strategy. So when the Council of Cardinals distributed a questionnaire asking dicasteries what activities could be passed from them down to local dioceses around the world they were uncooperative in their response. A middle-ranking official in one dicastery told me: 'Every department in the Curia received a letter asking, "What can you do to devolve matters down to dioceses?" The cardinal read it out to staff, and before anyone could speak, he said: "Well, in our case, there's nothing really, is there?" He was not asking a question which required an answer. I suspect the same thing happened in many other departments.' The Church would lose its universal unity if too much was passed out to local bishops, they argued. But could nothing at all be devolved, the cardinal advisers asked. No, was the curial reply.

It was to counter that kind of foot-dragging that Pope Francis turned to the whole body of cardinals. He presented his reforms to the consistory in February 2015, hoping it would unblock some of that lack of curial cooperation. Yet he found opposition even there. Vatican reporters began to detect that conservatives and traditionalists felt they were winning the battle to slow down the momentum of reform. 'There's more resistance than I had expected,' one of the Pope's allies told me.

Francis himself made out that he was unsurprised and undismayed. 'Resistance is now evident. And that is a good sign for me, getting the resistance out into the open, no stealthy mumbling when there is disagreement,' he told *La Nación*. 'It's healthy to get things out into the open; it's very healthy. To me, resistance means different points of view, not something dirty. It is connected to some decisions I may occasionally take, I will concede that. I am not worried. It all seems normal to me. If there were no difference of opinions, that wouldn't be normal.' But he admitted that the pushback was slowing down reform to the extent that he did not expect it to be completed by the end of 2015. 'It's a slow process,' he said. 'We're tackling it step by step.' But the truth was that work on the drafting of the new constitution had not even begun. The C9 had not even nominated a drafting committee to work on the changes. Members of the C9 were privately talking about a process that would take years.

* * *

Pope Francis may have been playing a much craftier game than the enthusiasts for change appreciated. Certainly there was an apparent consistency in the behaviour of the Argentine Pope. Some of the decisions Francis made, like the creation of the C9 and boosting the importance of the Synod of Bishops, fitted the template of radical reform set out by Quinn and others. But other acts moved in the opposite direction, such as continuing to make bishops of people given jobs in the Curia and in the enlarged offices of the synod secretariat. This may have been inconsistent. But others saw the Pope as playing a long game. 'Francis is playing softly softly catchee monkey,' one Vatican insider said. 'Keeping people guessing is part of his management technique. He keeps people off balance. It is part of his destabilizing the Curia.' 'He's a Jesuit,' said the Argentinian journalist Alberto Barriaga. 'He doesn't move directly on an objective. He will surround it and when it is the right moment, he will pulverize it.'

Francis may not have been able to get the cardinals collectively to agree upon fixed terms but that did not stop him implementing the idea in practice. Dozens of Curia officials – from cardinals to lowly monsignors – were dispatched back to their home countries having been thanked for their service over the past five or six years. Overturning the old way of doing things, bypassing the usual channels and preferring the unofficial to the official, emerged as the quintessential Francis way of getting things done. He promoted certain individuals, leapfrogging them three or four grades in the curial pecking order. When he wanted to get a message to China, instead of using a Vatican diplomat, he sent it via some Argentinian missionaries whom he knew had good contacts with the Chinese government. 'He's very happy to use unconventional channels,' one foreign ambassador told me. He was untroubled about overturning precedent, as when he lifted the diplomatic immunity of a papal nuncio who had been accused of sexually abusing boys in Santo Domingo and ordered he should be put on trial in a Vatican court.

Nor was he afraid to upset official systems and sentiments when he saw a greater good. In Argentina he had struck up a personal friendship with an evangelical pastor, Tony Palmer. Early on as Pope he decided to send a message through Palmer to the Charismatic Evangelical Leadership Conference in the United States. Francis told Palmer to get out his iPhone and recorded a message of greeting to men he described as 'brother bishops'. After it was played on a giant screen at the conference, Vatican officials in the department responsible for Christian unity received a peeved communication from Lambeth Palace, the office of the Archbishop of Canterbury, pointing out that as Palmer and the other evangelical bishops were not Anglicans it was not appropriate for the Pope to refer to them as 'brother bishops' that way. 'We had spent ages under the previous pope trying to keep Palmer out of the Vatican on the grounds that he wasn't an Anglican but had a rather dubious background in the Gospel of Prosperity,' said a former official from the Pontifical Council for Promoting Christian Unity. (The Gospel of Prosperity asserts that God will give material riches to Christians who are faithful.) 'Palmer's presence wouldn't have been conducive to good relations with the Church of England or the Anglican Communion. But Francis wasn't bothered about all that. Friendships mean a lot to him. He uses his friendships, as he did with Rabbi Skorka in Israel. To Francis the message of brotherhood, unity and love was more important than denominational niceties.'

But the most significant area in which Pope Francis used unilateral papal action to shape deeper reform was in the appointment of cardinals – the men who would chose his successor as Pope. Francis created two batches of cardinals; 19 in February 2014 and 20 more a year later in 2015. Again the Pope's approach was unorthodox; those appointed were not given the usual advance warning from the Vatican but heard it from an unexpected public announcement by the Pope. Some learned it only at second-hand because of texts and calls of congratulations from friends who had heard the Pope speak. On both occasions commentators pored over the lists of new cardinals and tried to figure out an overall message from the Pope. What became clear was that those who had been given the new red hats were not all of a particular view. In the 2015 batch there were some like John Atcherley Dew of New Zealand and Ricardo Blázquez Pérez of Spain who were open to change on the totemic issue of allowing remarried Catholics to take Communion. But in the same batch was also Berhaneyesus Demerew Souraphiel of Ethiopia, who had called homosexual behaviour 'the pinnacle of immorality'.

Nor were the new men all friends of the Pope; he struggled to pronounce the names of some of them. Nor was he looking for men of a particular age bracket; Bishop Soane Patita Paini Mafi of Tonga was only 53 but several other of the new men were close to the bishops' retiring age of 75 already.

What was immediately striking was the geographical spread. Only a few were from Europe and none were from the United States – two regions already over-represented in the College of Cardinals compared with a map of where the world's Catholics actually live. But there were significant numbers from the developing world including cardinals from some of the poorest places on earth – Burkina Faso, Haiti, Nicaragua, Panama, Ivory Coast, Cape Verde, Tonga, Vietnam and Myanmar. Many of these countries did not have cardinals before. Clearly the first Pope from outside Europe for 1,300 years was seeking to redress an imbalance in a church where two-thirds of its 1.2 billion members live outside the West – a proportion that is set to grow to three-quarters by the end of the century. For the first time Europe now has less than half the world's cardinals and 41 per cent are from the developing world compared with 35 per cent when Francis was elected. They would be, the new Ethiopian cardinal said, 'the voice of the voiceless' in the global Church. The first Pope from the global South was orchestrating a shift that could change Catholicism for ever.

Francis's selection of cardinals created another transfer of power and struck a blow against the disease of clerical careerism which he sees as such a problem in the Church, and in the Vatican in particular. In the past there was a clearly defined route to becoming a cardinal. A priest would rise through the ranks to become a bishop's secretary, spend some time as an official in a national bishops' conference or get a middle-ranking job in the Curia in Rome, before being appointed an auxiliary bishop. Next he would become the bishop in a small diocese, before being promoted to a large metropolitan archdiocese, which, a few years later, would result in an automatic red hat. Certain big archdioceses – like Venice or Paris or Los Angeles – were always led by a cardinal.

No longer. Pope Francis passed over archbishops in several of these 'automatic' dioceses and appointed men from much smaller places. He twice bypassed the Patriarch of Venice and the Archbishop of Turin and gave red hats to the bishops of the much smaller Italian dioceses of Perugia, Ancona and Agrigento.

And he created no US cardinals at all, ignoring the unwritten tradition that big dioceses like Chicago, Los Angeles and Philadelphia have always been led by a cardinal in recent times. That may simply have been because in each case the retired archbishops were still voting cardinals. Or it could have been an attempt to redress the imbalance of the fact that Americans comprise just 6 per cent of the global Church and yet have 9 per cent of its cardinals. Either way, the Pope's actions undermined the prevailing assumption about the way to become a cardinal. 'Clerical careerists who thought they knew the road to becoming a cardinal,' wrote Tom Reese, 'now find that "the first will be last, and the last will be first".'

That was reinforced by another signal. Only one cardinal in the two batches was from the Curia – Archbishop Dominique Mamberti, who had taken over Cardinal Burke's position as head of the Vatican's supreme court, the Apostolic Signatura. 'This has not gone down well with many in Rome,' said one long-serving middle-ranking member of the Vatican civil service. 'The old system has been broken and Francis has given every indication that this is permanent. In *Evangelii Gaudium* he clearly states that we have to get out of the idea and mentality that we do things this way because we've always done them this way. Francis wants to get the Curia out of the Italian mentality.' Pope Francis had already abolished the honorific priestly title Monsignor (My Lord) for priests under the age of 65 because he felt it smacked of medieval flummery. (He kept it for members of the Vatican diplomatic corps only.) And he was said to have declared an end to another *onorificienza*, the courtly post of Papal Gentleman, a group of often aristocratic dignitaries who officiated at public ceremonies. Francis was said to believe the title was 'archaic, useless, even damaging'. Now he appeared to be suggesting that the bureaucrats who ran the Vatican civil service didn't need top clerical titles either.

Two characteristics united the individuals chosen by Pope Francis to be his new cardinals. Many were, or had been, presidents of their national or regional bishops' conferences. Clearly working well with other bishops was a characteristic Francis valued highly. But the overwhelming common factor was that each man seemed to see himself as a pastor who was close to his people, and worked closely with those who were most in need. In Uruguay, Archbishop Daniel Sturla Berhouet was working in the slums of Montevideo when he learned he had been made a cardinal. In Panama, Bishop José Lacunza Maestrojuan was an activist for social justice for indigenous people – 'the poorest of the poor' – affected by mining conglomerates. In Mexico, Archbishop Alberto Suárez Inda had spoken out powerfully on immigration and violence around the drug trade. In the small Italian diocese of Agrigento the archbishop, Francesco

Montenegro, had been a tireless advocate for the migrants in Lampedusa, which was in his diocese, and had stood up against the Mafia, refusing a grand church funeral for a gang leader. Francis's choices were all, said Gerard O'Connell, the Rome correspondent of the Jesuit magazine *America*: 'prayerful, courageous, open-minded, humble men with a simple lifestyle, not careerists or ideologues, pastors committed to the culture of encounter, not men of confrontation'. They were, as the Pope had said in that first Spadaro interview, 'ministers of the Gospel...who can warm the hearts of the people, who walk through the dark night with them, who know how to dialogue and to descend themselves into their people's night, into the darkness, but without getting lost'. The people of God, Pope Francis had said, 'want pastors, not clergy acting like bureaucrats or government officials'. And that was what he wanted for the College of Cardinals. They must not, he warned them, 'become a closed caste' but must 'serve Jesus crucified in every person who is marginalized...even in those who have lost their faith, or turned away from the practice of their faith, or who have declared themselves to be atheists'. This would be scandalous to some people, Francis said, but 'Jesus is not afraid of this kind of scandal!'

Francis wanted more here than simply to bring the voices of the peripheries to be heard at the centre of the Church. The new cardinals would be the men who would, sooner or later, elect Francis's successor. The new conclave had a distinctly different bias to those which went before it. The geographical spread of cardinals was still unrepresentative of the location of Catholics around the globe. But it was less so. Europe still had the biggest number, 57, but that was for the first time less than half the 125 eligible to participate in the election of the next pope. Of these, 26 were still Italian, but that was the lowest figure on record. The next biggest group were the 18 cardinals from North America, then Africa with 15, Asia with 14, South America with 12, Central America with 6, and Oceania, which had 3. One traditionalist website spoke with alarm about the prospect of a 'Third World conclave' but the numbers were still some way off that being possible, though Francis has asked a senior cardinal to prepare a document on the implications of his idea of expanding the conclave of electors from its current notional limit of 120 to 140. With curial cardinals at an historic low the impact of the Curia on the conclave would be even further reduced.

For the Pope from Argentina, however, this is not simply about loading the odds in favour of another leader from the developing world next time. He thinks that younger churches have the potential more generally to revitalize the Church centred in a continent which – as he told the European Parliament when he visited it in 2014 – is now like 'a grandmother, no longer fertile and vibrant' but rather 'elderly and haggard', which risked 'slowly losing its own soul'. As he had told Spadaro: 'The young Catholic churches, as they grow, develop a synthesis of faith, culture and life...different from the one developed by the ancient churches. For me, the relationship between the ancient Catholic churches and the young ones is similar to the relationship between young and elderly people in a society. They build the future, the young ones with their strength and the others with their wisdom. You always run some risks, of course. The younger churches are likely to feel self-sufficient; the ancient ones are likely to want to impose on the younger churches their cultural models. But we build the future together.'

* * *

From early 2015 Pope Francis gave his College of Cardinals a new role. He invited them at what was called an 'extraordinary consistory' in February that year to act, de facto, as a kind of Senate for the Catholic Church, much as the cardinalate acted in the first millennium of church history. Francis asked Cardinal Pell to report to them on the state of church finances and the progress of the reforms to the Vatican Bank and other finances in four audio-visual presentations. It was the first time that the College had received such a report and been given the chance to interrogate officials on it. The Pope also asked them for their views on the reforms to the constitution of the Curia and on proposed devolutions of power from the central to the local churches, which were presented to the cardinals by the Secretary of the C9, Archbishop Marcello Semeraro.

At the same time Francis signalled his own views on the direction of reform he wanted by changing the church ceremony at the heart of the relationship between Rome and the senior dioceses around the world. In the past the symbol of office of those senior archbishops known as metropolitans and primates was a band of cloth known as a *pallium*. In church history it is more ancient than the mitre or the crozier as an episcopal symbol. Traditionally it was bestowed on the prelates by the Pope in Rome. But Francis ordered that from January 2015 the bishops should be invested with the garment by the papal nuncio back in their home dioceses. The move was designed, a Vatican spokesman announced, to enhance 'the participation of the local church in an important moment of its life and history'. It was to signal major steps along what Pope Francis told 34 candidates for the *pallium* was the Church's 'path of collegiality'. It was another break with the trajectory of the previous 150 years. It signalled what, as we shall see in Chapter 15, is the first step in a shift of power from the Roman bureaucracy to the Synod of Bishops – the biggest shift for over 400 years, according to the church historian Eamon Duffy.

But would that happen? Some, like the Franciscan friar and international author Father Richard Rohr, believed that the changes Pope Francis had instituted have already changed the Church permanently. 'Francis's very manner of talking is unpapal and scary for any who feel a pope owes them absolute answers and perfect certitude about everything. We now have a Pope who knows his role: to be a pastor, a friend, a companion on the journey, and a surgeon in the field hospital after a battle. Francis has become a living and happy invitation to all of humanity, even beyond the too-tight boundaries of Christianity. In that alone, he has changed the papacy. We can never go completely backward.' Others disagreed. The conclusion of John Wilkins, a former editor of *The Tablet*, was very different. 'If the Curia could nullify key parts of Vatican II in ten years, they could nullify Pope Francis's legacy in ten days,' said Wilkins. 'So here is the $64,000 question: can he institutionalize all this? That was Vatican II's failure. Can he redress it?'

Again Francis was elusive, telling the cardinals in that extraordinary consistory that 'the reform is not an end in itself' but a means to better spread the message of the Gospel and to put the peripheries at the centre. Spiritual rather than structural reform was his greatest concern 'right now', the Pope said in a newspaper interview at the end of 2014. One of the C9, Cardinal Sean O'Malley, revealed that the Pope was worried about the spiritual welfare of the people in the Curia. 'He wants them to feel that they are there not just for a job, but they are part of a mission and that mission comes from Christ,' said O'Malley. 'To be able to carry it out we need to attend to our own interior life so that we have a sense of vocation and that we are being led by God's grace to seek God's will and to embrace it joyfully and generously in our lives.'

To address this, Francis introduced compulsory five-day retreats for all Vatican officials. In the past the annual Lenten retreat was held inside the Vatican and curial officials would attend the two prayer sessions and attend a reflective talk by a retreat director but would fit them into their work diary. Some did not attend at all. But Francis made them all go off to a monastery for five days – and he went with them. Structural reform will achieve nothing without spiritual change, the Pope argued, an attitude he said must cascade out to dioceses, parishes, communities and the ordinary faithful across the Catholic world. The question was: would that foster the kind of constitutional change needed to tackle the clericalism and careerism which had beset the Curia? Or would spiritual renewal divert attention from the continuing need for a change in Vatican organization?

'I don't think he has a plan of the exact outcomes he wants, he just wants to unleash the unruly freedom of the Spirit,' said one long-term close-up observer of the Vatican. One of the Jesuits closest to the Jesuit Pope agreed. 'Pope Francis doesn't likes visions rather than projects,' Father Antonio Spadaro told me. 'He likes to discern the will of God from inside history. Sometimes that means he learns what God wants for the Church, step by step, by walking the paths.'

14

The War over Sex Abuse

It was 6.30 a.m. Unusually, a Swiss Guard stood by the chapel in the Casa Santa Marta as guests made their way down to an early breakfast. The soldier was not in his plain blue fustian everyday tunic. He was wearing the full yellow-and-blue-and-red dress uniform – the Medici colours of the sixteenth-century Pope, Leo X – which these men have worn since the Renaissance. The coloured stripes and the baggy pantaloons make the guards look appurtenances of a quaint tourist-attraction Vatican. But the comic-opera costume belies an operational purpose. These men are there to guard the Pope.

'Sorry,' said the guard at the door, when one of the visitors tried to enter the chapel to say their morning prayers before breakfast, 'you can't go in. The chapel is occupied.'

Inside, Pope Francis was praying alone. Normally others were permitted to join him before the tabernacle containing the Blessed Sacrament early in the morning. But today was different and he wanted to be alone with God before the others arrived for his 7 a.m. daily Mass.

It would be a smaller crowd than usual. The main guests were six survivors of the sexual attacks by priests whose conduct – and the conduct of thousands of other priests and members of religious orders – had deeply shamed the Catholic Church in the closing decades of the twentieth century.

The shame was far from a thing of the past. Now Francis was about to come face to face with some victims of the predator priests whose conduct had tarnished the moral authority of the Catholic Church all across the world. It would be the first such meeting in his 54 years of ministry. Indeed, victims of clerical abuse from Argentina were claiming, that very day, that he had been avoiding such a meeting – despite their repeated requests – for more than two decades.

Now Francis had screwed up his courage to say a private Mass for six survivors – and would then meet them, one by one, in a morning of personal encounters. It was a big day for them. It was a big day for him too. He needed to pray.

* * *

Given the speed with which Pope Francis had acted on the reform of the Curia, the Vatican Bank, and on pivotal appointments at the top of the Church, he seemed to have been extraordinarily slow to address the issue of the thousands of paedophile priests whose behaviour had scandalized the world – as had the way that their behaviour had been covered up by many bishops. Nothing had done more to damage the credibility of the Church in recent decades and to undermine the message it strove to communicate. It was not just the problem itself. It was also, as the British ambassador to the Holy See, Nigel Baker, boldly noted on an official UK government website, the Church's 'failure to understand the seriousness of the problem, and to grasp the need to do so much more to stop it'. The previous pope, Benedict, had met with sex abuse victims in various countries on his travels but despite that, the diplomat noted when he arrived in post in 2011, for the church hierarchy 'the collective response still appeared to be one of denial'. Far more needed to be done, the ambassador said in an unusually public criticism.

Little seemed to have changed with the arrival of Pope Francis. Almost a year had gone by without this most talkative of popes properly addressing the subject of sex abuse. Behind the scenes he had been no more active. At the first meeting of his council of eight cardinal advisers, the C8, in October 2013, sex abuse was not even on the agenda – despite the huge damage that it had done to the reputation of the Catholic Church. It took him almost a year before he announced he was creating a Pontifical Commission for the Protection of Minors. It took him another three months to decide who would serve on it. And only after 16 months of his pontificate had elapsed was he getting round to meeting survivors – something Pope Benedict had already done half a dozen times. 'He has been extraordinarily slow,' one cardinal confided in me. What explained the delay?

The world had long before lost patience with the Catholic Church's foot-dragging on the issue. That was underscored in January 2014 when the Vatican was summoned before the United Nations Committee on the Rights of the Child to explain how it had handled the issue of paedophile priests. The truth was that under Benedict XVI the Catholic Church had done a lot to address the issue. In his later years as Cardinal Ratzinger, he had insisted that all clerical abuse cases were sent to him personally from all over the world. Reading the files had horrified him. When he became Pope he defrocked 848 abuser priests. But his instinct was to handle matters behind closed doors. It was only in 2010 that he allowed dioceses around the world to report suspect priests to the police and ordered local bishops to draw up new guidelines to protect children in churches. Many bishops had ignored both edicts.

So the UN report, when it was published, was scathing. It indicted the Catholic Church with tens of thousands of crimes by priestly abusers over several decades in a dozen countries. It called on the Church to remove all abusers from active ministry, report them to the police and open the church archives on the 4,000 cases which had been referred to the Vatican. The case against the Church was clear but the UN experts, either naïvely or ideologically, could not resist extending their attack to include Catholic teachings on contraception, homosexuality and abortion – telling the Church that it encouraged the persecution of homosexuals and transgendered people with its doctrine on the complementarity of the sexes. The extension of the agenda allowed Vatican officials to respond with a forceful counter-attack, claiming the UN had gone beyond its proper area of competence – and had violated the safeguards on religious freedom in its own Universal Declaration of Human Rights.

A month later, in March 2014, Pope Francis also hit back. In an interview with *Corriere della Sera* he complained that, when it came to putting in place guidelines to protect children, 'the Catholic Church is perhaps the only public institution to have acted with transparency and responsibility'. He continued: 'No one else has done more. Yet the Church is the only one to have been attacked.' More children were abused by family members, he said, than by priests.

The Pope's response sounded out of touch and ill-judged. It was true that the Catholic Church had made some improvements. In countries like Britain, Ireland and the United States tight child protection guidelines had been put in force. The procedures set in place in the UK after a report by Lord Nolan, the former chairman of that country's Committee on Standards in Public Life, had become the worldwide best-practice benchmark on child protection. In the US background checks on adults and safe environment education, for millions of Catholic children and church workers, had seen new cases of clerical sexual abuse fall significantly. But in many other countries no such measures had been put in place. Despite the Pope's words it was just not true that the Catholic Church had 'moved with transparency and responsibility'.

Francis had been badly briefed. Certainly in 2010 Pope Benedict had instructed bishops that henceforth they must obey civil laws requiring the reporting of offenders to the police. But most countries in the world did not have laws that actually make the reporting of such crimes mandatory. Where there was no such civil law bishops remained subject to a church law that required them to keep allegations of clergy abuse secret. That was what was laid down in a 2001 *motu proprio* of Pope John Paul II, *Sacramentorum Sanctitatis Tutela*, confirming a 1974 instruction of Pope Paul VI, *Secreta Continere*. Pope Benedict's 2010 revision of the rules, telling bishops to comply with civil law, had not reversed that. The legal framework was still in place for an institutional cover-up by the bishops. The wriggle-room it allowed was exploited just a few weeks later when the Italian bishops' conference, at the end of March 2014, announced 'with backing from the Vatican' that its members would cooperate with any police inquiry – but would not be reporting predator priests to the police because they had no 'juridical obligation' to do so. The statement by Francis that things had got better – and lamenting that the Church was getting no credit for that – sounded defensive. Instead he should have been apologetic at what priests had done, and bishops had covered up. The new Pope seemed to be reading from the Church's same old script. 'No change' was the message received by the rest of the world.

* * *

Something was going on behind the scenes, but painfully slowly. One of the Pope's eight cardinal advisers, Cardinal Sean O'Malley – who had spent a decade trying to clear up hundreds of sex abuse cases in the Boston archdiocese – had raised clerical sex abuse when he saw it was not on the agenda of the first meeting of the C8. But the Pope, and the other cardinals, did not seize on the idea that something needed to be done immediately. O'Malley persisted. After ten months of private badgering Francis finally took him aside from the other advisers and said: 'OK, what do we need to do?'

The very next day O'Malley called a press conference and announced that Pope Francis was setting up a Pontifical Commission for the Protection of Minors. The Vatican was taken unawares. The usual protocol was to consult within the Curia on such a new body. There would then be turf wars to decide which department should oversee it. Then a legal constitution would have to be drawn up. Then various factions in the Curia would have their say on who should be the members. Only then would it be announced. That day in December 2013 O'Malley turned all that upside down. He announced it first. The specifics, he told the media, would be worked out later but the members would be 'experts in the work of safeguarding children' and would include those with practical experience of taking care of children. The commission would therefore include outsiders. And, like the lay experts brought in to reform Vatican finances, they would report direct to the Pope.

* * *

One afternoon, three months later, the phones rang, in close succession, in homes in England, Ireland, France, Germany and Italy. The man making the calls was Monsignor Bob Oliver who had been, for the previous two years, the chief prosecutor at the Congregation for the Doctrine of the Faith in the Vatican. Almost all his work there had been investigating predator priests. Before that he had spent ten years working with Cardinal Sean O'Malley in Boston helping clear up one of the worst clerical sex abuse portfolios in the history of the US Church. He was ringing a collection of psychologists, psychiatrists, psychotherapists and lawyers – and asking them all the same question. Would they be interested in joining the Pope's new commission into sex abuse? A quick decision was needed, he told them. Pope Francis wanted to announce the membership of the body the very next day. Quite why it was such a rush, after months of inactivity, was not clear.

Several of those calls broke new ground. Four of them were to women, which would mean that half the experts summoned to the panel were female. That was unprecedented for a Vatican committee. But one call was even more unusual. It was to someone whose expertise in the subject of sex abuse was rooted in personal experience. Marie Collins was a survivor of sexual molestation by a priest. She was the only survivor to be invited to join the Pontifical Commission for the Protection of Minors in those early days.

Five decades earlier, at the age of just 13, she had been taken into hospital. There she had been raped by the Catholic priest who was her hospital chaplain. The experience was so traumatic that it took her 25 years to summon up the courage to report him. It had added hugely to the confusion in her mind that her abuser was a priest. The fingers that abused her body the night before were the next morning holding and offering her the sacred host, which Catholics believe to be the very body of Christ. Eventually, decades later, she went to see the Archbishop of Dublin, Cardinal Desmond Connell, who told her the abuse was 'historical' and so felt it would be unfair to tarnish the priest's 'good name' so many years later. Collins complained to the police and her abuser, Father Paul McGennis, was jailed for the offence 37 years later. She was not his only victim, it transpired.

Marie Collins was only one of thousands of children abused by Catholic priests and nuns in Ireland over half a century according to the report of an Irish government inquiry published in 2009. As public outrage built, Marie Collins became the spokesperson for the victims demanding that Connell should resign along with another Irish cardinal, Sean Brady, who had also turned a blind eye to abuse. When a new Archbishop of Dublin, the strict reformer Diarmuid Martin, was appointed in 2003, Collins became one of his main advisers, helping him design anti-abuse systems that were put in place throughout the Irish Church. In 2011 she set up the Marie Collins Foundation, a charity to help victims and their families to recover from abuse. A year later she was invited to an international conference on clerical sex abuse organized by the Vatican at the Gregorian University. It was the first time the Church had ever organized such an event, and was supported by the Vatican's highest office, the Secretariat of State. It was the first official acknowledgement at that level of the scale of the problem.

Marie Collins flew to Rome. There she told representatives from 100 bishops' conferences and 30 religious orders around the world her personal story and explained that her abuser had told her that as a priest 'he could do no wrong'. This, she said, 'added weight to my feelings of guilt and the conviction that what had happened was my fault; not his. When I left the hospital I was not the same child who had entered. I was no longer a confident, carefree and happy child. Now I was convinced I was a bad person and I needed to hide that from everyone.' She also told the assembled bishops and superiors how the church hierarchy had responded. The Irish survivor of sex abuse told the conference how important it is to listen to victims, who may only be able to confess an act of abuse a long time after it has taken place. The English psychiatrist and psychotherapist Baroness Sheila Hollins, who had worked with victims of sexual abuse, explained to the senior prelates present that 'not being believed – or even worse, being blamed for the abuse – adds hugely to the emotional and mental suffering caused by sexual abuse'. The failure of an abuser to admit his guilt further compounded the damage. So did the failure of the abuser's superiors to take appropriate action. 'In the case of a priest there is an extra layer of trust and deference, which makes a disclosure of abuse even harder in my experience,' the Catholic psychiatrist stressed. Indeed she believed that the lack of an admission of guilt and of an apology is usually the biggest barrier to healing and recovery. 'As a person of faith,' she added, 'I am a great believer in the power of forgiveness as a healing agent. But forgiveness is rarely achieved without confession and reparation.'

The two women were encouraged by the response of some of the church leaders present but came up against the refusal of others to accept the scale and depth of the problem. Marie Collins told me: 'It was good to hear someone say, "I hadn't realized this was such an issue. I will go back to my diocese and put something in place." But it was also extraordinary to hear bishops saying, "We don't have this problem in our country." The room was divided into three groups: those who understood the problem, which was people from countries where it has been a high-profile issue; the deniers, who said it was all a media plot or survivors looking for money from the Church; and the third group, who had their eyes opened.'

Strikingly, though the conference was held in Rome, the Italian bishops' conference – one of those groups inside the Church that remains in denial of the problem – did not send a representative. But others were convinced. After the conference a Centre for Child Protection was founded under a German Jesuit and professor of psychology, Dr Hans Zollner. Based in Munich, but moving to Rome in 2015, it began to conduct inter-disciplinary research on abuse prevention.

Zollner, like Hollins and Collins, was among those who, almost two years later, got the call from Monsignor Oliver asking if they would join the new Pontifical Commission for the Protection of Minors. The next day the Vatican announced the membership of the body. Hollins and Zollner had agreed to join. So had Collins, despite knowing that in doing so she would come in for a lot of criticism from other survivors who accused her of 'colluding with the Church'. A French child psychiatrist, psychotherapist and expert on child sexual abuse, Dr Catherine Bonnet, had accepted. So had Hanna Suchocka, a former prime minister of Poland and a human rights lawyer so tough she had been nicknamed the Polish Mrs Thatcher. Another member was a long-standing personal friend of Pope Francis, Father Humberto Miguel Yáñez, a moral theologian from Argentina. It was to be chaired by Cardinal O'Malley. It looked a strong group.

But the forces of denial in the Vatican were strong too. When the voluminous Pontifical Yearbook – the annual handbook to Vatican Affairs – was published, the Pontifical Commission for the Protection of Minors did not rate a mention in its 2,300 pages even though its establishment was announced three months before the book's publication deadline. At the first meeting of the commission, in May 2014, Cardinal O'Malley made a startling confession to the members gathered in the same room in the Casa Santa Marta in which the C8 met. Despite having the backing of Pope Francis for the work of the commission, and despite being one of the Pope's C8 advisers, O'Malley had run into serious opposition to the whole enterprise from a group of officials within the Curia. O'Malley told his fellow commissioners that there was only one group to which there was more resistance within the Vatican – the economic commission.

'The truth is there is a real camp of deniers in the Curia,' one commissioner told me. 'At first they kept their heads down, hoping all the fuss would go away when the press stopped talking about it. But they do not like the idea of the commission. They think it will add to the risk of the Church being tainted by the issue – as though that has not happened already.'

Many Italians in the Curia were seized with the notion that sex abuse is a peculiarly Irish problem. They claimed that it is to be found only in Ireland and in countries to which Irish priests had emigrated, like England, the United States and Australia. This is not a new prejudice on the part of the Curia; in the tenth and eleventh centuries officials in the Vatican complained that they could not manage celibacy among Anglo-Saxons as they were 'too hot-blooded'. On the twentieth-century sex abuse scandal, one non-Italian curial official told me: 'There was no sense among my colleagues that the Vatican had got anything wrong on sex abuse. It was seen as an Irish problem and the problem of the Irish diaspora, a foreign problem.'

The experts on the new commission were dismissive of this position. 'It is total nonsense that this is an Anglo-Saxon or an Irish problem,' one commissioner said. 'I have had people contact me from Africa, South Africa, Nepal, India, Japan, Ecuador, Bolivia. It is in every country on earth and in every community. But it is covered up'. Taboos on talking were far greater in other countries, the experts told O'Malley. In Africa, for example, it was young mothers who were most vulnerable to the abuse of power and authority by priests. One of the psychologists insisted: 'It's worldwide. It's a human problem. There are issues of cycles of abuse; with those who are abused going on to abuse others. There's a victim inside every perpetrator but that doesn't mean we shouldn't crack down on them. There is complete consensus on that within the commission.'

There was another form of denial within the Curia. It took the form of the argument made to Nigel Baker, the British ambassador to the Holy See, that 'this is essentially an historical problem' but 'now that better controls on the selection of candidates for the priesthood have been implemented, it should not reoccur'. A significant body of Vatican officials took this line. So much so that the head of Vatican finances, Cardinal George Pell, told one member of the commission: 'Your Pontifical Commission won't take long or need much of a budget because all the work is virtually done.' That showed, another commission member told me, that 'he doesn't understand the sex abuse crisis, and he didn't really understand it when he was Archbishop of Sydney, where he made a poor job of handling it. The reality is that the Commission for the Protection of Minors is going to have to be around for many years. That's how big the problem is and many in the Curia are still part of it.'

Some suggested that the problem extended beyond the Curia and was present in local churches around the world. Father Dominic Allain, the director of Grief to Grace, a Catholic ministry which seeks to offer spiritual and psychological help to sex abuse victims, said in response to the criticism of the British ambassador: 'The Holy See has consistently stressed the need for the healing of victims to be the priority, but I am afraid this has yet to result in much action from bishops' conferences who still tend to see the problem in terms of liability and scandal. When they do think of help for victims of clerical abuse they think in narrow terms of some "talking therapy". All the studies show that this is insufficient, even from a psychological point of view, for treating the cases where there is serious Post Traumatic Stress Disorder.' Bishops in the US and the UK were reluctant to fund or even publicize the required treatment, he claimed, saying that because victims groups are very vociferous it 'isn't the right time' to have such a ministry. 'It seems as if the bishops do not want people banding together in case they recover more memories or correlate stories.'

The idea that abuse will not occur in future because the problem has been addressed is fanciful, according to one abuse victim, Peter Saunders, of the National Association for People Abused in Childhood in the UK. 'There are lots of existing priests who are abusers,' he said. 'There are lots of existing priests who have not had an awareness of sex abuse as part of their training for the priesthood. And it is very difficult in practice to screen out certain people who have malign intentions on children.'

At its first meeting the Pontifical Commission for the Protection of Minors was told by Cardinal O'Malley that it would have a broad mandate but that this would not include dealing with individual cases. Pope Francis had been privately to the Congregation for the Doctrine of the Faith (CDF) a few months earlier and told the doctrinal watchdog that the commission was tasked with finding an exemplary model for child protection but that the job of investigating and prosecuting abusers would remain with the CDF. The role of the commission, O'Malley told its members, was to propose initiatives to encourage local responsibility around the world and the mutual sharing of best practices for the protection of all minors, including programmes for training, education, formation and responses to abuse. Some of the commission's members were happy with that brief. 'It is realistic,' Baroness Hollins told me. 'We are dealing with a lot of issues, some of them very small, some big. Some of it is very practical, like what kind of methods should we use for the gathering of evidence. Our job is to try to make sure that the Holy Father leaves no stone unturned.'

But others voiced unhappiness with the idea that they would avoid individual cases. One commission member raised the case of Bishop Robert Finn of Kansas City – the first church official to be convicted by a court in the United States of failing to report to the civil authorities a priest suspected of abuse who was subsequently sentenced to 50 years in prison. The Church spent $1.4m on Finn's defence but in 2012 the Opus Dei bishop was found guilty of shielding a paedophile and given a two-year suspended jail sentence. Almost two years later, the commissioners complained, Finn was still in office, a state of affairs which made it look as though – for all the words of papal apology – the Church was not serious in dealing with those who covered up clerical sex abuse. 'We raised the issue of Bishop Finn at every meeting,' one commissioner told me. 'Cardinal Sean wanted to move on this but it was clearly not within his capability. It was all bogged down in the Congregation for Bishops and the CDF.'

What most alarmed the commissioners was the discovery that Pope Francis knew nothing about Bishop Finn. 'That amazed me,' another commissioner said. 'One of the things the commission has said needs to be put in place is a reporting mechanism so the Pope gets to know things like that.' Dealing with abuser priests – even if behind the scenes and rather slowly – was nowhere near enough. The lay commissioners insisted at this first meeting that mechanisms needed to be put in place to discipline – and remove – bishops who took part in cover-ups. They also asked Pope Francis to meet some survivors of predator priests.

The other area of concern to the lay members was the speed at which the Vatican seemed set upon working. 'The Church has a completely different idea of pace,' one commissioner said. 'It famously thinks in millennia. Senior clerics have no idea how normal people do things. We wanted to set deadlines and produce an interim report quite quickly. They wanted to meet only twice a year. So we insisted on setting up working parties on specific issues which will work in between those meetings.' Marie Collins said at a press conference after a commission meeting in 2015: 'I have spent the last year feeling quite frustrated about the slowness. I always knew that the Church worked slowly but when you are on the inside it seems even slower.'

But the biggest disappointment to many of the outside members was that Pope Francis did not attend their first meeting. He had greeted the members in the Casa Santa Marta at dinner the night before but was not present for their first session. He would be there for the first full meeting of the body, they were told; they had agreed to expand the membership of the body to bring in those with expertise from a wider geographical area. It was a promise that was not to be kept; Francis did not attend that meeting either.

As the first meeting concluded the outsiders got their first direct glimpse of how unseen forces in the Vatican intrigued to steer events to their own opaque ends. The press release that was issued after the meeting was written in very woolly terms. 'Everyone in the Vatican is afraid of plain language,' one commissioner told me. They were beginning to learn the way the Vatican worked.

The secular world, with its much more black-and-white view of sex abuse, kept up the pressure on Rome. At the end of that same month, May 2014, a second United Nations body, the UN the Committee on Torture issued a report criticizing the Vatican's handling of the clerical sex abuse scandal over the preceding decade during which more than 3,400 cases of abuse had been reported to the Holy See. The Vatican had responded with legal rather than moral arguments. It had admitted that clerical sex abuse was 'an egregious betrayal of trust and a violation of the innocence of the victims' which had caused 'untold suffering and scandal'. But the Vatican insisted abuse did not fall under the UN definition of torture. More reprehensibly, in the eyes of abuse survivors, Rome had resorted to a legal technicality, saying that, strictly speaking, the Holy See did not have legal responsibility for the actions of Catholic priests and bishops throughout the world. Under international law it was responsible only for the tiny Vatican City State. It was a shamefully legalistic argument which was deeply unconvincing not only to the UN committee but to most of the outside world.

Pope Francis seemed to be getting some sense of the scale of the problem. During an in-flight press conference, returning from the Holy Land, Francis let slip that he would be meeting some sex abuse survivors. This was another change. Under Pope Benedict such meetings were only made public after they had happened, but Pope Francis was announcing it in advance. He also spoke of the need for 'zero-tolerance' of sex abuse – a phrase which the commission had discussed at length, exploring the different way in which that was interpreted in difference countries and cultures. That was a sign of real progress to the lay commission members. 'The Pope might not have been present at our discussions,' one said. 'But it was clear evidence that our recommendations were getting through to him and that he was resolved to act upon them.'

Francis also sent another revealing signal. He told journalists on the plane that a priest who was guilty of sex abuse 'betrays the body of the Lord' as grievously as if he had participated in 'a satanic Mass'. To the secular media it seemed a peculiar comparison. But the Pope's message was to priests across the world for whom it ought to have been a shocking comparison, for it was linking sex abuse to an evil which inverted, opposed and mocked the Mass at the heart of everything for which the Church stood. Inside the Church it was the toughest language imaginable. Not just priests but now three bishops, he told reporters, were under investigation for sex offences.

It was not clear which three individuals he had in mind. A Belgian bishop, Roger Vangheluwe, had 'resigned' in 2010 after admitting to molesting his young nephews. The Scottish cardinal, Keith O'Brien, had also been forced to stand down a year later after being accused of sexual harassment by a number of seminarians and priests. Perhaps Bishop Finn was the third. Or perhaps it was Archbishop Józef Wesołowski, who had been recalled from his post as papal ambassador in the Dominican Republic in August 2013 after being accused of paying young shoeshine boys to perform sex acts. It was unclear at that point whether he had been brought back to Rome to escape scandal in the Caribbean country or because the Vatican intended to prosecute him. What had added to the ambiguity was that church spokesmen initially gave shifting, even contradictory, statements as to the reason for the decision – and the former nuncio had been allowed to move freely in Rome, with no restrictions, until a visiting bishop from the Dominican Republic saw him on a Roman street and tweeted: 'The silence of the Church has hurt the people of God.'

But the Pope was still primarily addressing the issue of those who abused; he did not seem to have taken on board the need for action against those who protected the abusers – whether out of a desire to protect individuals, avoid scandal or shield the Church from potential legal liability and claims for compensation. Pope Francis may have had a blind spot to that because of the way he had handled sex abuse cases when he was Archbishop of Buenos Aires. That was what was suggested by the main survivor group in the United States when it heard that Francis was planning to meet survivors. David Clohessy, the director of the Survivors Network of those Abused by Priests (known as SNAP), claimed that at least five victims of paedophile priests had approached the then Cardinal Bergoglio in Buenos Aires and had been ignored or rebuffed. Some parents of abuse victims said they were turned away by his office. Others were offered rosaries blessed by Pope John Paul II instead of being given a meeting with Bergoglio. One even claimed to have been manhandled by the cardinal's staff. An Argentinian lawyer said he represented dozens of victims in Argentina. A campaign group named BishopAccountability.org published a database listing, over the two decades of Bergoglio's time as a bishop, 43 alleged predator priests in Argentina – seven of them still in ministry.

All this stood in stark contrast to Francis's own account. In a book of conversations with the Argentine rabbi, Abraham Skorka, in 2010, Bergoglio had suggested that sex abuse was not a problem in his time in Buenos Aires: 'In my diocese it never happened to me, but a bishop called me once by phone to ask me what to do in a situation like this and I told him to take the priest's faculties, not to permit him to exercise his priestly ministry again, and to initiate a canonical trial.' Many survivors' support groups felt that this was not enough; the priest should have been reported to the police, not merely subjected to a church trial. But Bergoglio had insisted in 2010 that church attempts to cover up the problem were both wrong and counter-productive. 'I do not believe in the positions that some hold about sustaining a certain corporate spirit so as to avoid damaging the image of the institution,' he said. 'The solution ... of switching them to other parishes is stupid, because the priest continues to carry the problem in his baggage.' The answer was 'zero-tolerance'. Elsewhere he repeatedly condemned the broader issue of the sexual exploitation of children in society, describing the city of Buenos Aires as a 'meat grinder' because of its prostitution and trafficking in sex-slaves.

Those close to Bergoglio at the time support his account. Father Guillermo Marcó, who was for eight years his press spokesman, insisted: 'There were no sex abuse cases in Buenos Aires when Bergoglio was archbishop. The two infamous cases did not occur in his jurisdiction but in the dioceses of Moron and San Isidro.' As Archbishop of Buenos Aires Bergoglio had no canonical authority over those areas. 'Even as president of the Argentine bishop's conference he had very limited power and could not intervene in such cases. Bergoglio was always very firm when there was any suspicion that a child had been abused: he supported the family and avoided cover-up though he also believed that the presumption of innocence was essential to avoid false accusations against priests.' Even so, there was an ambiguity to Bergoglio's position despite his firm rhetoric with Skorka. Both Moron and San Isidro dioceses were within the Buenos Aires archdiocese, of which Bergoglio was metropolitan. And in his time as president of the conference the Argentine bishops missed the Vatican's 2010 deadline to create safeguards against new abuse.

Yet if there was anything equivocal about Bergoglio's position it seemed confined to the past. In June 2014 Archbishop Józef Wesołowski was defrocked as a result of the charges of molesting under-age boys during his diplomatic assignment to Santo Domingo. It was an unusual and dramatic penalty; he was stripped of his status not only as a bishop but as a priest. The Vatican also announced that he had been stripped of his diplomatic immunity, opening the way for the Dominican Republic to begin extradition proceedings against him. It was just over a week later that Pope Francis prepared himself, early one morning in the first week of July, to come face to face with a group of sex abuse survivors for the first time in his life.

* * *

It was a delicate task, negotiating the six survivors – two from Britain, two from Ireland and two from Germany – through the clerical labyrinth of the

Vatican to find the Pope at its centre. Some were angry, some afraid, all were apprehensive. One of the women, even years after her abuse, still became distressed at the sight of men in black, wearing dog collars. The two Irish survivors were happy for their identities to be known by those they met, as was one of the English victims, but the other and both Germans did not want their names made public. One of the women survivors still hadn't told her family about the abuse even though it happened years before, and she didn't want them to find out through a leak to the press. 'We had to tell the Monsignor who is in charge of the Casa Santa Marta to take great care in how he spoke to them,' Baroness Hollins said. 'Any suggestion that he was telling them what to do could have been taken very badly.'

The survivors arrived in the Vatican guesthouse, where the Pope now lived, the night before the meeting. The woman who was still traumatized by clerical dress had to be guided into the dining room at the Casa Santa Marta by one of the commissioners and given a seat at a table by the edge with her back to the room so that she would not be overwhelmed by the sight of all the clerical collars. The event, after all, was supposed to be a healing experience, not something which would add to the survivors' trauma.

The Pope's informal personal style helped with that. One of the survivors, the Englishman Peter Saunders, saw Francis enter the cafeteria as the survivor group were eating. Saunders, who had been sexually abused by two priests and a lay teacher at a Catholic School in Wimbledon from the age of 8 until he was 13, said afterwards: 'He came into the refectory as we were having dinner, and he was just tossing food on his plate like any mortal would. I told the person sitting next to me: 'There's the Pope!' As he was standing up to leave, I caught his eye and waved to him and he came over. I was pinching myself, thinking: 'Is this really happening? Is the Pope coming towards us?' Francis greeted them all and shook hands with every individual. Saunders joked with him about the soccer World Cup which was being played at the time and told the Argentine pontiff that he hoped his native team would win. It broke the ice. Saunders said he went to bed having had his unease laid to rest.

In discussing the preparations for the private Mass with the Pope, great care had to be taken over the camera angles in the broadcasting set-up to televise the service, as is routinely done with his 7 a.m. homily. 'Before the Mass we had to negotiate to make sure that the camera which was filming him did not move off the Pope,' one commissioner said. 'Some survivors were concerned about being identified. So the camera focused only on Francis.' The Vatican employees who normally attend the morning Mass were excluded.

One of the survivors had developed an immense anger against the Church. He announced that he was boycotting the Mass because he had learned that he wasn't to be allowed to hold a press conference afterwards. The man tried to persuade one of the other survivors not to attend either. Inside the chapel, after the Pope had arrived in a simple green chasuble, the day's texts from Hosea and St Matthew's Gospel were read by Marie Collins and Baroness Hollins. Another commission member then left the chapel and persuaded the two survivors outside to enter. There they heard Pope Francis describe what had happened to them as 'despicable acts' through which some priests and bishops had 'violated their innocence' and sacrificed young children 'to the idol of their own lust', profaning the very image of God in whose likeness we were created. He continued:

Before God and his people I express my sorrow for the sins and grave crimes of clerical sexual abuse committed against you. And I humbly ask forgiveness. I beg for your forgiveness, too, for the sin of omission on the part of the Church leaders who didn't respond adequately to reports of abuse. This led to ever greater suffering...and endangered other minors who were at risk.'

None of this was new. Pope John Paul II had voiced sorrow for the sins of 'some ministers of the altar'. Benedict XVI had met with victims six times and had personalized the apology with the direct words: 'I'm sorry.' But Francis now went a step further, saying: 'All bishops must carry out their pastoral ministry with the utmost care in order to help foster the protection of minors, and they will be held accountable.' Holding bishops accountable – and introducing changes to canon law which would allow them to be removed from office for failing to deal with sex abuse properly – was the central demand that the commission had made from the outset if the Church was really to change. There must be consequences for the cover-up as well as the crime. Pope Francis seemed to have heard. 'Let no wolf enter the sheepfold,' he concluded.

What was noticeable was that in the sermon he did not speak in Italian as he usually does in his daily homilies. He spoke in his native Spanish, the language to which he always reverts when he has something to say from deep within his heart. 'We had all been given copies of what he was to say in our own language,' said Marie Collins. 'He didn't preach; he talked to us. The way he was speaking was gripping. Real sincerity came through.' Francis stuck to his prepared text, but departed from it occasionally to become more direct and personal. There were translators on hand to render the Pope's words in the native languages of the six survivors. 'I got the feeling it came absolutely from his heart,' said

Collins. 'It wasn't an act. There was no sense he was trying to impress anyone. He gave us Communion himself, something he doesn't normally do.'

After Mass, and breakfast, Pope Francis went directly to the room where the meetings were to take place. The lay commissioners, with their experience of working with survivors, had made some suggestions about the format. When Pope Benedict had met survivors he had had a line of priestly aides sitting around the room. The setting had been very unnerving for some survivors. 'One of the things we negotiated in advance,' said Marie Collins, 'was that Francis would see them on their own, one at a time, with no-one else present apart from a translator.' The encounters took place in a room in the Casa Santa Marta in which visitors usually watched television. It contained just a television and four chairs. 'There was nothing to give any aura of power. It was very simple.' The sessions began at 9 a.m. and carried on until 12.30 p.m. 'He gave each person as much time as they liked,' said Collins, who sat in as emotional support for one of the Irish survivors. 'Each finished only when they had said everything they wanted to say. He listened, rather than speaking. He did not look at his watch or give any indication that the session should be governed by anything other than what the person who was talking wanted.'

The group of six were mixed. Some had become survivor advocates; others just wanted to tell him their personal story. Peter Saunders told the Pope how, growing up in a devout Catholic home, it had been so difficult to cope with the shame that it had taken him 24 years to acknowledge what had happened. Long after the physical abuse had ended, he told the pontiff, 'it remains in your head as though it was yesterday'. And he spoke of the London-based National Association for People Abused in Childhood (NAPAC), which he founded 19 years before to provide a support system to help other victims deal with the aftermath of abuse. An Irish survivor, Mark Vincent Healy, presented the Pope with a dossier which suggested that official state figures were significantly under-reporting abuse by priests. It also raised the issue of the high levels of self-harm and suicide among abuse victims. And another Irish survivor, Marie Kane, asked Pope Francis to remove Cardinal Sean Brady as Archbishop of Armagh and Primate of Ireland for his lack of action over a predator priest who continued to abuse for a further 19 years.

The lay experts of the commission were impressed. 'I was very impressed with Pope Francis,' Marie Collins said. 'He listened very well, genuinely paying attention. He didn't come out with any of the glib platitudes or patronizing stuff that survivors normally get from church leaders. The survivors were not a homogeneous group; all survivors are at different stages of healing. But after-wards they all said it had been very helpful. I did not tell my own story. I was only there to support another survivor but, I can't explain why, I also found it a healing experience.' Another commissioner told me: 'He was really interested in the stories of each person. I suspect he got as much out of listening as they got out of telling him their stories.'

The Pope's informality and ordinariness played a big part in putting the survivors at ease. One abuse victim told me: 'He is so down to earth. He is really ordinary in an extraordinary way. He likes to give a rosary to people he meets. When he realized he had forgotten them he didn't call a flunkey but said, "Hang on a minute", and popped back upstairs to get them himself and came down swinging them in a bag.'

At the end of the day Peter Saunders told the media: 'I left feeling I had been heard. It was a life-changing moment for me.'

* * *

At first something seemed to change too for Pope Francis after his face-to-face encounters with those abused by priests. Perhaps the meetings had been for him something similar to the experience of Pope Benedict, who had once been found by an aide in tears reading the accounts of child abuse victims after he demanded in 2001 that all such cases be sent to his office in Rome when he was head of the Congregation for the Doctrine of the Faith. The idea was to speed up action against abusers. Certainly there appeared to be a gear change in Rome once again.

A catalogue of activity followed. A month after the meetings Pope Francis made one of his cold phone calls to a member of Opus Dei in the Spanish diocese of Granada who had written to him to describe the abuse he had suffered at the hands of priests when he was a teenage altar boy. Francis apologized to him on behalf of the Church and told him to go to the local archbishop. The Pope then rang the archbishop and the Congregation for the Doctrine of the Faith and told them to act. (Two months later Francis rang the man again and – annoyed at how little the church authorities had done – told the man to go to the police. As a result a Spanish judge charged 10 Catholic priests, some of them members of a conservative group called Los Romanones, with sex abuse.) A month after the Pope's first call to Granada, the Vatican announced a visitation – an official investigation – in the Kansas City diocese where Bishop Finn was still in office despite his 2012 criminal conviction for failing to report a paedophile priest to the police – an act clearly outlawed by the sex abuse charter issued by the US bishops' conference in Dallas in 2002. The Archbishop of Ottawa, Terrence

Prendergast, was sent by Rome to the US diocese to interview more than a dozen important local church figures and asking whether Finn was fit to be a leader. Finn's divisive episcopal style – he had made many high-handed changes in Kansas when he arrived – was reported. His years of ignoring the advice of key figures in the diocese who had been in place before his arrival told against him. It revealed a tendency to set his own judgment above that of others which may have been what led him to ignore the requirement within the Dallas charter which mandated the reporting of child abuse to the civil authorities. Prendergast then sent a report on his findings to the Congregation for Bishops.

Two days later the Pope authorized the arrest of the Archbishop Józef Wesołowski, ordering him to face criminal charges over sex with children; Wesołowski announced that he wanted to appeal against his defrocking but was still placed under house arrest. Next day the Pope sacked Monsignor Rogelio Livieres Plano as bishop of Ciudad del Este in Paraguay. But there was an interesting difference with this case. Livieres, another Opus Dei prelate, had been accused of protecting a priest suspected of sexually abusing young parishioners. But the Vatican spokesman Federico Lombardi took pains to explain to journalists that the Paraguayan bishop was not being sacked for this reason. 'Let's not confuse Wesołowski and Livieres; one is a case of paedophilia, the other is not,' Lombardi told the Catholic News Service. 'Paedophilia was not the principal problem' with Livieres but rather 'there were serious problems with his management of the diocese, the education of clergy and relations with other bishops,' Lombardi said. Livieres was alleged to have repeatedly clashed with more moderate members of his diocese. So the Pope had removed Livieres, a Vatican statement said, and Francis had named another bishop to run the diocese as an administrator for the time being. Some evidence of the sacked bishop's belligerence was demonstrated in his reaction. Pope Francis 'must answer to God' for his removal, he declared.

The dismissal raised a challenging question for the Pontifical Commission for the Protection of Minors. Pope Francis had moved fast, only months after he was elected, to oust Bishop Franz-Peter Tebartz-van Elst, whom the media dubbed the Bishop of Bling after he spent €31 million luxuriously renovating his official residence – spending €2m on bronze window frames, €250,000 on an ornamental fishtank, €200,000 on a spiral staircase and €15,000 on a freestanding bath created by the French designer Philippe Starck featuring – very oddly for a celibate priest – headrests at both ends. He also had to pay a German court a fine of €20,000 after lying on oath over a first-class flight to India on a charity trip. The bishop was summoned to see Pope Francis and within two days he was removed. The question this raised for commission members was this: how could the Vatican act so swiftly to axe bishops when issues of mismanagement were raised – and then be so slow when the issue was a bishop shielding sex abusers?

And yet despite all this resolute action from Pope Francis, the manoeuvring continued out of the public eye inside the Vatican, with various departments in the Roman Curia vying for control over the supposedly independent Pontifical Commission for the Protection of Minors. The body had had its second meeting in July. Again the Pope did not attend. And the lay members had repeatedly to fight subtle attempts by one Vatican department after another to put the Commission under its control. At first it was individuals inside the doctrinal watchdog, the CDF, who tried to bring the commission under their sway. Forces seemed constantly at work behind the scenes. Odd things would happen such as press releases which had been agreed by the commission appearing the next day with parts mysteriously deleted by some unknown individual.

The intrigue continued. At the July meeting the commission discussed where they should site their office. Some members wanted one in the Vatican, to be closer to the seat of power and send the signal to bishops that they needed to take notice of what the commission said. Others wanted an office outside the Vatican to make it easier to maintain contact with the wider world and give commissioners and survivors easy access to the office. In the end they decided on an office just outside the Vatican in the Via della Conciliazione, which leads from central Rome to St Peter's Square. At their next meeting they were unilaterally informed that they had been found a better office – inside the Vatican in the Department of the Secretary of State.

It was not the only trick the Curia pulled. At the October meeting the external commissioners discovered that the statutes for the constitution of the commission – which they were supposed to draft and agree – had already been drawn up by someone else. The lay members on the commission staged a revolt. This was unacceptable and they insisted that the statutes be scrapped.

One of the measures in the statutes which someone had tried to foist upon them included a provision which said: 'Local churches should make their own decisions.' That sounded innocuous, since part of Pope Francis's general programme of reform for the over-centralized Curia was that power should be devolved from Rome out to the world's bishops. But the commissioners were alarmed. On the issue of sex abuse local dioceses making their own decisions had been part of the problem. It had led to institutional cover-up on a massive scale because each bishop had sought to avoid the kind of public scandal, or financial liability to victims, which would have blemished their reputation in

Rome. 'Many local bishops did nothing, or tried to protect the institution,' one commissioner said. 'That has been the whole problem up until now.' Local decision-making produced very variable results. Combating sex abuse, and retraining those who were disposed to cover it up, would only work if stringent systems were put in place from the top down.

To square this circle the commission proposed that every national bishops' conference around the world should appoint a liaison officer to act as a two-way conduit between the local diocese and the commission. 'It would give the local church some input into the working of the commission but allow the commission to set best-practice for the whole universal Church,' one commissioner said. 'It will give some balance between the central and the local. Local churches will be able to input into the process without being allowed to use arguments about collegiality to get off the hook.' They asked the Pope to write to every bishop requiring them to cooperate with the Pontifical Commission for the Protection of Minors in full – which he did before the commission's next meeting in February 2015. At that next meeting they junked the statutes the Curia had tried to impose upon them. They wrote their own interim constitution and sent this to the Pope, who agreed it on a three-year trial basis.

The 'two steps forward, one step back' dynamic, which had come to characterize the way sex abuse was being handled inside the Vatican, continued. After the meeting, the commission's secretary, Monsignor Bob Oliver, gave an interview to the conservative US periodical the *National Catholic Register* which summed up the ambiguity of the whole process. 'The commission itself has a position within the Curia, where it does have autonomy; it reports directly to the Holy Father,' the monsignor summarized, but added, 'but it does so in collaboration with all of the other dicasteries.'

The struggle to get bishops held accountable for their actions, and disciplined for their failures, continued in the same tortuous fashion. In November 2014 Cardinal Sean O'Malley launched a surprisingly bold attack on the lack of action over Bishop Finn in a television documentary for a major US programme, *60 Minutes*. Finn's conviction for failing to report suspected child abuse would disqualify him even from teaching in Sunday school in the Boston diocese, he declared. 'It's a question that the Holy See needs to address urgently,' said O'Malley, adding, 'there's a recognition of that from Pope Francis.' This was a measure of the determination of the cardinal from Boston whom the Pope had brought in to head the child abuse commission. But it also revealed how circumscribed was O'Malley's power. It seemed that this was one area in which Francis seemed reluctant to cut across existing procedures within the Curia.

Why was this? The survivor support group SNAP in the United States had suggested that the Pope's record of rebuffing sex abuse victims and their families in Buenos Aires suggested some equivocality on his part. The man who was Bergoglio's press adviser for eight years in Argentina, Guillermo Marcó, offered a hint. The most infamous case of clerical child abuse in Argentina in Bergoglio's time was that of Father Julio César Grassi, the well-known founder of a national charity to shelter street children. Grassi was accused of sexually abusing at least five boys. He was eventually jailed for 15 years. But throughout a six-year appeal process Bergoglio defended Grassi, complaining there was a media campaign against the celebrity priest. Grassi later said that throughout the long criminal trial Bergoglio 'never let go of my hand'. Church officials led by Bergoglio commissioned a lengthy private report arguing that Grassi was innocent; it was submitted as part of his defence but in 2013, with his third appeal rejected, the priest was jailed. 'Grassi continued to insist he was innocent,' said Marcó, 'and Bergoglio thought that one should believe in his innocence. Bergoglio was always very firm when there was any suspicion that a child had been abused: he supported the family and avoided cover-up. But he also believed that a presumption of innocence is essential.' Pope Francis has not altered that view. One cardinal who is close to Francis, and recently discussed sex abuse with him, said that in private conversation 'the Pope clearly enunciated four principles: that victims should come first; that robust procedures must be put in place throughout the Church to protect children; that the Church should cooperate with the civil authorities to bring offenders to justice; and that there should be fairness for priests, to prevent false accusations'. It is this final principle which perhaps explains the slow pace of action by Francis on sex abuse. 'People say that Pope Francis is dragging his feet over the sex abuse issue,' said one commissioner, Baroness Hollins. 'But the Pontifical Commission for the Protection of Minors is taking longer to set up because it is so complex. It's not simple like the Vatican Bank. I like the fact that he's not looking for quick fixes. It's complicated and we're going slowly because we don't want to fall flat on our face.'

That was not all. There were other complexities. In December 2014 Pope Francis met the Attorney General of the Dominican Republic, Francisco Domínguez Brito, in the Vatican to discuss the Wesołowski case. The trial of the disgraced archbishop could not proceed until his appeal against his defrocking was held. That should have been done in October 2014 but six months later it had still not been heard. The discussions with the Santo Domingo law chief centred on whether Wesołowski should be extradited to face charges in the Caribbean or whether his trial should take place in the Vatican. 'The problem is that the Dominican Republic don't want him back,' an insider in the Holy See claimed. 'The case would be too embarrassing.' There are too many photographs and stories of senior politicians and officials in the overwhelmingly Catholic country ingratiating themselves with the former nuncio before he fell from grace. 'They'd rather not have them all republished with the suggestion that they associated with someone on trial for being a paedophile. So he'll probably end up being tried in the Vatican and then, if found guilty, sent to a jail in Italy.' For all that, said the abuse survivor Peter Saunders, the public disgracing of Wesołowski is progress: 'It wouldn't have happened a decade ago.'

Later that month Saunders was named as one of eight new members of the Pontifical Commission for the Protection of Minors along with experts from Colombia, the Philippines, New Zealand, Australia, Zambia and South Africa. The announcement came as Pope Francis approved the commission's suggestion to double its members to widen its geographical experience and also its inter-disciplinary strength to include a professor of pastoral psychology and experts on professional standards, family protection, social work, education, human trafficking and the psychological treatment of clerical offenders. David Clohessy, the director of the US abuse survivor's group SNAP, was unimpressed. He praised Saunders and Collins as 'smart and compassionate individuals who are brave to take on this role' but he feared they could 'end up feeling used or betrayed' if the commission does nothing, as Clohessy expected. Saunders was clear-eyed but determined. 'We will not be a fig-leaf for inaction,' he said. 'I admire the risk the Vatican has taken in having people like me on the commission.' The new members sounded robust. But the Vatican officials tasked with managing the commission still felt the need to smooth ruffled feathers among curial resisters. Its secretary, Monsignor Oliver, again went to the media in a diplomatic attempt to calm the fears of those still opposing the work of the commission. Among its tasks, he said, was 'assisting the Congregation for the Doctrine of the Faith in its effort for new guidelines for the response to abuse'. Clearly there were those in the Vatican who were disconcerted, or even alarmed, at the Pope allowing so many outsiders into the Roman fortress.

For their part the commissioners remained wary but determinedly constructive. 'One needs to be aware of the kind of manoeuvring that goes on in the Vatican,' one said. 'But there is a lot of good work going on in the commission. Its members have an excellent range of skills and all the right intentions. If it was left alone then it would do a good job. Vatican power struggles are the only thing that might threaten it – that and the fact that the CDF has only seven officials to handle the thousands of cases referred to them every year, which is very odd considering that this is supposed to be one of the Pope's top priorities.' Such paradoxes abounded. The Vatican's money men seemed determined to starve the Commission of proper funding. The commissioners knew that they would have to remain vigilant and watch for Vatican resistance and inertia.

Another key appointment in January 2015 seemed to justify their optimism. Charles Scicluna was named Archbishop of Malta and also the head of a new body designed to speed up the hearing of appeals by priests disciplined by the Church for sex abuse. Scicluna had been the tenacious canon lawyer who had worked with Benedict XVI, both before and after he became Pope, on hunting down and prosecuting paedophile priests. He had been the man behind the investigation into the priest who was perhaps the Catholic Church's most notorious abuser, Marcial Maciel Degollado, the founder of the ultra-conservative movement the Legionaries of Christ. For decades Maciel had abused young boys but had been protected by his close association with Pope John Paul II, who admired his staunch Catholic orthodoxy. Maciel had also channelled vast sums of money to allies in the Curia. (Cardinal Ratzinger was once offered an envelope stuffed with cash but handed it back.) The original investigation into Maciel had been shelved on the orders of Pope John Paul in 1998. But Scicluna had persisted and in 2006 one of the first acts of Pope Benedict was to remove Maciel from office and in 2010 denounce him for 'a life without scruples or authentic religious sentiment'. In the dying days of the Benedict era the energetic Scicluna was shunted off to become an auxiliary bishop in his native Malta. Now the Church's most aggressive scourge of sex abuse was back at the heart of the Vatican process to clean up abuse. 'He is just the right man to do that,' one commissioner told me, 'especially since there are a lot of conservative cardinals on the panel too. But Scicluna is an excellent man. Clerical abuse is black and white to him, as it should be.'

The accelerated pace continued. In February Pope Francis wrote the letter which the commission had requested he should send to every Catholic bishop. It encouraged them all to follow his example by meeting survivors, something many had never done. 'There are far too many bishops around the world who have refused to meet with survivors,' said Peter Saunders afterwards. But most importantly the Pope's letter ordered bishops across the globe to cooperate fully with the commission in its work. He told them: 'Everything possible must be done to rid the Church of the scourge of the sexual abuse of minors and to open pathways of reconciliation and healing for those who were abused.' Bishops must abandon old priorities 'such as the desire to avoid scandal'. There was, he said, 'absolutely no place in ministry for those who abuse minors'.

The letter was sent on the eve of the first full meeting of the expanded Pontifical Commission for the Protection of Minors. At last, members of the commission felt, real progress was beginning to be made at their meetings. At their February meeting they finalized the statutes which would govern their proceedings, which were subsequently approved by the Pope. They discussed the arguments often raised against the idea of making it compulsory for every bishop to report a suspected abuser to the police – and concluded that it was not true that the risk to victims would be increased by mandatory reporting. They made a recommendation to the Pope that this requirement be made universal throughout the Church, even where it was not required by the civil law of the land. The diverse input from the old and new members raised a wide variety of topics. They discussed whether priests should be advised that during the sacrament of confession – when Catholics privately acknowledge their shortcomings and sins before an individual priest – the priest should instruct an individual confessing to child abuse that they must report themselves to the police before the forgiveness of God known as absolution could be given. They discussed what can be done to stop bishops being pressured by their insurers and financial advisers to cover up clerical abuse. There was a suggestion that Pope Francis should be asked to wash the feet of sex abuse survivors during a future Holy Week.

A major difference began to emerge between the lay outsiders and the clerical members more accustomed to Vatican ways. Peter Saunders expressed fears about the commission's schedule, now it had an expanded membership, only convening twice a year. 'We should be meeting every six weeks,' he said. Vatican officials appeared to think that getting things done in months rather than years was speedy. 'They think things can't move any faster,' said another commissioner. 'When we wanted to appoint new members to expand the commission we were told the new people would have to be approved by the papal nuncios in their own country. They all were written to – but three months later they still had not replied. In the secular world this could've been done in a week. That is why it is such a good idea to have so many outside members on the commission. They know how things are done in the real world. We are trying to keep them to the mark but the pace is glacial.'

As a compromise the commission set up a series of working groups to meet and gather evidence between official meetings. They covered: the care of survivors and their families; guidelines on how to make the Church safe for children; Church attitudes to corporal punishment; better training in seminaries for men about to become priests; guidelines for priests on how they should deal with sex abuse in confession; training for both new and existing bishops; mechanisms to hold local churches accountable to civil law; the changes that were needed in canon law to combat sex abuse; new guidelines on the gathering of evidence against accused priests; and a study of how offender priests should be treated and cared for. Pope Francis immediately authorized actions in some of the areas. Every church leader – from members of the Curia down – is now going to have to undergo training on sex abuse. New bishops would henceforth have to participate in training, as would existing bishops as part of their regular official *ad limina* visits to Rome.

The working group on corporal punishment was insisted upon by new members of the commission after Pope Francis, the day before the February meeting, had told pilgrims gathered in St Peter's Square that it was permissible for parents to smack their children so long as the dignity of the child was maintained. The Pope recalled, approvingly, the words of a father who had said: 'At times I have to hit my children a bit, but never in the face so as not to humiliate them.' Pope Francis commented: 'How beautiful! He knows the sense of dignity! He has to punish them but does it justly and moves on.'

The new members of the commission were undaunted about taking issue with the Pope on this. 'The Pope is wrong on smacking,' declared Peter Saunders. 'There may be something refreshingly honest and human about the way he expresses his opinions. But his remarks on smacking were a real howler, particularly the fact that he said that a father smacking a child, not on its face, was "beautiful". That was very unfortunate. Smacking is physical abuse. It can never be permissible. All the evidence suggests it does not work.' Another new commissioner spoke out just as boldly. There was no type of corporal punishment for children that was acceptable, said Dr Krysten Winter-Green who works in the United States with abused young people. 'There has to be positive parenting, in a different way,' she said.

Saunders was equally outspoken in other areas. He told church officials they must stop using the word 'historic' about abuse. 'No-one speaks about historic bank robbers,' he said acidly. 'So why talk about historic child abuse. The abuse may be over but the effects of it live on in the present. It's still very much alive, which is why the Church still needs to be very much involved in healing.' He persuaded the commission to take evidence from Father Tom Doyle, a US priest, canon lawyer and addictions therapist who has been scathing in the past about the Church's treatment of the victims of clergy abuse. 'It was brave of them to agree that,' Saunders said afterwards, 'and this is very encouraging.' Emboldened, he also suggested the commission should study links between priestly celibacy and sexual abuse. Cardinal O'Malley disagreed, and said so at the press conference after the meeting. 'I personally don't believe that celibacy is necessarily what causes sexual abuse', he said, citing studies done on behalf of the US Bishops' Conference on the issue. But Saunders was undeterred. 'There's nothing in the Bible about celibacy', he later said. 'The Church should reconsider its position.'

But the most significant development at the meeting was an agreement among the commission that the top priority for action by the Pope was a measure to make bishops accountable for their actions – and mechanisms to discipline, demote and if necessary remove bishops who did not report allegations of sex abuse. 'You can have as many guidelines as you like in place, but if the men that are supposed to be implementing don't implement them, there has to be some sanction or you're wasting your time,' Marie Collins said after the meeting. 'It has to be something that doesn't depend on what pope or bishop is in place. It has to be a firm, fixed structure that will be immovable and will remain in place no matter who the leadership are and what their views are.'

Four months later, in June 2015, Pope Francis accepted the committee's recommendations in full. The world's bishops were told that they had a duty to report child abuse to three key Vatican departments. A new judicial section was set up inside the Congregation for the Doctrine of the Faith to bring to trial bishops who failed to report abusers. A new CDF No 2 was to be created to head it. The Pope would delegate to it his authority to sack bishops. Set against that success was the frustration of several commission members that Pope Francis had not participated in their first full meeting in February 2015 as they had been promised he would. 'He has been to several meetings of the Economic Commission,' another commissioner said, 'but he's still not been to one of ours. That is disappointing.'

Could neglect of sex abuse victims in Buenos Aires in Cardinal Bergoglio's past be responsible for some ambivalence now in Pope Francis's present? 'It may be that he handled things the wrong way in the past,' said Marie Collins. 'I do not know. But what I can tell you is he is not like that now. The man then is not this man now. Perhaps he can be criticized for what he did then. We all live and learn. If he had that attitude before he wouldn't be alone in that.' Looking back to her long session in a small room with him when he met survivors, she added: 'As a survivor I have developed pretty strong instincts over the years. Insincerity jumps out at me. But he wasn't putting on a performance. He was listening as a man, not as Pope, he was just a man. I will trust him completely. That's not to say it's not complex. He could be conflicted, but he is still trying to get it worked out and do the right thing now.'

Peter Saunders, the other survivor on the commission, shared her instincts. 'I think the Church is changing – it certainly needs to – and Francis is the right man for the job. I believe him to be sincere. I don't think he will let us down.

He's a different kind of pope.' But Saunders too had reservations. 'I think it is brave of the Church to have started this commission but it needs to move a lot faster.' The Vatican tended to 'operate in a slightly different time dimension' where the definition of 'quick' may be months or years. 'When it comes to time,' Saunders said, 'children only get one stab at childhood.'

A reminder that this is a present rather than a past problem has come to Saunders, as to other commission members, from the flood of correspondence which had deluged him since it was announced he was joining the Pontifical Commission. 'I am getting stuff from all over the world – people sharing their pain and the depth of depravity of some Catholic priests,' he said. 'And they are not just cases from the past but cases which are still going on. People are writing to me to complain of bishops who still refuse to listen to what they have to say and who refuse even to communicate with them.' Saunders insisted the commission must do more to support survivors of abuse. He wrote to fellow members proposing they extend their remit to deal directly with such cases. The Pontifical Commission for the Protection of Minors, he said, should become 'the FBI of the Church, staffed by laity, so that people can come to me and other members rather than referring them somewhere else'. By 'somewhere else' he means the Congregation for the Doctrine of the Faith, which he asserts is not up to the job.

Those writing to Saunders were coming up against the same problem that members of the commission realized was confronting them. There is a serious split inside the Vatican, as there is throughout the Church, on sex abuse. There are those who are trying to change things. But there is an influential camp who are doing their best to block change on this, and on a range of other issues on which Pope Francis wants movement. 'Some of these people have absolutely no scruples about getting their own way,' one commissioner told me. 'No doubt they will say they are acting for the greater good of the Church but their vision of the Church is not a healthy one.' The nearer campaigners got to the seat of power in the Church the more they realized that a civil war is being waged inside the Vatican over sex abuse.

Several commissioners fear that tackling sex abuse recidivists inside the Vatican may prove too great a challenge for Pope Francis. Moreover, one commissioner said, 'though the pontiff is sincere in his desire to address the child abuse crisis, it is far from his first priority'. Reform of church governance, of the synod, and of the Vatican finances all seem to have a higher command on his attention. 'An incoming Pope has an enormous amount on his plate,' said Peter Saunders. 'Even so, sex abuse should be near the top of his list. It is what has undermined the credibility of the Catholic Church around the world most seriously in recent decades. What worries me is that there are still people around Pope Francis who are not trustworthy, people who don't want to see progress on this matter, because they have something to hide, because they had been part of the cover-up or simply because they have other priorities. I have reservations about how far the Vatican will really address the problem. But I am open-minded. So let's give the process a chance. But after getting involved I feel the more I know, the less I know.'

All the lay members of the commission were clearly being robust behind the scenes, but it was the two survivors who were the most uncompromising. On the eve of the February meeting Marie Collins gave an interview in which she said: 'Survivors and everyone else are waiting to see if this commission achieves anything. We certainly don't want to be waiting 20 years to find out if there's anything to come out of it that's worthwhile.' At the press conference after the meeting Peter Saunders set a deadline. 'If we do not see serious progress in the next two years then I, and the other survivor and some lay members, will walk out.' Marie Collins backed him, telling reporters she also would leave if no progress was seen soon.

Later one of the other members of the commission said privately to Saunders: 'You have the commission by the balls on that.' The Vatican was afraid that they really might quit – which would be a public relations disaster at the very least.

'We're not here for lip service or to be token "survivors" for PR cover,' Mr Saunders replied. 'We're here to protect children. And if we conclude that we really can't do that, we'll walk.'

15

Synod and Schism

It was an authentic eighteenth-century English country manor house in the Palladian style, but it had been spruced up to such high-tech modern standards – pale pine floors and under-lit spa pool – that it looked like a modern replica. The large meeting room to the side was new but, by contrast, it had been built to look as though it might be old, with its bare brick walls and dark wooden beams. The chandeliers suspended from the high ceiling, made of circular black iron, looked anachronistically medieval. The hotel was a jumble of genuine tradition and unhistorical fakery on the edge of the Roman city of Chester in the north of England.

At a table, in the middle of this *mélange* of the authentic and the faux, sat Cardinal Raymond Burke, the implacable standard-bearer for the Catholic Church's fiercest opponents to the reforms of Pope Francis. The cardinal is known through the Church for his combination of unflinching doctrinal conservatism and his love of lacy liturgical old-form finery – on high days he even wears a *cappa magna*, the 20-yard-long red silk cape discarded decades ago by most prelates but which has come to be regarded as the emblem of restorationists and revivalists in the Catholic Church. He was there to give a talk on marriage, which he had entitled 'Remaining in the Truth of Christ on Holy Matrimony'. The room was packed with an audience as varied as the architecture. Clean-cut young men with short hair sat alongside eccentric-looking professorial figures with bow-ties and voluminous hair. There were clerics of all shapes and sizes. An elegant young priest with high cheek-bones sat – in a dashing calf-length double-breasted black coat – behind a red-faced rotund cleric, whose dog-collar seemed tight-set against his bulging neck. Women in tweedy twin-sets sat cheek by jowl with matronly housewives from working-class districts of Liverpool wearing the little golden feet lapel-pin that is the symbol of the Society for the Protection of Unborn Children (SPUC), which was sponsoring the event. One of the women peered suspiciously around the room and said to her companion: 'There are people here I've never seen at an SPUC event before.' There were more than just seasoned pro-life campaigners present. The room was filled – it was revealed when the time came for questions – with unreconstructed tradition-alists who thought the Catholic Church had lost its way at the Second Vatican Council and who felt it was now dangerously adrift under the papacy of Francis. Behind me sat a middle-aged couple with cut-glass upper-crust accents which would not have seemed out of place in the stately home Downton Abbey. 'This is a battle for the soul of the Church,' one said to the other in a whisper so loud that everyone around could hear.

The cardinal stood up and moved to a transparent podium. It did not take him long to get into full culture-warrior confrontation mode. Within the first minute he was attacking modern culture for being 'profoundly confused and in error'. Two minutes later he was attacking by name Cardinal Walter Kasper, who had expressed 'the confusion and error' during an Extraordinary Consistory of Cardinals a year earlier, in February 2014, after Pope Francis invited Kasper – the man described as the theologian of this pontificate – to address his fellows on the subject of the forthcoming Synod on the Family. Kasper had suggested, in what Francis later described as 'a beautiful and profound presentation', that it was time for the Church to allow Catholics who had divorced and remarried to receive Holy Communion. Burke offered to the Chester meeting his own vision which was as remarkable for what it omitted as for what it said.

The cardinal spoke about 'the fundamental truth of marriage' for almost an hour without once mentioning love in its most commonly understood sense. There were references aplenty to 'the integrity of the conjugal act' and 'the essence of the conjugal union'. He spoke of 'the faithful, indissoluble and procreative union of marriage' and even of 'the faithful and enduring covenant of divine love'. But it was abstract philosophical theology. There was, in it, no recognition of the secret language of human love: of intimacy and care, of softness and openness, of empathy and warmth, of creativity and companionship, of kindness and cleaving, of mutual support and friendship, of weeping together and laughing together, of giving and sacrifice, of touch and affection, or of emotional and psychological closeness. Cardinal Burke's view of marriage was something clinical and cold. The love-making of a couple using contraceptives was 'a tool for personal gratification', in the Burke lexicon. At times his language was even violent, as when he said that with contraception 'the procreative nature of the act has been radically violated'. It was language of a kind which fell oddly on the ear from a man who, at the same time, accused gay men and women in the Church of having an 'incredibly aggressive homosexual agenda'. There was only one mention of mercy – and that was to disparage it.

But there was something else that was even more striking. Throughout the hour in which he spoke, he quoted Pope John Paul II no fewer than 25 times. He quoted Benedict XVI some 22 times in all. He even quoted Pope Paul VI three times. But he did not quote Pope Francis once. Indeed the word 'Francis' did not so much as pass his lips. 'It was quite extraordinary,' one member of the audience observed to me afterwards. It was as if he could not bring himself even to pronounce the name of the current pontiff. And when once he spoke of 'the Holy Father' he meant John Paul II.

The questions he was asked after his speech, with only one exception, seemed to come from unequivocal traditionalists. Indeed they were not questions so much as laments for the old ways. They asked about the abandonment of Thomist philosophy, inadequately catechized priests, hermeneutics of rupture and discontinuity, a crisis in reverence for the Eucharist, and the implicit blasphemy of priests who say they want to make the liturgy interesting. Only one questioner dared to be different, asking about dialogue, being open-minded, thinking outside the box, and the open discussion. Cardinal Burke replied that 'deepening our understanding of the tradition of the Church is not being not open'. To think otherwise was to be naïve. 'We have to speak truth in charity,' he said, drawing his biggest round of applause from an audience who did not sound as if they were being particularly charitable. 'That was long overdue,' said the Downton woman behind me. It was an instructive evening, for it lifted the veil on the kind of opposition which Pope Francis is up against.

Cardinal Burke ended by telling his faithful followers that they should take Saint John Fisher and Saint Thomas More as models. They were martyrs who died defending the integrity of the fidelity and indissolubility of marriage. The cardinal was clearly ignorant of the historical facts of what happened when Sir Thomas More was confronted with the Oath of Succession – which declared Henry's child by his first marriage illegitimate so that the children of his second would succeed to the throne. More said he would swear it, if it were worded differently. It was not the issue of whether the first marriage of Henry VIII was valid – or, as the monarch claimed, invalid – which was the point of principle for which More died. What he objected to was the fact that the Oath abjured the Pope and laid the ground for schism between the Church of Rome and the Church in England. The irony was lost on Cardinal Burke. But Thomas More was martyred not to defend the indissolubility of marriage. He gave up his life to defend the authority of the Pope.

* * *

Had Pope Francis been a fly on the wall at the Chester event he might merely have smiled wryly. The previous two popes may have regarded all disagreement as dissent. But Francis had set out to allow different views within the Church to flourish. Indeed fostering vigorous debate was central to the biggest of all the reforms he was planning to transform the Catholic Church.

The new Pope's decision to set up the Council of Cardinal Advisers, which became his C9 cabinet, had been an extremely bold step. It brought cardinals into the decision-making process of the Church over the heads of the Curia officials who had for centuries run the Vatican, often as a law unto themselves. But Pope Francis could claim that he had been given a mandate for that. Cardinal after cardinal, during the discussions before the conclave that had elected him, had said the Curia needed to be a servant not a master to local churches round the world. But the Pope's next – and potentially most far-reaching – change was one that was made on his own authority alone.

One of the top issues on the agenda of the first meeting of that cabinet was how a Francis papacy could allow bishops around the world to have a greater say in how the Church was run. The church jargon for that was episcopal collegiality, and the main vehicle for this ought to have been the Synod of Bishops, the body set up by Pope Paul VI in the last year of the revitalizing Second Vatican Council. The presence of so many bishops in Rome for the great Council inspired Pope Paul to create a body which would 'make ever greater use of the bishops' assistance in providing for the good of the universal Church'. The pontiff would enjoy 'the consolation of their presence, the help of their wisdom and experience, the support of their counsel, and the voice of their authority'.

The word *synod* derives from the union of two Greek words, *syn* which means 'together', and *odòs* which means 'path or journey'. The concept of synodality is an ancient one within the Church, even if in the second millennium of church history the popes began to rule like medieval kings – and synodality became a word which fell upon stony ground. But if Pope Paul VI enabled it in the modern Church he shied away from implementing the idea, so, from the outset, the synod had never been what the Vatican II bishops desired. Where Paul VI was nervous about releasing the potential of the synod, Pope John Paul II had no time for sources of authority to rival his own and effectively closed it down. Benedict XVI was less autocratic but did not change the formula of the synod as an occasional gathering of bishops, delegated from episcopal conferences around the world, called to advise the Pope on a particular subject. Popes reverted to a monarchical model of government. Synods became formal rubber-stamping bodies meeting every two or three years, their debates circum-scribed by the Curia and their conclusions pretty much decided in advance by the Vatican. Francis remembered, all too well, his experience as the relator (secretary) of the 10th Ordinary General Assembly of the Synod of Bishops in 2001. 'A Vatican official came and told him what to do,' one Argentine theologian told me. 'That will not happen any more.'

The revitalization of the synod was to be, according to the church historian Massimo Faggioli, Francis's most important reform. The eminent papal historian Eamon Duffy, went further. 'If the weight is to shift from the Roman bureaucracy to the Synod of Bishops,' he said, 'it will be a restructuring on a scale not seen since that of Pope Sixtus V in the late sixteenth century.'

* * *

Francis wasted no time in setting about his top priority. He began working privately with Cardinal Lorenzo Baldisseri, the man he had appointed as secretary-general of the synod not long after becoming Pope. Baldisseri had been secretary to the conclave that had elected Francis. Three months later Baldisseri announced that the Pope was looking to transform the synod, which met occasionally, into 'a dynamic permanent synod' that would create 'an osmosis between centre and periphery'. In August 2013 Pietro Parolin, the Pope's newly-appointed Secretary of State, in his first interview, revealed that Francis had made it one of his objectives to create a more democratic atmosphere in the Church. 'It has always been said that the Church is not a democracy,' Parolin said. 'But it would be good during these times if there could be a more democratic spirit, in the sense of listening carefully.' What the Pope wanted was 'a collegial movement of the Church, where all the issues can be brought up, and afterwards he can make a decision'.

Pope Francis began to translate those words into action. He doubled the office space of the synod's permanent secretariat, a body which worked entirely outside the Curia. He authorized the hiring of more staff. He met several times with Cardinal Baldisseri to reform the procedures used at synods. In October 2013 Francis was reported as saying in another interview: 'This is the beginning of a Church with an organization that is not just top-down but also horizontal.' And he sent out another radical signal by mentioning his fellow Jesuit, the late Cardinal Mario Martini, who as Archbishop of Milan had been seen as the liberal pole of authority in the time of Pope John Paul II. 'When Cardinal Martini talked about focusing on the councils and synods he knew how long and difficult it would be to go in that direction.' He would proceed, Francis said, 'gently, but firmly and tenaciously'. Those words were to be a blueprint of what was to follow.

Pope Francis spent two days in early October meeting with Baldisseri and his Synod Council. The Pope brought to the table the 'see-judge-act' method that Latin American bishops had adopted from Liberation Theology. A three-stage process was needed: to examine the lived experiences of ordinary Catholics, and reflect upon them, and then to decide what actions were needed for change. A new vehicle was needed, the Pope said, to revive synodical government and return to the way it was conducted in the early Church and was still practised in the Orthodox Church. Then he hit upon the idea. He would turn the next meeting of the Synod of Bishops – on the subject of the Family, scheduled for October 2015 – from a two-week meeting into a two-year process. He decided that the Ordinary Synod in 2015 should be preceded by an Extraordinary Synod in October 2014 which could decide the questions that should be the basis of discussion at the regular meeting. In between the two synods, the wider Church could offer views on the issues based on its lived experience and prayerful reflection. But that was not all. He wanted wider consultation and stimulation even before the bishops got to the subject in the first place. That required input from both above, from the College of Cardinals, and below, from ordinary Catholics all round the world. Francis took the idea to the first meeting of his council of cardinal advisers in October.

The project moved swiftly. In November he ordered a study designed to reduce the number of dioceses in Italy – which numbered more than two hundred – and a reform of its governance structures to redress the imbalance between Italians and the bishops of the rest of the world. That month he published *Evangelii Gaudium*. In it he said he wanted to promote a 'sound decentralization' of church government. And he added: 'Since I am called to put into practice what I ask of others, I too must think about a conversion of the papacy. It is my duty, as the Bishop of Rome, to be open to suggestions which can help make the exercise of my ministry more faithful to the meaning which Jesus Christ wished to give it.' Pope John Paul II had said something similar almost twenty years before but, said Francis, 'we have made little progress in this regard'. The Second Vatican Council had called for a return to the way synods had worked in the early Church – 'to contribute in many and fruitful ways to the concrete realization of the collegial spirit'. Yet this had not happened and the devolution of 'genuine doctrinal authority' to the national conferences of bishops had not happened sufficiently. Instead 'excessive centralization' was hindering the ability of local churches around the world to reach ordinary people. And the lack of synodal government in the Catholic Church was a huge obstacle to any future moves towards Christian unity with Constantinople and Moscow. Diversity and debate was not a problem but a blessing: 'Differing currents of thought in philosophy, theology and pastoral practice, if open to being reconciled by the Spirit in respect and love, can enable the Church to grow.'

This would be a seismic shift. The Curia, including the guardians of doctrinal orthodoxy at the Congregation for the Doctrine of the Faith, would become subordinate to the synod. They would be servants rather than masters. The change in the pecking order became apparent when, in January 2014, Pope Francis announced his first new cardinals. Top of the list was Pietro Parolin, as we noted previously, the Secretary of State. But where the old protocol would next have named Gerhard Müller, the head of the CDF, his name was only third. Above him had been placed Lorenzo Baldisseri, the secretary of the synod. The significance was not lost on Vaticanologists. 'The message was unambiguous,' said one leading Vatican-watcher, Robert Mickens: 'the CDF is to be at the service of the College of Bishops, not its doctrinal minder'.

There was another dimension to the thinking of Pope Francis. Government by synod would remove one of the major obstacles to Christian unity so far as the Orthodox Church was concerned. In his first interview as Pope, with Antonio Spadaro in September 2013, he had said:

> We must walk together: the people, the bishops and the pope. Synodality should be lived at various levels. Maybe it is time to change the methods of the Synod of Bishops, because it seems to me that the current method is not dynamic. This will also have ecumenical value, especially with our Orthodox brethren. From them we can learn more about the meaning of episcopal collegiality and the tradition of synodality. The joint effort of reflection, looking at how the Church was governed in the early centuries, before the breakup between East and West, will bear fruit in due time. In ecumenical relations it is important not only to know each other better, but also to recognize what the Spirit has sown in the other as a gift for us.

The Pope's thinking was revealed more explicitly when he appointed Enzo Bianchi as a consultant to the Pontifical Council for the Promotion of Christian Unity. Bianchi was the prior of the monastery of Bose, a community of monks and nuns belonging to different Christian Churches. Soon after his appointment he told the *Vatican Insider* website: 'The Pope wants to achieve unity also by reforming the papacy.' He wanted to make it a papacy which 'is no longer feared', to quote the words of the Orthodox Church's ecumenical patriarch Bartholomew, 'with whom Francis has a bond of friendship'. That would require 'a new balance between synodality and supremacy', Bianchi said. 'The Orthodox Church exercises synodality but not primacy, we Catholics have papal primacy but we lack synodality. There can be no synodality without primacy and there can be no primacy without synodality. This would help create a new style of papal primacy and episcopal government.' He later added: 'No-one has spoken like this for a thousand years.' Conservatives greeted his words with alarm.

The process Pope Francis had conceived was set in train. In October 2013 a 38-point questionnaire was sent out by Cardinal Baldisseri to national bishops' conferences across the world with the instruction that they should use it to ask ordinary Catholics what they thought of the Church's teachings on the Family. Baldisseri also announced that ordinary believers could also write directly to his office with their views. The questionnaire – which some bishops' conferences put online for grassroots Catholics to answer directly – did not shy away from controversial issues like premarital sex, contraception, divorce, remarriage, same-sex relationships, *in vitro* fertilization and adoption by gay couples. It was a revolutionary act by Francis. The direct global survey of lay people was unprecedented. Indeed, previous popes had made it evident that they did not want to know what the people in the pew thought. They should just pray, pay and obey. That had been made very clear in previous years to senior British clerics Cardinal Basil Hume and Archbishop Derek Worlock, who held a National Pastoral Congress of 2,000 bishops, clergy and lay people in Liverpool in 1980. When the British prelates handed the report of the event to Pope John Paul II, pointing to one paragraph and asking him to read it there and then, he put it aside without even looking at it. Pope Francis's initiative to send a questionnaire to the laity was without precedent since Cardinal John Henry Newman had written, in the nineteenth century, his famous essay, 'On Consulting the Faithful in Matters of Doctrine', suggesting a two-way process between the taught and the teacher.

The questionnaire was far from perfect. Its wording was opaque and clumsy. It asked why ordinary people did not understand church teaching rather than enquiring what they found difficult or out of line with the Gospel. 'It was a classic Roman document laying the blame on the failure of the laity,' an official in one bishops' conference told me. Some commentators even suggested that it had been deliberately badly written by conservative Vatican officials to subvert the intentions of the reforming Pope. One middle-ranking Curia official laughed at that notion and told me: 'The language just reflects the way people here think.' What was remarkable, he added, was not that it was done badly but 'that it was done at all – that was what people here found astonishing.' They were to be further amazed when they discovered the things ordinary Catholics dared to say in reply – and what Pope Francis intended to do with the results.

If the questionnaire was the view from below, Pope Francis knew that he had to contend with opinions from around him in the Vatican from indivdiuals who were accustomed to see their views holding sway. How would the College of Cardinals react to the idea of empowering the college of bishops? Francis decided to test the water with a subject which was both close to his own experience of dealing with chaotic families in the slums of Buenos Aires – and which had also been a neuralgic issue at the 2005 Synod on the Eucharist. He selected one man to light the gunpowder fuse.

* * *

When the cardinals gathered in Rome for their seven days of discussions before the conclave that chose Francis, they all lodged in the Vatican hostel where the Pope now lives, the Casa Santa Marta. The then Cardinal Bergoglio had a room right across the hallway from that of Cardinal Walter Kasper. The German cardinal had, by coincidence, just received from his publisher two copies of the Spanish translation of his latest book, *Mercy: The Essence of the Gospel and the Key to Christian Life*. He gave one to Bergoglio.

'Ah, mercy!' the Argentine cardinal exclaimed when he saw the title. 'This is the name of our God!'

It was not – in the words of David Gibson of Religion News Service, who interviewed Kasper afterwards – 'just one of those *pro forma* compliments you might give to an acquaintance at a book party'. Mercy, as decades of Bergoglio's life had shown, had long been a guiding principle for the former Jesuit Provincial's later life and ministry. He devoured Kasper's book in the days leading up to the voting. Four days after the conclave ended the new Pope was addressing a large crowd in St Peter's Square. Kasper, who was watching on television, was staggered when Francis mentioned the book, praised Kasper as a 'very sharp theologian' and told the world: 'That book has done me so much good.'

Ever since the time of Pope John Paul II, Kasper had been arguing that it was time to lift the ban on remarried Catholics taking Communion if their first marriage had not been annulled by the Church. (An annulment is a declaration that when a couple married, one or more of the Catholic tests for validity of marriage was not met.) Kasper was not advocating a change in the Church's dogma on the sanctity of marriage, but an amendment in the 'pastoral practice' about who can receive Communion. He said: 'To say we will not admit divorced and remarried people to Holy Communion? That's not a dogma. That's an application of a dogma in a concrete pastoral practice. This can be changed.'

Even a murderer can confess and receive Communion, he frequently noted. His attempt to persuade John Paul to allow the change had been thwarted by conservatives in Rome, led by the then head of the CDF, Cardinal Joseph Ratzinger. Over the years the two German cardinals had sparred over the issue in the pages of theological journals. Though Ratzinger's view had prevailed the conservatives still did not like Kasper. After Francis praised his book from the balcony, one of them went to the Pope and admonished him: 'Holy Father, you should not recommend this book! There are many heresies in it!' Kasper knew this because the Pope himself later told him, telling Kasper not to be concerned and adding with a smile: 'It goes in one ear and out the other.'

Kasper was the man Pope Francis decided should address a gathering he had called of the cardinals for February 2014 to discuss the two forthcoming synods on the Family. To the wider world the issue of remarried Catholics and Communion might have seemed fairly arcane. But, with Catholics now getting remarried at a similar rate to the rest of society, it is a huge pastoral crisis in those parts of the Church which do not simply turn a blind eye to the issue. Some hoped the problem could be eased by making it easier to get an annulment. But three individuals close to the Pope, two of them cardinals, have told me that Francis does not see this as the solution. Kasper warned the Pope that if he addressed his fellow cardinals on the subject there would be a heated response. 'Holy Father, there will be a controversy afterwards,' Kasper said. The Pope laughed and told him: 'That's good, we should have that!'

Kasper was right. The discussion which followed his presentation was impassioned, with heavyweight conservatives lining up against the German advocate of reform. But Francis rejoiced in the exchanges. 'I would have been more worried if there hadn't been an intense discussion,' he said afterwards. 'The cardinals knew that they could say what they wanted, and they presented different points of view, which are always enriching. Open and fraternal debate fosters the growth of theological and pastoral thought,' he said. 'I'm not afraid of this; on the contrary, I seek it.'

Two key insights about Pope Francis arose from all this. The first was about the specific issue of Communion for the remarried. But the second – and almost certainly the more important understanding – was about how anxious he was to change the way the Church makes decisions.

It was overwhelmingly clear that Pope Francis wanted a more compassionate approach to remarried Catholics taking Communion. In public he dropped massive hints. In his first airborne press conference in July 2013, when asked about the issue, he said: 'I believe this is the time of mercy. The Church is a mother: it must reach out to heal the wounds. This time is a *kairos* of mercy.'

The word *kairos* denotes a special moment in history in which God's purposes can be seen at work in a particular way. He quoted with approbation his predecessor as Archbishop of Buenos Aires, Cardinal Quarracino, as saying 'half of all marriages are null...because people get married lacking maturity, without realizing that it is a life-long commitment, or get married because society tells them they have to get married'. The Pope then placed the issue on the agenda for the very first meeting of the C8, where he suggested studying the Orthodox practice of blessings for second marriages. Next, in *Evangelii Gaudium* he had written: 'The doors of our churches must always be open and the sacraments available to all', adding that the Eucharist 'is not a prize for the perfect, but a powerful medicine and nourishment for the weak'. He had, remember, described Kasper's presentation as 'beautiful and profound'.

He appeared to have gone further in 2014 when he was reported as having telephoned a woman who had written to him from Argentina to say that her parish priest had denied her Communion because, though she had never been married before, she had now wed a man who had previously been divorced. She afterwards told the media that the Pope had counselled her simply to find another priest who would allow her to receive the Eucharist. That had caused a furore, with conservatives saying the Pope was undermining church teaching on marriage and also complaining that he should have consulted the woman's priest and bishop before calling her. The Vatican press office rushed to tell the media that this was a private conversation which 'did not form part of the magisterium' – church jargon for official teaching. But Francis was untroubled by the criticism, I was told by one cardinal close to the Pope. 'In talking to the woman he's acting as if he were parish priest to the world,' the cardinal said. 'Conservatives say he doesn't give enough thought to the implications of the advice he gives to individuals being applied to the wider Church. And he knows that what he is doing in such situations is a double-edged thing to do. But he feels the spirit of God is present in it – and that the instinct of the People of God will find what is right in any given situation.' He took the same attitude to a group of individuals in what the Church calls 'irregular' family situations just a month before the first October synod. He conducted 20 weddings in the Vatican, a number of them couples who were already living together, contrary to church teaching on premarital sex – 'living in sin' as several newspapers put it. At least one of the couples had a child. Once again the message was that the Church welcomed all – not only those who embrace its sexual ethics perfectly.

As the months passed, the results of the questionnaire began to leak to the media, despite requests from the Curia that they should be passed to Rome without being published. Bishops in some countries had refused to issue the survey to their flock; in Italy, for example, they had done almost nothing to engage ordinary Catholics with the questions. But it gradually became clear that in many of the 114 countries that had replied – from Germany and Ireland to the Philippines and Japan – a tectonic gap had opened between official teaching and what Catholics in the pew believe and do. The Canadian bishops respected the Vatican request not to publish the details but announced that their survey had found 'a huge gap' between theory and practice, according to Archbishop Paul-André Durocher, president of the Canadian Conference of Catholic Bishops. Conservatives in the Curia became increasingly alarmed. Cardinal George Pell said that 'substantial doctrinal and pastoral changes are impossible' and the sooner 'the wounded, the lukewarm, and the outsiders' realized that the better; the irony that the wounded, the lukewarm, and the outsiders were precisely the kind of people Pope Francis was trying to reach was clearly lost on the Australian cardinal. The Vatican's most senior arbiter on doctrine, Gerhard Müller, had the Vatican's official newspaper reprint one of his essays, which insisted that the Church only allow married couples to separate for 'compelling reasons', such as physical or psychological violence. In all other cases, he said, 'the marriage bond of a valid union remains intact in the sight of God, and the individual parties are not free to contract a new marriage, as long as the spouse is alive'. The CDF chief insisted, citing Pope Benedict XVI, that the argument for withholding Communion from remarried Catholics was rooted in 'sacred scripture'. There was, he averred, 'no possibility of admitting remarried divorcees to the sacraments'.

But this was the pontificate of Francis, not Benedict. The days were gone when the head of the CDF spoke and his word was taken as final. Müller, as we saw in Chapter 13, was rebuffed by members of the C8. Cardinal Marx responded that the synod was perfectly free to change pastoral practice on Communion for the remarried. When Müller hit back – insisting that changing practice implied changing doctrine, and that neither synod nor Pope were free to do that – the chairman of the C8, Cardinal Rodríguez Maradiaga, slapped down Müller for rigid thinking. The battlelines were being drawn.

What happened next was that Pope Francis made it clear that he wanted the lived experience of the lay Catholics set out in the questionnaire to be the starting point for the discussion among bishops at the Extraordinary Synod. Their views were to be the basis for the *instrumentum laboris* – the working document on which the approaching synod would be based. This was far from normal practice. Again, said one mid-ranking curial official, Pope Francis 'was striking out into new territory'.

* * *

Pope Francis wanted major change. He wanted the Church to become more compassionate in the way it treated Catholics excluded from full Communion because of their 'irregular' sexual situations. But he wanted much more. He did not want to decree change like an old-style papal monarch. He wanted the Church to find a better way to agree its decisions.

On 1 April 2014 he wrote a letter that received little attention from the world's media. It was to Cardinal Baldisseri, Secretary of the Synod. It was even ignored by most Vatican analysts at the time. But the great church scholar Father Ladislas Orsy wrote of it: 'That brief letter may well be to date one of the most significant documents of the present pontificate.' In it Pope Francis told Baldisseri of his intention 'to raise the undersecretary of the synod, Fabio Fabene, to the dignity of bishop'. The formality of the wording was a clue. The letter used the solemn sentences normally reserved for major papal proclamations, Orsy observed. No undersecretary to the synod had ever before been made a bishop. But there was more to the Pope's signal of intent even than that. Orsy deconstructed the letter in an article for the Catholic weekly, *The Tablet*. Francis had written that he had made the decision 'after having deeply examined the signs of the times' – a signal, said Orsy, that Francis was aware he was seizing an historical moment. It also spoke, rather mystically, of the origin of the synods lying in the 'inexhaustible expanse of the mystery and of the horizon of the Church of God'. Once 'mystery' is the measure, wrote Orsy, 'the riches waiting for discovery cannot be exhausted'. What Pope Francis was signalling was a change which, in his view, was both historic and profound.

The reason he had chosen Baldisseri to supervise the process became clear a month later. 'The Church is not timeless, she lives amidst the vicissitudes of history and the Gospel must be known and experienced by people today,' the Secretary to the Synod told a Belgian Christian magazine, *Tertio*. It was time to update church marriage doctrine in connection with divorce, the situation of divorcees and people who are in civil partnerships. The response of ordinary faithful Catholics to the questionnaire was significant, Baldisseri said, seeming to echo the old Bergoglio line that the holy faithful people of God 'are infallible in believing'. Cardinal Baldisseri said that the bishops 'must recognize that the faithful perceive the truth'. The two-synod process, he said, 'will allow a more adequate response to the expectations of the people'. He also announced a significant change to synod procedures. Where previously bishops had made prepared speeches in succession, with almost no interaction or dialogue, they were now to be asked to submit their presentations two weeks before the meeting opened. 'This is not to limit the discussion, but to help organize it,' the cardinal said. The synod would begin with a summary of those presentations by cardinals rather than, as in the past, a rephrasing of the working document drawn up by the Curia. The drawing of the agenda would thus pass from Vatican bureaucrats to bishops out in the dioceses. All this had been agreed in detail with the Pope, as had another big Francis gesture – the announcement that the synod proceedings would, for the first time, not be conducted in Latin but in Italian. To the horror of the traditionalists, Pope Francis was dragging the Catholic Church kicking and screaming into the fifteenth century, which is when the rest of Europe set aside the dead language for the common vernacular.

But the true extent of the change Francis had planned only became evident when he stood up to speak. On the opening morning of the Extraordinary Synod the 191 bishops were told by the Pope: 'One general and basic condition is this: speak out ... Nobody should say: "I can't say this or they will think this of me ... "' After the heated discussion in Feburary when the cardinals debated the Kasper presentation, one cardinal had written to the Pope saying: 'Some cardinals didn't have the courage to say certain things out of respect for the Pope, believing that the Pope may have thought differently.' That was not good, Francis said. 'This is not what synodality is about. We must say everything we feel we need to say, in the spirit of the Lord, without pusillanimity and without fear. At the same time, we must listen humbly and embrace with an open heart what our brothers tell us. These two attitudes express synodality.' They should speak with *parrhesia* – the Greek word (meaning to speak candidly, boldly, and without fear) which was used of the way the disciples spoke after the Resurrection. The bishops, he concluded, should speak boldly and listen with humility, safe in the knowledge that 'because the synod always takes place *cum petro et sub petro* [with Peter and under Peter] ... the Pope's presence is a guarantee for everyone and protects the faith'.

It was a dramatic contrast to previous synods, which under previous popes had been stage-managed as carefully as Soviet party congresses, where Vatican officials went around privately telling participants not to mention certain subjects or make particular remarks. This time, the Pope said, there should be no such taboos.

The shocks continued. During the opening speech of the synod, Cardinal Péter Erdő of Hungary said that 'many marriages celebrated in the Church may be invalid' because couples did not go into them with the intent of making a lifetime commitment. Erdő had been appointed relator, or secretary to the sessions, so his comments carried particular weight. Annulments should be made easier, he implied, suggesting that bishops could grant them, avoiding the necessity of a courtroom procedure. Many bishops' conferences around the world had already backed such an idea. But though Pope Francis had already indicated his eagerness for speeding up annulments – he had set up a commission in August to study it – both reformers and resisters knew that annulments were a side-issue. The debate over ending the exclusion of remarried Catholics from Communion had become a symbol of a deeper disagreement between the two sides.

The division was aired again with further remarks of Erdő suggesting that the debate should be seen through the lens of the principle of graduality. This was a piece of theological terminology that had been popular three decades earlier but that had been squashed by Pope John Paul II after the 1980 Synod. It says that morality is not all-or-nothing; rather, moral progress comes in stages and it is necessary to start 'where people are' and then move them towards being better rather than demanding instant perfection. So it is better to encourage individuals where they are doing good than chastise them for what they are getting wrong. It seemed an effective summary of the overall approach of Pope Francis. Cardinals at the synod began to speak up for it. Gradualism could help the Church find a new way of talking about sex, said Cardinal Marx, one of the C8, which by this point had become the C9 with the addition of Cardinal Parolin to its ranks. Cardinal Vincent Nichols of Westminster said the idea 'permits people, all of us, to take one step at a time in our search for holiness in our lives'.

A similar pragmatism was reported to the synod from the grassroots. One of the married couples invited to attend was Ron and Mavis Pirola of Sydney, Australia, who had been married for 55 years and had four children. They told the synod of a dilemma from their own lives. Family friends had a gay son who told them he wanted to bring his partner home for Christmas. The Pirolas' friends were faithful Catholics who understood the Church's opposition to homosexual partnerships. But they were also loving parents who resolved their dilemma on whether to invite the gay couple into their home with three simple words: 'He's our son.' The case, the Pirolas said, showed how the clergy might have something to learn from the ordinary faithful on how to strike a balance between upholding church teaching but also showing 'mercy and compassion'. The synod responded 'very warmly, with applause', said Cardinal Nichols afterwards. The Nigerian Archbishop Ignatius Kaigama – who earlier in the year had thanked God and praised Nigeria's president for signing a new anti-gay law that imposes a 14-year prison sentence for homosexuality – commented: 'If the son is part of the family it is only natural that the family should be together. You cannot exclude a family member from a feast, from a meal. Our arms should be open.'

Such a change of tone from Africa was just one indication of how the leadership of Pope Francis was working through the synod. There was a new warmth, veteran observers said. 'Laughter was heard in the synod for the first time,' said one senior Curia member. The vocabulary changed, noted another seasoned official, expressing surprise at the meeting's general wish to tone down the use of terms such as 'living in sin', 'contraceptive mentality' and 'intrinsically disordered', which were previously common. The word 'gay' was heard for the first time in a synod. But as well as a shift in tone there was a far greater sense of a genuine conversation between the synod fathers than on previous occasions.

But a vocal minority of conservatives in the synod became increasingly concerned. They saw the new openness of Pope Francis as an unwelcome departure from the clarity of the approach of the previous two popes, which had valued orthodoxy over debate. It was too reminiscent of the mood and tone at the Second Vatican Council, whose enthusiasts they blamed for subsequent excessive liberalism. This was exactly the wrong time for the debate on Communion for the remarried, they believed, because it would weaken the Church's defence of the sanctity of marriage at a time when it was under attack from campaigners for gay marriage, which was becoming increasingly acceptable all across the developed world. Five conservative cardinals had, on the eve of the synod, produced a book, *Remaining in the Truth of Christ: Marriage and Communion in the Catholic Church*, arguing against Kasper on the issue of Communion for the remarried. It included contributions by cardinals Müller and Burke, with a blunt foreword by Cardinal Pell.

But it was the methods as much as the message of the synod that prompted their growing anxiety. They claimed that an attempt to deliver a copy of the book to every member of the synod had been thwarted by the synod administrators. Cardinal Burke had disapproved of the testimony of the married couple from Australia, saying that the friends involved of the Pirolas had scandalously exposed their grandchildren to the bad example of a 'disordered relationship'. But it was the production of an interim summary, halfway through the synod, that led the conservative faction to break out into open revolt.

The midway document – known as the *relatio post disceptationem*, or report after the debate – was supposed to be a summary of the first week's debates before the members broke into smaller different-language groups to discuss it. When it was produced, the media greeted it as a revolutionary document overturning many of the attitudes of the John Paul/Benedict era. Communion for the remarried should be allowed on a case-by-case basis, it said. Gay Catholics should be 'accepted and valued' by the Church. Pastors should seek to emphasize the positive rather than the negative elements of the lifestyles of remarried or gay Catholics. Mercy should be advanced alongside doctrine. The 'law of gradualness' should be applied to help guide couples towards the ideal. All this was described as a 'pastoral earthquake' by the veteran commentator John Thavis. The document was received very differently by opposing factions within the Church. Joshua McElwee, the Vatican correspondent for the liberal *National Catholic Reporter*, commented on Twitter: 'It feels like a whole new church, a whole new tone, a whole new posture. Wow.' And the leading Jesuit commentator of *America* magazine, Father James Martin SJ, tweeted: 'Today's stunning change in tone from the Catholic bishops on LGBT people shows what happens when the Holy Spirit is let loose.' But the ultra-conservative Voice of the Family coalition branded it a 'betrayal' of the Catholic faith. It was, said the organization's founder, John Smeaton, 'one of the worst official documents drafted in church history'.

A heated row broke out, with angry and raised voices. It was not just the hardline conservatives who were indignant. More mainstream members of the synod accused Archbishop Bruno Forte, the secretary of the committee selected by Pope Francis to draft the interim report, of inserting his own views into the document and presenting it as a draft of the synod's final document. Bruno was, reported Associated Press, 'an Italian theologian known for pushing the pastoral envelope on dealing with people in "irregular" unions while staying true to Catholic doctrine'. Cardinal Napier of South Africa spoke out at a Vatican press conference. It was not enough, he suggested, to say that the synod's final document could be rewritten to more accurately reflect the views of the meeting. The story had flashed around the world with headlines like: 'At last, the Catholic Church changes its mind on gays'. That was almost impossible to retract, he complained. 'We're now working from a position that is virtually irredeemable,' he said. 'It's not what we were saying (in the synod hall). It's not a true message!'

The arch-conservative Cardinal Raymond Burke went further. The interim document was not just unrepresentative, he said, but wrong. 'The document lacks a solid foundation in the Sacred Scriptures and the Magisterium,' he proclaimed. For the first week of the synod Pope Francis had not spoken. It was time for him to break his silence, Burke pronounced. A statement from the Pope was 'in my judgement...long overdue', Burke said. 'I can't speak for the Pope,' he later added, though many felt that was exactly what he was trying to do. 'And I can't say what his position is on this, but the lack of clarity about the matter has certainly done a lot of harm.' In fact the Pope's position was quite clear. He had seen the interim report in advance and had approved it.

Behind the scenes the authors of the interim report tried to make out that it reflected the views that cardinals had outlined in their longer written presentations to the synod as well as what they had said in their four-minute speeches in the hall. But many cardinals were not placated. Some objected to the fact that the synod secretariat had refused to release texts of their speeches to the synod; they claimed that the summaries outlined at the synod's daily press conferences were exercises in spin rather than accurate accounts of the breadth of the discussion. When the cardinals congregated in their language groups, one synod father opened the discussion by pointing to the section on gay couples in the interim report: 'Did you hear any of this last week?' He got a negative reply all round. The interim report was severely criticized in seven of the ten language-based discussion groups.

'The old Vatican manipulation behind the scenes is still at work, this time from the other side,' one church historian based in Rome told me. 'Those on the liberal wing, who feel they have the backing of the Pope, have been manoeuvring the agenda so that it advances what they want, leaving the conservatives feeling their opinions are being given insufficient weight. But that has been a tactical mistake, because by broadening the debate from Communion for the remarried to include homosexuality they have shifted the synod on to a disagreement on which the battlelines are even more deeply entrenched.'

The staunch conservative, Cardinal Pell, detected a plot in that. Communion for the divorced and remarried was, for some liberal cardinals, 'only the tip of the iceberg'. Pell continued: 'It's a stalking horse. They want wider changes, recognition of civil unions, recognition of homosexual unions. The Church cannot go in that direction. It would be a capitulation from the beauties and strengths of the Catholic tradition, where people sacrificed themselves for hundreds of years, to do this.' In the synod he demanded that the reflections of the language groups should now be published too. He slammed his hand on the table and said to the officials of the secretariat: 'You must stop manipulating this synod.'

The Pope certainly got the frank debate he wanted. The synod ended with a vote on a final document which toned down some of the conciliatory language on gays and remarried Catholics. Almost all the document was approved by an overwhelming majority of bishops. But three sections – one on how the Church should deal with those in same-sex relationships and two calling for further study on Communion for the remarried – failed to receive the two-thirds majority that constitutes formal approval by the synod. The secular media reported the vote with headlines like: 'Pope suffers synod setback on gays'. But the Jesuit magazine *America* showed there was another way to interpret the outcome. Its Rome correspondent, Gerard O'Connell, who is close to Pope Francis, wrote:

> The Final Report of the Synod on the Family revealed that the Synod has closed no doors, all the main questions are still on the table, and an absolute majority of the synod fathers are with Pope Francis, in favour of a Church that like the Good Samaritan reaches out to care for all her 'wounded children'.
>
> At the same time it showed clearly that a significant minority totally opposes the admission of the divorced and remarried to the sacraments of reconciliation and the Eucharist, and wants the Church to move with great caution in its pastoral approach to homosexual persons lest Church teaching be compromised.

Like the interim report, it encouraged pastors to identify and take advantage of 'the positive elements' in civil marriages and cohabitation, with a view to leading those couples towards the Christian ideal of marriage.

If it was a setback the Pope responded to it by publishing, unusually, the full final report, including the three paragraphs that did not get a two-thirds majority. Beside each of those paragraphs he noted the voting figures, showing that they just fell short of two-thirds approval (on remarried Communion by just 9 votes, on the gays paragraphs by 20 votes). But their inclusion in the final document ensured the issues would stay in the debate at the next synod. The full document was sent to bishops' conferences throughout the world to promote discussion on the issues among bishops, clergy and lay Catholics at local church level. To add to the complexity, a number of reform-minded bishops voted against the final text because it was too conservative rather than too liberal. The Archbishop of Westminster, Cardinal Vincent Nichols, said he did not vote for the final wording on gays because it did not include the words 'welcome', 'respect' and 'value'. And Archbishop Joseph Kurtz, head of the Conference of Bishops in the US, made a point of using the language of welcome that the final text had rejected.

But the synod ended with a masterly address from Pope Francis in which he praised the frank exchanges in which the synod fathers had engaged. He made it clear that he was untroubled by the level of disagreement. 'Personally, I would have been very worried and saddened if there hadn't been these temptations and these animated discussions,' the Pope said, 'if everybody had agreed or remained silent in a false and quietist peace.' Debate did not mean that the Church's unity was in danger, Pope Francis added. But he concluded by warning traditionalist and conservative bishops against zealous literalism and 'hostile rigidity' and by cautioning progressives and liberals against 'destructive do-goodism' and a 'misguided mercy' that wants to bind up wounds without first treating them. The speech won him a thunderous four-minute standing ovation from the vast majority of the 191 synod members. 'It was the kind of speech that both a Raymond Burke and a Walter Kasper could walk away from feeling as if the Pope understands them,' wrote John Allen in the *Boston Globe*, 'and it seemed to allow what had been a sometimes nasty two-week stretch to end on a high note.' One curial official expressed astonished admiration to another veteran Vatican-watcher, Robert Mickens, telling him over dinner: 'They have repeatedly taken the Pope to the brow of Vatican Hill, intending to throw him off the cliff, but he always passes through their midst and walks back to Casa Santa Marta.'

* * *

Vatican analysts hailed the 2014 Extraordinary Synod as a new chapter in the history of Catholicism. A first step had been taken in significantly shifting the way the Church governed itself. Bishops had openly discussed ideas for which they could have been investigated, censured, silenced or removed from office under previous papacies. The climate of conformity and fear that had gripped Catholicism had lifted. But the price of that was that it allowed the first mainstream public opposition to Pope Francis to emerge. In the months that followed, that criticism grew into a vocal backlash.

The most vociferous of Francis's public critics was Cardinal Raymond Burke. He was a man who now felt he had nothing to lose. He had already been stripped of his position on one of the Catholic Church's most influential bodies, the Vatican committee that oversees the appointment of new bishops throughout the worldwide Church. Before the synod the Pope had summoned him to a private meeting, where the pontiff had told him that he was to lose his job as head of the highest-ranking legal body. He has served there for six years, which was longer than most men kept that post. The Church needed a 'smart American', the Pope would later say in explaining the decision publicly, to be head of the chivalric Order of Malta. But neither man believed that. It was a largely ceremonial job usually given to cardinals as they approached retirement. Burke, the apotheosis of the culture-warrior bishop from the fortress Church of the John Paul/Benedict era, was being given the sack. His confrontational condemnatory approach to the wider world summed up everything Pope Francis wanted to change in the Church.

The gloves were now off for Burke. The thin code in which he began to speak of the pontiff was decipherable to everyone – though it suited some conservatives to pretend to believe Burke's shallow assertions of loyalty to the Pope. It was, said Professor Eamon Duffy, 'a dramatic departure from the protocol that inhibits cardinals from public criticism of living popes'. Burke's distaste for Pope Francis and what he was doing was evident to all. He made it clear to any media outlet that wanted to interview him.

'There's really just a growing confusion about what the Church really teaches,' Burke told the Irish television channel RTÉ. He did not need to say who he thought was responsible for spreading it. 'You can't have this dichotomy between doctrine and the discipline by which we're disposed to follow it. That isn't the way church doctrine is formulated and it's not the way discipline is formulated. The Church is not a democracy. The Church is not about revolutions. This talk about finding good elements in homosexual acts, that simply is a contradiction for us.' 'Who am I to judge?' was not a question disposed to fall from the lips of Cardinal Raymond Burke. In an interview with the Spanish Catholic weekly *Vida Nueva* he went further in another attack on the Pope's leadership. 'Many have expressed their concerns to me. At this very critical moment, there is a strong sense that the Church is like a ship without a rudder,' Burke said. 'Now, it is more important than ever to examine our faith, have a healthy spiritual leader and give powerful witness to the faith.' The implication was clear; the current leadership was not spiritually healthy. 'I do not want to seem like I am speaking out against the Pope,' he said, disingenuously, in the interview. But the ordinary faithful 'are feeling a bit seasick because they feel the Church's ship has lost its way'. Commentators like the traditionalist Damian Thompson in the British conservative journal the *Spectator*, who before the synod had been lamenting 'a degree of chaos unprecedented in recent Catholic history' which was all 'the Pope's fault', now began to write about 'the Catholic civil war' having begun.

Mainstream cardinals dismissed talk of a conservative backlash as sensationalist. 'There's some opposition, but it is a very small if voluble minority,' one cardinal close to the Pope told me. 'It's just not serious. The vast majority of people in the Church are very happy to have a pope with this inclusive style.' That may have been true in the broader Church. And certainly, even among conservatives, outright hostility was at first confined to a tiny traditionalist minority. The Georgetown University academic Paul Elie, in an article for *New Atlantic* magazine on the cloistered retirement life of Pope Benedict, described the opposition as 'certain Catholics who object to the direction in which

Francis is taking the Church' who had turned to look to Benedict, the Pope Emeritus, as their standard-bearer. 'They are the seminarians with crew cuts striding in groups around Rome, cassocks swishing at their ankles,' he wrote. 'They are the devotees of the Latin Mass and the advocates of reunion with the fascist-friendly schismatics of the Society of St. Pius X.' So the addition of Cardinal Burke to the opposition was significant. He may also have been an arch-conservative devotee of the old forms of the Latin Mass but he was closer to the mainstream and a cardinal who had been at the heart of church governance in the Ratzinger era.

In the first months of the Francis papacy conservative Catholics had been unsure what to make of the new Pope. At first they tried to seek out and emphasize all the points of continuity between him and his predecessor Benedict. But gradually it became clear that there were also many points of contrast and of change. This bemused them. It also caused them a particular problem because part of their traditionalist ecclesiology insisted that the Pope was always right. One of the most reactionary British Catholic websites had been called Protect the Pope in the Benedict era. Under Francis it would have had to change its name to 'Protect the Pope – from Himself'. That was a thought which the conservative Catholic columnist Ross Douthat was later to articulate in the New York Times, writing that 'this Pope may be preserved from error only if the Church itself resists him'.

But in the early months of the Francis pontificate most conservatives kept their heads below the parapet. Some hoped he would reveal himself to be more the kind of pope they wanted. Others decided to wait out what many conservative bishops in the United States privately began to call 'the Jesuit Experiment'. The Vatican correspondent of the National Catholic Register, Edward Pentin, who has good contacts among the traditionalist right-wing in the Church, told me just after the synod: 'They feel that Pope Francis is causing confusion in the Church by not upholding the Church's teachings properly. They think he has socialist leanings and that he brought division through his silence in the synod rather than uphold traditional doctrine and practice.' Those close to Francis insisted, 'He's not silent; he's listening.' But conservatives were unimpressed. 'Just listening and remaining silent implies he consented to the general innovative theology presented at the synod, they feel,' said Pentin. 'They see him as ushering in a period of confusion, uncertainty and concern. Those fighting on life issues felt they had their back covered by the last Pope. Now they are not so sure. After Francis's remarks about the Church being obsessed with abortion, and his albeit misquoted "who am I to judge?" on homosexuality, they feel like their general has deserted them. They are concerned about his theological approach.' They see it as a theological vagueness and lack of precision. A liberal Jesuit inside the Vatican said something similar: 'For the past three decades progressive Catholics have felt excluded. Now it's the traditionalists' turn. Benedict was like a father to them. Now they are fatherless.'

At the end of 2014 one of Italy's best-known Catholic writers, Vittorio Messori – who had been a Vatican insider since 1984 when he conducted a rare book-length interview with the then cardinal, Joseph Ratzinger – wrote an article in *Corriere della Sera* which claimed to have detected a turning point for Pope Francis. Doubts about the new Pope had spread to 'some of the cardinals who were among his electors' who were now having 'second thoughts'. Another prominent right-wing Catholic intellectual Professor Robert de Mattei publicly suggested that developments under Francis were leading down 'a road that leads to schism and heresy'. And the Catholic controversialist Antonio Socci floated the wild idea that the resignation of Benedict XVI might not have been valid under church law – meaning that Francis was not really pope.

Burke and Pentin had used the same word: 'confusion'. It became conservative code for the resistance to Pope Francis which surfaced most boldly in the United States – the part of the world where the 'culture wars' between conservative and liberals had become most engrained and embittered. Men as clever as Archbishop Charles Chaput of Philadelphia and the late Cardinal Francis George, then the retired Archbishop of Chicago, announced themselves to be confused too.

Confusion was a euphemism for anything the Pope said that conservatives did not like. Archbishop Chaput had signalled his suspicion of Pope Francis within weeks of his election. Chaput was in Rio de Janiero for World Youth Day. He had booked the trip assuming Pope Benedict would be presiding. It was long before Francis gave his interview saying the Catholic Church had been too obsessed with abortion and gay marriage – two of Chaput's key badges of Catholic identity. It was even before the defining remark: 'Who am I to judge?' But as early as July 2013 Chaput was cautioning that 'the right wing of the Church' generally had 'not been really happy about his election'. He warned the Pope that he needed to 'take care' of conservatives. To reinforce the point he then published, on his diocesan website, extracts from emails he had received from 'confused' catechists, parents and everyday Catholics. One mother of four children who had opened pro-life clinics and spent years counselling pregnant girls 'wanted to know why the Pope seemed to dismiss her sacrifices'. Another, which Chaput said came from a priest, complained that Francis was accusing priests 'who are serious about moral issues of being small-minded'. Another email he published bemoaned the fact that the Pope 'makes all of the wrong people happy, people who will never believe in the Gospel and who will continue to persecute the Church'.

At the end of it all the archbishop posted: 'We can draw some useful lessons from these reactions.' He did not need to spell out what he thought they were. They were lessons, not for Pope Francis, who presumably was not a regular reader of catholicphilly.com, but for those of Chaput's flock who needed guidance on what to think about the new Pope. After the synod Chaput went further while giving a lecture in Manhattan, saying that 'confusion is of the Devil' and that 'the public image that came across [of the synod] was one of confusion'. Again the subliminal message was clear, as David Gibson, a Catholic convert who reports for Religion News Service, put it: 'Confusion may come from the Devil, but the synod came from Pope Francis.' Chaput, the man scheduled to host Pope Francis at the World Meeting of Families in Philadelphia in September 2015, went on to suggest that US Catholic bishops should consider refusing to sign civil marriage licences for all couples in protest at the introduction of legalization allowing gay marriages. Justifying this characteristically confrontational suggestion, he said: 'Conflict always does two things: it purifies the Church, and it clarifies the character of the enemies who hate her.' It was the sight, one US commentator observed, of 'a culture warrior in full battle array'. The opponents of Pope Francis had entered the field.

There were two issues here. One was what Vatican veteran John Allen perceptively has called the Pope's older-son problem. It was a reference to the Parable of the Prodigal Son. 'Over his first eight months, Francis basically has killed the fatted calf for the prodigal sons and daughters of the post-modern world, reaching out to gays, women, nonbelievers, and virtually every other constituency inside and outside the Church that has felt alienated,' Allen wrote. 'There are an awful lot of such prodigals, of course, which helps explain the Pope's massive appeal. Yet there are also a few Catholics today who feel a bit like the story's older son, wondering if what they've always understood as their loyalty to the Church, and to the papacy, is being under-valued.' Allen continued: 'In the Gospel parable, the father eventually notices his older son's resentment and pulls him aside to assure him: "Everything I have is yours." At some stage, Pope Francis may need to have such a moment with his own older sons and daughters.'

But the other problem was with a smaller, but more influential, group. The loudest resistance to Pope Francis did not simply come from those who had felt smiled upon in the Benedict years and who now felt pushed to the kerb. Most of the bishops in the United States had been appointed in the John Paul/Benedict era and were men in the mould of the popes who had elevated them. A few 'social justice' moderates, like Blase Cupich, Archbishop of Chicago, had slipped through the net, but the bulk were pastorally minded conservatives. A smaller number, perhaps a fifth of the total, were ideological conservatives; the leading figure among these was Chaput. (Burke is regarded even by fellow hardline conservatives as embarrassing in his belligerence – 'Burke is the leader of the Catholic equivalent of the Tea Party', as one seasoned observer of the scene put it, 'whereas Chaput is at the head of the Church's neo-con Republicans.') It was with these theo-cons that Pope Francis's problem lay. They were clerics who adopted the rhetorical trope of 'confusion' but they were not confused at all. They simply disagreed with the Pope's instruction to include, encourage and accompany, preferring instead to prohibit, judge and condemn. Some of them took the view that, since the Pope was aged 76 when he was elected, they could afford just to ignore him, keep their heads down and wait for him to die. 'Popes come and go but the Curia lasts forever,' they say, and many in the Curia don't think he's going to last long,' one insider told me. But others could not resist the temptation to be obstructive or obtuse.

To convey their unhappiness with 'the Jesuit Experiment' they engaged in activities which in the military would be described as dumb insolence. Bishop Morlino of Madison, Wisconsin, adopted a dismissive tone towards *Evangelii Gaudium* in an interview on the conservative EWTN TV network, suggesting Pope Francis's exhortation was just his personal opinion and not a proper teaching document. Others were downright disrespectful, like the zealous anti-abortion campaigner Thomas Tobin, Bishop of Providence, Rhode Island, who said that instead of kissing babies the Pope should be reaching out to embrace and kiss unborn children. Others tried patronizing the Pope, as with the interview with Cardinal George on the eve of his retirement from Chicago, in which he asked a series of condescending questions of the Pope, each beginning: 'Does he not realize ... ?' George ended by saying of Francis: 'He says wonderful things, but he doesn't put them together all the time, so you're left at times puzzling over what his intention is. What he says is clear enough, but what does he want us to do?' Had a liberal spoken like that about Pope John Paul II or Pope Benedict XVI he would have been hauled to Rome for a severe dressing-down.

The problem for conservative bishops was that, even as they voiced all their reservations and 'confusion' about Francis, the Pope's popularity among ordinary Catholics rose to soaring levels. The authoritative Pew Forum survey in March 2015 showed that, two years after becoming the leader of the Catholic Church, his favourability ratings among US Catholics were at the same high levels as those of Pope John Paul II in the 1980s and 90s, and far surpassing those of Pope Benedict. Nine out of ten approved of him. The survey showed that Pope Francis continued to grow more popular – and that conservative Americans approved of him even more than did moderates or liberals. His popularity was also climbing steadily – by 13 points since he was elected – among the non-Catholic population. Men and women, Republicans and Democrats, were united in their esteem for the pontiff. 'The constant cry of conservative bishops may be that people are confused by Pope Francis,' said David Gibson of Religion News Service. 'But all the evidence is that people are not confused. It is the conservative bishops who are confused because they do not know how to interpret him. There is no real confusion in the pews. The *sensus fidelium* is clear,' he said, referring to the Catholic doctrine that church teaching is only accounted to be completely true when it has been universally accepted by the whole Church, which incudes ordinary Catholics in the pews.

Despite the Pope's enormous popularity there were some in the Catholic Church who began to talk openly about the possibility of the Church being split by a formal schism in reaction to Francis's 'confusing' messages. The notion was floated by a number of prominent conservatives, most notably by the *New York Times* columnist Ross Douthat. Not long after the Extraordinary Synod, Douthat issued a warning to the Pope not to 'break the Church' to promote his goals. If Francis continued to alienate conservative Catholics, he warned, it could lead to 'a real schism'. The subtle threat that conservatives might splinter off was echoed by a number of other conservatives and secular commentators. But these dark warnings did not come from Catholic churchmen. They were almost all from lay conservatives who were probably influenced by uninformed talk among the secular conservatives they knew. There was widespread outrage in neo-con circles at Pope Francis's denunciations of capitalism. They were further stung by the news that he was preparing to throw the Church's weight behind calls for action on climate change. It was also perhaps significant that Douthat was a convert to Catholicism who perhaps lacked an intuitive understanding of the priority which Catholics place on unity. Senior Catholic clerics, after long careers working within a complex sophisticated and wealthy hierarchical institution like the Catholic Church, were unlikely to easily countenance the idea of breaking away and having to set up a new church structure from scratch. Catholics have always seen schism as a Protestant rather than a Catholic proclivity. As David Gibson rather tartly put it: 'That's a lot of infrastructure to create, and pay for; it's not like a zealous Baptist who can start a new congregation with a Bible, a river and maybe a tent.' More importantly those talking of schism were a tiny if noisy minority said the Pope's chief theological adviser, Archbishop Victor Manuel Fernández. In May 2015 he told *Corriere della Sera*: 'The overwhelming majority of the people are with Francis and they love him. His opponents are weaker than you might think. Not pleasing everyone does not mean provoking a schism.'

But the talk of schism was important even if it was just sabre-rattling. 'It was an emotional release valve which gives you a sense of how unsettled the conservatives are,' Gibson said. 'These are people who have had the inside track for so long they feel disorientated now to be on the outside.' Cardinal Burke was the only clerical outlier on this. Asked by the Catholic website *Aleteia* whether there was 'a real risk of schism' he replied: 'If in some way the Synod of Bishops was seen to go contrary to what is the constant teaching and practice of the Church, there is a risk'. But Burke was already out in the cold and physiologically may have felt he had nothing more to lose. Other senior conservative clerics avoided such wild talk.

Pope Francis needed to do three things if he was to make his changes stick. The first was to replace ideologue bishops with more moderate men. Francis had begun to do that, but it would not bring change quickly, said Gibson. The second was to give cover to those bishops who were always closet Francis types but who kept quiet in the shadow of fierce ideological conservatives. And that too had begun, with a number of individuals clearly emboldened. 'The third is to convert and convince the pastoral conservatives,' said Gibson, 'and there is a significant amount of that going on. One centre-right bishop said to me the other day: "Francis has reminded me of what's important."'

* * *

Pope Francis was unfazed by the backlash he had provoked. When I asked a Jesuit close to the Pope, Father Antonio Spadaro, whether Francis was privately pleased or concerned with the outcome of the first synod he replied: 'He's never pleased, or upset; he's consoled. I have never seen him anxious or preoccupied. He says that the sense of peace which descended upon him soon after his election has never abandoned him. Everything is in the hands of the Holy Spirit.' Francis took the example of a previous pope, John XXIII, who used to wake up at night thinking about some problem but then would say to himself: 'Giovanni, why are you so worried? Whose Church is it, yours or God's?' And then he would answer his own question: 'It's God's; so go back to sleep.'

Francis, likewise, had a simple answer to the question asked by Cardinal George in Chicago: 'What does he want us to do?' The Pope gave the reply just a month after George had asked it. In an interview with the Argentine newspaper

La Nación he said: 'Look, I wrote an encyclical and an apostolic exhortation. I'm constantly making statements, giving homilies. That's magisterium. That's what I think, not what the media say that I think. Check it out; it's very clear. *Evangelii Gaudium* is very clear.' It was a tart rebuke to George's dissimulation. 'Francis knows exactly how power is spelled,' said Bernd Hagenkord, a Jesuit who works for Vatican Radio. 'He's a communicator in the same league as Mother Teresa and the Dalai Lama. They say he's being unclear, but we know exactly what he means.'

The *La Nación* interview two months after the synod was notable for the bold questions asked by the reporter Elisabetta Piqué – and for the directness of the Pope's replies. Resistance to his reforms was now becoming more evident, she observed. 'You said it,' he replied. 'Resistance is now more evident. But that's a good sign for me. It's out in the open and there is no stealthy mumbling when there's disagreement. I am not worried. It all seems normal to me. If there were no difference of opinions, that wouldn't be normal.' The interview continued:

Elisabetta Piqué: At the recent Extraordinary Synod of Bishops on the Family, two different visions of the Church surfaced, one sector open to debate and the other refusing to hear anything about it. Is this the case? What do you think?

Pope Francis: I wouldn't say that's quite so... What we benefited from was the synodal process, which is not a parliamentary process but rather a protected space so that the Holy Spirit can work. Two clear qualities are needed: courage to speak and humility to listen. And that worked very well. There are, indeed, positions more inclined this way or that way, but in the pursuit of truth. You could ask me, 'Are there any individuals who are completely obstinate in their positions?' Yes, there surely are. But that doesn't worry me. It's a question of praying for the Holy Spirit to convert them, if there are such people. The prevailing feeling was a brotherly one, trying to find a way together to tackle the family's pastoral issues.

Piqué: Conservatives, especially in the United States, fear that the traditional doctrine will collapse. They say the Synod caused confusion because it mentioned the 'positive nuances' of living together, and gay couples were mentioned in the draft...

Pope Francis: The Synod was a process... The first draft was merely a first draft meant to record it all. Nobody mentioned homosexual marriage at the Synod; it did not cross our minds. What we did talk about was how a family with a homosexual child goes about educating that child, how the family bears up, how to help that family to deal with that somewhat unusual situation. That is to say, the Synod addressed the family and the homosexual individuals in relation to their families, because we come across this reality all the time in the confessional: a father and a mother whose son or daughter is in that situation. This happened to me several times in Buenos Aires. We have to find a way to help that father or that mother to stand by their son or daughter. That's what the Synod addressed. That's why someone mentioned positive factors in the first draft. But this was just a draft.

Piqué: Some people fear that the traditional doctrine will collapse.

Pope Francis: You know, some people are always afraid because they don't read things properly. Or they read some news in a newspaper... They don't read what the Synod decided... I think some Synod fathers made a mistake when they talked to the media. We decided that each one of us would grant as many interviews as he liked, with total freedom. No censorship was imposed. We chose transparency.

The synod issued briefings rather than publishing speeches word for word, he said, because some members of the synod sent written presentations in advance and then said something slightly different at the meeting. Also, Francis said, he was anxious that individuals felt free to say what they liked without keeping anything back, as they might have done if they knew their speech was to be reported *verbatim* and attributed to them. 'Different bishops had different approaches, but we will all move on together.' Pope Francis said he was not afraid of doing that 'because it is the road that God has asked us to follow'. It was not, he stressed, about doctrine but about how to look after people. That had been a key point in his concluding address to the synod, the Pope recalled:

I pointed out that we had not addressed any part of the doctrine of the Church concerning marriage. In the case of divorced people who have remarried, we posed the question, what do we do with them? What door can we open for them? This was a pastoral concern: will we allow them to go to Communion? Communion alone is no solution. The solution is integration. They have not been excommunicated. But they cannot be godparents at baptism, they cannot read the readings at Mass, they cannot give Communion, they cannot be catechists. There are about seven things they cannot do. It seems that they are excommunicated *de facto*! So let us open the doors a bit more.

Pope Francis continued that he saw no reason why remarried Catholics could not be godparents. The presence of a remarried Catholic at a christening amounted to them saying, the Pope said: 'I made a mistake, I was wrong here, but I believe our Lord loves me, I want to follow God. Sin will not have victory over me, I want to move on.' That was a Christian witness, he said. So why was that disallowed when the Church's rules would permit someone to be a godparent who was a crook, so long as he had been properly married in church? What kind of testimony did that give to their godchild?

'A testimony of corruption? We must change things a little. Our standards need to change.'

A few days later Pope Francis published the preparatory document for the 2015 Synod. It consisted of the final document from the 2014 Synod – including the three controversial paragraphs – along with a new set of 46 questions to be delivered to bishops' conferences, Eastern Catholic synods, religious superiors and dicasteries, as well as academic institutions and ecclesial movements. The team that put together this *lineamenta* was the same as the one behind the Extraordinary Synod. Francis had not heeded calls from conservatives to change the men whom they had accused of trying to manipulate the outcome of the 2014 gathering. Rather, he had given a vote of confidence to Cardinal Péter Erdő as the synod's relator, or secretary, and also to Archbishop Bruno Forte, who had drafted the conciliatory paragraphs on homosexuality which conservatives had found so contentious. Forte was again named special secretary to the 2015 Synod. But one man had been added to the team. Cardinal Wilfrid Napier – the South African prelate who had forcefully complained that the 2014 interim report did not reflect the first week of the synod debates – was added as a fourth president of the 2015 October assembly. Bishops around the world were told to prepare for the Ordinary Synod by focusing on the pastoral care of families without seeing it merely in terms of doctrinal issues. They were urged to do everything possible to avoid 'starting over from zero', but rather to take account of what already happened in the first synod.

The 2015 Synod promised to be as fiercely contested as was the 2014 one. At the start of 2015 the General Secretary of the Synod, Cardinal Baldisseri, defended the controversial part of the 2014 final report and revealed that Pope Francis endorsed the controversial mid-term report from the meeting before it was published. 'All of those points have been personally approved by Pope Francis,' he said. Some critics seemed mollified by the way the process was working through. 'Some were very upset and disturbed that the cardinals were arguing in public,' said Cardinal Napier. 'But most of us are saying: Isn't that what a debate is about. You try winning people with your arguments.' But others maintained their original stance. Cardinal Angelo Scola, the man who had been the favourite to be Pope when Francis got the job, declared that Communion for the remarried risked 'almost a functional separation among doctrine, pastoral practice and discipline'. Archbishop Anthony Fisher of Sydney said something similar, and said that those building expectations of change were doing everyone a disservice. 'People have said Francis has caused confusion because he hasn't been clear enough,' Fisher said. 'I think he wanted a discussion, he wanted points of view. It's a dangerous strategy, no doubt.

There can be a lot of emotion and polarization'. That was exemplified in March 2015 when one in ten priests in Britain signed a letter to the *Catholic Herald* calling on the synod later that year not to admit remarried Catholics to Holy Communion.

For all that, no one was sure what Pope Francis's intentions were at the end of the two-year two-stage synod process. 'The first synod was a way of breaking up the soil,' said one senior priest in Rome outside the Vatican. 'The whole process has been very clever. As we approach the second synod it's still not clear whether Francis has been pursuing a particular agenda by stealth. Or whether the whole process of opening up discussion is more important to him than the eventual outcome. That way he keeps everyone involved and engaged. No one can be quite sure so they have to go along with the procedure he has put in place.' A seasoned Vatican diplomat suggested that Pope Francis wanted the best of both worlds: 'He wants a synodical process but in the end he'll also want a decision and a clear course. The second synod may set that course but without taking a decision. I suspect that the decision will come from Francis alone in the post-synod document he draws up.'

One conservative Jesuit church historian in Rome, who asked not to be named, offered a more Machiavellian insight: 'It was interesting that on the opening morning of the 2014 Synod the Pope stressed that the synod always takes place *cum petro et sub petro* – with Peter and under Peter. That phrase implies consultation and collegiality. He wanted people to feel reassured that the Pope's presence was a guarantee for everyone and protected the faith. But the phrase cuts two ways. It is *with* Peter, so the Successor of Peter is just a first among equals. But it is *under* Peter, which means that in the end, even after a synodical process, it is the Successor of Peter who decides. Perhaps Francis meant that ambiguity intentionally. It may be, of course, that I am thinking in this suspicious way only because I am a Jesuit. But then the Pope is a Jesuit.' Another member of the Society of Jesus, from the Americas, offered a gloss on that: 'There's a Jesuit expression from the ancient Greek *speûde bradéōs* which means 'make haste slowly'. Francis is learning from the mistakes he made before, when he presided over some deep divisions within the Jesuits in Argentina. When he was 36 he tried running an organization top-down and it didn't work very well. What he himself called his authoritarian way of making decisions without consultation backfired. So, if he can now move the synod at least partly in what seems to be his direction, it will enable him to say, when he announces a change, 'as the synod fathers have deliberated and taught'; that, in other words, he is acting on the back of the opinions of many synod fathers – much as he said when he set up the C8, that he had a mandate from his fellow cardinals to do it. Ultimately his position is greatly strengthened if he has the Church with him, including the C9 as it now is, and the synod. It's really important to him to bring people along. But even more basically, as a friend of his told me recently, he is completely open to the process. He's fine with letting the Holy Spirit guide things. That's essential for understanding what he's doing.' The papal historian Michael Walsh, the former Librarian at Heythrop College, suggested that Francis would strike a balance on that: 'He does not want a split in the bishops. He wants to try to reach consensus,' said Walsh. So the move forward may be smaller than he personally wants. But the unity of the Church is important in Catholicism.' The head of one Roman seminary agreed. 'This isn't a tactic – to maintain unity,' he said. 'It is a principal – to usher in collegiality'.

Behind the scenes Francis conducted a series of private meetings over the following months in the Casa Santa Marta. Those who received individual summons to go to see him told me that the subjects which were so controversial at the synod were at the top of the list of issues he wanted to discuss. The head of one Rome-based religious order had a one-to-one with Francis to discuss the issue of the pastoral care of divorced and remarried Catholics. 'It was clear he wanted change,' the religious leader told me. 'His question was how? I told him that in the third century some Christians were excluded from Communion because they had once offered worship to the Emperor. It was very harsh. The Pope at the time changed the discipline to readmit them, I told Francis.' The Pope nodded.

Another of his private meetings was with Erwin Kräutler, Bishop of Xingu in the Brazilian rainforest. The Pope wanted to talk to him about his forthcoming encyclical on the environment, *Laudato si*. But Kräutler's big anxiety was the desperate shortage of priests in his huge diocese, which had 700,000 Catholics in 800 church communities and only 27 priests. Could married men be ordained? 'You tell me,' the Pope replied. Local bishops, through their regional and national conferences, the pontiff said, should make proposals based on their lived experience and then bring them to Rome. It was consistent with Francis's general desire to make bishops take more responsibility for the direction of the Church without waiting for initiatives from Rome or from the Pope personally. But it also reflected the Pope's shrewd sense that he could not tackle everything at once. When one of his advisers later asked him about married priests, Francis replied: 'One thing at a time.' Another senior curial official confirmed that, saying: 'He understands you need to pick your battles.' Nevertheless in November 2014 the Brazilian bishops set up a task force to study the idea.

The position of homosexuals in the Church was also on the agenda for his private talks. Again his approach was not doctrinal. 'He wanted to know about people's lived experience,' one Vatican insider told me. 'He wants to know where God is already active in people's lives. That was why he began the two-synod process by asking the laity of their experience of life through the question-naires.' On the principle of 'one thing at a time' Francis knew that finding a place for gays and lesbians in the universal Church is a massive task. His limited experience of Asia, and what he had begun to learn about Africa, taught him that the local churches were in very different places on the issue. 'On homosex-uality he does want change,' said one of those who had private meetings with the Pope, 'but he sees pastoral care as a fulfilment of the teaching rather than a contradiction of it. Part of the Catholic approach is to yoke together two inconsistent views in a way which is consistent.' A senior figure in the Curia said: 'Francis is trying to find a solution that uses both poles in the tension. The tension cannot be resolved but it can be lived with. It is time over place,' the official added, referring to one of Pope Francis's four guiding principles. 'And Francis is sharp. He knows not to move too quickly.'

None of those who had had these private meetings with Francis wanted to break confidence by speaking publicly. But Father James Alison, a priest and theologian who has written much on gay and lesbian theology, said it was a significant step forward for the pontiff to allow discussion of the dilemmas posed for families with gay relatives. 'I think that the Pope was very brave even allowing the issue to come up at the synod at all, given how much of a psychological factor it is in the lives of many clergy and in particular the higher clergy,' he said. 'A lot of them are gay; the notion that somehow all the gay people are weeded out before they become bishops is nonsense; I was never in a minority as a gay person when I lived in a formal religious setting, never.' Alison was a member of the Dominican order for over a decade. His advocacy for the acceptance of homosexuals in the Church is rooted in Catholic teaching concerning nature, grace and original sin. 'The structure of holiness that has given them their jobs depends on a notion of goodness, which includes denying who they are. And some of them think that that's a sacrifice made to God and that they're doing something good. Whereas in fact it means that they're constantly demanding sacrifices of other people to be like them. And so you can see why it requires a great deal of courage for any of them to even start talking about it.

'They can talk about an issue like Communion for the divorced and remarried because that is essentially theological (and depends on issues concerning the sacraments, and the words of our Lord which are genuinely theologically complicated). But the gay issue, which is theologically quite straightforward, is immensely difficult for many bishops psychologically,'

Alison continued. 'And that's why it's such a relief when the pontiff appears to be straight because it means that it's not a particular problem for him. He just let people know they could talk frankly and boldly – and that they needn't be frightened of expressing their opinions. There was a predictable backlash but the Pope handled it very well.'

One Jesuit close to Francis, Father Antonio Spadaro, thinks the point that Alison makes about Francis and homosexuality is true more widely. The backlash over the synod has been wider, deeper and more visceral than the resistance to Francis's reforms within the Curia, because it touches on doctrine, which for many clerics lies at the heart of Catholicism. The criticisms made of the Pope by some conservatives are so sharp that Spadaro views the 'anguish' of the Pope's foes 'as more of a psychological problem' than a question of doctrine. And he added that Francis's emphasis on mercy 'provokes in some Catholics a panic, the fear of a lack of certainty that stuns me'.

Yet other perceptive commentators on the Catholic Church think that Pope Francis does not have a stealthy private agenda at all. His plan, so far as it goes, is to open up the Church more to allow the Holy Spirit to blow more freely through the institution, eddying in what were once airless corners. 'What the Pope most wants is not for one side to win, but for both sides to recognize the need to encounter one another', wrote the prominent US Catholic writer Michael Sean Winters, who normally takes a liberal perspective in his award-winning columns. 'He has called the Church to a 'culture of encounter' and that call pertains not only to those outside the Church but also within. The Pope's own advisers tend to agree. Cardinal Marx said: 'The Synod cannot have winners and losers. That is not the spirit of the Synod. The spirit of the Synod is to find a way together. Not to say: "How can I find a way to bring my position through?" Rather: "How can I understand the other position, and how can we together find a new position?" That is the spirit of the Synod.'

The former Master of the Dominican Order, Father Timothy Radcliffe, saw Francis working at a deeper level even that that. 'The Pope is also undoing the mechanisms of control; he's an uncontrolling person,' he said. Radcliffe cited the eminent Catholic philosopher Charles Taylor and his great work *A Secular Age*. 'Taylor thinks that secularism is fundamentally about control because once you cease to believe in the providential presence of God working in the world then humans have got to take over and control everything. And the Church has been affected by this desire to dominate and to rule. What Pope Francis is doing is systematically undoing that in ways that are deeply liberating.' Radcliffe sees the Pope's extended synod process, beginning with the questionnaire, as part of that. 'He wants to know what ordinary Catholics

Newly elected Pope Francis waves to the waiting crowd from the central balcony of St Peter's Basilica (*above*) on March 13, 2013. Pope Francis bows his head (*below*) to receive the blessing of the ordinary people before he gives his first blessing as Pope.

Francis rejects a golden papal cross in favour of his old metal one (*above left*).
The Pope greets the crowd at the end of his weekly general audience at
St Peter's, February, 2015 (*above right*).

Audacious humility: the Pope prays in the back pew (*below*)
in the chapel of the Casa Santa Marta before saying Mass for the
Vatican cleaners and gardeners a week after his election.

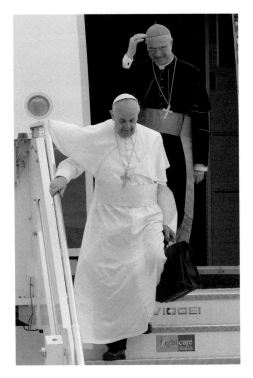

Francis breaks another papal precedent by carrying his own bag
as he disembarks in Rome on his return from Brazil in July 2013.

Francis and US President Barack Obama developed a good rapport in a private
audience which lasted twice as long as expected at the Vatican in March 2014.

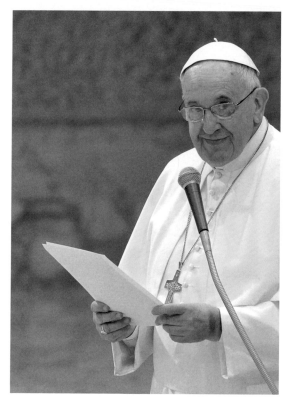

Francis speaking during an audience with families at
the Paul VI hall at the Vatican, December 2014.

Francis dons a red nose to joke with a newly-wed couple who use
'clown therapy' in their work with sick children in Italian hospitals.

Francis prays at the separation barrier between Israel and Palestine in May 2014 (*above*) after his visit to Bethlehem on the West Bank, and then prays at the Western Wall in Jerusalem's Old City, May, 2014 (*below*).

Francis hugs and then kisses Vinicio Riva, a man disfigured by
neurofibromatosis, during a general audience in St Peter's Square.

The Pope dispenses with the old papal protocol that a visiting monarch should wear black
if she is not a Catholic when he meets Queen Elizabeth II at the Vatican, April 2014.

The smiling Pope: Francis at the start of his homily during Mass
at Manila Cathedral in the Philippines, January 2015.

People of all ages and backgrounds, like this child at one of the Pope's general audiences
in the Vatican, are put at ease by the warm down-to-earth style of Francis.

Francis surprised his aides by going to Confession in public during Holy Week, March 2015.

The Pope refused an umbrella and insisted on wearing the same poncho as everyone else in the rain-soaked crowd in Tacloban, Philippines, January 2015.

think. His fundamental concern is that together as a church we must be responsible. He wants to devolve a lot of responsibility from his own position to the college of bishops – and he hopes that bishops in the dioceses will give more responsibility to the ordinary people.' But that is not all. 'He also wants each of us to take responsibility for our own lives because in the end that's what being grown-up is about. What Pope Francis wants is a church for grown-ups.'

The paradox for the Pope is that establishing such a model has empowered those in the Church who are as opposed to change as Francis is open to it. Cardinal Raymond Burke, now liberated from his posts and responsibilities in the Vatican, seems intent on making himself the centre of the opposition. In an interview with French television in February 2015 he raised the stakes yet again – saying that he was prepared to 'resist' the Pope in a public challenge that had no precedent in the John Paul/Benedict era. This was the key part of the exchange with the FranceTv.info interviewer:

Cardinal Burke: I cannot accept that Communion can be given to a person in an irregular union because it is adultery. On the question of people of the same sex, this has nothing to do with marriage. This is an affliction suffered by some people whereby they are attracted against nature sexually to people of the same sex.

Question: If perchance the Pope will persist in this direction, what will you do?

Cardinal Burke: I shall resist, I can do nothing else. There is no doubt that it is a difficult time; this is clear, this is clear.

Question: Can we say today that the Catholic Church as an institution is threatened?

Cardinal Burke: The Lord has assured us, as He has assured St. Peter in the Gospel, that the powers of evil will not prevail, '*non praevalebunt*' as we say in Latin, that the forces of evil will not have victory over the Church.

At this point the camera lighted upon a portrait of Pope Francis and the interviewer asked:

Is the Pope still your friend?

Cardinal Burke (with a smile): I would not want to make the Pope an enemy for sure. That is enough for now.

It certainly was. He was indicating to the interviewer that she had asked enough questions. But it also could easily have meant that Cardinal Burke would have more to say in the future. He did. In March 2015 he compared gay couples and remarried Catholics to murderers. A month later he gave an interview to the

Italian Catholic website *Nuova Bussola Quotidiana* in which he claimed that his 'I shall resist' declaration was not a criticism of Pope Francis but of some hypothetical pontiff but few were persuaded by his protestations.

Many in the College of Cardinals shrugged off the rhetoric of bellicose rigorists like Burke as expressing the views of a small minority on the extreme fringes of the Church. 'There's opposition for every change so I do expect if he makes any change there will be opposition,' said one of Francis's C9, Cardinal Oswald Gracias, Archbishop of Bombay. 'There are a lot of voices that are very loud [in opposition], but I don't think they represent the mainstream,' said Cardinal Donald Wuerl, Archbishop of Washington. 'There's some opposition but it's just not serious,' one cardinal close to Francis, Cardinal Cormac Murphy-O'Connor, told me. 'The challenge for him is to ensure that collegiality becomes enstructured. How? The synod is very important. He said that to me. The synod was set up to implement the collegiality of Vatican II. It has never properly done that.' Indeed, said the church historian Michael Walsh: 'Cardinal Joseph Ratzinger, the future Benedict XVI, said you could only have collegiality if the Pope was present'. By contrast with that, Cardinal Murphy-O'Connor continued, 'true collegiality is what he's restoring. He came in not with a plan but with an instinct – but an instinct which had been formed. It was formed in Aparecida where a model was established for collegiality among the Latin American bishops which he is bringing now to the universal Church.'

It was a Latin American who set out what Pope Francis wants to unfold for the college of bishops worldwide if he is given the time. At the beginning of 2015 Cardinal Oscar Andrés Rodríguez Maradiaga, coordinator of the C9 advisers, gave a lecture about the reforms of the Church of Mercy at Santa Clara University. 'True ecclesial renovation,' he said, cannot occur without a transformation of institutions but also a focus on the quality of the Church activities, practical, spiritual and mystical. He continued: 'Usually, renovation begins with pastoral activities. For it is there where the inconsistencies of a certain "model" of the Church and reality are primarily experienced. The missionaries, the evangelists on the "margins" of the Church, are the first ones to notice the insufficiency of the "traditional" ways of action; the pastoral criticism begins with the experience of the mission in the "peripheries". Changes and adjustments begin there.' This required simultaneous changes in institutions, organization, attitude and approach, he said. Reforms must encompass all levels of the Church: the religious congregations, missionary societies, dioceses; the Vatican Curia, bishops' conferences, synods, parishes and lay movements; and also the teaching of theology, seminaries, Catholic schools and so forth. 'Everything in the Church changes consistent with a renewed pastoral model,' he said, and concluded: 'The Pope wants to take this church renovation to the point where it becomes irreversible. The wind that propels the sails of the Church towards the open sea of its deep and total renovation is Mercy.'

What this means for the Synod of Bishops is that Pope Francis wants it to become a permanent part of the structure for governing the universal Church. That means that the Pope will continue to revamp and expand the synod. So much so, predicted the commentator Michael Sean Winters, that the October 2015 Ordinary Synod would probably have to be extended. 'People say this is new but that is how the Church was in the first millennium,' said the Jesuit, Father Norman Tanner SJ, who is Professor of Church History at the Gregorian Pontifical University, in Rome. 'And women played a role there. Those who pretend that the Church has always been as it was in the Pope John Paul II and Benedict XVI era are either ignorant or dishonest.'

Others went further. Cardinal Napier advised that if the Pope was going to make changes in the governance of the Church that would last, he would have to 'put structures in place that are going to make those changes carry through regardless of who is in the seat'. For change to be effective what was needed was a synod with more teeth. 'Better consultation is not the same as sharing in decision-making,' said Mary McAleese, who served as president of the Irish Republic from 1997 to 2011 and who, after leaving politics, completed a doctorate in canon law. In a lecture to the Von Hügel Institute in Cambridge she explored the three ways in which the Vatican II document *Lumen Gentium* suggested that the College of Bishops could exercise more power over church governance. None of them had been tried in practice. The most effective of the three, she suggested, was involved turning the Synod of Bishops into a decision-making body. 'Reforming the Curia is a meaningless exercise unless you reform church governance,' she said in an interview with RTÉ. 'That means that there has to be a decision-making body working with the Pope – decision-making, not advising, not collaborating, not being asked [their] opinion – but being directly involved in governance'. The Synod of Bishops was the obvious body to do that, though there were some canonical issues to sort out about the relationship of the synod to all the bishops worldwide, she said. Under canon law, the Pope can give decision-making powers to any synod, though no pope has ever done so. It would be, she said, 'a template for the kind of noisy, messy, argumentative Church the Vatican Council envisaged and that Francis seems comfortable with: not top-down, control-driven and passive, but a healthy, vibrant *communio* of the diverse engaged in active listening and talking top-down, sideways and bottom-up, unafraid of bad news, unafraid of healthy debate'.

That is exactly what traditionalists and conservatives like Cardinal Burke fear.

'I don't think Pope Francis has a plan of the exact outcomes he wants,' said Father Timothy Radcliffe, 'he just wants to unleash the unruly freedom of the Holy Spirit and let it blow where it will.'

16

A Weakness for Women

'The boys played the girls – and for once the girls won.' Sister Simone Campbell spoke with her usual easy grace and charm. But it was not a particularly smart thing for a lawyer to say, even with a smile. The girls might have won one round, but there was a longer game being played. And the boys could play quite dirty.

As well as being a lawyer Sister Simone was a member of a religious order, the Sisters of Social Service. She was speaking on the CBS News flagship US documentary *60 Minutes* about the long war conducted over the past decade between activist nuns and conservative bishops in the United States. But her words had a wider resonance, for they spoke to the unsettled relationship between women and men throughout the Catholic Church all across the world – a relationship which has taken a new, but no less complicated, turn since the election of Pope Francis. The struggle for the soul of Catholicism continues, though there has been a tectonic shift in the fault-lines between the two sides.

The subject under discussion was Obamacare – or, more formally, the Affordable Care Act, the legislation with which President Barack Obama sought to provide some measure of healthcare to the poorer citizens of the United States. The US bishops had opposed the measure, arguing that it would be used to channel government money to fund abortion. The US nuns had argued that it would be good for the poor and that the bishops had been misled by their staff on the abortion issue. 'How do you know that?' she was asked. 'Because I read the bill,' she replied. 'The fact is I'm a lawyer. I read the bill. I saw what it said. It made sense. I could see that it said "no federal funding of abortion" which is what the bishops' staff was concerned about.' The bishops' staff clearly hadn't read the bill properly, was the implication. The insult did not go unnoticed.

The battlelines between the nuns and bishops, the women and men, had been drawn years earlier. But Obamacare was a tipping point. Sister Simone wrote an open letter supporting the legislation. Dozens of prominent nuns signed it. The Catholic Health Association – the largest healthcare group in the United States, with more than 2,000 health facilities – took the same view. So did a crucial number of anti-abortion politicians and the bill was signed into law in 2010. That date was significant, as we shall see. A number of Catholic politicians who voted for the bill later said: 'The sisters gave me cover to vote for Obamacare.' Affordable healthcare might never have been passed were it not for the stance taken by Roman Catholic nuns. The bishops were not pleased. Things were not helped by Sister Simone's subsequent remark: 'The boys are upset. It's way more politics and culture than it is faith.' The feisty sister may have been joking. But the bishops were not amused.

* * *

A significant shift in the attitude to women in the Church was signalled by Pope Francis from the very start of his pontificate. Within the first two weeks of his election he spoke no fewer than three times about women's 'special and fundamental role in the Church'. He scandalized conservatives by washing the feet of two women, one of them a Muslim, in his first papal Maundy Thursday service. The first witnesses of the Resurrection were women, he noted in his Easter sermon, adding that women had 'a special role in opening doors to faith in Christ'. He dedicated the second general audience of his papacy to highlighting what Vatican Radio called 'the fundamental role of women in the Church'. It was a theme to which he was constantly to return throughout the first two years of the pontificate, saying 'we need to create still broader opportunities for a more incisive female presence in the Church'.

What did that mean? The coordinator of the Pope's council of cardinal advisers was in no doubt. Within a week of the new body being formed, Cardinal Oscar Rodríguez Maradiaga of Honduras announced that it meant more women in top jobs in the Vatican. 'It is a natural step – there is a move towards putting more women in key roles where they are qualified,' he said. Pope Francis seemed repeatedly to agree. The role of women in the Church must not be limited to being mothers, wives, workers, cleaners, flower arrangers or altar servers, teachers of the catechism or even the heads of big Catholic charities. 'There is more. We need to develop a profound theology of women.' Women 'have to be more, profoundly more, even mystically more'. But two years later the world seemed no clearer as to what practical change would come as a result.

* * *

What the old theology of women said was fairly well understood. Theoretically it rested on the dubious claim that Thomas Aquinas, the father of Catholic philosophical theology, had defined women as 'defective males'. (That was, in fact, a notion which the Church had inherited from Aristotle – and which Aquinas argued *against* no fewer than six times.) But as late as 1976 Pope Paul VI's Curia was still arguing against women priests using the argument that women do not look like Jesus. By 1996 Pope John Paul II had switched to arguing that if Jesus had wanted to ordain women, he would have begun with the best of them, his mother – ignoring the fact, said the maverick Catholic intellectual Garry Wills, 'that Jesus in the Gospels ordained no priests, male or female'. Yet whatever argument was used against the ordination of women, in practice the Church had traditionally insisted that the place of women was primarily to fulfil the role of spouse and mother.

But the stand-off between the nuns and bishops in America was rooted in something deeper than the theology of women. It was a totem which represented an altogether bigger issue. In the 1960s a revolution had been wrought in the Catholic Church by the Second Vatican Council. It had attempted to throw open the windows of a church that had been for over a thousand years turned inwards on its own sacramental life, in a rejection of the profane world. Vatican II wanted to turn the Church outwards to face the world. But it also wanted to strip the Church of the trappings and systems of governance it had acquired over the centuries in which popes had ruled as lords of the territory of the Papal States as well as spiritual leaders. Vatican II wanted to return the papacy to the more simple and collegial ways of the first thousand years of the Church. It had called for a deepening of Catholic spirituality. Social justice, rather than charitable piety, was seen as the vehicle through which to spread the good news of Jesus Christ. The religious sisters of the United States were one of the groups which most ardently embraced this new understanding of the Gospel.

But many in the Church were less enthusiastic. More conservative figures in the Roman Curia swiftly developed reservations. Pope Paul VI was conflicted over the speed and extent of the changes being introduced in the name of Vatican II. His successors, John Paul II and Benedict XVI, formed the view that many of those advocating more change in the name of 'the spirit of Vatican II' were taking Catholic doctrine and practice too far from the essential core of the faith. These two popes set up what was in effect a counter-reformation to Vatican II. Their chief tactic in this was the appointment of conservative bishops. Pope John Paul II – and the man who was for 25 years his guardian of doctrinal orthodoxy, Cardinal Joseph Ratzinger, who succeeded him as Benedict XVI – chose as the shibboleths of Catholic identity the issues of abortion, gay marriage and the ordination of women. No accommodation could be made for those matters with the relativist tolerance of modern secular culture.

Throughout the Catholic Church fault-lines were established between those who embraced the Council and those who wanted to row back from it. The division between the *conciliarists* and *restorationists* – what the secular world more crudely calls liberals and conservatives – was nowhere so stark, and so embittered, as in the United States. Both sides insisted that they were in true continuity with the real tradition of the Church. Both accused the other of creating rupture with the authentic past and replacing it with something invented more recently.

For decades there was an uneasy coexistence between the two groups. The US nuns embraced a Vatican II mission among the poor and among groups who were socially excluded or marginalized, including immigrants and the gay and lesbian communities. The US bishops backed a more conservative preoccupation with issues of human life – from conception to death – which focused most publicly on opposition to the sins of artificial contraception, divorce, homosexuality, euthanasia and above all abortion. These issues became, for them, key emblems of Catholic witness and identity. Undergirding both sides were very different theologies of women. The two were on a collision course.

The irresistible force met the immovable object when the nuns at the head of the Leadership Conference of Women Religious (the LCWR) were told at a meeting in Rome that they were to be subjected to a Vatican investigation. In April 2008 they were summoned to a meeting with Cardinal William Levada, the American archbishop who was Benedict's successor as head of the Congregation for the Doctrine of the Faith – the post in which he had been nicknamed God's Rottweiler. Levada was articulating the thoughts of his conservative colleagues back in the US bishops' conference who had conducted an investigation of the US nuns which they passed to Rome. Now the nuns' leaders were told that a 'doctrinal assessment' of their activities was to be undertaken by the Vatican. It would examine complaints that some of their meetings had been addressed by speakers who 'moved beyond the Church' and even beyond Jesus; that their attitudes to women priests and to homosexuality were contrary to Vatican teaching; and that they embraced 'certain radical feminist themes' incompatible with the Catholic faith. They were also not doing enough anti-abortion campaigning. The CDF appointed Archbishop Peter Sartain of Seattle to work with the LCWR to correct the group's perceived failings. But the investigation was not made public. The CDF kept its inquisition secret for four years.

But the nuns knew that the gloves were off when, later that year, another Vatican department – the Congregation for Institutes of Consecrated Life and Societies for Apostolic Life, the body responsible for supervising religious orders – announced that it too was organizing a probe into all US female religious orders. The process, which had been authorized by Benedict XVI, was to be called an 'Apostolic Visitation'. An American nun who was the head of a religious order based in Rome, Mother Clare Millea, was to engage in 'respectful sister-to-sister dialogue' in inspections of 341 communities, involving 50,000 women, in the largest such investigation in church history. The Vatican maintained that the two investigations were unrelated but few of the nuns involved believed that.

'They missed the whole point of what we've been about for the last 50 years of renewal,' said Simone Campbell, 'taking the Gospel to the streets.' The Vatican had not missed it, so much as rejected it according to another nun, Sister Sandra Schneiders, a professor at the Jesuit School of Theology at Santa Clara University, Berkeley, California. The nuns were the biggest, best organized and probably most effective promoters of the vision of the Second Vatican Council, Schneiders wrote. They were therefore the 'most serious danger' to those trying to restore 'the pre-conciliar Church'. They were being used as a 'symbolic scapegoat' in a power struggle between those who favoured the renewal and reforms promoted by Vatican II and those who did not.

An email was sent around her fellow sisters by Schneiders. It said:

I am not inclined to get into too much of a panic about this investigation – which is what it is. We just went through a similar investigation of seminaries, equally aggressive and dishonest. I do not put any credence at all in the claim that this is friendly, transparent, aimed to be helpful, etc. It is a hostile move and the conclusions are already in. It is meant to be intimidating.

Her advice was that the nuns should receive the Vatican inspectors 'politely and kindly'. But she noted pointedly that 'uninvited guests should be received in the parlour, not given the run of the house'. There was no obligation to answer questions from people asking 'questions they shouldn't ask'. She advocated what she called non-violent resistance. 'This is a fake war being stirred up by the Vatican at the instigation of the frightened. Let's not get into it.' Some communities refused to cooperate at all. When Mother Clare sent round an initial questionnaire, several groups returned it blank or with a copy of their order's constitutions attached; she would find that the answers were already contained in their official documents, they suggested.

Across the nation the Vatican investigation was met by religious sisters with shock, confusion and anger. The bishops began briefing the press that the LCWR, which spoke for 80 per cent of US nuns, did not really represent its members. There was an irony in that, for the majority of US Catholics did not seem to share the confrontational approach of their hard-line bishops. Large numbers of lay Catholics voiced support for the nuns who had educated them and their children and who had cared for them in hospitals which had been built by the sisters. Various support groups sprang up to back the sisters. They were fuelled by a sense of outrage summoned up by one supporter who said incredulously: 'Let me get this straight. Some priests committed sex abuse. Bishops covered it up. And so they're investigating nuns?' Press comment, over the months that followed, was overwhelmingly in support of the sisters – and highly critical of the Vatican.

Rome was so rattled that it broke its usual silence. A year into the visitation the man behind the second inquisition, Cardinal Franc Rodé, head of the body informally known as the Congregation for Religious, tried to reinforce the Vatican's case. He announced in a carefully written English-language statement that the purpose of the investigation was to 'to identify the signs of hope, as well as concerns, within religious congregations in the United States'. But he then blew his cover with an interview with Vatican Radio in Italian in which he said Mother Clare would be investigating complaints of 'a certain secularist mentality that has spread among these religious families, perhaps even a certain "feminist" spirit'.

It now became apparent that the Curia were far from united. The next year, 2010, the leadership of the Vatican office running the public investigation changed. Cardinal Rodé's second-in-command retired and was replaced by an American, Joseph Tobin, a former superior general of the Redemptorist Order, who said he wanted to move the process towards a genuine dialogue with the US nuns. Tobin said that Rome needed to acknowledge the 'depth of anger and hurt' provoked by the visitation. A 'strategy of reconciliation' was now needed, he said. The next year Pope Benedict replaced Rodé with another more concil-iatory figure, the Brazilian Cardinal João Bráz de Aviz.

However, over at the Congregation for the Doctrine of the Faith, Cardinal Levada – who had been the doctrinal chief of the US bishops before moving to do the same job for the whole Church in Rome – ploughed on. He was determined to push through the doctrinal investigation of the US nuns' leaders before his imminent retirement. In April 2012 the CDF went public, disclosing that it had been investigating the Leadership Conference of Women Religious and had found 'serious doctrinal problems'. These included promoting 'radical feminist themes incompatible with the Catholic faith'. The nuns were also found guilty of focusing their work too much on poverty and economic injustice, while keeping 'silent' on abortion and same-sex marriage.

Back at the Congregation for Religious, Archbishop Tobin was unhappy – both at the content of the CDF's findings, and also at its failure to consult him before releasing the report. A month after Levada retired in July, Tobin launched an extraordinary public attack. He lambasted 'unscrupulous canonical advisers' in the Vatican who had built up animosity between Rome and the nuns, sowing fear among them that they were facing penalties or even the dissolution of their communities. And he criticized his predecessor Cardinal Rodé, saying: 'A visitation has to have a dialogical aspect, but the way this was structured at the beginning didn't really favour that.' So outspoken was he that Pope Benedict removed him from the job and sent him to become Archbishop of Indianapolis back in the United States. The crackdown on the US nuns had become, in the words of Cardinal Sean O'Malley of Boston, a 'debacle'.

When the *60 Minutes* team decided to put together a documentary on all this they went to a down-and-out section of Brooklyn to get a glimpse of a religious sister at work. In a soup kitchen there they filmed Sister Judy Park, working among some of the poorest people in the world's richest country. 'Isn't the Vatican's point that you should be emphasizing the role of the Church and what is right and what is wrong instead of just serving soup?' the reporter, the late Bob Simon, asked. Sister Judy replied: 'My role is not to judge. My role is to accompany people.'

A few days later the Catholic Church had a Pope who said exactly the same thing. The world had turned upside down. Or so the nuns imagined.

* * *

It was a shock, therefore, after all Pope Francis's early rhetoric, that one of his first administrative acts was to endorse the crackdown on the American nuns. Two weeks after his election the nun's leaders were invited to the Congregation for the Doctrine of the Faith once again. There they found Levada's successor as head of the Vatican's doctrinal department, Archbishop Gerhard Ludwig Müller, a German theologian who had been a protégé of the man who later became Pope Benedict. The two men were so close that Benedict had asked Müller to edit his collected theological works. With Müller the nuns found Archbishop Peter Sartain – the man who had been appointed by the Vatican to 'correct' their inadequacies. Müller told the nuns that he had discussed the 2012 guilty finding against them with the new Pope. Francis had reaffirmed the document's criticism – and the programme of reform which had been set out for them under the guidance of Sartain. In the face of all that had happened – and all Francis had said – how could this make sense?

Their puzzlement was compounded the very next day. Pope Francis announced a replacement for Tobin in the department which supervised religious orders. Nuns and brothers and monks around the world had been braced for a hardliner when Tobin was removed for criticizing the crackdown. But Pope Benedict, in the turmoil surrounding his resignation, had not filled the post. Now Pope Francis appointed a Franciscan who was much respected among other orders. He was the Spaniard José Rodríguez Carballo, who was serving in Rome as the minister general of the Orders of Friars Minor – an order that traces its roots directly to St Francis of Assisi. His appointment looked like an optimistic sign. Yet it sat oddly with the Pope's endorsement of Müller's continuing tough line with the nuns.

Another perplexing contrast was to follow. Soon after, Francis addressed 800 women from different religious orders in 70 countries. His message to them was: 'It is an absurd dichotomy to think of living with Jesus but without the Church, of following Jesus outside of the Church, of loving Jesus without loving the Church.' This was a coded message to those US nuns who had responded to the Vatican investigation by saying they might leave the Catholic Church and set up their communities outside it. Clerics may make promises of obedience to their ecclesiastical superiors, but nuns were not clerics, some of them had argued. They made their vows to God alone. So they had no need to become agents of the institutional Church.

But if the Pope's message to them was orthodox the language he employed was not. It was particularly peculiar considering that he was addressing women who had given up the chance of motherhood to pursue their religious vocation. Nuns, he said, must not end up as 'old maids'. Rather they must become 'spiritual mothers' with a 'fertile' chastity, generating 'spiritual children in the Church.' It did not sound much like the language of a new theology of women. He did the same thing in Brazil a few months later, mixing a new message with old vocabulary when he told the country's bishops that he wanted them 'to promote the active role of women in the ecclesial community'. Again he couched the command in curious gendered imagery – without women, he said, the Church 'risks sterility'.

Pope Francis was admonished for his choice of language from an unusual quarter. Ulla Gudmundson was a Swedish Lutheran. But she was one of the few female ambassadors to the Holy See. She told one of the Pope's intimates that she was disappointed that he had no words of praise for the 800 top nuns other than couched in terms of traditional female virtues like motherliness. Why not praise them for their intelligence and leadership qualities, she complained, and thank them for putting those at the service of the Church? Her remarks were

conveyed to the Pope who wrote a note to a mutual friend a few days before
he left for World Youth Day in Brazil. In it he said he very much agreed with
the ambassador and added: 'I'm thinking hard of how I can introduce this
theme.' On the flight back from Brazil he found an opportunity. Responding
to a reporter's question he gave his fullest exposition to date of the need for a
different relationship between the Catholic Church and women. He was asked
if women could become deacons, the step below being a priest in the clerical
hierarchy. Or if they could become the head of a department in the Vatican
bureaucracy. He sidestepped both questions. Instead his response ventured into
more mystical territory. 'The Church without women is like the college of the
Apostles without Mary. The role of women in the Church is not simply that of
maternity, being mothers, but much greater: it is precisely to be the icon of the
Virgin. Our Lady is more important than the Apostles!' he said, adding that in
the Italian language the word for the Church is feminine – *la chiesa* – as is the
case in the theological concept of the Church as the Bride of Christ. 'The Church
is feminine. She is bride, she is mother. We have much more to do in making
explicit this role and the charism of women. This needs to be better explained.
We need to develop a profound theology of women.' And he added: 'It can't just
be about their acting as altar servers, heads of Caritas, catechists... No! They
have to be more, profoundly more, even mystically more.' (Pointedly the official
Vatican translation of this differs from what Francis actually said; he literally
said 'theology of the woman' but the Curia version is 'theology of womanhood',
which carries a less radical nuance.) Asked about the possibility of women
priests in the Catholic Church he baldly replied: 'As far as women's ordination
is concerned, the Church has spoken and said: "No." John Paul II said it, but
with a definitive formulation. That door is closed.' And again he returned to
his main point: 'Women, in the Church, are more important than bishops and
priests; *how*, this is something we have to try to explain better, because I believe
that we lack a theological explanation of this.'

A month later he was pressed on this, in his first big interview as Pope, and
replied by saying what he was *not* talking about. 'I am wary of a solution that
can be reduced to a kind of "female *machismo*", because a woman has a different
make-up than a man. But what I hear about the role of women is often inspired
by an ideology of *machismo*,' he told his Jesuit interviewer, Antonio Spadaro.
'We must not confuse function with dignity.' Women and men were equal in
dignity, he suggested, but had different roles to play – a distinction which many
in the Church question, as we shall discuss below. 'We have to work harder to
develop a profound theology of women,' Francis told Spadaro. 'Only by making
this step will it be possible to better reflect on their function within the Church.

The feminine genius is needed wherever we make important decisions.' What he seemed to be hinting at was that the issue was not the need for women to hold more offices or positions in the Church. The issue was how to find ways to assign greater value to the roles women already play.

Advocates for the ordination of women tried to gloss this. They suggested Pope Francis was not saying that he agreed with the Church's stance. He was merely being clear about what the official position was, and hinting that it was not politically realistic to make women priests at present. Perhaps the closed door could be opened in the future, and Francis was the man with the keys. But that idea looked unrealistic when, later the same month, the Pope approved the excommunication of a prominent supporter of women priests. The Australian priest Father Greg Reynolds, who also publicly supported same-sex unions, was expelled from the Church for continuing to say Mass publicly after being stripped of his priestly faculties by his local archbishop. There were even bizarre reports, denied by Reynolds, that he had been present at a Mass where a blessed host had been given to a dog.

Francis held to the same nuanced line in his signature teaching document *Evangelii Gaudium*. Again he came back to a traditional view of feminine qualities. He wrote of 'the indispensable contribution which women make to society through the sensitivity, intuition and other distinctive skill sets which they, more than men, tend to possess'. These included 'the special concern which women show to others, which finds a particular, even if not exclusive, expression in motherhood'. Many women already shared pastoral responsibilities with priests, he said. And female theologians offered 'new contributions to theological reflection'. But there remained a 'need to create still broader opportunities for a more incisive female presence in the Church'. What he called 'the feminine genius' was needed in the workplace, in social structures and in the Church', he said. And again he reiterated: 'Men and women are equal in dignity' and insisted that 'male priesthood sacramental power should not be too closely identified with power in general'. Sacramental power was about 'function not dignity or holiness'. A priest should be a servant; his calling 'does not imply an exaltation which would set him above others'.

Ulla Gudmundson was not impressed. The Swedish Ambassador to the Holy See was about to come to the end of her tour of duty in Rome. She continued to maintain that it was impossible for a woman not to feel alienated by the way men at the top of the Church spoke on the subject. As a woman, she wrote in an article for *The Tablet*, she felt she was a person who was curious about the world, impatient to explore it and eager to do what she could to make it a better place. So she felt diminished when men in the Church reduced her to the mission of emulating Mary in being 'motherly, gentle and tender'. When the Pope said that Mary was more important than popes, bishops and priests, she said, it sounded like an alibi for not making room in the Church for living women. At the end of November, as she was leaving her ambassadorial post she had a farewell audience with the Pope.

'Ah,' said the Pope as she was introduced. 'It was you who worried about the state of women in the Church!' At the end of their conversation she handed him a list with the names, emails and phone numbers of 50 Catholic women theologians with a letter. 'It said that I hoped he would have the time to meet and listen to the women of his Church who for many years were working on a renewed Catholic anthropology, and who were also deeply committed to social justice,' she said to the Pope. 'Women, I pointed out respectfully, could be the Pope's best allies in combating corruption and greed, not because women are nicer people but because women seldom have a stake in the structures as they exist today.' She also gave Pope Francis a book entitled *Half the Sky: Turning Oppression into Opportunity for Women Worldwide*.

The Pope replied: 'Yes, women can bring something new to the Church. They think differently from men.' He went to hand the envelope with the list to Archbishop Gänswein who was standing at his side, but the pontiff held on to it, saying: 'This is important'. Gudmundson is ambivalent about the way the Pope is handling the whole issue. 'I think Pope Francis deserves huge credit for having released spiritual energy in his Church,' she said. 'During the seven years I have followed developments in the Vatican and the Catholic Church, I have never seen such activity around the question of women's position in the Church as this spring.' Having said that, she noted, somewhat wearily a year later: 'Not so much has happened since then.'

Francis continued to send mixed signals on what he meant about giving women a greater role in the Catholic Church. At the end of 2013 Maria Voce, the president of Focolare, one of the lay movements in the Church of which the Pope approves, suggested that Francis should institute a Council of Lay Advisers to complement his C9 of cardinal advisers. Women could be part of it. The proposal was met with deafening silence. Then the Pope was asked by an interviewer from the Italian newspaper *La Stampa* whether he might appoint female cardinals in the future, since there were cardinals in the past who were not priests. Francis replied: 'I don't know where this idea sprang from. Women in the Church must be valued not "clericalized". Whoever thinks of women as cardinals suffers a bit from clericalism.' Clericalism – the idea that priests are exalted or special rather than servants of their people – is one of the principal diseases of the Catholic Church in

Pope Francis's opinion. Instead, the month after, in January 2015, he told an Italian women's group, Centro Italiano Feminille, of his hope that 'the spaces for a more capillary and incisive feminine presence in the Church will be enlarged'. He did not say what that would mean in practice. But, again, he emphasized the female gifts of 'delicateness, special sensitivity, and tenderness'. Cardinal Stanisław Ryłko, the president of the Pontifical Council for the Laity, was, the Pope had said at one point, working 'in this direction with many women experts in different areas'. But no more was publicly heard of that in the months that followed.

Some small signs of change did occur. When the membership of the Pontifical Commission for the Protection of Minors was announced in March 2014, half of its members were women. And when the membership of the CDF's main advisory body, the influential International Theological Commission, was revised, five women theologians became members, compared with just two under Pope Benedict. They were all regarded as conservatives. 'But they are women, and that's a start,' said the British-Zambian theologian Tina Beattie. 'It's encouraging to see more women in these roles.' And when the Queen visited the Pope she was told that she could ignore the old protocol of having to wear a black dress and mantilla. She turned up wearing one of her signature brightly coloured pastel outfits. The significance of this was not lost on the Catholic commentator Joanna Moorhead writing in the *Guardian*. It was, she said, 'yet another of those subtle but hugely significant signs coming out of the Francis pontificate'. At one level, of course, it didn't 'matter a fig whether an elderly woman meeting an elderly man in Rome wears black or lilac'. But on another level it denoted a rethink in 'that ancient and pernicious mindset within the Vatican that women are somehow unclean temptresses and must be attired in black to sanitise them when they're allowed into the presence of a saintly celibate churchman'.

But elsewhere the mixed messages continued. In May 2014 the Congregation for the Doctrine of the Faith again summoned the leaders of the US sisters to Rome. In what the head of the CDF, Cardinal Müller, described as 'blunt' language he accused them of not abiding by the reform agenda the Vatican had imposed on their leadership organization two years before. The nuns' leaders, Sisters Carol Zinn, Florence Deacon, Sharon Holland and Janet Mock, did not reply in kind. Rather they described the encounter as a 'dialogue that was respectful and engaging' and the Vatican pronounced it 'a very helpful meeting'. But the gap in comprehension remained wide. When a group called Women's Ordination Worldwide held a rally in Rome that month, Pope Francis did not engage with the issue but resorted to making jokes. He gave an interview to Franca Giansoldati of *Il Messagero*, who became the first female journalist to engage him on women's issues. The exchange between them made many in the Church think again about Pope Francis's attitude to women:

> **Interviewer**: You speak little of women, and when you do, you address the argument only from the point of view of maternity, the woman as spouse, the woman as mother, etc. And yet now women lead states, multinationals, armies. In your opinion, what position do women occupy in the Church?
>
> **Pope Francis**: Women are the most beautiful thing God has made. The Church is woman. Church is a feminine word. Theology can't be made without this feminine dimension. You are right about this, we don't speak enough about it. I agree that more work must be done on the theology of women. I have said so and work is being done in this regard.
>
> **Interviewer**: Do you perceive a certain underlying misogyny?
>
> **Pope Francis**: The fact is that woman was taken from a rib ... [the Pope laughs heartily]. It's a joke, I'm joking. I agree that there must be more reflection on the feminine question, otherwise the Church herself cannot be understood.
>
> **Interviewer**: Can we expect historic decisions from you, such as a woman head of a dicastery [Vatican department]?
>
> **Pope Francis**: [The Pope laughs] Well, so many times priests end up under the thumb of their housekeepers ...

Afterwards Vatican officials stressed that the Pope had been joking. But many observers suggested that a truth was being spoken within the jests. Ultra-conservative websites celebrated what they saw as a refusal by Pope Francis to make any concessions to feminism. At the other end of the spectrum there was an increasing impatience from women's groups at jokes they had ceased to find funny years before. Not long afterwards, Francis addressed the European Parliament in Strasbourg. Again he used an eccentric metaphor, comparing Europe to a haggard grandmother who was 'no longer fertile and vibrant'. Commentators, inside and outside the Church, seized upon the incongruity of the image. The Vatican spin doctors had to spring into action yet again, insisting that the Pope 'had nothing but the deepest love and respect for all grandmothers'. There was a general puzzlement at the Pope's choice of vocabulary. It seemed bizarre from a man who had previously referred to women, and particularly older women, as 'the backbone of the Catholic Church'– and who, at the age of 77, was clearly intellectually and spiritually fertile and vibrant himself. One secular wag described it all as a classic example of 'the dexterous feminism for which the Holy See is famed'.

Vatican official did their best to reinforce the conservative side of the Pope's ambivalence. In May 2015 Francis had his first high level meeting with a top woman bishop. The Pope received Archbishop Antje Jackelen of Uppsala, the first woman to head the Lutheran Church of Sweden. It was the first time a senior female bishop had been invited into the Vatican for a personal audience with the pontiff. Yet instead of celebrating the fact Vatican officials damped down the publicity and did their best to ensure that photographs of the event were not widely circulated.

* * *

How was the world to make sense of this twisting papal slalom through the obstacle course of gender relations? What did Pope Francis really think about women and their role in the Church?

As a man nearing his eightieth year, whose familial and religious upbringing was shaped by women, most particularly by his beloved Grandma Rosa, he had a high view of womankind. But it was essentially an idealized vision of woman as wife, mother and home-maker. To that was added an upbringing in a macho Latin American culture which he had rarely left throughout his adult life. That, together with his warm avuncular papal personality, put him at ease with women. But it produced all kinds of unarticulated assumptions about women which younger generations no longer shared – and which seemed particularly alien in Europe and North America. His odd and old-fashioned metaphors were rooted in that. They made him seem out of touch even when he trying to sound sensitive. When he increased the number of women theologians on the Vatican's top advisory body from two to five he said that this was insufficient and that more women would be appointed. But that fact was overshadowed by him describing the women on the committee as 'the strawberries on the cake'. The phrase was seized upon by the media as a Freudian slip which revealed that he really thought women were nothing but sweet and decorative. One celebrated female theologian, Elisabeth Schüssler Fiorenza, riposted: 'If the women are the strawberries then the men are the nuts'.

The former president of the Republic of Ireland, Mary McAleese, was much harsher. McAleese, who moved to Rome to study canon law after leaving politics, blamed the clerical culture which had formed Francis. 'There is a blindness here that comes from a kind of a priestly formation that leaves so many good decent gentlemanly men like Francis still carrying a residual element of misogyny,' she said. It closed him off to the dangers of not facing up to the fact that women felt excluded and were leaving the Church in droves. 'I don't think that he gets it, or that anybody around him fully understands. Why would they? They are all clerical male celibates who are just used to women kissing their hems, handing them their meals, polishing their tables.' When the Pope issued his pre-synod questionnaire before the Extraordinary Synod on the Family in 2014 McAleese revealed: 'I wrote back and said I've got a much simpler questionnaire, and it's only got one question, and here it is: "How many of the men who will gather to advise you as Pope on the family have ever changed a baby's nappy?" I regard that as a very, very serious question.' Of Pope Francis, she said: 'He's a lovely person, everybody likes him and women like him. We love his smile, we love his openness, we love his accessibility, we love his frankness, we love the ease of him. But we also know that that's not enough.'

Unlike previous recent popes Francis has worked as a pastor among the ordinary folk he calls the holy faithful people of God. From his 18 years as a bishop and an archbishop he knows that it is women who run the day-to-day operations of the Church. Without them, parishes, schools, hospitals and a variety of Catholic social-service organizations would cease to function. But, said another prominent feminist theologian, Dr Elizabeth Johnson, of Fordham University: 'Francis is a kindly old gentleman from Latin America. He's chivalrous and profoundly prayerful but he's never had much experience of women as intellectual equals. He doesn't understand the struggle for equality that women have been through.'

That is only partly true. Francis is probably the first Pope in the Catholic Church ever to have had a woman as a boss. As we saw in previous chapters he has commented on how much he learned from Esther Balestrino de Careaga, the shrewd communist who ran the chemistry laboratory in which he had his first job. He grew up as a Peronist in a country where Eva Perón – Evita – was one of the most powerful Argentines of the twentieth century. As leader of the Jesuits one of his chief political friends and interlocutors was a female human rights lawyer and judge, Alicia Oliviera. As an archbishop he spent long hours in the homes of poor women in the slums, drinking *mate* and learning of their experiences of life. Every Sunday he would debate with another friend, Clelia Luro, the fiery feminist widow of the maverick Argentine bishop, Jerónimo Podesta. Francis has never been afraid of smart women, said his fellow Jesuit Father Tom Reese. He recounted the story of a female lawyer who had teamed up with Bergoglio in Buenos Aires when he was campaigning against organized sex trafficking in Argentina. Reese met her in Washington and asked: 'What was it like working with Bergoglio?'

'It was wonderful,' she responded. 'He did whatever I told him!'

Francis may have been at ease working with clever and forceful women – or debating with them about equality or on social issues like same-sex relationships. But gender has been his Achilles' heel, according to Father Augusto Zampini, a theologian from Buenos Aires who now works in Britain. 'We have feminist theologians in Argentina, but the feminist movement in the US and Britain started earlier, and in the UK has more freedom within the Catholic academic environment. So Bishop Bergoglio has never been confronted on gender issues in the way he is being challenged today as Pope,' Zampini said. 'He doesn't feel at all surefooted on the issue of women. Every time he speaks about women, the Vatican needs to come to his rescue, clarifying his statements and, probably, providing some piece of advice for the future. Francis doesn't need that clarification or advice on other social issues such as economic marginalization. It would be interesting to see what would happen if he connects his zeal for social inclusion with gender marginalization.' One conduit for that advice is said to be Archbishop Victor Manuel Fernández, Rector of the Catholic University in Buenos Aires, who is close to a number of women theologians. Fernández was Bergoglio's right-hand theologian in drafting the seminal document for the Latin American bishops at Aparecida and also wrote the first draft of *Evangelii Gaudium*.

But Papa Bergoglio is also rooted in a tradition of particular papal interaction with feminism. Pope John Paul II called for 'a new feminism' that would reject the temptation to imitate male models of psychology and behaviour. Benedict XVI critiqued the tendency for some feminists to see equality in terms of a struggle for power. Pope Francis was drawing on this when he spoke of female machismo – or in his Italian, *machismo in gonnella*, machismo in a skirt.

The elephant in the room, on all this, is power. 'I have been amazed to hear worthy cardinals admonish women religious leaders not to crave power,' Gudmundson wrote in *The Tablet*. 'One rather feels they are barking up the wrong tree. Pope Francis, by contrast, barks up the right one when he directs his admonitions to the cardinals themselves and instructs apostolic nuncios to look for bishops with pastoral qualities rather than careerists.' But empowering women was not the same thing as discouraging careerism. Those in favour of the ordination of women were yet more critical. It was all very well, they said, for the Pope to play down the importance of power when he was the one wielding it. And there was a contradiction about him telling priests that the priesthood was not about power but service – and then accusing women of seeking power when they too wanted to serve as priests.

Francis stumbled further into the minefield in February 2015 with comments in an interview with two Italian journalists in which he compared 'gender theory' to nuclear war and genetic manipulation. All were plots to destroy the natural order of creation. It was clearly not a subject in which he was completely at home. He appeared to be attacking the notion that there is a spectrum of sexual identity rather than a simple polarity of male and female. The idea of a spectrum, he said, did not 'recognize the order of creation'. But gender theory is more nuanced and subtle than that. It examines how people learn to identify themselves sexually – and examines how they can become stereotyped into certain roles based on societal expectations. The Catholic Church has had problems in the past with fluid notions of gender, most particularly at the United Nations where some groups have used gender as a codeword for reproductive health rights which are deemed to include abortion. But it is quite possible to accept elements of gender theory without buying into the radical concept that gender is a pure social construct – and that sexual identity can be adapted indefinitely. Gender theory can seek to separate cultural aspects of femininity and masculinity from biological realities. 'The Church now has this terror of what it calls gender ideology,' said the theologian Tina Beattie, Professor of Catholic Studies at the University of Roehampton in London. 'It is threatened by the idea that gender is fluid and that we are all now going to go through life endlessly reinventing ourselves. That is the position of a few American feminist academics. But there are hundreds of feminisms which don't say that – and the Church can't just dismiss them all.'

But, as ever, though Pope Francis may have been uncomfortable with the ideology, the pastoral experience was a different matter. 'Reality is superior to ideas' is one of his repeated catchphrases. In keeping with that, after giving his 'gender theory' interview, he offered a private audience to a transgender man who was being victimized in his parish church in Spain. Diego Neria Lejarraga, who was born as a girl and raised as a devout Catholic, was invited to the Vatican after many people spurned him in church in his hometown of Plasencia in western Spain. He had undergone a sex-change operation eight years earlier at the age of 40 after years of living in 'a body that felt like a prison that absolutely didn't correspond with what my soul felt'. Catholic doctrine holds that sex change procedures do not change a person's gender in the eyes of the Church. One priest called him a 'daughter of the Devil'.

Francis rang Neria twice. In the first call the Pope told him that God loves all his children 'as they are'. He went on: 'You are a son of God and the Church loves you and accepts you as you are.' Neria was surprised but thrilled. He was even more surprised when, in the second call, Francis invited him to go to the Vatican for a personal meeting – and offered to pay for the flight for Neria and his fiancée. By way of thanks, the couple took the Pope a small package of local produce, including olive oil, paprika and cherry jam. The man's supporters speculated that the invitation was not a gesture of pastoral care so much as an attempt by Pope Francis to learn about the transgender experience first-hand. But Neria was left in no doubt by what happened. During the meeting, Neria asked the Pope if, after his gender reassignment, there was 'a place somewhere in the house of God for him'. Francis responded by embracing him. 'The meeting was a wonderful intimate unique experience that changed my life,' Neria said afterwards. 'Now I am finally at peace.' Back home Neria told a Spanish newspaper: 'This man loves the whole world. I think there's not – in his head, in his way of thinking – discrimination against anyone. I'm speaking about him, not the institution. If this Pope has a long life, which all of his followers hope, I think things will change.'

Turning the whole debate on its head Ulla Gudmundson offered a radical thought at an event known as Voices of Faith. It was held in the Vatican to hear women's stories on International Women's Day in March 2015. The concept of 'the feminine genius' as applied by men to women, Gudmundson said, carries the subliminal message that a woman's place is in the home. The phrase, like that of 'sexual complementarity' – the idea that men and women play different but complementary roles in life and in the Church – is all too often, in the words of Sister Sandra Schneiders, 'code for the theory and the programme of sexual apartheid and female subordination in the Church'. Another theologian, Elizabeth Johnson, a professor at Fordham University in New York, was one of a number of feminists who offered another more radical thought: 'Pope Francis says we need a new theology of women; but this has already taken shape over the last 50 years,' she said. 'Many people would say that we do not need a theology of women – women should not be singled out. What may be needed is a new theology of the layperson,' she proposed. In the long run, said Father Tom Reese, 'having this conversation in the Church is probably more important than the Pope simply mouthing some statements that feminists like'.

But what if, asked Gudmundson, 'the feminine genius' is seen as a quality that can exist in men as well as women. That is how the medieval mystics saw it. Surely 'feminine' qualities – gentleness, compassion, sensitivity, empathy, consideration for others, reluctance to use violence – are desperately needed in today's world. Just as women need the opportunity to be strong, courageous and intelligent, she said, 'I would also like to see men have the opportunity to be tender, patient, sensitive.' Isn't Pope Francis himself, she said, with his constant refrains of love, mercy, forgiveness, peace, a splendid example of 'the feminine genius'? The shame was that, though the Voices of Faith event was in the grounds of the Vatican, there was not a single cardinal present to hear the women's stories. Had there been they might have realized that a woman's place is not in the home. A woman's place is in the Vatican.

* * *

Into the third year of the Francis pontificate there had been significant progress in a wide range of areas. The Church and the world had become used to a different style of papacy. Substantial progress had been made in reordering church finances and clearing out the mess inside the Vatican Bank. Changes had begun within the Curia. The Synod of Bishops was alive and in a state of gloriously messy revitalization. There were even faltering steps on sex abuse. But on the place of women in the Church, for all the rhetoric, little had really changed. Then, in December 2014, the Vatican published its report into the biggest investigation ever conducted in church history – the Apostolic Visitation on the US nuns – the unprecedented and highly controversial Vatican inquisition of every community of Catholic sisters in the United States.

Anyone predicting the outcome at the outset would have foretold fire and brimstone. The visitation had been triggered in 2008 by a massive decline in the membership of female religious orders in the US – which dropped from 181,421 in 1966 to 56,000 in 2010. Numbers had declined in men's orders too but the Vatican did not deem it necessary to investigate that. The high-octane rhetoric from Curia conservatives about the nuns at the outset revealed the real concerns: 'irregularities or deficiencies' in their lifestyle, a 'secularist mentality', 'radical feminism', too much working with the marginalized and not enough campaigning against abortion. The investigation had been expected to conclude with the disciplining or silencing of individual nuns or communities. The reordering or even dissolution of some groups had seemed in prospect. So did the general imposition of oaths of loyalty similar to those imposed upon the leaders of the Catholic aid and international development confederation Caritas in 2012 after it was accused of working alongside secular aid agencies which promoted contraception in family planning.

But by January 2012, when the chief investigator, Mother Clare Millea, passed her final report to Rome, the hardliners had been removed from the Vatican department which had initiated the investigation. Curia wheels, as ever, turned so slowly in processing it that by the time it was ready for release – nearly two years later – there was a new Pope and a new mood.

The final document published by the Congregation for Institutes of Consecrated Life and Societies for Apostolic Life in December 2014 was just 5,200 words long. It said almost the opposite of what its instigators would have wanted, expressing the Vatican's gratitude for the selfless service of women in the religious orders. It began:

> Since the early days of the Catholic Church in their country, women religious have courageously been in the forefront of her evangelizing mission, selflessly tending to the spiritual, moral, educational, physical and social needs of countless individuals, especially the poor and marginalized. Throughout the nation's history, the educational apostolate of women religious in Catholic schools has fostered the personal development and nourished the faith of countless young people and helped the Church community in the USA to flourish.

And it concluded by expressing 'the profound gratitude of the Apostolic See and the Church in the United States for the dedicated and selfless service of women religious in all the essential areas of the life of the Church and society'. The work of the nuns, it noted, was especially apt to 'resonate with Pope Francis' insistence that "none of us can think we are exempt from concern for the poor and for social justice"'.

Strikingly, terms like 'crisis', 'dissent', 'doctrine' and 'hierarchy' did not appear in the document, which mentioned the term 'obedience' only in the context of obedience to Jesus Christ rather than to the Church's power structure. The report contained no disciplinary measures or new controls. The decline in religious vocations, it noted, was from a short-term peak in the 1960s 'that was not typical of the experience of religious life through most of the nation's history'. Talk of a crisis, it thereby implied, was overstated. The praise-filled document was irenic in tone. It brought an unexpectedly pacific conclusion to an episode of tension and high anxiety precipitated by the Church's male-dominated power structure. Mother Clare had clearly brought 'the feminine genius' to bear upon the five-year-long inquiry with which she had been charged.

The reaction of the religious sisters was one of enormous relief. Sister Sharon Holland, a respected canon lawyer who had served in the Vatican and who was now president of the Leadership Conference of Women Religious, described the Vatican document as 'affirmative and realistic'. She praised its 'encouraging tone'. Other nuns were more combative, perhaps with an eye to the fact that the second Vatican confrontation with them – via the doctrinal policemen of the CDF – was still to be resolved. Sister Sandra Schneiders highlighted the report's assertion that a visitation was a 'willingness to share burdens and seek answers together' rather than a 'threat of reprisal or act of coercion'. This, she said, was an implicit acknowledgement that the approach of Cardinal Rodé had been misconceived in setting up the visitation. 'Five years of suspicion, threat, judgment, accusations, mutual distrust and justified anger at rank injustice cannot be abolished with a few pages of appreciative acceptance, no matter how sincere', she wrote. As long as the threat of action by the CDF against the nuns continued to hang over their heads the women would be 'ill-advised to adopt a naïve stance of "let's just all forget about this nasty little event and move on"'.

The fact that the second Vatican crackdown against the nuns was still in place prompted a variety of reactions. The long-serving Vatican reporter John Thavis wondered if a 'good cop, bad cop' dynamic still lingered on in the Vatican Mother Clare's review had praised the nuns while Cardinal Müller's had been distinctly critical and had demanded that the nuns made major changes in their attitude to women priests, homosexuality, abortion and euthanasia. There was another possibility. It was that the Latin American Pope felt an ambivalence towards the North American nuns. 'A Latin American in the United States is like an Irishman in England,' one senior member of the Curia told me. 'He combines both a sense of respect and a feeling of resentment at the economic and cultural dominance of his bigger neighbour. There is something of that in Pope Francis. It may well be that he sees the American nuns as Americans first and nuns second.'

There seemed some grounds to suggest that. Not long after his election Francis had had a private meeting with the leaders of the nuns and male religious orders in Latin America, the Confederation of Latin American and Caribbean Religious. He had told them that if they got a letter of criticism from the CDF they should not worry but carry on with the work which their experience of real life dictated to them. But he also shared with them a concern he had about progressive nuns who flirted with a New Age spirituality which seemed to leave Jesus Christ behind. The Pope told them: 'I knew of one superior general who encouraged the sisters of her congregation not to pray in the morning, but to give themselves a spiritual bath in the cosmos.' This was precisely one of the accusations laid against some US nuns by the CDF. 'The nuns' leaders had just the year before brought in a Jewish agnostic as their keynote speaker,' one senior Vatican official told me. He was referring to the futurist Barbara Marx Hubbard, who spoke to at the LCWR annual meeting in 2012. Her topic was her concept of 'conscious evolution', a pantheistic notion which includes talk of the nervous system of the planet and the 'birthing' of humanity. The head of the CDF, Cardinal Gerhard Müller, had condemned conscious evolution as old gnosticism dressed in new language. The advice Pope Francis was getting from within the Curia only reinforced that sense.

'The perception inside the Vatican in Pope Benedict's time was that the US nuns were a pretty wild bunch who were out of control,' said one middle-ranking

Curia official who served in Rome at that time. The American sisters were doing their best to play against that stereotype. They decided that rather than take a confrontational approach, they would engage in robust dialogue with Archbishop Sartain and the other Vatican overseers. The used the same dialogue techniques the sisters employed among themselves to settle disagreements and make decisions. The approach was reflected in the public statements of Sister Sharon Holland, the leader of the nuns, who struck a conciliatory note. 'The CDF isn't finished, but we're working well with the delegates who have been appointed [by it],' she said. 'Mainly we're working with Archbishop Sartain, who's been very helpful, very available. We've developed a good working relationship. We're hoping not to need the whole five years to bring that process to a good conclusion.'

That proved to be precisely the case. Pope Francis, it seemed, was simply taking one step at a time. Four months later the CDF also did an abrupt about-face on its seven years of inquisition. The earlier concerns about 'serious doctrinal problems' and 'radical feminist themes incompatible with the Catholic faith' seemingly evaporated. The document announcing the dramatic development, which was agreed jointly by the nuns and the three American bishops who had been appointed to oversee them, said: 'Our extensive conversations were marked by a spirit of prayer, love for the church, mutual respect and cooperation. We found our conversations to be mutually beneficial.' Individual statements by the two sides went out of their way to emphasize reconciliation. For the nuns Sharon Holland said: 'We are pleased at the completion of the mandate, which involved long and challenging exchanges of our understandings of and perspectives on critical matters of religious life and its practice.' Archbishop Sartain, striking a similar tone, said: 'Our work together was undertaken in an atmosphere of love for the Church and profound respect for the critical place of religious life in the United States, and the very fact of such substantive dialogue between bishops and religious women has been mutually beneficial and a blessing from the Lord.' Despite the emollient words the media was in no doubt this was a massive Vatican climbdown.

But Francis's position, as with so much else on his attitude to women in the Church, remained unclear. The report on the Apostolic Visitation of the nun's communities was widely seen as an olive branch from the pontiff to the sisters. But a careful reading of the text revealed that all was not resolved. It gently asked the women to 'carefully review their spiritual practices and ministry' to ensure that they are 'in harmony with Catholic teaching about God, creation, the Incarnation and the Redemption.' This seemed a veiled indication that Francis still had reservations about some nuns giving themselves a spiritual bath in the cosmos when they should be focusing on Jesus. Another sentence in the report suggested that many nuns 'wish to be externally recognisable as consecrated women'. The wording was mild but it was a clear challenge to those orders whose members had adopted secular clothing that they might need to accommodate the wishes of those with other views. Some members felt they were disenfranchised inside orders which had become more progressive than they found comfortable, it reported. It noted an 'ongoing need for honest dialogue with bishops and clergy' to clarify the sisters' role and strengthen 'their witness and effectiveness as women faithful to the Church's teaching and mission'. That was code for saying that the nuns still needed to make some compromises with the CDF in its disciplinary process. And, although the tone of the public report was overwhelmingly positive, separate documents had been sent privately to communities about which Mother Clare had particular areas of concern.

It was the same with the agreement between the nuns and the Congregation for the Doctrine of the Faith. Hidden among the placatory words was an agreement that the nuns' leadership would take care in selecting the speakers and programmes at its conferences, and have 'competent theologians' review its publications. It did not specify who would select the theologians. Some sisters later suggested the reviewers would be nuns since women's religious orders are full of distinguished theologians. But there was, nevertheless, an agreed intention in the report 'to promote a scholarly rigour that will ensure theological accuracy and help avoid statements that are ambiguous with regard to Church doctrine or could be read as contrary to it'. Speakers at LCWR events would use the 'ecclesial language of faith' in their remarks rather than skiing off the theological piste. Was this a theological figleaf to cover curial embarrassment since, as one waggish commentator put it 'there is no Latin word for Ooops'? Or might it have been a gentler indication of some residual concern?

The language had become far more conciliatory, but differences remained. 'Pope Francis and the nuns share the same approach on getting out on to the streets and working with the poor and marginalized,' one cardinal said privately, 'but he is orthodox on doctrine and he's going to deal with the nuns in quite an open way.' That may well also have encapsulated the attitude of the Argentinian Pope to women more generally.

* * *

Throughout the first two years of the Francis pontificate his cardinal advisers – and other senior figures in the Curia – repeatedly insisted that they and the Pope were eager to see women take a more prominent place in the Catholic Church.

At the consistory of cardinals in February 2015 many others said the same thing. But it was slow to happen. Partly the problem was that the men could not agree the details. Cardinal Sean O'Malley said he wanted to see women at the heads of Vatican congregations. But the head of the CDF, Cardinal Müller, said that could not happen, because the heads of congregations, which had the power to make laws, had to be led by an ordained man. Müller said women could lead at only the next level down – in the Pontifical Councils, particularly those responsible for the laity, the family or for healthcare. But there was no great influx of women on to Pontifical Councils either. Only at the next level down, on the recently created Pontifical Commission for the Protection of Minors, were women being appointed in numbers – and, even there, the women had to fight hard to maintain an equal gender balance when the commission's membership was expanded. The only other place where more women were appointed was on another advisory body, the International Theological Commission, where 5 women were outnumbered by the 25 male members.

There were reports that Pope Francis had told Cardinal João Bráz de Aviz, who ran the Congregation responsible for male and female religious orders, that half his staff should be women, but there was no sign of it happening. Around the Vatican Cardinal Müller let it be known that he opposed the introduction of such set quotas of women. Another senior member of the Curia – the No. 2 in one Vatican department – said, rather optimistically, 'if the Curia is changed so that it becomes based on competence it will automatically bring women into positions of leadership'. Change will come 'as soon as the reforms of the Curia kick in', a cardinal close to Pope Francis told me. 'The Pope is aware of the issue of women in the church. There will be changes, or rather not changes so much as developments. People should expect some more top women appointments.'

After two years of words without action most women in the Church were not holding their breath. In April 2015 the Pope provoked headlines like 'Francis the Feminist' after a speech which backed equal pay for equal work for women. Christians had a duty to fight to make sure that women receive equivalent compensation for doing the same jobs as men. But his call for increased social justice in secular society – which, despite the headlines, was only reiterating what Pope John Paul II had previously said – underscored for many a discrepancy what the Church preached to the world and what it practiced at home. It would have been comparatively easy, for example, as the theologian Tina Beattie argued, for Pope Francis to have boosted the representation of women at the Extraordinary Synod on the Family in October 2014. It was within his personal gift to name delegates. But instead of half, or even a third, of those discussing the Family being women, the Synod comprised 183 male clerics, 12 married couples and 1 nun. That meant 195 men and just 13 women. 'We are told that the question of ordination is ruled out,' Beattie told the Vatican's International Women's Day event in 2015. 'If we're asked to accept that and respect it, we have to see that in every single other situation, there is full and equal participation of women's leadership in the Church – that every single position that does not require ordination is filled equally by men and women.'

There were some women – not just conservatives – who were prepared to defend Pope Francis in all this. Alice L. Laffey, who teaches feminist theology at the College of the Holy Cross, Worcester, suggested that too many Western women look at Pope Francis through a rich-world perspective. 'No matter what efforts Pope Francis makes with respect to women, if he refuses to move the ordination question forward, many, including Catholics, will consider his efforts toward women as insufficient or even hypocritical,' she said. 'But the ordination of women is not the most pressing question for most Catholics or even for most Catholic women. Throughout the world, women and their children make up the greatest percentage of human beings living in destitution. Their main concern is not women priests but food, health, education and physical safety. Francis's genuine concern for the real lives of the poor and suffering warmly embraces women.' Pope Francis, she said, was charting new territory. His emphasis on the poor was a challenge for the rich world to move beyond its current ethical preoccupations and shift its priorities to the care of those who are vulnerable and on the margins.

'He is a Latin American male, patriarchal and paternalist,' said Father Tom Reese. 'He doesn't know about academic feminist gender theory. But he is concerned about women's lives in the slums – and that highlights the gap between the rich world/poor world perspectives. In the slums women are not bothered about women's ordination but about their husband's job, putting food on the table, the drug-gang preying on their sons or their daughters' safety from sexual trafficking. And those are all things Pope Francis speaks about.'

There was some evidence of these conflicting perspectives in the way that Pope Francis handled the issue of the Catholic ban on contraception during his visit to the Philippines. The Pope seemed to make a series of contradictory statements. On the one hand he opposed artificial contraception, describing *Humanae Vitae*, the document Pope Paul VI wrote on the subject, as 'prophetic' and 'beautiful'. But then he quoted population experts as saying that three was the ideal size for a family and said that Catholics should not breed 'like rabbits' but should exercise 'responsible parenthood'. He announced he had 'rebuked' a woman who had 'irresponsibly' had eight children by caesarean section. Later, after the Italian Association of Large Families complained to the Vatican, he had his aides put out a statement insisting that big families were 'a gift from God'.

At the root of all this was an attempt by Francis to set his pastoral compassion for individuals against the kind of population programmes the rich world wants to encourage or coerce the poor world to adopt. Previous popes had seen contraception as something that violates the natural law set out in philosophical theology. Francis saw it as another way in which the rich try to impose their will on the poor. He was happy for exceptions to be made to the ban on contraception in the light of the needs of individuals and the pastoral care that the Church owed to them. In those circumstances he preferred not to judge. But what he had in his sights was what he called neo-Malthusian policies of family planning – on which he was perfectly happy to issue scathing judgement. He was attacking the way birth control programmes were imposed on poor people by rich nations, who wanted to eliminate poverty by eliminating poor people. *Humanae Vitae*, in Francis's estimation, was a far-sighted defence of the poor. There is enough food in the world, he repeatedly said, for everyone. The reason the rich wanted fewer poor people was so that the affluent could keep more for themselves. The equation was need *versus* greed. The proper response was not population control but a fairer distribution of the earth's resources. As a Tweet by the Pope's spin doctor Greg Burke put it: 'Poverty is not caused by big families, but by an economy that favours profit over people.' Such an economy was not only exploitative of the poor but often nakedly bullying.

There may still have been contradictions in the Pope's flurry of comments. Many would argue that, despite all he said, it was unfair to deprive women in any part of the world of the right to take control of their own lives. But unpacking Francis's underlying thinking in this way suggests that when he talked of 'a profound theology of women' he may have had in mind something that to others looked very indirect or elliptical. Either way, it was not a message that women in North America or Europe were well attuned, or well disposed, to receive.

Nor, even if had been accepted, might it have been enough. There were many other issues in the Church that would have benefited from a female perspective. Lucetta Scaraffia, the editor of the monthly women's insert in the Vatican's house newspaper, *L'Osservatore Romano*, suggested a major one. Many of the shameful cover-ups during the sexual abuse scandal were rooted, she believed, in 'the masculine law of *omertà*' – the Mafia codeword for complicit silence. This could not have functioned if women had been present at different levels of the Church in 'non-subordinate' positions.

But there were many other ways, it was suggested to Pope Francis from a variety of Catholic sources, in which the contributions of women could enrich the life of the Church. In parishes women could – with a simple change in canon law – become deacons, baptizing, visiting the sick, ministering in schools and hospitals and prisons, preaching, officiating at Benediction, preparing couples for marriage, and conducting weddings and funerals. In dioceses they could sit on tribunals as well as administering diocesan property and finances as they do at present. Nationally they could act as secretaries to bishops' conferences as well as in other policy and administrative roles. Internationally they could be appointed papal ambassadors – nuncios – or represent the Vatican on multilateral bodies like the International Atomic Energy Agency, the International Telecommunication Union, the Organization for Security and Co-operation in Europe, the Organization for the Prohibition of Chemical Weapons, or the World Council of Churches. A woman could be the permanent observer of the Holy See at the United Nations General Assembly, the Council of Europe, Unesco, the World Trade Organization, the Food and Agriculture Organization, or the United Nations High Commissioner for Refugees. Pope Francis could convene a council of women advisers to complement his council of cardinal advisers. There could be a Synod of the Laity, half of whose members could be women, alongside the Synod of Bishops.

As Pope Francis entered the third year of his pontificate his continuing failure to translate his words on women into some form of action became increasingly problematic for many Catholics. 'There was a time not so long ago when all institutions in the world were run by men,' said the theologian Tina Beattie. 'But the world has changed and we are now in a time and place where the Catholic Church looks ridiculous in embracing attitudes which can otherwise be found only in some of the most fundamentalist and unpleasant regimes on earth.' The Church's attitude to women is the single most corrosive influence on the evangelical ability of Catholicism to reach the modern world, she said. Rome would always seem deficient in authority and integrity so long as it speaks from the lived experience of only half the human race. Pope Francis appeared to understand that. But he did not know what to do about it.

Many women in the Church were happy to advise him. 'There's huge richness in the Catholic tradition on women but we've gone down a narrow fearful dogmatic road on this under Popes John Paul II and Benedict XVI,' said Beattie. 'In a reaction against feminism, and women's ordination in other Churches, they refused to enter into dialogue. Pope Francis has said he is prepared to do that but shows no sign of knowing how to go about it. He said in one of his interviews: "I know we need a theology of women and we're working on it." But who is we? Because women have been working on it for a long time. So the Vatican doesn't need to work on it; it just needs to read what women theologians have been writing for the past 50 years.'

There are some small grounds for optimism, she feels. In April 2015 a one-day conference was held at the Pontifical University Antonianum in Rome, entitled "Women in the Church: Prospects for Dialogue". The event was the initiative of the Roman institution's new rector, Sister Mary Melone who is the first woman every appointed as rector of a pontifical university. As well as presentations from women from all five continents the conference heard from Cardinal Gianfranco Ravasi, president of the Pontifical Council for Culture, who quoted extensively from the texts of women's writers. Among the topics discussed were the idea that the Church's traditional notion of 'complementarity' might be replaced with a concept like 'reciprocity' or 'relationality'. The conference agreed to produce an anthology of new writings on the place of women in the Church for publication just ahead of the Synod on the Family in October 2015. 'It is only a small step,' said Professor Beattie, 'but it is a step in the right direction'.

There is a long way to go. Rethinking the role of women in the Church, Professor Melone suggested, inevitably also involves men rethinking their role in the Church too. Unless Francis can stimulate that – and persuade men in the Church to act upon it – then, for all his aspirational words, it is clear that this is one area in which Pope Francis risks being adjudged by many to be a grave disappointment.

17

Prophet or Politician?

President Barack Obama was smiling broadly when he left his private meeting with Pope Francis. What was he so pleased about? Only a very few people knew. Those who guessed got it wrong. Ahead of the meeting, conservatives in the US bishops' conference had briefed Vatican officials that the Pope should give Obama a roasting. His affordable healthcare legislation would, in the eyes of the American Right, result in public funding of abortion. The Pope did not agree. Indeed Pope Francis, according to one source high inside the Roman Curia, actually approved of the President's signature healthcare legislation. Francis felt it would help the poorer citizens of the world's greatest power. But it was not Obamacare that brought the smiles.

Nor were they produced by agreement over the issue of poverty and inequality, at home and around the world, on which the Pope was well to the left of the President. That was clear from the searing criticisms of global capitalism contained in the copy of Francis's manifesto *Evangelii Gaudium*, which he gave Obama to take away. The President took the denunciation of a global economic system that excludes the poor and said he would keep it in the Oval Office to read when he was feeling frustrated. But he was not smiling about that either.

The copy of the communiqué issued after the meeting said that the two men – who talked for almost twice as long as the half-hour that had been scheduled – spoke about 'the exercise of the rights to religious freedom, life and conscientious objection, as well as the issue of immigration reform'. Pope and President seemed to find a rapport, though they spoke through interpreters. They pledged to work together on their common commitment to eradicate human trafficking. They also discussed 'current international themes'. It was in this last bald phrase that the clue lay.

The Pope's diplomatic network had briefed him that Obama, after his re-election in 2012, had fixed on Cuba as an area in which he could do something that would be part of his legacy when he left office. Francis, though he was not a big international traveller in his time as Archbishop of Buenos Aires, devoured newspapers and journals on global politics. And he had a particular interest in Cuba, having been there as part of the Catholic Church's official delegation when Pope John Paul II visited the island in 1988. Indeed, the then Cardinal Bergoglio had edited a book on the dialogue between John Paul and Fidel Castro. It saw the Church as the vehicle to rescue Cuba from communism. So in his meeting with Obama in March 2014 he raised the subject. The Pope returned to the matter several times in their 52 minutes together. By the end of the meeting Francis had agreed to broker a deal to restore diplomatic relations between Washington and Havana, which had been frozen for five decades.

As soon as Obama left, the Pope summoned Cardinal Jaime Ortega, the Archbishop of Havana, to see him. They had known and respected one another for decades. Ortega was the man who had asked Bergoglio for a copy of the speech that convinced cardinals in their pre-conclave meetings that the Argentine should become Pope. The Cuban cardinal had then posted it on his website ahead of the papal election for all the world to see. Ortega began to set up secret meetings between Washington and Havana. The Canadian government agreed to host them but its officials took no part. Vatican diplomats were the mediators. They shuttled back and forth to Toronto and Ottawa, where most of the clandestine meetings took place. Pope Francis was, apart from the American and Cuban presidents, the only head of state involved in 18 months of undercover negotiations. When the talks were about to break down, over the exchange of prisoners, the Pope wrote personal letters to the two presidents urging them to take the risk and swap. He offered to act as personal guarantor of the good faith of each side in the deal. It worked, bringing an end to the last remnant of the Cold War that had dominated world history for over half a century. When the President of the United States and his counterpart in Cuba, Raúl Castro, simultaneously announced the reopening of diplomatic relations between their two countries, both named – and effusively thanked – Pope Francis for his part in bringing it about.

It was a process that benefited all sides in the Rome-Washington-Havana triangle. The first Pope ever from Latin America offered the US President a degree of Catholic cover from the wrath of Republicans, most particularly the large Cuban émigré population in Florida. The Cuban leader Raúl Castro looked to the Catholic Church – to which 60–70 per cent of Cubans still belonged – to provide stability and continuity in the transition from communism now that Cuba could no longer rely on a daily subsidy of 80,000 barrels of oil from Venezuela, as it had once done. And Pope Francis himself saw it as the first major fruit of the strategy he had set out in his first address to the Vatican Diplomatic Corps after his election when he said that peace, the fight against poverty and 'building bridges' should be its three main goals. 'Pontiff' comes from the Latin for bridge-builder.

Pope Francis managed to accomplish something that had long eluded some of the world's finest diplomats for half a century. 'It was classic Francis spontaneity, a real bit of papal creativity,' one ambassador to the Holy See told me. 'The Pope told his diplomats not to be afraid to take risks. Francis does, and sometimes they pay off. He is ready to put his prestige on the line with anybody where he thinks he has a realistic prospect of success. But he is not naïve. He also understands the limitations of political power.'

For decades before the Cuba deal, Vatican diplomats had been nurturing good relations with both sides. Diplomacy may need grand gestures, but as Francis said after helping to broker the Cuba agreement, it also needs *piccoli passi* – baby-steps. Inching the needle forward was what the Pope was doing earlier that year when he invited the Israeli and Palestinian presidents to a prayer summit at the Vatican after his visit to the Holy Land. Nothing would come of it, sceptical political analysts predicted. But the fruits of peace do not fall suddenly.

Pope Francis was a pragmatist as well as a risk-taker. He had also surrounded himself with those with very different skills to his own. One of the diplomats who had played a key role in the Cuba negotiations was his Secretary of State, Cardinal Parolin, a career diplomat who had previously been responsible for some of the Vatican's most delicate relationships – with Venezuela, Israel and China. Parolin, now the man in charge of all the Holy See's foreign affairs, called the Cuba deal a model for future ambassadorial efforts. Parolin's dexterous diplomacy and the Pope's prophetic pragmatism made them a formidable duo. As one Vatican official put it: 'What came together here was the flower of one of the finest, oldest and most refined diplomatic corps in the world and someone who comes completely from outside of that. And they worked brilliantly together.'

The pair put in place a similar long-term strategy with China, with which the Holy See has been locked in a decades-old impasse over the control of China's 12 million Catholics – half of whom are members of underground churches loyal to Rome and half of whom belong to a government-sponsored church with bishops appointed by the Chinese Communist Party. Relations with Saudi Arabia were similarly delicate. And despite Francis's fondness for big gestures he also knew when he should listen to advice. The Pope told his staff that, on the way back from Korea in August 2014, he would like to stop off at Ibril in Iraqi Kurdistan, where hundreds of thousands of Christians and other religious minorities have fled from the advance of the ruthless fundamentalists of the so-called Islamic State. Despite his reputation for being a maverick, the Pope listened to the advice of his security staff who said that, with Islamist militants within fifty miles of the city, it would be too dangerous, not just for the Pope, but also for those who would flock to see him.

But what the Cuba deal showed was that the Church should expect the unexpected from its unpredictable pontiff.

* * *

The Pope nodded. Cardinal Gianfranco Ravasi had just told him that what he liked about Francis was that he generally used straightforward coordinate clauses when he spoke rather than the sprawling subordinate clauses often favoured by intellectuals.

The Pope just nodded.

Ravasi was a high-brow if ever there was one. He was the president of the Vatican's Pontifical Council for Culture and had spent many years running the famous Ambrosian Library in Milan. He was a friend of Umberto Eco – the semiotician, essayist, philosopher, literary critic and novelist who was perhaps Italy's most celebrated intellectual. He was, according to the doyen of daily Rome-watchers, John Allen, the 'Noam Chomsky of the Vatican – an intellectual who's become a star through a combination of brain power and media savvy, not to mention a remarkably entrepreneurial spirit for an egghead'.

Pope Francis pondered Ravasi's words and then, a little while later, waved the cardinal over and asked him: 'What does that mean?'

The response was characteristic of Francis. It spoke of his self-confidence – and his sense of humour. Being Pope helped with the self-assurance. But the sense of comedy came naturally.

'Pray for me every day,' Francis said to the head of the Jesuits when he came to visit.

'I do,' said the Jesuit Superior General, Father Adolfo Nicolás.

'Ah, but do you pray *for* me or *against* me?' the Pope laughed.

The naturalness was what ordinary people admired. Discombobulated cardinals, like Francis George or Raymond Burke, may have claimed they couldn't understand the Pope but the plain people understood him well enough. Perhaps the cardinals were just too clever, which may be why Pope Francis warned against cleverness at the opening of the Extraordinary Synod on the Family when he said: 'Synod assemblies are not meant to discuss beautiful and clever ideas, or to see who is more intelligent ... They are meant to better nurture and tend the Lord's vineyard, to help realize his loving plan for his people.'

Lay people seemed to understand Francis – the only Pope ever to take the name of a saint who was a layman rather than a priest – when he boiled down his message to say: 'Let's be the Church of Yes, not No.' When the people in the pews were asked what they liked about Pope Francis, their answers were revealing: his warmth, his smile, his simplicity, his humility, his audacity, his joy, his sense of liberation, his respect for people of other faiths and even for atheists. Above all, people cited his ordinariness, his extraordinary ordinariness. 'He is one of us,' they said. It is why in Rome they coined the phrase: the scandal of normality. 'Though the faithful respected and admired Pope John Paul II and Benedict XVI they did not feel the extraordinary warmth we detect now,' one Vatican insider said. Pope Francis was bypassing theological discussion and aiming straight to the heart of the people.

Even when he addressed a crowd of three million people in Brazil, and of six million – a papal record – in the Philippines, Pope Francis sought to maintain the same approach. He described it in this way: 'I manage to look at individual persons, one at a time, to enter into personal contact with whomever I have in front of me. I'm not used to the masses.' When he gave interviews his choice of recipients revealed the same desire for connection; he gave them to a Jesuit journal, an Argentinian newspaper, a community magazine from a shanty town, an atheist intellectual, and several newspapers in Rome, of which he frequently declares himself bishop, rather than describing himself as universal pontiff. But his scattergun sayings went beyond interviews, or his uninhibited in-flight press conferences. What grabbed the public imagination was not his set-piece addresses to important international bodies but odd lines from his folksy unscripted daily homilies in the Casa Santa Marta chapel – or the one-to-one phone calls to people who had written to him to share their troubles. The details of those were invariably leaked. Francis did not seem to mind. As mentioned in Chapter Eleven, when the atheist Eugenio Scalfari interviewed Francis, he arrived without a voice recorder or even a notebook. When he offered to send Francis his write-up of their encounter the Pope told him not to bother, saying, 'I trust you.' This was not the act of a holy innocent; it was the sophisticated calculation of a man who was trying to change the way that papal utterances were heard. It was part of his strategy to demystify the papacy and make the Pope a first among equals.

Again and again he sent out the message that he wanted to be one with the people. When he landed in the typhoon-devastated Philippines the weather was so bad that his advisers wanted him to celebrate Mass in the cathedral at Palo. Immediately he said no. The cathedral could accommodate only a few hundred people and the crowd was immense. He had come to be with them, not to shelter from the weather. And when local church officials offered him a giant umbrella to protect his vestments, Francis said he wanted a plastic yellow hooded poncho exactly like those being worn by the crowds. He had been due to deliver a prepared speech in English but set it aside and spoke from his heart in Spanish. 'When I saw in Rome that catastrophe, I felt I had to be here. And on those very days, I decided to come here. I'm here to be with you.' He had been advised to call off the trip the day before but had insisted on travelling from Manila to Tacloban on a turbulent flight in a tropical storm, which had turned to a Category 2 typhoon by the time he finished Mass and had to leave. Unless he went to the worst-hit area, he said, there was no point to his trip to the Philippines at all.

Ordinary Catholics, in the Philippines and people all around the world, knew how to read that. What they perceived in Pope Francis was a deep personal integrity. 'He walks the walk, as well as talking the talk,' a pilgrim in St Peter's Square told me one day. 'He's a priest who practises what he preaches.' The common man is more astute than elites give credit for, wrote the award-winning Catholic commentator Michael Sean Winters, adding: 'The man on the street can spot a person who is comfortable in his or her own skin and sniff out a phony a mile away.' The Catholic provocateur Garry Wills was hinting at the same thing when he said, mischievously: 'It's a bit disorienting to have a Pope who is actually a Christian.' An old inter-faith colleague, a rabbi from Latin America, Abraham Skorka, told me that this had always been part of the Bergoglio he knew as Archbishop of Buenos Aires: 'He is genuine; he is the real thing. What you see is what you get. You can't fake authenticity.'

Clever clerics may have chosen to be bemused but the Catholic faithful knew exactly what the Pope meant when he said: 'If a gay person seeks God, who am I to judge?' and later added that marriage must be 'between a man and a woman' but also insisted that the Church needed to look at the issue of civil unions to protect the legal rights of people in 'diverse situations of cohabitation'. He saw no contradiction in that; only complexity. What he learned at Aparecida was that life comes before reflection and action. Law follows life, not vice versa.

A Vatican insider offered an interesting reflection on that. 'Francis is the first Pope to come from a city, so he understands both modernity and diversity,' he suggested. 'Previous popes grew up in villages, so they are more disposed to try to recreate the past, to feel nostalgia for what they feel has been lost. So Francis, being the first Pope of the City, accepts plurality and accommodation where Popes of the Village valued conformity and convention. People who live in cities see the power of symbols, whereas in the village and in the country they value something which is more direct.'

Certainly Francis was the first Pope in recent times who had formerly been an ordinary diocesan bishop rather than a diplomat or a theologian. He brought with him a sense of engagement with the real lives of ordinary people. 'He knows that a sense of touch is often what is missing from the life of the city,' said that same Vatican insider. 'He understands the physicality of human touch, the washing of the feet, the kissing of the disfigured man, the embrace of the transgendered man cold-shouldered by his parish priest.' Francis was adept at putting people at their ease. At a conference on human trafficking in the Vatican's Pontifical Academy of Sciences, a stately sixteenth-century villa in the middle of the Vatican gardens, the Pope encountered a prostitute who was giving a verbally graphic account of how she had been raped. What could the Pope do to help, he asked. 'Give me a hug,' she said. He did.

One of the characteristics that most irked panjandrum prelates was precisely what most endeared Francis to plain people – his tendency to shoot from the lip. Violence was not to be condoned, he said after the *Charlie Hebdo* killings, but anyone who insulted his mother ought to expect a biff on the nose. The lack of linguistic precision, which horrified the elite with its philosophical untidiness, was what communicated so colourfully to ordinary listeners. The people in the pews could feel a common sense in sentences that reporters delighted as seeing as self-contradictory or controversial:

- There is no Catholic God.
- Flattery was 'the leprosy of the papacy'.
- Atheists can go to heaven.
- God is not afraid of new things.
- Communists have stolen Christianity's flag.
- I would happily baptize a Martian.
- Catholics do not need to breed like rabbits.
- Proselytism is solemn nonsense.
- Let's not talk about the perfect mother-in-law.
- Argentina was undergoing a 'Mexicanization' by drug gangs.
- Women are the strawberries on the cake.
- Sometimes a father must hit his child, but never in the face – that's beautiful.
- Clerical careerists had 'spiritual Alzheimers' because they got so caught up in ambition and self-importance they forgot why they became priests in the first place.

Time after time Pope Francis found a flamboyant phrase that was provocative – and sent his press officers into overdrive trying to explain that he did not really mean what he seemed just to have said. It did not convince those who thought that

Francis lacked papal dignity and should realize that his pronouncements ought to be more carefully considered as they would be minutely scrutinized by those who had become accustomed to analysing the significance of every pontifical word. Francis's chief spokesman, Father Federico Lombardi, a fellow Jesuit, must have felt like the man with the shovel after the Lord Mayor's Parade, constantly following behind to sweep up the mess. The Pope did not seem bothered. 'From the point of view of style, I haven't changed from the way I was at Buenos Aires,' he told one Italian newspaper. 'To change at my age would be ridiculous.' On the second anniversary of his election a Mexican television interviewer put to him the criticism that he talked too much, and too spontaneously. The Pope replied: 'I talk the way I talk, like a parish priest, because I like to talk that way. I've always spoken that way. Always. For some it's a defect; I don't know. But I think the people understand me.'

They did indeed. Perhaps they could not quite articulate his message and repeat it back to him. But they understood it, and so did the clever clerics who feigned not to comprehend because they did not like what he was saying. Nor did they like what their flocks were saying as a result. 'The bishops are unsettled because the faithful are asking "why are our bishops not more like Francis?"' said one prominent Jesuit in Rome. 'One of the most significant aspects of Francis's papacy so far is that he is holding up for people the "face of Christ" ... which is loving, merciful, patient, rather than obsessing about particular moral issues,' said another US Jesuit, Father Pat Kelly, a theology professor at Seattle University. That was a massive shift of emphasis from the kind of message many US bishops had been stressing. 'Pope Francis has turned out to be an extremely skilful political player,' said a British Jesuit. 'Those who are uneasy with the radical things he says have to face up to his world popularity.' Francis has turned his popularity into a powerful tool for taking on entrenched interests.

Francis is at the heart of a struggle for the soul of Catholicism, and his greatest allies are the ordinary Catholics in the pews. Public opinion polls, like the Pew Forum survey in the United States, showed that the popularity of this pope had grown steadily over his first two years in office. Nine out of ten American Catholics gave him favourability ratings as high as those of Pope John Paul II, who visited the US five times. And that was even before Pope Francis set foot on US soil. More than that, analysis by Georgetown University showed a Francis Effect: the number of Catholics who said the strength of their religious affiliation had increased under Pope Francis had risen by 7 per cent – a figure which Georgetown's Mark Gray said was a 'significant bounce'. Interestingly, 94 per cent of conservative Catholics gave the Pope a thumbs-up, seven points higher than his 87 per cent approval among Catholics who described themselves 'moderates or liberals'.

* * *

As his papacy entered its third year the old debate about whether Pope Francis was a conservative or a liberal began to look irrelevant. What was emerging was that this Pope was orthodox on doctrine but revolutionary in his application of it. He put the Gospel – and a vividly merciful expression of it – before dogma. He had an openness in his attitude to liturgy – another issue which polarized so many in the Church. And he had about him a simplicity which was calculated, and an asceticism which was joyful, rather than puritanical, despite its severity. He rejected the papal palace in favour of living in the Vatican guest house, the Casa Santa Marta, not only out of a distaste for luxury but because he needed to chat to other people in the cafeteria rather than live in regal isolation.

He espoused traditional Catholic teachings, but gave new reasons for them or added new dimensions to them. He lauded the ban on artificial contraception. But he did so not by deferring to philosophical theory about natural law. Rather he saw it as a defence of the poor in the face of an assault by the rich who wanted to impose population control to grab an even greedier share of the world's resources. He opposed gay marriage, but defended civil unions on human rights grounds. Yet he disapproved of gay adoption because he said it put the rights of adults to be parents above the right of a child to have a mother and a father.

He said that mercy was a higher Gospel virtue than judgement or condemnation. In his very first Angelus address, just days after becoming Pope, he highlighted the Gospel story in which Jesus saves a woman whom the authorities wanted to stone to death for adultery. In the story, Francis said, Jesus did not use words of contempt or condemnation, 'but only words of love, of mercy, that invite us to conversion'. Elsewhere he said: 'Truth is like a diamond; when you show it to people in your hand it glitters and attracts; but if you throw it in their face, it is hard and it hurts.'

He proved generally tolerant of the use of the Latin Mass for those who wanted it (having discouraged it as Archbishop of Buenos Aires). He even used Latin in the modern form twice himself in the Vatican and again in Korea where he and the people shared no common liturgical language but Latin. Tolerance and inclusion emerged as two of his hallmarks. When an interviewer once asked him what phrases he had picked up in the Roman dialect since becoming Pope he replied: *'Campa e fa' campa* [live and let live]'. Having said that, he made clear his own preference for the changes ushered in by the Second Vatican Council, which dropped Latin for the language of the local people in each place. He said Mass in Italian at the parish of All Saints in Rome on the 50th anniversary of the first Mass ever said in the vernacular by Pope Paul VI after Vatican II. And in doing so he said: 'Let us thank the Lord for what he's done in the Church in these 50 years of liturgical reform. It was quite a courageous act of the Church to draw close to the People of God so they could understand well what they are doing. And there is no going backward, we must always go forward, always forward. Those that go backward are mistaken.' Francis's approach to liturgy, because it had not restricted the use of the Latin Mass, as he had in Buenos Aires, was thus described as 'good news for traditionalists' by the British Catholic conservative commentator Damian Thompson, while the US liberal, Michael Sean Winters, pronounced: 'For the first time in my adult life, there is the sense that the wind is at our back in the Church, not in our face.'

In all this, Pope Francis exploded the old polarities. Previously the Catholic Church had divided along four planes – but into two sides. On politics, those to the left emphasized Catholic Social Teaching on issues of social justice and the need to side with the poor while those to the right down-played that and enthroned their opposition to abortion, women's ordination and gay relationships as the key tokens of Catholic identity. On doctrine, rigorists said no change was possible in what the Church taught, whereas progressives said teaching could be modified in the light of the changing insights of the times. On liturgy, the traditionalists preferred lace and Latin as against modernists' liking for contemporary music and the language of the living room. On governance, centralizers favoured a clear authoritarian monarchical style while decentral-izers wanted the wider Church to take part in the way decisions were made.

Pope Francis has revealed that the dynamics inside the Catholic Church are rather more complex than the secular media often portrays. The old stereo-types were that political conservatives were also doctrinal rigorists, liturgical traditionalists and uncompromising centralisers. Under Francis it was possible to be a political conservative and a determined decentraliser. Enthusiasts for social justice might also reveal a fondness for the Latin liturgy. A doctrinal conservative could speak loudly on behalf of the poor. Pope Francis dissolved old boundaries. In doing so he has left senior figures in the Church grasping for new metaphors to express the Francis style. 'He's not changing the lyrics but only the melody,' said one of the pontiff's inner circle, Cardinal Sean O'Malley, adding: 'The Church's message was perhaps too harshly presented to people and out of context. He is trying to show us the whole context ... God's love and mercy and desire to accompany us and to forgive us when we fall and to help us overcome our weaknesses. And to have a sense of connectedness to the Lord and to one another.'

The cardinal who said to me: 'Francis plays on the same team as us but he kicks the ball in an entirely different direction,' meant that Pope Francis sees the same world through a different lens, the lens of mercy. 'His differences with the mainstream Vatican are as much temperamental as ideological,' said one senior Curia official. That is why there is no common doctrinal character in his appointments to senior positions in the Curia, and the men he has made new cardinals or bishops. 'What matters is that they should see themselves as pastors before all else; the doctrinal positions they hold are secondary. And they should have a collegial style rather than an authoritarian one.'

I asked a number of cardinals the same question: 'Is Francis a conservative or liberal?' 'Neither, he's a Catholic,' said one. 'Neither, he's a radical, in the sense of going back to the sources, to the idea that above all God is love and mercy,' said another. 'Neither, he's a revolutionary,' concluded a third.

* * *

Pope Francis has shown himself to be both a prophet and a politician. The qualities needed for both have been manifest, in differing combinations, in many of the key areas of activity we have examined in the past chapters.

He brought a prophetic eye to the task of cleaning up the Vatican Bank. If the secrecy went, so would the shady dealing, he insisted. But he also brought to the task both sophisticated administrative skills and political shrewdness – and showed resolute insistence that he would not be blinded by banking technicalities. Those whom he grew to perceive as obstacles were ruthlessly removed.

On the reform of the Curia he again had a clear vision – of transforming the Vatican bureaucracy from the master to the servant of the wider Church. And there too he demonstrated considerable political subtlety, working simultaneously on a number of levels. He replaced the most recalcitrant of the old guard and attempted a reform in the attitudes of those who remained. Encountering resistance to structural reform he sought to shift the balance of power within the Curia away from the dominance of the Congregation for the Doctrine of the Faith. To shape longer-term change he tried to appoint a different type of cardinal, from different parts of the world, to tilt the balance within the conclave which will elect the next pope. Again, he wanted pastors to dominate. And for the first time, Europeans are now outnumbered by the rest of the world.

A similar balance has been evident in his reshaping of the synod process. He began with a prophetic vision – that the Church should be transformed from a creaking feudal monarchy into an institution where decisions are made by a much wider group. But again he brought a political pragmatism to the process, consulting the world's lay people as part of a two-year two-synod process which could transform the synod into a body more continually in session. And again he brought his political wiles to bear on the process. Indeed some said he may have been too Machiavellian in packing the committee that wrote the Extraordionary Synod's controversial interim report with those who shared his own conciliatory views on the treatment of the remarried and gays.

Only in two areas did his blend of the prophetic and political seem to falter. On sex abuse he understood that action was needed to bring predator priests to justice and that systems needed to be set in place to prevent sex abuse in the future. But he seemed more enthusiastic about the prevention than the prosecution. He did not appear to put the same effort or urgency behind the Pontifical Commission for the Protection of Minors that he showed on the Vatican finances. The issue of how to hold bishops to account for their failures in reporting seemed difficult for him to push through a wilfully obstructive curial bureaucracy. He also seemed privately anxious about whether the new 'zero tolerance' procedure on abuse might lead to false accusations against priests; in March 2015, the month in which he stripped the disgraced Scottish cleric Keith O'Brien of his 'rights and duties' as a cardinal, he also controversially promoted a bishop in Chile, Juan Barros, who was enmeshed in a cover-up scandal – having received assurances in private from the man and his superiors that he was guiltless. As if to counter-balance that, a month later the resignation of Bishop Robert Finn was abruptly announced in a single terse paragraph from the Vatican. It said that Finn had resigned under Article 2 of Section 401 of Canon Law which refers to a situation when 'a diocesan bishop who has become less able to fulfill his office because of ill health or some other grave cause is earnestly requested to present his resignation from office'. Finn had been summoned to Rome weeks before to a meeting with Cardinal Marc Ouellet, the Prefect of the Congregation for Bishops, who had made clear to the Opus Dei bishop that his position was untenable. Finn's supporters, Cardinals Justin Rigali and Raymond Burke, were no longer members of the body.

The decision was widely welcomed across the spectrum of Church opinion. Even more conservative journals concurred. In Britain the *Catholic Herald* said Finn's 'clinging on to office was a scandal' and in the US the *National Catholic Register* described his resignation as 'a bitter but necessary reckoning'. But the move did little to lessen the growing sense of crisis inside the sex abuse commission over the Barros affair. Four of its lay members publicly expressed alarm at Pope Francis's decision to make a bishop of a man who had previously been accused of covering up for a clerical child abuser. Barros denied the accusation and Pope Francis, after reading all the papers in the case, decided to override protests – including those of three victims who said Barros witnessed their abuse. 'I am very worried,' said one commission member, Dr Catherine Bonnet, a French child psychiatrist, calling for a meeting with Cardinal O'Malley on the issue. She and the commission's other psychiatrist, Baroness Sheila Hollins, and its two sex abuse survivors, Marie Collins and Peter Saunders, flew to Rome to express their concerns to O'Malley, who promised to pass them on to Pope Francis. The appointment of Barros went completely against what Pope Francis had said in the past about those who protect abusers, said Collins. 'The voice of the survivors is being ignored,' she said. 'The concerns of the people and many clergy in Chile are being ignored and the safety of children in this diocese is being left in the hands of a bishop about whom there are grave concerns for his commitment to child protection.' Saunders was even more blunt: 'The Pope cannot say one thing and then do another,' he said. Local people were so worried that almost half of Chile's members of parliament, 30 priests and 1,300 ordinary Catholics wrote to the Pope. But the appointment went ahead. Francis also seemed to have difficulty reconciling theory and practice.

And on the place of women in the Catholic Church the Pope seemed to understand the vision – 'we need a new theology of women' – but appeared to have no idea what to do about it in practice. One of the most outspoken critics, Ulla Gudmundson, who spent five years as Sweden's female ambassador to the Vatican, said: 'I think the attitude to women is the last remnant of the pre-Vatican II Church.' Father Timothy Radcliffe, whom Pope Francis appointed as a consultor to the Pontifical Council for Justice and Peace in May 2015, believes that 'the single biggest challenge that the Pope faces is how he is to give voice and authority to women'.

* * *

It is characteristic of both prophets and politicians that they look forward rather than back. President Barack Obama wondered, ahead of the first visit by Pope Francis to the United States, who would turn up in Washington in September 2015: the prophet or the politician? The American President tried to anticipate both. He praised the prophet for a moral example that 'shows us the importance of pursuing the world as it should be, rather than simply settling for the world as it is'. But he also took the precaution of announcing the subjects the two men would discuss at the White House – 'a broad range of issues' including poverty, the environment, welcoming and integrating immigrants and refugees into our communities, and protecting religious minorities and religious freedom around the world. That, he hoped, would prevent the pontiff from springing any unexpected surprises. The US bishops tried to exert a measure of influence too. Cardinal Daniel DiNardo, the vice-president of the US bishops' conference, tried to steer Pope Francis on to the turf of the old US culture wars. 'Some people say that he hasn't said much about the unborn or about pro-life,' the cardinal said. 'But when he talks, he's very strong on it. So I know he's going to do that when he comes,' he predicted.

Both as a prophet and a politician Francis continued his unpredictability. On the plane back from the Philippines he had quipped that he'd love to enter the United States from its border with Mexico to pay homage to the country's immigrants but then thought he could not pay a fleeting visiting to the homeland of Our Lady of Guadalupe and promised to go there for a full week on another occasion. Neither politicians nor church leaders could be quite sure whether Francis would speak to their agenda. One wit predicted that when Francis stood up as the first Pope ever to address a joint session of Congress – around 30 percent of whose members are Catholics, more than belong to any other religion – he could turn out to be 'an equal opportunity annoyer'. After all, when the European Parliament had invited Francis to speak he had taken their breath away with those remarks comparing Europe to a haggard old grandmother who was no longer fertile or vibrant.

For all his famous 'who am I to judge' remark on homosexuality, Pope Francis was happy enough to make withering judgements on global capitalism as an idolatrous ideology promoting the 'economics of exclusion' which kept the young without jobs and neglected the elderly. He was just as capable of saying something equally acerbic in the nation which prided itself on being the home of free enterprise. Similarly the US bishops knew, or ought to have known, that though Francis was an uncompromising opponent of abortion he was just as likely to include opposition to the death penalty in his definition of what it meant to be pro-life. And he might also include in the same category a broad sweep that included everything from the care of children and their education, to unemployed young men and young women trafficked for sex, to the poor and marginalized, to the infirm and elderly. This was not quite what was envisaged by those bishops for whom life begins, and all too often seems to end, with conception. Where Pope John Paul II used to talk about the 'culture of death' Pope Francis had a more far-reaching concept with his notion of a 'throwaway culture' that incorporates everything from the waste of food to old folk robbed of dignity 'because they're no longer useful'.

Previous popes, including John Paul II and Benedict XVI, had included similar condemnations of unregulated capitalism in their social encyclicals, though John Paul in particular had included caveats about the need to respect wealth creation. Pope Francis's genuflection to that in *Evangelii Gaudium* was perfunctory. But Francis's predecessors had not provoked major Catholic businessmen to threaten to withhold big donations from the Church as they did with Francis. 'The people with the money are upset,' said David Gibson, a long-time observer of the US Catholic scene. 'They are used to the perks that come with writing big cheques. John Paul and Benedict made the same kind of statements on economic issues but it did not seem to be a high priority for them.' For Francis it was personal. He had seen half his flock plunged below the poverty line when the International Monetary Fund had flown in from Washington during Argentina's massive debt default crisis in 2001. His empathy with migrants was not ideological; he was born of migrant parents. 'Not to share one's wealth with the poor is to steal from them,' Francis disdainfully wrote in *Evangelii Gaudium*. 'Economics, immigration and the death penalty were secondary issues for John Paul and Benedict and their closest allies in the US,' said Gibson. 'So wealthy conservative Catholics could make a prudential judgement. But Francis will not let the rich off the hook on economics. What they don't like about Francis is that he takes this stuff seriously.' The shift from sex to money was particularly discomfiting for many conservatives who had felt safe with a generation of bishops appointed by Popes John Paul II and Benedict XVI who were happy to see sexual ethics as the shibboleth of Catholic identity. The idea that the Church might now shift focus from sex to the ethics of economic justice was deeply disconcerting to those who sat comfortably atop the hierarchy of the distribution of the world's wealth.

Conservative commentators reacted by saying that Pope Francis did not understand US capitalism because he was 'a creature of his background in Argentina' where a corrupt crony capitalism ruled the roost and was very different from red-blooded US capitalism. That was only partly true. Francis, like many Latin Americans, had an ambivalent attitude to the United States which mixed respect and resentment at its economic dominance of the Americas. 'Francis is not friendly to the Anglo-Saxon world,' one senior Jesuit in Rome told me. 'The Argentinian mind-set sees the US as anti-Latin American.' A senior Englishman in the Curia said: 'Francis is anti-American when it comes to aspects of US foreign policy as well as its corrosive influence as the crucible of consumerism and materialism.' The British economist Maurice Glasman, who was invited by Francis to participate in a Vatican seminar on Catholic Social Teaching, traces the roots of that firmly to Bergoglio's personal experience of the devastating impact of global capitalism on the poor. 'He became bishop of Buenos Aires in the 1990s during a period of Washington-led free-market economics that ended in a spectacular and devastating crisis,' Lord Glasman has written. 'Argentina experienced austerity and a financial crash nearly two decades before the rest of us, and the bishop was witness to the destitution and institutional breakdown involved.'

Whatever the origins of this, it is undeniable is that this Pope has switched the Catholic focus from what he has privately called 'below the belt' issues of sexual ethics to focus on money – an altogether less comfortable subject for wealthy Christians. He has been clear that the Church has been too 'obsessed' with abortion, gay marriage and contraception. And has called for a poor Church for the poor. By constantly returning to the theme of the poor, the marginalised and the excluded he has reminded Catholics that the issue of the relationship between poverty and riches was Jesus's most common theme throughout the Gospels (apart from the Kingdom of Heaven). Jesus mentions the poor literally hundreds of times. By contrast his references to sexual ethics are few. That has been Francis's emphasis too. In *Evangelii Gaudium* he also warned clerics against getting moral issues out of perspective. In a section headed 'From the Heart of the Gospel' he wrote:

> In preaching the Gospel a fitting sense of proportion has to be maintained. This would be seen in the frequency with which certain themes are brought up and in the emphasis given to them in preaching. For example, if in the course of the liturgical year a parish priest speaks about temperance ten times but only mentions charity or justice two or three times, an imbalance results, and precisely those virtues which ought to be most present in preaching and catechesis are overlooked. The same thing happens when we speak more about law than about grace, more about the Church than about Christ, more about the Pope than about God's word.

A vivid example of Pope Francis's determination to shift the Catholic Church's agenda from sex to money was clear to Lord Glasman from his visit to the Vatican. In a seminar in the presence of the Pope he outlined what he saw as the central features of Catholic teaching on capitalism, emphasising its incentives to virtue over vice, its stress on the dignity of labour, on a vocational economy, and on the representation of the workforce in corporate governance. It was the kind of capitalism more typically found in somewhere like Germany rather than in the more red-blooded Anglo-Saxon model of the US and the UK. Unrestrained capitalism created incentives to sin against the dignity of individuals and their families. Glasman later wrote: 'There were audible rumblings of discontent in the audience, and a visiting American put the view plainly that my argument, with its implied interference in managerial prerogative and the sovereignty of capital, was "communist". It all felt a bit uncomfortable. But Pope Francis interjected with a question. He asked my interrogators – for there was more than one – "What is your idea? That the banks should fail and that is the end of the world, but the workers starve and that is the price you have to pay? You exploit the parents and then buy pencils for their children in school?"'

The acolytes of the free market, who had been taken aback by the vehemence of the Pope's condemnation of capitalism in *Evangelii Gaudium*, were not going to take the risk of waiting before they reacted to Pope Francis's much-trailed encyclical on ecology and the environment. The fact that Francis wanted to write such a document had been known in the first few months of his papacy when the leading liberation theologian, Leonardo Boff, told friends he had been contacted by the Pope. Boff was by now Emeritus Professor of Ethics, Philosophy of Religion and Ecology at Rio de Janeiro State University. He had broadened his reach to look at creation as well as liberation. Francis asked to see Boff's writings on eco-theology. Boff at the time declared: 'Francis is more than a name – it's a plan. It's a plan for a poor Church, one that is close to the people, Gospel-centred, loving and protective towards nature which is being devastated today. Saint Francis is the archetype of that type of Church.' A key moment in the conversion of the great saint from Assisi, Boff recalled, came when he heard a voice from the crucifix at San Damiano calling: 'Francis, rebuild my house, which is falling into ruins.' That call, according to Boff, is today a metaphor for much more. 'What is in ruins is not just the Church but the whole of Creation, for the modern world has ceased to see it as sacred. The planet has instead become a place that we master and abuse rather than "our Sister, Mother Earth", as St Francis called it, which instead ought to be cherished, preserved and healed.' Understanding that is the most radical form of humility, grounded in the very humus of the earth, said Boff. The Pope took the name of his eco-encyclical, *Laudato si*, from a 13th century prayer attributed to St Francis, The Canticle of the Sun. It was the first papal encyclical ever – another Francis innovation – not to have a title in Latin. The title, like the subtitle, 'on the care of our common home', was in Italian.

But the encyclical was a long time in preparation because of a split inside the Vatican. Some wanted it to keep humankind as the focus of creation, as Pope John Paul II had done in his writings. He had stuck with the traditional Catholic understanding of the relationship between humans and the natural world which saw man as separate from nature. Man was expected to use his intelligence, and exercise his freedom, to dominate and subdue the earth. But others in the Curia argued that this anthropocentric understanding was part of the mind-set which had led to the careless and casual exploitation of the earth's resources in unsustainable ways. Pope Benedict, in his encyclical *Caritas in Veritate*, had diluted the language of domination and shifted church teaching more clearly towards environmental protection. The inclination of Pope Francis seemed to be to move further in Benedict's direction. 'God always forgives, man sometimes forgives, but nature never does,' Francis told one journalist. 'I don't know if humans who mistreat nature are fully responsible for climate change but they are largely responsible for it,' he added later.

While all this internal debate was going on in the Vatican a raft of 'prebuttals' began to appear in conservative journals. Writing in the right-wing philosophical monthly *First Things*, Professor Robert P. George of Princeton University proclaimed: 'The Pope has no special knowledge, insight, or teaching authority pertaining to matters of empirical fact of the sort investigated by, for example, physicists and biologists, nor do popes claim such knowledge, insight, or wisdom. Pope Francis does not know whether, or to what extent, the climate changes (in various directions) of the past several decades are anthropogenic – and God is not going to tell him.' Quite why Professor George, a law professor rather than a scientist, should be thought to have any more expertise than the Pope was not clear. Over at the business magazine *Forbes* the free-market economist Steve Moore was even more biting: 'Pope Francis – and I say this as a Catholic – is a complete disaster when it comes to his public policy pronouncements. On the economy, and even more so on the environment, the Pope has allied himself with the far left and has embraced an ideology that would make people poorer and less free.' Perhaps rudest of all was a blast from the controversialist columnist Maureen Mullarkey, who wrote: 'Francis is not a fool. He is an ideologue and a meddlesome egoist. His clumsy intrusion into the Middle East and covert collusion with Obama over Cuba makes that clear. Megalomania sends him galloping into geopolitical – and now meteorological – thickets, sacralizing politics and bending theology to premature, intemperate policy endorsements.'

Francis was not to be diverted. Fighting inequality and protecting the environment were long-standing core components of Catholic Social Teaching. Deniers may have wanted to ignore the full force of the consensus of the 800 scientists who make up the Intergovernmental Panel on Climate Change but it was inescapable that the planet was getting warmer and that Christians had a duty to care for God's creation, irrespective of the causes of climate change. The brunt of that change was being borne by the poorest people in the world who were, theologically and politically, Pope Francis's invariable starting point. 'It's not Marxism,' said Father Augusto Zampini, the Argentinian moral theologian. 'It's the Gospel.'

* * *

In the run-up to the Second World War, on a number of occasions, the Russian dictator Joseph Stalin made a joke when discussing the relative strengths of Europe's armies. 'How many divisions has the Pope?' mocked Stalin, suggesting that moral authority meant nothing in the face of the supremacy of brute force. He was so pleased with his quip that he repeated it several times to several politicians, including Sir Winston Churchill. Ironically the dictator Stalin and his Soviet state socialism are long gone but the Pope and his power are still with us.

The moral authority of popes is manifest in the secular world through what political scientists call soft power. Soft power is what Pope John Paul II used to help bring about the collapse of communism and the fall of the Berlin Wall. That remade the political map not just of Europe but of the world. Benedict XVI used his moral authority to envision a war between an ideologically pure Church and a secular culture which was in thrall to an acquisitive consumerism and materialism – in a world wallowing in a hedonist quagmire in which all moral certainty had been lost. Pope Francis turned that notion on its head: the reason the Church was in decline was not the power of self-indulgent secularism; the Church was fading because it was weak and weary and turned in on itself. It was failing to get out to change the world by inspiring it with the joy of the Gospel. The tide had turned, he felt: it was time for the vibrancy of the Church in the poor world – Latin America, Asia and Africa – to revitalize the flagging churches in the rich world of North America and Europe. He had said as much in his first interview as Pope when he told Antonio Spadaro:

> The young Catholic churches, as they grow, develop a synthesis of faith, culture and life, and so it is a synthesis different from the one developed by the ancient churches. For me, the relationship between the ancient Catholic churches and the young ones is similar to the relationship between young and elderly people in a society. They build the future, the young ones with their strength and the others with their wisdom. You always run some risks, of course. The younger churches are likely to feel self-sufficient; the ancient ones are likely to want to impose on the younger churches their cultural models. But we build the future together.

But how would Francis use the new soft power that had been placed in the hands of the Pope from Argentina? A line in the statement from President Obama, on what he and the Pope would discuss in the White House, mentioned 'protecting religious minorities and religious freedom around the world'. One of the new challenges facing the world in Pope Francis's time was a change in the form of Islamic fundamentalism. In the previous decade, its most extremist adherents had threatened the peace of the world mainly through acts of terror. But the rise of the so-called Islamic State in Syria, which then spread to Iraq, transformed the threat into a standing army on the ground which seemed initially capable of taking large swathes of land with relative ease. Any peoples who did not share their narrow and distorted view of Islam were killed, crucified, beheaded, burned alive or driven from their homes. Terror became a weapon of conventional war. Millions became refugees as chaos spread across the Middle East. Religion became a key determinant. Christians, Yazidis and all other Muslims – Shias, Sunnis and Alawites – became victims of their ruthless wave of persecution.

The beheading of hostages – in orange jumpsuits designed to echo those worn by Muslim inmates in US detention in Guantanamo – shocked the world with its callous gleeful brutality. Pope Francis was particularly shaken by the grisly ritual in which a line of Islamic terrorists in black hoods created a line of 21 Egyptian Coptic Christians whose only crime was to have crossed from Egypt into Libya in search of work. Their last words were 'Jesus, help me', Francis said in a private audience with another Christian leader. 'The blood of our Christian brothers and sisters is a testimony which cries out to be heard,' he said in Spanish and without a script, always a clear sign that a message comes direct from the heart of the pontiff. 'It makes no difference whether they be Catholics, Orthodox, Copts, or Protestants. The martyrs belong to all Christians.' Elsewhere he coined the phrase 'the ecumenism of blood' to describe this common martyrdom as the Islamic jihadists proceeded with their aim to create 'Christian-free' zones in the region that was the cradle of the faith. That, along with the militancy of Boko Haram and others in Africa and Asia, was turning Christians into the world's most oppressed religious group.

Francis knew he had to strike a balance in his response to this. When the United States first threatened airstrikes on Syria in 2013 the Pope had responded by staging a global prayer and fast for peace. But when refugees began to flee the Islamic forces in 2014 Francis sent a personal envoy, Cardinal Fernando Filoni, to northern Iraq to find what assistance they needed. Questioned by journalists about the situation, the Pope conceded that efforts to stop Islamic militants from attacking religious minorities were legitimate. 'In these cases, where there is an unjust aggression, I can only say that it is licit to stop the unjust aggressor,' Francis said. 'I underscore the verb "stop". I'm not saying "bomb" or "make war", just "stop". And the means that can be used to stop them must be evaluated.' But he added that the international community, including Muslim communities – under the umbrella of the United Nations – should orchestrate the initiative and must act in accordance with international law. The United States should not act alone. 'Terrorism' cut both ways. The word could also be used to describe the way some national governments used military force unilaterally. When an individual nation decided to strike on its own, feeling it has 'the right to massacre terrorists and with the terrorists many innocent people fall', that could be 'state terrorism'.

For all those caveats it seemed that the Vatican's position hardened as the so-called Islamic State advanced and tensions rose. In the same month that the 21 Copts were beheaded, human rights organizations warned that the terrorists were trying to completely eradicate Iraqi minority groups from large areas of the country. Archbishop Silvano Tomasi, the Vatican's permanent observer at the United Nations, said jihadists were committing 'genocide' and must be stopped. 'What's needed is a coordinated and well-thought-out coalition to do everything possible to achieve a political settlement without violence,' he said. 'But if that's not possible, then the use of force will be necessary.' That statement crossed a line for the Vatican, which has traditionally opposed the use of force in the region. 'We have to stop this kind of genocide,' the archbishop said. 'Otherwise we'll be crying out in the future about why we didn't do something, why we allowed such a terrible tragedy to happen.'

There was, and is, grave danger in such talk. It risked creating a truth out of the jihadists' delusion that Christendom is engaged in a Holy War against them – a perception which had not been helped by President George W. Bush's careless use of the word 'crusade' after 9/11 when he launched the 'war on terror'. Pope Francis was alive to the perils. For decades he had carefully cultivated good relations with Muslims when he was Archbishop of Buenos Aires as part of a wider effort to create a friendly inter-faith atmosphere in Argentina. There he had visited mosques and Islamic schools. In the Buenos Aires Islamic Centre he had written a greeting in the visitors' book using an Islamic prayer title: 'I give thanks to God, the Merciful'. He became a friend of the centre's president. He had fallen out with the Vatican after he condemned Pope Benedict's gaffe in his Regensburg lecture where he quoted a Byzantine emperor as saying the only new things produced by Islam were 'evil and inhuman'. Bergoglio had responded by organizing an inter-faith meeting.

As Pope he had written in *Evangelii Gaudium*: 'Authentic Islam and the proper reading of the Qur'an are opposed to every form of violence.' On his trip to the Holy Land in May 2014 he had taken with him two old friends, Argentine Rabbi Abraham Skorka and a Muslim leader, Omar Abboud, president of the Institute for Interreligious Dialogue in Buenos Aires. Later that year on his trip to Turkey he had expressed sympathy for Muslims defending the Qur'an as 'a prophetic book of peace' and had prayed facing Mecca in the Blue Mosque in Istanbul. At the end of the trip he called on moderate Muslims to combat religious extremism. He had also said that he would 'never close the door' on the possibility of dialogue with the Islamic State if that might bring peace. 'I never count anything as lost,' he said. 'Never. Never close the door. It's difficult, you could say almost impossible, but the door is always open.'

All this has placed Pope Francis in a unique position to 'weigh in diplomatically', according to Francis Rooney, the former US ambassador to the Holy See. But the US diplomat wanted the Pope to speak in favour of war. Francis should promote, Rooney said, a 'just' force to combat Islamic extremists consisting of 'a broad community of nations'. Such a force may be needed. But it is by no means clear that the Pope should be the one calling for it. Endorsement by the Pope could turn necessary international policing into a Crusade against Islam, in the rhetoric of terrorist recruiting sergeants. Pope Francis's visit to the United Nations General Assembly in September 2015 had been timed to coincide with the fiftieth anniversary of the 1965 address by a previous pontiff. Then, with the Vietnam War being waged, Pope Paul VI had famously declared: 'War never again, never again war.' No Pope since then had contradicted that resolution. Should Francis go down in history as the Pope who reversed that? And called for what would be seen by many Muslims, if he gave a military force his blessing, as a Holy War?

Ambassador Rooney was right about one thing. Pope Francis was in a unique position. But it was a position in which he could make clear, while condemning the brutal violence of a tiny minority of extremists, that he wanted to make common cause with the moderate Muslim majority. Only they could effectively counter the men of violence within their faith. But the support, rather than the condemnation, of the Pope was what they needed.

* * *

The story of Jorge Mario Bergoglio that has unfolded throughout this book has been a story of change. He changed himself and, when he became Pope, he set about changing the Church in the same way. The journey from Argentina to Rome, from Bergoglio to Francis, uncovered a pope of paradox – a man who has turned out to be a radical but not a liberal, an enabler with an authoritarian streak, a self-confident man in constant need of forgiveness, and a churchman who combines religious humility and political wiles. It has also been the story of a man who has undergone a deep inner transformation – growing out of that 'great interior crisis' he underwent in Córdoba – which wrought such a profound and long-lasting change in both his personal and political vision.

As leader of the Jesuits of Argentina he had determined to revive older church practices and was content to live with the political status quo. For almost two decades he resisted the work of those Jesuits striving to empower the poor and place their destiny in their own hands rather than in the hands of government or employers. And, though he always had a deep love for the popular piety of the poor, and was assiduous in providing charity to them, until he was near the age of 50 he avoided addressing the economic and social circumstances which made, and kept, people poor. Rather he was the hammer of Liberation Theology. But his great interior crisis, and his prolonged contact with the poor as Bishop of the Slums, reshaped him. It turned him from an authoritarian reactionary into a model of humility, listening and consultation. And it reshaped his politics too. Instead of merely reprimanding the rich and telling them to treat the poor more fairly he began repeatedly to denounce political and economic systems as structures of sin – making use of the language of the Liberation Theology he had once rejected. Oppressing the poor and defrauding workers of their wages, he now said, were sins 'that cry out to God for vengeance'. And he went on to become the Pope who has shaken up the complacencies and self-certainties of the Vatican – deconstructing the monarchical model of papacy, stripping away its rococo affectations and accretions, and declaring his desire for 'a poor Church for poor people'.

The story of Bergoglio's life shows how a man who made mistakes had, through a difficult time of personal transformation, become aware of his own frailties and devised, after prolonged prayer, a strategy to handle them. Acutely conscious of the forgiveness and mercy of God, he determined that his future should make redress for the mistakes of his past. It made him both tender and strong. He was humbled but steeled for the task. After he became a bishop, said one of those he trained, Father Rafael Velasco SJ, there was 'huge change in his pastoral outlook'. 'His speeches denouncing injustice and those who oppress the poor, were,' said Velasco, 'something new'. He added: 'I was pleasantly surprised by it, because that was not the Bergoglio I knew. But I can only judge Pope Francis on the actions he takes as Pope and I like what I see.'

The transformation in Córdoba appears to have had its roots in the pivotal Spiritual Exercises set out for the Jesuits by their founder, Ignatius of Loyola. One of the key Exercises is called The Two Standards meditation. It sets the Standard of the Enemy (riches, honour, pride) against the Standard of Christ (poverty, dishonour humility). Father Pat Kelly SJ believes it is crucial to know that to appreciate the Jesuit Pope. 'I think it is helpful for understanding Francis to recognize that humility is a part of the Standard of Christ. So it is the "way of Jesus"'. Another US Jesuit Father James Martin, editor-at-large of *America* magazine, explained: 'In another Exercise St Ignatius sets out three degrees of humility, each harder but more desirable than the one before. The first is the humility of the person who resolves not to do anything wrong and be obedient to the law of God, which is hard enough. The second is where the individual develops a sense of spiritual detachment so they do not feel any preference for wealth or poverty, or a long life or a short one. That would be like someone being asked to choose between flying business class or economy and feeling such spiritual freedom that they genuinely had no preference for one over the other. The third degree, which is the most perfect way of being humble according to St Ignatius, is to intentionally choose the hardest option – poverty, discomfort, contempt – in deliberate emulation of Christ.' In Córdoba, it seems, Bergoglio worked through to this third degree. 'To admit publicly, as he later did, that he made rash and authoritarian decisions is an amazing thing,' said Martin. 'Usually people would say something like: "Looking back, perhaps I might have done things differently". But there is a searing honesty about what Pope Francis admitted in the interview he did with Fr Spadaro for our consortium of Jesuit magazines. Imagine the humility that takes. So Francis is clearly a very free man. And he learns from his mistakes. As a young Jesuit provincial, he tried running things from the top down and it didn't work very well so as Pope he is trying a different way entirely.' The Pope's insistence on collegiality and synodality is a massive learning from experience. The Argentinian Jesuit Father Michael Petty, who knew Bergoglio throughout his Jesuit leadership years, agreed: 'I always think that this is the great lesson he takes to the papacy: he can't bash into those who think differently from him.' The Dominican Father Timothy Radcliffe said: 'One of his greatnesses is that he has the capacity to realize he was wrong.'

But that was not the end of the transformation. The man who later became the smiling Pope was known as a dutiful but rather dour character as a bishop and archbishop in Buenos Aires. So much so that the locals called him Horseface. Jesuits said he was the man who never smiled. Friends said his face lit up only when talking about his football team, San Lorenzo. An Argentine photographer who followed Bergoglio around for a decade in Buenos Aires rarely got a picture of the camera-shy Bergoglio smiling. His press secretary Guillermo Marcó was constantly trying to persuade him not to look so glum in front of the cameras on the very rare occasions he was prepared to give interviews to the media. As Pope, Francis never stops smiling and gives interviews at the drop of a papal zucchetto.

What changed? It was not just the smile. In Buenos Aires he was preparing himself for retirement having reached the age of 75. He looked worn-out, worried and rather sad. Today, Argentinians say, he looks ten years younger. His sister Maria Elena says there is definitely something different about her brother since he became pontiff; 'I get the impression he's very happy,' she said. One cardinal who knew him well in Buenos Aires said to the Pope rather bluntly when the two met privately: 'You're not the same guy I knew in Argentina.' Something has rejuvenated him. But it is more than all the cafeteria food in the Casa Santa Marta, which has made him put on a fair bit of weight since becoming Pope (his doctors have told him to lay off the pasta). 'He's got a billion people praying for him,' laughed James Martin. 'Also, as we like to say, it's the grace of office: the spiritual help that God gives you to carry out your ministry.' Being made Pope has liberated him to be the person he feels God meant him to be. There is a joy and a sparkle about him. He is warm and engaging. 'He comes across to people in private like every family's friendly uncle,' one member of the papal inner circle told me. 'He is kindly, reliable, and direct. You intuitively trust him.'

The change came, miraculously it would seem, at the very moment he was elected Pope. 'During the vote I was praying the rosary – I usually pray three rosaries daily – and I felt great peace, almost to the point of not being aware of myself,' he told Mexican television in an interview to mark his second anniversary in office. 'It was the very same when everything was resolved,' he said, referring to the moment when he was elected Pope. 'For me this was a sign that God wanted it. Great peace. From that day to this I have not lost it. It is "something inside", it is like a gift. I do not know what happened next. They made me stand up. They asked me if I agreed. I said yes. I do not know if they made me swear on something; I forget. I was at peace.' Francis said the same thing in private to friends. A cardinal close to Francis, Cardinal Cormac Murphy-O'Connor, told me: 'He's told me he's at peace, that he doesn't find the job alarming.' His friend for 40 years, the human rights lawyer Alicia Oliveira, told me just before she died: 'He's having a great time. Every time I speak to him I tell him: "Be careful Jorge, because the Borgias are still there in the Vatican." He laughs and says he knows. But he's very, very, very happy. He's having fun with all the people in the Vatican telling him he can't do things – and then doing them.' One of his C9 cardinal advisers, Cardinal Reinhard Marx, said: 'He is very authentic. He is relaxed, calm. At his age, he does not need to achieve anything or prove he is somebody. He is very clear and open and without pride. And strong. Not a weak person, but strong.' That strength, and the self-mocking confidence which grows from it, was evident in his final remarks to the Mexican TV interviewer who teased him by asking about the reputation Argentinians have for thinking they are superior to the rest of Latin America. The Pope replied: 'Do you know how an Argentine commits suicide? He climbs to the top of his ego and jumps!'

Members of the Society of Jesus, above all, are clear as to the source of that strength. It comes from his 13-year formation as a Jesuit and the disciplines St Ignatius drilled into the training of members of the order. Father Juan Carlos Scannone, who was one of his teachers, said: 'I think he's very Ignatian and it helps him not only in his interior life but also in his way of governing.' Father James Martin agreed: 'The key to understanding him is that he's a Jesuit. He is, as we Jesuits say, a man of the Exercises. The hallmark of the Jesuit is freedom. He doesn't have to live in the Apostolic Palace because he's free from what Ignatius called "disordered attachments"; so he doesn't feel bound to practices he feels are no longer essential. The way he governs is also very Jesuit; his nine cardinal advisers are just like the council of consultors which every Jesuit provincial has, made up of senior men who are not currently holding any other office in the province, and who can speak their minds. The way he's running the synod is basically like a big Jesuit group discernment.'

Discernment is a central Jesuit characteristic. The word describes a process of reflection, prayer, talking, listening and debate which allows different perspectives to emerge. The Pope's opening instruction to the synod fathers – to speak with boldness and listen with humility – were classic Ignatian instruments of discernment, explained the South African Jesuit Father Russell Pollitt. His closing speech at the synod, Pollitt noted, was peppered with Jesuit terms, speaking of the process being 'a journey' with moments of 'consolation' and 'desolation'. His warnings to conservatives not to be 'hostile' and 'inflexible' were drawn from Jesuit vocabulary. So was the admonition to liberals not to succumb to the temptation of 'binding wounds without first healing them'.

Outsiders might not have recognized all the vocabulary but they understood the spiritual dynamic. 'What he has got going for him is his spiritual formation as a member of a religious order,' said the American theologian Sister Elizabeth Johnson, who is herself a member of an order, the Sisters of St Joseph. 'He's tapping into a very deep vein of relationship with God which makes him both comfortable and profound. It comes from deep in his soul.'

'I feel like I'm still a Jesuit in terms of my spirituality, what I have in my heart,' Pope Francis told reporters early in his papacy. 'I think like a Jesuit.' His former Argentine confrère, Michael Petty SJ, agreed, insisting that his Jesuit training made him more than a match for the intrigue of the Curia. 'He can deal with the politics of the Vatican with his little finger,' Petty said simply.

The man who was born Jorge Mario Bergoglio has been, over the past two years, attempting to put the Church through the same kind of transformation he underwent himself in Córdoba and thereafter. Just as he went from a strict authoritarian approach to a consultative and collegial style, so he wants the universal Church to mutate from a monarchical model of the papacy into a more participative paradigm in both the College of Cardinals and Synod of Bishops. The transformation requires a shift in behaviour but also, more profoundly, a change of attitude. Conservatives in the Catholic Church, in resisting Pope Francis, have routinely resorted to talking about what Cardinal Burke has called the 'unchanging and unchangeable truths' of church teaching. But this is a misleading trope, as the internationally acclaimed expert on church councils, Father Norman Tanner SJ, Professor of Church History at the Gregorian, earlier explained when he said: 'Those who pretend that the Church has always been as it was in the Pope John Paul II and Benedict XVI era are either ignorant or dishonest'. The theologian Elizabeth Johnson spelled out some of the ways in which the Church has developed and reformed. 'The Church has over the years changed its teaching on slavery, the right to usurp other people's land, usury, contempt for the Jews, freedom of religious practice and the right to follow your own conscience,' said Johnson. Once again law often follows life, not vice versa. 'Changes in doctrines about Mary – the Immaculate Conception and the Assumption – were the Church catching up with the ideas which the laity had already accepted,' said another theologian, Tina Beattie. And change is not always advertised as such. As the church historian Michael Walsh put it: 'Popes depend upon tradition. Even when they change something they often preface it by saying "as my venerable predecessors have always taught…"' 'Change can happen but I think at this point it must come from top,' said another church historian, Massimo Faggioli. 'It's one of the paradoxes of this papacy.'

There are paradoxes aplenty. Pope Francis is a monarch who wants to abolish the papal monarchy. He is a decentralizer who wants everything to pass across his desk. He is the first among equals who issues unilateral instructions about collegiality. He wants to demythologize the papacy and is the Pope that masses of the faithful love because of it. He is the Jesuit who took a vow never to strive for high office who occupies the highest position in the universal Church. He is a pontiff whose homely imprecision is his antidote to infallibility. Perhaps, some suspect, it has been his plan all along – from the moment he refused the red ermine-trimmed cape symbolizing papal authority and had the raised papal throne replaced by a chair on the same level as everyone else. Perhaps. Or perhaps he is just untroubled by inconsistency and wants to let the Holy Spirit blow where it will. Perhaps, in the end, changing the way the Church makes decisions is more important to him than what those decisions turn out to be. If so, there is a downside to that.

Pope Francis has set up massive expectations of change on issues like Communion for the remarried. He has taken the risk that huge disillusion will set in if there is no change on an issue which has become emblematic and which is of significant importance in the pews. Of course, if there is no change, the official teaching may be disregarded; many remarried Catholics may just continue to take Communion even as many married Catholics allow their consciences to override the Church's official teaching on contraception. But for Francis to resile from his indications that he wants a more compassionate pastoral practice could be as damaging to his authority as *Humanae Vitae* was to that of Pope Paul VI. Even if he suggests that he is deferring to the wishes of a more conservative Synod of Bishops his personal standing could be severely damaged.

Those expectations are high. A Pew Forum survey in 2014 showed that 56 per cent of US Catholics thought that the Church would allow birth control by 2050 and 51 per cent believed priests would be allowed to marry. Note they said 'would' not 'should'. The latter figure was significantly up since the election of Pope Francis. Some 42 per cent even thought there would be Catholic women priests by the same year and 36 per cent thought the Church would recognize same-sex marriage by that year. Conservatives were horrified by the figures but a number also said that the Pope could be hoist on a problem of his own making. 'When that finally becomes clear,' wrote one moral theologian, Professor Christian Brugger, 'there is going to be disappointment, anger, and, I fear, intransigence.' If Francis has overplayed his hand that might so dent his authority as Pope that it could endanger the important reforms and initiatives he has set in train in so many other areas.

* * *

Can the reforms of Pope Francis outlast his papacy? How far are Francis's changes to date reversible? What can he do to lock them in?

Some of the changes Pope Francis has made seem already unlikely to be reversed. The clean-up of the Vatican Bank has imported principles of transparency and accountability which are standard practice in all walks of public life and in most private companies. It is hard to see what justification could be made for returning to the secrecy and opacity which earned the bank such a scandalous reputation in recent years. Likewise, though the reformed structure of the overall Vatican and Holy See finances could be reshuffled by a future pope, it seems unimaginable not to retain the orthodox budgeting and auditing procedures that have dragged the curial finances into the twentieth if not the twenty-first century.

Formal reform of the Curia has proceeded at snail's pace. The Pope's new C9 Council of Cardinal Advisers were set the task of devising a totally new constitution of the Curia. But all that their first two years of work produced was the merging of six or seven pontifical councils into two new super-congregations. Resistance to even that limited idea was immediate and wide-ranging. It is unclear whether something far more radical may yet be in the pipeline. There is, however, more to the reform of the Curia than restructuring. Important changes of personnel have taken place. There have been moves to demote the Congregation for the Doctrine of the Faith to a more equal ranking with other Vatican departments. Pope Francis has announced he wants a change of attitude. But a new pope could undo all that with a wave of the hand.

Francis has moved swiftly and decisively to alter the composition of the College of Cardinals. Many of those in big metropolitan sees who expected red hats have not got them. Cardinals have been appointed from far and wide, including from places on the peripheries which have never before had a cardinal. Francis has placed an emphasis upon the developing world but also on choosing men who are both pastoral and collegial. For the first time more than half the cardinals are from outside Europe, with 41 per cent from the poor world. That is already likely to have an impact on the balance within the conclave that will elect Francis's successor. 'The Eurocentrism of the past few centuries has definitely come to an end,' declared the Pope's favoured theologian, Cardinal Kasper.

The Pope's changes in revitalizing the Synod of Bishops are perhaps the most far-reaching of his changes, and yet they are to date the least institutionalized. The synod is no longer the rubber-stamping body for policies devised by the Pope and the Curia as it was under Pope John Paul II and, slightly less so, under Benedict XVI. It is a place of genuine debate. Bishops have stopped talking through veiled allusions and it might take them a while to shed that freedom were Francis to be succeeded by a policeman pontiff. But a hardliner would doubtless silence them before too long. 'Unless Francis changes the way bishops are appointed then nothing is reversible,' said Dr Nicholas Lash, Emeritus Professor of Divinity at the University of Cambridge.

In other areas reform has been so negligible that it makes little sense to talk about whether it might be reversed. Very little progress has been made in overhauling the Vatican's incorrigible secrecy in handling sex abuse. Reforms on the current and future protection of minors are patchy, with enormous variation from one country to another. In some countries, like Italy, bishops' conferences are dragging their feet disgracefully. There are dark forces within the Curia seeking to block progress on the bringing to book of predator priests and on the disciplining of bishops who persist in covering up such scandals. Francis talked of zero tolerance and then appointed a bishop in Chile whose track record on cover-ups is so controversial that his service of installation was violently disrupted by protestors. On the place of women in the Church there has been talk but almost no action. That is the area in which zero tolerance is most effectively in place.

If the progress which Francis has made is to be locked-in, both the Pope and his cardinal supporters know that institutional changes are needed to ensure that the reforms to date are not reversed by some centralizing successor. The Council of Cardinal Advisers, the C9, needs to be institutionalized in the curial constitution. A less drawn-out and, ironically, less consultative process needs to be imposed to transform the curial court into a modern civil service. Statutes need to be drawn up to ensure that consistories of cardinals are more routine and function like a senate, overseeing the Curia and acting as a revising chamber for legislation from the Synod of Bishops. Pope Francis needs to delegate decision-making powers to the synod, which needs to meet more regularly. The Synod of Bishops should be empowered to supervise and vet all future appointments of personnel to the Curia. Democratic governments around the world offer a variety of models that the C9 could study in pursuit of Pope Francis's overriding ambition that whatever decisions are taken by the Church should be made by a consensus of Catholics – bishops, clergy and laity – all around the world.

Reform-minded cardinals, both conservative and liberal doctrinally, understand what is required. 'If you're going to make change and it's going to stick,' said Cardinal Napier, 'you've got to put structures into place that are going to make those changes follow through regardless of who's in the seat.' The key principle for Pope Francis, said Cardinal Kasper, is that 'he must set in motion a process which is irreversible'. At present, another cardinal close to the Pope told me, 'reform is a bit like the kingdom of God; it is both already here and yet a future promise'. The reform has certainly not passed the point of no return, one member of the Pope's inner circle said. 'There is every chance, given the intensity of the opposition, that the pendulum could swing back. What we need for Francis is another four or five years.'

But will Pope Francis be given the time?

* * *

There were two Swiss Guards by the door of the elevator. The American cardinal said 'Buona sera' as he approached. Pope Francis had asked the cardinal to come up to see him privately after dinner in the Casa Santa Marta. The guards saluted. 'Are you going to see the Holy Father?' one asked. The cardinal nodded. 'Would you mind telling him something? Tell him he's really got to move out of this place; we can't guard him properly here. Will you tell him?' The cardinal said he would and entered the lift. At the second floor the doors opened. Pope Francis was waiting by the doors to greet his guest. As they walked down the corridor to the Pope's room, Francis asked: 'Did the Swiss Guards tell you to tell me to move?' The cardinal looked surprised. The Pope laughed. 'Don't listen,' he said. 'They say that to everyone.'

The guards were not merely hankering after the old ways. There had, after all, been a serious attempt on the life of a previous pope, John Paul II. Noises were made about threats from the Mafia after Pope Francis had taken firm stances against them on several occasions. Most dramatically, on one occasion, he declared that Mafia bosses had excommunicated themselves from the Catholic Church.

Now death threats are being routinely made against Pope Francis by the propaganda outlets of the so-called Islamic State. Its magazine has run a cover photo of the militant group's flag flying above the obelisk in St Peter's Square. The terrorist organization has claimed Francis was 'in the crosshairs of ISIS'. In the video it released of the beheading of the 21 Coptic Christians in Libya it claimed that jihadist forces were now 'south of Rome'. Then it announced that they would one day drop homosexuals from the leaning tower of Pisa. In 2015 it described Italy as 'the nation signed with the blood of the cross'. Vatican security chiefs were treating it all as much more than terrorist bluster. In the run-up to the Pope's trip to the Philippines special forces there had foiled an incipient plot to explode a bomb as the papal motorcade began to move through Manila.

But when security chiefs met him, Pope Francis was calm in his response. 'On the horizon we see shadows and dangers which worry humanity,' he told them. 'As Christians we are called not to lose heart or be discouraged.' His was a ministry of proximity, he said. He needed to be able to touch people and them to touch him. Those around him knew that already. Francis had declined a bulletproof vehicle on his visit to the Holy Land with the words: 'At my age I do not have much to lose'. And in Brazil his head of security had told a reporter that he did not even dare to suggest the pontiff wore a bullet-proof vest. 'He would've fired me!' he joked. At the time the Pope had said: 'I am reckless, but

I am not afraid. Nobody dies before their time comes. When my time comes it will be the will of God.' That was before the threats from the terrorist jihadists began. But those did not change the Bergoglio line. In 2015 he told his old friend, the Buenos Aires slum priest Padre Pepe: 'I have said to the Lord: take care of me. But if your will is that I should die or that they do something to me, I ask you one favour: that they don't hurt me.' And boldly – considering that he knew Padre Pepe was writing it up for the shanty-town's community newspaper *La Cárcova News* – he added: 'I'm a real scaredy cat when it comes to physical pain!' But he was genuinely calm. One of his close friends told me: 'He is distinctively Jesuit. He has already given his life to God; when God takes it is up to the Lord.' That may be a religious truth. But it would be mistake to underestimate Pope Francis's considerable personal bravery.

In any case, other intimations of mortality felt more pressing to the pontiff. Entering the third year of his papacy, in which he would be 79, he told another interviewer: 'I have the feeling that my pontificate will be brief: four or five years; I do not know, even two or three. Two have already passed.' It was not the first time he had hinted at such a thing. The year before he had said, in one of his airborne press conferences, that as Pope: 'I try to think of my sins, my mistakes, not to become proud, because I know it will only last a short time,' before adding, 'Two or three years and then I'll be off to the Father's House.' It was, as so often, hard to know how seriously to take such remarks. Was Francis thinking aloud? Was he floating ideas to see what reaction he would get? Was it part of his wider strategy to wilfully devalue the coinage of papal utterances to make them less imperial and more part of the cut-and-thrust of conversation within the Church? Some commentators even speculated that he was raising the idea to confuse those who were resisting his reforms. If his opponents thought Francis's time as Pope might be limited they might be more tempted to sit back in the hope of riding out the storm and returning to business-as-usual under a pontiff they found more congenial, the argument went. Whereas if the resisters thought he might be around for longer they might be more inclined actively to try to sabotage the Francis reforms now. That sounded very tortuous thinking but then the Vatican has specialized in that kind of behaviour for centuries.

The fact of the matter is that in his late seventies, despite his arthritis and his sciatica, Pope Francis seems amazingly sprightly and very active. His aides repeatedly press him to slow down but he takes no notice. The older he gets, the more in a hurry he appears. And although he praised his predecessor Pope Benedict for setting a modern precedent in resigning – adding, 'Benedict should not be considered an exception, but an institution' – he said he did not approve of the idea of popes resigning at a fixed age, such as 80. That would make him in the years he approached the fixed retirement deadline a lame duck pope who could be successfully ignored by his opponents. Francis is enjoying himself and is willing to continue so long as God sees fit. 'No resignation on the horizon for the Argentinian Pope,' was the perceptive conclusion of one Veteran Vatican-watcher, Andrea Tornielli of *La Stampa*, after the interview. What is more likely is that Francis is worried he might run out of time before he has completed the tasks he has set himself. According to Marco Politi, author of *Francis among the Wolves*, the Pope had told a Latin American friend at the end of 2014: 'The only thing I ask of the Lord is that the changes for which I am making so many personal sacrifices will not be like a light that goes out.' One of those closest to Francis thinks that if the Pope does sense that time is running out for him he will accelerate the pace of change. Archbishop Victor Manuel Fernández, who wrote the first draft of the Pope's manifesto *Evangelii Gaudium*, said in the middle of 2015: 'The Pope goes slow because he wants to be sure that the changes have a deep impact. The slow pace is necessary to ensure the effectiveness of the changes. He knows there are those hoping that the next pope will turn everything back around. If you go slowly it's more difficult to turn things back ... You have to realize that he is aiming at reform that is irreversible. If one day he should intuit that he's running out of time and he doesn't have enough time to do what the Spirit is asking him, you can be sure he will speed up.'

But it would be a mistake to look at the first years of the Francis pontificate and judge it by the mechanics of structural change – or even by the extent it had fulfilled Papa Bergoglio's aspirations for what he might eventually achieve. Pope Francis has already changed something massive in the Catholic Church. It is far more than what business leaders, who have cited the Pope as a model of transformational management, call a fundamental corporate restructuring. It is more even than what the marketing men called 'an extraordinary global rebranding'. Pope Francis has set free a new spirit within the Church and one which establishes a new paradigm of what it means to be a Catholic in the twenty-first century.

'It will be hard to go backwards after Francis's papacy,' wrote Father Richard Rohr, the Franciscan friar and international best-selling spiritual author. 'He has forever changed the Catholic conversation. No-one can ever say a validly elected pope, with all that implies in anyone's mind, did not say the things Francis [has] said. They will be quoted for a long time to come. It is now a part of the authoritative data, like the Gospels themselves, and must be reckoned with.' Many agreed. One senior figure high inside the Vatican told me: 'Bishops have acquired the habit of saying what they think. They have stopped talking in code.' An eminent Rome-based church historian added: 'Differences of opinion are now not just allowed but encouraged. The next Pope could roll that back but he would not be able entirely to disavow the Francis inheritance.' The Pope's chief theological adviser came to the same conclusion. 'No, there's no turning back,' said Archbishop Victor Manuel Fernández. 'When Francis is no longer pope, his legacy will remain strong. The Pope is convinced that the things he's already written or said cannot be condemned as an error. Therefore, in the future anyone can repeat those things without fear of being sanctioned. And then the majority of the People of God with their special sense will not easily accept turning back on certain things.'

Others were more world-weary. 'That's the triumph of hope over experience, I fear,' wrote that great enthusiast for the Second Vatican Council, John Wilkins, who was for decades editor of *The Tablet*. 'If the Curia could nullify key parts of Vatican II in ten years, they could nullify Pope Francis's legacy in ten days.' Several pessimists quoted to me the words of the great Jesuit historian Fr John O'Malley: 'What's done can be undone.' All that is true up to a point. In the unlikely event of someone like Cardinal Burke becoming the next pope, much would change with a snap of the fingers. Yet even so, something of Francis would linger in the collective Catholic consciousness and the people in the pews would say to themselves: Hang on, didn't we just hear the opposite? 'The great twentieth – century theologian Johann Baptist Metz speaks of something he calls "dangerous memory"', said Professor Elizabeth Johnson. 'Even after he has gone Pope Francis's legacy will remain as a dangerous memory for he has shown that it is not disloyal to disagree. He has put a different meaning out there of what it means to be a Catholic in good standing.'

A shift in mind-set has taken place. Pope Benedict proceeded from the premise that a solid theological background is necessary if the Church's pastoral practice is to be correct. By contrast Pope Francis insists that it is possible to set aside theological preoccupations and instead to seek first direct contact with people in need of pastoral care and compassion. Neither approach replaces the other; both are complementary, but Francis's insight had been, until now, too long forgotten.

Francis sees the most formidable challenge for the Church today not as the preservation of unchanging doctrine but as the imitation of Jesus Christ in the changing context of a contemporary world. He is neither conservative nor progressive, but he has adopted an approach that uses a discourse which values tradition and yet moves the conversation forward. The genius of Pope Francis is that he combines tradition and modernity with a freshness of expression that is perfectly suited to the times. He both values the treasury of the past and yet moves beyond it. He has given Catholics and non-Catholics alike a vision of what the Church might look like, and in which it can thrive, in the modern world. Despite what traditionalists would claim, the Catholic Church throughout its history has adapted to different cultures and countries. But in many ways it retreated into a nostalgic cul-de-sac under popes John Paul II and Benedict XVI. Pope Francis has re-envisioned it in a form which remains challenging but which gets its message across in a way that connects with contemporary culture. 'Francis has created a new level of expectation for how the Church should go about her work,' said Cardinal Donald Wuerl, the Archbishop of Washington, 'and I don't think you can change that.'

Earlier this year Pope Francis invited a large group of Rome's homeless people on an exclusive private tour of the Vatican Museums and the Sistine Chapel followed by dinner. It was not a publicity stunt – the Pope banned cameras from the event as he arrived to greet the homeless in person. But it embodied the change he has brought to the Catholic Church. It was not the action of a philosopher or a theologian. It was the act of a pastor whose radical change is a change of style, persona and emphasis – and ironically of great substance. It was not the act of a pope who has all the answers but one who knows that the greatest act of a Christian is to be a companion on the journey. He was not, in Richard Rohr's words, telling us *what* to see, so much as teaching us *how* to see – through the eyes of love and mercy.

It has been a journey for Francis too. The man whose first job was as a club bouncer, keeping out the undesirables, has become the gatekeeper of a celestial establishment at whose doors he has declared everyone welcome. After two papacies of philosophically precise rigidity, Pope Francis, in just two years, has legitimized an alternative. No one can say that the only way to be Catholic is to be dour and rules-based. He has shown that another kind of Catholicism is possible. Those who have lived through his papacy will never forget it. Pope Francis has not just demonstrated a different way of being a pope. He has shown the world a different way of being a Catholic. And he has said to people of all faiths, and of none, that in our troubled times the Gospel is indeed good news which – if embraced with mercy and humility and joy – really can make the world a better place.

Bergoglio Timeline before the papacy

Year	Life of Jorge Mario Bergoglio	Jesuit Provincials in Argentina
1936	Born 17 December in Flores, Buenos Aires	
1939		
1940	Starts kindergarten run by Sisters of Mercy who prepare him for his First Communion at the age of eight	
1946		
1949	Sent as a boarder to Wilfrid Barón de los Santos Ángeles secondary school	
1950	Starts six-year vocational course at the Escuela Nacional de Educación Técnica, leading to a diploma as a chemical technician	
1953	Recognizes vocation during Confession on 21 September	
1957	Nearly dies from lung infection	
1958	Enters Society of Jesus on 11 March Last time Bergoglio votes in an election	
1959	Asks to be sent to Japan as a missionary	
1960	Takes first vows as a Jesuit Studies humanities in Chile	
1961	Begins two years of philosophy at the Colegio Máximo	
1962		
1963		
1964	Teaches at the Colegio de la Inmaculada Concepción high school in Santa Fé for two years	
1965		
1966	Teaches at the Colegio del Salvador in Buenos Aires	

Argentina politics	Jesuit Superior Generals	Popes and Vatican
		Pius XI, since 1922
		Pius XII elected (1939–58)
Juan Perón, President of Argentina (1946–55)	Fr Jean-Baptiste Janssens (1946–64)	
Arturo Frondizi, President (1958–62), overthrown by the military on 29 March 1962		John XXIII elected (1958–63)
		Second Vatican Council (1962–65) Paul VI elected (1963–78)
	Fr Pedro Arrupe (1965–83)	
Juan Carlos Onganía, dictatorial President (1966–70)		

Year	Life of Jorge Mario Bergoglio	Jesuit Provincials in Argentina
1967	Studies theology for three years at the Colegio Máximo	
1969	Ordained a priest, 13 December	
1969		Fr Ricardo 'Dick' O'Farrell (1969–73)
1970	Tertianship at the University of Alcalá de Henares in Spain until 1971	
1971	Becomes Novice Master, continuing until 1973	
1973	22 April: takes final Jesuit vows 31 July: becomes Provincial	Fr Jorge Mario Bergoglio (1973–79)
1974		
1975		
1976	Two of Bergoglio's Jesuits, Orlando Yorio and Franz Jalics, are seized by the military, tortured and illegally detained for five months	
1977	The father of a kidnapped pregnant woman, Elena de la Cuadra, appeals to Bergoglio for help	
1978		
1979	Becomes Rector of the Colegio Máximo, serving there until 1986	Fr Andrés Swinnen (1979–85)
1980	Visits Ireland for three months	
1981		
1982		

Argentina politics	Jesuit Superior Generals	Popes and Vatican
Juan Perón, President (1973–74, second term) Isabel Martínez de Perón, President (1974–76)		Vatican counter-attack on Liberation Theology begins
	Jesuit's watershed 32nd General Congregation in Rome votes to embrace the option for the poor	
Military junta seizes power; thousands of political opponents are rounded up and killed in what becomes known as the Dirty War (1976–83) General Jorge Videla, dictatorial President (1976–81)		
		John Paul I elected; in office for 33 days (26 August–28 September) John Paul II elected (1978–2005)
Leopoldo Galtieri, dictatorial President (1981–82) Falklands War (2 April–14 June) Galtieri orders invasion of the British-held Falkland Islands; more than seven hundred Argentinian soldiers are killed; Argentinian junta falls		

Year	Life of Jorge Mario Bergoglio	Jesuit Provincials in Argentina
1983		
1985	Organizes an international conference with Fr Juan Carlos Scannone on Faith and Culture	Fr Victor Zorzín (1985–91)
1986	Finishes as Rector and visits Germany for six months to work on his PhD; returns to Argentina to teach part–time in Buenos Aires	
1987	Elected Procurator of Argentine Jesuits	
1989		
1990	Exiled to the Jesuit community in Córdoba as an ordinary priest	
1991		Fr Ignacio Rafael García-Mata (1991–97)
1992	Becomes Auxiliary Bishop of Buenos Aires	
1994	Attends the Synod of Bishops in Rome	
1997	Becomes Coadjutor Archbishop of Buenos Aires	Fr Álvaro Restrepo, a Columbian and former assistant to the Superior General in Rome (1997–2003)
1998	Becomes Archbishop of Buenos Aires, 28 February	
1999		
2000	Argentine bishops make a weak Millennium Jubilee apology for the Dirty War	
2001	Made a Cardinal, 21 February Appointed realtor at the Synod of Bishops in Rome	
2003		
2004		

Argentina politics	Jesuit Superior Generals	Popes and Vatican
Civilian rule returns to Argentina, and investigations into human rights abuses begin	Fr Peter-Hans Kolvenbach (1983–2008)	
Raúl Alfonsín, President (1983–89)		
Carlos Menem, President (1989–99)		
Amnesty laws passed to prevent prosecution of the military junta		
Fernando de la Rúa, President (1999–2001)		
Massive economic crisis in Argentina		
Poverty soars		
Néstor Kirchner, President (2003–07)		
Amnesty laws repealed and prosecutions recommence		

Year	Life of Jorge Mario Bergoglio	Jesuit Provincials in Argentina
2005	April: attends conclave for the election of a new pope; Bergoglio is runner-up November: elected president of the Argentine Bishops' Conference until 2008	
2006		
2007	At Aparecida, a conference of all bishops of Latin America, Bergoglio is elected to write the key document. It gives a central place to 'poor people's culture'	
2008	Re-elected president of the Argentine Bishops' Conference until 2011	
2009		
2010	Appears as a witness at the ESMA trial into crimes committed during the Dirty War	
2012	Argentine bishops make another apology for the Dirty War but take no institutional blame	
2013	Becomes Pope on 13 March and takes the name Francis	

Argentina politics	Jesuit Superior Generals	Popes and Vatican
		Benedict XVI elected (2005–13)
Abortion legalized in some cases		Regensburg lecture
Cristina Fernández de Kirchner, President (2007–present)		Pope Benedict attends Aparecida conference in Brazil
	Fr Adolfo Nikolaus (2008–present)	Launches CDF investigation into leadership of US nuns
		Launches wider investigation into all US nuns – the biggest in Vatican history
Same-sex marriages legalized		
Thirtieth anniversary of the Falklands War		CDF finds 'serious doctrinal problems' with 'feminist' US nuns
Videla is sentenced to 50 years for overseeing the systematic theft of the babies of political prisoners		
President Cristina Kirchner gives a cool welcome to Bergoglio's elevation; then cranks up her enthusiasm for Argentina's first pope		Francis 2013–

Pope Francis Timeline

	Key events	World	Pope says
2013			
March	13 March 2013, Francis elected Pope, aged 76		'How I would like a poor church for the poor'
	Pays own hotel bill and declines to live in papal palace		'Mercy is the Lord's most powerful message'
	Gives first press conference and blesses atheists		'Authentic power is service'
	In his first Sunday Mass and Angelus preaches on what is to emerge as his key theological theme: mercy		Tells priests they must be shepherds who 'smell of their sheep'
	Installation Mass on the feast day of St Joseph, 19 March		
	Washes feet of women, including a Muslim, on Holy Thursday		
April	Council of Cardinal Advisers (C8, later C9) set up to advise Francis on church governance and reform of the Vatican bureaucracy		
	Francis canonizes Pope John XXIII and Pope John Paul II		

Vatican finances	Curia	Synod of Bishops	Sex abuse	Women in the Church
	Benedict hands over Vatileaks dossier to Francis			
Francis ends the annual €25,000 paid to cardinals on the Vatican Bank supervisory board	Francis confirms that posts of top Vatican bureaucrats will be reappointed only provisionally	Francis authorizes hiring more synod staff	Francis asks the CDF for 'decisive action' on sex abuse	Francis reaffirms Vatican criticism of US nuns
Invites top banker, Peter Sutherland, of Goldman Sachs, to discuss Vatican finances with the C8	Superior of the Franciscans, Fr José Rodríguez Carballo, is first big new appointment Francis axes €1,500 'papal transition bonus' for Vatican staff			Says he might give women more important tasks

	Key events	World	Pope says
May	Francis denounces unregulated capitalism after a thousand people die in a Bangladesh sweatshop Hears first confessions as Pope, in ordinary Roman parish	German Chancellor Angela Merkel calls for more controls on financial markets after meeting the Pope	'Slave labour' from unbridled quest for profits 'goes against God' Pope attacks growing chasm between rich and poor
June	On UN Environment Day, Francis attacks the world's waste of food		
July	Publishes first encyclical, *Lumen Fidei* (The Light of Faith), mostly written by Pope Benedict XVI Begins key bishop appointments by selecting a moderate for Cologne	Francis visits Lampedusa to mourn the deaths of African migrants Travels to World Youth Day, Brazil	'The world has forgotten how to cry' for refugees 'Who am I to judge?' – (on gays) 'This is the time of mercy – a *kairos* of mercy'

Vatican finances	Curia	Synod of Bishops	Sex abuse	Women in the Church
		Francis authorizes more offices for synod staff		Francis says the world's nuns must be spiritual mothers
		Tells Italian bishops he wants to cut their numbers		not 'old maids'
Francis names Fr Battista Ricca as his eyes and ears inside the Vatican Bank	Francis says that the courtly post of Papal Gentleman is 'anachronistic'	Francis tells synod staff he wants a radical change in the working of the Synod of Bishops		
Senior Vatican accountant, Fr Nunzio Scarano, is charged with money smuggling				
The president of the Vatican Bank gives up his office to US consultants to overhaul the Bank's 19,000 accounts				
The bank prepares a dossier on Scarano for Italian police		Francis says his predecessor in Buenos Aires believed 'Half of all marriages are null'	Announces that Vatican employees can now be tried in Vatican courts for crimes against children	Reiterates that women cannot be Catholic priests but says that the Church needs a 'new theology of women'
Francis sets up CRIOR to report on Vatican Bank reform				
Sets up COSEA with top global financiers to reform wider Vatican finances		Right wing of the US Church are unhappy with Francis, says Archbishop Chaput of Philadelphia		
Italian press exposes Ricca's homosexual past. Francis refuses to sack him from the Bank				

	Key events	World	Pope says
August	Career diplomat Archbishop Pietro Parolin is appointed new Secretary of State		
September	Francis gives his first interview, to Fr Antonio Spadaro, for 16 Jesuit magazines around the world Pietro Parolin says 'Reform of celibacy could be discussed'		Francis says that the Church has been too obsessed with abortion, gay marriage and contraception
October	Francis visits Assisi to pray at the tomb of St Francis. Spends most of his time there with disabled children		'This is the beginning of a Church...that is not just top-down, but also horizontal'
November	Publishes *Evangelii Gaudium* (The Joy of the Gospel), setting out the programme for his pontificate	Francis embraces Vinicio Riva, a man covered in disfiguring growths	The Eucharist 'is not a prize for the perfect, but a powerful medicine for the weak'
December	Pope replaces conservatives with moderates on the Congregation for Bishops. Cardinals Burke and Rigali are removed Invites three homeless men and their dog to his birthday breakfast	*Time* magazine names Francis its Person of the Year	

Vatican finances	Curia	Synod of Bishops	Sex abuse	Women in the Church
COSEA invites six top international consultancy firms to scrutinize aspects of Vatican finances	Top conservative worship official, Cardinal Cañizares, sent back to Spain to be Archbishop of Valencia		Papal nuncio Wesołowski recalled to Rome from Dominican Republic, accused of paying boys for sex	
	Conservative Cardinal Piacenza removed as head of the Congregation for Clergy	Reformer Lorenzo Baldisseri appointed Secretary General of Synod of Bishops		Fr Greg Reynolds is excommunicated in Australia for supporting women priests
The Vatican Bank publishes an annual report for the first time in its history	Parolin takes over from Bertone as Secretary of State First meeting of C8	Francis spends two days with synod officials to reform processes He approves a questionnaire to ask the world's Catholics about church teaching on the family and sex	Sex abuse not on the agenda for the first meeting of the C8	Francis tells a Vatican symposium that women are 'close to my heart'
		Francis orders a study on how to reduce the number of bishops in Italy		
3,300 Vatican Bank accounts have now been closed down	The head of the CDF is not asked to become a member of Congregation for Bishops	Reformer Nunzio Galantino chosen by Francis as head of Italian bishops conference	Francis sets up a Commission for the Protection of Minors to prevent future sex abuse	Female head of Focolare proposes lay men and women advisers Pope says no to female cardinals

	Key events	World	Pope says
2014			
January	Abolishes title of Monsignor for priests under 65		
	Joins March for Life via his 11 million followers on Twitter		
February	Creates 19 new cardinals, including many from poor countries, at his first consistory		
			Kasper presentation is 'beautiful' and 'profound', says Pope
March		President Obama meets the Pope	The Pope says he is not 'a superman' but 'a normal person'
			Paul VI was prophetic in *Humanae Vitae*

Vatican finances	Curia	Synod of Bishops	Sex abuse	Women in the Church
Francis sacks four of the five cardinals in charge of the Vatican Bank Appoints known reformer, Bishop Giorgio Corbellini, as head of the AIF, the Vatican financial watchdog		Few Curia officials are included in the list of new cardinals announced by Francis	The Vatican is summoned before the United Nations Rights of the Child Committee over the issue of paedophile priests	
		Francis asks Cardinal Kasper to address cardinals on lifting the ban on remarried Catholics taking Communion	The UN publishes a scathing report on the Church's record over sex abuse and cover-ups Appoints anti-sex-trafficking pioneer Vincent Nichols, of Westminster, as a cardinal	
	Francis introduces compulsory five-day retreats for all Vatican officials	Results of the global questionnaire show a wide gap between church teaching and what ordinary Catholics believe and do	Francis criticized for saying that the Church gets no credit for changes over sex abuse Members announced for the sex abuse commission include a victim Italian bishops refuse to report abuser priests to the police	Women don't need specific jobs in the Church but must be deeper in our thinking, says the Pope Half of the Pontifical Commission for the Protection of Minors are women

	Key events	World	Pope says
April	Francis rings a woman in Argentina and tells her to receive Communion elsewhere after her parish priest refuses to give it to her because her husband was previously divorced		'May no one abuse the name of God through violence' – (addressed to Jewish and Muslim leaders)
May	Tells bishops from Brazil they should investigate allowing married men to become priests	Francis visits the Holy Land – Jordan, Palestine and then Jerusalem	Sex abuse by a priest is as bad as a satanic Mass
June	Hosts the presidents of Israel and Palestine at a prayer summit in the Vatican Archbishop of Canterbury visits Rome	In Calabria, Francis tells the Mafia that they are excommunicated Islamist terrorist persecutions surge in Iraq and Syria	
July	Creates a new super-ministry for Vatican finances, the Secretariat for the Economy; Cardinal George Pell appointed as finance supremo New Vatican Asset Management body is announced. Vatican Bank limited to transferring money abroad for missionary work		

Vatican finances	Curia	Synod of Bishops	Sex abuse	Women in the Church
CRIOR reports. Francis decides not to abolish the Vatican Bank but to remove church investments from its control	C8 becomes C9 as Parolin joins advisers The Pontifical Yearbook is already out of date when it is published; it can't keep pace with the Pope's reforms	Francis breaks with tradition by making the synod undersecretary a bishop to signal the importance of synod reform	Sex abuse commission omitted from the Pontifical Yearbook	Francis abolishes the old strict dress code for women visitors when he meets the Queen of England
Bank investigators report to AIF a 'suspicious transaction' by Cardinal Bertone, Pope Benedict's No. 2		Synod secretary Baldisseri says the 'Church is not timeless' and 'practice could change with circumstances'	The commission's first meeting is told of serious resistance to reform on sex abuse within the Curia	Worldwide women's ordination rally in Rome
Francis sacks the entire board of AIF after a year of in-fighting with the watchdog's modernizing director René Brülhart. Five Italians are replaced by top international financiers			Victims' groups publish a dossier accusing the Pope of ignoring sex abuse when he was in Buenos Aires Wesołowski is defrocked as a priest and bishop	Francis makes 'spare rib' and 'housekeeper' jokes about women
Francis strengthens the powers of the Vatican financial watchdog, the AIF The president of the Vatican Bank quits. Francis appoints Jean-Baptiste de Franssu, from COSEA, to the job	C8 becomes C9		Second meeting of sex abuse commission Francis meets six sex abuse survivors	Five women appointed to the CDF International Theological Commission

	Key events	*World*	*Pope says*
August	Francis lifts block on canonization process for Oscar Romero	Francis visits Korea for Asian Youth Day. Beatifies 124 Korean martyrs	
		Pope sends envoy to Iraq	
September	Conducts 20 weddings in the Vatican, including of couples 'living in sin' Appoints moderate Blase Cupich to be archbishop in the key US diocese of Chicago	Francis visits Albania and addresses Muslims invited to the cathedral	
October	Extraordinary Synod on the Family in Rome Pope beatifies Pope Paul VI		Francis tells cardinals at synod to speak boldly and listen with humility

Vatican finances	Curia	Synod of Bishops	Sex abuse	Women in the Church
Francis gives the AIF the authority to monitor the accounts of all Vatican departments			Francis rings a clerical sex abuse victim in Granada, Spain, and tells him to go to the police	Francis visits Korea, stressing the important role of lay people in the Church
Pell brings in top Australian layman, Danny Casey, as his right-hand man			The Vatican finally launches a probe into Bishop Robert Finn, convicted in 2012 of sex cover-up by a US court. Wesołowski is arrested by Vatican prosecutor	
Scarano tells the *New York Times* he 'trusted the wrong people'		Interim synod report uses conciliatory language on the divorced and gays Final document is watered down after conservatives rebel Cardinal Burke attacks Francis for spreading 'confusion'	Vatican departments jockey for control over the sex abuse commission at its third meeting The commission doubles its membership to cover the whole world	

	Key events	World	Pope says
November	Brazilian bishops establish Commission on Married Priesthood Francis prays in a mosque with a senior Islamic cleric in Istanbul	Francis visits the European Parliament in Strasbourg Visits Turkey and asks Muslim leaders to speak out against extremism	'The Qur'an is a prophetic book of peace' It would be 'beautiful' if Islam's political, religious and academic leaders spoke out clearly to condemn terrorism
December	Francis comments on synod debate over gays. It was about families with gay members, not gay relationships, he tells *La Nación* interviewer Pope gets top popularity ratings in Pew Forum survey		Francis says he is not worried about 'obstinate individuals' who oppose him; it is all part of free debate

Vatican finances	Curia	Synod of Bishops	Sex abuse	Women in the Church
	Archbishop Paul Gallagher is made Vatican foreign minister	Cardinal George of Chicago says he doesn't understand 'what the Pope wants us to do' Francis removes Cardinal Burke as Vatican's top judge. Burke warns of 'a real risk of schism'	Sex abuse commission chairman, Cardinal O'Malley, attacks lack of Vatican action over Bishop Finn	Francis compares Europe to a haggard infertile old grandmother The Swedish ambassador to the Holy See hands Francis a list of 50 top Catholic women theologians
Vatican regulator reports 200 suspicious transactions. Two former Vatican Bank managers are charged with embezzlement Cardinal Pell discovers 'hundreds of millions of euros' in undisclosed Vatican accounts	Cardinals who voted for Francis are having 'second thoughts' says top Vatican reporter Francis outlines the 'spiritual ailments' of cardinals in a withering Christmas pep talk	Archbishop of Sydney, Anthony Fisher, warns of dangerous expectations of change on remarried Communion Preparatory documents for the 2015 synod include paragraphs on gays and the remarried Pope appoints same team to run 2015 synod	Francis meets the Attorney General of the Dominican Republic over prosecution of Wesołowski	Francis calls women theologians 'the strawberries on the cake' The Vatican offers an olive branch to US nuns at the end of the big Visitation investigation. Second CDF process remains in place

	Key events	World	Pope says
2015			
January	After *Charlie Hebdo* massacre, Francis condemns religious violence but says anyone who insults his mother should expect a punch Francis invites a Spanish transgender man and his fiancée to the Vatican – and pays for their flights	Francis visits Sri Lanka and the Philippines	Francis backs *Humanae Vitae* and the Catholic ban on artificial birth control but says priests must interpret it with compassion
February	Creates 20 new cardinals. Europe is for the first time ever in a minority in the conclave to elect the next pope.		Being made a cardinal is a call to greater service; cardinals should 'not be boastful or puffed up with pride'

Vatican finances	Curia	Synod of Bishops	Sex abuse	Women in the Church
Pell introduces new rules requiring all Vatican departments to draw up monthly budgets. All accounts are to be audited independently	Members of the Council of Cardinal Advisers publicly criticize the head of the Congregation for the Doctrine of the Faith, Cardinal Müller	Cardinal Burke says that the 'Church is like a ship without a rudder' under Francis	Former top sex abuse prose-cutor, Charles Scicluna, made Archbishop and takes over top Vatican abuse tribunal	'Mothers are often exalted with praise and poetry,' Francis says, but 'they often get very little concrete help and appreciation' 'Mothers are the strongest antidote to the spread of selfish individualism'
Italians plant 'Dirty Tricks' stories to discredit Pell in the media Pell reports in detail on Vatican finances to a two-day meeting of all cardinals	Cardinals meet up for two days to review Vatican finances and discuss structural reforms of the Curia The old guard plot to curb Pell's power	Cardinal Burke says he will 'resist' Pope Francis if he lifts the ban on remarried people receiving Communion	Francis writes to the world's bishops, instructing them to cooperate with his sex abuse commission Fourth meeting of the commission. Pope again does not attended. Lay members are frustrated at the slow pace of action	Voices of Faith women meet in the Vatican for International Women's Day. No cardinal attends

	Key events	World	Pope says
March	In a second-anniversary interview the 78-year-old Pope says he feels his pontificate will not last long and that he is open to following Benedict in resigning; but he hints that he is not planning to retire at the age of 80	Francis's worldwide popularity soars, with 95 per cent approval ratings being measured in the US	The developing world's 'ideological colonization' is trying to destroy marriage and the family Catholics should not breed 'like rabbits': 'Responsible parenthood!'
April	Francis's Easter message calls on the international community not to stand by as a 'humanitarian tragedy' unfolds in the Middle East. He also focuses on violence in Kenya, Syria, Iraq, Libya, Nigeria, South Sudan, Sudan and the Congo		Francis praises a framework nuclear agreement with Iran as an opportunity to make the world safer
May	Romero beatified in San Salvador		
June	*Laudato si*, encyclical on creation, the environment and climate change	Francis visits Bosnia and Herzegovina	
July		Francis visits Ecuador, Bolivia, and Paraguay	
August			

Vatican finances	Curia	Synod of Bishops	Sex abuse	Women in the Church
Francis confirms Pell's powers and backs his reforms		10 per cent of UK priests sign a letter calling for the ban on remarried people taking Communion to remain	Sex abuser Keith O'Brien is stripped of his cardinal's privileges Members of the Commission express alarm at the Pope's decision to appoint a Chilean bishop accused of a sex cover-up	
			Four members of sex abuse commission fly to Rome to protest over Chilean bishop Bishop Finn finally resigns	
	Council of Cardinal Advisers meets			

	Key events	World	Pope says
September	Francis visits Cuba and the United States	Addresses joint session of Congress	
	World Meeting of Families in Philadelphia	Visits the White House Addresses UN General Assembly	
October	Ordinary Synod on the Family		
November		UN Climate Change Conference, in Paris	
December	Holy Year of Mercy begins		
2016		Francis to visit Argentina and also Krakow in Poland for World Youth Day 2016	
2017		Francis to visit Brazil and also Indonesia	

Vatican finances	Curia	Synod of Bishops	Sex abuse	Women in the Church
	Council of Cardinal Advisers meets			Female theologians publish book on role of women in the Church
		Synod meets in Rome		
	Council of Cardinal Advisers meets			

Timelines by Thomas Vallely

Acknowledgements

For a man the world regards as an icon of simplicity Jorge Mario Bergoglio has an immensely complicated back story. In one sense that is inevitable when someone comes to the attention of the wider world only at the age of 76 as he is elected Pope. But the intellectual and spiritual journey of the man who became Pope Francis has been a story of twists and turns. There have been knots aplenty in the ribbon of the life of a priest who has now admitted to 'having many faults' in his authoritarian style of leadership until he was in his fifties. He has acknowledged 'hundreds of errors' in his life before he became Pope. Since then he has moved with a pace and energy that have filled every week – and sometimes every day – with noteworthy events and newsworthy initiatives. His aides have lamented their inability to keep up with this whirlwind pope, and a biographer can easily experience the same sensation. I am therefore grateful to the large number of people who have assisted me with the task of picking a path through all this complexity.

Staying abreast of the Pope's wide range of activities is no small task. Even more tricky has been analysing and interpreting papal pronouncements and actions which are sometimes elliptical or ambiguous. That task is complicated by the determination of many commentators to reshape Francis as they desire him to be rather than report him as he is.

There has been wilful confusion, too, among biographers writing about the early life and ministry of the man. Accounts of Bergoglio's time as leader of Argentina's Jesuits from 1973 to 1986 have been clouded by two contradictory impulses. On the one side are interpretations from critics who seem tainted with a bitterness that is perhaps inevitable in a country like Argentina, which still has not come to terms with the legacy of what was a particularly nasty civil war. On the other side are the instincts of hagiographers who want to highlight only the saintly qualities in Bergoglio's past and apologists who want to cram Francis into a mould to fit their particular ideology of the Church. To all this is added the fact that the memories of some of those who knew Bergoglio in the past have been judiciously revised since he became Pope, for both good and ill motives.

I could not have managed to make sense of all this without the assistance of many people. In Argentina I was lucky to find as a *vade mecum* Cecilia Macon, a lecturer in the Philosophy of History at the University of Buenos Aires with a special interest in the politics of memory from the particular perspective of trials of crimes against humanity. She guided me through the maze of Argentine politics, and the peculiar puzzle of Peronism, and was also both an unflagging proxy interviewer, 'can do' travel agent and translator. She remained my eyes and ears in Argentina while I was researching in Rome and the United States or writing back in the UK.

In Rome Robert Mickens, formerly of *The Tablet* and now editor-in-chief of the globalpulse.com website, was unstintingly magnanimous with his time, knowledge, intuitions and contacts – and also happy to share his considerable acquaintance with Rome's little-known *ristoranti*. Mgr Rod Strange was most generous in allowing me to use the Beda College as a base and unfailingly insightful in explaining the finer and more arcane points of the Roman way of doing things. In the United States I was grateful for the hospitality of the Jesuits of Seattle University and its enterprising Dean, Mark Markuly, and in New York of the head of Bloomsbury US, George Gibson.

Others whose knowledge and perceptions helped me in both editions of this book included: Rabbi Abraham Skorka, Alessandro Speciale, Alexander des Forges, Alicia Oliveira, Fr Antonio Spadaro, Fr Augusto Zampini, Austen Ivereigh, Fr Bernd Hagenkord SJ, Clelia Luro, Catherine Pepinster, Clifford Longley, Cardinal Cormac Murphy-O'Connor, Daniela Frank, David Chibanda, David Gibson, Fr David Oakley, Professor Eamon Duffy, Edward Pentin, Professor Elizabeth Johnson, Dr Emilce Cuda, Fr Eric Genilo SJ, Federico Wals, Dr Fernando Cervantes, Professor Fortunato Malimacci, Francis Campbell, Francis McDonagh, Cardinal George Pell, Gerard O'Connell, Gregory Burke, Fr Guillermo Marcó, Fr Gustavo Antico, Fr Gustavo Carrara, Hugh O'Shaughnessy, Dr Ian Linden, Fr James Alison, Jack Valero, Cardinal James Harvey, Rt Rev James Jones, John Allen, John Cornwell, Fr John O'Brien CSSp, Professor John Pollard, John Wilkins, Fr José María Di Paola (Padre Pepe), Joshua J. McElwee, Fr Juan Carlos Scannone SJ, Julian Filochowski, Lisandro Orlov, Margaret Hebblethwaite, María Elena Bergoglio, Marie Collins, Mgr Mark Langham, Martin Pendergast, Fr Michael Campbell-Johnston SJ, Fr Michael Downey, Michael Walsh, Miguel Mom Debussy, Fr Miguel Yanez SJ, Professor Nicholas Lash, Ambassador Nigel Baker, Fr Norman Tanner SJ, Mgr Paul Tighe, Peter Saunders, Fr Peter Verity, Philip Pullella of Reuters, Archbishop Philip Tartaglia, Mgr Philip Whitmore, Fr Rafael Velasco SJ, Fr Ricardo Aloe, Mgr Roderick

Strange, Fr Roger Taylor, Baroness Sheila Hollins, Professor Stewart Hoover, Tim Livesey, Professor Tina Beattie, Fr Timothy Radcliffe OP, Mgr Tony Currer, Ambassador Ulla Gudmundson, Cardinal Vincent Nichols, Cardinal Walter Kasper and Cardinal Wilfrid Napier. My apologies for anyone inadvertently omitted.

I'd also like to thank the considerable number of cardinals, bishops, theologians, diplomats and Jesuits who spoke but asked for their names not to be listed here. Thanks also to all those I quote anonymously who talked on condition that their names were not made public, either in order to speak more frankly or because their positions did not permit them to talk openly for publication.

Particular thanks for the second edition must go to the Dutch historian René Fraters, who wrote initially to me to comment on the first edition and then remained in contact with a flow of interesting material on Pope Francis for which he constantly trawled from myriad sources. The diligent and perceptive Louise Hall and Sonia Soans also provided invaluable assistance in meticulously combing through the first edition to prompt me to additional information and explanation. I am grateful to Markus Wieser of the *Istituto per le Opere di Religione* for taking me on a tour of the Vatican Bank and talking me through the Pope's reform process there – and to those inside the Curia who did the same thing, perforce anonymously, with regard to Francis's work inside the Vatican bureaucracy. In the United States I was helped immensely by David Gibson of Religion News Service, who was generous in sharing both information and insights into the US religious scene which has become the most public battleground between rival factions in the struggle for the soul of the Catholic Church in the Francis era.

I would also like to acknowledge my debt to the Pope's various newspaper interviewers: Antonio Spadaro, Andrea Tornielli, Eugenio Scalfari, Henrique Cymerman, Fr Jose-Maria de Paola (Padre Pepe), Ferruccio de Bortoli, Franca Giansoldati, Valentina Alazraki, and Elisabetta Piqué, whose biography *Francisco: Vida y Revolución* is filled with stories from Bergoglio's time in Argentina that are not to be found elsewhere. I profited greatly from Rachel Sanderson's *Financial Times* investigation into the Vatican Bank, which was an excellent introduction to the issues. John Laurenson's courageous BBC World Service programme on The Church and the Mafia offered new material as did Mick Peelo's and Birthe Tonseth's RTÉ documentary *Pope Francis – The Sinner*. As ever I learned much from the perceptive reporting of the veteran Vatican-watchers – John Allen, Massimo Faggioli, Robert Mickens, Sandro Magister, Fr James Martin SJ, Philip Puella, Fr Thomas Reese SJ, John Thavis, Andrea Tornielli and Gianni Valente.

The book-length interview of Bergoglio before he became Pope, by Sergio Rubin and Francesca Ambrogetti in their book *El Jesuita* (2010), remains a mine of primary material for any research on Jorge Mario Bergoglio, though we may now read his own words and self-justifications with different eyes. The same is true of his conversations the same year with Rabbi Abraham Skorka in *Sobre el cielo y la tierra* (On Heaven and Earth), which are shot through with revealing moments.

Thanks for the help in translating from Spanish and German to Isabel de Bertodano, Catherine Ramos and Barbara Fox – and to Ilenia Cuvello who deciphered the cursive nineteenth-century Italian handwriting on the wedding certificate of Bergoglio's Grandma Rosa. Brother Mario Rausch SJ took considerable time to show me around the Colegio Máximo, including the section of the seminary in which Bergoglio hid fugitives from the Argentine military death squads during the Dirty War and the old garage where Bergoglio as Provincial kept his car. Roger Williamson made available his copious research into the future Pope's conduct in the years of military dictatorship. And Mark Dowd and Charlotte Pritchard of BBC Radio 4 were most generous in allowing me to hear all their unedited research tapes of extensive interviews with Horacio Verbitsky, Luis Zamara, Fr Ernesto Giobando, Rodolfo Yorio, Fr Tony Panaro, Fr Andres Agare and Estela de la Cuadra before I set out for Argentina.

Carl Bernstein's research on the links between the CIA and the Vatican was important as was John Pollard's *Money and the Rise of the Modern Papacy: Financing the Vatican, 1850–1950*. Jeffery L. Klaiber's *The Jesuits in Latin America 1549–2000: 450 Years of Inculturation, Defense of Human Rights and Prophetic Witness* was very useful, as was Norman Tanner's *New Short History of the Catholic Church*. *Inside the Jesuits: How Pope Francis is Changing the Church and the World* by Robert Blair Kaiser offered a number of insights. On background for the Dirty War I drew on Emilio F. Mignone's *Witness to the Truth: The Complicity of Church and Dictatorship in Argentina* (*Iglesia y Dictadura*) and Iain Guest's *Behind the Disappearances*. On Liberation Theology – both its diluted variant *teología del pueblo* which attracted Bergoglio in the 1980s, and its more full-blooded social justice imperative which Bergoglio embraced after Argentina's massive financial crisis in 2001 – I am grateful for the assistance of Francis McDonagh, Fr Augusto Zampini, George Gelber, Ian Linden and Fr Juan Hernández Pico SJ of the Romero Pastoral Centre in El Salvador. Thanks too for the acumen of Professor Mario I. Aguilar, author of *Pope Francis: His Life and Thought* and editor of the De Gruyter three-volume *Handbook of Liberation Theologies*. Ian Linden's *Global Catholicism: Diversity and Change since Vatican II* was invaluable. Monika K. Hellwig's *What are the Theologians Saying Now?* was illuminating, as were the two key Vatican texts: *Instruction on Certain Aspects of 'Liberation Theology'*, 1984, which bears all the hallmarks of the style of Joseph Ratzinger, and the more positive 1986 *Christian Freedom and Liberation* clearly influenced by the Pontifical Council for Justice and Peace. On the spirituality of Pope Francis I have been assisted by the writings of Fr James Hanvey SJ and Fr James Martin SJ.

My editors Robin Baird-Smith and Jamie Birkett at Bloomsbury UK and George Gibson at Bloomsbury US, and their assistants and staff, were unfailingly understanding, unperturbed by my shifting deadlines and ready with sage suggestions when needed. Thanks to my copy-editor Nick Fawcett of Proof Positive for his amazing eye for detail. My son Thomas, an historian in the making, produced a Timeline to guide me through various parallel chronologies while I was working on the first edition; it proved so useful that I included it in the book. He repeated the task with a willing enthusiasm for the second edition as an immensely useful précis of the early years of the Francis papacy. Many thanks to him for that.

But my most heartfelt gratitude goes to my wife Christine Morgan whose judgements about institutional politics and human psychology seem infinitely subtle and intuitively correct. She brought them to bear on the range of delicate issues which arose during the research and the writing. She is also the best and most affirming editor with whom I have ever worked; her discerning insights are couched so gently that I would find myself happily rewriting a section after she had begun by telling me how good it was. And she uncomplainingly took up all the domestic slack during the many months of research, travel and writing, through two editions. My thanks are boundless.

Despite all this help from so many quarters any errors or omissions I acknowledge are mine. But I have had such sterling assistance from so many experts that I dare to hope that this book will go some way to unravelling the knots in the ribbon of Jorge Mario Bergoglio's life and offer some elucidation of the early years of the ministry of the man who became the first Pope Francis.

Index